Mike's
Best of
history
book

jaime
RYAN

Test
232-260

ODYSSEY THROUGH THE AGES

▼▼▼▼▼▼▼▼▼▼▼▼▼▼

Garfield Newman
Senior Author and Editor
York Region Board of Education

Christine De Geer
Associate Author and Editor
York Region Board of Education

Contributing Authors

Christopher Crowder   *Queen's University*
Elizabeth Graham   *York University*
Richard Guisso   *University of Toronto*
David Pendergast   *Royal Ontario Museum*
James Reilly   *University of Toronto*
Gerald Schaus   *Wilfrid Laurier University*
Christopher Simpson   *Wilfrid Laurier University*
Narendra Wagle   *University of Toronto*

McGraw-Hill Ryerson Limited
Toronto Montreal New York Auckland Bogotá Caracas
Lisbon London Madrid Mexico Milan New Delhi Paris
San Juan Singapore Sydney Tokyo

Odyssey Through the Ages

Copyright © McGraw-Hill Ryerson Limited, 1992.
All rights reserved. No part of this publication may be reproduced or transmitted in any form or by any means, or stored in a data base or retrieval system, without the prior written permission of McGraw-Hill Ryerson Limited.

ISBN 0-07-551107-X

4 5 6 7 8 9 10   BP   0 9 8 7 6

Printed and bound in Canada

This book was manufactured in Canada using acid-free paper.

Sponsoring Editor: Janice Matthews
Associate Editors: Denise Shortt and Nancy Christoffer
Senior Supervising Editor: Marilyn Nice
Copy Editor: Elizabeth Bolton
Cover and Interior Design: Stuart Knox/Matthews Communications Design
Cartography: Deborah Crowle

Canadian Cataloguing in Publication Data

Newman, Garfield
   Odyssey through the ages

Includes index.
ISBN 0-07-551107-X

1. Civilization, Ancient. 2. Civilization, Medieval.
I. De Geer, Christine. II. Title.

CB311.N48 1992   930   C91-095191-8

Care has been taken to trace ownership of copyright material contained in this text. The publishers will gladly accept any information that will enable them to rectify any reference or credit in subsequent editions.

Contents

Preface		*v*
Acknowledgements		*vii*
CHAPTER 1	*Understanding the Past*	*1*

UNIT 1 — Civilizations of the Near and Far East — 22

CHAPTER 2	*Humanity Before Civilization*	24
✓ **CHAPTER 3**	*Egypt and the Near East*	51
✓ **CHAPTER 4**	*Ancient India*	94
CHAPTER 5	*Chinese Civilization*	129
Skills Focus		**167**

UNIT 2 — Civilizations of Greece and Rome — 170

✓ **CHAPTER 6**	*The Rise of the Greeks*	172
✓ **CHAPTER 7**	*Classical Greece*	200
✓ **CHAPTER 8**	*The Rise of Rome*	231
✓ **CHAPTER 9**	*The Roman Empire*	263
Skills Focus		**298**

UNIT 3 — Civilizations of the Non-Western World — 300

✓ **CHAPTER 10**	*The Islamic Middle East*	302
CHAPTER 11	*Japan: Land of the Rising Sun*	335
✓ **CHAPTER 12**	*The Ancient Maya*	367
✓ **CHAPTER 13**	*The Ancient Aztecs*	397
Skills Focus		**430**

UNIT 4 — *The Resurgence of Western Civilization* — 432

✓ **CHAPTER 14**	*Europe in the Dark Ages*	434
✓ **CHAPTER 15**	*The High Middle Ages*	460
✓ **CHAPTER 16**	*The Late Middle Ages*	493
✓ **CHAPTER 17**	*The Foundations of Early Modern Europe*	517

Skills Focus — **544**

Epilogue: The Emergence of the Global Village — 546

CHAPTER 18	*Towards the Modern Age*	548

Illustration Credits — *562*

Acknowledgements — *564*

Glossary — *565*

Index — *571*

Preface

▼ ▼ ▼ ▼ ▼

In this age of rapid technological advancements the study of ancient civilizations can seem remote to high school students. Yet much of what affects them in their everyday lives is a product of the past. Even those civilizations that have not laid the foundations for modern cultures can teach us a great deal. The primary focus of *Odyssey Through the Ages* has been to prepare students for future studies of the past and to focus their interest on history. If we, as teachers, can convince students of the relevance and fascination which the past holds, students will continue to study history both formally and informally, thereby broadening their horizons and enriching their lives.

From the book's conception it has been our intent to draw upon the expertise of a variety of leading Canadian scholars. In doing so, we have been able to compile a comprehensive text which provides a refreshing look at past civilizations based on the most up-to-date research. At times teachers may find long held beliefs challenged, as recent discoveries and interpretations alter our understanding of history.

A common complaint about textbooks which attempt to cover broad spans of history is that the material presented overwhelms the student. Our approach in this text has been to develop fewer concepts and ideas, and to develop those presented in enough detail so as to make them understandable. This has meant making concessions in some areas, for example not covering a particular artist or battle that some may consider significant. What we have gained from this approach is the ability to cover the civilizations in sufficient detail that the book can stand on its own as a learning resource.

Odyssey Through the Ages opens with a general introduction to the study of history. The intent of this chapter is to act as a lengthy preface to the students explaining the scope of the work and introducing them to the discipline of history. As well we hope to whet the student's appetite for the past by touching on a variety of topics relating to the study of history. The text concludes with an epilogue which is designed to bring the study of ancient civilizations full circle. By dealing with the age of exploration, students are introduced to a variety of concepts including acculturation and the global village. This chapter provides numerous opportunities for further studies and can serve as a bridge to courses in more recent world history.

Our efforts to enliven the study of history has led us to incorporate a number of new features in a high school textbook. Among these features are numerous recipes from ancient sources and selections of historical fiction. The skills components of the book are designed to challenge students on a variety of levels as well as to provide several opportunities for extension activities. In the end, we hope that both teachers and students will find *Odyssey Through the Ages* an enjoyable book to read and a valuable learning tool.

Garfield Newman
Christine De Geer

Acknowledgements

▼ ▼ ▼ ▼ ▼ ▼ ▼ ▼ ▼ ▼ ▼ ▼ ▼

The task of compiling a textbook which covers as many civilizations over as long a time period as *Odyssey Through the Ages* has been an arduous one. Such an undertaking could only succeed with the assistance of a number of people to whom we are greatly indebted. Our contributing authors provided superb texts for us to work with as well as invaluable insights and ideas around which to build units. Their enthusiasm for the project from the outset is much appreciated.

We need also to thank those who assisted in our research. To Mary Timms, the librarian at Dr. G.W. Williams Secondary School thanks for your patience and your unfailing willingness to help. An equally large debt is owed to the Royal Ontario Museum, whose vast collections were readily accessible to us. We are especially indebted to Cathy Pagani and Jack Howard in the Far Eastern Department at the ROM and to Emil Hustiu who supplied the exquisite drawings for chapters 12 and 13. Charles Wing-hoi Chan, of the University of Toronto, supplied the calligraphy for chapters 5 and 11.

A very special group of young people played an instrumental role in the development of this textbook. The following students from Dr. G.W. Williams Secondary School were with us throughout the project in the capacity of student editors, helping to ensure that *Odyssey Through the Ages* was both interesting and readable: Steve Jackson, Kier McManus, Jennie Metcalfe, Paula Clark, Ann Michelle Stretch, Wendy Heming, David Shuh, Renée Gallant, Sandra Eley, Neil O'Higgins, Neil Gregory, Christa Gregory, Jill Hewlett, Brenda Rice, Matthew Salhani, Sherri Owen, Carrie Giles, and Adam Kunopaski.

Other reviewers of the text who made valuable suggestions are: Sharon Adams of Central Kings Rural High School, Nova Scotia; Russell Green of Sussex Regional High School, New Brunswick; Marc Keirstead of York Separate School Board, Ontario; Paul Rexe of Crestwood Secondary School, Ontario; Carmon Stone of Queen Elizabeth High School, Nova Scotia; and John Watkins of Bloor Collegiate Institute, Ontario.

Undoubtedly, those who have made the greatest sacrifice for us have been our families. Our spouses, Phyllis Newman and Harold De Geer, have tolerated late nights and have sacrificed weekends over the past year, while Mathew Newman has had to share his father with numerous ancient civilizations. To Phyllis, Mathew, and Harold we wish to express our love and heartfelt thanks.

We of course cannot forget to thank McGraw-Hill Ryerson who made this dream a reality. Thanks to Terry Seary for bringing the idea to the attention of McGraw-Hill Ryerson and to Janice Matthews for having the patience to work with two idealists. Any success we have had in bringing new innovations to the teaching of history is due to Janice's support of our ideas. We would also like to thank Denise Shortt and Nancy Christoffer for their efforts throughout.

Far more people than have been mentioned here have been involved at some point in the creation of *Odyssey Through the Ages*. To all those who have not been mentioned we wish to express our sincerest gratitude.

Garfield Newman
Christine De Geer

CHAPTER 1

Understanding the Past

Chapter Highlights

- archaeologists and historians at work

- legends to help us understand the past

- estimating the age of ancient artifacts

- fact and fiction behind the story of King Arthur

- the challenge and rewards of underwater archaeology

To some people, the past seems remote and irrelevant to their lives. History, they argue, is nothing but a collection of names, dates, and events that happened long ago. But history is much more. It is a record of our triumphs and defeats, of great achievements of humanity and it is also a window on the day-to-day lives of those who lived in the past. The study of history enables us to understand and appreciate festivals and traditions from countries throughout the world. One of the lures of travel is the opportunity to experience different cultures and festivities and the chance to gaze upon great achievements of humanity, be it art, architecture, or technological innovations. However, Canada today is a multicultural nation whose strength and vitality is enriched by a diversity of culture and tradition, and one need not travel abroad to experience the richness of the world's cultures. Whether celebrating the Acadian heritage in the Maritimes, partaking in the revelry of St. Jean Baptiste Day in Quebec, or shopping in Kensington Market in Toronto, one is caught up in the celebration of Canada's rich ethnic past.

The Roman philosopher Cicero wrote, "Not to know what took place before you were born is to remain forever a child." Imagine knowing nothing of what had gone on before you were born, with no idea of the type of life your parents or grandparents had lived, and having no understanding of the development of the Canadian nation nor the foundation of your culture. Holidays such as Christmas and Canada Day would have no meaning; the struggles of people such as Martin Luther King and Mahatma Ghandi would have no relevance. In essence, you would suffer from "cultural amnesia" as you would be unaware of your heritage, and your cultural past. Moreover, you would be totally ignorant of the world around you, oblivious to the great civilizations that have come and gone. Such ignorance can be the seedbed of prejudice, as those unaware of the cultures of others often show a lack of tolerance and understanding.

The study of history can also be a vital tool in developing skills critical to success in many walks of life. The student of history must learn how to find, analyze, and present information. There are few professions that do not require some kind of research, analysis, and good communication skills. Hence, the study of history has a practical application. It both fascinates us and enriches our lives while at the same time develops a variety of skills that can be drawn on for a lifetime.

Key Concepts

history

primary source

secondary source

legend

archaeology

primary data

stratigraphy

radiocarbon dating

historical fiction

*W*hat Is History?

Too often **history** is seen simply as a chronology of events that happened in the past. In fact, history is a discipline which focuses on the study of change over time and is most concerned with the question *why*. Without change historians would have nothing to study. Historians gather facts in order to understand why events occurred and the impact these events had on society. History is not solely about political power-struggles and military campaigns. This type of history ignores the vast majority of the people who make up the past as it focuses on those with wealth and power. For us to have a full picture of the past, history must also include the study of religious events, economic trends, technological change, artistic achievements, and the social fabric (the homes, clothing, food, festivals, and music of the people). Social history must endeavour to reflect the lives of men and women from all classes, for the poor as well as the rich have a past. Because records generally deal with the powerful and wealthy and tend to ignore aspects of daily life, the historian often relies on the work of archaeologists to determine a complete picture of earlier living conditions. For those societies that left little or no written record, the work of the archaeologist is vital to the historian who hopes to glimpse into the lives of earlier civilizations.

*D*ifficulties In Writing History

The path to understanding the past is littered with difficulties. The first task facing the historian is the gathering of data which is unprocessed and would mean little to the untrained eye. Data is often sparse and limited, especially when dealing with those people without rank or power. **Primary sources**, which are written accounts recorded at the time of an event, may include diaries, eye-witness accounts, government records, ships' logs and so on, seldom reveal much about women, the labouring poor, or the plight of children.

The second task facing the historian is to work with the limited information available in an attempt to reconstruct the past as accurately as possible. This requires a great deal of analysis and interpretation. Thus history both exists and must be interpreted. Reconstruction of the past is referred to as a **secondary source** for it is an account of the past based on research and analysis.

Those who feel history never changes are wrong. Our understanding of the past is continually changing and expanding as the result of new interpretations and an ever increasing wealth of knowledge. Historians are not alone in the quest to reconstruct the past. Other disciplines such as archaeology, **anthropology**, **ethnology**, economics, geography, and the sciences play a vital role.

The study of the past can be broadly broken down into three phases. First, to unearth the past. This entails locating the data, be it the written or physical remains of a society. Once the data have been gathered, the data must be analyzed and interpreted. The final step is the challenge of reconstructing the past. The balance of this chapter is designed to explore the various facets of understanding the past in order to prepare you for a journey through history.

*U*nearthing the Past

*L*egends and History

At some point in our lives we have all been enchanted by an enduring **legend**. Whether the story is of King Arthur or Robin Hood, the lure of King Solomon's Mines, the Epic of Gilgamesh, or the search for Atlantis, we are drawn by the excitement and intrigue of legends. Unlike **myths**, which deal with the divine, and humanity's relationship with the divine, the central characters of legends are human and the stories have a basis in fact. Often legends deal with the achievements of great leaders, the exploits of great warriors, or the wisdom of great sages and magicians. Despite the fact that the characters take on superhuman qualities and the events get distorted, legends remain more than fanciful stories. Legends can act as sign posts to historians and archaeologists by capturing the imagination and preserving the essence of the character, event, or society portrayed. From there the great challenge is to separate fact from fiction in an attempt to understand the past.

While some people perceive legends as little more than a good story, others have dedicated much of their lives to unearthing the history underlying the legend. In some cases the rewards have been astounding, while in others the quest continues. One of the most famous examples of the overlap between legend and history is the search for Troy.

Schliemann and the Search for Troy. The lively and fascinating stories of Homer's epic poetry have come alive for many readers and have led some to believe that such tales were not simply created, but must have evolved from colourful accounts rooted in past events. Heinrich Schliemann, a wealthy German, was among those romantics caught up in the accounts of the Trojan War and firmly believed in the existence of these legendary cities and events. He was known as a sharp and sometimes unscrupulous businessperson and, when delving into his life and beliefs, one must be aware of the inconsistencies of his own biographical accounts in his notes on the excavations and in the discovery of artifacts. This enigmatic character, often referred to as "the father of archaeology" may also be described by the less glorious title of the "teller of tall tales."

His passion for discovering Troy took him to Turkey in 1868 to a mound known as Hisarlik on the plateau of the ancient city of New Ilium. Upon acquiring permission from the owner of the mound and agreeing to pay the costs Schliemann began in 1870 to dig with a ferocity that destroyed many structures which he deemed unimportant. He found evidence of ancient cities built one atop of another and was certain Troy was the second last city. His critics thought Schliemann was blinded by his enthusiasm since the city found was indeed too small to be Troy.

Schliemann, not to be daunted, pushed on, finding a vast cache of gold, silver, and bronze items, and thousands of pieces of exquisite jewelry, which he immediately claimed to be the treasure of Priam, King of Troy. This find gave Schliemann credibility again, although Schliemann and his critics were still bothered by obvious inconsistencies. After Schliemann's death in 1890, conclusive proof was found that this "Troy" was 1000 years too old. One of Schliemann's associates recognizing the merit of Schliemann's discovery continued the search, and subsequently unearthed a city with magnificent walls, watchtowers, and gates. In the debris he found evidence of violent destruction. Had the magnificent Troy of Homeric legend finally been found? It is unfortunate that Schliemann could not have participated in this discovery, because the doubts that plagued him until his death would have been dispelled.

The Nature and Purpose of Archaeology

Archaeology provides scholars with the **primary data** necessary to answer certain questions. As archaeology is a means to an end, rather than an end in itself, it is most often problem oriented. An excavation takes place in order to solve a problem or test a hypothesis, and the artifacts gathered become the primary source for anthropologists, ethnologists, paleontologists, scientists, and historians. In short,

At the Ball site, where a large Huron Indian village was discovered, archaeologists are working on a feature. The feature in this case is a stain in the soil that was left by the decaying posts from the longhouses. In unearthing, the archaeologist must be careful not to distort or destroy; therefore, the work in uncovering and recording the feature is always meticulous and slow.

archaeology is the methodology by which information regarding the past is extracted from the earth.

The Ball Site: A Case Study

Not all archaeologists triumph with discoveries on the scale of Troy nor do they lead a life of adventure such as Hollywood's Indiana Jones. While the work of the archaeologist can be challenging and immensely rewarding, the process requires meticulous care and great dedication. Perhaps the best way to create a vivid picture of the archaeologist at work is to trace an excavation from the time of the selection of a site through to the cataloguing of the artifacts. The site chosen for our example is called the Ball site and is located near Orillia, Ontario.

The excavations here have unearthed a Huron village dating to the last decade of the sixteenth century. The Ball site represents the first time an entire Huron village has been excavated. The 16 years of digging have provided site directors Dean Knight and Isobel Ball with a wealth of knowledge concerning Huron life on the eve of contact with Europeans and will undoubtably force a rethinking of what we believe about some aspects of Huron culture. For example, the Ball site challenges two beliefs regarding Huron villages: that they covered two to two and one-half hectares and that the size and design of the Huron longhouse was relatively consistent. The four hectare Ball site has already revealed 64 longhouses of widely varying sizes and design.

Several factors come into play when deciding where to carry out a dig. Knowing that a particular site may yield important information is often a matter of luck. In the case of the Ball site, notes by a turn-of-the-century amateur archaeologist regarding native artifacts found in the area were used in the site selection. The next step in choosing a site is to consider what questions are to be answered. The Ball site was chosen because it represents a Huron village in a period of transition, at a time when European trade goods were beginning to appear, thereby radically altering native technology. Another factor to consider is obtaining permission to carry out the excavation. This is often much easier in open areas such as fields than in urban centres. Finally, the archaeologist must assess the potential size of the site and weigh this against available resources.

Before the excavation can begin, a "dig team" must be assembled. The team will consist of: a field director who is a trained and licensed archaeologist, a number of supervisors who have some training and experience, and the crew which is comprised of people with minimal experience. Depending on the site, other professionals such as photographers

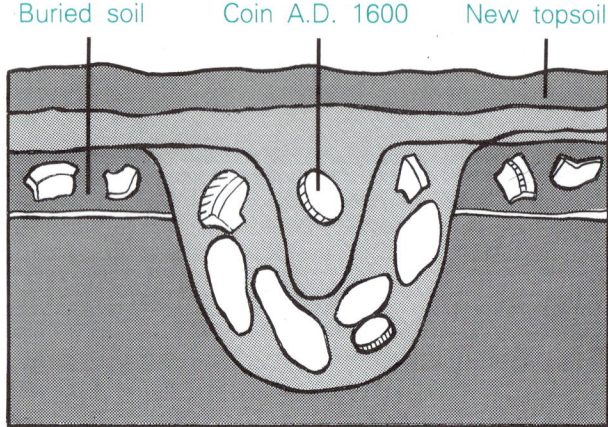

Before excavating, the site is prepared by establishing a grid system over the entire area. This allows the archaeologists to accurately record where artifacts or stains in the soil were found. The first task is to remove the topsoil while watching for artifacts or changes in the colour of the soil. The technique used is called shovel shining, which involves carefully scraping the soil away using the edge of the shovel. Once artifacts begin to appear, a more meticulous method called troweling is used. Troweling is done by carefully scraping the edge of a trowel along the earth so as to remove the soil slowly.

and/or surveyors may also be brought in. For the analysis of the artifacts the talents of a wide variety of people are drawn on. Faunal experts examine the bones, floral experts examine plant remains, geographers do soil analysis, and even pathologists may be called in if a body is unearthed.

While the top layers of earth are removed an eye is always kept on the soil in case a stain or an artifact appears. Stains are left in the soil by a variety of sources. At the Ball site longhouses are identified by a series of round stains, which mark the former walls. These stains were left by the decaying posts that formed the frame of the structure. Other stains include hearths and middens, or garbage pits. Often middens yield bits of pottery, carbonized seeds, bones, and other remnants of daily life. As stains and artifacts are discovered, they are recorded in field notes and the location placed on graph paper. The artifacts are placed in bags, which are labeled while the stains are cross-sectioned. When features such as middens or hearths are discovered, the soil is screened to ensure that no artifacts are accidentally discarded.

Archaeology is essentially destruction: once a site has been excavated it can never be reworked. Therefore accurate and meticulous notes are essential. Throughout the dig each member of the team maintains a field journal in which they record the date, the square being excavated, any finds, and their impressions. Graph paper is used to map each square which, when plotted on a master map, helps to create an accurate picture of the whole site. The information gathered each day by members of the team is collated at the end of the season by the field director and assistants. The work in the field represents about one quarter of the archaeologists' work, with three-quarters of the time spent in the laboratory analyzing the mountain of primary data collected each season.

The analysis of artifacts will vary greatly depending on the nature and purpose of the site. At the Ball site, analysis falls within anthropological lines. The presence of at least 64 longhouses and a palisade encircling the site indicates that the people who lived in the village were not migratory. Pottery found reveals a relatively advanced level of technology, although the discovery of brass arrowheads suggests that trade was occurring and bringing a rapid change from Stone Age weapons. Finally, the carbonized remains of corn and bones of various animals provide some insight into the diet of the Huron at the end of the sixteenth century.

For the work of the archaeologist to be of value, the primary data and the completed analysis need to be published so that the information can be disseminated to all interested parties. Ontario law requires that any archaeologist granted a licence must prepare a site report at the end of each season in order to get their licence renewed for the following year. The site reports, which include a description of the artifacts and the areas excavated, are printed and distributed by academic presses, thereby becoming available to scholars. In this way the work of the archaeologist contributes to the body of knowledge collectively held by society. Just as the Ball site has greatly added to what we know of Huron culture and society, countless similar digs worldwide have contributed to our knowledge of past cultures.

Underwater Archaeology: A Unique Challenge

Treasures of the past are found under water as well as on land. For as long as people have used waterways as a means of transportation there have been shipwrecks. Many of these well preserved shipwrecks and their contents are still lying at the bottom of a sea, an ocean, or a lake. While the rewards of underwater archaeology can be great, the challenges of the work can be daunting. Essentially the same archaeological principles are applied in underwater projects as on land sites, although the environment imposes several restrictions. First and foremost, conventional diving can be used only to a depth of about 35 m and even then dives must be for a relatively short period of time. On average, underwater archaeologists spend about four hours a day in the water. Another factor underwater archaeologists contend with is limited mobility. A fully equipped diver working underwater lacks the dexterity of someone on land. This problem is compounded by the limited visibility resulting from sediment in the water or simply the lack of light rays reaching the site. Finally, the recovered artifacts require immediate treatment to prevent them from decomposing after being removed from the protection of the silt. Despite the challenges faced in underwater archaeology the magnificent finds of the past 35 years have convinced archaeologists that the effort is indeed worthwhile. One of the most famous underwater archaeological projects in the world is that of the warship *Mary Rose*. The story of the *Mary Rose* clearly illustrates the value of underwater archaeology.

The Recovery of the Mary Rose.

The *Mary Rose* was built in 1509–1510 in Portsmouth, England and was named after Henry VIII's younger sister, Mary. As one of the first ships built for battle the design of the *Mary Rose* was revolutionary. The use of heavy guns and watertight gunports was evidence of the shift in the nature of naval warfare that was occurring at the beginning of the sixteenth century. Originally the ship carried 43 heavy guns and 37 lighter weapons although after being rebuilt and rearmed in 1536 a total of 91 heavy guns were aboard. For 35 years the *Mary Rose* played a significant part in Henry VIII's navy; then on a summer day in 1545 disaster struck.

In the summer of 1545 the French launched an attack on England as part of an on-going war. The attack came at Portsmouth, the home of the Royal Navy and the site of the Royal Dockyard. As the English sailed into the Solent (the body of water between the mainland and the Isle of Wight) the *Mary Rose* began to sink. The French believed they had sunk the ship by gunfire, but in fact the English had been the masters of their own misfortune. Despite being designed for a complement of 415 people there were 700 crew on board and the ship was heavily laden with guns and ammunition. Negligence also contributed to the disaster. The lower gun ports were left open after firing, and when the *Mary Rose* began to turn, the excessive weight caused the ship to lean, allowing water to flood in through the gun ports. The ship heeled over on its starboard side and sank quickly in the shallow waters of the Solent. Of the 700 people on board fewer than 40 managed to escape; the rest accompanied the *Mary Rose* to its watery grave. The loss of the *Mary Rose* was a serious blow to the English but they were able to rally and successfully resist the French invasion.

INNOVATIONS

Underwater Archaeology on the Great Lakes

The Story of the *Hamilton* and *Scourge*

When the War of 1812 broke out between the Canadas and the United States, the Great Lakes quickly became a vital theatre of operation. Control of the waterways was essential if troops and supplies were to be moved quickly and easily. To build up their fleets on the lakes both sides enlisted merchant schooners which were converted to armed vessels. Two of these were the schooners *Diana* and *Lord Nelson* which, after refitting, were renamed the *Hamilton* and *Scourge*.

Early in the morning of August 8, 1813 an American squadron sat anchored, off present day St. Catharines, Ontario, waiting to press the British at first light. Suddenly and without warning, a violent squall came up capsizing the *Hamilton* and *Scourge* sending 53 of a crew of 72 to a watery grave. The two schooners came to rest on the bottom of the lake, 91 m below the surface. For the next 160 years the two vessels lay lost and undisturbed in the dark, cold waters of Lake Ontario.

Until recently the search for the *Hamilton* and *Scourge* was beyond the realm of possibility. At 91 m the water is too deep, dark, and cold for divers to explore using standard underwater archaeological methods. With the development of deep-water photography by remote control, access to depths formerly unattainable became possible. In 1973 a brief exploration using a ROV (remotely operated vehicle) and sonar revealed that the vessels were still intact and in a remarkable state of preservation. The fresh water, constant near-freezing temperatures, and utter darkness were all key factors in the preservation of the ships and their artifacts. In 1982 a detailed survey of the *Hamilton* and *Scourge* was carried out by the Hamilton-Scourge Society in conjunction with the National Geographic Society. Using cameras mounted on a remote controlled vehicle, 1900 still photographs and 26 hours of videotape were recorded. The wealth of information gathered in 1982 was further supplemented by the Jason Project; a state-of-the-art ROV, which allowed for outstanding mobility, versatility, and almost unlimited endurance.

The *Hamilton* and *Scourge* Project is one of the most important underwater archaeological projects in the world. The state of preservation of the ships and the numerous artifacts will ultimately provide researchers with an abundance of documentation on the construction of schooners in the early nineteenth century. Among the incredible cache lying with the vessels are cannons still on the deck, cutlasses crossed above the guns, shot resting in the shot racks and boarding axes in their racks just as they were over 175 years ago when the vessels sank. Drawing on techniques developed for the raising of the *Mary Rose* and the preservation of artifacts recovered from the sea the Hamilton-Scourge Society is examining the means by which these treasures can be made accessible to the public.

Jason Meets the *Hamilton* and *Scourge*

The robot Jason II, which is a second generation of the ROV technology, was developed for the deep waters of the Mediterranean yet was first used here in Canada. The Jason, containing cameras, lights, laser imaging equipment, and fibre optic cables, is attached to its companion vehicle the Medea. This ROV system is connected to an operations barge on the surface of the lake.

In the control centre of the barge, the famed oceanographer Robert Ballard directed Jason's exploration of the lake bottom with the guidance of archaeologist Dr. Margaret Rule.

The operations barge controls, monitors, and operates all aspects of the ROVs. The pilots used joysticks to manoeuvre Jason, or entered commands into the computer which were relayed to the Medea via a fibre optic cable. These commands were relayed through another cable to the computer within Jason which then reacted accordingly.

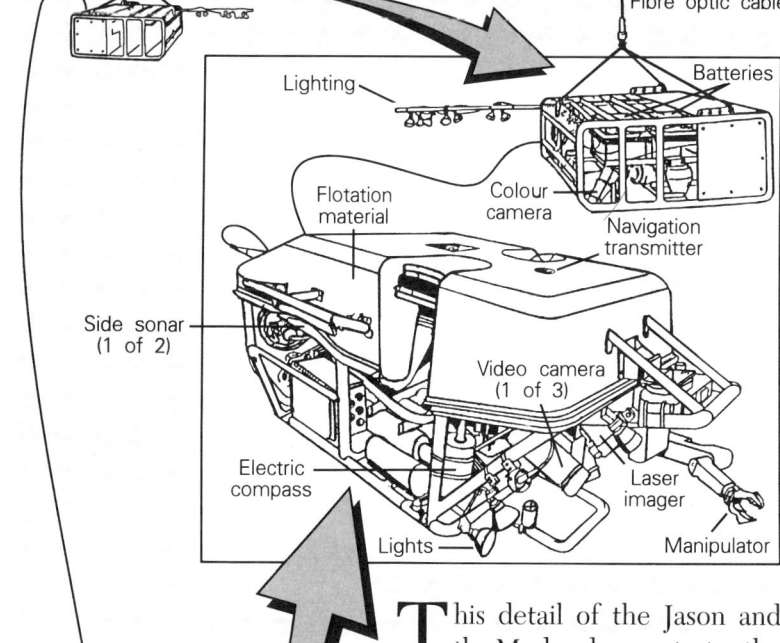

This detail of the Jason and the Medea demonstrates the technology carried by these specially designed remotely operated vehicle systems. Using this technology, scientists can explore up to six kilometres underwater. The Jason and Medea are equipped with video and still cameras that record data and computers which receive the information from the pilot on the barge.

William Bishop's painting of Henry VIII's flagship, the Mary Rose, *is based on evidence gathered through the unique techniques of underwater archaeology. Clearly evident in this illustration are the open gun ports, which contributed to the sinking of the ship, and the netting, which trapped many of the men.*

Immediately after the sinking, several attempts were made to recover the *Mary Rose* but all proved futile. In the years following, some of the spars, rigging, and guns were recovered although in time the remains of the ship and its contents were completely covered by sediment. In 1836 a diver attempting to free a fishing net found a Tudor gun—he had inadvertently rediscovered the *Mary Rose*. The diver recovered a few of the guns and longbows from the ship but his discovery was soon forgotten.

Modern attempts to find the *Mary Rose* began in 1971 when the Mary Rose Committee, headed by Alexander McKee and Dr. Margaret Rule, completed the first dive. The survey and excavation of the site began in 1979 and required 3 years and over 24 000 dives to complete. After the excavation was completed, and more than 17 000 artifacts had been recovered, the *Mary Rose* was raised and returned to Portsmouth where it had been built more than 470 years earlier.

The numerous artifacts recovered provided archaeologists with invaluable insights into Tudor shipbuilding and warfare as well as the social divisions on a sixteenth century English vessel. Among the weapons found were 138 yew longbows and 3000 arrows. Prior to the excavation of the *Mary Rose* only one arrow dating to the Tudor period was known to exist. Also recovered were several beautifully decorated bronze guns in excellent condition and 1800 rounds of ammunition ranging from small iron shot to large stone shot. The navigational equipment recovered included a compass, a slate protractor and dividers, and pocket sundials. Among the most interesting artifacts found were the various personal items such as wooden combs, a bone manicure set, ink pots, wooden tankards, plates and knives, leather book covers, musical instruments, games such as backgammon, coins, and leather bottles. Even a flea and an oak leaf had been preserved by the sediment!

The conservation of such a large number and variety of artifacts was, itself, a major task. Many of the artifacts were remarkably well preserved by the water and sediment but needed immediate treatment once removed from their resting place. Metal objects had to be treated to remove salt and to stabilize oxidized metal. Wood and leather were preserved by first saturating the artifacts with a soluble wax and then freeze-drying them. Pottery and glass were thoroughly washed with fresh water. As each artifact was recovered it became part of a comprehensive picture. Details of each object were fed into a computer. As each object was drawn, photographed, conserved, and displayed the information was added to the computer.

Of course the biggest challenge was the raising, preserving, and displaying of the remains of the *Mary Rose*. The *Mary Rose* is now on display in the specially constructed Mary Rose Hall where *misting* installations maintain a high level of humidity and every hour the ship is sprayed with 27 000 L of chilled water.

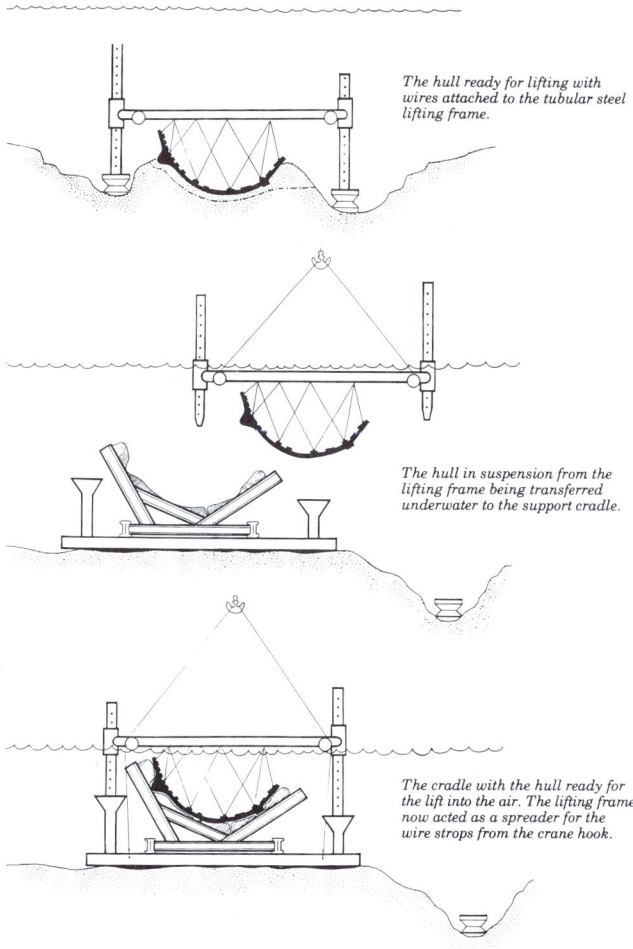

The hull ready for lifting with wires attached to the tubular steel lifting frame.

The hull in suspension from the lifting frame being transferred underwater to the support cradle.

The cradle with the hull ready for the lift into the air. The lifting frame now acted as a spreader for the wire strops from the crane hook.

The hull of the Mary Rose was lifted to the surface using a specially constructed apparatus. This series of diagrams illustrates how the Mary Rose was successfully raised.

The excavation and raising of the *Mary Rose* is the largest underwater archaeological project ever undertaken. Many of the recovered objects are fascinating and rare, and provide important information for historians. The hull of the ship remains a clear illustration of the skills of Tudor shipwrights while the rigging is a vivid display of Tudor technology. The artifacts give insights into life on board English vessels in the Tudor period, highlighting the social divisions that existed. The books, pewter plates, and elegant wine flagons of the senior officers contrast sharply with the crude wooden plates and tankards of the regular mariners. Finally, the *Mary Rose* represents a link between the ships of the late medieval period and the swift galleons of the late sixteenth and seventeenth centuries.

The Search for King Arthur

One of the clearest examples of the overlap of legend, archaeology, and history is the search for proof of the existence of King Arthur. Inspired by the stories of King Arthur and the Knights of the Round Table, both historians and archaeologists have supplied pieces to the puzzle. While historians have examined the written records, archaeologists have excavated sites that are mentioned in the legends.

Few legends of the world have captured people's imagination as much as the story of King Arthur. From Arthur's conception to death, the Arthurian legends are filled with magic, heroism, and romance. Characters such as Merlin the magician, the beautiful Guinevere, the remarkable Sir Lancelot, and the mysterious Lady of the Lake have made the stories of King Arthur and the Knights of the Round Table some of the most inspiring legends of the western world.

According to legend, Arthur was conceived when Uther Pendragon, filled with desire for Igraine, had himself transformed into a replica of her husband, the Duke of Cornwall, and entered her bedroom. While Uther lay with the unsuspecting Igraine, the Duke of Cornwall was fighting his last battle. Upon hearing of the death of the Duke, Uther immediately married Igraine.

When Arthur was born, the magician Merlin, who had assisted Uther in his seduction of Igraine, took the child and had him raised by a peasant and his wife. Following the death of Uther Pendragon the leadership of the Britons was in question. To redress this problem Merlin invited Lords and Knights to London and here he provided a great stone in which a sword was firmly anchored. Inscribed on the sword were the words; "Whoso pulleth out this sword of this stone…is rightwise King born of all England." Much to everyone's surprise the young Arthur drew the sword from the stone and was consequently crowned king.

King Arthur took up residence in Camelot where he lived with his wife Guinevere. Guinevere was reputed to be the most beautiful woman in Britain. Throughout the 16 years of his reign Arthur proved to be a capable administrator, a fierce warrior, and a great leader. Some legends go so far as to suggest that Arthur built an empire that included Britain, Scotland, Ireland, Iceland, Norway, Denmark, and France. Of great assistance to Arthur throughout his reign was the magical sword Excalibur, which he received from the Lady of the Lake. Arthur also founded the Order of the Knights of the Round Table, an order that included the knights Sir Lancelot and Sir Galahad.

King Arthur's final resting place remains a mystery. He is believed to have been mortally wounded near the River Camel in Cornwall. According to legend Arthur left the battlefield and went to Avalon, which was an earthly paradise, and here he died.

As with all legends, the story of King Arthur is largely fictional. Much of the Arthurian legend is the product of two very imaginative minds, Geoffrey of Monmouth and Sir Thomas Malory.

Geoffrey of Monmouth wrote the *History of the Kings of Britain* in 1136 while he was a cleric and teacher at Oxford. It contains an account of the life and times of Arthur, King of the Britons. Geoffrey's story is replete with dragons, magicians, and chivalrous knights in armour. While it is unlikely that dragons and magicians ever existed, the rules of chivalry and knights in armour reflect the period in which Geoffrey lived, not Arthurian England. Nevertheless, Geoffrey's version of King Arthur has endured as one of the great pieces of medieval English literature.

Sir Thomas Malory's *Le Morte d' Arthur* was completed about 1469. This version of the Arthurian legend was not intended as history but rather had a social purpose. *Le Morte d' Arthur* was a fresh and powerful work of prose that provided a striking contrast between the Golden Age of King Arthur and the disarray England was experiencing during the civil war, which is known as the Wars of the Roses.

Neither Malory nor Geoffrey of Monmouth provided a historically accurate account of Arthurian England. Instead, both made significant contributions to the legend of King Arthur. Both accounts were based to some degree on earlier Celtic legends that had some basis in fact.

Historical records tell us that the Romans had withdrawn from Britain by the late fifth century. This left a void that was soon filled by marauding Saxons. Eventually the Saxons began to marry British women and establish settlements, which brought them increasingly into conflict with local tribes. There is little doubt that during the sixth century a warrior and great leader united the Britons in their resistance of the Saxon invaders. Thus, the context of the Arthurian legend can be verified through historical records.

The work of archaeologists has helped to further verify some aspects of the legend of King Arthur. For example, Tintagel is generally considered the birth place of Arthur. Excavations at Tintagel have unearthed fragments of pottery imported from the eastern Mediterranean region during the sixth century. This would suggest that a wealthy household, able to afford imported luxury goods, existed at Tintagel at the time of Arthur's birth. Although no conclusive evidence of King Arthur's existence has been discovered there are enough tantalizing bits of the story that have been verified to keep the search alive.

Analyzing Data

Methods of Dating Artifacts

When an archaeological find occurs, the first secret to be unlocked is the age of the artifact and the site. The key to this puzzle can be found in many forms.

Stratigraphy is the study of the layers of a civilization. It is based on the principle that the most recent archaeological items are found at or below ground level and as the dig goes deeper the items found become progressively older. The consecutive layers of a civilization can be distinguished and differentiated, each layer representative of the inhabitants. What is limiting in many methods of dating is the necessity to consider the location and the context of the artifact. These limitations were raised in 1949 by Professor Willard F. Libby, an American chemist who discovered the principles of **radiocarbon dating**.

Radiocarbon, or C-14, dating measures the age of organic material by gauging the level of the radioisotope carbon 14. Carbon 14 is formed by neutrons interacting with the earth's nitrogen. This process creates radiocarbon that is equally distributed throughout the atmosphere. All living things take in radiocarbon throughout their lives and at the moment of death the process is reversed and the radiocarbon begins to decay at a constant rate. It is the rate of decay that accurately measures the age of material up to 40 000 years old. When 5730 years have passed after the death of an organism the radiocarbon level is at exactly one-half of the original level, after another 5730 years it is, again, exactly half. Decay of the radiocarbon will continue according to this formula. After measuring the radiocarbon one can establish the stage of decay and this will indicate the amount of time elapsed since the death of the organism. Radiocarbon dating is the most popular technique used on organic materials and is probably the most effective.

There are a variety of techniques available for the archaeologist to choose from. While few of these methods allow for absolute dating, estimated ages can be obtained with relative ease. Furthermore, recent improvements in dating techniques have made them an invaluable tool in unmasking historical forgeries.

Exposing Frauds

Forgeries and fakes, although relatively rare, have sometimes made significant impacts on the archaeological community. Some of these frauds have been successfully executed and were given immediate and long lasting credibility whereas others were exposed immediately. Some of the reasons for the appearances of forgeries and fakes include attempts to earn personal fame or prestige or a desire to demonstrate the faults in archaeological methods. Private collectors, some of whom know very little about their collections, have also opened up a big business of creating ancient artifacts from new materials, re-using ancient materials, or converting genuine artifacts into ones of greater value. Due to the number and accuracy of dating methods available today it is a lot more difficult to outsmart the archaeological world with a forgery than was the case in the past.

In the early 1900s one of the main quests in archaeology was to find the *missing link*, which was believed to be an ape-like humanoid that bridged the gap between humans and apes. This set the stage for one of the greatest and most successful frauds, which lasted several decades before it was exposed. In 1912 the *link* was found in a gravel pit in Piltdown Common in southern England. The find, consisting of a fragment of a skull and a jawbone, was sent to the British museum by Charles Dawson. Upon examination this find was proclaimed as a breakthrough since it consisted of a human-like skull and an ape-like jawbone. Evidence provided by this find added credibility to the theory that humans had evolved from apes. The Piltdown find enjoyed many years of fame until modern dating methods demonstrated that the bones were much younger than had been alleged, and that the bones had been stained and filed down. No one claimed responsibility for this famous hoax and until today it remains a mystery as to who so successfully deceived the archaeological world and why. Fakes, frauds, and forgeries elicit many questions that cannot be answered even by today's modern techniques. Yet, they do belong to the world of archaeology as a fascinating category of their own.

Analyzing Artifacts

To an archaeologist, the artifacts recovered during an excavation represent primary data, much like a diary is a primary source to a historian. Artifacts are the key to a wealth of information regarding the society being studied, but to unlock the information requires careful analysis. Artifacts can be broken down into two main categories: organic remains that are the remnants of living things such as plants and animals, and inorganic remains such as stone tools or pottery.

The best preserved organic artifacts are found in dry, hot regions, such as deserts; in freezing conditions, such as arctic regions; or in waterlogged places, such as peat bogs or the bottom of the sea. Decay caused by micro-organisms destroys underwater artifacts unless the objects lie in water that is near freezing or have been covered in silt. Interesting finds have been made in peat bogs, which are acidic in nature. The acid causes bones to decay while the flesh is preserved by the moisture and the peat. Consequently bodies are sometimes found in bogs that are remarkably well preserved but have no bones.

One of the tasks in analyzing organic material is to determine its source: Was it from the local environment or was it a product of human activity and brought to the site? For example, people are selective in the type of wood used for building and in the wood gathered for a fire. Consequently wood used in buildings may have been brought from some distance while firewood is more likely to represent the local environment.

Human remains present a special challenge to the archaeologist. Much can be learned about a people by the study of their skeletal remains. The first object in the analysis of human remains is to determine the age and sex of the person being studied. The age of young children and teens can be determined within one year by examining the teeth present in the jawbone while the age of young adults is determined by the fusion between the heads and shafts of long bones. Determining the age of adults is much less precise as it is done by studying tooth wear, which can be affected by several factors. The sex can be determined by bone structure. Males tend to have heavier and larger bones while the pelvis of a female is structurally different from a male's in order to facilitate child-bearing.

A special area of study is paleopathology or the study of ancient diseases. Childhood diseases often leave lines of slowed growth in the bones or changes in the skeleton. For example, rickets causes bow legs, a pigeon chest, and brittle bones. Other diseases such as syphilis, tuberculosis, and leprosy cause noticeable deformation and destruction of the bones in the head, spine, and limbs. Bones that show abnormal wear often reveal the occupation of a person or injuries associated with specific activities. Weapons also leave specific marks; swords leave narrow cuts, spears leave clearly defined holes, and clubs leave crushed and shattered bones.

Upon close inspection a great deal of information can be gleaned from both stone tools and pottery. A microscopic examination of the edges of stone tools will often reveal evidence of its use. For example, tools used for cutting plant stems may have a residue of silica gloss on them from the silica present in plants. The stones used in making tools were not randomly selected, but were quarried to obtain the proper type and quality. Flint, chert, and obsidian are all popular types of stones from various regions of the world. In some instances stone quarried hundreds of kilometres from a site has been found even though similar types of stone were found locally. The most plausible explanation for this is that high quality stone was prized and eagerly traded.

Pottery, the most common of all archaeological finds, has been used for over 10 000 years. The abundance of pottery sherds is because it preserves well and was a cheap everyday commodity that was discarded when broken. Even a few pieces of ancient pottery can supply a great deal of information. The degree to which the clay was worked, the techniques used in manufacturing and decorating, the firing conditions, the artistic ability of the potter, and much more can be determined by a careful examination of a few pottery sherds.

Science, Anthropology, and History

These three disciplines also belong to the world of archaeology. In applying scientific data to an archaeological find, and by using anthropology to interpret the results, a very complete historical picture can be created. This approach was used by teams working in Herculaneum, who have brought this ancient Roman city back to life. The city of Herculaneum has slumbered beneath 20 m of volcanic mud and ash, complete with buildings, furnishings, livestock and citizens—each item with a story to tell. Combining archaeology with a scientific and anthropologic interpretation, these stories are being unearthed, recovered, and retold.

Both Herculaneum and Pompeii suffered a similar fate when Mount Vesuvius unleashed its volcanic wrath in A.D. 79. The hurricane speeds of the volcanic mud and ash imprisoned residents of both cities during their rush to safety. When the excavations of the seafront chambers in Herculaneum began, skeletons and artifacts were discovered depicting a series of haunting tableaux-like scenes. These finds are of more value than similar ones in Pompeii since the wet earth and mud sealed them better than the dry pumice covering Pompeii. Many rooms and items reflecting daily life in Herculaneum remained intact. Surprising finds have been made, such as a cradle, beds, cupboards, table and chairs, fishnets, and a most valuable discovery of a Roman boat. Foodstuffs such as cereal, eggs, and vegetables have also been found. It is the interpretation of these artifacts that offers a reasonably complete picture of life in Herculaneum before the disaster and during the terrifying seconds before the victims' deaths.

To find out more detail about a skeleton, an artist, Jay H. Matternes, and a physical anthropologist, Dr. Sara Bisel have combined their talents. Dr. Bisel interprets the bone structure and Jay Matternes puts muscles and other anatomical elements on the diagrams of these skeletons. The final product would be a drawing depicting the person's appearance. The following example of one such skeleton traces this process. The soldier's bones indicated that the 37 years of his life were eventful. He had three teeth missing, which were probably lost in a fight. The top bone of his leg, the femur, gave several clues. A lump indicated a stab wound, the rounded shape indicated much exercise and that he was well fed. The bottom of the femur (at the knee) was enlarged and this may have come from horseback riding or from holding lumber between the knees, as this soldier-carpenter might have done. This "biography by bones" gives a lively and complete picture of these once-living skeletons in Herculaneum.

So what is the story told by Herculaneum? The refined houses, the size of the theatre, and the number of baths indicate that the general population consisted of a cultured and affluent people. There is a resort-town atmosphere in the orientation of the buildings overlooking the bay. Common labourers are zot as evident as are crafters and artisans, indicating more specialized occupations. Generally people were wealthy and well fed, save for the overworked and undernourished slaves.

Analyzing Historical Research

The data gathered by archaeologists is only one of the sources the historian draws on when attempting to reconstruct the past. As has been outlined previously, legends can be a rich source of inspiration and a basis from which to begin. Societies that have left written records provide the historian with a wide variety of sources to draw upon. Written accounts recorded at the time of an event are referred to as primary documents. Primary documents include such things as government documents, court transcripts, medical records, ships' logs, personal diaries, newspaper accounts, and so on. The fact that these accounts were written by eyewitnesses does not always mean they can be accepted at face value. For example, John Lok recorded in 1554 on a voyage to Guinea that he saw elephants and dragons locked in mortal combat, but withheld telling of how his men hid in a tree when an anteater appeared. The explanation for this seemingly odd report lies in the *mental baggage* of the explorers and the audience they were writing for. (Mental baggage refers to the preconceived ideas that someone has that lead them to interpret events or draw conclusions in a way consistent with their expectations.) The merchants who funded the voyage would never have believed the story of the anteater as none had ever been reported, but they fully expected dragons to be encountered in far-away exotic lands. To ensure funding for future voyages of exploration, the report told of events that the merchants could conceive of, and avoided aspects of the truth that might be unbelievable. What can be learned from this example is that the historian must take into account the mental baggage, the intended audience, and the special interests of the writer when analyzing primary documents.

Bias is another factor historians must be aware of. In the past the records of events have often been written by the victors. Richard III of England is considered by many to be a much maligned character. After losing his throne during the Wars of the Roses, Richard III was portrayed as an evil and corrupt monarch. The accounts of Richard's reign must, however, be carefully scrutinized for they were recorded by chroniclers working for his archrival Henry Tudor. Similarly, diary entries and newspaper accounts, while preserving the details of an event, may reflect the particular bias of the writer. Therefore, when dealing with primary documents the historian must carefully analyze both the facts and the source.

Aside from drawing on archaeological information and a variety of primary sources, historians also rely on secondary sources. Secondary sources are accounts written after an event, and are generally based on information contained in primary documents. Secondary sources allow the historian to establish a framework from which to begin. By drawing on the work of other historians the task becomes manageable. Secondary sources can vary from ancient texts to recent publications. Herodotus' *Histories* is a historical account of the Greek-Persian wars and is thus considered a secondary source—even though it was written over 2400 years ago!

History is like a puzzle for which we have only some of the pieces upon which we must base our conclusions. Regardless of the missing pieces, historians are often faced with the difficult task of choosing what to stress and what to ignore. The aim of all historians is to objectively interpret the events in order to reconstruct the past as accurately as possible. Despite the best efforts to remain objective the writing of history is always infused with the historian's bias. In choosing to stress one cause over another, or to focus on an aspect of history while overlooking another, historians reveal their bias. It is impossible for anyone to stress equally all causes and events or to even know and incorporate all facts into their writing, therefore, bias must remain a part of the writing of history. Thus, the challenge falls to the student of history to know the bias of the author whose work they are consulting. We must always keep in mind that our knowledge of the past is based on fragmentary evidence and the interpretation of historians and archaeologists who are fallible. It is because historians can never be absolutely certain of the past that the study of history is alive with controversy. Students should join in the controversy and the elusive quest to know the past by exploring, challenging, and questioning.

*R*econstructing the Past

The final step in the study of history is to attempt to recreate the past as accurately as possible. This requires the historian to act much like a detective, piecing together the events of the past based on limited bits of information. The process of unearthing and analyzing data provides the historian with the necessary information to reconstruct past events; however, as there are always pieces of the puzzle that are missing, a great deal of interpretation and speculation is involved. Whether it is a museum curator, a historian, an anthropologist, or a writer of historical fiction no one can ever know the past with complete certainty. Instead all of those who deal with the past attempt to present as complete a picture as they can based on available facts and conjecture. Whether reading a history book, touring a museum, or exploring a reconstructed historical site we are benefiting from the years of research, analysis, and interpretation of many professionals. Their work allows us to

Historic sites recreate the past as a living museum bringing the past to life. Sainte-Marie Among the Hurons near Midland, Ontario is one of Canada's best known historic sites. The site is a reconstruction of a Jesuit mission which was burned in 1649. The reconstruction of Sainte-Marie was based on archaeological evidence as well as written records.

glimpse the past and acquire a vivid picture of earlier societies.

Historical Fiction

Wouldn't it be nice if reading history books was as enjoyable as reading your favourite novel? The genre of **historical fiction** often makes this possible. A well researched novel can bring history to life by setting historical facts within the framework of an entertaining story.

In choosing a work of historical fiction it is important to know the author's reputation for accuracy. Even then, always remember that historical fiction is fiction, and some things in the novel may be a product of the author's imagination. If in doubt, do a little research to see if the story can be verified—there is no better way to learn history than to be inspired by a good book.

Understanding the Past CHAPTER 1

HISTORICAL FICTION

MEDIEVAL HISTORY FROM A WOMAN'S PERSPECTIVE

A Vision of Light set in fourteenth century England is a tale of joy and sorrow narrated by Margaret of Ashbury; an unforgettable character who wanted to record her experiences and thoughts in a book. The very notion of a woman writing a book was considered by many men of the fourteenth century to be arrogant and heretical. Consequently, three clerics brusquely rejected Margaret's request to be her scribe. Finally, a young cleric named Brother Gregory accepted her offer and she was able to record a story of astonishing resourcefulness; surviving the Black Death and accusations of witchcraft and of a vision of light that illuminates Margaret's soul and gave her a miraculous gift of healing.

A Vision of Light serves a timeless purpose reminding us that all people, rich or poor, male or female, have a past worth recording. While women of the Middle Ages were generally without power or influence the tale told by Margaret of Ashbury illustrates the value of studying the history of all classes. Her story is not of triumphs on the battlefield or in the political realm, it is the story of triumphs in life. Hence Margaret's story is every bit as rewarding and insightful as any told by crusading knights or warring kings. In the excerpt below the reader is introduced to Margaret of Ashbury and Brother Gregory and the stage is set for a fascinating story to unfold.

In the Year of Our Lord 1355, three days after the Feast of the Epiphany, God put in my mind that I must write a book.

"I am only a woman," I said to the voice in my mind. "I have no letters, and do not know Latin. How shall I write a book, and what shall I put in it, since I have never done any great deeds?"

The Voice answered:

"Put in it what you have seen. There is nothing wrong with being, and doing ordinary things. Sometimes small deeds can show big ideas. As for writing, do as others do: get someone to write it for you"...

It seemed like a good idea to me. The more I thought on it, the better it was. I like to hear books read, I thought, but I have never heard one about women. Sometimes my husband reads to the household from a book of travels, about the marvels that lie in far places. Sometimes we have a priest to read high thoughts and worthy meditations for the improvement of our souls. I would like to hear a book read such as the one the Voice told me about.

I told my husband that a Voice in my mind which was clearly from God told me to have a book. He answered, "Another voice again, eh? Well, what is my money for, but to indulge my sweet poppet? If you wish a book, you may have it, as far as I'm concerned. But I must warn you

The Writing of History

Historians, much like the curators of museums and historic sites, attempt to reconstruct the past. Much of this chapter has focused on the gathering and analyzing of information whether it be archaeological or historical data. The historian's craft is one of that it will be no easy thing to find a priest to write for you."

... The first priest I asked grew angry and refused all money for such a task. He looked at me with his sharp eyes and said, "Who put this in your mind, the Devil? He often plants improper desires in women. Women have no reason to write anything at all. They do not take part in great deeds, nor do they think sublime thoughts. These two things are the only proper reasons for writing books. The rest are all vanity, and will lead others into sin. Go home and serve your husband, and thank God that He has made you humble."

I was very discouraged.

"Voice," I said, "you've got me a tongue lashing, and I'm sad."

The Voice said, "Keep at it Margaret. I didn't think you were the sort of person who gave up so easily."

"It's really too much for me this time. Everyone's always telling me what's impossible, and maybe this time they're right. No man wants to write down what a woman has to say."

"You just haven't found the right one yet," said the Voice. "Keep on looking."

... The woman hesitated for a moment, looking Brother Gregory up and down, and then said firmly, "I need a clerk who can write."

"That is self-evident," responded Brother Gregory, inspecting her more closely. Rich, very rich, he concluded. And self-willed too.

"I mean write, really write." They've played a joke on me, those cathedral clerks, thought Margaret. The man's a beggar—one of those vagabond thieves who dress up like friars to get money..."

"I can write," said Brother Gregory, with calm arrogance. "I can write Latin, French, and common English. I will not, however, write in German; it is a barbaric tongue that curdles the ink."

He speaks properly, thought Margaret. Not like a peasant or a foreigner. I'll try him. So she plunged on: "I need a clerk who can write a whole book."

"A copyist for a book of prayers? I can do that."

"No—a book, a book about women? A book about me."

Brother Gregory was shocked. ... She was spoiled to the bone. What foolish rich man was indulging these insane fantasies?...

Brother Gregory lifted the heavy brass door-knocker. In a few moments he had been shown to a place where he might wait in the great hall. As he sat on a bench, inspecting the painted seal on the chimney over the great hearth, his matted sheepskin cloak beside him, he wondered how long it would be before she tired of the project...

..."Where do you wish to begin?" asked Brother Gregory.

"At the beginning, when I was little," answered Margaret.

"So you've been hearing voices since you were little?" Brother Gregory's own voice was bemused.

"Oh no, when I was little I was just like everyone else. The only voices I heard were mother's and father's. They didn't like the way I was turning out. But that is the way it is with parents. Some children just work out better than others. So I thought I'd start there—with my family, and how things began differently than they ended..."

research, analysis, and synthesis. Using the information they have managed to gather, historians present their version of what happened in the past.

History is in many ways a strenuous discipline, it is not simply a matter of remembering names, dates, and events. Historical studies involve gathering information from a variety of primary and secondary sources, analyzing the information, and finally synthesizing the material in order to present the finds in a coherent fashion. Many skills are required to be successful in studying history. Students of history must develop good research skills in order to gather the necessary information. This entails knowing where to look for information, how to read efficiently, and how to make good notes. Organizational skills are also essential. Information is gathered randomly and must be organized if an intelligible essay or seminar is to be presented. Even the notes taken day-to-day in a classroom need to be well organized if students hope to survive the deluge of information they face.

For the hard work of research to pay off the student of history must be able to effectively analyze and evaluate the information gathered. Often far too much information is available and choices must be made as to which facts are necessary and which can be overlooked. Analysis requires good thinking skills. Thinking divergently and creatively allows the historian to see patterns where none seem to exist and to come up with innovative and new interpretations of the facts.

Finally, the gathering and analyzing of information is of limited value if it is not clearly presented. Presenting a lucid picture of the past requires a synthesis of the information. Also essential is the ability to write and speak effectively. If the information and analysis is not presented in an effective manner then the effort may have been wasted.

The aim of *Odyssey Through the Ages* is to enrich your understanding of the past as well as of a variety of cultures from around the world. Vivid descriptions of many of the world's great civilizations are brought to life with numerous photographs, illustrations, and feature studies. Be sure to pause long enough to enjoy the various selections of historical fiction or to imagine the festivities and banquets enjoyed by diverse people throughout the ages and around the world. *Odyssey Through The Ages* will broaden your knowledge of the past and the world around you, while assisting you in the development of skills that will be critical for your success in education and in future careers.

Suggested Sources for Further Research

Adkins, Lesley and Roy Adkins, *An Introduction To Archaeology* (New Burlington Books, 1989).

Carr, E.H., *What is History?* (Penguin Books, 1981).

Cavendish, Richard, *Legends of the World* (Schocken Books, 1982).

Lockery, Andy, *Marine Archaeology and the Diver* (Atlantis Publishing, 1985).

MacIntosh, Jane, *The Practical Archaeologist* (Facts on File Publications, 1986).

Marwick, Arthur, *The Nature of History* (The Macmillan Press Ltd., 1970).

Thorndike, Joseph J. Jr., *Mysteries of the Past* (American Heritage Publishing Co., 1977).

Focus Your Knowledge
▼▼▼

1. What are the major difficulties historians face in writing history?
2. Why can it be said that archaeology is a means to an end but not an end in itself?
3. Briefly outline the stages archaeologists go through in preparing and executing a dig.
4. What additional factors must the underwater archaeologist contend with in their work?
5. How have improved dating techniques assisted in exposing frauds?

Apply Your Knowledge
▼▼▼

1. How have legends assisted in our understanding of the past? What legends can you think of which may provide clues to the past? What aspect of the legend would you focus on in attempting to unearth the past?
2. Which method of dating ancient artifacts do you feel would be more reliable; stratigraphy or radio-carbon dating? Why?
3. Prepare a chart as follows to summarize the information that can be obtained from various artifacts.

Organic Remains	Human Remains	Tools and Pottery

4. Using Herculaneum as an example, explain how science and anthropology are helping us to understand the past.

UNIT 1

Civilizations of the Near and Far East

CHAPTER 2
Humanity Before Civilization

CHAPTER 3
Egypt and the Near East

CHAPTER 4
Ancient India

CHAPTER 5
Chinese Civilization

Common to most societies is the question of human origins. This unit begins by addressing this very question: Where did we come from and what is our place in the world? By comparing a variety of stories of creation and examining the evidence for evolution, Chapter 2 provides a fascinating look at the origins of humanity. The chapter concludes with a focus on the Neolithic Revolution and its significance to the emergence of the first civilizations.

The remaining three chapters of this unit provide a look at some of the earliest civilizations of the world including Mesopotamia, Egypt, China, and India. The common thread throughout these chapters is the role that major rivers played in the development of the civilizations. While the rivers around which each civilization settled allowed for permanent cities to arise and the development of complex societies, each region produced a unique culture which was the product of the environment and the people.

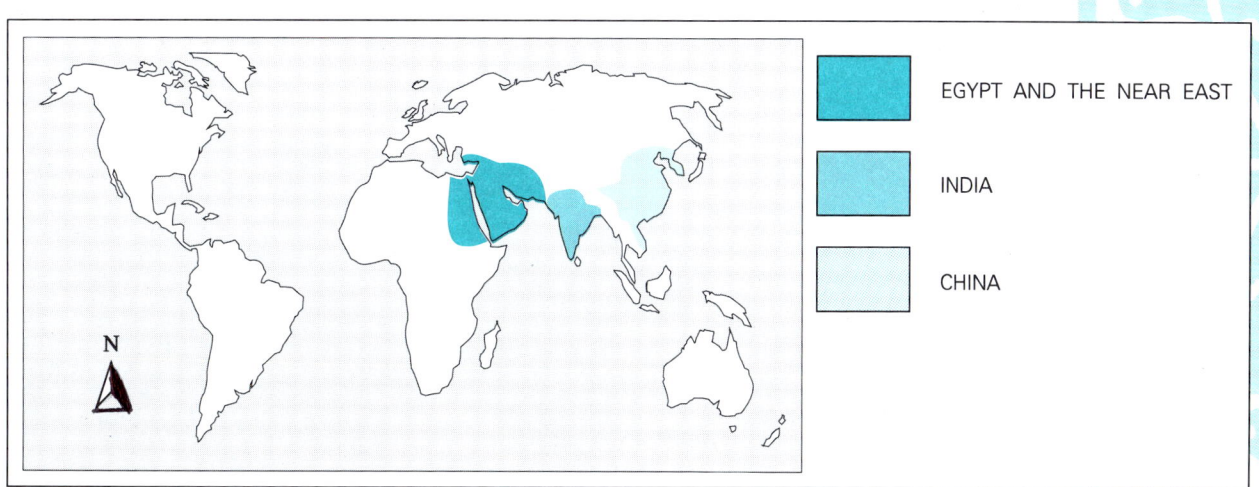

CHAPTER 2

Humanity Before Civilization

Chapter Highlights

- stories of creation from around the world

- Charles Darwin's theory of evolution

- our 3-million-year old ancestor named Lucy

- the role of science in unravelling the past

- Neanderthals, who they were and what happened to them

- living in the Upper Paleolithic Age

- the Neolithic Revolution

Have you ever pondered how old the earth is? Scientists estimate the age of the earth to be between 4.5 and 5 billion years old. For most people the concept of deep time is difficult to grasp. How old is 5 billion years? Perhaps by using an analogy we can begin to appreciate how old the earth really is.

We consider the Upper Paleolithic Age, which began about 50 000 years ago with the appearance of the first fully modern humans, the very distant past. Relative to the history of the earth, the time from the Upper Paleolithic Age to the present represents about four minutes out of a year. So you see, the earth is almost incomprehensibly old and human history is but a minuscule part of the history of the earth. Similarly, the history of **civilizations**, which is the focus of this book, is but a fraction of the history of humanity. Before immersing ourselves in the story of civilization it will be useful to examine humanity before civilization and to ponder our origins.

Common to all cultures and societies is a story of creation. A story that explains the origin of the earth and all its inhabitants. Many stories of creation establish a hierarchy in which humans are given dominion over the animals. Over the past century and a half scientists have provided an alternate explanation, one that seriously challenges long held religious beliefs. They have shown that humans, like all animals, have evolved over millions of years and suggest that all living things share a common ancestor. Thus, science suggests that humans are not the result of a separate creation, but are simply more advanced intellectually than other animals. Furthermore, the earth is not the private domain of humans but belongs to all living things. People, therefore, have an obligation to protect the environment and endangered species.

The focus of this chapter is the period of time from the origins of humanity to the eve of civilization. The first section of the chapter is a comparative look at various stories of creation and is followed by a discussion of the theory of evolution. The remainder of the chapter traces the history of humanity from the earliest hominids to the eve of civilization including a look at life in the **Paleolithic** and **Neolithic** Ages.

Key Concepts

civilizations
Charles Darwin
natural selection
chance mutation
Homo sapiens
"Lucy"
Neanderthal
Lascaux Caves

Stories of Creation

The summaries of these creation stories chosen are representative of the civilizations covered in this text. The beliefs and ideas held by these civilizations about the origins of humanity and the earth appear in various forms, from a simple account listing events in the order of occurrence to a complex narrative that details the creation of humans, their environment, and the rest of the cosmos. Many of these stories were not intended as factual accounts and were not intended for a literal interpretation. Yet, they are valid accounts, if even only in a symbolic or spiritual sense and are important as part of the beliefs of a civilization.

Mesopotamia

The oldest written records of a religion and of the story of creation date back to ancient Mesopotamia, which is today modern Iraq. The creation of the universe was conceived in human terms explaining life to the Mesopotamians as they knew it; hence, it was a depiction created by people for people. The main creation roles were played by four gods: An, the god of heaven; Enlil, the air god; Enki, the water god; and the mother-earth goddess who had various names. These supreme deities planned out and created the main components of the universe and then delegated these components to their offspring to rule.

Nammu, the **primeval** goddess, gave birth to the heaven, the sea, and the earth. Enlil, the lord of the gods and the king of the universe, gave the heavens to the father An and the earth to the mother Ki. An's domain took the shape of a great domed roof containing the sky, the stars, the moon, and the sun, which lighted Ki's realm and the cities in it. Beneath the earth swirled the underworld, the fearsome home of the demons and the kingdom of the dead.

The children of the heaven-god An were called the Anunnaki. They were unhappy, hungry, and without clothes. They did not know how to make and eat bread, nor did they know how to wear clothes. They ate plants and drank water like animals. To provide for these divine children, Enlil, the air god, and Enki, the water god, created cattle, sheep, plants, the yoke and plow, and the pickaxe. Enlil and Enki expected them to become active, well fed, and happy. Enlil also provided *me* (pronounced may), a set of universal laws governing everything that existed. These laws ensured that the universe would operate in an orderly and effective manner. Enlil himself broke one of these laws by exhibiting human weakness. He was banished to the underworld for committing rape; the product of this encounter was the moon god Nanna.

Enki organized the earth by assigning various degrees of prosperity to lands and cities and by supplying everything necessary to make the earth fruitful. He poured pure water into the rivers, filled the marshes with fish and reeds, made the rain fall, put the grain in the fields, and built stalls for the livestock.

Two versions recount what happened next. One version relates that the divine Anunnaki remained unskilled and hungry and could not make use of the bountiful resources of the earth. The other version tells that the lesser gods protested and struck because they had worked too hard digging irrigation trenches and labouring in the fields. In both cases the solution to the problem was to create another being to take over earthly tasks and to serve the gods. Humans were fashioned from clay, and perhaps the blood of a god slaughtered for that purpose. Human beings were quite conscious of their role as slaves and servants to the gods: their work allowed the gods freedom from the drudgery of everyday life. The structure of Mesopotamian society clearly reflected this frame of mind, since Mesopotamians were quite content providing for their gods first of all and then themselves.

Egypt

The Egyptians, as the Mesopotamians before them, had their most important gods responsible for creation. This is the case with most creation stories since making something out of the primordial chaos is a job befitting only the most important and influential gods. Several different versions of the creation story exist, hence it is necessary to specify that only the most popular stories, from Heliopolis and Memphis, will be discussed.

The earth was created when a primeval hill, the first solid matter, emerged from the waters of chaos. This was a natural assumption for ancient Egyptians as they often saw islands of mud appearing in the Nile, or existing areas becoming islands during the annual inundation. The myth from Memphis differs slightly in detail. The earth emerged from a lotus flower, which was born from the same chaotic waters. Atum, the creator god, simply emerged standing on the first hill that rose from the water. Atum, "the perfect one" was self-begotten. He then ejected from his being Shu, the air, and Tefenet, the moisture. Next he separated the sky from the earth and Geb, the earth, and Nut, the sky, came into being. Geb and Nut then joined and had children who were the gods Osiris, Isis, Seth, and Nephthys. This group of deities formed the first unit in the divine hierarchy of gods worshipped in Heliopolis.

The story from Memphis tells that the artisan-god Khnum sat at his potter's wheel fashioning living beings out of clay and at the same time created their *ka*, which was their spiritual duplicate. In this story the creation of the gods is prominent. Other Egyptian deities exist without identification to a particular story: instead they are associated with a particular aspect of the world such as crafts, the sun, or a city.

China

China is unique among the major civilizations in that for the first 2000 years of its existence, it lacked a creation story. In fact, compared to those traditions whose pantheons are filled with gods and goddesses, heroes and heroines, epics, and battles, the Chinese pantheon is scant, impoverished and episodic. In the early accounts of history the earth's existence is taken for granted and is not explained. The creator of the universe does not appear until much later.

It was not until the third century A.D. that Chinese literature mentions a creator-figure. Pan Gu was a legendary giant whose axe, or whose rapid growth, separated the heavens from the earth. At about the same time, there appeared the figure of Yi, the divine archer, who shot down six of the seven suns in the sky. Yi's wife, fleeing his anger when she stole his elixir of immortality, became the Lady in the Moon. These legends, however, are folkloric traditions and the more official versions of the beginning of history are quite different and more rational in approach.

According to China's first historical work, dating from the first century B.C., the universe was originally a cosmic egg with the heavens above and the "four-cornered" earth below. China was thought to be the centre of the earth. Three earthly rulers, over the space of 54 000 years, gave the world its natural features. They were followed by the Five Sage-kings who ruled, traditionally, from 2750–2250 B.C. It was these five men, altruistic though not heroic, who provided the Chinese people with the essential aspects of civilization: writing, agriculture, medicine, music, family and marriage laws, and even taxes. The best known of them is the Yellow Emperor, Huangdi, who later came to be the ruler of Heaven, and whose wife, the sole prominent female in Chinese mythology, gave her people the gift of **sericulture** (cultivating silkworms).

India

Nearly all of our understanding of the origins of Indian beliefs is derived from the Vedas. The Vedas are books of knowledge containing all the sacred lore of the early period. Earlier versions of the creation stories are entertaining and colourful accounts of folklore. The Hindu creation story evolved much later and explained the origin of the earth and of the *triad*. The *triad* represents the three aspects of the Supreme Being; Brahma, the creator, Vishnu, the preserver, and Shiva, the destroyer.

The Spirit of the Supreme Being was personified by a golden lotus on a great sea. From Vishnu, the first element of the Hindu Trinity, the "lotus navelled," came a lotus on which sat Brahma the lotus-born creator. Brahma is the second element, the creator god and also the father of gods and humanity. According to the story he had always existed without distinct parts, and then suddenly appeared. He produced the waters and put his seed into them and they became a brilliant golden egg, and he was born out of this egg as Brahma, the first father of the world. He then divided the egg in two and made heaven and earth out of the two halves. Brahma first created a woman from himself and she was so lovely that he fell in love with her. They married and lived together creating all kinds of living things. Shiva, the third element of the Hindu trinity, probably the Vedic storm god, became the lord of the cosmic dance of creation and destruction, this being necessary so the world could be created again. From this story of creation comes not only the creation of the world and its occupants, but also the explanation for the Hindu Trinity who are ever present and who represent the Supreme Being in different roles.

Greece and Rome

Among the most timeless and memorable stories are those of ancient Greece. So inspiring were the tales of the Greek gods that the Romans saw fit to adopt the mythology of the Greeks in all but name. Hence, in recording the story of creation for these two great civilizations, we refer to the Graeco-Roman stories. To avoid confusion and to credit the rightful originators the Greek names have been maintained throughout this account.

In the beginning there existed only a formless swirling chaos. All the materials that would be utilized in creation swirled around in disorder in the cosmic dust. Suddenly Gaea, the great earth-mother, emerged from the chaos. In succession behind her came Erebos, the darkness; Aether, the light; Pontus, the sea; and Eros, love. In her first sleep Gaea gave birth to her mate, the lord of the heavens, Uranus. With the help of Eros, they blessed the world and created trees and bushes, flowers and gourds, and all the creatures that crawled, ran, and flew. Uranus contributed by providing the rain that filled all the hollow basins in the world and into these set all swimming animals. The first children resulting from the union of Uranus and Gaea were the horrific Hundred Handed Monsters who had fifty heads and arms, which swirled in every direction. Gaea was pleased since they were well suited to perform the tasks she assigned. The next set of children were not much handsomer; they were the three Cyclops, thunder, lightning, and brightness. These children were incredibly clever and began building sturdy stone walls and hammering weapons immediately. Uranus, the father, was afraid of their rebellious spirit and banished them to the underworld of Tartarus immediately.

Gaea's next three children were the towering Titans, among them the shrewd Cronus who led his brothers and sisters to overthrow his father Uranus.

Cronus, his brothers and sisters, ruled the world with Cronus as the leader. The Titans married and had children, among these Helius, the sun, Silene the moon, and Eos the dawn. The Titans, Coeus and Phoebe had children who provided the model upon which humanity was based. Cronus feeling secure on his throne took a fellow Titan, Rhea, as his wife. He remembered his father's prophecy, "One of your own children will seize your sovereignty from you, as you have done from me." To prevent the prophecy from being fulfilled he swallowed his five children. Rhea was shocked and designed a clever plan to save the next child. Rhea went to Arcadia and under the dark mantle of night gave birth to her son Zeus who she protected by hiding him in a cradle in a tree. When Zeus was full grown his mother told him about the circumstances of his birth. In vengeance Zeus gave Cronus a mixture to drink that caused him to spit forth all his children who were now fully grown. The children rebelled and took up arms against Cronus.

Zeus, his brothers and sisters, the Giants, and the Cyclopes waged war against Cronus and the Titans. The Titans were terrified by the deluge of attackers and weapons. Once vanquished, Zeus sealed them all in Tartarus.

Zeus became the father of humanity and ruled over the three levels of existence; the airy bright world of the gods on Mount Olympus, the earth and all who resided there, and the dark menacing world of Tartarus.

*I*slam

The common heritage shared by all Islamic countries is the Koran, the written record of the word of God as revealed to the prophet Muhammad during the early seventh century A.D. Many of the ideas and characters that appear in the Koran are equivalent to those appearing in the Judaeo-Christian religions, for example, the story of Adam.

God moulded Adam's body from the dust of many colours that came from all over the earth. He left Adam inert for 120 years between Mecca and Taif. During this time an angel known as Iblis or Satan crept up to the lifeless mould and left a black spot. God returned and breathed the Holy Spirit into the body, giving it life, and set this creation above the angels. Stubborn Iblis refused to bow down to Adam and for this was expelled from paradise. Paradise was guarded by a peacock and Iblis bribed the bird to allow him to enter. Together with the serpent he acted out his plan for revenge. Adam and Eve were fascinated by the forbidden fruit and succumbed to the serpent's suggestion to try it. Once they did, their shell-like covering split open and everything fell off except their fingernails and their toenails.

God expelled both Adam and Eve from paradise and they fell to earth. Adam dropped on Mount Sarandib in Sri Lanka. This being the highest of mountains Adam was still able to reach heaven and talk with the angels. Furious, God reduced his height to about 30 m. Eve fell at Jedda in Arabia, Iblis and the peacock fell into India, and the serpent fell into Iran. Adam lived at Sarandib for 200–300 years where he was taught many skills by the angel Gabriel. He learned farming, spinning, weaving, mining, medicine, music, and geometry.

God finally accepted Adam's repentance and sent him to Mecca to live in a house carved out of a ruby. He was reunited with Eve and became the father of humanity, teaching his children all the techniques and skills he had acquired. This story is characterized by the fact that it assumes the existence already of a God and of earth and deals exclusively with the creation of humans and the establishment of a lifestyle on earth.

*J*apan

Japanese mythology, first written down in the Kojiki, Record of Ancient Matters, in A.D. 712, is colourful

The Japanese children Zzangi and his sister Izanami are creating an island by stirring the waters of the sea with their heavenly lance. Then they descend to live on the beautiful island that they have created. Their offspring are the other islands, the mountains, the rivers and the flora and fauna, as well as other deities. (From the William Sturgis Bigelow Collection. Courtesy of the Museum of Fine Arts, Boston.)

and much concerned with nature. According to the legends, a god and goddess, brother and sister, created the earth by stirring the oceans until land masses formed. Impressed by the beauty of the Japanese islands, they descended from the Plain of High Heaven to dwell there, and their offspring became the mountains and rivers, and flora and fauna of the earth. While giving birth to fire, the goddess died and her brother, like Orpheus in Greek mythology, unsuccessfully tried to rescue her from the Land of the Dead. After his return to earth, he bathed to purify himself and from his eyes were born the goddesses of the Sun and the Moon, and from his nose, their brother, the god of Wind and Storm. Amaterasu, the Sun Goddess often the object of insults from her quarrelsome brother, finally refused to shine her light unless he were tamed. The other deities exiled him from their midst, and thus Amaterasu became supreme. Her grandson's grandson, a man called Jimmu, became the first emperor of Japan in 660 B.C.

Although the first emperor exists only in legend, later Japanese rulers all claimed direct descent from him. The imperial line of Japan, therefore, is considered the longest unbroken succession of rulers in world history. Even today, the emperor of Japan carries out worship of the Sun Goddess and possesses as his crown jewels the regalia of Amaterasu, a mirror, a sword, and a jewel.

Maya

The Maya believed that creation had already occurred several times prior to the most recent creation. Each time the earth was destroyed by a calamity, only to be created again. The supreme being in charge of this was Itzamn'a; he was the creator of human life, the inventor of books and writing, and the patron of science and learning. He ruled over day and night, the heavens, the earth, and the sky. His rather unflattering portrait shows him as being old, having a large nose, toothless jaws, and hollow cheeks. Below him exist a multitude of gods, among them Ah Kindril, the sun god, Ah Puch, the lord of death, Ek Chua, the guardian god of merchants and travellers, Xaman Ek, the ruler of the North Star, and Chac who ruled over the four domains of rainmaking, thunder, lightning, and storms.

The Maya developed in detail the concept of cosmology. Rather than constructing elaborate stories about the creation of the gods, the world, and humanity, they designed a very complex integration of these elements into a world view. The world was believed to be resting on the back of a giant crocodile floating on a lily pond. The world was divided into three levels of existence on a vertical axis, the underworld, the earth, and the sky. There were 13 heavens and 9 underworlds arranged in layers, with the earth resting as a flat four-sided plane (defined by the geographical directions) between them. Humanity was believed to exist at the centre of this three-fold vertical axis and the four-sided horizontal plane.

The Judaeo-Christian Story of Creation

The Biblical story is taken from Genesis, the first book of the Old Testament. Again, the ultimate being, God, is instrumental in the creation of the earth and of humanity and it is interesting to note that as in other stories he is also creating from primordial chaos. In the Judaeo-Christian story of creation the chaotic darkness had no shape and was submerged in water. God saw this chaos and began separating elements. First he created light to divide the darkness into night and day. Then he made dry land appear that parted the oceans and the seas and on this land he placed all kinds of grasses, fruits, and trees. God created more lights to divide day and night and also to be the indications used for separating seasons and for counting days and years. The largest light, the sun was used for the day; the rest, namely the moon and the stars, were used for the night. Into the sea, onto the ground, and into the air God placed an abundance of animals of every kind and he bade them to be fruitful and to multiply. Then God created a man out of the dust of the ground in his own image, and gave him life by breathing into his nostrils. He placed this man in a garden called Eden, which God had planted, and gave him control over all the animals of the earth. God brought all these animals to Adam who named them. Adam did not find a companion among these animals and God saw that Adam felt lonely so God caused him to go into a deep sleep. He took one of his ribs and made a woman. When God brought her to Adam, he said that because she was of his flesh and bones he would call her woman. God blessed the couple and encouraged them to be fruitful and to multiply and again gave them authority over the earth and the animals that he had created.

It is interesting to note that in ancient civilizations the question of origin was as pressing and as important to people as it still is today. The approach to the question has developed over the centuries from creating mythological explanations to research and interpretations using very sophisticated scientific methods. The answer to the question "Where are we from?" has moved from stories and beliefs to very complex and not always compatible scientific theories.

The Theory of Evolution

For centuries a literal interpretation of the biblical story of creation went unchallenged. James Ussher, an eighteenth century Irish archbishop, carefully retraced the events of the Bible to determine the year of creation. His calculations, which agreed with those of another cleric who was working independently of Ussher, placed the time of creation at 9:00 am on October 23, 4004 B.C. Aside from accepting Ussher's date for creation most nineteenth century Europeans believed in the *Great Chain of Being* whereby all living organisms were created in their ultimate form and ranked from the simplest to the most complex. Of course, at the top were humans. There was no doubt in people's minds that the world operated according to a divinely inspired plan.

In 1859 **Charles Darwin** published his highly controversial book, *The Origin of Species*, which presented a direct challenge to the biblical account of creation. Although the concept of evolution had been prominent in intellectual circles for some time, it was Darwin's work that brought the debate of evolution to the foreground.

Charles Darwin

Charles Darwin was born in 1809 to parents from two of England's most distinguished families. His father was a doctor and his grandfather, Erasmus Darwin, was a prominent doctor and biologist. His mother was the daughter of Josiah Wedgewood who was the founder of the famous Wedgewood pottery. Darwin first entered Edinburgh University with the intention of becoming a medical doctor. He soon found medicine not to his liking and moved to Cambridge with the intention of becoming an Anglican priest. While at Cambridge, Darwin became fascinated with science and biology in particular. With the help of his mentor and friend, Professor John Stevens Henslow, Darwin was able to secure the position of naturalist on the H.M.S. *Beagle*. For five years, from 1831 to 1836, the *Beagle* circumnavigated the globe. This period was of profound significance to Darwin and ultimately to the western world. Darwin himself wrote; "The voyage of the *Beagle* has been by far the most important event in my life and has determined my whole career...." Prior to 1830 Darwin believed that God had made an organic world and a physical world in which the organic was perfectly adapted to the physical. By 1837 his experiences on the *Beagle* voyage had caused Darwin to change his views. He came to believe that the direct action of the physical world induced biological adaptations. This new belief focused on change as an essential feature in the survival of a **species**. The one thing missing was the mechanism of change. Darwin stumbled onto the answer of this riddle while reading Thomas Malthus's *Essay On Population*. Malthus had concluded that because population increased in a geometric progression (1,2,4,16,246...) while food production increased arithmetically (1,2,3,4,5...) the resulting conflict would produce natural laws of struggle. Darwin picked up on Malthus's idea of a struggle for survival and applied it to plants and animals. This provided him with the concepts of natural law and natural pressure that he used to formulate his theory of evolution by **natural selection**.

Absent from Darwin's theory of natural selection was the negativism of the Malthusian view. Darwin's idea stressed the progress and improvement of a species created by over-population and the struggle for scarce resources: a struggle that eventually leads to the survival of the fittest. Those with favourable variations would be better suited to the environment; they would survive and thus pass on, through heredity, those favourable variations. Those with variations detrimental to their well-being would die thereby preventing negative mutations from being passed on. For example, a giraffe born with a longer neck could more easily reach leaves and was, therefore, better equipped than a short-necked giraffe to access food. In the competition for food the long-necked giraffe would survive and pass on this positive variation while the short-necked giraffe would die. In this way Darwin explained how species progressively evolve through natural selection and are, at any given time, the best suited to the environment.

After 20 more years of gathering massive amounts of facts and observations to substantiate his theory, Charles Darwin published *The Origin of Species by Means of Natural Selection, or the Preservation of the Favoured Races in the Struggle For Life* in 1859. The public's reaction was immediate and vigorous. The first printing of the book sold out in one day. Suddenly the theories of evolution and natural selection became central to the lives of everyone, as heated debates broke out in newspapers, magazines, and scientific assemblies. Darwin's work presented the first serious challenge to the biblical view of creation. He had provided the mechanism for change and backed up his theory with hundreds of pages of facts and observations. Furthermore, the theory of natural selection denied the existence of a divine plan and suggested instead that competition for scarce resources determined who would survive.

Since the publication of Darwin's *The Origin of Species* the theory of evolution has been further developed and refined. The first major addition to Darwin's work came in 1865 when Gregory Mendel theorized on the laws of genetic inheritance after studying changes in the colour of pea flowers over successive generations. Mendel's discoveries led to a new science called genetics. Although Mendel had identified genes as the carriers of traits he did not know exactly what genes were or how the genetic information was carried. The answer to these questions was supplied by James Watson and Francis Crick in 1953 when they showed that genetic information was carried on chromosomes that are long thread-like molecules composed of DNA (deoxyribonucleic acid). Each link, or gene, in the chromosome is composed of thousands of bits of genetically coded information. The order of the genes provides the code that determines all inherited characteristics within an individual. Theoretically DNA molecules should be duplicated with 100% accuracy, but they are not. Random errors in DNA occur in all living forms. Although the errors are often meaningless, they sometimes produce variations or mutations in the offspring. The result of negative mutations is that survival is more difficult and hence the variations often die out. Positive mutations, however, are passed on as they result in the organism being better suited for survival.

The concept of **chance mutation** supplemented Darwin's work by explaining the process by which changes occur in a species. The theory of natural selection through chance mutation is the synthesis of many years of work by many scholars. Summarized it states that over millions of years chance mutations have altered the traits of species. Changes that have benefited an organism have made it better suited for survival while changes detrimental to an organism have led to its demise. Through this process of natural selection, or survival of the fittest, the plants and animals that inhabit the earth have changed and diversified. While some species have become extinct, others have changed beyond recognition. For example, the ancestor to the modern horse, Eohippus, which lived 50 million years ago, measured about 25 cm high and weighed less than 5 k!

In the nearly century and a half since Darwin published *The Origin of Species*, numerous discoveries of fossilized bones of creatures neither fully human nor ape have led many to conclude that the world is billions of years old and that our human ancestry extends millions of years into the past. Others remain unconvinced of the theory of evolution, citing gaps in the fossil record as proof that science does not hold all the answers to the origins of humanity.

The History of Human Evolution

Our Early Ancestors

The quest to trace our human ancestry has intensified in the past 30 years, as major new fossil finds and advances in science have unlocked secrets of the distant past. As a result scientists can now trace our lineage as bipedal creatures back four to five million years. What still remains a mystery is the point at which **hominids** diverged from **primates** and began the long journey to becoming a modern *Homo sapiens*. There are many questions regarding our early ancestors. The answers being supplied by archaeologists, anthropologists, and scientists are sketchy and remain shrouded in controversy. Until 1980 most experts believed that man and ape diverged from a common ancestor about 15 million years ago. This belief was based on jawbones of a small-brained primate called Ramapithecus that was believed to have human traits. The discovery of two complete skulls of Ramapithecus in Pakistan have convinced **paleontologists** that Ramapithecus is in fact the precursor to the orangutan not humans. Other fossil finds and genetic research support this conclusion that the suggested split came about eight million years ago. Many of the finds, and the theories they have generated, have shed much light on our evolutionary past while at the same time generating a great deal of controversy.

One of the most important and controversial finds was made by Dr. Donald Johanson in 1974. At Hadar, Ethiopia, Johanson and a team of international specialists unearthed a nearly complete skeleton of a 106 cm tall female that was three million years old. The diminutive skeleton was nicknamed **Lucy** after the Beatles song "Lucy In The Sky With Diamonds," which happened to be playing on the camp radio the day she was discovered. The discovery of Lucy as well as bits of more than 60 other individuals dating to the same period led to the naming of a new species, Australopithecus afarensis. Johanson considers Lucy a pivotal link between humans and apes as he believes she was completely bipedal, meaning she could stand and walk upright. According to Johanson, Lucy was "without question a hominid—a member of erect-walking primates to which we, Homo sapiens, belong and of which we are the sole surviving representatives." The discovery of Lucy was a shock to many experts who had believed that a large brain was the key to human development. Despite having a brain the size of a small chimpanzee, Lucy's pelvic structure was similar to that of a modern woman.

Four years after the discovery of Lucy, bipedalism was pushed back a further 500 000 years by the discovery of footprints in the Laetoli Beds in Tanzania. The discovery was made by Dr. Mary Leakey. The Laetoli Beds are a plain that were repeatedly covered with a thin layer of ash spewed from an ancient volcano, called Sadiman. During the rainy seasons of 3.6 million years ago the ash was moistened as it fell and then hardened, preserving in remarkable detail the footprints of the creatures who roamed this area. Among the footprints found by Mary Leakey were those of guinea fowl, elephants, giraffes, ostrich, hares, and most significantly a double trail of hominid tracks; all frozen in time 3.6 million years ago! These footprints confirmed two very important points; that human ancestors walked upright as early as 3.6 million years ago, and that the form of their feet was identical to ours.

On the Laetoli plain in Tanzania, tracks of hominids and many animals were discovered. The footprints made in the dampened ash spewing from an ancient volcano remained hidden, only to be discovered by Dr. Mary Leakey over 3.5 million years later. This scene is an artist's conception of what this moment, captured only in these footprints, might have looked like.

Bipedalism was of fundamental importance in the evolution of humanity. It freed the hands, allowing for a multitude of tasks to be carried out including carrying, toolmaking, and intricate manipulation. Essentially all modern technology stems from the freedom hominids gained by walking upright. So where do the hominids of Laetoli fit into the rise of modern humans? This question provokes one of the most spirited debates in **paleoanthropology**. Some scientists, such as Donald Johanson, believe the footprints belong to the Australopithecus afarensis species and are, therefore, earlier relatives of Lucy, while others believe the footprints belong to the Australopithecus africanus species. Like all of the other debates related to the study of paleoanthropology, the controversy will only be resolved through further discoveries and analysis.

In 1984 Richard Leakey and Alan Walker unearthed the most complete Homo erectus skeleton ever found. The discovery, made on the west shore of Kenya's Lake Turkana, was of a 12 year old boy from 1.6 million years ago. The boy, at 160 cm tall was surprisingly large for his age and would probably have reached a height of 180 cm had he not died prematurely. Other than a low forehead and a beetle brow, Homo erectus were similar in appearance to modern humans. Their brains were smaller than ours and their build was heavier, but otherwise if dressed appropriately they would not look out of place in a crowd today. As early as 1.4 million years ago Homo erectus had learned to use and control fire. This allowed them to spread into the temperate regions of Europe and Asia, making them the first hominids to live outside of Africa.

The finds of Donald Johanson, Mary Leakey, and Richard Leakey are but a few of the numerous discoveries that have contributed to our understanding of our human ancestry. New discoveries are being made all the time and are challenging the theories of experts. With each new discovery, each challenge to a theory, and the application of recent scientific innovations, we edge closer to answering the riddle of our family tree.

Human Evolutionary Theory

What if we were to attempt a brief synopsis of the human evolutionary path based on current knowl-

PRIMARY DOCUMENT

THE SCOPES' MONKEY TRIAL

Darwin's theory of evolution created a furor that was eventually felt by pupils and teachers. In 1925 the Tennessee state legislature passed a law banning the teaching of evolution in public schools. When John T. Scopes challenged the law by continuing to teach evolution he was charged, found guilty, and fined $100. The trial drew national attention as Clarence Darrow and William Jennings Bryan debated the states' role in education. Darrow, acting in defense of Scopes, argued in favour of intellectual and religious freedom and against the states' interference. Bryan, an evangelical Christian and staunch opponent of evolution, argued that evolution was not fact and that it undermined students' faith in Christianity and their Christian morals. Below are excerpts from the arguments presented by both Darrow and Bryan.

Clarence Darrow

The Bible is not one book. The Bible is made up of 66 books written over a period of about 1,000 years, some of them very early and some of them comparatively late. It is a book primarily of religion and morals. It is not a book of science. Never was and was never meant to be. Under it there is nothing prescribed that would tell you how to build a railroad or a steamboat or to make anything that would advance civilization. It is not a textbook or a text on chemistry. It is not big enough to be. It is not a book on geology; they knew nothing about it. It is not a work on evolution; that is a mystery....

And along comes somebody who says "we have got to believe it as I believe it. It is a crime to know more than I know." And they published a law to inhibit learning. Now, what is in the way of it? First, what does the law say? This law says that it shall be a criminal offense to teach in the public schools any account of the origin of man that is in conflict with the divine account in the Bible. It makes the Bible the

edge and theories? Such an attempt would be as follows. The earliest primates, which is the order of mammals that humans belong to, appeared approximately 65 million years ago. Sometime around 33 million years ago a small fruit-eating animal called Aegyptopithecus inhabited the forests that covered northern Africa. Scientists believe Aegyptopithecus was the first of the higher primates and a direct ancestor of the great apes and humans. At some point over the next 29 million years the ancestral lines of humans and apes split. When exactly this occurred no one is sure. Various primates dating from 8 to 20 million years ago have been put forward as the likely intermediary between Aegyptopithecus and hominids although none have been accepted as the direct ancestor of humans. The dearth of fossils and lack of complete specimens from this period leave this chapter of our past largely in the dark.

Beginning about 4 million years ago the fossil record is more complete, allowing for a more detailed treatment of the evolution of humanity. From the evidence gathered there is little doubt that human origins lie in Africa. The Great Rift Valley, which is a Y-shaped scar in the earth's crust running north through Tanzania, Kenya, and Ethiopia, has produced the most concentrated and earliest fossils yardstick to measure every man's intellect, to measure every man's intelligence and to measure every man's learning. Are your mathematics good? Turn to Elijah 1:2. Is your philosophy good? See II Samuel 3. Is your astronomy good? See Genesis 2:7.... Every bit of knowledge that the mind has must be submitted to a religious test.

William Jennings Bryan

Evolution is not a theory, but a hypothesis.... Today there is not a scientist in all the world who can trace one single species to any other, and yet they call us ignoramuses and bigots because we do not throw away our Bible and accept it as proved that out of two or three million species not one is traceable to another. And they say that evolution is a fact when they cannot prove that one species came from another, and if there is such a thing, all species must have come, commencing as they say, commencing in that one lonely cell down there in the bottom of the ocean that just evolved and evolved until it got to be a man. And they cannot find a single species that came from another, and yet they demand that we allow them to teach this stuff to our children, that they may come home with their imaginary family tree and scoff at their mother's and father's Bible.

How can any teacher tell his students that evolution does not tend to destroy his religious faith? How can an honest teacher conceal from his students the effect of evolution upon Darwin himself? And is it not stranger still that preachers who advocate evolution never speak of Darwin's loss of faith, due to his belief in evolution? The parents of Tennessee have reason enough to fear the effect of evolution on the minds of their children.... It is belief in evolution that has caused so many scientists and so many Christians to reject the miracles of the Bible, and then give up, one after another, every vital truth of Christianity.

The use of the masculine pronoun in this passage reflects the language accepted at this time in western history.

related to human evolution. Australopithecus, the earliest biped dating to 4 million years ago and the larger brained Homo habilis dating to 1.8 million years have both been found only in Africa.

According to some theories our ancestors diverged from apes between 6 and 10 million years ago and were initially just another species of ape. Over the next few million years three key changes occurred that set these creatures on the road to evolving into modern humans. The first, and arguably the most profound change was the development of bipedalism. The second change was that the lineage split so that there were at least three separate species of hominids. It must be remembered that different species that interbreed produce infertile offspring and that today all humans belong to the same species, Homo sapiens. The separate species that existed about 3.5 million years ago belong to the genus Australopithecus and included Australopithecus robustus, Australopithecus africanus, and Australopithecus afarensis. The third change was that tools were used on a regular basis by 2.5 million years ago.

There is much disagreement over what happened next although it is certain that the Australopithecines disappeared and a larger brained hominid called Homo habilis (man the handyman) appeared. It is worth noting that most scholars believe Homo habilis evolved from one of the Australopithecines and that the changes were significant enough to warrant scientists placing Homo habilis in the same genus as modern humans. By 1.7 million years ago the increased brain size and body size as well as other changes were significant enough to suggest another species, Homo erectus.

By 1.2 million years ago all hominids but Homo

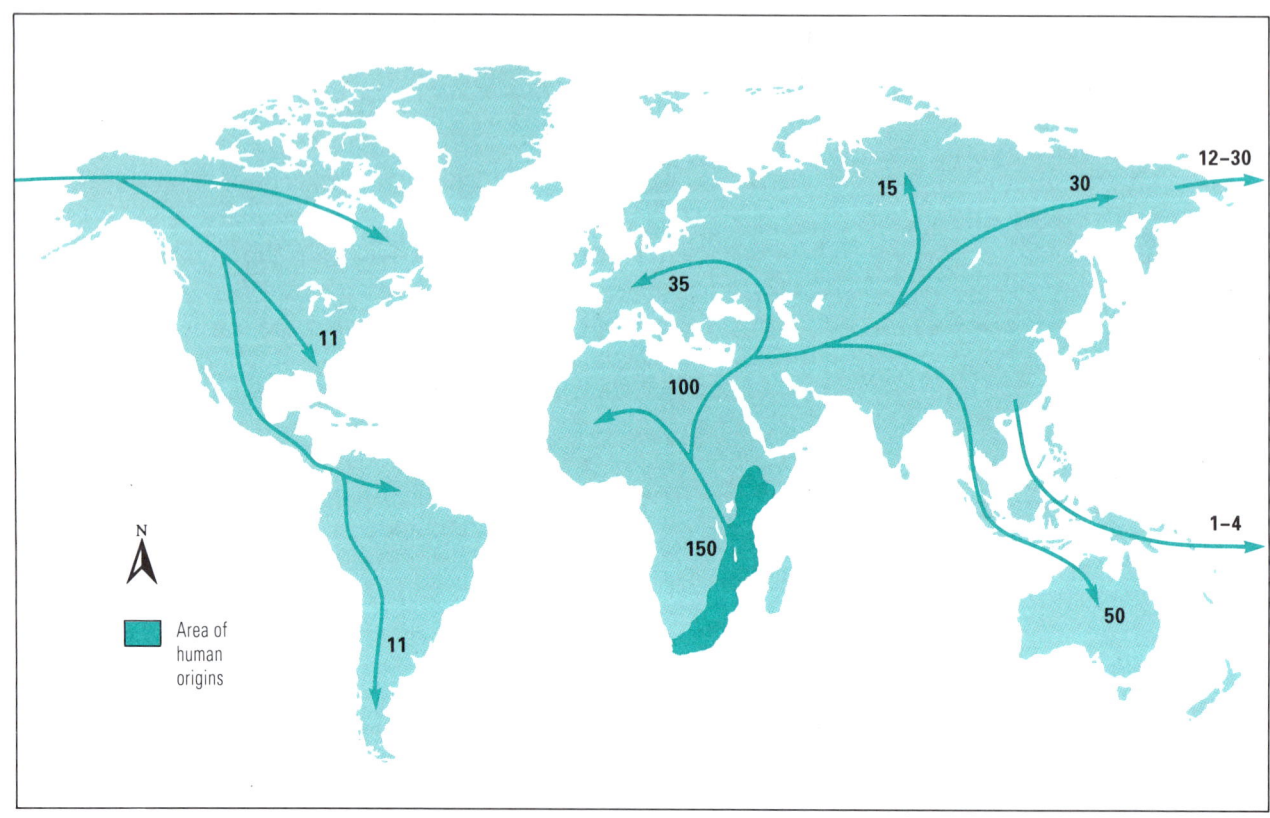

Early Human Migrations

Current research suggests that modern humans arose in Africa about 150 000 years ago. From there, populations fanned out into the rest of the world, leaving Africa about 100 000 years ago. The map above illustrates the likely route of human migrations and the dates indicate, in thousands of years, the approximate time of arrival of humans in the various regions of the world.

erectus were extinct. Its larger brain and omnivorous diet made Homo erectus the best suited to the environment as they could more easily obtain food than the other species. Over the next 500 000 years Homo erectus continued to evolve in the direction of modern humans acquiring a larger brain and rounder skull although they still had thicker skulls and brow ridges than we have today. By 400 000 years ago the changes were again significant enough for Homo erectus to be reclassified as Homo sapiens (the wise man).

By 100 000 years ago humans had settled in three distinct populations, all of which were Homo sapiens. In Europe and the Near East were a people we call (Homo sapiens neandertalensis) **Neanderthals**. Africa was populated by anatomically modern humans (Homo sapiens sapiens) and in Asia were yet another group of people although there are too few fossils to clearly define these people. Sometime around 50 000 years ago the anatomically modern Africans began to invade Europe. Initially it was believed that the Neanderthals had evolved into Homo sapiens sapiens but scientists are now quite certain that the invasion of Homo sapiens sapiens led to the assimilation if not extinction of the Neanderthals. Eventually the Homo sapiens

sapiens, who are direct ancestors of ourselves, inhabited all parts of the world reaching Australia 40 000 years ago, the Americas 12 000 years ago, the Arctic 10 000 years ago and the Pacific Islands a scant 2000 years ago.

Towards Modern Humans

The Neanderthals

The people we call Neanderthals lived between 100 000 and 40 000 years ago at a time when Europe and Asia were in the grips of the last ice age. The Neanderthals, who were named after Germany's Neander Valley where the first skeleton was found in 1856, were a powerfully built people of limited intelligence. If it were possible to meet a Neanderthal person their physical appearance would immediately reveal that they were not anatomically modern humans. From a distance you would notice that Neanderthals were heavy set people with an average height of 160 cm and weighed about 73 k. Their arms and legs would seem stubby as their forearms and lower legs were shorter than ours and they were heavily muscled especially at the shoulders and neck. As you drew nearer you might be taken aback by their facial features. Neanderthals' eyebrows rested on prominently bulging bony ridges while their nose, jaws, and teeth protruded forward. The lower jaw sloped back in such a way that Neanderthals had no chin and their eyes lay sunk in deep sockets. Finally, if you were to shake hands with a Neanderthal you could not help but be impressed by the firm grip of his or her large and powerful hands.

So, what happened to the Neanderthal people? It is quite likely that the invasion of anatomically modern humans from Africa led to the demise of the Neanderthals. The Homo sapiens sapiens possessed superior weapons and tools, products of their superior intelligence and ingenuity. After inhabiting Europe and the Near East for 60 000 years the Neanderthals were wiped out within a couple of thousand years by the murder, disease, and displacement brought by Homo sapiens sapiens. It has been suggested that the Neanderthals were assimilated by the invading people from Africa. This would appear unlikely as there is no fossil evidence of a Homo sapiens sapiens-Neanderthal hybrid. In fact, the fossil evidence shows that within 2000 years the Neanderthals had been completely replaced by Homo sapiens sapiens. Also, it is quite unlikely that the Homo sapiens sapiens, who were fully modern in appearance, would want to mate with the Neanderthals considering their strikingly primitive appearance. Even if interbreeding took place there is some evidence to suggest that the offspring would not have survived as the pelvic structure of the female Neanderthals suggests a 12 month gestation period. In the end, as harsh as it may sound, the invasion of the modern humans into Europe and Asia appears to have caused the extinction of the Neanderthals.

The Great Leap Forward

Sometime around 35 000 years ago, a process of monumental significance began. Jared Diamond aptly described this process as "The Great Leap Forward." Two fundamental changes occurred to facilitate this event; the development of modern anatomy, and the beginning of innovative behaviour.

After millions of years during which the changes in hominids were imperceptibly slow, suddenly and very rapidly changes began to occur that would clearly set humans apart from all other animals. Accompanying the arrival of anatomically modern humans was a burst of innovations and creativity. The curiosity and ingenuity first displayed 35 000 years ago set in motion progressive technological and artistic developments that would eventually put people into space. The achievements of humanity in the past 35 000 years are truly astounding especially when we consider that in the previous 60 000 years Neanderthal culture remained virtually unchanged.

The curiosity, ingenuity, and creativity of Homo sapiens sapiens produced a vast array of crafted materials. Tools were made of thin stone blades struck from larger stones and some were mounted on wooden shafts. Most tools of the Homo sapiens had a specific purpose: there were needles and awls for making clothing, mortars and pestles for preparing food, and axes for cutting wood. Eventually more sophisticated weapons were developed such as barbed harpoons, darts, spear throwers, and bows and arrows. The development of these more advanced weapons allowed them to hunt large and vicious animals such as wild pigs, reindeer, horses, and bison. Watercraft may also have appeared since places such as Australia were settled for the first time. Perhaps even more significant than the advances made in tools and weapons was the development of trade and expressions of aesthetic appreciation. The long distance trade that developed was not only for raw materials but also for ornaments. Aside from the objects of personal adornment, sculpture and painting began to appear. For the first

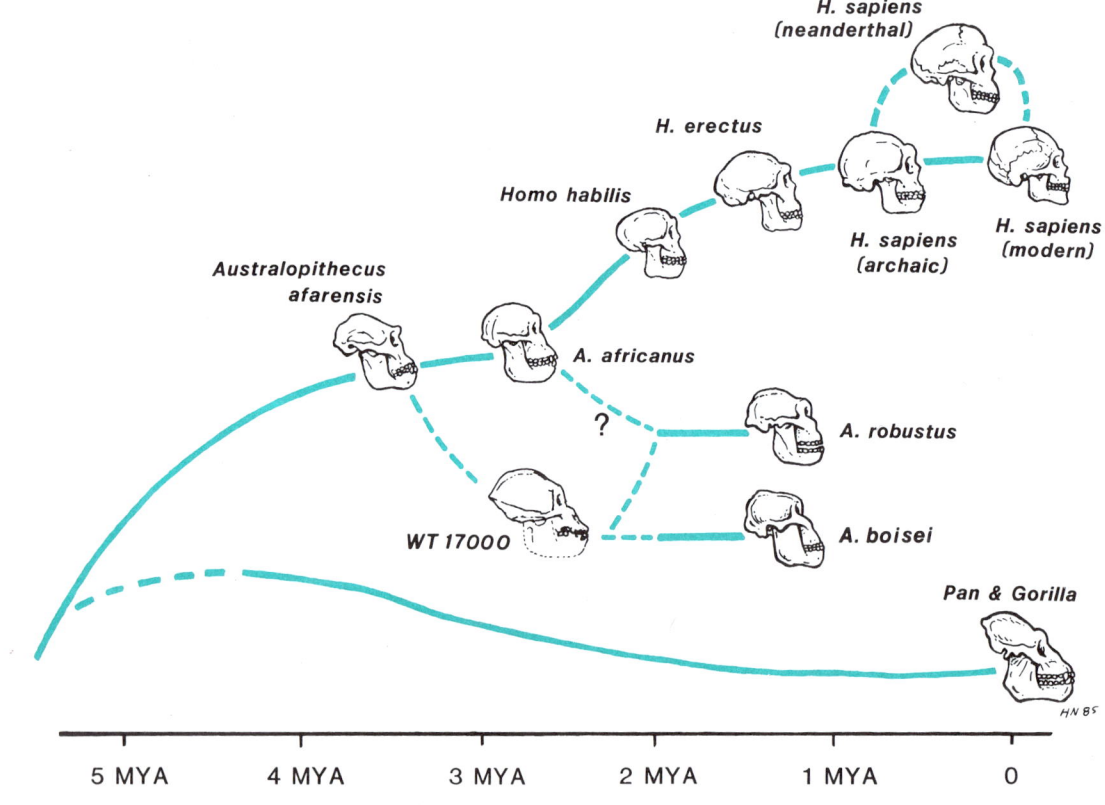

This timeline of evolution traces the likely development of hominid species over the past 4 million years. It begins with our ancestors diverging from the apes 6 to 10 million years ago. Three million years ago, key changes took place; bipedalism and a split of hominids into three separate species belonging to Australopithecus. By 1.7 million years ago, Homo erectus appeared. By 400 000 years ago, Homo sapiens appeared. By 100 000 years ago, three distinct populations existed; the Neanderthals in Europe and the Near East, the anatomically modern humans in Africa, and a little known group in Asia.

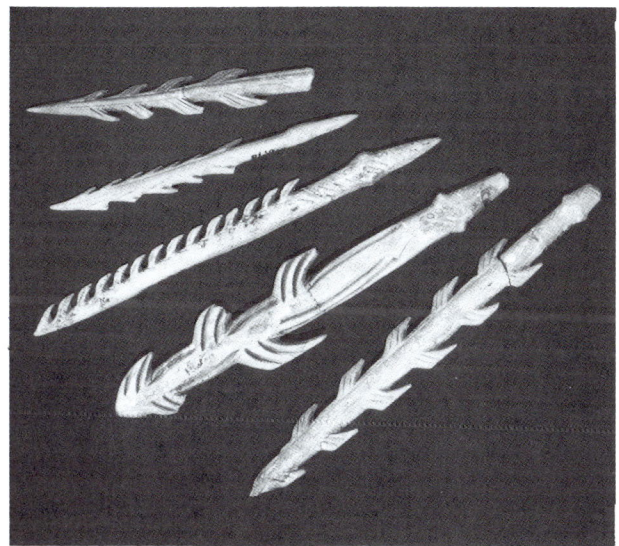 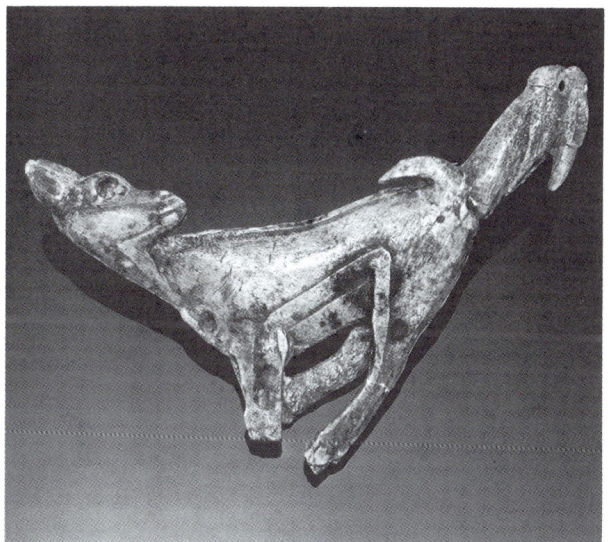

These items demonstrate evidence of a great surge of creativity, innovativeness, and an appreciation of aesthetics demonstrated by the carving of figures and the ornamentation of tools and weapons. Great advancements in technology are demonstrated by the harpoon heads (left) and the spear thrower (right). The harpoon heads, used 11 000 years ago, were fastened to wooden shafts and could easily be replaced.

time in history there is evidence of an appreciation of beauty. Modern humans had arrived!

Daily Life in The Upper Paleolithic Age

During the Upper Paleolithic period (50 000 years ago to 10 000 years ago) people lived in small groups or bands of five to ten families that were related by blood or marriage. As the people were nomadic or semi-nomadic and lived by hunting and gathering, they were very aware of their surroundings and in tune with nature. Also, as success often depended on a communal effort the social relationships within the band were very close. Every so often various bands would join together to hold tribal gatherings or ritual ceremonies. In order to keep the blood line strong it was important that the young people marry outside of their own band, and at these gatherings, which often numbered several hundred people, marriages were arranged.

The men of the Upper Paleolithic period were supreme big-game hunters. The game stalked, varied according to the region. In Europe mammoths, aurochs, bison, reindeers, wild cattle, horses, and red deer were pursued while llamas, giant sloths, and an ostrich-like bird called a rhea were hunted in South America. In Australia, emus, wallabies, kangaroos, and mega-marsupials were the prized animals. These early hunters used a variety of techniques to capture large game including driving the animals into natural enclosures or driving them over cliffs, into marshes or tar pits. The appearance of the bow and arrow about 20 000 B.C. allowed hunters to stalk animals with even greater success. Despite their success at hunting big game we must be careful not to overemphasize the importance of hunting and consequently man's role in society. Weapons, which preserve better than leather bags or baskets used in gathering, and the paintings of heroic hunts have coloured our view of Paleolithic society.

The gathering of food was done mostly by women

HISTORICAL FICTION

DAILY LIFE IN PALEOLITHIC ENGLAND

In the first chapter of Rutherfurd's novel, *Sarum*, a family of hunters and gatherers from the tundra in northern England (this chapter is set in the time of the retreat of the last ice age) make an epic journey south in search of better hunting grounds. Upon reaching southern England the family from the north meets up with a family of hunters and gatherers who have been cast out of the local bands. This meeting proves somewhat fortuitous as the two families are able to learn from each other. The excerpt below provides a clear example of the differences between the hunters and gatherers of various regions.

Thus began the curious relationship between the hunter from the tundra and the hunter from the southern woods. Tep had four children. His woman had died, so he had traveled to the west and stolen another from a band of hunters, when she was little more than a girl. Her name was Ulla and two of the children were hers. She was a round-faced creature with large brown eyes that wore a perpetually frightened look, and a scrawny body. The children all resembled their father, running swiftly through the woods on their long-toed feet and catching small animals with a ferocious dexterity that was frightening....

In the open tundra, where game was so scarce, men hunted in groups and followed their prey for days, wearing it down before moving in for the kill. But Tep hunted alone, in woods where game was plentiful and varied. Roe deer, the swift wild horse, hare, grey partridge, swans, and geese were easy prey. More dangerous were the wild boar and brown bear; and fellow hunters were the polecat, the fox, the wolf, badger, stoat and weasel. Blackberries grew on the edge of the clearings, and juniper berries. There were edible fungi and grasses. All these animals and plants, the narrow-faced man with the bent back understood. He knew everything that was edible and where it could be found.

His weapons were more varied too. In the tundra Hwll had carried a single spear and a bow and arrow. The ends were made of flint, carefully chipped to a razor-sharp serrated edge, and bound to the shaft with twine. But Tep's weapons had many different heads, each one for a different animal. They were smoother, usually chisel-ended rather than pointed; his arrow heads fitted neatly into a notched shaft, and some of his spearheads had a socket into which the handle could fit snugly. The spear he used to catch fish had barbs so that the fish would not slip off; in particular Hwll admired the delicate, lancet-like arrows Tep used to kill the fox so that its fur remained undamaged.

Nor were these the only differences. Tep's clothes, unlike his, were close-fitting and sewn together with twine made from animal gut. He wore a single jerkin and loincloth in summer, and added long leggings in the winter.... And Ulla made baskets of osier and beautifully carved bowls of wood superior to anything Akun could have attempted.

... Hwll was one of the last of his kind ... the Paleolithic hunters, the wanderers of the tundra, were gradually being displaced as the warm forests crept northwards and more sophisticated Mesolithic forest hunters like Tep took over the land.

and children and accounted for approximately 80 percent of the diet in the Upper Paleolithic period. Women were virtually assured of returning from their foraging with a sackful of food while the men could never be certain whether the hunt would be a success. No wonder there was such rejoicing when a major kill was made. Women would have spent a large portion of their time gathering food, which included various roots, potatoes, fruits, sweet berries, honey, and shellfish. Studies of the teeth of Paleolithic skeletons suggest that the bulk of the diet was vegetables.

Paleolithic Art

The clearest expression of the creativity and ingenuity of the Upper Paleolithic people lies in their art. During the Upper Paleolithic period a cultural explosion occurred. Tools began to be carved for beauty as well as utility; pendants were made from horse teeth, jewelry made of shell was worn by the living and the dead, and sculptures of plump, large breasted women, perhaps symbolizing fertility, abounded. The most stunning artistic development of the Upper Paleolithic period were the vibrant cave paintings that often depicted animals now extinct.

Among the most famous of the cave paintings are those of the **Lascaux Caves**, located in south-central France. The paintings, dating to 15 000 B.C., are the work of experienced artists. The painters often made use of irregularities in the cave walls to add a three-dimensional effect to their art. For example, a concavity has been used to form the belly of a pregnant cow. In other instances the animals were intentionally distorted to give the viewer a more striking perspective. Scaffolding, as high as five metres, was used to allow the artists to paint the ceilings of the caves. After first outlining a silhouette of the figure using charcoal, the artist then created the picture using paint made from charcoal, clay, minerals, **ochre**, and other materials. The work, deep in the caves, was executed by the light of animal-fat lamps. No one is certain as to the use of the caves, although some believe they were used in rituals relating to hunting magic. The significance of the paintings for us is that they capture and preserve the creativity of the Paleolithic people. Despite the primitive nature of the paintings, they manage to capture the elegance and strength of the subjects and by using a variety of artistic techniques are able to convey movement and depth.

Little concrete evidence of Paleolithic religions has been found, although paintings, such as those found at Lascaux, certainly indicate a special reverence and awe for certain animals. Further evidence of religion comes from another cave in France called Trois-Frères. Here, in what is called the Chapel of the Lioness, a cave lion engraved on a stalagmite shows marks of being repeatedly hit as if to kill it. Nearby the image of a sorcerer is painted and engraved on the cave wall. The sorcerer, depicted as being half man and half animal and wearing a great set of antlers, dominates the chamber much as a religious icon dominates a church. It is thought that perhaps the Chapel of the Lioness was a ritual meeting place of Paleolithic hunters.

The technological innovations and artistic expression of the people of the Paleolithic period clearly sets them apart from the earlier Neanderthals. After millions of years of evolution humans acquired the knowledge and ability to adapt the environment to their needs.

The Neolithic Revolution

The Neolithic Revolution, or New Stone Age, refers to the period after 9000 B.C. when ground and polished tools were primarily used. This is one of the greatest revolutionary periods in the history of

BELIEFS

Stonehenge
A NEOLITHIC RELIGIOUS MARVEL

▼▼▼

The advent of the Neolithic Revolution brought several significant changes to early religions. Due to the rise of agriculture, Neolithic farmers were able to spend less time in the pursuit of food than the earlier hunters and gatherers. This permitted a priestly class to develop to look after spiritual needs and for members of the community to devote time to large, permanent building projects. Finally, and perhaps most significantly, the early farmers were in tune with the changing seasons and aware of the need to trace the movement of the sun and moon.

The most famous of all Neolithic religious sites is Stonehenge on the Salisbury Plain in southern England. The arrangement visitors see today is actually the result of several phases of construction dating from about 3100 B.C. to about 1100 B.C. The stones used in the construction of Stonehenge came from two areas. The bluestones, which form the earliest semicircle, were brought from the Preseli Mountains some 385 km away. The larger sarsens, weighing up to 45 t, were brought to the site from the Marlborough Downs 30 km north of Stonehenge.

The Construction of Stonehenge

No one is certain as to how the massive stones were brought to Stonehenge and erected. One hypothesis is that the stones were dragged on massive sledges and rollers and hauled with ropes of leather or cow hair. Once at the site the most probable method for raising the sarsens and lintels is the one depicted.

Raising a sarsen stone into an upright setting.

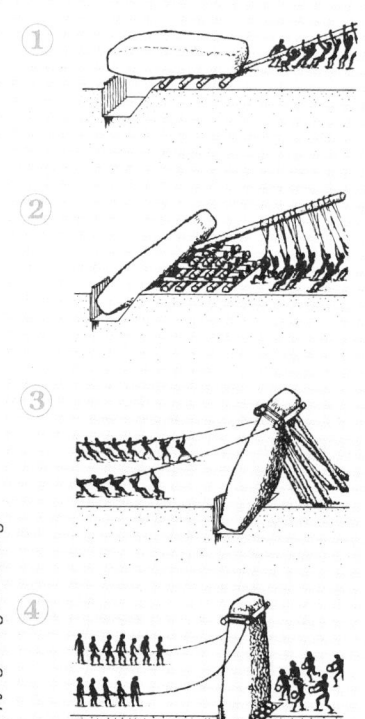

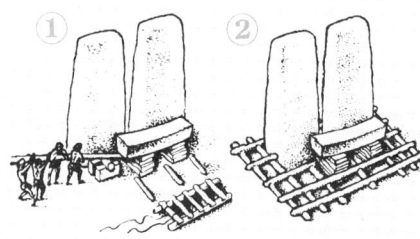

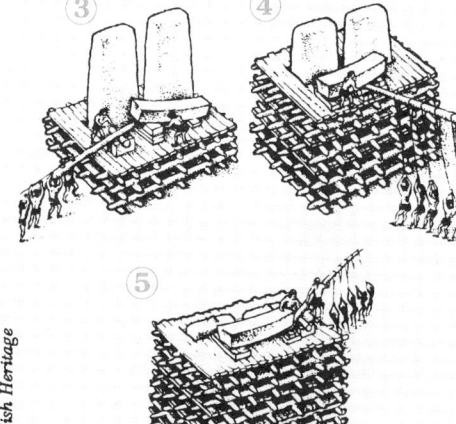

Raising a lintel to the top of two sarsens.

What Was the Purpose of Stonehenge?

There is no doubt that Stonehenge was a massive religious site. It also appears that it was a giant Neolithic calendar capable of predicting eclipses. The design of Stonehenge allows for the marking of the summer and winter solstices. If you were to stand at the centre of Stonehenge on June 21st you would see the rising sun aligned with the avenue and perfectly bisecting the stone circle. Many theories abound as to the other purposes for Stonehenge; however, many of the secrets of this awe-inspiring site remain a mystery.

humanity for it is at this time that people began to abandon a semi-nomadic lifestyle to begin farming. For the first time a monumental sociological shift occurred that was the result of human innovation rather than an evolutionary development. The agricultural revolution was a further manifestation of the Great Leap Forward that has allowed modern humans to gain ascendancy. Using the same innovative and creative spirit, people learned how to harness nature by planting crops and domesticating animals. What were the factors that contributed to the shift from hunting and gathering to agriculture?

The first and most obvious factor is that by the end of the last ice age, around 9000 B.C., people had learned a great deal about plants and animals. After observing animals at a water-hole or caring for injured animals men may have decided to corral some of them. Women, meanwhile, may have tried to grow some of the wild grains they gathered. Perhaps they noticed that where a basket of grain had spilled new stocks began to grow or noticed shoots sprouting from a midden (garbage pit). Whatever the process, men and women learned that they could control their food supply rather than relying on luck. Another factor contributing to the rise of agriculture was that the ice age had ended resulting in a warmer, wetter climate. This led to a widespread abundance of wild grasses including the ancestors of today's grains. Accompanying the end of the ice age was a rise in population. The increase in the density of the population led to increasing competition for land which would eventually give the edge to agriculturalists. On average, hunters and gatherers require 16 km^2 per person whereas the same 16 km^2 can accommodate 100 agriculturalists. Thus the early farmers would be able to gain numerical superiority and eventually displace the remaining hunter-gatherers.

The animals first domesticated were cattle, sheep, goats, and pigs. Of these, cattle were the most important as they supplied meat, leather, and milk from which cheese and butter were made. When animals were slaughtered nothing was wasted. Dishes were prepared using the udder, tripe, brains, bone, head, feet, tails, blood, and even gristle. Similarly, the weeds that grew in the grain fields were harvested along with the grain and and often incorporated into the **pottage** (thick soup). Two of the drinks enjoyed by neolithic farmers were beer made from barley and mead. Mead is an alcoholic beverage made by allowing honey and water to ferment. It was often flavoured with wild fruit and herbs.

Improved tools allowed for better and more efficient agriculture. Using a sickle made of flint bladelets, placed in a curved segment of an antler, a family could harvest enough wheat in ten days to last them six months. Land could also be cleared more quickly with the improved tools. Axes made of flint could cut down in five minutes, a pine tree having a diametre of 17 cm. As well, the invention of the hoe allowed for the tilling of the soil. During the late Neolithic period the development of metallurgy produced a wider range of tools. Using copper, sharper knives, elegant drinking vessels, spits, buckets, and cauldrons were made.

The Neolithic Revolution resulted in a profound shift in society. People abandoned their semi-nomadic lifestyle and instead built permanent towns and cities. Some left the fields altogether, choosing to specialize in a certain craft. As people began to take up different positions, society became more hierarchical; and a class system developed. The domestication of animals and the planting of crops freed people from the endless pursuit of food thereby allowing for the development of arts, music, sports, and other leisure activities. It also allowed for the development of more complex religions as society could afford to maintain a priestly class that made no material contribution to society. The establishment of permanent cities and complex religions brought about elaborate religious sites and burial tombs. In the process of shifting from hunting and gathering to farming, people laid the foundations for civilization.

What is a Civilization?

The term civilization is difficult to define. What makes one group civilized and another not? Put this question to a group of people and you will no doubt find that a consensus cannot be reached. There are, however, certain elements that are generally agreed upon as being fundamental to a civilization. The first of these is permanence. Before we consider groups civilized they must live in permanent cities and towns. Secondly, there must be an organized system of government and law that unites the people and a system of writing by which laws can be recorded and knowledge passed on. Civilizations are also characterized by the existence of specialized tradespeople and a system through which goods and services can be exchanged. While there are several other elements that can be argued as essential to a civilization, these five are the pillars on which all civilizations rest.

Several elements that some may consider essential for a civilization would be more appropriately labeled by-products of a civilization as they are the result of a highly organized and specialized society. A complex and highly organized religion, for example, is not essential to a civilization nor is a rigid class structure. Similarly, refined art and music, advanced architecture and even systems of education are not essential for a society to be considered civilized. They are, however, the hallmarks of great civilizations.

Rivers and Civilizations

The earliest civilizations, found in Mesopotamia, Egypt, India, and China all shared one thing; they developed along a river valley. Mesopotamia grew up along the banks of the Tigris and Euphrates rivers, Egypt drew its life from the benevolent Nile, India's earliest civilization sprung from the Indus River Valley, and Chinese civilization originated along the mighty Yellow River. All of these civilizations relied on the rivers for a steady source of water, fertile soil, and fish to supplement their diet. In most cases the rivers also served as an easy means of communication, thus facilitating trade and the exchange of ideas.

The decision of the early farmers to settle in the river valleys and to attempt to control and utilize the rivers had profound implications for the rise of early civilizations. The fertile soils allowed for larger populations to develop and for more material goods to be produced. A centralized system of government evolved to coordinate projects such as irrigation, to administer the land, to govern the people, and to organize defence. Writing was developed initially to keep records; later it became a vital tool for preserving the valuable knowledge that was being acquired. As people developed specialized skills they left the fields to become expert craftspeople. Finally, as wealth increased and people had more leisure time they were able to spend more time on the arts, music, and sports. The great river valleys of the world provided the key ingredients necessary for the world's first civilizations to flourish.

Suggested Sources For Further Research

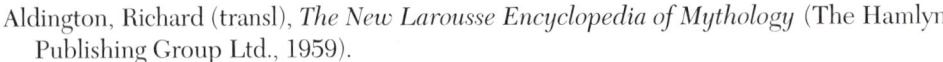

Aldington, Richard (transl), *The New Larousse Encyclopedia of Mythology* (The Hamlyn Publishing Group Ltd., 1959).

Cavendish, Richard (ed.), *Legends of the World* (Schocken Books, 1982).

Darwin, Charles, *The Voyage of the Beagle* (NAL Penguin Inc., 1988).

Diamond, Jared, "The Great Leap Forward," in *Discover*, May, 1989

Eaton, S. Boyd, Melvin Konner, and Marjorie Shostak, *The Paleolithic Prescription* (Harper & Row Publishers, 1988).

Howard, Jonathan, *Charles Darwin*, Past Masters Series (Oxford University Press, 1987).

Johanson, Donald and James Shreeve, *Lucy's Child* (William Morrow & Co., 1989).

Leakey, Mary D., "Footprints In The Ashes Of Time," in *National Geographic*, Volume 155, No. 4, April 1979.

Leakey, Richard and Alan Walker, "Homo Erectus Unearthed," in *National Geographic*, Volume 168, No. 5, November 1985.

Lewin, Roger, *Human Evolution* (Blackwell Scientific Publications Inc., 1989).

Marshack, Alexander, "An Ice Age Ancestor," in *National Geographic*, Volume 174, No. 4, October 1988.

Morell, Virginia, "My Brother the Ape," in *Equinox* (Equinox Publishing, September/October 1983).

Putman, John J., "In Search Of Modern Humans," in *National Geographic*, Volume 174, No. 4, October 1988.

Rigaud, Jean-Philippe, "Treasures of Lascaux Cave," in *National Geographic*, Volume 174, No. 4, October 1988.

Wallace, Douglas, "The Search For Adam and Eve," in *Newsweek*, January 11, 1988

Weaver, Kenneth F., "The Search For Our Ancestors," in *National Geographic*, Volume 168, No. 5, November 1985.

Focus Your Knowledge

1. How did James Ussher arrive at a date for the creation of the world? Why is this date now challenged by many people?
2. What is the significance of the footprints discovered by Mary Leakey in the Laetoli Beds?
3. Why are we virtually certain that human origins lie in Africa?
4. What physical features suggest that the Neanderthals are not our ancestors? What happened to the Neanderthals?
5. Briefly describe life in the Paleolithic Age.
6. How did rivers play an important role in the early civilizations of Mesopotamia, Egypt, India, and China?

Apply Your Knowledge

1. Prepare an organizer that allows you to compare the similarities and differences of the creation stories found in this chapter. Consider the creator-figure, why the world came into being, and the explanation of the creation of humanity and nature. Note the factors that are common to most stories around the world. Speculate as to why these similarities exist.
2. Briefly explain Charles Darwin's theory of evolution and state why his theory was so revolutionary. How do you think the people of Darwin's society would have reacted?
3. What was the "Great Leap Forward"? How do the artifacts depicted both in the colour plates and in the text reflect this revolutionary change?
4. Describe and assess the importance of the woman's role in Paleolithic societies.
5. What factors contributed to the Neolithic Revolution? How did the Neolithic Revolution pave the way for the first civilizations?

Extension Activities

1. Do a cave painting in the style of the Lascaux Cave paintings. This can be done by first creating a template of the figure to be painted. Place the template on a large piece of brown paper and proceed to dab paint using a sponge. Several different figures can be placed on one large sheet thereby capturing the visual effect of the caves.

2. Using one of the recipes found in the chapter or one found through further research prepare a Neolithic dish to share with the class.

3. Using a bone or piece of wood, create a decorative weapon such as a spear thrower or a harpoon head. Or, by using clay or plasticene, construct a model of a Neolithic religious site such as Stonehenge.

4. Having read a variety of stories relating to creation try your own hand at coming up with an explanation for the origins of the world. Write your myth as if you are telling it to a Neolithic audience who do not have the benefits of modern science.

5. Present one of the creation stories found in this chapter or your own story of creation to the class. You could use a skit, a comic strip, a bulletin board display, or a video taped production to present the story.

CHAPTER 3

Egypt and the Near East

Chapter Highlights

- writing cuneiform script and Egyptian hieroglyphics

- ziggurats: temples to the gods

- the Egyptian practice of mummifying the dead

- the story behind the pyramids

- living among the ancient Egyptians

- the foundations of Judaism, Christianity, and Islam

Sometime between 6000 and 7000 years ago nomadic hunters and gatherers abandoned their wandering lifestyle and settled along the fertile banks of the Tigris, Euphrates, and Nile rivers. The exact process by which these people learned farming methods and made the crucial decision to form permanent settlements can never be known. Regardless, the Fertile Crescent, a broad well-watered area stretching from the Mediterranean to the Persian Gulf, became home to the world's earliest civilization, Mesopotamia. Meanwhile the Nile Valley was home to the impressive Egyptian civilization.

An understanding of the history of ancient Egypt and the Near East is critical for a true appreciation of the development of later western civilization. The early civilizations of Egypt and the Near East profoundly influenced many aspects of Greek and Roman culture from the alphabet to the wheel. Not all facets of these ancient cultures have been passed on to us. In many respects the cultures of Egypt, Mesopotamia, and other kingdoms of the Near East are preserved only in art, written documents, or the remains unearthed by archaeologists. Throughout this chapter we will explore various elements of several of the ancient civilizations of the Near East. Egypt has been selected as the primary focus of the chapter to allow for a detailed study of one of the civilizations.

Key Concepts

Tigris and Euphrates rivers
levee
Sumerians
Hammurabi
Assyrians
cuneiform
ziggurats
Hyksos
maat
canopic jars
mastaba
Valley of the Kings
Hittites
Canaanites, Phoenecians, and Hebrews
Moses
Covenant
Yahweh
The Temple of Jerusalem

Mesopotamia: The Cradle of Civilization

The earliest of all civilizations arose in a land the Greeks would later call Mesopotamia. Mesopotamia means "land between the rivers" and refers to the area between the **Tigris and Euphrates rivers**. It was in this region that humans first abandoned their nomadic lifestyle and began to form permanent settlements. The changes that occurred in the river valleys of the Tigris and the Euphrates were truly revolutionary and formed the pillars of western civilization. Codified laws, the concept of kingship, the building of places to worship the gods, writing, and even the wheel were first developed by the Mesopotamians. In tracing the roots of western civilization we must turn to the ancient Mesopotamians.

Geography

Mesopotamia is defined as the area in the lower Tigris-Euphrates Valley stretching northwest from the Persian Gulf to just north of Baghdad. In modern terms this would be the eastern part of Iraq. In ancient times the southern part of Mesopotamia was known as Sumer and the northern area was referred to as Akkad. Eventually the two regions were unified under Babylonian leadership and henceforth were known as Babylonia.

The land of Mesopotamia is essentially a bleak **alluvial plain** which receives too little rainfall to allow crops to mature. The climate is hot and dry and the soil is arid and sterile if not cared for. Furthermore, the land contains no minerals and almost no stone or timber for building. On the surface, life in the Tigris-Euphrates Valley would seem somewhat foreboding. The soil was baked by the long, hot summers causing vegetation to wither and die. During the winter, stormy south winds brought unpredictable downpours that turned the river valleys into a slippery mess. Spring was the most tenuous time for those living in Mesopotamia. Spring rains combined with the melting snows from the neighbouring Zagros Mountains swelled the Tigris and Euphrates rivers often causing catastrophic flooding.

So what attracted settlers to this seemingly inhospitable region? The answer to this question lies in the natural **levees** that occur along the meandering course of the Euphrates River. Natural levees are embankments produced by the sediment that builds up after thousands of years of flooding. The levee surface slopes gently downward away from the river. Thus the highest and safest ground on a flood plain is along the portion of the levee adjacent to the river. Aside from the protection, the silt and sediment of the levees was fertile, easily drained, planted, irrigated, and cultivated. Adding to the richness of the area around the levees were the swamps that teemed with fish and waterfowl and produced an abundance of reeds. In the spring the reeds provided excellent forage for sheep and goats and in maturity were an important building material. Hence, it was around

MAJOR EVENTS IN MIDDLE EASTERN HISTORY

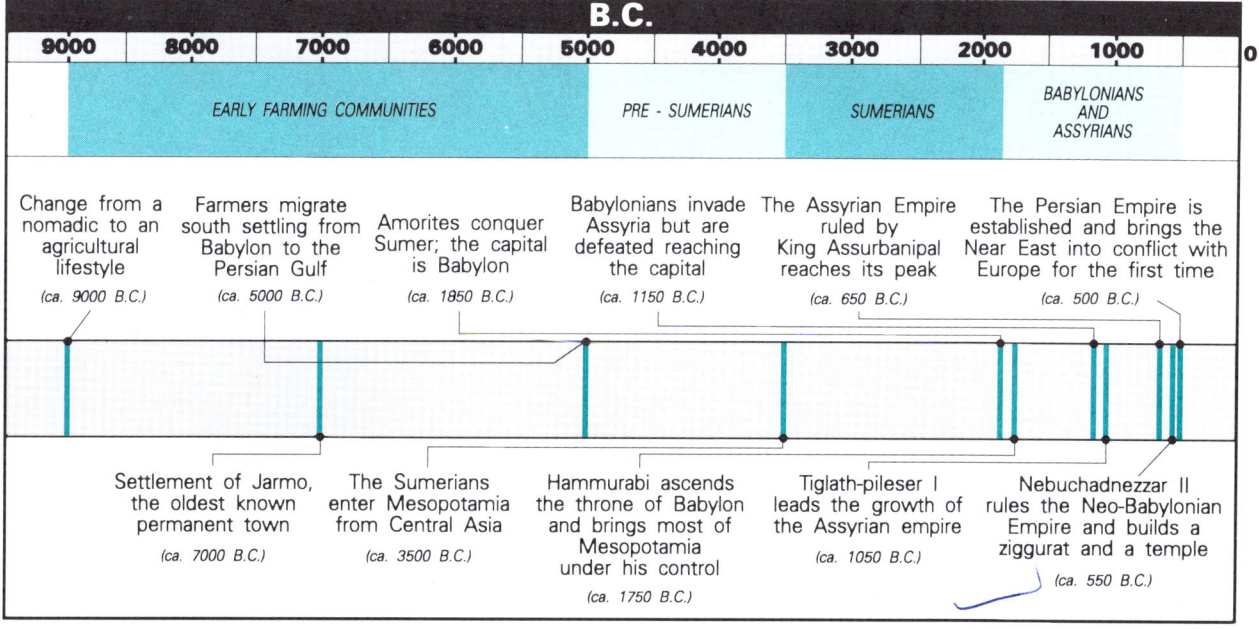

Egypt and the Near East **CHAPTER 3**

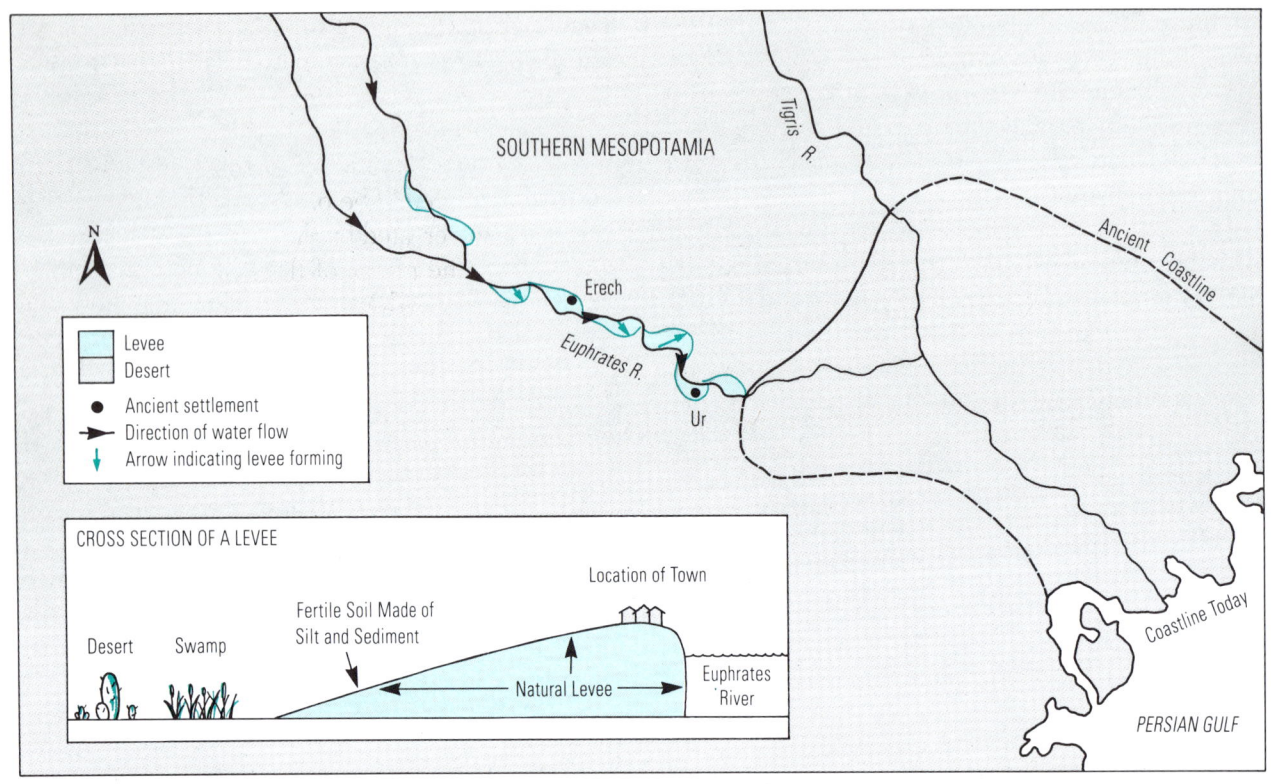

Settlement Areas in Ancient Mesopotamia
The cross section (insert) shows the settlement pattern of ancient Mesopotamia. Towns were established on the high point of the embankment, while farming took place on the fertile soil of the levee. These regions represented pockets of productive land as much of Mesopotamia was inhospitable desert.

these natural levees that the first settlers in Mesopotamia saw promise and established permanent settlements.

While the natural levees held great promise it was a promise that could be realized only with irrigation and good drainage. Furthermore, the land between the rivers and streams was inhospitable desert and swampland. This would prove to be a great hindrance to the unity of Mesopotamia as communication was difficult and dangerous. Unlike the predictable Nile River in Egypt, the Tigris and Euphrates were givers of both life and death. Sudden floods often ravaged Mesopotamian villages without warning. The isolation and vulnerability of Mesopotamia profoundly influenced life along the Tigris and Euphrates.

The People

Mesopotamian civilization was the product of the cross-fertilization of four distinct ethno-cultural groups. The **Sumerians**, who arrived about 3000 B.C. from central Asia, were the first to develop writing and large social organizations, which constituted the first cities of the world. Throughout the history of Mesopotamia Semitic-speaking peoples arrived from the Syrian desert. Two groups who were of particular significance were the Akkadians, who arrived ca. 2600 B.C. and the Amorites, who arrived ca. 2200 B.C.. The third major cultural group to settle in Mesopotamia were the Indo-Europeans, represented by the Luvians and the Hittites. These migrations took place around 2000 B.C. Finally, the Hurrians were a people from the Caucasus who began migrating to Mesopotamia around 1800 B.C. Thus the study of ancient Mesopotamia is not that of a single cultural group but is the study of several different peoples who settled the area.

The Growth of the Empire

For much of its history, Mesopotamia was a collection of independent city-states as geography made it a difficult area to unify. Although Mesopotamia would eventually become unified it was much later than neighbouring Egypt and the unity was tenuous at best.

The early government of the towns and villages was democratic. An administrative bureaucracy was established to look after an increasingly complex society. Roads and canals were built and maintained, laws enforced, and disputes adjudicated. As the towns grew and prospered rivalries developed that led to intermittent wars. During the time of war many Mesopotamian villages found it necessary to appoint one of their strongest and ablest men to lead them to victory. In fact the Sumerian title for king was *lugal* and means "big man." Although the appointment was initially temporary, the frequent recurrence of wars led to the eventual decline of democratic government and the rise of a monarchical system in which the kingship was hereditary and **despotic**.

Sumerian Society. The Sumerians were the dominant culture in Mesopotamia between 2900 B.C. and 2400 B.C.. Their society was divided into four main classes. The top class was the nobility, which was comprised of the king and his family, the chief priests, and the high palace officials. The king's prominent position in society was further enhanced when it was given a religious dimension. Although the king was never **deified**, the institution of kingship was believed to be one of the basic institutions of human life created by the gods. Thus, it could be argued that the power of the king was not derived from brute strength but was divinely ordained. The king and the other members of the nobility owned the most and best land.

Those men and women who worked for the nobility in exchange for the use of their land were known as *free clients*. This group of people were dependent on the nobility for their livelihood and made up a good portion of Sumerian society. Commoners were free citizens who were not dependent on the nobility as they owned their own land. The fourth group in Sumerian society were the slaves.

The Akkadians. During the period of Sumerian domination the basic social, economic, and intellectual framework of Mesopotamia was established. However, despite repeated attempts to attain mastery over lower Mesopotamia the Sumerians were never successful. Instead the unification of lower Mesopotamia was accomplished by a **Semitic** chieftan named Sargon. After conquering the Sumerians in 2331 B.C. Sargon established his capital at Akkad, from which the Akkadians took their name. Sargon's greatest achievement was to finally unify Mesopotamia and to spread Mesopotamian culture throughout the area known as the Fertile Crescent. (The Fertile Crescent is a belt of rich farmland that stretches from Mesopotamia northeast to Syria and southwest to Egypt.) The dynasty established by Sargon was short-lived. By 2200 B.C. the Akkadians fell to invading barbarians.

The Babylonians. Mesopotamia was eventually reunited by another Semitic people known as the Babylonians. The Babylonians used their central location to dominate trade and eventually establish control over all of Mesopotamia. Guiding Babylon's rise was the talented king **Hammurabi**. Hammurabi, who came to the throne ca. 1750 B.C., established Babylon as the leading power in Mesopotamia by conquering both Akkad and Assyria, thereby gaining control of both the north and the south. The most lasting element of Hammurabi's reign was his law code. Hammurabi's code was inscribed on a stone pillar and set up in public for all to see. On the pillar Hammurabi is depicted as receiving his authority from the god Shamash. Thus, the laws of ancient Babylon were not only considered divinely inspired but were clearly written out to form a consistent body of laws. The laws themselves tell us much about life in ancient Mesopotamia. The penalties were designed to fit the crimes. This law code was the original embodiment of the concept an eye for an eye and a tooth for a tooth. For example, if a son struck his father the son's hand was cut off, or if someone were to break another's bone they would have the same bone broken. These laws, however, differed according to rank. Members of the nobility faced much more lenient penalties, often being required to only pay a fine.

Despite the talents and efforts of Hammurabi, Mesopotamia was not to remain united for long. By 1550 B.C. the Babylonian kingdom was in decline and the unity of Mesopotamia was again crumbling.

The Assyrians. For the next seven hundred years Mesopotamia experienced turmoil and uncertainty. The invasion of the warlike Hurrians was but one of the events that contributed to the centuries of chaos. Finally, in the tenth century B.C., Assyria began to emerge as the dominant force. Led by Assurnasirpal II and drawing on the best army in the Near East, Assyria was able to reunite Mesopotamia and to establish the first true empire the world had ever seen. Using boasts such as: "I built a pillar over against his city gate, and I flayed all the chief men... and I covered the pillar with their skins; some I walled up within the pillar, some I impaled upon the pillar on stakes...and I cut off the limbs of the officers" the Assyrians soon became the most feared army in the Near East. By the seventh century B.C. the Assyrians had established an empire stretching from the Persian Gulf north and west to Syria, Palestine, and Egypt.

The power of fear was not enough to hold together the Assyrian empire. The Assyrians had overextended themselves and had terrorized all that they conquered. It was only a matter of time before the subjected states rose up in revolt. The revolts began to occur in the late seventh century B.C. and by the end of the century the collapse of the Assyrian empire was complete. Although Babylon would enjoy a short-lived resurgence the cradle of civilization had passed its prime and was in decline. By 539 B.C. Mesopotamia had become a part of the vast Persian empire.

Writing

The greatest contribution of Mesopotamia to the rise of western civilization was the invention of writing. Writing allowed for the transmission of wisdom and knowledge, for laws to be codified, and for records to be kept thereby facilitating trade. The earliest writing found dates to 3500 B.C. and was discovered at the ancient Mesopotamian city of Uruk.

The written language of the Mesopotamians was developed by the Sumerians and is called **cuneiform**, which means "wedge-shaped." Writing was done by pressing a wedge-shaped stylus into soft clay. Other writing materials used included stone and chisel, metal and chisel, and paint on glazed terracotta. Before the development of cuneiform script written communication was in the form of pictograms. At this point writing was used only for record keeping and therefore only concrete words such as ox, grain, or sheep were needed. As society became more complex the language evolved allowing for signs to be used to depict homonyms and eventually abstract thoughts. This shift from pictograms to ideograms allowed for the development of a true system of writing in which conventionalized signs symbolized ideas. For example "*" could mean star but also could be used for heaven, sky, or god depending on the context. The system of cuneiform writing eventually spread to Persia and Egypt and for centuries was the only international script. It became a great vehicle for the growth and spread of civilization and the exchange of ideas between cultures.

Science and Technology

Writing was only one of the many advancements credited to the ancient Mesopotamians. By developing a variety of tools and techniques the Mesopotamians were the first to derive a prosperous life based on large-scale agriculture. The earliest and probably most significant development came in the fourth millennium B.C. when a Sumerian crafter built the first known wheeled vehicle. His design, using solid wooden wheels, allowed oxen to pull three times as much weight as before. Aside from the use of wheeled vehicles, Mesopotamian farmers developed seeder-plows and pickaxes to make their work easier and more efficient. The Mesopotamians became talented bakers, brewers, weavers, and tanners. Even some of their buildings, constructed of mud-brick and tile, were so well built that they have survived the ravages of time.

Beliefs

Mesopotamian religion is the oldest in the world for which written records exist. It was a **polytheistic** religion comprised of a variety of gods and demi-gods totalling 3600. This vast number of deities reflects the diversity from region to region as no one could worship this many gods. Despite the differences in the representation of the gods and the varieties found in the local towns all of Mesopotamia shared essentially the same religion. The five most prominent deities were; Enlil, the supreme god and god of the air, Ishtar, the mother-goddess of fertility and life, An, the god of heaven, Enki, the god of the underworld and the water, and Shamash, the sun god and the giver of law. The names used here are the Sumerian names. Throughout Mesopotamian history the names would change but the essential function remained the same.

Several of the myths of ancient Mesopotamia have interesting parallels with the Old Testament. Consider, for example, the story of Utnapishtim.

> There was a time when Enlil, the most powerful of the gods, was displeased with humankind and decided to send a flood that no living being could survive. But the verdict seemed too harsh to Ea, a fellow-god, who forewarned his favourite mortal, Utnapishtim, in a dream. Taking heed, Utnapishtim built a boat for himself and loaded it with his family and "the seed of all living creatures...the game of the field, and all the craftsmen". The boat weathered the storm, which raged for six days and six nights. On the seventh day, as the waters receded, he disembarked and sent forth his passengers, humans and beasts. Then, grateful for his survival, he made an offering to the gods, who reproached Enlil for his harsh decision. Enlil, in a gesture of atonement, conferred the gift of immortality upon both Utnapishtim and his devoted wife.[1]

The similarities between Utnapishtim's ordeal and the story of Noah's Ark are striking but not totally surprising when one considers the regularity of floods in ancient Mesopotamia and the influence of

---

[1]*Samuel Noah Kramer, Cradle of Civilization (New York: Time-Life Books, 1967) p. 116.*

INNOVATIONS

THE DEVELOPMENT OF *Writing*

Writing is one of the pillars of civilization as it allows for the transmission of knowledge. The first stages of writing developed in response to society's need to maintain records related to commerce and government. The Mesopotamians were the first to develop a written language. Their script is known as cuneiform meaning wedge-shaped.

Top view demonstrating position of stylus and possible orientation and angles of impression.

Early Means and Methods of Writing

Two items are required in any system of writing: something to write with and something to write on. The Mesopotamians used clay and a reed stylus. By pressing the stylus into the clay at various angles and by varying the lengths of the impression, a variety of marks were possible.

From Pictographs to Ideograms

Initially, only concrete words such as the names of plants, animals and objects were needed. As the society became more complex the demands on the written language became greater. Eventually, the pictographs evolved into stylized symbols which allowed for the writing of abstract words and complete sentences thereby becoming a true written language.

PICTOGRAM	TURNED 90° TO LEFT TO FACILITATE WRITING CA. 3100 B.C.	CUNEIFORM CA. 2400 B.C.	IDEOGRAM CA. 600 B.C.	MEANING
				BIRD
				OX
				SKY HEAVEN GOD

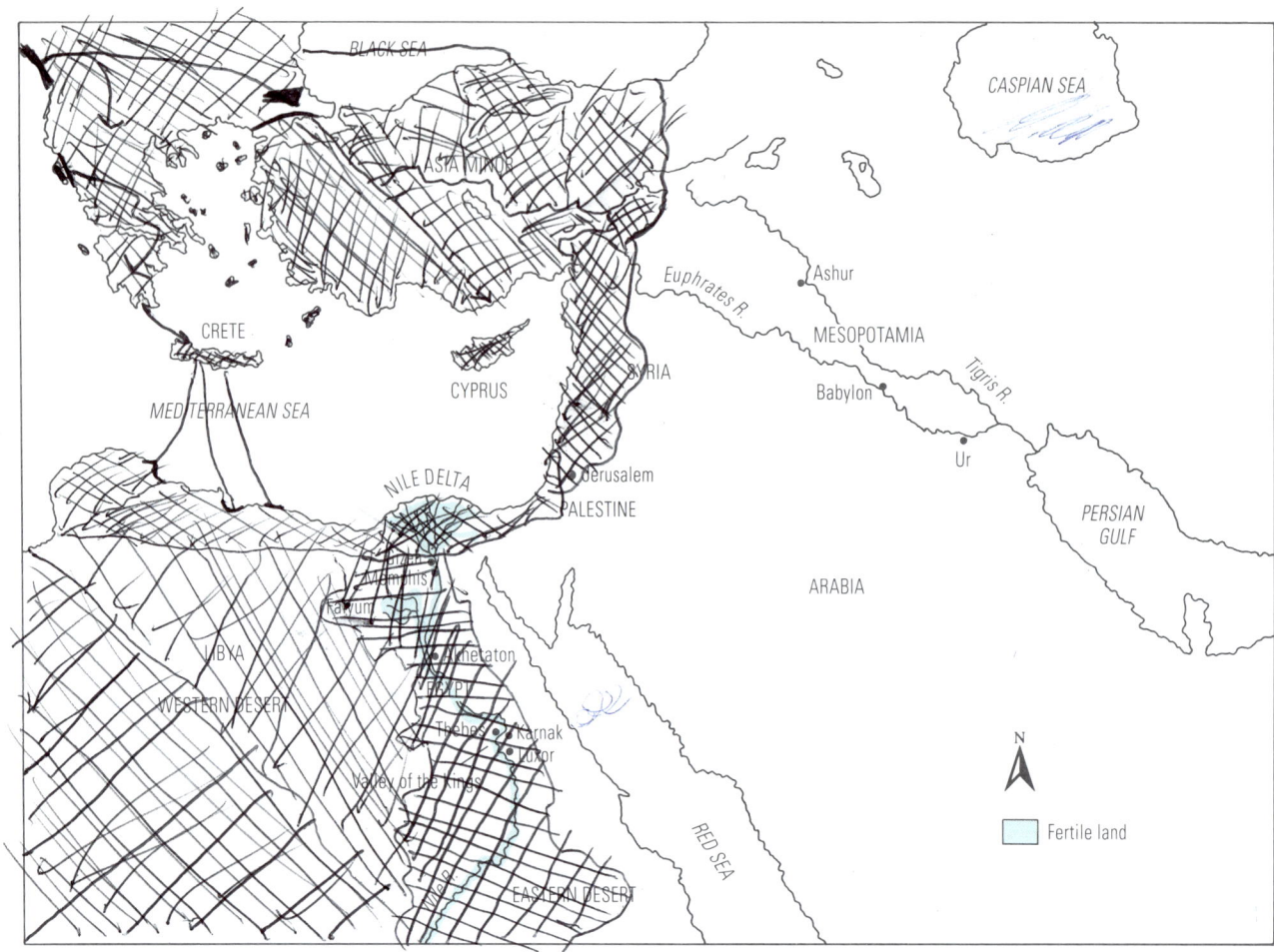

Ancient Egypt and Neighbouring States

Mesopotamian culture on other societies.

The religion of the Sumerians reflected the degree to which their lives were subject to the whims of nature. They believed that humans were helpless in the face of the gods' wrath and that life was wrought with uncertainty and plagued by insecurity. Furthermore, the Sumerians were convinced that humans were created to be the slaves and servants of the gods, and therefore accepted the hardships and catastrophes that occurred as being expected.

Despite the fatalism of their religion, it did play a central role in the everyday life of the ancient Mesopotamians. They believed that humans resembled the gods in appearance and intellect with the essential difference between them being the immortality of the gods. The gods brought order and understanding to the otherwise perplexing and unpredictable natural forces around them. Their religion also provided the Mesopotamians with spiritual and ethical guidance and an explanation of the mysteries of life and death. Thus Mesopotamian religion became

The great Ziggurat at Ur was built by Ur-Nammu. It was a massive structure with a base measuring approximately 60 by 40 m. Supported by this base are proportionally smaller structures with the chapel at the top. It was accessible by flights of steps set into the structure at an angle.

the inspiration for magnificent temples, sculptures, and works of art.

Ziggurats: Temples to the Gods

According to the beliefs of the ancient Mesopotamians it was vitally important that the gods be honoured by religious ceremonies. These ceremonies were performed by the priests in sacred temples. The temples, like most Mesopotamian architecture, were constructed of mud bricks. The constant threat of flooding forced the builders of the temples to place them on platforms. Over time the temples, which had begun as small shrines, evolved into the imposing structures known as **ziggurats**. A ziggurat was a series of platforms decreasing in size as they were placed on top of each other. The structure resembled the step pyramids of the Egyptians except that a small chapel sat on top of the ziggurat. Ziggurats ranged from one to seven platforms and were decorated with painted stucco and coloured glazed bricks. To further enhance their appearance the structures were often planted with flowers, shrubs, and trees.

One of the most famous ziggurats was the Tower of Babel. The original structure had been destroyed and rebuilt several times. The final restoration was undertaken by Nebuchadnezzar who hoped to raise the tower so that it would rival heaven. Once completed the Tower of Babel's size made it one of the great wonders of the ancient world. Its temple was perched three hundred feet atop the multi-layered ziggurat. The base measured 91 m on each side and covered half a square kilometre. Surrounding the massive structure were storehouses and apartments for the priests who served the temple.

Lasting Influence

There is no doubt that Mesopotamia deserves the title of cradle of civilization. For it was in the river valleys of the Tigris and Euphrates that people first abandoned their nomadic way of life and began to build permanent homes and villages. Such permanence led to an increasingly complex society that developed the concept of kingship and the city-state. Mesopotamia was also the birthplace of writing, astronomy, which led to the discovery of seasonal equinoxes, and of a written law code. Even the wheel, one of the most revolutionary technological advancements in history, was the product of the ingenuity of the ancient Mesopotamians. Of all this and much more we are the inheritors. Later civilizations would borrow heavily from the Mesopotamians, taking their ideas and building upon them. One such civilization was that of ancient Egypt.

Egypt: A Land of Many Wonders

What images are evoked by the mention of the name Egypt? If towering pyramids, ancient mummies, and long lost tombs containing unimaginable wealth spring to mind then you share with countless others a fascination with ancient Egypt. The sense of awe and grandeur that we feel today has been felt by visitors to Egypt for over two thousand years! The ancient Greek historian Herodotus exclaimed that Egypt "has more wonders in it than any country in the world and more works that are beyond description than anywhere else."

The Egyptians were much more than Pharaohs, pyramids, and elaborate burials. They were a living, breathing society who experienced many of the joys and sorrows we today encounter. In many ways the people of ancient Egypt are not as far removed from us as the four thousand years separating our societies would suggest. In examining this civilization of untold wonders, we must be careful not to allow the grandeur of its monuments to hide from us the people and the society that produced such treasures.

Geography

flip back to p. 47 importance of a river.

Nile Valley. There were several important geographic influences that shaped Egyptian culture and civilization. The most important of these was the Nile River. The wealth of Egypt depended entirely on the water from the Nile and thus has often been referred to as the gift of the Nile. Rainfall in the Nile Valley is negligible while rainfall in the Nile Delta is only 100–200 mL. Hence it was the flooding of the Nile upon which the fortunes of Egypt depended.

The waters of the Nile River come from the convergence of the White Nile and the Blue Nile. The Blue Nile, fed by the summer monsoons in Ethiopia, led to the flooding of the Nile. This flooding occurred annually between July and October. The receding waters left behind a rich alluvial soil which made the Nile Valley a fertile and productive region.

Unlike other major rivers such as the Tigris and the Euphrates whose flooding was often violent and unpredictable, the Nile was usually a **benevolent** and predictable ally. The Egyptians were able to plan with some certainty the planting and harvesting of crops. However, if the water levels were higher than usual serious damage could occur and water levels that did not reach their usual heights could lead to drought and famine. Thus the Nile was a force both revered and feared by the Egyptians.

Nile Delta and the Faiyum. Aside from the Nile Valley there were two other regions in Egypt that were extensively cultivated and settled. The area where the Nile empties into the Mediterranean Sea is known as the Nile Delta. The Nile Delta is the largest area of fertile land in Egypt and consequently contained many of the major centres of ancient Egypt. Lake Moeris lies at the end of a branch of the Nile. Around this lake lies an oasis known as the Faiyum. The Faiyum was the third largest area of settlement and cultivation in Egypt. Through extensive irrigation the ancient Egyptians were able to make this area a significant agricultural region.

Deserts. Perhaps the greatest irony of Egypt is the fact that the very lush and fertile Nile Valley is sandwiched between two inhospitable deserts, the Western Desert and the Eastern Desert. The isolation created by the deserts served to protect Egypt from invasion while also insulating Egyptians from outside influences. It is therefore hardly surprising that the civilization that developed would be conservative in nature and reflect incredible stability for most of its long history.

The significance of the deserts went beyond acting as a buffer against outside influences. The deserts were an important source for minerals and building supplies. Among the resources extracted

UNIT 1   *Civilizations of the Near and Far East*

from the deserts were copper, gold, tin, alabaster, limestone, amethyst, and natron, which was used in the mummification process.

The Mediterranean. Another geographic feature that significantly shaped Egyptian history was the Mediterranean Sea. It was the Mediterranean that was Egypt's major outlet for trade. The extensive trade routes that were established allowed Egypt to obtain a diversity of items. More importantly trade was the key facilitator of **cultural diffusion**. One cannot help but notice the tremendous influence of the Egyptians on the **Bronze Age Greeks** (the Minoans and Mycenaeans).

The Rise of the Egyptian Nation

With the unification of Egypt, under King Menes in about 3100 B.C., began the history of one of the world's great civilizations that would last over three thousand years. Egyptian history is generally divided into three eras each characterized by their own accomplishments. The Old Kingdom, lasting from about 2700 B.C. to about 2200 B.C. was the age of the pyramids; the Middle Kingdom, from about 2000 B.C. to about 1800 B.C. was a time when Egypt greatly expanded its political and economic boundaries; and the New Kingdom, spanning the years of about 1600 B.C. to about 1100 B.C. represented the Golden Age of Egypt.

The Old Kingdom. Prior to 3100 B.C. Egypt was likely a collection of unorganized societies. Lower Egypt or the Delta Kingdom was ruled by a monarchy symbolized by the red crown while the white crown represented the power of Upper Egypt. The legendary King Menes is believed to have been the first to unite Egypt and wear the double crown symbolizing the unity of the two kingdoms. Between 3100 B.C. and 2700 B.C. Menes and his heirs were able to consolidate their power and achieve absolute rule in Egypt. By the time of the Old Kingdom the king was ruler of all of Egypt and had been deified as well. Thus, he was the supreme ruler of all affairs, be they secular or religious.

The Old Kingdom reached its peak during the Fourth Dynasty. By engaging in trade throughout much of the Mediterranean and by mining copper in

MAJOR EVENTS IN EGYPTIAN HISTORY

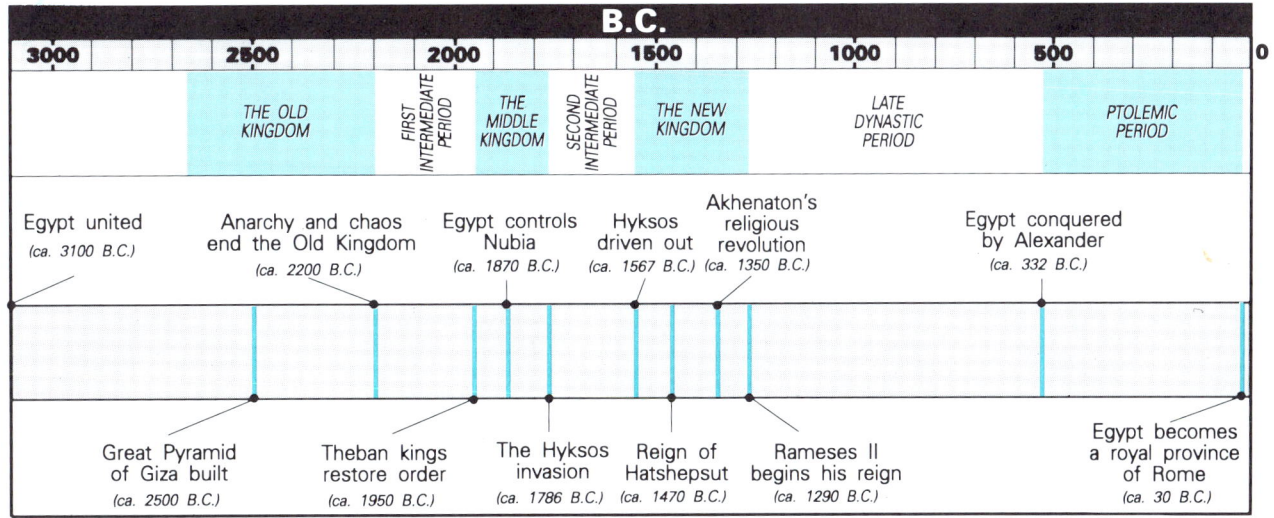

the Sinai Peninsula, the Egyptians had acquired tremendous wealth both in material goods and in new ideas. Timber from Syria, wine and oil from Crete, and the potter's wheel from Mesopotamia were all introduced to Egypt during the Old Kingdom. The greatest symbols of the wealth of the Old Kingdom were the three massive pyramids at Giza. Built between 2600–2500 B.C. the pyramids at Giza were the chief undertaking of the kings of the Fourth Dynasty, Khufu (also known as Cheops), Khafre, and Menkure. To this day these monumental structures stand as testimonials to the greatness Egypt achieved during the Old Kingdom.

The Middle Kingdom. Egypt was unable to avoid the internal dissension that can accompany prosperity. The strong central government that had allowed Egypt to flourish broke down at the end of the Old Kingdom period as local and provincial officials became increasingly more powerful. The resulting civil wars thrust Egypt into 150 years of anarchy and disorder known as the First Intermediate Period. By 2050 B.C. Egypt had been reunited under the rule of the Theban kings. For the next 250 years Egypt was to be ruled by Theban monarchs, who initially ruled at Thebes and eventually moved the capital back to Memphis. Theban supremacy was also reflected in the rise to national prominence of the god Amon. Amon had been a local deity whose principal seat of worship was Thebes. During the Middle Kingdom he was merged with the sun god Re to become Amon-Re, an Egyptian national god.

Throughout the Middle Kingdom the economic and political boundaries of Egypt were expanded. Through wars with Palestine, Libya, and Nubia the Egyptians were able to extend their influence. By encouraging social mobility through the promotion of members of the middle class the rulers of the Middle Kingdom were able to curtail the ambitions of the local princes. As a result Egypt experienced two centuries of peace and stability during which the nation prospered.

Egypt's success was to be punctured by the **Hyksos** invasion. The Hyksos were a war-like people, most likely from the area of Syria and Palestine. While the Egyptians were culturally equal or supe-

EGYPT'S MOST MEMORABLE PHARAOHS

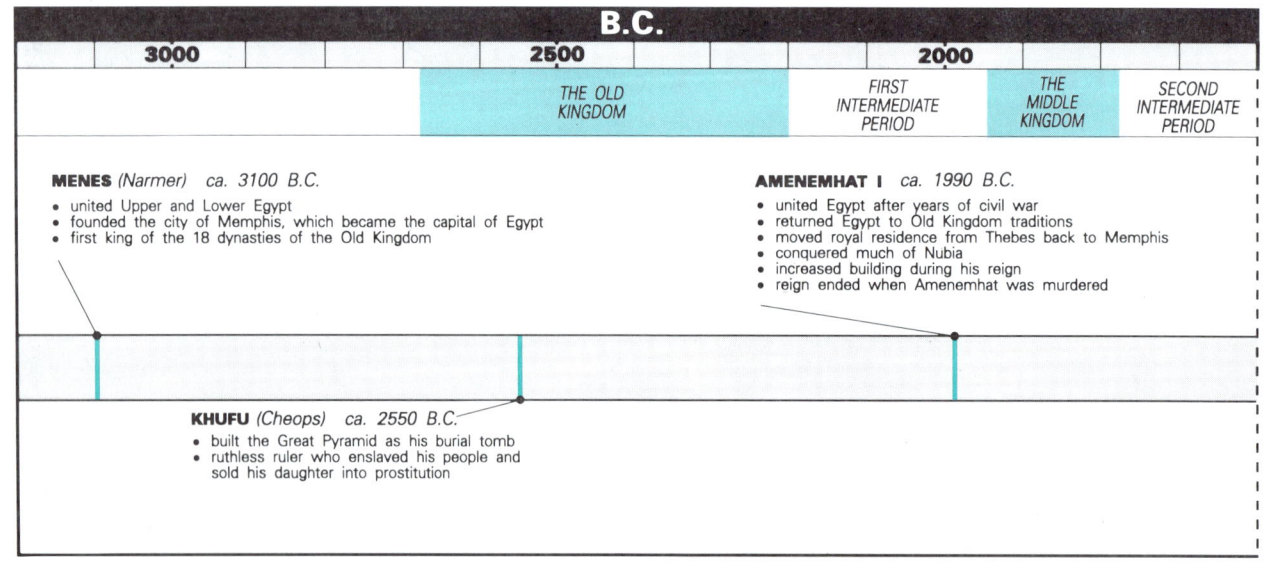

64 UNIT 1   *Civilizations of the Near and Far East*

rior to any of the civilizations of the Mediterranean they lagged behind the peoples of Anatolia in technological developments. The Egyptian army, using copper weapons, was no match for the improved bows, the horse-drawn chariots, and the bronze weapons of the Hyksos. Although the method of conquest is uncertain, the superior technology of the Hyksos was surely a factor and they were able to take over the administration of Egypt. For 150 years the Hyksos, using the existing infrastructure, ruled Egypt. In the end the Egyptians came to master the new weapons introduced by the Hyksos and were able to drive them out of Egypt. Egypt emerged from the Second Intermediate Period strengthened and revitalized.

The New Kingdom. Egyptian civilization reached its apex during the New Kingdom. It was during these five centuries that Egypt experienced its Golden Age, building an empire and producing fine works of art. The New Kingdom was also a period dominated by several larger than life characters.

Hatshepsut has been referred to as history's first powerful female leader. When her husband Thutmose II died, Hatshepsut became regent for her young stepson. Rather than govern in his name until he was old enough to assume the throne, Hatshepsut declared herself the female king of Egypt. Statues and paintings often show Hatshepsut wearing a beard to symbolize her power. The reign of Egypt's most famous woman has been described as a period of peace, stability, and prosperity.

Hatshepsut was succeeded by the stepson she had earlier deposed. Thutmose III, known to historians as the Napoleon of Egypt, is best remembered for his numerous military campaigns into Anatolia. Much of the wealth of the New Kingdom was derived from **tribute** paid by the people subjugated during Thutmose III's conquests.

In the midst of unparalleled wealth and power the Egyptians faced an attempted religious revolution from which they never fully recovered. Amonhotep IV, who changed his name to Akhenaton, concentrated his energies on reforming Egyptian religion. Akhenaton opposed the worship of Amon-Re, traditionally the supreme god of the Egyptians. In place

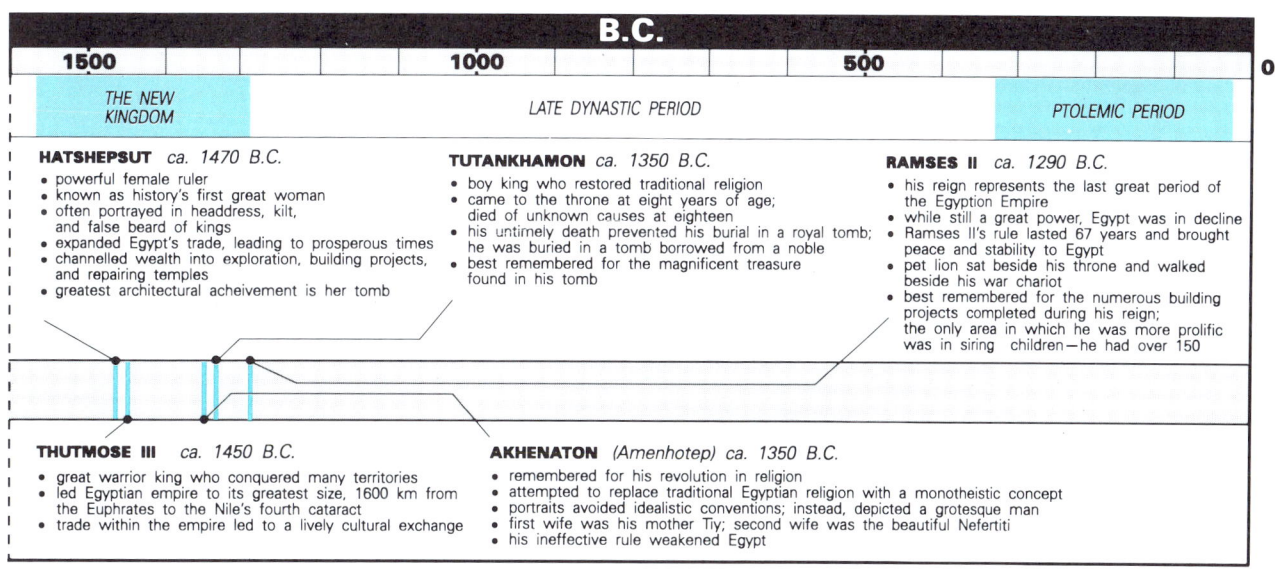

Egypt and the Near East CHAPTER 3

A Tomb Fit for a Queen
The wealth and power of Hatshepsut's reign are reflected in her burial tomb. Of all the tombs found in the Valley of the Kings, none are as impressive as hers. The imposing colonnaded façade creates a sense of grandeur appropriate for one of Egypt's greatest rulers.

of Amon-Re Akhenaton sponsored the worship of Aton. To promote the new cult he took the name Akhenaton, meaning "he who serves Aton" and built a new capital city called Akhetaton ("Place of the Glory of Aton"). Akhenaton also had the temples of other gods closed and their possessions confiscated. These actions have since caused Akhenaton to be referred to as the first **monotheist**. This term is somewhat anachronistic as the Egyptian people were still expected to worship the pharaoh while the royal family worshipped Aton.

Akhenaton's preoccupation with reforming Egyptian religion left him little time to govern the empire built up by his predecessors. By the time of his death the Egyptian empire was crumbling from neglect. While still a dominant power Egyptian civilization had begun its long decline. Tutankhamon came to power as a young child. He should best be remembered as the pharaoh who, under the guidance of his advisors, restored traditional Egyptian religion. As successor to Akhenaton, it was Tutankhamon and his advisors who destroyed the cult of Aton. He is, however, better known for the incredible wealth found in his tomb. As the only royal tomb found virtually intact, Tutankhamon's name has come to be associated with the long-lost treasures of ages past. The treasures found by Howard Carter in 1922 included gold inlaid furniture, lavish jewellery, and a solid gold coffin.

By the time of Ramses II, 60 years later, Egypt was in its twilight years. The 67 years of Ramses II's reign represents the final grandeur of Egyptian civilization. During his time Ramses II constructed more buildings and colossal statues than any other Egyptian king. Among his greatest monuments are the two huge temples at Abu Simbel, which were the focus of a massive undertaking in the 1960s to save them from being submerged beneath the artificial lake that was created with the construction of the Aswan High Dam. The salvage operation involved dismantling the temple facades by cutting them into huge blocks and moving them 210 m further from the river, where they were placed in a simulated environment. The operation took 4 years and cost 40 million dollars to complete.

It was not long after the reign of Ramses II that Egypt was invaded and eventually fell under the rule of foreigners. During the next thousand years Nubians, Assyrians, Persians, Greeks, and Romans would govern the state of Egypt. The once grand and

UNIT 1   *Civilizations of the Near and Far East*

mighty Egyptian civilization was in decline. Yet, despite being subjected to the rule of foreigners for the next three millennia the grandeur that was Egypt has never been lost. All those who have gazed upon the remnants of ancient Egypt have felt a sense of awe and reverence for a once great civilization.

Egyptian Beliefs

In attempting to understand Egyptian culture and society no factor is more significant than religion. The Egyptians were a deeply religious people for whom the sacred and the secular were inseparable. Religion was an integral part of all aspects of Egyptian life.

Societies whose livelihood is closely linked to environmental factors often show a special reverence towards nature. Early Egyptian society was no exception. The religion of early Egypt had its roots in the worship of nature deities, and the first gods to arise were frequently represented in animal form. In time, as their religious concepts became more complex, the gods of Egypt became **anthropomorphic**. Gods in human form became fused with earlier ideas resulting in an interesting mix of human bodies with animal attributes.

The fact that Egyptian gods were portrayed in animal forms or a combination of human and animal traits should not be misinterpreted. Initially animals were used by towns as figureheads, serving as a rallying point for soldiers in battle. They were used to give a concrete form to a particular characteristic. For example hawks and falcons were especially favoured for their swiftness, crocodiles instilled fear into the hearts of enemies, and the ichneumon (Egyptian mongoose) represented the ability to devour one's enemies who were portrayed as snakes. Dogs and cats were also popular as they were seen as loyal. Hence, the gods were given the form or attributes of the animal whose characteristics they were believed to embody.

Another misconception regarding Egyptian religion is that they worshipped hundreds of gods. In fact each town or region had their own local deities and myths relating to various phenomena such as creation. Each local god usually had a goddess wife to whom the village women made their plea. The divine couple often had a son or daughter thus completing the family. Also included in the daily lives of Egyptians from the time of the Middle Kingdom were a number of **demigods**. These figures were not actually gods, but were believed to bring luck, divert anger and sadness, or help women conceive.

From the time of the Middle Kingdom national gods began to emerge. The most significant of these was Amon, the local god of Thebes and thus the favoured god of the Theban kings. The other deities common to the Egyptians were the gods of the dead including Osiris, Anubis, Horus, and Thoth.

The Egyptian Idea of Spirit. The Egyptians had a very complex explanation for their existence. Aside from the physical body each individual had a ka, ba, and akh. According to Egyptian beliefs infants were placed in the mother's womb after being created on a potter's wheel by the god Khnum. For each human crafted, Khnum also made a spiritual duplicate. This was called the ka. The ka was stored in the heart and at death was separated from the body. It would inhabit the tomb of the individual to be near the body in which it had spent its life. Like the living body from which it had come, the ka would need items such as food, clothing, perfume, and furniture.

The ba was a non-physical element unique to each person. It entered the body at the time of birth and left the body at death. The ba is best described as a person's character or personality and was depicted as a human-headed bird. When someone died their mummy needed to be transformed into a form that could exist in the afterworld. This form was called

BELIEFS

GALLERY of EGYPTIAN GODS

Although the Egyptians worshipped a number of local deities, several of these rose to national prominence. Illustrated below is a selection of the more significant gods with a brief description.

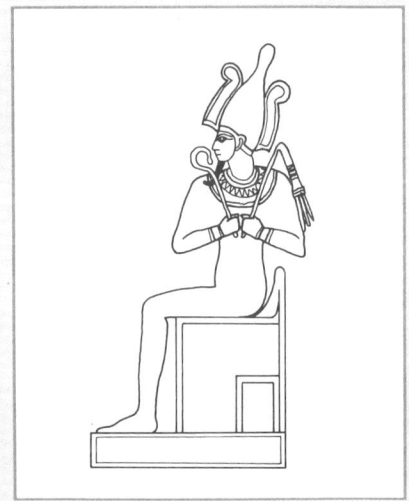

Amon rose to national prominence during the Middle Kingdom under the Theban rulers and became the king of the gods. He was portrayed as a human wearing a headdress with two plumes.

Re, the sun god of Heliopolis, was portrayed as having a sun disc on his head. He was often named as the creator of humans. Later on the gods Amon and Re were united as the god Amon-Re.

Osiris was the god of the earth and vegetation and was always portrayed in a mummified form. After having been murdered by his brother Seth he was reborn; this came to symbolize the yearly cycle of the Nile.

 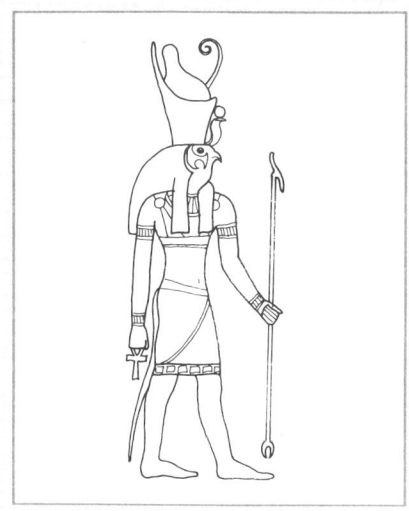 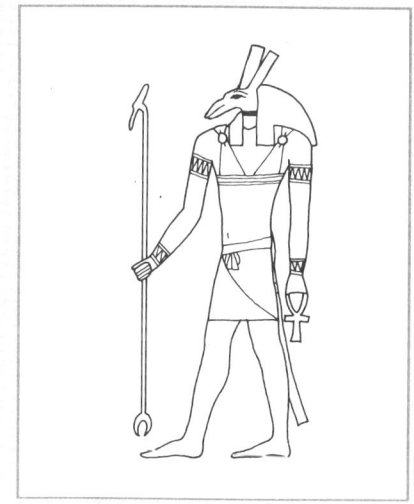

Anubis was the jackal-headed god of mummification and was portrayed as holding the divine sceptre of the kings and gods. Anubis presided over the bandaging of the dead and the weighing of the heart.

Horus was the son of Isis and Osiris. He was portrayed as the falcon-headed god wearing the double-crown of Egypt. Egyptian kings saw themselves as the physical manifestation of Horus on earth.

Seth was the Lord of Upper Egypt, and was portrayed as an imaginary animal resembling a donkey. Seth was associated with the desert and storms.

  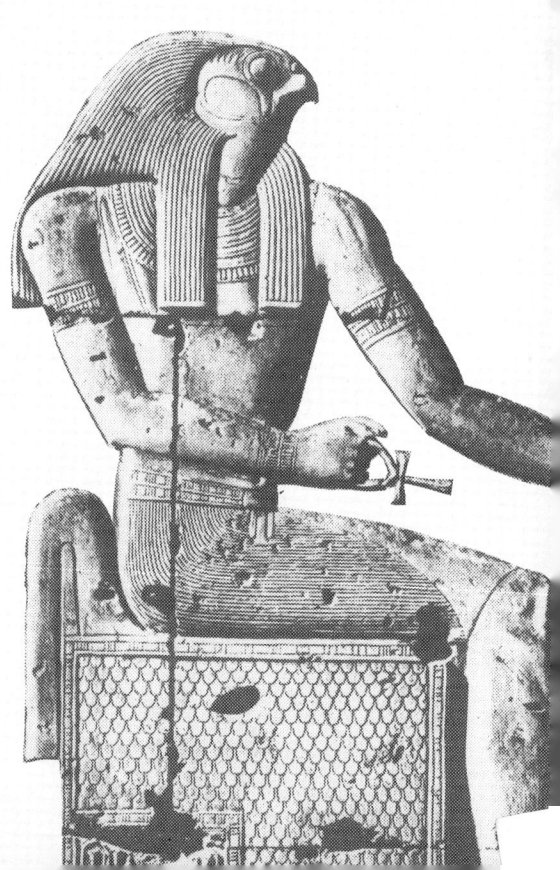

Thoth was the ibis-headed god of wisdom and writing and was associated with the moon.

Isis was the wife and sister of Osiris. Isis used her magical powers to protect children and was often portrayed as carrying a suckling child.

the akh. The transformation took place through the use of magical spells said over the mummy.

A final concept central to Egyptian religion was that of **maat**. Maat, which was essentially order, truth, and justice, was a quality Egyptians believed was put in the world at the time of creation. Individuals were supposed to act in accordance with maat as it represented the divine will. Only by living in accordance with the divine will could the Egyptians achieve harmony with the gods and be assured entry into the hereafter. Maat's physical representation was in the form of a woman wearing an ostrich feather on her head.

The Afterlife. Considering the elaborate rituals associated with death and the time and expense put towards preparing tombs it is not surprising that the Egyptians have mistakenly been viewed as a sombre and even morbid people. In fact the Egyptian concept of the afterlife is a reflection of their zeal for life and their optimistic outlook. The Egyptians saw the afterlife as a duplication of the best moments on earth. They expected that in their afterlife they would be engaged in the activities they enjoyed most such as fishing, hunting, feasting, or sailing. Thus death to the Egyptians was not an end but a beginning.

The concept of an afterlife was a basic religious belief common to all Egyptians regardless of their social status. The preparation for the afterlife varied considerably depending on whether the individual was royal, noble, or peasant. But for all, there were two basic requirements. First, the body must be preserved in a lifelike form and second, the deceased must be provided with the items necessary for a life in the hereafter. The goods provided ranged from a few simple possessions placed with a peasant to the elaborate storehouse of treasures which accompanied the kings and queens. Royal tombs commonly held large food supplies, furniture, tools, weapons, chests of clothes, jewellery, and games. All Egyptians, whether rich or poor, believed that the essence of the deceased continued to be tied to this world even after death. This essence, or the ka, returned via the preserved body and received its sustenance from the food and drink left in the tomb and continued to enjoy the material possessions placed in the tomb.

Egyptian Burial Practices. Central to Egyptian religious beliefs was the need to preserve the body. It is likely that mummification was a development in the evolution of Egyptian burial practices. The earliest people to settle in the Nile Valley buried their dead in pit-graves dug in the hot desert sands bordering Egypt. The rainless climate and the dryness of the sand around the body caused a natural process of **desiccation** whereby the bodily fluids were absorbed by the sand, preventing the body from decaying. Accidental exposure by shifting sands or by desert animals such as the jackal would have exposed some of the bodies to later generations making them aware of the preservation of the body. This in turn would have contributed to the linking of the afterlife with the need to preserve the body.

As Egyptian burials became more elaborate the body of the deceased came to be placed in a lined tomb. Since the bodies were no longer surrounded by the sand, desiccation did not occur naturally and the bodies decomposed. As a consequence, the Egyptians developed an artificial means to duplicate what had previously happened naturally. This process is known as mummification. Initially the Egyptians simply wrapped the body of the deceased in resin-soaked linens to preserve a life-like form. Eventually a more elaborate process was devised that enabled them to prevent the body from decaying. This process was lengthy and expensive and therefore the special reserve of royalty and the nobility. Peasants continued to rely on the natural desiccation that occurred when the deceased were buried in pit-graves in the sand.

INNOVATIONS

THE MAKING OF A MUMMY

Mummification was a complicated and lengthy process; lasting up to 70 days. It began with the body being delivered to the embalmer. The embalmer would bathe the body and lay it out. In preparation the priests would shave their entire bodies and the priest in charge would wear the mask of a jackal representing the god Anubis. Then, the following steps took place:

Step one
- brains removed through the nostrils using a hook-like instrument

Step two
- priest in charge turned body on its right side
- incision made and major organs removed
- heart (considered the seat of intelligence) left in place

Step three
- each organ dried using natron
- organs placed in respective canopic jars, representing four sons of Horus
- Hapi (baboon) guarded the lungs; Duamutefla (dog) the stomach; Imseti (human) the liver; Qebehsenuef (falcon) the intestines

Step four
- body cleansed with wine
- cavity stuffed with linen
- body covered with natron and dried for 70 days

Step five
- once body fully dried, anointed with spices and herbs
- mouth cleansed and stuffed with linen
- nostrils cleansed and stuffed with wax
- linen placed under each eyelid which was drawn over linen
- incision closed
- wires of gold fastened over nails to hold in place

Step six
- body wrapped in 150 m of linen
- deceased's name written on cloth to preserve identity
- amulets and jewellery hidden in the folds of the wrappings

71

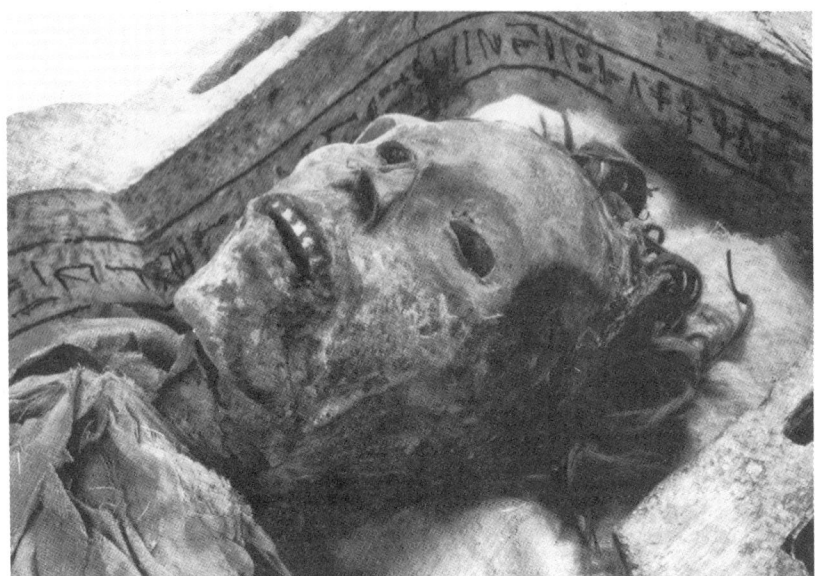

An-tjou, who is from the ROM collection, was mummified around 600 B.C. As he had no titles, little is known about An-tjou other than the fact that he was descended from a Libyan mercenary chieftain and was wealthy enough to be mummified.

An Egyptian Funeral. The funerals of Egypt's elite were lengthy and elaborate affairs. When someone died a period of loud mourning took place. The female relatives of the deceased, as well as paid mourners, would bare their breasts and walk through the streets crying out in grief. They would be followed by the male relatives who were also bare to the waist and who pounded their chests in sorrow. Later there would be a more composed procession in which the body was transferred from the home to the embalmers where the mummification took place. This process took about 70 days to complete. Once the process of mummification was completed the mummy was returned to the family and the final procession to the tomb would begin. In this procession the mummy was placed on a sledge drawn by oxen. This was followed by a second sledge drawn by men that carried the **canopic jars** containing the deceased's preserved internal organs. At the rear of the procession were the servants who carried objects the deceased would need in the afterlife. Upon arrival at the tomb a priest would touch the mummy's eyes and the grave goods were lowered in place through the roof as there was no entrance. Once everything was in place the entire structure was roofed over. Some **mastaba** tombs were massive and elaborate structures designed to imitate palace facades. Later mastabas built for royalty were surrounded by smaller tombs containing the bodies of their followers. They also may have contained mortuary chapels to which offerings were brought. By the beginning of the Old Kingdom Egyptian kings were assumed to be the living embodiment of Horus, the son of the god Osiris. Obviously a person of such stature had to be laid to rest in a tomb that suited their status. The pyramid was such a tomb. The choice of the pyramid shape may have been an attempt on the part of the Egyptians to recreate the mound they believed had emerged from the waters of chaos at the time of creation. Over 40 pyramids have been discovered in Egypt dating primarily from the Old Kingdom although some from the end of the Middle Kingdom and the New Kingdom have also been found.

The earliest pyramids were in fact a series of mastabas stacked one on top of the other. For example the famous Step Pyramid at Saqqara built for King Djoser began as a single mastaba on which five additional mastabas descending in size were placed. The burial chamber of the king remained underground as was customary.

Pyramid construction reached its climax with the building of King Khufu's tomb at Giza. Known as the Great Pyramid, this structure rose 146 m in the air and had sides 238 m long. In total the base of the Great Pyramid covers six hectares! The Great Pyramid is constructed of two-and-a-half million stone blocks weighing on average two-and-a-half tonnes each and to this day is the largest stone structure in the world. All this was completed during the 23 years of Khufu's reign and without the aid of the wheel, lifting devices, or draft animals.

By the time of the New Kingdom the pharaohs had come to realize the folly of building the massive pyramids. Nothing could better advertise to grave robbers the location of a deceased pharaoh and his riches than these monuments rising majestically from the desert. In hopes of eternal security the pharaohs of the New Kingdom chose two quiet and hidden valleys, which they believed would be safe since they were isolated and could be easily guarded. These valleys near Luxor we now call the **Valley of the Kings** and the Valley of the Queens. Here the pharaohs had elaborate tombs cut deep in the valley walls. The tombs had high corridors brightly painted with inscriptions from various religious texts such as the *Book of What is In the Underworld*. These corridors led to the burial chamber and a side chamber that contained the royal grave goods. The burial chamber was covered with scenes from the life of the deceased designed to convince the gods that they had led a good life in accordance with maat. The ceiling of the burial chamber was often covered with an astronomical map of the heavens.

Temples. Not all of the time and effort of the Egyptians went into building tombs for the pharaohs. A great deal of time was devoted to the

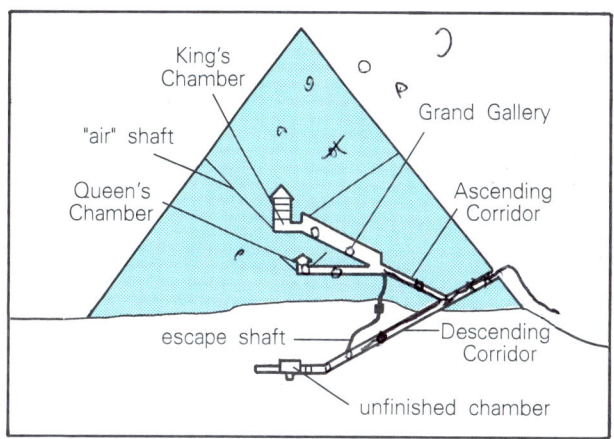

Few monuments are as impressive as the Great Pyramids of Giza. To this day, Khufu's burial tomb is the largest stone structure in the world. The interior of the pyramid is as impressive as its size. The design was altered twice during its construction leaving the Queen's chamber and an underground room unfinished.

construction of temples dedicated to the gods. These massive structures usually made of sandstone were designed to be enjoyed from the inside during a ceremony rather than as an accent to the landscape. All Egyptian temples had the same basic features: a monumental gateway, a roofless colonnaded court, a great hall with a ceiling resting on massive sandstone columns, and a private sanctuary of the god. The massive temple was in turn part of an even larger complex that included living quarters, workshops, a school, a sacred pool, granaries, and other storehouses. Thus the religious complex contained all the necessary facilities to support a community dedicated to serving the god. The largest and most famous of these temples is the Temple of Amon at Karnak. In this temple 134 pillars, all depicting scenes of the king worshipping Amon, stand like massive tree trunks.

Egyptian Art

Art is often a mirror of the society that produced it. It reflects their hopes and fears, joys and sorrows. The

THE ARTS

CONVENTIONS of EGYPTIAN ART

Egyptian artists painted for religious reasons, not to realistically depict the subject. The intent was to portray the character of the deceased and to illustrate the activities to be enjoyed in the afterlife. The art was governed by many conventions and it is these customs that gave Egyptian art its characteristic appearance.

❶ **Profile**
- head painted in profile
- side view of eye and eyebrow in face
- eye never looking straight ahead

❷ **Colour**
- men painted in red ochre
- women painted in yellow ochre

❸ **Stance**
- hips had a three-quarter turn
- chest and shoulders shown at their full width
- both feet, legs, arms and hands had to be showing

❹ **Scale**
- size of figures indicated social standing
- central figure noticeably larger than the rest
- men much larger than their wives
- wives and children often portrayed as crouching below with arms around calves

❺ **Proportions**
- hands and feet often disproportionally large

NOTE:
- Commoners were often portrayed with more realism as they were not subject to these conventions.
- More formal depictions of nobility often contained symbols of power such as the crook and flail.

art of the ancient Egyptians reveals a very conservative people. This conservatism was one of the three key factors that shaped the nature of Egyptian art. The other two factors were that virtually all art was produced for religious purposes and that the pharaoh was the chief patron and main subject of the arts. As a consequence Egyptian art was not innovative but sought to remain unchanged by following traditions established at the outset of the Old Kingdom. The resistance to change inherent in Egyptian art was a product of their quest for eternity. Their preoccupation with permanence produced an art of conventions and idealization. The fact that Egyptian art followed these conventions, remaining virtually unchanged for over three thousand years, is in itself impressive.

The artistic conventions adopted by the Egyptians were not to limit the artist but to ensure that each work possessed clarity, harmony, and balance. For example, the fists were often clenched so as to make the forearm muscles visible, or the face showed no signs of age or illness. Art for the Egyptians served to capture for eternity the ideal form of the individual represented.

Sculpture. The most majestic and imposing works of art produced by the Egyptians were their statues. Egyptian sculpture ranged in size from small models to colossal statues such as the Sphinx (20 m high and 73 m long) and the statues of Ramses II (20 m high). Egyptian statues generally looked straight ahead and were not engaged in any activity. The result of such a pose is that the statues are very rigid and lacking in emotion. While Egyptian sculpture may not have had the life-like qualities of later Greek statues they did capture the majesty and character of the pharaohs for eternity.

Carved Relief and Painting. Two artistic forms commonly found in the tombs of the pharaohs and the nobility were **reliefs** and wall paintings. Both served a similar purpose; to convey to the gods the character of the deceased, or to illustrate the activities they looked forward to enjoying in their afterlife. Carved reliefs are pictures that are cut into the stone walls. They were either raised with the area around the figures being removed or sunk, or the figures themselves were carved into the surface. Paintings were generally considered second best and most often used in tombs where poor rock surfaces made relief work difficult. In some cases paintings were selected over reliefs as they were a less costly and time consuming alternative.

Perspective was not a primary concern to ancient Egyptian artists. Instead they produced mathematically precise paintings and reliefs that were concerned with relaying the necessary information. Realism was the least of the artist's concerns. Aside from the contrived stance and the disproportionate size of the figures, the Egyptian paintings show many other examples of the conveyance of information taking precedence over reality. For example, Egyptian artists often used what is called false transparency to relate the necessary information. In a picture of a man dipping a ladle into a pot the viewer should not be able to see the contents of the pot or the ladle; the Egyptians, however, in their painting made both the contents and the ladle visible as if the pot were made of glass.

In the study of Egyptian art it is important to view it from their perspective not ours. The task set before the ancient Egyptian artist was to capture for eternity the essence and the character of the deceased. In this conservative society the artists were not supposed to be innovators. Theirs was a much loftier task, to speak to the gods through their works of art. Viewed in this light, the Egyptian artists were not only successful but also played a vital role in a vibrant society.

Life Among the Ancient Egyptians

History is often a record of the lives and exploits of the powerful and the wealthy. Battles were won by them, tombs were created for them, they were the focus of society and they reaped its benefits. The life of the masses has, in recent years, become of greater concern to historians. Ethnohistory is a new and challenging field that combines various disciplines such as archaeology, anthropology, and historical studies to unearth a part of our past that has often been neglected. To do a civilization justice we must look at all the strata within a society and all the elements that make up the daily life and routines of this civilization.

The bountiful harvest that was collected annually in the Nile Valley and the security afforded by Egypt's relative isolation ensured all Egyptians, regardless of their station in life, a comfortable existence. Recent studies on Egyptian daily life offer a fascinating perspective of a lifestyle from well over 3000 years ago. This perspective was supplied by the wealth of funerary offerings placed in the tombs, agricultural implements, domestic items, colourful and lively paintings, and small figurines engaged in all sorts of activities representative of everyday Egyptian life. Imagine stepping back in time and taking the role of one of these characters portrayed in Egyptian art during the New Kingdom.

What would it have been like to be a member of one of the great civilizations of antiquity? Had you been an artisan, a merchant, a trader, or a common labourer in ancient Egypt you would have lived in a one-storey mud-brick home which looked no different from the outside than the rest of the dusty yellow houses on the crowded street. These houses had four square rooms with only window slits to ensure privacy and cool shelter from the hot midday sun. Furnishings would have been simple, reed mats and cushions, sometimes a wooden chest or a table. This was home to the ancient Egyptians.

The Family. The home was the refuge and the gathering place for the family—a place to escape from the noisy confusion of the village, a place to wash the dust away, and to eat and sleep when not labouring out in the endless fields alongside the Nile.

Children were fed and dressed simply and allowed few extravagances. Mothers or elder sisters cared for the children until they were four to six years old, when they were sent off to be educated either in a teaching room by a priest or by the father who would pass on all the knowledge about his trade or occupation.

The Role of Women. The interpretation of ancient Egyptian life comes mainly from tomb decorations, and this includes what is known about the role of women in society. It seems women were respected in their sphere of domestic life. The female flesh colour in the paintings and models (yellow, instead of the much darker flesh-tones of the male) may indicate a sheltered life out of the sun. In early tomb decorations women are often absent from heavy or culturally important work. At times their role seems decorous, since they are usually depicted in the ideal, slender and young. Later women were depicted much more often and in more elaborate clothing. Still, they didn't hold important titles, had little political power, were usually illiterate, and were barred from intellectual aspects of government or society. In marriage, within the domestic sphere, a woman's role was important and she had the right to make a will or to ask for a divorce. By contrasting what is known of Egyptian men the lives of women seem to be very limiting, but one cannot be sure of this.

The Role of Men. The husband was the head of the family and passed on the inheritance to his children. Marriage property was agreed upon by a marriage settlement, and did not necessarily follow a rigid pattern. He was not restricted to the number of wives he could have, but economics usually dictated that he take only one wife. The priests also exerted a powerful moral influence and although harems and concubines existed, sexual excesses were not evident in everyday social life. The man of the household was the labourer, the craftsman, or the official. Since he was the holder of the office or the occupation, this was hereditary through the male line of descent. It took many generations to acquire skills and secrets of the trade and sons were expected to continue the tradition. Change was not encouraged since this was a risk. Instead the sons and after them their sons continued within their specialized professions.

Formal Education. The sons of priests, pharaohs, and administrative families were educated in a more formal manner, and in these classes the son also inherited the father's position. Literacy was of paramount importance in the running of the highly bureaucratic Egyptian society. Therefore it was a priority to teach children to read and write and, once obtained, these skills were highly valued. The children learned two types of writing, rewriting existing poetry and prose, and business writing. Business writing was required for the numerous and varied tasks that gave the scribe his rank and importance to society.

Clothing of the Commoner. A day in the fields would begin early, making use of the best part of the day. The labourer would wear as little as possible, a pleated or knotted loincloth made of very light material or perhaps nothing at all. They may have worn their wig, if they had one, to protect their head from the sun. Children and servant girls often wore only an amulet around their necks or a string of beads around their waist. The women wore long, narrow robes made of a light, almost transparent linen that was easy to clean and good protection against the heat. Among the commoners, it was felt that footwear was unnecessary and that going barefoot was preferable.

Agriculture. As much as they depended on the Nile it also dictated the labourer's life. At the beginning of the year when the Nile flooded, dams and canals had to be maintained and repaired. It was necessary to retain as much of this valuable water as possible after the Nile receded. The river also left fertile soil on the fields and after the surveyors had marked out the land with their ropes the labourers sowed the land as soon as possible. Grains such as barley and wheat, vegetables such as onions, leeks, lettuce, radishes, gourds, melons, peas, and lentils grew well in these fertile areas. Planting did not take much time as the soil was usually soft. Children and labourers drove herds of animals over the saturated earth to churn up the ground and to stamp in the seeds. During the rest of the growing season the crops were cultivated and the livestock was herded to the fields to graze.

Then the tax collectors and scribes descended on the fields to calculate the yield and to assess taxes. The harvest would end up in the landowner's

This miniature, found in a tomb, depicts several activities surrounding the harvesting and processing of grain. Figures such as these were arranged in a wide range of activities and were meant to accompany and serve the deceased in the afterlife.

kitchen, or in the town market, or perhaps be given to the labourers as payment.

Foods and Festivals. The next season was a time for festivals since food had been assured until the next year. The people were relieved from their agricultural duties, but were involved in community jobs such as building temples and tombs. Festivals were a joyous occasion for young and old, rich and poor. Reasons for celebrating may have been religious, political, the butchering of an ox, or to end a successful hunt in the marshes.

A banquet or a festival would require some preparation. The room needed to be decorated with flowers and perfumed, the food needed to be prepared and the entertainment arranged. The kitchen would be full of servants busily preparing the festival fare, a freshly slaughtered ox, an assortment of roasted or boiled game such as wild goat, gazelle, quail, duck, or fish, and vegetables that were in season such as leeks, melons, onion, beans, chick peas, lettuce, and radishes. Seasoning for the meat and vegetables would include garlic, onions, beer, milk, and wine. There would also be a wide selection of wild and cultivated fruits, among these grapes, figs, dates, and pomegranates. The pastries and cakes were shaped and decorated with preserves and sweetened with honey. The guests could help themselves directly from the heaping plates placed on tables or offered to them by servants. Food would be eaten using many different types of bread to mop up the plate afterwards.

The guests would arrive in their brightly coloured clothes often bringing their pet dogs, cats, or monkeys. In the spirit of the decorations and scents of the house, they would be annointed, offered a flower, and given a cone of fat that they would place on their head, it would melt and produce a perfumed scent. The Egyptians loved to enjoy themselves; harp, flute, tambourine, or castanet music accompanied the professional dancers. There may have been acrobats, board games, ball games, or wrestling matches. Wine and beer flowed freely throughout the evening. Since Egypt had an abundance of grapes and effective methods of wine production they created refreshing wines that were much more popular than the dull inexpensive beer. As these drinks were plentiful there was always the danger of excess—sometimes these festivals turned rather bawdy and raucous. The priests could not limit the behavior at the banquets but encouraged the rather sobering custom of reminding the guests of their approaching death; every guest was shown a little statue of a mummified corpse—usually Osiris—and this achieved the desired effect!

Housing and Furniture of the Upper Classes. These festivities may have taken place in the house of a member of the aristocracy, or a public official such as a vizier, or a scribe, or a wealthy landowner or farmer, or perhaps an officer of the military. This house or villa was spacious, opulent, and luxurious, alive with a richness of detail and colour. The interior of the house was clean, airy, and decorated with vases of flowers and floral patterns on the walls. The furniture contributed to the impression of tasteful ornamentation. The imported timber from Lebanon and Syria was crafted carefully into beautiful pieces inlaid with semi-precious stones, ivory, and **faience**. Upon examining these masterpieces more closely it is evident that the Egyptian crafters possessed remarkable skills in joinery and veneering. Much of the furniture was covered in gold or silver overlay creating functional opulence fit for pharaohs.

The rooms were pleasantly arranged in two levels opening up on an ornamental courtyard with trees, fountains, and a pool. The terrace, which was on the roof, looked out on the courtyard as well and was a pleasant escape from the heat of the night. The most impressive feature of the house was its size. Ceilings were high and rooms were numerous enough to accommodate servants and family. The occupants

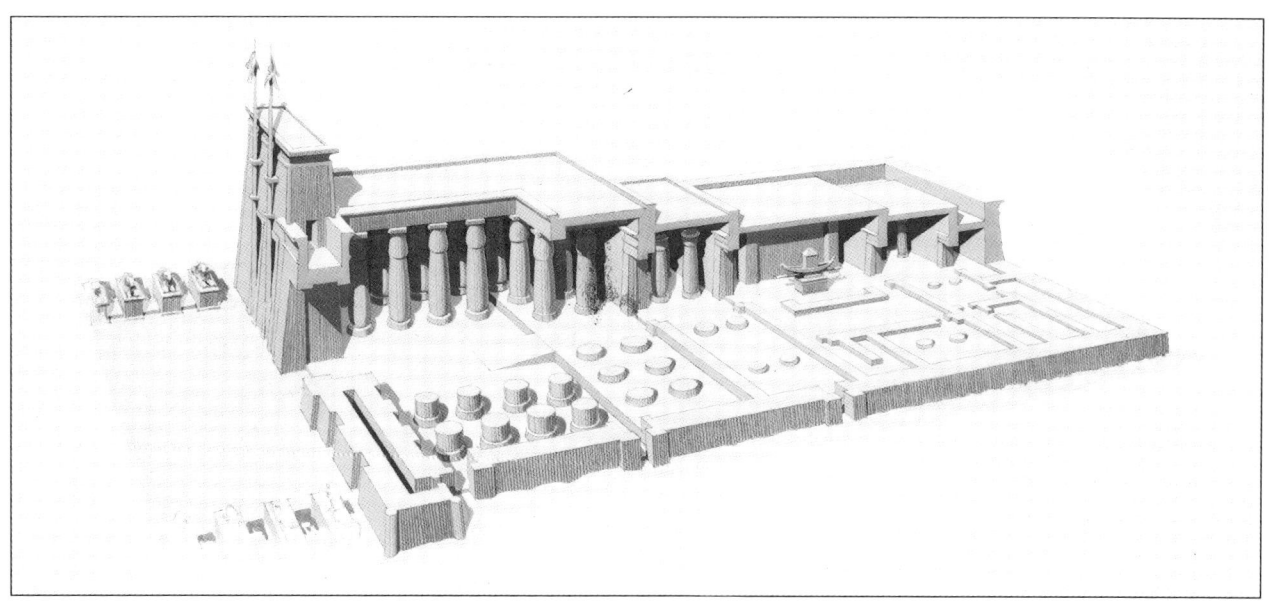

A typical Egyptian temple was a massive complex containing all that was necessary for a sanctuary to survive independently. The colonnades used by the Egyptians were brightly painted, depicting scenes from various religious texts. Some of the rooms were designed to throw off grave robbers with false doors and entrances. The burial chamber was surrounded by several smaller chambers which contained the various grave gods.

appreciated this home for its efficiency but most of all for the fact that it was perfectly designed for their relaxed and comfortable lifestyle.

Clothing and Jewellery of the Upper Classes. This love of functional ornamentation was also obvious in the clothing they chose to wear—it was practical yet elegant. Their jewellery was their means for personal expression. The sophistication in dress and in the jewellery increased with the importance of rank or the family.

The men would wear the loincloth common to the lower classes but would cover this with a full linen tunic with sleeves secured with an elegant belt. Footwear was indicative of aristocracy even though sandals were not very comfortable. Pharaohs often wore pictures of their enemies on the soles of their shoes to insult them by stepping on their faces.

The women wore similar clothing to the women of the lower classes although the cloth might have been finer and decorated with lively patterns and bright colours. The finest, softest cloth was of course kept for the queen. This elegant simplicity was highlighted with an assortment of finely crafted jewellery such as earrings, rings, bracelets, necklaces, breastplates, anklets, and belts. This jewellery reflected a break from the traditional Egyptian art as the artist was less bound by convention and rules. Their craft demonstrated a skill that has never been surpassed. Using gold, silver, agate, jasper, garnet, amethyst, and turquoise in fanciful engraved or twisted forms the Egyptians fashioned exquisite accent pieces. This jewellery was stored in finely crafted boxes of ivory or wood covered in gold.

Cosmetics. Beside the jewellery box would be another box of materials and utensils necessary to apply cremes and make-up. Fashionable eyes were almond shaped with eyebrows and eyelids made up in blue, green, or dark grey. This heavy make-up was

An Egyptian pharaoh, preparing to sacrifice to the gods, is appropriately attired in the pleated kilt and long, sheer skirt of the nobility. His upper body is adorned with magnificent jewellery, which complements the simple outline of his clothing.

applied for two reasons, beauty and protection from the glare, dust, and infection. They would smooth a red fat-based paint over their lips and after frequent baths would apply perfume. The barber would come during this time to shave their heads as short hair was much easier to keep clean and more comfortable in the confines of their own homes.

The wig worn in public, would be made from real hair or dyed black wool. The women would wear longer, shoulder-length hair that was braided and usually ornamented with a band or jewellery. The impression they wanted to create with their appearance was one of elegant attractiveness. Appearance was important and they attempted to look like those tall well-proportioned characters depicted in their art.

It is easy to piece together a picture of Egyptian society. The paintings, models, and literary texts all bring to life a collection of fascinating but very ordinary men and women who were hard working, who appreciated the comforts of home and family, and who liked to find many occasions to supplement their daily life with celebrations and banquets.

Science and Technology

The conservative mentality, practicality, and the reluctance to take risks or to change underlying Egyptian thought and education is evident in their achievements in science and technology. They created what was needed, refined it until it was practical and could be used efficiently and further modification or inventiveness was not necessary, nor encouraged. Examples of this reluctance to grow and experiment can be seen in the development of Egyptian writing, arithmetic, astronomy, and medicine.

Writing. The ancient Egyptian form of writing, known as **hieroglyphics**, dates back to the earliest periods of their history. It is thought likely that the Egyptians borrowed from the Mesopotamians who had developed cuneiform script—a script that had evolved from a series of pictographs. The Mesopotamians had developed a more comprehensive system of writing that replaced the pictographs, but Egyptian hieroglyphics never lost their pictographic nature. By about 3100 B.C. the Egyptians had a fully developed written language that used a combination of ideograms, symbols that express a whole word or idea, and phonograms, symbols that suggest a phonetic sound.

INNOVATIONS

Unlocking the Mystery of the Hieroglyphics

The key to unlocking the hieroglyphic code was found in the Rosetta Stone in 1822. This famous piece of black basalt (Figure 1) was unearthed by Napoleon's army while they were digging trenches near Rashid, (Rosetta) Egypt in 1799. The soldiers, realizing the uniqueness of this find, brought the stone to Napoleon. He was fascinated by the discovery and immediately ordered impressions to be made and sent to scholars throughout Europe. The scholars compared the three types of text (hieroglyphics, demotic, and Greek) in an attempt to break the hieroglyphic code. The first breakthrough came with the translation of a single word. The hieroglyphic text had symbols within an outline called a cartouche, which was the scribe's means of noting the name of royalty. This they matched up with the name of Ptolemy found in the Greek text (Figure 2).

This was as far as the deciphering went until Jean Francois Champollion reconstructed the symbols as sounds and applied these sounds to cartouches found in other texts. To his surprise he found that he was able to identify other names such as Cleopatra (Figure 3). After 23 years of testing his hypothesis on a variety of hieroglyphs Champollion was able to break the ancient secrets of the hieroglyphic code. In the end Champollion's success owed much to the Rosetta Stone which had allowed for the comparative study of the ancient Egyptian hieroglyphics with the known Greek writing.

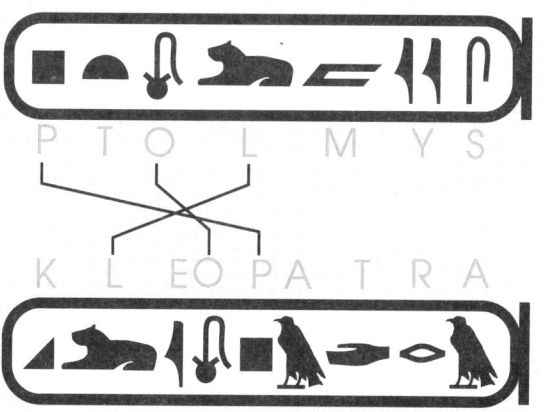

At the time of the New Kingdom there were about seven hundred hieroglyphs in common use, of which about one hundred remained strictly visual while the rest were phonograms. The system of hieroglyphic writing, while aesthetically pleasing and well suited to the adornment of temples and tombs, proved somewhat impractical for day-to-day use. From the earliest period, scribes rounded off hieroglyphic symbols creating a handwriting known as hieratic writing. This simplified form of hieroglyphics was more suited to rapid writing, such as a brush on wood or a reed pen on papyrus. A further refinement of hieratic script occurred around 700 B.C. creating the demotic or popular script that was used primarily for secular matters such as letters, accounts, and record keeping.

As ancient Egyptian civilization waned the use of hieroglyphics faded from use. The last recorded use of hieroglyphics is found on the Temple of Isis at Philae dating to A.D. 394. By this time hieroglyphics were a mysterious text used only by a few priests who kept their meaning secret. It was not until the nineteenth century when the work of Jean François Champollion cracked the hieroglyphic code that we were able to unlock the secrets of ancient Egypt.

Medicine. Names marked on Egyptian tombs clearly indicate the existence of doctors in Egyptian society. It was a literate profession and medical knowledge was recorded from a very early date, the oldest text dating back to 2000 B.C.. These accumulated texts were a mixture of observation, medical and surgical descriptions, diagnosis, and prescriptions. Evident in these texts is sound medical observation mingled with nonsense, magic, and religion. Some of the inaccuracies inherent stem from an inadequate anatomical knowledge and the belief that disease was imposed as a punishment by the gods.

Some common medical problems that appear in the texts and that can easily be verified by examination of mummies are worm infestation, arthritis, smallpox, tuberculosis, and gallstones. The medicines that were concocted were made of beer, milk, oil, plants, herbs, and animal substances. Bandages, splints, and disinfectants were used and they usually treated and stitched open wounds.

The texts comprised a sacred and unchallengeable wisdom that was greater than the abilities of the doctors. This resulted in a stagnation of the development of medicine since no further research or modification was found to be necessary. Being resourceful and practical was part of the Egyptian mentality, as was the confining conservatism. They created the tools necessary to live a comfortable life in the Nile valley. Whether calendars, canals, or medical cures, all were developed to enhance the lives of the Egyptian people.

Trade

By the time of the New Kingdom, Egypt was engaged in a vast trading network that centred on the Mediterranean Sea but spanned as far as northern Europe, subtropical Africa, and the Near East. A recently discovered and excavated trading vessel dated to the fourteenth century B.C. has contributed greatly to our understanding of the cosmopolitan world of the late Bronze Age. The ship found at Ulu Burun was discovered off the coast of modern day Turkey by a Turkish sponge diver in 1982. The vessel was found to carry diverse items including copper ingots from Cyprus, Mycenaean pottery from Greece, tin ingots from Asia Minor, amber beads from the Baltic, and glass and ivory from Syria. It is believed that ships such as the one found at Ulu Burun followed a circular pattern as they plied the waters of the Mediterranean. Setting out from Egypt, such a vessel would have travelled first to Syria and Palestine then on to Cyprus, the Aegean sea, and occasionally as far west as Sardinia before heading back towards North Africa and Egypt.

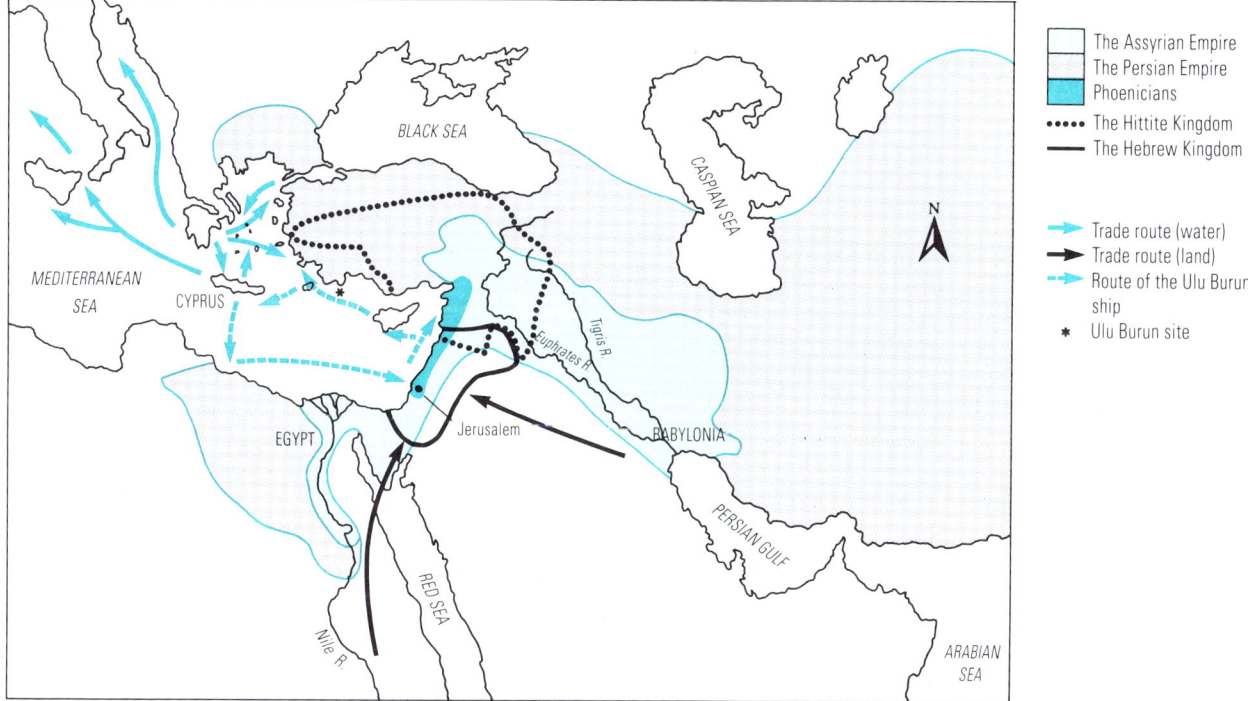

Early Kingdoms of the Near East
The circular trade route that existed during the Bronze Age brought a multitude of goods to Egypt, giving a cosmopolitan feeling to many of the major cities.

The interchange of such a variety of cultures had a far greater significance than simply the exchange of material goods. It was through trade that ideas, forms of artistic expression, technology, and building methods were spread. It is because of this cultural diffusion that it is not surprising to find that the Egyptians owed a great deal to the Mesopotamians for their concepts of mathematics and writing, that early Greek art and medicine owes a great deal to the Egyptians, or that the calendar we use today is derived from the Roman (Julian) calendar that was in turn borrowed from the Egyptians. Although Egypt was a conservative society where change was slow, trade and the exchange of ideas ensured that Egyptian history would not be completely static but always evolving.

One of the great achievements of Egyptian culture was its longevity. For over two thousand years Egypt remained a dominant political and cultural force in the Near East. In fact its influence spread throughout the Mediterranean helping to shape first Minoan culture and later the culture of mainland Greece. As one of the world's first civilizations and one of the earliest powers to dominate the eastern Mediterranean, Egypt played a critical role in the development of the Near East. Although conservative in nature the ancient Egyptians made significant advances in many fields including art, architecture, and technology. In the end, although we may marvel at the pyramids and be intrigued by the tombs and treasures of the pharaohs we must not lose sight of the ancient Egyptians as a people. They had a rich and vibrant society whose customs and traditions reflected their dependence on nature and a very positive view of the afterlife.

Egypt, although long the most powerful and influential state in the Near East, was by no means the only significant civilization in this area of the world. Several other kingdoms and empires rose and fell over the centuries prior to the emergence of the Roman Empire. Among these were the **Hittites,** the **Phoenicians, the Canaanites,** and the **Hebrews.**

The Hittites

The Hittites were an Indo-European people who settled in Asia Minor, which is today Turkey. Indo-European refers to the family of languages including English, French, Spanish, Latin, Greek, Persian, and Sanskrit (the ancient language of India). It is believed that the Hittites migrated to Asia Minor from southern Russia around 2700 B.C. at a time when Indo-Europeans were migrating en masse into Italy, Greece, Iran, India, and Central Asia. The Hittites, like the Egyptians, established one of the strongest kingdoms of the Near East and were one of the last great kingdoms of the Bronze Age.

The Hittites had established themselves as a prominent force by about 1650 B.C. at which time they had established a capital at Hattusha. With the sacking of Babylon in about 1595 B.C. the Hittites established themselves as a force to be reckoned with in the Near East. Over the 200 years between 1400 B.C. and 1200 B.C. the Hittite empire reached its greatest extent. Under King Suppiluliumas (1380–1340 B.C.), whose reign paralleled Akhenaton's in Egypt, the Hittites managed to seize Egyptian territory in northern Syria. While Akhenaton was preoccupied with religious reform, Suppiluliumas was able to successfully invade a disoriented Egypt. Later, towards the end of the fourteenth century B.C., the Hittites and the Egyptians agreed first to peace and then to the forming of an alliance. The Hittites, realizing the limits of their strength and the extent to which they could endure attacks from their many hostile neighbours, began to search for diplomatic and political solutions to avoid war. After fighting the army of Ramses II to a standstill in Syria about 1300 B.C. the Hittites agreed to end their wars with the Egyptians. Although this brought an end to war between the two great powers of the Near East neither were to savour the benefits of peace for long. Within a century both empires would be destroyed by invaders.

Hittite culture and society shared some customs with other states of the Near East. This was in part due to the fact that they readily adopted aspects of the cultures they conquered. Mesopotamian culture undoubtedly had the greatest impact on the Hittites as can be seen by the fact that both societies believed the king became a god after death.

Hittite society was divided along rigid class lines. At the head of society were the king and queen, the king being recognized as the head of the army, the chief judge, and high priest. He personally led the army into battle and handled diplomatic affairs with foreign powers. The queen was also highly regarded, playing a role in some diplomatic affairs as well as having some religious duties to perform. Beneath the king and queen were the members of the aristocracy. The aristocracy was composed largely of the king's relatives and served as royal administrators. Despite the family connections to the crown the aristocracy posed a constant threat to the king. Ambitious members of the aristocracy led repeated revolts against the king hoping to seize the throne for themselves. The numerous plots against the king bred instability within the government. The third important class in Hittite society were the warriors. This group met in their own assembly (the *pankus*) to hear the king's will. Although they could not vote on government policy they did serve as a court of law with the power to punish criminals. Aside from these divisions Hittite society was further divided according to one's profession. The Hittites were a largely agricultural society in which local affairs were handled by the Elders. Aside from the farming community there were numerous artisans who made pottery, cloth, leather goods, metal tools, and a number of other goods needed by society. The merchants, who peddled goods from community to community, also formed an important part of Hittite culture. At the bottom of the social and economic scale were slaves, who were often captured in war.

The Canaanites and Phoenicians

Among the most important of the smaller kingdoms of the Near East were the Canaanites and Phoenicians. The Canaanites were a semitic tribe who first settled in the area of Palestine. They developed a thriving urban civilization with Jericho and Jerusalem as their major cities, which were established at about the same time of the Old Kingdom of Egypt. By 1200 B.C. the Canaanites were driven from Palestine to a narrow strip of land along the Mediterranean called Phoenicia, there developing a new culture that was called Phoenician. Phoenician culture was a blending of Mesopotamian and Egyptian culture with innovations by the Phoenicians. Perhaps their greatest innovation was a vastly simplified alphabet. The Phoenician alphabet used one letter to designate a sound, thereby simplifying reading and writing to the point that many more members of society could learn to read and write. The Phoenician alphabet was later adopted by the Greeks and would become the ancestor to the alphabets of the west.

The Phoenicians also became extensive traders and established colonies that served as trading posts. The most famous and powerful of these was Carthage in North Africa, which was established in 813 B.C. Carthage would become a major power in the Mediterranean, rivaling Rome in the third and second centuries B.C. Among the most important trade articles of the Phoenicians was a reddish dye which the ancients called purple. Clothing dyed in this colour was considered a luxury and became a symbol of royalty.

The extensive trade networks of the Phoenicians allowed for the spreading of their alphabet and culture. As a result, despite never having had the numerical strength to establish a mighty kingdom, the Phoenicians made a significant contribution to western culture and civilization.

The Israelites

Of all the kingdoms of the ancient Near East the Israelites are the most familiar to us today. Most of our information regarding the early Hebrews comes from the Old Testament, a considerable amount of which has been verified through archaeological finds. According to the Old Testament nomadic tribes wandered into Palestine from the east about 1900 B.C. Each tribe was led by a patriarch, of which Abraham is the most famous. In the Old Testament God is said to have appeared before Abraham at a place called Harran, a city east of the Euphrates River, and given him the following instructions: "Leave your own country, your kinsmen, and your father's house, and go to a country that I will show you. I will make you into a great nation." When Abraham arrived at the city of Shechem in Canaan God again appeared to him and said: "I give this land to your descendants."

Later, Abraham's grandson Jacob, who took the name Israel meaning "God ruled," organized the

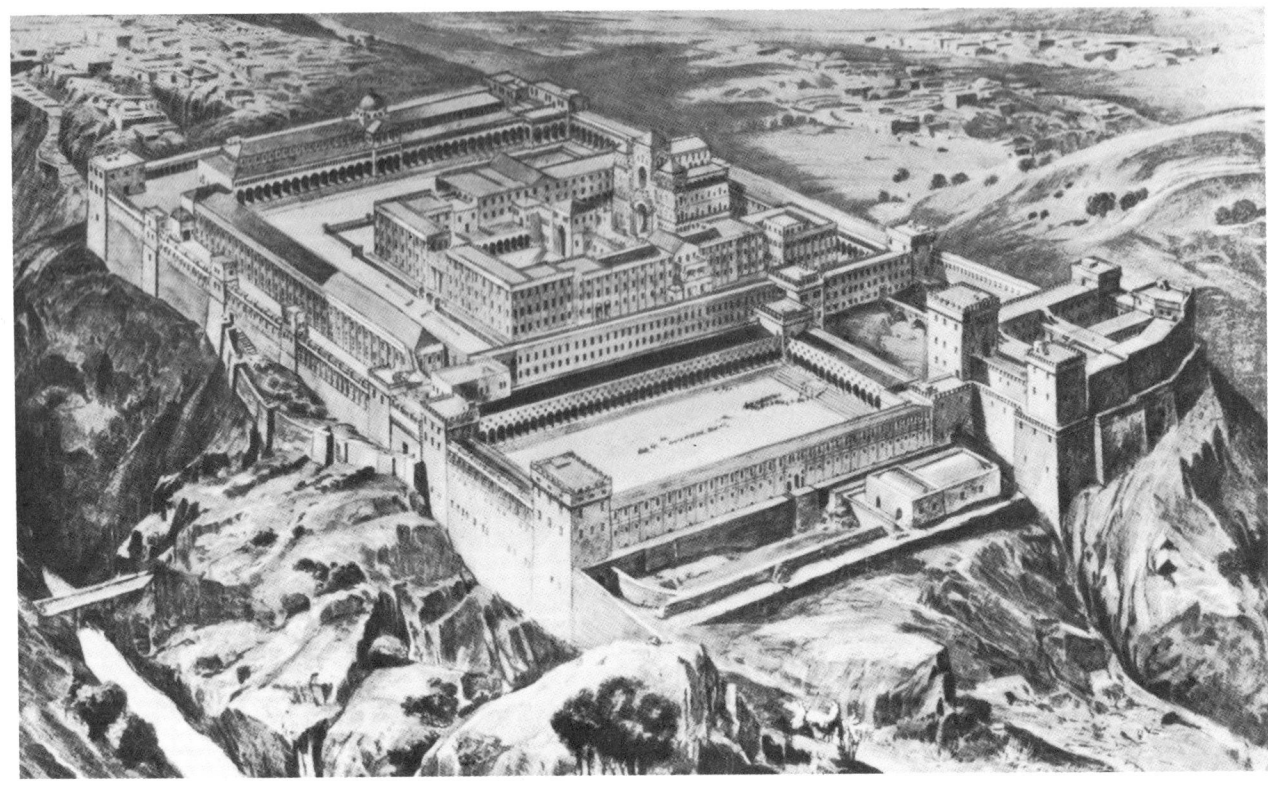

The greatest architectural feat of the ancient Israelites was built during the reign of King Solomon. The Temple of Jerusalem, depicted here in an artist's reconstruction, must have been an awe-inspiring sight to those Israelites who came to worship their god. All that remains today is a portion of the west wall, known as the "Wailing Wall."

people into 12 tribes. Some of these tribes remained in Canaan while others, perhaps fleeing drought and famine, settled in Egypt becoming subjects of the pharaohs. To these numbers were added numerous slaves taken captive by the Egyptians during their conquest of Canaan in the fifteenth through thirteenth centuries.

Among the most famous of the biblical stories is that of **Moses** leading the Israelites out of bondage from Egypt. The oppression suffered by the Israelites was considerable. Under Ramses II Egypt underwent its most ambitious period of construction since the days of the pyramids. Much of the labour required by the Egyptian empire was supplied by conscripted foreigners. They were forced to serve in the army, till the fields, pave the roads, build temples, assist in the construction of a new palace, and two virtually new cities. In the face of such ill treatment many sought to flee the enslavement of the Egyptians. Sometime around the end of the thirteenth century B.C. a mass exodus of Israelites from Egypt occurred led by a man with the Egyptian name of Moses. Moses organized the tribes of Israel into a confederation bound by a **Covenant** to a god named **Yahweh**. According to the Old Testament, Moses received instructions directly from Yahweh including the Ten Commandments that prescribed a body of laws based on ethically right conduct and that stated: "Thou shalt have no other gods before me." For the first time the Israelites were united under one God and the foundations were laid for the monotheistic religion which would profoundly shape western civilization.

The Israelites, led by Moses, established themselves in Palestine and in 1230 B.C., guided by Joshua, Moses' successor, invaded Canaan capturing the city of Jericho by siege. Despite being delivered from Egypt by Moses and led to victory by Joshua, the Israelites still lacked a central government and over the years the tribes drifted apart. Eventually about 1020 B.C. Saul became the first king of the Israelites and led them against their greatest enemy, the Philistines. Under David, Saul's successor, the Israelites captured Jerusalem and extended the kingdom's boundaries to their greatest extent.

David's son Solomon is best remembered for his wisdom and skillful administration. He has also been credited with writing some of the books of the bible including Proverbs, Ecclesiastes, and the Song of Solomon although it is quite certain that they were written much later. Solomon ruled at a time when many of the Near Eastern powers were weak and he was able to maintain peace through a series of alliances and by increasing the size of the standing army which he equipped with chariots. The greatest monument to Solomon's rule was the **Temple of Jerusalem** which he had built to house the Arc of the Covenant. The temple has been described as "a marvel of cedar beams, cast-bronze pillars, ivory-paneled doors, golden vessels, and carved stone ornaments..." This magnificent temple was destroyed during the Babylonian invasion, rebuilt in the sixth century B.C. and destroyed again in A.D. 70 by the Romans. All that remains today is a part of the western wall of the outer court which is called the Wailing Wall. Solomon's other great building was his new palace which was said to be large enough to house his 700 wives and to have stables for 12 000 horses!

Following the death of Solomon the Kingdom of Israel split in two. While the northern part of the kingdom retained the name of Israel the southern half, with Jerusalem as its capital, became known as Judah. Weakened by internal divisions, Israel was conquered by the powerful Assyrians in 722 B.C. and its leaders dispersed throughout the Assyrian empire. The scattered people became known as the ten lost tribes of Israel. This left Judah as all that remained of the former kingdom of Israel and it too was to fall. In 586 B.C. Judah fell to Chaldean or New Babylon and the captives were deported to Babylon. Slowly, the Israelites trickled back into Palestine but the period of a Jewish kingdom had passed.

The Evolution of the Jewish Faith

Although the ancient Israelites may not have established a vast empire nor have left a great deal of monumental architecture, their spiritual ideas have profoundly influenced much of western culture and continue to exert tremendous force on the modern world. Central to understanding the development of the Jewish faith is the concept of the Covenant. The Covenant was a formal agreement between the Hebrews and their God Yahweh that was first made at the time of Abraham and later renewed under Moses. According to this contract the Hebrews were to worship Yahweh as their only God and they in turn were to be his chosen people and were promised the land of Canaan.

Initially Yahweh was likely just one god among many who were worshipped in the Near East. As the main god of the Hebrews, Yahweh would have faced competition from other gods such as Baal, Enlil, Marduk, and Amon-Re. Over time the Hebrews came to regard Yahweh as the only true God, thus laying the foundations for a monotheistic religion. Yahweh, as he appears in the Old Testament, is an all powerful and all knowing God who created the world and then stood outside of it. He is at times portrayed as a jealous, vindictive, and intolerable

PRIMARY DOCUMENT

The Old Testament as a Historical Source

For many the Old Testament is a revered book. For historians the Old Testament is an invaluable research tool which provides numerous insights into the past. Because of the Old Testament more is known about the daily lives of the Israelites than either the Romans or the Chinese. While it is primarily a religious document one can gain a great deal of knowledge from the Old Testament by carefully reading passages and reflecting on the topics covered. Below are a few extracts from the Old Testament focusing on laws of the ancient Israelites. As you read these selections reflect on what they tell us of life in ancient Israel. You may wish to peruse the Old Testament for further evidence concerning daily life among the Israelites.

Dietary Laws
(Leviticus 11:1-22)

And the Lord said to Moses and Aaron, "Say to the people of Israel, These are the living things which you may eat among all the beasts that are on the earth. What ever parts the hoof and is cloven-footed and chews the cud, among the animal, you may eat. Nevertheless among those that chew the cud or part the hoof, you shall not eat these. The camel, because it chews the cud but does not part the hoof, is unclean to you. And the rock badger, because it chews the cud but does not part the hoof, is unclean to you. And the hare, because it chews the cud but does not part the hoof, is unclean to you. And the swine, because it parts the hoof and is cloven-footed but does not chew the cud, is unclean to you. Of their flesh you shall not eat, and their carcasses you shall not touch; they are unclean to you.

These you may eat, of all that are in the waters. Everything in the waters that has fins and scales, whether in the seas or in the rivers, you may eat....Everything in the waters that has not fins and scales is an abomination to you.

And these you shall have in abomination among the birds, they shall not be eaten, they are an abomination: the eagle, the carrion vulture, the osprey, the kite, the falcon according to its kind, every raven according to its kind, the ostrich, the nighthawk, the seagull, the hawk, according to its kind, the owl, the cormorant, the ibis, the water hen, the stork, the heron according to its kind, the hoopoe, and the bat.

All winged insects that go upon all fours are an abomination to you. Yet among the winged insects that go on all fours you may eat those which have legs above their feet, with which to leap on the earth....

Various other Laws
(Deuteronomy 21:1-29)

If in the land which the Lord your God gives you to possess, anyone is found slain, lying in the open country, and it is not known who killed him, then your elders and your judges shall come forth, and they shall measure the distance to the cities which are around him that is slain; and the elders of the city which is nearest

> to the slain man shall take a heifer which has never been worked and which has not pulled in the yoke. And the elders of that city shall bring the heifer down to a valley with running water, which is neither plowed nor sown, and shall break the heifer's neck there in the valley. And the priests the sons of Levi shall come forward, for the Lord your God has chosen them to minister to him and to bless in the name of the Lord, and by their word every dispute and every assault shall be settled. And all the elders of that city nearest to the slain man shall wash their hands over the heifer whose neck was broken in the valley; and they shall testify, Our hands did not shed this blood, neither did our eyes see it shed. Forgive, O Lord, thy people Israel, whom thou hast redeemed, and set not the guilt of innocent blood in the midst of thy people Israel; but let the guilt of blood be forgiven them. So you shall purge the guilt of innocent blood from your midst, when you do what is right in the sight of the Lord....
>
> If a man has two wives, the one loved and the other disliked, and they have borne him children, both the loved and the disliked, and if the first-born son is hers that is disliked, then on the day when he assigns his possessions as an inheritance to his sons, he may not treat the son of the loved as the first-born in preference to the son of the disliked, who is the first-born, but he shall acknowledge the first-born, the son of the disliked, by giving him a double portion of all that he has, for he is the first issue of his strength; the right of the first-born is his.
>
> If a man has a stubborn and rebellious son, who will not obey the voice of his father or the voice of his mother, and though they chastise him, will not give heed to them, then his father and his mother shall take hold of him and bring him out to the elders of his city at the gate of the place where he lives, and they shall say to the elders of his city, 'This our son is stubborn and rebellious, he will not obey our voice; he is a glutton and a drunkard.' Then all the men of the city shall stone him to death with stones; so you shall purge the evil from your midst; and all Israel shall hear, and fear....
>
> A woman shall not wear anything that pertains to a man, nor shall a man put on a woman's garment; for whoever does these things is an abomination to the Lord your God....
>
> If a man is found lying with the wife of another man, both of them shall die, the man who lay with the woman, and the woman; so you shall purge the evil from Israel....
>
> If a man meets a virgin who is not betrothed, and seizes her and lies with her, and they are found, then the man who lay with her shall give to the father of the young woman fifty shekels of silver, and she shall be his wife, because he has violated her; he may not put her away all his days....

God and yet despite his often harsh nature, Yahweh was a God for everyone; a God who cared for all classes and was not too aloof to care for the individual. The Hebrews believed that their God intervened in human affairs and forgave those who truly regretted their wrongs.

What made the Jewish faith stand apart from other faiths at the time of Moses was that it was a religion of the people that was deeply and passionately felt from within and was not imposed from above. It must be remembered that the prophets such as Moses were not kings and therefore could not force the people to obey laws. Yet these men of ordinary status were able to exert tremendous influence on the ethical behaviour of a society—an influence that has lasted for over three thousand years!

Critical to the success and development of Judaism was the passion of the prophets who emerged throughout Israel's history. Of all the prophets Moses is the most significant and all others looked back to him. A theme common to all of the prophets was the corruption of society and God's forgiveness if people repented. They declared that God would prove his love for his people by providing a Messiah (a person with divine power) to lead the Israelites. From about 200 B.C. on, Jewish thought maintained that a king would someday appear to lead the people of Israel and restore their power and glory.

Despite the dispersion of the Jewish people throughout Europe and around the world beginning with the **Diaspora** in A.D. 70, their culture and religious beliefs have been by far the most influential of all the ancient cultures of the Near East. Many of the traditions of the Israelites live on today not only among the Jewish but among several other major religions. It has been said that without Moses there could have been no Jesus or Muhammad. To what degree this is true is difficult to ascertain but what is certain is that three of the world's most dominant religions, Judaism, Christianity, and Islam all derive their roots from the spiritual beliefs of the ancient Israelites.

Suggested Sources For Further Research

Baines, John, and Jaromir Malek, *Atlas of Ancient Egypt* (Facts on File, 1985).

Bass, George, F., "Oldest Known Shipwreck Reveals Splendors of the Bronze Age" in *National Geographic*, Volume 172, No. 6, December, 1987.

Carter, Howard, *The Tomb of Tutankhamen* (E.P. Dutton, 1972).

Casson, Lionel, *Ancient Egypt* (Time, Inc., 1965).

David, Rosalie, *Cult of the Sun* (J.M. Dent & Sons Ltd., 1980).

Durant, Will, *Our Oriental Heritage* (Simon and Schuster, 1954).

Edwards, I.E.S., *The Pyramids of Egypt* (Ebury Press, 1972).

El Mahdy, Christine, *Mummies, Myth and Magic in Ancient Egypt* (Thames and Hudson, 1989).

Hamilton-Paterson, James and Carol Andrews, *Mummies, Death and Life in Ancient Egypt* (William Collins Sons & Co. Ltd., 1978).

Herodotus, *The History* (translated by David Greene) (University of Chicago Press, 1987).

Hobson, Christine, *The World of the Pharaohs* (Thames & Hudson, 1987).

James, T.G.H., *An Introduction To Ancient Egypt* (Harper and Row Pub., 1979).

Kamil, Jill, *The Ancient Egyptians* (The American University in Cairo Press, 1984).

Lucas, A., *Ancient Egyptian Materials and Industries* (Histories & Mysteries of Man Ltd., 1989).

Moorey, P.R.S., *Ancient Egypt* (Ashmolean Museum Publications, 1983).

Osborn, Charles (ed.), *The Israelites* (Time Life Books, 1975).

Patterson, James Hamilton and Carol Andrews, *Mummies* (Penguin Books Ltd., 1978).

Romant, Bernard, *Life in Egypt In Ancient Times* (Editions Minivera, 1981).

Saggs, H.W.F., *Civilization Before Greece and Rome* (Yale University Press, 1989).

Tompkins, Peter, *Secrets of the Great Pyramids* (Harper and Row Pub., 1971).

Focus Your Knowledge

▼▼▼

1. Why did a unified kingdom develop earlier in Egypt than in Mesopotamia?
2. What contributions to western civilization did Mesopotamia make?
3. How did geography influence Mesopotamian and Egyptian history and society?
4. What features distinguish the Old Kingdom, the Middle Kingdom, and the New Kingdom?
5. Why did Pharaohs abandon pyramids in favour of the rock-cut tombs in the Valley of the Kings?
6. How did the conventions of Egyptian art influence their style of painting?
7. List and describe three achievements of the Egyptians in science and medicine.
8. Why did the Egyptians and the Hittites form an alliance? How successful was this alliance at preserving their empires?
9. What contributions to western civilization did the Phoenicians make?
10. Why were the prophets critical to the development of Judaism?
11. Using the Egyptian timeline as your guide, create a similar one for the Hebrews.

Apply Your Knowledge

▼▼▼

1. Prepare an organizer that compares and contrasts the religious concepts of the ancient Mesopotamians, Egyptians, and Hebrews with a present day religion. Be sure to include attitudes towards death and the preparation for the afterlife.

2. What features of the New Kingdom earned it the title of the Golden Age of Egypt? Use specific examples in your answer.

3. Briefly describe the Egyptian social structure. Evaluate the role women played in Egyptian society.

4. Choose five important individuals from Mesopotamian, Egyptian, or Hebrew history and explain their contribution.

5. Identify examples of influence on our society from the ancient Near East. Prepare a list of items/ideas that are in your home and community that reflect these influences.

6. Compare and contrast the spiritual beliefs of the Hebrews to Egypt and Mesopotamia. Speculate as to why the Hebrew faith survived while the others did not.

Extension Activities

▼▼▼

1. Using either clay or plasticene and a wooden stylus, write a message in cuneiform script. To do this you may wish to develop your own script or do further research on cuneiform writing.

2. Following the conventions set out in the Feature Study on Egyptian Art, create an Egyptian-style wall painting of a day in your school.

3. Using the information on Egyptian society, write a sketch of a "Day in the Life of…" To do this you should choose a position in society and describe the daily routine in a first person narrative.

4. Working in groups of three to four, select a topic from the following list on which to do a short seminar presentation. Remember to work closely with your librarian in gathering your research.

Topics:

A famous pharaoh
Tutankhamon's Tomb
The Great Pyramid at Giza
The Hyksos invasion
Egyptian hieroglyphics

King Hammurabi
A Mesopotamian ziggurat
Dead Sea Scrolls
Women in ancient Egypt
Moses and the Exodus

5. Working in groups of three to four attempt to discover the secrets behind the building of the Egyptian pyramids. First, hold a brief brainstorming session during which your group attempts to create their own hypothesis. Following the brainstorming share your ideas with the class and discuss the plausibility of each hypothesis. Groups should then research the construction of the pyramids and use their findings to (a) create a cross-section of the Great Pyramid at Giza and (b) explain the process by which the stone blocks were quarried, transported, and put into place.

CHAPTER 4

Ancient India

Chapter Highlights

- preparation and presentation of food in the Hindu culture

- Gotama the Buddha and the founding of Buddhism

- Taj Mahal's construction and purpose

- cross-cultural influences in Indian culture

- arts and literature of India's classical period

Indian civilization has endured continuously for over five thousand years, maintaining its place as one of the great civilizations of the world. India is a subcontinent consisting of many regions. Like Europe, the regions in India have developed their own food, dress, mannerisms, language, and history that distinguishes them from one another. India is known in Asia as the land of the **Buddha**, as Buddhism is perhaps its greatest contribution to other cultures of the world. Thousands of Hindu temples, with their images of gods and goddesses, also exist throughout India. Aside from these two major religions, India is home to *yoga* (the art of meditation) and *gurus* (spiritual teachers), making it a land where the search for spiritual happiness and salvation is paramount.

Throughout its long history, India has always been in contact with other great civilizations. In the very ancient past, India had contacts with Mesopotamian civilization, while later, from the sixth century B.C., it interacted with ancient Iranian and Greek civilizations. In medieval times India encountered the great Middle Eastern Muslim civilization, and in relatively modern times it was influenced and affected by modern European civilization. India provides a good example of how civilizations interact and learn from each other without losing their own individualities. Indian civilization is best studied by focusing on the distinct values, lifestyles, religions, and technological and scientific advances that were experienced, catalogued, and described by the people of that civilization in the span of its four thousand years of recorded history.

Key Concepts

Buddha
Mohen-jo-daro and Harappa
Aryan
Vedas
Brahmin
Uphanishads
Maurya
nirvana
Hinduism
Sanskrit
Gupta
karma
Delhi Sultanate
bhakti

Geography

The cultural and historical geography of India has been described by some scholars as falling into three kinds of zones: nuclear zones, zones of relative isolation, and route zones. The nuclear zones are self-contained, socio-cultural regions while zones of relative isolation are those areas that are located some distance from main cultural centres. The final type of zone, known as route zones, are the key strategic areas and trade routes between nuclear zones. In India the nuclear zones are located in the plains and river basins, and of the three zones they are the most important to ancient India. The settlements in the nuclear zones in the river valleys and upland plains of the rivers in the North and South sustained India with a stable agriculture and pre-modern, industrial belts, which supported the large population.

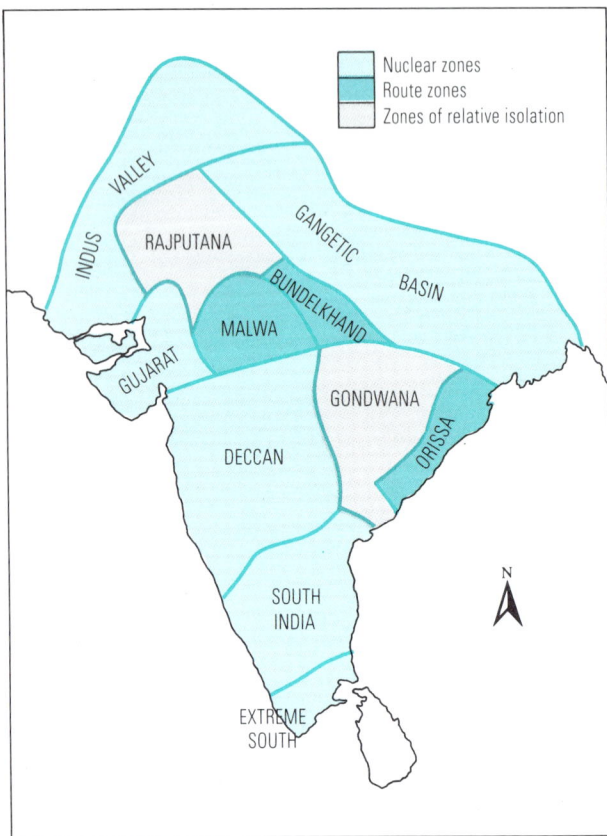

Zones of Ancient India

The Indus Valley Civilization

The earliest civilization in India dates to ca. 2500 B.C. and is referred to as the Indus civilization. The two major cities of the Indus civilization were **Mohen-jo-daro**, which is in Sindh, Pakistan, on the banks of the Indus proper and **Harappa**, situated four hundred miles north of Mohen-jo-daro on the banks of the river Ravi, a tributary of the Indus. Some scholars regard Harappa and Mohen-jo-daro as twin capitals of the Indus Empire. Both cities, situated in what is now Pakistan, had citadel walls situated on their western boundaries. In the vicinity of the citadels were impressive buildings: large municipal or temple granaries, a sacred tank, and an assembly hall. The big storage houses were accompanied by one-room **tenements**, which could have been houses of slaves, judging from Mesopotamian examples. The great houses in the eastern section of the city had thick walls of burnt brick and entrances that were almost always in a narrow side lane, not on the main street.

The quality of the town planning is an outstanding feature of this civilization. The streets were laid out in a grid pattern with the main streets running from north to south and the cross streets and lanes running at right angles to them. Baked bricks, rare at this time in the Near East, were used for wells, bathing platforms, and drains, which provided the cities with excellent drainage for rainwater and sewage. Indus town planning suggests an efficient municipal government, which placed a high priority on hygiene.

An average house consisted of a courtyard around which were located four to six living rooms, a bathroom, and a kitchen. Some of the larger houses had up to 30 rooms while all private homes had impressive bathrooms and often their own wells. The presence of staircases in many of the homes indicates a second storey.

Indus Culture. Much of what we know of the culture of the Indus civilization comes from seals that have been discovered. The writing of the Indus people is preserved on square and rectangular seals cut out from steatite, a variety of soft stone. Brief legends are found carved on these seals although very little information is given. The script found on the seals, which were used for stamping, remained unchanged for over eight hundred years. This is in sharp contrast with ancient Sumerian and Egyptian practices, where the changes in the script indicate the emergence of new dynasties. The script has not yet been deciphered despite the intensive use of computers.

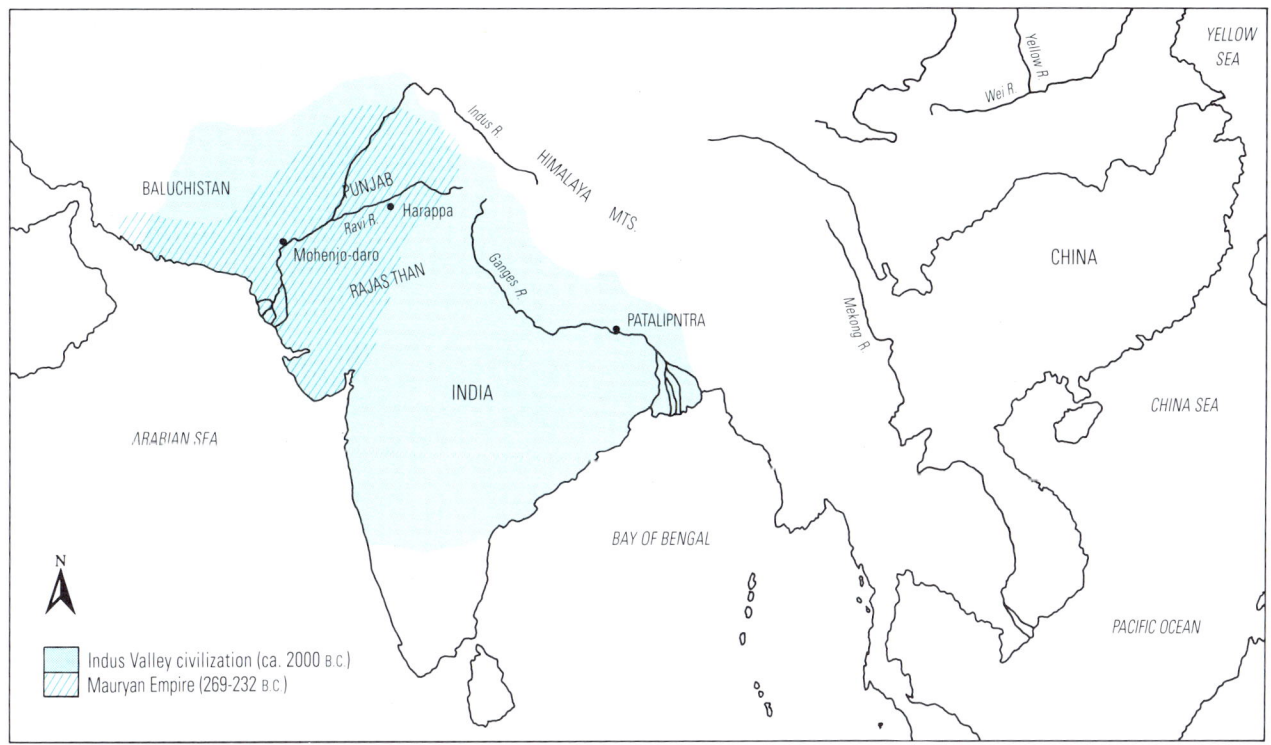

Ancient India
The development of India (ca. 2500–250 B.C.) from the Indus Valley civilization to the rise of the Mauryan Empire.

The pictures carved on the seals are regarded as masterpieces in miniature art form. Noteworthy are the beautiful renderings of the humped bull and rhinoceros. The seals provide a useful clue for our understanding of the religion of the Indus civilization. Perhaps more tantalizing for the students of Indian history is the fact that many of the religious signs found on the seals reappear as sacred objects and symbols in later Indian religions such as Hinduism and Buddhism. The seals depict animals like tigers, water-buffaloes, deer, and chimaeras (fantastic, hybrid animals) who were combinations of part bull and part elephant, part goat and part fish; or sometimes a composite of three or four animals including humans were used. There are scenes depicting animal sacrifices, the worship of the sacred pipal tree, the bull, and the Indian god Shiva. Many of the Indian gods of classical antiquity are half human and half animal, such as the god Ganesh who has the face of an elephant and the body of a human. The yogic (meditative) position of the gods and the svastika signs that appear on the seals are recurrent features of later Indian religions.

Some seals indicate Mesopotamian contacts. For example, the naked, bearded, lion-killing hero called Gilgamesh has a representation in the Indus motif as a naked hero fighting two tigers with his bare hands. Indus seals found in Ur dated from 2300 B.C. indicate trade in cotton and other goods while ivory combs listed in Babylonian documents, have been found at Mohen-jo-daro.

Dating to 4000 years ago these carved seals were used by merchants to stamp possessions. The inscriptions are all very different so it is likely that these seals, pressed on clay tags, were used as identifiers or trademarks. They have provided a vivid record of life, customs, rituals and animal life.

Decline of the Indus Civilization. One of the puzzling features of the Indus Valley civilization is that the culture was static for at least 800 years. This is evidenced in the technology and methods utilized throughout the civilization. For example, the potters' forms and techniques remained constant till the end of the Indus Valley civilization. The bronze tools also retained older forms, for example the **adze**, without an inserted shaft. The Indus script shows no variation from the earliest to the latest discovered **strata** whereas every century following saw its own characteristic script.

The cities that came into their own around 2500 B.C. began to decline at around 1700 B.C., becoming vast slums in the end. Constantly recurring floods, foreign invasions, changes in climate, geological changes at the mouth of the Indus, population growth, and disease are all cited as causes of the decline. Recent analysis indicates that the city phase of the civilization, noticeable by structural differentiation; trade, writing, and specialized skills in producing goods gradually disappeared. The Indus society gradually merged into other cultures. This appears to be a plausible explanation since civilizations do not simply die and vanish.

With the decline of the Indus civilization, we find

MAJOR EVENTS IN THE HISTORY OF INDIA

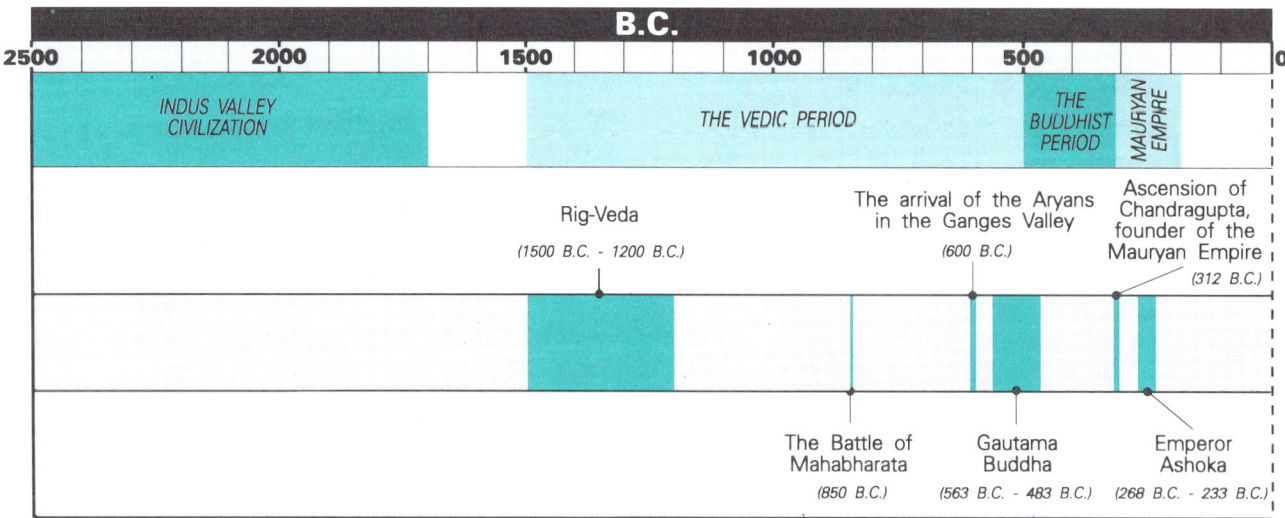

the arrival of the **Aryans**, who brought new regions under the plough and opened further territories in regions to the east of the Indus River. Until the discovery of Mohen-jo-daro and Harappa in 1923, the Aryans were credited with bringing the first civilization to India. It is now known that the Aryans were not city dwellers and that India's second city civilization, which arose at the time of the Buddhist period, was a product of a slow process of the amalgamation of the Indus civilization with the new culture brought by the Aryans. The period following the decline of the Indus civilization is commonly referred to as the Vedic Age.

The Vedic Age

Although many scholars hold the Aryans responsible for the destruction of the Indus cities, recent work suggests that by the time the waves of Aryan tribes came to India from central Asia the cities had already been in decline for some time. This time period takes its name from the Aryan literature called the **Vedas**, which is the earliest existing literature of the Aryans. The Vedas are still considered sacred and are revered by the Hindus. From the earliest times, the Aryan priest class called **Brahmins** preserved the Vedas by memorizing and orally transmitting the texts to other Brahmins. Since the Brahmins regarded them as secret and sacred, the Vedas were not actually written until the fourteenth century A.D.

In modern India the hymns from the Vedas are recited by the Brahmins during Hindu household and temple rituals. Hindu sacraments of birth, marriage, and death are blessed by the chanting of verses from the Vedas, which contain invocations to the gods to descend from their heavenly abodes to the earth to sanctify the ritual and to consume the foods offered to them. The gods are supposed to protect the worshippers and bless them.

The Rig-Veda. The *Rig-Veda* questions the origins of the gods and the universe. It was also during the Vedic period that the Brahmins first articulated

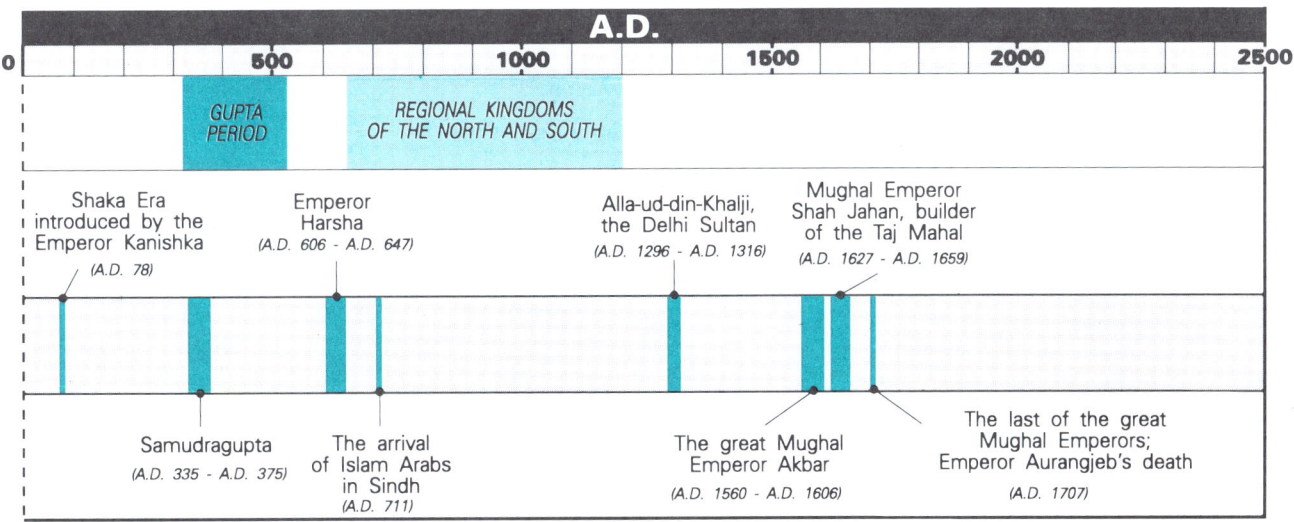

Ancient India CHAPTER 4 **99**

This Vedic village has been reconstructed according to the Vedas and other sources. These clusters of huts were usually protected by a fence or a palisade, in this case a bamboo railing. The entrance was in the form of a projecting gateway with a portcullis-style gate for livestock to pass through on the way to the fields.

the theory of the origin of humans and the emergence of the class system. According to a hymn in the Rig-Veda (tenth chapter) the Purusha, the primeval man, sacrificed himself and out of his head emerged the Brahmin, from his arms the Kshatriya, from his thighs the Vaishya, and from his feet the Shudra. Thus, Brahmin is the thinker, Kshatriya the defender and protector of humanity, Vaishya the producer, and the Shudra the labouring class.

In later periods the Brahmins proposed a colour scheme to complement their theory of the origin of the classes. The Brahmin is to be associated with white, the colour representing purity and calmness of mind; Kshatriya with red, the colour of activity, indicating his duty to fight and shed blood in defending others; Vaishya is to be identified with yellow, the colour of gold and ripened corn; and Shudra with black, the colour of the soil, which this class had to cultivate for other classes.

Such assumptions regarding high and low status, if based on the criteria of birth alone, result in an unfair, rigidly-stratified social structure. The right to chant the Vedas was confined to three classes of Vedic society: Kshatriya the warrior; Brahmin the priest; and Vaishya the cultivator, cattlekeeper, trader, and artisan. The Shudra, the fourth class (the workers, labourers, and servants) were considered low and impure, and were denied access to the Vedas. One of the curses of a Brahmin law-giver, called Manu, recommends unusually harsh treatment for the Shudras: "If a Shudra should hear the Vedas being chanted, then molten lead should be poured in his ears. If he should recite them his tongue should be cut off." This was never implemented, but shows how the Brahmins regarded the Vedas as pure and that the lower classes of the Aryan society were not entitled to rituals sanctified by the Vedas. This discrimination on the basis of birth in the Shudra class has been the ongoing practice of the Brahmin class.

The Brahmins. From the Vedic times the Brahmins became specialists in conducting elaborate sacrifices to the gods, sacrifices that often involved the killing of animals. The Brahmins acquired the monopoly to conduct consecration rituals for the kings of ancient and medieval India. Many sacrifices that the Brahmins performed were reserved for the warrior classes, and were designed to ensure their successes in war, long life, and happiness. The patrons, of course, had to pay fees for the Brahmins' services. Moreover the Brahmins received special concessions such as land grants, and gifts of moveable and immovable properties; in certain instances they also had immunity from paying taxes.

The position of the Brahmins as an elite class with claims to a higher, ritual status is based on their self-assumed purity and control of the sacred literature. This is a part of the Indian reality to this day. Although their position has been constantly challenged by the Buddhist and Hindu reformers through the millennia, they were never dislodged from their key position as the upholders of the Hindu religion and rituals. Thousands of important temples with their accompanying gods and goddesses continue to be serviced by the Brahmins.

Early Vedic Society. Early Vedic society, as cited in the Rig-Veda (1500–1000 B.C.), presents the Aryan, meaning the nobleman or respectable person, as a member of a semi-nomadic peoples. They travelled about in their chariots, with herds of cattle, which they considered their wealth and means of exchange. A modern carpenter could build a passable replica of the Aryan chariot by the description provided in the text. A modern brick-layer could replicate the elaborate sacrificial platforms used by the Vedic Aryans to worship and offer sacrifices to their gods, but we do not know what the Aryan houses looked like, as they lived in semi-permanent, make-shift settlements.

Their gods such as Agni (fire), Varuna, Mitra, Aditi, and Indra were nature gods that had to be appeased periodically. The description of the gods in the Rig-Veda appears to be descriptions of Aryan heroes, but magnified. The warrior god, Indra, is described in the text as pot bellied with a tawny beard. He likes to drink mead and soma and fight the enemies of the Aryans, destroying their fortifications. Later Vedic texts find the Aryan settlements are on the upper Ganges regions (the land between the Indus and the Ganges). By this time the Aryans have made the transition from a semi-nomadic life to a peasant society. The Aryans called their newly occupied territory the aryavarta (the region of the Aryans). During this period, new regions came under extensive cultivation, fields being cultivated with teams of animals, teams as large as 12 oxen. Wheat, barley, and rice became the staple food of the people. In about 1000 B.C. the Indians started using iron tools along with copper.

Also, a phenomenal growth took place in the Aryan beliefs in sacrificial rituals and magic. The sacrifices, ministered by the Brahmins, assumed the central stage in Aryan religion. The Brahmins asserted that the cosmos was controlled by sacrifice and the Brahmins, with their superior knowledge of the sacrifices, could, therefore, control the cosmos. They even claimed that they were the gods on earth.

The Late Vedic Society. By the late Vedic period (approximately 1000–500 B.C.) the formation of states with kings materialized, gradually undermining the tribal and clannish political organization of the earlier Rig-Vedic period. The rudiments of speculative and mystical thought that were apparent in the Rig-Veda are found in abundance in the later texts, culminating in the emergence of Indian philosophy and mysticism in the texts known as the **Upanishads**. The Upanishads focus on the philosophical questions such as what happens after a person dies, and the search for individual salvation. They reveal the identity of the individual soul (atman) in relation to the soul of the universe (brahman) and various **metaphysical** states that ultimately lead to total happiness. One mystical formulation was expressed in the equation "that you are" (tat tvam asi), which suggests that people are an integral part of the whole universe and by knowing oneself one can come to understand the universal mystery. Another Upanishadic statement reads: "Lead me from darkness to light; from ignorance to knowledge." The rigid class structure characteristic of Vedic Society was challenged by the teaching of Gotama the Buddha.

The Buddhist Period

The centuries immediately preceding the founding of Buddhism witnessed a shift in the main centres of Indian civilization to the central and eastern Gangetic Plains. Buddhist texts mention 16 geographic and cultural regions spread from the northwest to the northeast and central India. Several kingdoms of the region were engaged in territorial wars and by the time of Gotama, the Buddha (563 B.C.–483 B.C.) (enlightened one), the kingdoms of Magadha and Kosala in the northeastern area had emerged as the wealthiest and most powerful rival states of the region. In time the kingdom of Magadha, under the **Maurya** dynasty (312–184 B.C.), would become India's first empire.

The Buddhist period is described as the second period of urbanization as several urban centres had emerged after 500 B.C. As Max Weber, a well known sociologist, accurately observed, Buddhism presented itself as a product of urban development, urban kingship, and the city nobles. The urban centres in northeastern India were characterized by a high degree of occupational specialization, including craftspeople, servicepeople, professionals such as doctors, accountants, and money changers, as well as entertainers, merchants, and those in the king's service such as warriors, civil administrators, and servants.

Gotama the Buddha. Gotama the Buddha (the enlightened one) belonged to an aristocratic warrior clan of the Shakyas. The clan territory, with its capital Kapilvatthu, was located in the northeastern part of India near the foothills of India's Himalayan mountains. At the age of 29, the Buddha left his wife and his infant son to find for himself true happiness, and leave behind human suffering. After seven years of wandering in search of knowledge and being a disciple of the well-known philosophers of his time, he sought the truth himself by sitting under a tree and meditating. He supposedly saw the light of truth and became the Buddha, the enlightened one.

After achieving the state of enlightenment, he gave his first sermon to the five monks who became his disciples. The sayings of the Buddha were collated and classified immediately after his death and further elaborated over the next one hundred years. The early Buddhist literature is vast, consisting of the Buddha's sayings and the rules of discipline that had to be followed by the monks and nuns who accepted the Buddhist philosophy as the way to attain total freedom from suffering. Why did the Buddha's teachings hold such a wide appeal for his lay followers and his monks? What was there in his teachings that his lay followers and monks found relevant to their mode of livelihood and thinking?

Buddha's Teachings. The Eightfold Path is central to the Buddha's teaching. This path includes: proper discipline of the body, abstaining from taking life, stealing, and committing adultery; correct speech, to speak the truth, avoid cursing, backbiting, idle chatter; proper thought, including belief in rebirth as the fruit of good and evil deeds; not coveting wealth; and absence of hatred. Proper means of gaining a livelihood should not include poison, humans, weapons, alcohol, and butchering of animals for food. The last three requirements, proper exertion, self control, and cultivation of correct thoughts, were for those who had joined the Buddhist monastic order. The content of the last three involve meditation on the goals that will lead to **nirvana**, the ultimate state of happiness.

One of the fundamental messages of the Buddha was that a person should actively cultivate an attitude of compassion, friendliness, and joy towards all beings in the universe. Buddhism was part of the rationalist tradition of the age which did not believe in a personal, all-powerful creator.

The Buddha's teachings were open to all classes in society, undermining class distinctions based on birth. The Buddha stressed the virtues of honest living, and contrary to the general impression that Buddhism stood for renunciation, Buddha's advice to his followers who were householders was very practical. It even included advice on acquiring and managing money in what was considered to be an ethically correct manner. The Buddha once said: "The lay disciple with money obtained by hard work, gathered by strength of arm, earned by sweat and legitimately acquired, makes himself happy and cheerful, and he makes his parents, wife, children, slaves and labourers happy." This is the first reason for acquiring money. Second, he makes his friends and acquaintances happy. Third, he makes himself secure against misfortunes as may happen by way of fire, water, kings, robbers, and ill-disposed heirs. Fourth, he is able to give a share to his relatives, guests, the king, and to the gods. Fifth, and from the Buddhist point of view perhaps most important, with his money he is able to give offerings for the deserving people of all religions. As a reward individuals attained heaven after death. In his famous advice to the son of a rich householder, the Buddha advises that one should amass money by correct means, like a bee gathering honey from flowers.

But for the monks, the Buddha insisted that money is not conducive to happiness, and is an obstruction to true spiritual advancement. On one occasion Buddha said to the monks that the loss of such a thing as money is a trifling matter, whereas the loss of wisdom brings utter misery. The monks were not allowed during the early days of Buddhism to own houses, fields, or cattle, to touch gold or silver, or to engage in trade and agriculture. They neither took part in production nor had control over the means of production. For their survival the monks had to depend solely on gifts (dana) from the lay followers.

The Buddha had much to say about the political and social institutions created by people to safeguard their interests. The Buddha said that when the world reached a stage of moral decay, strife, and insecurity, there was a need to restore order out of anarchy. People assembled and elected the best person from among their group to protect their interests and in return for these services they would pay taxes. This is one of the earliest known examples of the **social contract**. Kingship for the Buddha was a human institution created out of a collective human will. The Buddha told the story of a king who was advised by his wise minister that he should make his subjects prosperous and abolish criminal activities. According to the minister, the king should provide seeds to the farmers, capital to the traders, and suitable jobs to those who want to serve the state. In this manner, all the subjects would be happily occupied with their own duties, there would be no revolt, and the people would be glad to pay taxes. The Buddha thus offered a solution to a very modern problem.

The Buddha regarded the world to be without a soul; constantly changing, it is impermanent and full of suffering. To be attached to this world is to invite suffering, which he calls dukkha. The Buddha explains the way to end the suffering. Through discipline of body and training of mind, and following the correct ethical and philosophical path taught by the Buddha, one can reach nirvana, the stage of total freedom from suffering. The Buddha's dying words to the monk, Ananda, were that a person should become her or his own light and not rely on help from others for salvation. Buddha's overriding concerns for the welfare of humanity, his ideas on compassion, equality, social justice, and non-injury to all living beings, were adopted by Indians and became a part of India's humanist tradition. As Buddhism spread throughout Asia his message of compassion, love, and respect for all living beings became a part of Asia's heritage also.

Mauryan Empire

Magadha emerged as the dominant state during and immediately after the Buddha's death. But the Mauryan Empire of the Magadha (312–184 B.C.) gave India political and cultural unity. Chandragupta, a member of the Maurya clan, became the founder of the empire, and his accession is placed about 312 B.C.

Megasthenes, the ambassador of Seleucus Nikator of Syria, visited Pataliputra the capital of Chandragupta Maurya. Megasthenes wrote a book called *Indica*, which is now lost, but was quoted extensively by classical Roman scholars, and Megasthenes' eyewitness record is still an important source for the study of the Mauryan Empire. Megasthenes gives us a description of the city of Pataliputra that contained the emperor's palace, which had 80 pillars. The walled city had 570 towers and 64 gates and was surrounded on all sides by ditches filled with water. It was about 14 km in length and 2.5 km in breadth and had a circumference of about 33 km. Judging by this description of Pataliputra, it was twice as large as Rome under Emperor Marcus Aurelius.

Megasthenes observed seven levels of Indian society consisting of philosophers, agriculturists, herders, soldiers, traders and artisans, inspectors and spies, and, the seventh, advisors and officers of the emperor. He was surprised not to find slavery of the Greek type in India. "All the Indians are free and not one of them is a slave," he wrote. Megasthenes praised the treatment given to the foreigners living in Pataliputra. Whenever a foreigner died in the city, the officers of the state would set aside his property in trust, inform his next of kin and turn over the property to them.

Another complimentary remark was that the Indians carried on their transactions honestly. This was a sharp contrast to the practices of the Greek states, where legal quibbles, litigations, and frauds were frequent occurrences. He also relates that Chandragupta lived guarded by Amazon women with drawn swords. An even more detailed picture of Mauryan administration is found in the book *Arthashstra* ("the science of political economy") a book written by Kautilya, Prime Minister of Chandragupta.

The *Arthashstra*. The *Arthashstra* is an extraordinary book; it instructed the kings and princes on how to administer the empire through a highly centralized and well-paid bureaucracy. The book became the model for the bureaucratic organization of public life and the economy, not only for the Mauryan Empire but also for other kingdoms in ancient and medieval India. Kautilya described the duties of the king and of the heads of departments, these departments included accounts and audit, war, the mint, mining, and the department to manage gambling and harlotry, which were state monopolies. The *Arthashstra* advises kings on how to control economic activities such as mining, trade, crafts, and agriculture. Defining the duties of the king, the *Arthashstra* observes: "In the happiness of his subjects lies his happiness; in their welfare his welfare....Whatever pleases himself he shall not consider as good, but whatever pleases his subjects he shall consider as good." The *Arthashstra* also describes a municipal government, possibly that of the city of Pataliputra, including prescribed fire prevention methods:

> Vessels filled with water shall be kept in thousands in rows, without cluttering them, in big streets and at places where four roads meet....Any house owner who does not run to give his help in extinguishing the fire of whatever is burning shall be fined 12 *panas* (coins) and the renter of the premise refusing to do so shall be fined 6 panas. Whosoever carelessly sets fire shall be fined 54 panas, and he who intentionally sets fire to a house shall be thrown into fire.

Kautilya, *Arthashstra*, bk. II, 34.

About the city's health precautions it is said:

> Whoever throws inside the city the carcass of animals, those of cat, dog and snake shall be fined 3; ass, camel, mule and cattle 6 panas; and human corpse shall be punished with a fine of 50 panas...

Whoever throws dirt in the street shall be punished with a fine of one-eighth of the pana; whosoever is responsible for water collected in the street shall be fined one-fourth pana.
Kautilya, *Arthashstra*, bk. II, 34.

The Reign of Ashoka. Ashoka (268–233 B.C.), the grandson of Chandragupta, inherited his grandfather's vast bureaucratic government, but modified it to include the social and ethical practices of Buddhism. Ashoka had a crisis of conscience when he conquered the country of Kalinga in 261 B.C. He became remorseful of the tragic consequence of the war in which "100 000 were killed and wounded and 150 000 were forcibly taken as captives from their homes." Deeply touched by the miseries caused by the war, Ashoka declared that he would change his policy of outright conquest by means of wars, and, instead, practice and teach by his personal example, the policy of *dhamma* (justice and righteousness). His aim was to be compassionate and just towards others and to look after their welfare and happiness. He immortalized his policy of dhamma by having it inscribed on pillars and rocks. These royal proclamations were autobiographical in nature and recorded the details of his rule.

Ashoka asserted that he was like a father to his people and would care for them as he would his own children. To do so, he instructed his officers to strictly implement his dhamma policy. Included in Ashoka's policy of dhamma was a command to respect one's father and mother, relatives, teachers, and philosophers. To care for his people he built rest houses and hospitals, which were supplied with medicinal plants. He also planted trees for shade, and had wells dug to provide water. Throughout his empire, he instituted medical treatment for people and animals. In a remarkable confession he explained how hundreds of animals were killed daily for food in his kitchens. Ashoka, out of compassion for the animals, stopped eating meat and became a vegetarian.

This illustration shows the dry-field cultivation process in three panels. In the top panel, the sowing is being done, in the second panel, oxen are being used as the draught animals and in all panels, the women carrying the children are working in the fields beside the men.

He appointed special commissioners of justice who toured the countryside teaching people to follow a path of righteousness and to look to the needs of the religious **mendicants**. Some scholars say that Ashoka used Buddhist social ethics to bind the people to a common purpose, to raise the ethical and moral standards of his subjects, and to promote internal harmony in his vast empire.

His policy of dhamma became a norm for subsequent dynastic rulers of ancient and medieval India. The inscriptions of the kings of ancient India who succeeded Ashoka asserted that in their kingdom

Ashoka, ruler of the Mauryan Empire, became religious after bloody campaigns to expand the empire. He ordered that pillars be erected throughout India engraved with instructions to the people to behave in a virtuous manner. These pillars were made of polished sandstone and stood over 10 m high.

they cared for widows and orphans, instituted free hospitals for cattle and people, built rest houses with free food, constructed canals and irrigation ditches, and supported the Brahmins, the Buddhists, and other religious sects with the gifts of land. Recorded are the kings' intentions to maintain and protect the laws and regulations of social groups living in their kingdoms.

Further, the Indian kings loved to proclaim, as state policy, the superiority of dhamma, which is justice and social ethics, over brute force. There can be no doubt that Ashoka's deliberate attempt to impress ethical norms on his subjects had a lasting effect on Indian political behaviour. In the inscriptions, Ashoka by virtue of his righteous (dhamma) policies, addressed himself as "beloved of god," which he was.

The Formative Period

The Mauryan Empire deteriorated gradually after Ashoka's death, and by 184 B.C. rule passed into the hands of the various interlocking, regional powers in the northwest, south, and northeast. In central India and in the southwest and southeast along the coastal areas, the Shatavahana kings ruled from the first century B.C. to the beginning of the third century A.D. Their empire extended from the east coast to the west coast and their control facilitated the international trade connection with the western countries and the east. Theirs was the strongest military presence in central and south India; however, they had to contend militarily with the Shaka in western India. The relationship between the two powers was not always hostile and they often established links between themselves by marriage. It is significant to note that both the Shakas and the Shatavahanas practised **Hinduism** and Buddhism with equal passion. Although the Shakas were a foreign presence in India, they had become Hindus and used **Sanskrit**, an Indian language of the elite, for record keeping. The Shaka rule lasted until A.D. 409 when they were finally conquered by the Gupta Emperor, Chandra Gupta II.

The Age of the Kushans. The conquest of northern India from the first to the third century A.D. was the work of the Kushans, a dynasty that united the Yue-Chi tribes of central Asia and established rule over the Shakas of Parthia and the people of the Punjab. Kanishka, their greatest king,

INNOVATIONS

THE HINDI LANGUAGE

Sanskrit, the classical language of India, is related to almost all the languages of Europe, including English. Hindi, modern India's national language is written in characters which originate from Sanskrit. Sanskrit is derived from the Indo-European linguistic branch, hence the similarities to Latin and also to English. For example, *Pitar*, which is the Sanskrit word for father, is similar to *pita*, the Hindi word and the cognate to the Latin *pater* and the English *father*. The following examples have been provided to further demonstrate this connection.

Hindi	Phonetic	Latin	English
माता	mata	mater	mother
अग्नि	agni	ignis	fire
शाला	shala	schole	school

---

replaced the Shaka rulers in A.D. 78. Like Ashoka, Kanishka adopted Buddhism as a state religion. The Kushan kings frequently adopted the Persian title, King of Kings and the Chinese title, Son of God, in their inscriptions and coins, indicating the introduction of divine kingship in India. By adopting such titles the Kushan kings were legitimizing their rule over petty kings and chiefs in newly conquered territories.

The age of the Kushans was prosperous. The great Asiatic trade routes crossed territories held by the Kushans in Bactriana and northwestern India. Through the Shaka chiefs they exerted control over the trade from the north to the western coast of India and to the Mediterranean and Rome. Control over international land and sea trade routes made the Kushan kings wealthy and powerful. The Kushans were the first Indian kings to introduce gold coins to the country and according to some scholars, they did this by melting Roman gold coins.

In the established tradition of Indian kings, the Kushans were eclectic in their religious practices. They were followers of Buddhism, but gave respect to the Hindu gods, Shiva and Vishnu, and the Persian cult of Mithras. Their King Kanishka is ranked with Ashoka as a great Buddhist ruler. Whereas Ashoka convened the third Buddhist Council, Kanishka held the fourth. According to the Buddhist tradition, at the end of the fourth Council, the entire Buddhist texts were re-edited and transcribed on copper plates and deposited in the Stupa, a Buddhist monument, at Peshawar. A Chinese monk who visited the Stupa in the fourth century A.D. said that it was 213 m high, and a wonder of the age.

The Kushans patronized Buddhist art forms, which combined elements of Greek and Roman art with Indian. The famous Buddhist philosopher, poet, and writer, Ashvaghosha, was in Kanishka's court, as was the physician Caraka, who wrote a brilliant book on Indian medicine that remains as one of the foundations of India's indigenous system of medicine known as Ayurveda.

There was a five-century gap between the disintegration of the Mauryan Empire in 184 B.C. and the beginning of the Gupta Empire in A.D. 320. This was considered a dark period in Indian history. For nearly five centuries short-lived kingdoms would rise and fall. Only the Kushans, Shatvahanas, and Shakas managed to establish kingdoms for a substantial period of time. The collapse of the Mauryan Empire, brought about when the last Mauryan Emperor was killed and replaced by a Shunga General, did not lead to cultural and economic decline, in fact it was a formative period of classical Indian civilization. It was also a period of cultural and economic interaction with the West and the East.

A new Indian art style emerged in the brief Shunga period which immediately followed the Mauryas. This period is noted for the creation of beautiful Buddhist monuments decorated with relief sculpture. In the Kushan period, the Buddhist art in the northwest of India had been influenced by Graeco-Roman style. In central India and in the north at Mathura, the Indian style continued and produced the classical Gupta style of art.

Indian Literature.
Many of the Hindu law-books, *dharma shastras*, of which the code of Manu is the foremost, laid down ethical and legal guidelines for the Hindus. Some of them were written in the second and third centuries A.D., at a time when India was supposedly in a dark period.

More importantly, India's two greatest epics were composed during this period. The epic *Ramayana* is the story of Rama, a prince who was exiled by his father Dasharatha. With his brother and his wife, Sita, Rama goes to the South in search of their livelihood. Sita is abducted by the demon king, Ravana of Lanka. Rama wages a mighty war against Ravana with the aid of an army of monkeys and rescues Sita, by defeating and killing Ravana. Rama is the archetype of an ideal king who rules justly and wisely. The kingdom of Rama, the Rama rajya, is considered by Hindus as a prototype of the golden age in which every man and woman lived happily under the protective custody of a wise ruler. Eventually, the hero Rama was elevated to the status of a god.

Another great epic tale is the *Mahabharata*, which is based on an actual battle fought in 850 B.C. The epic was recited orally for several centuries. The final inflated story consists of 106 000 verses and was composed over a period of two hundred years from A.D. 100–300. The 26 books of the *Mahabharata* narrate the story of a great war fought between two rival segments of the Bharatas clan. The five Pandava brothers with their allies collide with one hundred Kaurava brothers. Several sections of the *Mahabharata* deal with the ethics and morality of politics and social life. The most revered of the Hindu religious books, the *Bhagavadgita*, is a part of the *Mahabharata*. The *Bhagavadgita* ("the song of the Lord"), is to modern Hindus what the Bible is to Christians, and the Koran to Muslims.

The Spread of Buddhism.
Two centuries after the Buddha's death, Buddhism was split into 18 schools. In the post-Maurya period, Buddhism was separated into two schools, the Hinayana, the lesser vehicle, and the Mahayana, the greater vehicle. The historical Buddha, the great human teacher of the Hinayana, becomes a god figure in the Mahayana. The Buddha becomes saviour god of humankind. Through his grace, he saves all beings. Every

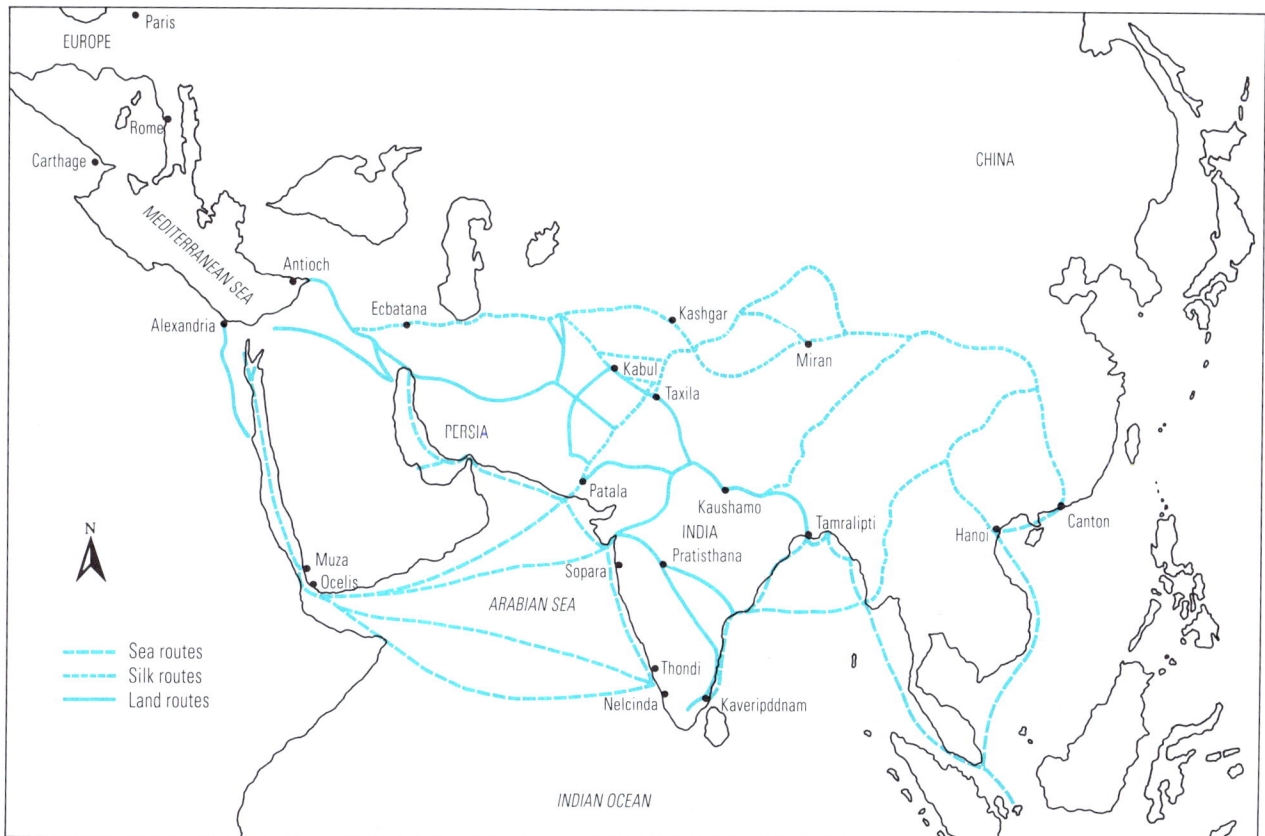

Ancient Trade Routes

Buddhist has a potential of becoming a Buddha, according to the Mahayana Buddhism. The Mahayana Buddhism, with new scriptures inspired by the earlier ones, spread through Central Asia to countries like China, Japan, Korea, and Tibet.

Trade. The period from 184 B.C. to A.D. 320 saw growth in India's trading and commercial connections with western and eastern civilizations. Spices and silk were the main items of trade. The Roman Senator Pliny (ca. A.D. 77) complained that Indian pepper drained the wealth of Rome: "There is no year in which India does not attract 50 million sesterces [coins]," he said. Greek sailors in the second century A.D. discovered the monsoon trade winds, which enabled them to sail to India by sea, avoiding the time-consuming coastal route via the Persian Gulf. The merchants sailed from Egypt in the month of July and arrived in 40 days at Muzaris on the west coast of India in Kerala. They stayed on the Kerala coast for about three months and began the return voyage from Muzaris in December or January. The Indian overland trade route was through Afghanistan to central Asia across the Hindakush Mountains where the route divided; one going towards the east and China and the other to the Mediterranean and Rome.

There were several Roman trading posts in south-

Ancient India CHAPTER 4 **109**

ern India. Roman coins, bronze statues, and amphoras have been found in various archaeological excavations carried out in the twentieth century. The Indian Tamil literature of the second century A.D. notes that in the thriving port of Muchris (Roman Muzaris) "the beautiful and large ships of the yavanas [Greeks and Romans] bringing gold, come splashing the white foam on the waters of Periyar [in Kerala] and return laden with pepper." The same literature describes the powerful yavanas clad completely in armour and acting as body-guards to the Tamil kings. The literature also raves about "the cool and fragrant wine brought by the yavanas in their good ships." Periplus, the author of *Periplus of the Erythraean Sea* (A.D. 100), was an experienced sailor who navigated the Red Sea, the Persian Gulf, the Kerala coast, and resided for many years at Barygaza (the modern city of Bhroach in Gujarat in western India).

Egyptians and Greeks were the principal carriers of the overseas trade with India. The Greek names, derived possibly from this contact, for rice, *oryza*; ginger, *zinziber*; and cinnamon, *karpion*, have a close correspondence with their Tamil equivalents *arisi*, *inchver*, and *karva* respectively. Pliny, as stated earlier, refers to the great demand for Indian pepper and ginger in Rome. An invader of Rome in A.D. 408 demanded and obtained, as part of the ransom, 1359 kg of pepper. We are told that the Kushan King, Kanishka, sent an Indian mission to the Roman Emperor Trajan on his accession. Trajan treated his Indian visitors with distinction, giving them senators' seats at the theatre.

The Gupta Empire

The imperial **Gupta** period is regarded as the golden age of ancient India, which lasted for two hundred years. The first king of the Gupta dynasty is Chandragupta I who began his reign in A.D. 320. His son Samudragupta (A.D. 335–375) was a great conqueror who brought much of northern India under his control. His invasion of southern India was even more interesting in that he did not annex the south, but instead collected tribute. His son Chandragupta II reigned from A.D. 375–415. He is known for the defeat of the Shakas in central and western India in A.D. 409. Chandragupta II is one of the few kings of ancient India whose memory is preserved in both the literary and folk tradition. Later Sanskrit literature preserves many tales about a great and wise king called Vikramaditya who ruled with justice and equanimity and who was a great patron of Indian art and literature. Vikramaditya is identified with Chandragupta II. A Chinese monk, Fa Xian (pronounced fa shen), who visited North India during the Gupta period (A.D. 390) observed:

> The climate of this country is warm and equable, without frost or snow. The people are very well off, without tax or official restrictions. Only those who till the royal lands return a portion of profit to the king. If they desire to go, they go; if they like to stop, they stop.... The king governs without the use of capital punishment; criminals are fined according to circumstances, lightly or heavily. Even in cases of repeated rebellion they only cut off the right hand.
> Fa Xian, *Buddhist Records of the Western World*.

Fa Xian's account reflects on the relatively mild manner with which the Guptas administered their empire. Chandragupta II's son Kumaragupta (A.D. 415–455) sustained rule without any additional conquests. His reign is noted for support, by means of land grants, to the Hindu temples and the Brahmins. Such grants were recorded on copper plates. Skandagupta succeeded his father Kumaragupta in A.D. 455. He had to contend with an increasing number of invasions from the northwest. Most of the empire's resources were spent in defending the Gupta frontiers. The Gupta Empire diminished in

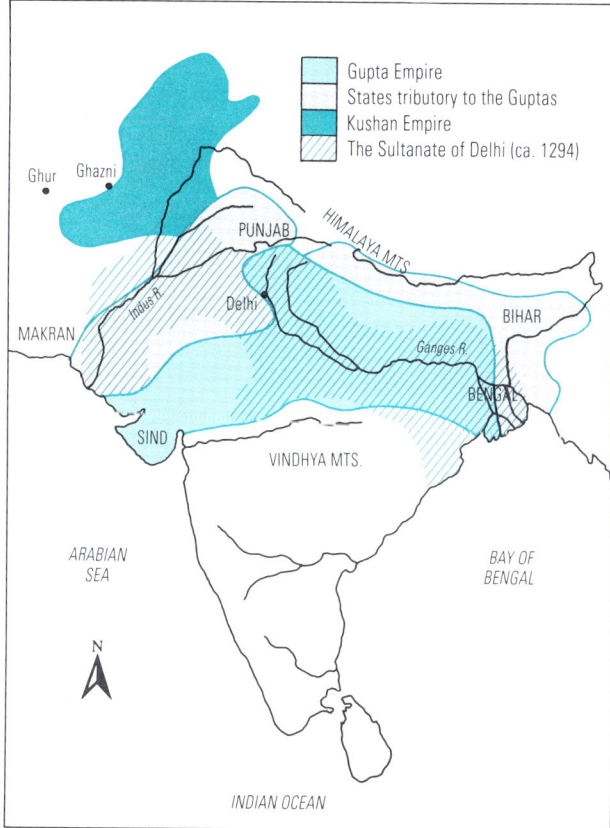

India: The Gupta Empire and the Sultanate of Delhi

This political map of India (ca. A.D. 400–1294) shows the political divisions of India from the time of the imperial Guptas to the arrival of the Muslim invaders.

size after Skandagupta's death in A.D. 467 but continued until ca. A.D. 520.

The decline of the Gupta Empire was hastened by attacks by the Hunas, central Asian nomads. Their leaders Mihirkula and Toramana controlled northwestern India for nearly fifty years from the beginning of the sixth century. Hunas were held responsible for destroying the cities and trading centres of northwestern India. They quickened the formation of a number of competing regional kingdoms in the north who engaged in constant intertribal wars. The Huna incursions into the Gupta Empire heralded the end of the Indian classical period and beginning of the medieval era.

Science and Technology

An Indian scientist, Brahmagupta, (A.D. 598–660) perfected the Indian decimal system for the notation of numerals, expressing tens and hundreds by position and employing a special sign for zero. This method of expressing all numbers by 10 symbols is perhaps India's greatest legacy to the world. The same Brahmagupta anticipated the gravitational theory. He said: "Things fall to the ground not because of any inherent force within but because of the pull from the earth." An earlier Indian scientist, Aryabhatta, (A.D. 476–520), a mathematician and astronomer, computed the math equation for **pi**, not derived in Europe until much later. Aryabhatta wrote that the earth, by its revolution (rotation on axis) produced the daily rising and setting of the sun, planets, and stars. The trigonometric sine function was not mentioned by Greek mathematicians and astronomers, yet it was used in India from the time of the Gupta period. A work on astronomy from that period called *Surya Siddhanta* provides a table of sine values.

In metallurgy, the proof of Indian advance in this field is to be found in an iron pillar ca. A.D. 415, now located in Delhi. The pillar is made of pure cast iron and weighs about 6 t and stands 7.3 m tall. It has stood without rust over 1500 years. There are records describing a copper image of the Buddha that was created at the close of the sixth century A.D. and was about 24 m tall. It was destroyed and melted by Muslim invaders in the twelfth century A.D. However, a 2.5 m bronze Buddha statue, also produced in the Gupta period, is still intact.

LITERATURE

SANSKRIT POETRY

The courtly poetry of the Gupta period created masterpieces in Sanskrit, the written and spoken language of ancient India. Sanskrit poets wrote verses in such a way that a mood was induced or an idea suggested, enticing the reader to come to the conclusion the poet intended. Often a particular detail or scene was chosen and the poet attempted to exactly recreate it. The appeal of Sanskrit is the precision of the language and the poet's playful use of puns, sounds and nuances.

The seasons served as an inspiration to Sanskrit poets. With spring comes harmony; it is not spring's beauty but its changes which stir the human heart. It is this harmonious reaction to and with nature that becomes the topic. Summer poems deal with the discomforts of the heat, the hot wind drying out ponds and wells and parching vegetation, creating both in humans and beasts a listlessness. Fall is a time for the harvesting of ripened sugar cane and rice. A harvest scene is described, creating an impression of golden prosperity and contentment. Some of the winter verses depicted scenes of peasant life. There is created a sense of comfort in having prepared well for the winter. Below is a selection of Sanskrit verse tracing this cycle of the seasons. The word Kāma in line 3 below means love.

As the mango puts forth shoot and leaf,
puts forth bud and flower,
so in our hearts does Kāma shoot
and leaf and bud and flower.

The day is miserably hot,
the night is worn and thin:
separated, with contradictory motion
like man and wife at odds.   [KĀLIDĀSA]

The wagon track, marked with juice from the crushed cane,
    carries a flag of saffron-colored dust;
a flock of parrots settles on the barley ears already bowed
    with grain;
a school of minnows swims along the ditch from paddy field
    to tank
and on the river bank the good mud cools the herd boy
    from the sun.   ABHINANDA

The warmth of their straw borne off by icy winds,
time and again the peasants wake the fire
whose flame dies ever back, stirring with their sticks.
From the smoking bank of mustard chaff,
noisy with the crackling of the husks,
a penetrating odor spreads
to every corner of the threshing floor.
                                 YOGEŚVARA

Education and University

Beginning with the age of the Guptas and further into the ninth and tenth centuries A.D., India was noted for its world famous Buddhist Universities. Nalanda University in Bihar, northeastern India was the most notable with 3000 students from Korea, China, central Asia, and from all over India. The Universities of Vallabhi in Gujarat, western India, Kanchi in south India, and Kashmir in north India were also famous. All the universities were well maintained with regular incomes from the ruling kings. Admission standards for the universities were high. Hiuen Tsiang who visited Nalanda University provides details for entrance at Nalanda:

> If men of other quarters desire to enter and take part in the discussions, the keeper of the gate proposes some hard questions; many are unable to answer, and retire. One must have studied deeply both old and new books before getting admission. Hiuen Tsiang, *Buddhist Records of the Western World*.

As it was a Buddhist University, the doctrinal works belonging to the 18 Buddhist sects were taught as compulsory subjects. Other subjects taught included logic, grammar and philosophy, medicine, systems of philosophy, works of literature, and general knowledge. The Chinese monk who visited the university wrote:

> The day is not sufficient for the asking and answering of profound questions. From morning till night they engage in discussion; the old and the young mutually help one another...There are eight halls and three hundred apartments in this monastery. Hiuen Tsiang, *Buddhist Records of the Western World*.

Hinduism

There are about six hundred million Hindus in the world today. In the area of religious development, the Gupta age saw the consolidation and crystallization of many of the classical features of Hinduism. Hinduism is a complex set of religious **ideologies** and practices. The worship of God in the image form and the belief in rebirth are key features of the Hindu religion. There is an assumption that a person is born again and again, and the status and rank of a person in this life depends on the good or evil actions performed in the past life. This is known as the law of action, **karma**, in Hinduism. If one violates the moral regulations (dharma) of society, and commits evil, then as a result of such evil actions, one gets to be born in a lower status in the next birth. Hinduism assumes that God comes down to earth periodically in various animal and human forms in order to save earth from falling into total anarchy. As an ancient Indian text on politics reads, under anarchical conditions, the law of fish prevails. The big fish eats the smaller ones. The good disappears and evil triumphs. God then restores order and morality in the world. The incarnation of God on the earth is called avatar. This concept existed in earlier phases of Hinduism, but the Gupta period saw it grow.

The literature that has made the greatest impact on Hindu's religious life is known as *Puranas*, ("ancient histories"). The *Puranas* describe the origin and the exploits of Hindu gods and goddesses. They contain Hindu myths, philosophical debates, ritual prescriptions, and **genealogies** of northern dynasties to the period of the Gupta kings. The *Puranas*, 18 of them, attained their final form in the Gupta age.

Hindus worship their gods in the form of images made of stone, wood, or metal. The texts composed in the Gupta period describe the elaborate rituals

Shiva, one of the most popular Hindu gods, is involved in the cosmic cycle of renewal and destruction as the destructive force. He is often depicted holding symbols of cosmic power such as fire, destroyer of any life. Often he is crushing a dwarf who represents the unenlightened person living in illusions.

followed by artists in making images of the gods. The texts also give detailed instructions for the priests on how, through ritual, they should breathe life into the image by inviting the deity to reside in the image. The household and temple ceremonies involved in the worship of God were in existence prior to the Gupta period, but in this period the rules were codified and standards established. The books written during the Gupta period tell us of the mode of worship of God in a Hindu temple. God, we are informed, is to be treated as the guest and lord of the house, to be awakened, bathed, fed, entertained, and worshipped by the devotee. Beautifully constructed Hindu temples that housed images of gods and goddesses became a wide-spread phenomenon from this time onwards. The texts were written in the Gupta period giving architectural blueprints for different temple constructions.

The books called the science of righteousness, the *dharma shastras*, deal with social, legal, and religious behavior of Hindus. They contain civil and criminal procedures and a list of punishments for breaking the laws. Secular laws dealing with trade regulations, contract, and debt appear as topics in the *dharma shastra* books. The books are also regarded as an instruction manual for the correct social behavior of all classes in Hindu society. Instructions cover the subjects of religious fasts, purifications, foods, marriage, and the rules governing the conduct of social classes. Although the *dharma shastra* literature dates back to the first century A.D., the majority of the *dharma shastras* known today were written during the Gupta period. The post-Gupta writers of medieval India merely commented on the *dharma shastras* written during the Gupta period. These commentaries offer us insights into the historical changes brought about in the social, legal, and religious behavior of Indians over the centuries.

Daily Life

Let us imagine the life of a wealthy young man and a woman in the Gupta age. At age six a young boy would receive a sacred thread in a ceremony that marked the beginning of his formal education. For the next decade the boy would attend a well equipped school, complete with an underground exercise room of magnificent proportions. These schools, which were outside the city, were staffed by a large number of specialists who were paid by the king. Throughout their education, boys played, studied, and were guided by mentors selected by their parents. At school boys were taught various arts (kala) and sciences (shastras). Training in the martial arts was also a part of the curriculum including the use of various weapons, hand to hand combat, giving and countering blows, and riding elephants and horses.

Girls of wealthy families received an education quite different from their male counterparts. They were taught reading, writing, painting, and dancing by female tutors. The tutors were well versed in legends and tales and were proficient in the arts and sciences, as well as being fluent in several languages and dialects.

The daily routine of a wealthy young man began in the morning with a series of exercises with wooden clubs and yoga to keep his body and mind alert. This routine was followed by an elaborate bath after which a fresh garment, fumigated with incense, and a turban-like hat were put on. Before leaving the house to attend to business young men would eat a mixture of powdered-dry mango, camphor, and cloves to freshen their breath. The daily schedule of men of the wealthy class included looking after business interests, although much of this work was left to their business managers. Before the midday meal men often played chess (which originated in India) or other board games. The midday meal may have consisted of game birds roasted on spits, wrapped in bitter leaves, and served with a sauce made of butter, mango juice, salt, and pepper. A soup prepared with beans, goat meat, fried eggplant, pieces of ginger, cumin, and lotus stalks fried in butter may also have been served. The meal would conclude with peaches and pears when in season (both of these were introduced to India from China in the first century A.D.) or with oranges, bananas, and mangoes. Churned buttermilk, mixed with sugar, honey, and the essence of flowers would normally be drunk with the meal, although Kapisha wine, from Afghanistan, would be drunk on special occasions. According to the Indian custom, the men would eat their lunch separate from the women.

Often a man of status had an art gallery that contained paintings which could be admired by his friends. The men of the wealthy class were also trained in art and literature, which they would display in the company of their friends by reading their poems or dramas. King Harsha wrote three plays while the emperor Samudragupta was an accomplished lute player and was referred to as the "king among poets." Occasionally men would visit the ganika, who were accomplished women entertainers who sang, danced, and engaged in literary conversations. Wealthy men and women enjoyed hosting dinner parties at which they would listen to music, make small talk, and sometimes sip imported Roman wines.

The Emperor Harsha

One king who sustained the glory of the Guptas was King Harsha (A.D. 606–647). His empire stretched from the Punjab in the northwest, northern Orissa in the east, and from the Himalayas to the banks of the Narmada River. A Chinese scholar and monk Hiuen Tsiang (pronounced yon chong) spent 13 years (A.D. 630–643) in India during Harsha's reign. He returned to China with 20 horses carrying 657 Buddhist texts and 150 relics associated with the Buddha. He describes Harsha's rule as honest and the people as living together in harmony. Hiuen Tsiang wrote that in the trials of the criminals no torture was used. Even the people who plotted against their superiors, after the facts were brought to light, were put into prison, but without any corporal punishment. Land tax was no more than one-sixth of the produce. Hiuen Tsiang compliments the people of North India on their "explicit and correct speech, harmonious and elegant expression and clear and distinct intonations" and notes that:

ASPECTS OF DAILY LIFE

FOOD and its Importance in INDIA

This painting depicts a couple about to partake in a meal. The food, which may have been similar to the meals outlined here, was presented in a pleasing fashion. Whether vegetarian or not, the meals included a wide variety of dishes prepared with numerous spices.

To offer food to a guest (*atithi*) is considered one of the five obligations of a Hindu family. God is the supreme guest in the Hindu household. Unlike giving thanks to God before eating, an orthodox Hindu *offers* his food to the gods before he eats. The cleansing of hands, feet, and mouth must be done before eating. The regulations concerning pure and impure food are many and are as old as the ancient Vedas. Eating food in the correct manner was prescribed during the age of the Buddha: he ruled that the whole hand should not be thrust into the mouth while eating; a person should not talk with food in his mouth, nor eat by tossing up balls of food, or stuffing his mouth. As well, Hindus should not shake their hands, scatter lumps of food, stick out their tongues, make a hissing sound, or lick their fingers or plate. Over the millennia, many more details of proper eating habits were added.

Muslims in India offer food to the needy, hungry, and guests as an integral part of their culture. Sharing of food is obligatory for all Muslims on their feast days. During the Mughal period, the Indo-Muslim cooking reached a high level of sophistication and maturity that is still unsurpassed, especially with regard to meat preparations. Even today, the best of meat dishes are called Moglai in India and Pakistan.

A traditional Indian meal is served with all of the dishes together and is concluded with fresh fruit. The serving of *paan*, which is a leaf heaped with chopped betel nuts and other scented ingredients folded up and secured with a clove, marks

the formal ending of the meal. Below are two sample menus, one vegetarian and one non-vegetarian, as well as a recipe from each of the menus.

Vegetarian Menu

Cauliflower soup

Chapati (a kind of bread)

Boiled rice

Toor dall (pigeon pea puree)

Fried okra

Stuffed aubergines (eggplant)

Papad (wafers)

Lemon pickle in vinegar

Banana satsuma pudding

Paan

Non-Vegetarian Menu

Meat soup

Tandoori chicken

Beef kofta curry

Batter drop raita (yogurt)

Chilli pickle in lemon juice

Kulfi (ice cream) for the princes

Paan

Bharwan baigan (Stuffed aubergines or eggplant)

6 eggplants

50 mL coriander seeds

25 mL aniseeds

15 mL cumin seeds

15 mL fenugreek seeds

5 mL turmeric powder

2 green chillies, finely chopped

5 mL salt

25 mL lemon juice

100 g ghee

1 large onion, finely chopped

Clean the eggplants and slit them lengthwise without halving them. Roast the first four spices together then grind them to a powder and add the turmeric; mix with the chillies, salt, and lemon juice to make a stuffing. Divide this mixture between the eggplants and tie them back together with cotton to stop the stuffing from escaping.

Heat the ghee in a large frying pan and fry the onion until light brown. Add the eggplants and cover tightly. Leave to cook turning occasionally until cooked, about 20–30 minutes.

Tandoori Murgha taangen (Grilled Drumsticks)

900 g chicken drumsticks

10 mL salt

50 mL special tandoori chicken powder

50 mL oil

25 mL lemon juice

2 medium onions

4 lemons, sliced in rounds

Remove the skin from the drumsticks and place them on a baking sheet. Now mix the salt and tandoori powder and rub half of it on one side of the drumsticks. Then turn them over and use the other half on the other side. Prick the meat on the drumstick using a fork.

Pour half of the oil over the drumsticks and put the baking sheet under the grill at a low heat. When the drumsticks get slightly brown, take them out, turn them over and pour the rest of the oil over them. Return to the grill once again; continue until chicken is cooked. Pour the lemon juice over the drumsticks.

Fry the onions in some of the remaining oil. Serve hot on a bed of fried onion rings and slices of lemon.

The people, although hot-tempered, are upright and sincere. They never take anything wrongfully and often yielded to others more than fairness required. The people are honest and sincere. They are noble and gracious in appearance. They apply themselves much to learning.
Hiuen Tsiang, *Buddhist Records of The Western World*.

Harsha devoted much of his spare time to building educational centres, and making provisions for highways. He built free rest houses, drink stalls, and planted fruit-bearing or shady trees. He arranged philosophical debates among scholars and patronized the performance of plays with moral themes. Harsha himself wrote three plays in the beautiful Sanskrit language. Hiuen Tsiang was impressed by the free hospitals built by Harsha, which were supplied with food, drink, and physicians. He writes:

> Here come all poor or helpless patients suffering from all kinds of diseases. They are well taken care of and a physician attends them. Food and medicine is provided according to their needs. They are made quite comfortable. When they are well they may go away.
> Hiuen Tsiang, *Buddhist Records of the Western World*.

An eyewitness account of Harsha states that "he forgot sleep and food in his devotion to good works." Harsha, like Ashoka before him, is in many ways an archetypical king of ancient India who was literate, and considered it his duty to support religious institutions and build hospitals as part of his social responsibility as a ruler. The king in his inscriptions gave a standard pledge to maintain order in society and to rule the subjects by the principle of dharma, that is, to rule by justice and righteousness.

Harsha spent, according to the Chinese visitor, one fourth of his state income on charity. He held five yearly assemblies to listen to debates among

One of the most representative examples of the Middle period and the regionalism expressed in Buddhist temple architecture is the Lingaraja temple at Bnubaneswar, dating from ca. 1000 A.D. The most impressive feature is the Sri Mandir, the tall beehive-shaped tower, which has intricately carved sections representing layers upon layers of heavens to house a multitude of gods.

various religious orders of the time, such as Buddhism, and Hinduism. At the end of the debates he gave away his accumulated personal fortune to charity. At one such assembly, witnessed by the Chinese monk, he distributed so much wealth that he was left with only his royal robes. Those too he gave away. In keeping with the spirit of ancient Indian kings, he was religiously tolerant and gave equal patronage to various religions. He himself was a Hindu, a devotee of the god Shiva, but his sister and brother were converts to Buddhism.

One must not forget, however, that Harsha was the most powerful ruler of northern India who conquered the "five indies, i.e. the whole of Northern and Central India" with 5000 elephants, 20 000 cavalry and 50 000 infantry.[1]

Harsha suffered defeat at the hands of Pulakeshin II, of the Chalukya dynasty of southern India in A.D. 630. The people of the country ruled by Pulakeshin are described by the Chinese monk:

> They are all very tall and of stern, vindictive character. To their benefactor they are grateful; to their foes they are relentless. If they are going to seek revenge, they first give their adversaries warning, then each being armed, they attack each other with lances; when one turns to flee, the other pursues him, but they do not kill a man down. If a general loses a battle, they do not inflict punishment but present him with a woman's clothes and so he is driven to seek death for himself.
>
> Hiuen Tsiang, *Buddhist Records of the Western World*.

*T*he Regional Kingdoms

The focus of Indian history from A.D. 650 to 1200 shifts from one empire to regional kingdoms in the north and south. Many of the northern dynasties were short lived. The more stable dynasties were found in the southern peninsula. From the seventh century to the fourteenth century India experienced several important and lasting dynasties in the south such as the Pallavas, Chalukyas Rashtrakutas, and Cholas, and, finally the dynasties of Vijayanagara, which ruled the southern part of the Indian peninsula from the fourteenth to the sixteenth century. The Cholas of southern India were a formidable power for nearly three centuries from A.D. 897 to 1120. As a great maritime power they had active trade and diplomatic contacts with China and other southeast Asian rulers; Cambodia, Java and Sumatra, and Malaya. Their naval armada successfully fought and won against the navy of Sailendra kings of Java and Sumatra (modern Indonesia).

*M*uslim Rule in India

The arrival of Muslims to the Indian subcontinent took place in A.D. 711 when Arabs led by Muhammad ibn Qasim captured the coastal city of Debal near modern Karachi in Pakistan. Muslim rule of Sindh was ushered in, and within a century, spread from the lower reaches of the Indus river to Multan in the Punjab. The Arabs were defeated by powerful Hindu rulers such as Chalukyas and Rastrakutas as they tried to extend their territories towards the west in Gujarat and central India. In the north their territorial ambitions were contained by the Gurjara Pratiharas. Muslims, however, continued to live along the west coast of India in trading colonies.

The next major Muslim inroad coming from northwestern Afghanistan, led to the permanent settlement of Muslims in the north, destruction of the Hindu rulers, and the establishment of the **Delhi Sultanate** in A.D. 1206. Qutub-ud-din, the general of Muhammad of Ghor, who had initiated the conquest of northern India from Afghanistan, became the first Delhi Sultan in A.D. 1206. The Delhi Sultanate lasted from A.D. 1206–1526. A number of Muslim dynasties made Delhi their capital, and consolidated their hold over the northern plain from the Sindh and Punjab to Bengal. During the Sultanate's zenith, the Sultans penetrated south, central, and western India, but could not control their southern possessions from Delhi. From A.D. 1206–1296, the Delhi Sultans consolidated their rule in the north, and more importantly, protected their northwestern frontiers from the Mongols. The Mongols had been united under the leadership of Chingghis Khan and his descendants had overrun

---

[1] Samuel Beal (trans.), *Buddhist Records of the Western World* (London: Trubner and Company, 1884).

much of central Asia, Mongolia, and northern China. The Mongol raids destroyed important Islamic cultural centres in Syria and Iraq. Northern India under the effective military leadership of the Delhi Sultans was able to contain the Mongol threat.

Alla-ud-din-Khalji (A.D. 1296–1320) was the first Delhi Sultan bold enough to invade the rich south. He raided it twice, each time his army returning with their elephants, camels, and horses laden with the gold and silver from the south. Alla-ud-din paved the way for the subsequent Islamic cultural and political entry into that region. Alla-ud-din is noted for his talents as a great administrator. His revenue demands, constituting as much as half of the produce of the peasants, was efficiently collected from the predominantly Hindu peasantry. With new access to the gold of the south and effective collection of land revenue, Alla-ud-din could maintain a well paid standing army of 100 000 men. The army was needed to protect the northwestern flank of his empire from the Mongols, who increasingly threatened the Delhi rule, and for his own conquests. Alla-ud-din had also to confront the discord within his own court. He controlled the nobility of the court by strong measures such as banning public drinking of liquor and not allowing social festivities among the nobles without his permission. He established a deadly spy network, who were so efficient in reporting conspiracies against the Sultan that his noblemen were afraid to speak aloud with each other in the open, choosing instead to communicate with each other by sign language. In order to meet the shortage of supply of necessary food supplies and rampant inflation in Delhi and other cities of the north, he introduced wage and price control, one of the earliest examples of the control of the economy through state intervention. To put it simply, he fixed the prices of all commodities, from slaves to horses. In order to stave off the shortage of food, he collected half of his taxes in grain, which was collected in state storehouses and redistributed to people at lower prices. His state officials, backed up by the secret police, hindered any malpractice on the part of the traders and merchants. If, for instance, a trader cheated in weights, Alla-ud-din's officers would make good the loss of weight by cutting off an equal amount of flesh from that offender's body.

Sultan Muhammad bin Tughluq, who was a brilliant general, and student of Islamic theology, built on the political and administrative infrastructure of Alla-ud-din-Khalji. Whereas Alla-ud-din was satisfied with raiding the south, Muhammad wanted to establish a permanent political presence in southern India, which he had begun to invade with his military expeditions. Towards that end, he built a new administrative centre at Daulatabad in south-central India. However, his move to shift the court and bureaucrats to the new city was roundly criticized by his contemporaries. In order to facilitate the collection of cash-revenue from his conquered territories, he introduced a copper currency, supported by reserves of silver. This was like the paper currency notes that were used in China during this period. The experiment failed, and silver coins were reintroduced. During the last ten years of his reign, the southern part of his empire began to disintegrate. After his death, the Sultanate rule was effectively confined to the northern plains of India from A.D. 1351–1526.

The Mughal Emperor Akbar

The political unification of the north stretching from the Bay of Bengal to Kabul and from the Himalyas to Gujrat and Malwa (central India) began with Akbar, the great Mughal emperor, whose career spanned from A.D. 1560 to 1606. Akbar's eclectic religious policy helped his empire to overcome Islamic insularity. Prior to Akbar, the Muslim rulers of India tended to look at their possessions as the land of Islam, and regarded non-Muslims as second-class citizens who had to pay a poll tax, called *ziziya*, to live in protective custody in a Muslim land. None of the Muslim rulers had appointed Hindus in their upper-echelon civil and military services, although the Muslim rulers were surrounded by the Hindu tributary chiefs. Akbar treated Hindus as equal partners in his empire venture. Hindus, particularly the warrior classes in the north, known as the Rajputs, were given access to the inner circles of Akbar's court. He married women of royal Hindu families, but instead of converting them to Islam according to the requirements of the Muslim law, he allowed these women to remain as practising Hindus. Akbar abolished the ziziya tax, another important signal to the Hindus that they were equal citizens of his empire. He abolished the pilgrimage taxes, which Hindus had to pay when they travelled to important religious centres such as Banaras. His new policy toward the Hindus was regarded with severe misgivings by some of the orthodox Muslim elite of his empire, but they were unable to change Akbar's policies.

Akbar enjoyed religious discourses in the house of worship which he built in his capital for that purpose. He would listen to the Hindus, Muslims, Sikhs, Jains, and Christians expound the teachings of their faith and engage in interfaith dialogues. Eventually, Akbar started an imperial cult of his own, with a set of rituals borrowed from Islam and other religions. People who joined his cult had to pledge to give up their faith, honour, property, and life to the service of Akbar. Akbar regarded himself as an almost semi-divine person. Perhaps, this image was important to sustain his hold on the subjects of his empire, who were mostly Hindus. Some modern historians regard Akbar as an **apostate** who had given up his faith and betrayed Islam.

Akbar reorganised civil and military bureaucracy. The officers of his new imperial service were divided into 33 ranks, and were responsible directly to him for the administration of his vast empire. He sur-

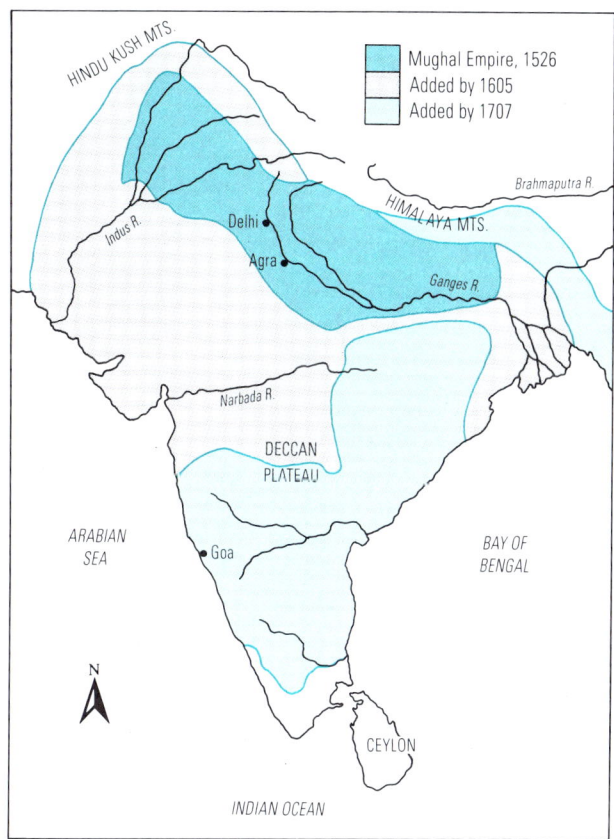

Mughal Empire 1526–1707
With a strong government the Mughal Emperors ruled most of the Indian subcontinent.

veyed the land under his control systematically over a ten year period and fixed the land revenue, based on its average yield. His taxation system was fair and brought in a steady flow of income to his empire.

Jahangir (A.D. 1606–1627), his son, sustained Akbar's policies: he did not conquer additional territories, but consolidated the gains of his father. Jahangir was fond of the good life, and was noted for his drinking bouts, philosophical dialogues, and his love for justice. His wife, Nur Jahan, a woman known for her beauty and wisdom, helped him administer the

ARCHITECTURE

THE TAJ MAHAL

The Taj Mahal represents a fulfillment of the dream of Mughal emperor Shah Jahan (1627–1659) to build an elegant white-marble mausoleum at Agra for his wife, Mumtaz Mahal. The Taj Mahal expresses the ultimate point of artistic perfection reached in the development of Indo-Muslim architecture in India. The building, which is a tomb garden, was well conceived and executed and was the outcome of coordination of skills of the master builders of Asia. The best masons from northern India were brought in. The calligraphers from Baghdad and Shiraz were invited. Specialists from Constantinople, Samarqand, Qandhar, Bokhara, and Kashmir designed and supervised building activities as well as planning the garden, which is an integral part of the Taj. The person who coordinated the work was Ustad Isa from Lahore.

empire, to such an extent that she almost took over the rule herself.

Shah Jahan, Jahangir's son, was a great general, prince, builder, and emperor. His masterpiece is undoubtedly the Taj Mahal, a monument he built to house his wife's tomb. When he died he was buried next to her. Shah Jahan built many impressive mosques, but his crowning achievement was an entirely new capital city in Delhi. The last of the great Mughal emperors, Aurangjeb (A.D. 1657–1707), was a puritan Muslim ruler who regarded India as the land of Islam and reversed the policies of his predecessors. He reimposed the ziziya tax on Hindus, discriminated against them in his service, and gave orders to demolish Hindu temples, which he considered a sacred act undertaken as a true Muslim. The latter half of his career was spent in the south where he conquered new territories. With his death in A.D. 1707, the Mughal Empire collapsed.

Hindu-Muslim Interaction

Alberuni, a Muslim author, wrote a book on India 150 years before the Muslims invaded northern India in the late twelfth century A.D. On the habits of the Indians, Alberuni states:

> The Hindus believe that there is no nation like theirs, no kings like theirs, no religion like theirs, no science like theirs. They are by nature miserly in communicating that which they know, and they take the greatest care to withhold it from men of another caste among their own people, still more, of course, from any foreigner.
> Alberuni, *Alberuni's India*, 17-22.

This excerpt is quoted by scholars to indicate the **insularity** of the Indians in relation to Muslims. The reality of Hindu-Muslim interaction in medieval India is much more complex than viewed by Alberuni.

The entry of Islam into the Indian subcontinent was bound to lead to a clash of the two civilizations. Islam introduced into India the cultural heritage of Islamic Arabia, Persia, and central Asia, with its distinct tradition of literature, languages, legal philosophy, and art. The differences between Hinduism and Islam are many. Muslims believe in conversion of others to their religion, Hindus do not practise conversion. Hindus worship images of gods and goddesses, Muslims are opposed to image worship. They associate image worship with the paganism of pre-Islamic Arabia and, whenever they are in a position to do so, they consider it a sacred duty to destroy images and the temples which house them. Some scholars are of the opinion that the mutual incompatibility of Hinduism and Islam was never resolved and the two went their separate ways with the creation of Pakistan as a sovereign Islamic state in 1947.

Islamic art with its penchant for domes, arches, simple and elegant geometric designs, and the use of marble stones in the buildings, enriched the existing ornate style of pre-Islamic Indian architecture. The Persian miniature painting styles popularized by the Mughals from the sixteenth century found ready acceptance in India. The formal gardens, the domed palaces, and mosques were also Islamic innovations in India.

The Muslim, west Asian and central Asian dress habits and military technology was adopted rapidly by the Hindus, as well as Persian-court etiquette. Persian, the language of Iran, became the language of diplomacy and political correspondence for both the Hindu and Muslim elites.

In the area of religion, the Hindu-Muslim influences on each other are complex and difficult to distinguish. Civilizations have the tendency to borrow the traits of civilizations they come into contact with. Before accepting those borrowed features they

ASPECTS OF DAILY LIFE

LIFE OF A MUGHAL GENTLEMAN

Mirzanama, an A.D. 1660 manual, portrays the lifestyle of a Mughal gentleman of honour, good taste, and good manners. Below are excerpts from that manual.

The primary requirement for a Mirza, a Muslim gentleman, is his birth in high family. In keeping with the dignity of his position, he should have a minimum high rank of a mansabdar of "one thousand" in the Mughal bureaucracy. Not all can become the Mirzas despite their wealth or high rank, if they do not possess the temperament of a Mirza. All his qualities are elegant as his appearance; on his stature his dress looks becoming; his disposition draws others to him. In generosity he is ahead of others so that his expenses sometimes exceed his income.

A Mirza should spend some of his time at day and night in the study of ethics. He should know *fiqh* (Islamic jurisprudence) and Quranic exegesis, works of history, the rules of prosody [verse] and rhyme. He should be expert in the use of various scripts.... He should be well versed in judging horses and the good and bad points of falcons. Swordsmanship and the archery should be his forte, but he should as far as possible not be inclined to use a matchlock musket, so that the unpleasant smell of its fuse may not reach his nose. On the battle front he should fight like a true soldier, even though he be killed. One who claims to be a Mirza welcomes such a death; for an honorable death is better than a dishonorable life.

Knowledge and understanding of music is a great art. The Mirza should acquaint himself with all the musical recitals and instrumental music. As a Mirza, he should confine himself only to knowledge of the harmony and musical tones words and their meanings, which cannot be regarded as disgraceful. He should under no circumstances indulge himself in singing, but leave this rather to the professional musicians. Singing can lead to dancing, and that necessarily to other disgraceful and ignominious actions.

If he has the bad habit of consuming alcohol, and cannot get rid of it by another alternative medicine, he should indulge in it wisely. He should not drink daily, as it is the habit of the rabble of the market-place. He should drink when the sky is cloudy in spring time and when it is drizzling. He should adorn his drinking feast with gold-embroidered table cloth, pleasing glass bottles and cups, jewel-studded jugs and golden goblets, as much as he can afford.

He should always provide perfumes in his parties; and try to keep his party fragrant with them. All sorts of vases full of flowers in every season should be on view. Without them, he should consider the luxury of living as forbidden.

He should regard boiled rice and tender *kabab*s as the diet of the Mirzas. Of the varieties of *pilaf*, he should prefer the ones made with *yakhni* (meat juice) or with the meat of a fat, healthy sucking lamb. The Mirza prefers *pilaf* because it does not grease the hand. Of all the varieties of *halwa* (sweetmeats) and Indian preserves, he should like the mango preserve with fresh, sweetened herb juice. He should consider drinking water without bidmushk (a fragrant ingredient) as a thing forbidden. Of the varieties of *halwa*, he should prefer that of nuts with fragrance and tablets of amber, and pieces of lemon and sandle wood perfume. Of the fruits, after melon and grapes, he should prefer mangoes, which can be obtained only rarely, as the best fruits.

He should form the habit of eating with the tips of his fingers. He should stop eating before he is full even though he is hungry; for it is not easy to be Mirza. He should not eat with someone who is ignorant of the manners of dining and who is gluttonous.

He should set a garden wherever possible in the compound of the house, for the Mirza is equal in numbers to a rose garden. In every corner of his garden there should be colourful chirping and singing birds like nightingales and parrots. The beauty of the flowers and birds is not merely for external view since the beauty of every bird leads one to the contemplation of its Maker, and its singing leads that heart to the anguish of divine love. For visiting gardens and viewing flowers and flower gardens, he should ride a flower-coloured or black and white horse. If he wants a flower to yield fragrance, he should himself pluck it from the bough. He should not accept it from the hands of the gardener, for there is no hand cleaner than the hand of a Mirza.

If he is hunting with a matchlock, he should not fire more than two shots. When he returns from the chase, he may rest by a pool or stream of water under the shade of a tree. After drinking coffee, he should distribute portions of the kill of the chase during the previous night and during the morning among all his companions, high and low.

---

strive to locate similar ideas, or sets of ideas, in their own traditions. This process is called **acculturation**. In Islam God does not manifest himself in an image whereas Hindus worship their gods in image form. Muslims assume that God is indistinct, has no attributes and is formless. Many Hindu religious leaders who had large followings in the Sultanate and Mughal periods, also emphasized the formless nature of God, but they found justification for such a view in their older Hindu texts, where God is described in that manner. Islamic insistence on the oneness of God is echoed in the medieval Hindu saints, but the idea of the oneness of God is also found in Indian theology and Indian philosophy. Thus, Hinduism in the medieval period internalized many religious traditions of the Muslims by digging into their own religious tradition. One such tradition was the mode of devotion, the worship and love of God on the part of a devotee, known as ***bhakti***. Bhakti doctrines emphasized direct access to God. They dismissed the Brahmins' role as an intermediary between God and a person. The reference to bhakti is as old as the *Bhagavatgita*. The doctrine of *bhakti* became a central theme of Hindus in Muslim dominated India.

India's contributions to the world are numerous and diverse. In the realm of agriculture India introduced the world to cotton, which the Greeks referred to as wool that grows on trees. Sugar is also a product of India and in fact its name is derived from the ancient Indian Sanskrit language, sharkara. Perhaps India's greatest food contribution to the world are spices such as pepper, cinnamon, cloves, cardamom, and mace. Even the term for rice is derived from the Indian term arisi. Many fruits such as oranges, lemons, bananas, and mangoes are also of Indian origin.

India's contribution to the world is also quite great in the area of science and technology. In mathematics, the earliest known record of the use of a zero symbol was in India. Europe came to know and use the zero through the Arabs who had learned it from the Indians, and in fact Arabic numerals are Indian numerals. Even the modern study of languages based on scientific principles owes its roots to the work of the Indian grammarian Panini who lived in the fifth century B.C.

Modern India is the product of centuries of traditions, as well as influences from many other cultures. While cross-cultural influences have been significant in the development of the Indian culture, India's impact on other cultures of the world has been extensive. Indian foods, textiles, languages, and religions have all been significant in many societies.

Suggested Sources for Further Research

Allchin, B. and R. Allchin, *The Rise of Civilization in India and Pakistan* (Cambridge University Press, 1982).

Basham, A.L., *The Wonder That was India* (London, 1954).

Basham, A.L. (ed.), *A Cultural History of India* (Oxford University Press, 1975).

Devahuti, D., *Harsha: A Political Study* (Oxford University Press, 1970).

Embree, A.T. (ed.), *Sources of Indian Traditions*, vol. I and II (Columbia University Press, 1987).

Embree, A.T. and S.M. Ikram, *Muslim Civilization in India* (Columbia University Press, 1973).

Schwartzberg, J. (ed.), *Historical Atlas of South Asia* (University of Chicago Press, 1978).

Thapar, Romila, *History of India*, Volume I (Penguin, 1966).

Wolpert, S., *A New History of India*, 3rd Edition (Oxford University Press, 1987).

Focus Your Knowledge

1. List the three types of Indian geographic zones and the regions that correspond to each.
2. Describe the towns of Mohen-jo-daro and Harappa.

3. Account for the disappearance of the Indus Valley civilization.
4. How did the Vedas influence the class structure of ancient India? Be sure to discuss the significance of the four elements of society: Brahmin, Kshatriya, Vaishya, and Shudra.
5. Why is it misleading to refer to the period between the Mauryan Empire and the Gupta Empire as a dark period in Indian history?
6. Why is the Gupta Empire called the Golden Age of India? Give specific examples.
7. What features distinguish the Hindu faith from others? Why is it important to those of the Hindu faith to live a morally sound life?
8. Why is Harsha considered an archetypical king of ancient India?
9. What contributions to Indian culture did the Muslims make?

Apply Your Knowledge
▼▼▼

1. Prepare an organizer that compares the ancient civilizations of India, Mesopotamia, and Egypt under the following headings: town planning, architecture, writing, the arts, and government. Where possible, account for the similarities and differences.
2. To what degree can it be argued that Buddhism was a product of its age? Give specific examples.
3. How did Buddhism challenge the rigid class structure of Indian society? Which elements of Buddhism would make it appealing to a number of other societies?
4. What does Megasthenes' description of Chandragupta Maurya and the Emperor's palace suggest about Indian civilization under the Mauryans?
5. What contributions to the governing of India did the Arthashastra make? Were the suggestions made to the kings and princes valid?
6. To what degree was the reign of Ashoka an example of Buddhism put into practice?
7. What examples of cross-cultural influences are evident in the development of Indian civilization?

Extension Activities

1. Using the Indus seals as a guide, prepare your own seal that uses writing and/or pictures to depict an aspect of modern daily life or religious symbolism.

2. Based on further research create a model of either Mohan-jo-daro or Harappa.

3. Carry out further research and create a map that illustrates the spread of Buddhism.

4. Using the feature study on Indian food, as well as further research, prepare and host an Indian meal. Try to incorporate appropriate rituals in the meal.

5. The period from 184 B.C. to A.D. 320 was a period of vibrant trade. Prepare a map that traces both sea routes and overland-trade routes and indicate which region the various goods came from.

CHAPTER 5

Chinese Civilization

Chapter Highlights

- the teachings of Confucius

- the Chinese calendar

- the reign of Shi Huangdi, China's first Empire

- foot binding in China

- the creation of the largest land empire the world has ever seen

- what made the China trade so desirable to Europeans

China is not the most ancient of civilizations. It does, however, possess the distinction of being the longest continuous civilization in human history. The Chinese Empire, whose basic configurations appeared about 1500 B.C., endured until 1911 when the last dynasty fell. The civilizations of Korea, Japan, and much of Indo-China drew a great deal of their cultural inspiration from the Chinese example. China also gave to the rest of the world many of the formative inventions of human history: the compass, the cross-bow, gunpowder, paper and printing, civil service examinations, paper money, silk, porcelain, and many other things that are part of daily life today. The Chinese did not invent everything, as some would have us believe, but the next time you have a game of cards or a dessert of peaches and ice cream, you might think of their origins in China! For much of recorded history, China was the wealthiest and most advanced of all civilizations.

Key Concepts

oracle bones
Confucius
filial piety
Daoism
Legalism
Shi Huangdi
Great Wall of China
Han dynasty
Mandate of Heaven
Buddhism
Song dynasty
Neo-Confucianism
foot binding
Chingghis Khan

▼▼▼

Prehistory

We do not know precisely when Homo sapiens first appeared in China. Fossils discovered in 1965 in southwestern China indicate that a **humanoid** may have lived in the region as early as a million years ago, but most scholars still use as their starting point the 1926 discovery of the so-called Peking Man, a **proto-human** who lived about 400 000 years ago and worked with chiselled tools and used fire.

From about 7000 B.C. Neolithic (New Stone Age) cultures developed in North China along the Yellow River. Cultural interchange among these settlements began the development of a distinctive civilization. From about 1600–1500 B.C., at a time when the civilizations of Mesopotamia, Egypt, and India were already well-established, Chinese civilization began to leave its earliest records.

Ancient China was not the China we think of today as the third largest country in the world, and the country with the world's largest population. In the earliest times, the geographic area of Chinese culture consisted only of a number of intensive farming communities scattered on the North China Plain, and not until the first century B.C. did it approach anything resembling its present geographical configurations. However, as elsewhere, the physical environment provided the challenges and

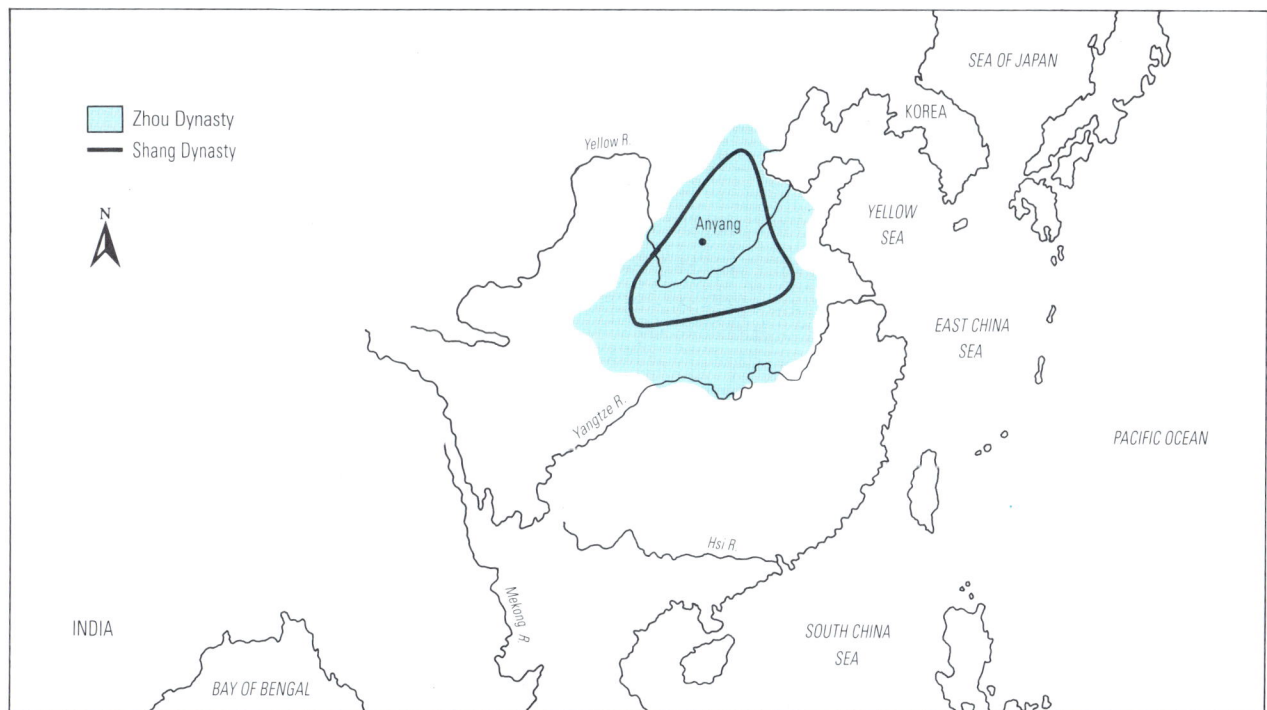

China: The Shang and Zhou Dynasties

opportunities for civilizational development, and to understand the directions of China's historical evolution, we must briefly examine the geographical context.

Geography

China today has a total land area of roughly 9 500 000 km², and its north-south extension (about 5500 km²) includes agricultural zones from temperate to subtropical. Thus, because of the wide range of crops they can produce, the Chinese have always considered themselves to be self-sufficient in food and other natural resources. Historically, they saw little need to trade with others, and tended to import only luxury goods.

In earliest times, Chinese civilization was centred on the Yellow River; a river often called China's Sorrow because its floods have claimed millions of lives over the ages. The Chinese also say that their civilization is the gift of the Yellow River, since it watered the North China Plain, a region of scarce rainfall, and made possible the cultivation of wheat, millet, and legumes. Along with pigs, chickens, and dogs these formed the diet of the early Chinese.

China's second major river, the Yangtze, is 5148 km long, (about 800 km longer than the Yellow), and though it was not fully developed as an agricultural region until long after the settlement of the North China Plain, it proved ideal for the intensive cultivation of rice that became the staple food of the East Asian diet.

The importance of rivers in the development of Chinese civilization has led a scholar by the name of

Chinese Civilization CHAPTER 5

BELIEFS

WHAT ANIMAL ARE YOU?

The Chinese Zodiac consists of twelve animals, mythical and real. These animals give colour to the New Year festivities and a title to each year. The animal has basic characteristics associated with it, although the Chinese view this information as related to their personalities or year of birth to be of little value.

The legend explaining why these creatures were chosen related to the Jade Emperor who wanted to hold a banquet for all creatures on earth. Invitations to all were sent out, but only these twelve turned up. They were honoured by being given a year. This is all part of the cyclical nature of Chinese time and the order of this cycle begins with the Rat and ends with the Pig. What animal are you? Do characteristics associated with this animal fit your personality?

Rat	Very smart and quick-witted.	Horse	Hardworking.
Ox	Grumbles a lot but is nevertheless big-hearted and long-suffering.	Ram	Quiet, restful, patient and gentle.
		Monkey	Full of energy and plans.
Tiger	Keeps promises and becomes very angry if others break theirs.	Cock	Keeps time well and is always punctual.
Rabbit	Clever and talented.	Dog	Keeps things to him or herself. Does not want to lead; prefers to follow.
Dragon	Full of energy and very direct.		
Snake	Never lets slip an opportunity.	Pig	Always comfortable and very home loving.

Karl Wittfogel to pose an interesting theory. He suggests that "oriental" civilizations—including Mesopotamia, Egypt, China, Japan, pre-Columbian America, and others—needed large-scale co-operation to build the dikes that protected them from floods and to irrigate, thus harnessing the productive capacity of water. This brought about the need for strong leadership and created a despotism in so-called hydraulic societies. Freedom, individualism, and democracy he believed, developed in Europe where water control was not so important a concern. His thesis has been criticized as racist in nature, and as too dependent on a single cause, but it raises some interesting questions.

YEAR	ANIMAL		
1972	Year of the Rat	1986	Year of the Tiger
1973	Year of the Ox	1987	Year of the Rabbit
1974	Year of the Tiger	1988	Year of the Dragon
1975	Year of the Rabbit	1989	Year of the Snake
1976	Year of the Dragon	1990	Year of the Horse
1977	Year of the Snake	1991	Year of the Ram
1978	Year of the Horse	1992	Year of the Monkey
1979	Year of the Ram	1993	Year of the Cock
1980	Year of the Monkey	1994	Year of the Dog
1981	Year of the Cock	1995	Year of the Pig
1982	Year of the Dog	1996	Year of the Rat
1983	Year of the Pig	1997	Year of the Ox
1984	Year of the Rat	1998	Year of the Tiger
1985	Year of the Ox	1999	Year of the Rabbit

Two other features of Chinese geography are worthy of mention. First, China is largely isolated from the rest of the world by high mountains, the deserts and steppelands of central Asia, and the great expanse of the Pacific Ocean. Internally, mountain ranges and river systems create provincial boundaries. These factors mean that in its formative years, Chinese civilization was largely isolated from the rest of the known world and that throughout its long history, China has been plagued by **regionalism** and provincial rivalries. Secondly, although famines have been common in Chinese history, the arable land has been able to support a large population. By the Christian Era in the West, the Chinese had already become the largest aggregate of human beings on earth, but for the next ten centuries or so, the population remained fairly static at around 50 million, not reaching 100 million until the tenth century. By 1949, the population was about 500 million, but it doubled in the next 30 years, causing the overpopulation problem of today. Now, with only 5 percent of the world's arable land, the Chinese support about 25 percent of the world's population!

Time and History in China

Chinese civilization measures time in a way very different from European civilization. Until the twentieth century, China used the lunar calendar exclusively; and even today, such Chinese festivals as the New Year are marked by this calendar. Secondly, the hours, days, months, and years were marked by a complex system in which *stems and branches* were named, and combined so that 5 times 12 equalled 60. Over time, animals came to be associated with these combinations so that one could speak of a year as the *X-stem Y-branch year*, or the *Year of the Horse*. Thus, there was no year one in Chinese history.

The Chinese never classified their history by such terms as ancient, medieval, and modern. Instead, they thought in terms of the reign of a particular emperor, or of a **dynasty**. In fact, traditional Chinese historians have always written their own history in terms of the *dynastic cycle*: a rhythm of rise, decline, and fall that seemed to them similar in all of China's 23 dynasties.

China has by far, the most complete and voluminous set of written records of any civilization, but because of the cyclical view of historians, its repeating patterns seem rather monotonous to the western reader. For instance, the pattern of the Tang dynasty was written to resemble that of the earlier Han dynasty. Chinese traditional historians have never been concerned with change, but rather with the eternal lessons of history. For them, history is a record of the consequences of good and bad actions, and serves ideally as a mirror in which rulers and their government officials might find reflected the most proper, advantageous, and humane ways to rule. The notion of historical progress is a western idea.

led modern historians to attempt to simplify the periodization of Chinese history by defining a number of stages of the development of the civilization and although none of these approaches is universally accepted, the following periods are widely used, and each had its distinctive characteristics.

The Formative Period—1600–1027 B.C.
The Classical Age—1027–221 B.C.
The First Empire—221 B.C.–A.D. 589
The Second Empire—A.D. 589–960
The Third Empire—A.D. 960–1368
The Last Empire—A.D. 1368–1911

The Dynasties of China

Of the 23 dynasties for which the Chinese have compiled official histories, some lasted less than 30 years and others endured for several centuries. Only seven or eight would be considered major. This has

The Formative Period

For the Chinese, the most important element of a civilization is writing; and indeed, the Chinese term for civilization (*wen-hua*) means literally "to trans-

MAJOR EVENTS IN CHINESE HISTORY

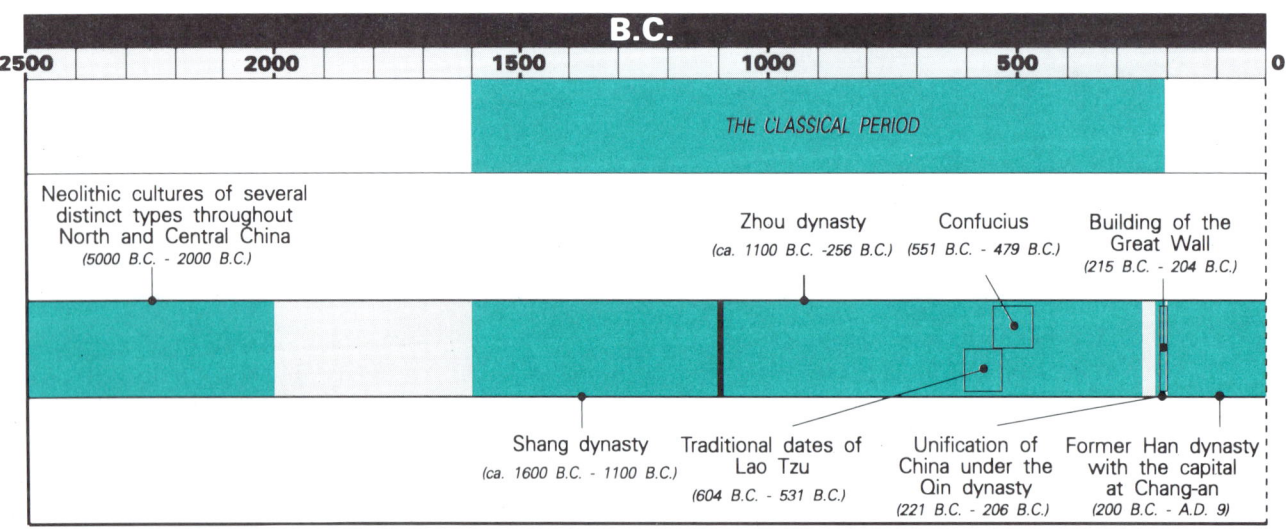

134 UNIT 1 *Civilizations of the Near and Far East*

form by writing." China's first historical dynasty, the Shang (1600–1027 B.C.), saw not only the creation of the written Chinese language, still used in a modified form today, but also, the creation of such other aspects of civilization as the development of cities, occupational specialization, complex societal organization, and distinctive artistic endeavours such as the crafting of jade and bronze.

The Shang people occupied an area about the size of modern France on the North China Plain and have left a rich archaeological record. This has enabled scholars to reconstruct a good deal of the history of the period. Most important of these archaeological remains are superb bronze vessels inscribed with useful historical information, and more than 100 000 **oracle bones**.

These bones, usually the scapular bones of cattle or sheep, were used for the purpose of divination. Scribes would use a sharp object to scratch into the bone a question—the probable outcome of a military campaign, the next day's weather, or the gender of the child of a pregnant queen—small holes were then drilled into the bone. When it was held over a fire, the bone cracked, and from the configuration of the cracks, the scribes or priests interpreted and recorded the answer. Sometimes we are even given the outcome. A sample inscription might say, "On Monday will the wife of the king have a boy?" "Yes."

On the same bone the outcome is recorded; "Monday." "Too bad." From this we can infer that the birth was that of a girl.

Shang society was well delineated. The king and his nobles lived in a series of walled capitals. Their houses were above ground, while those of the commoners seem to have been below ground. The king, while never a god like the Egyptian Pharaoh, had priestly functions, and worshipped Shanqdi (pronounced shong-dee), probably the ancestor of his family and the source of his power. This was the origin of the practice of **ancestor veneration** which is important even today in the lives of the Chinese people. Below the nobility were the social groupings of scribe-priest, farmer, artisan, merchant, and slave.

The order of these groupings is important. From the beginning of Chinese history, the ability to read and write has conferred high social status, and those who managed to obtain education were highly respected. Farmers were valued as primary produc-

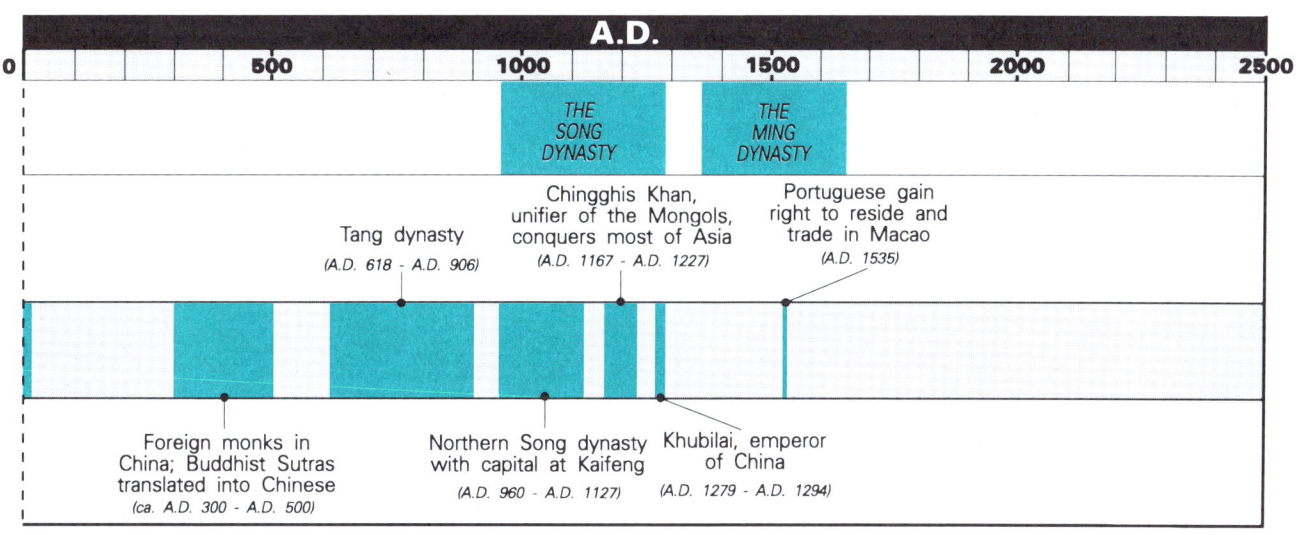

Oracle bones were used from about 1500 B.C. to foresee the future. A question was inscribed on the bone, then holes were drilled into it and it was held over a fire. When it cracked, it was from these cracks that the answer to questions could be divined. This particular oracle bone comes from the Royal Ontario Museum which houses one of the most extensive collections of these bones.

ers. The artisans, who produced so much of the art found in museums today, were considered nonessential but useful to society. Merchants were seen as parasitical and greedy and were an object of some contempt until modern times in China. It took several centuries for these class divisions to harden.

Slavery was legal in China until the twentieth century, but slaves, usually war captives and criminals, never seem to have made up any more than 1–2 percent of the population. Compared to the early Mediterranean civilizations, this was a tiny proportion.

In Shang society, women occupied a relatively high position, and at least at the beginning of the period, children probably took their surnames from their mothers. After marriage, young men often lived with their bride's family. Over time, however, there developed a distinct preference for male children because of their greater economic value in agriculture and because ancestral veneration could be carried out only by males. Without a son, parents were doomed to a gloomy existence in the afterlife.

The Shang rulers exercised only a loose political control over North China, and hence were easily overwhelmed in about 1027 B.C. by a warlike people who originated in Central Asia or northwest China and were called the Zhou (pronounced joe). Before its fall, however, the Shang distinctively marked Chinese civilization, bequeathing to later ages such features as their script, some enduring religious and social values, and the artistic principles seen in Shang bronzes, ceramics, and jades.

The Classical Age

Historians divide the Zhou period, which lasted until 256 B.C., into two segments. The first, or Western Zhou, lasted until 771 B.C. and carried on much of the culture of the Shang. There were, however, changes in burial customs, and military technology, and more importantly, in religion and politics.

In religion, divination by oracle bone became much less frequent, and Shanqdi, the supreme deity of the Shang, was replaced by Tian, or "Heaven." Tian was never seen as an anthropomorphic god and was never represented in art. Rather Tian was a divine force, a guardian of the Middle Kingdom (as the Chinese now began to refer to themselves), and of its ruling family. Chinese rulers in the Zhou began to call themselves Son of Heaven and used this term even into the twentieth century.

In politics, the Zhou established a decentralized system of rule with **lords**, **vassals**, **fiefs**, and **investiture**; a system of government similar to that which appeared in Europe almost 2000 years later. For this reason, some scholars call the Western Zhou a feudal system, but the differences between Egypt and China are as great as the similarities, and the term is best avoided. In any case, the system was not long in force, and its end is a romantic story.

Chinese historians have all been male, and through the ages, have shared the same **patriarchal** attitudes. Hence, when a state or dynasty falls, they have sought to find a woman to blame. In China, this is usually a femme fatale whose beauty leads her husband into folly and the neglect of state affairs. In this case the woman was called Bao Zi, a queen whose smile was so radiant that her husband spent all his time trying to make her laugh. When such diversions as the destruction of costly silks could no longer coax a smile from her, he found that she was amused every time he summoned his lords and vassals to come rushing to the capital to defend it against attack. He therefore called them frequently, even in the middle of the night when there was no threat. One fine day in 771 B.C. there was a real invasion and no defenders came to the rescue. To amuse his queen, the king had cried wolf once too often! The king was killed, and his son was forced to move the capital eastward to a safer location.

The Eastern Zhou

With the move of the capital from Xi'an (pronounced shee-on) to Loyang, the Zhou court lost all real power and endured for another five centuries only as the ritual and symbolic rulers of China. In fact, it is an error to speak of China in these centuries since there was no unity. Lords and their vassals immediately began to declare themselves independent, and this began an age of massive warfare, bloodshed, and violence with hundreds of small domains struggling for survival. By the third century B.C., seven huge states had gobbled up all the rest, and in 221 B.C., one of these defeated all its rivals and re-united the country.

Since interstate strife and competition were the dominant features of the Eastern Zhou, the various states had to be creative and innovative in order to survive. Progress was astonishing. At the beginning of the Eastern Zhou, China lagged behind the Mediterranean world by most of the material measures of civilization. By the end of the period, China had at least equalled them.

Progress was, of course, first seen in military technology. Better armour and weapons like the crossbow appeared. Iron technology finally surpassed that of Persia, and the cumbersome Shang war chariot was gradually replaced by swift cavalry. Generals wrote some of the world's oldest manuals on military strategy and tactics, and some states experimented with universal conscription. Many of them began to organize their people more tightly through direct agricultural taxation, law codes, and the promotion of a sense of shared loyalties and values.

At the same time, and in order to strengthen themselves, many states embarked upon programs to improve the livelihood of their people. They built walls, new dikes, irrigation works, and canals. Soybean came under cultivation and added protein to the diet, and new strains of wheat and rice were developed. Population grew along with interstate trade, and some states even experimented with wage and price controls.

In short, it was a fluid and lively time, and in the midst of all the violence and upheaval, few areas of daily life were unaffected. Music and poetry found new forms of expression, trousers began to replace the robe as everyday dress, and people cast off the "barbaric" use of knife and fork to eat with chopsticks. And above all, there took place the greatest outpouring of original thought in all of Chinese history.

Confucius

China's classical age, the age of the "hundred flowers" or the "hundred schools of thought," occurred in the sixth and fifth centuries B.C. This was perhaps the most intellectually fertile period in the history of the world. Roughly contemporary to the great names in China are many of the seminal thinkers in the other centres of civilization: Socrates, Plato, and Pythagoras in Greece, the Buddha in India, Zoroaster in Persia, and some of the greatest of the Hebrew prophets in Palestine. All of these thinkers left an indelible mark on human history, even though the questions they asked and the answers they offered were very different.

In China, the overriding concern of all the thinkers was the question of how to bring order to a disordered world. Moreover, lacking a salvationist tradition, they shared a common belief that order must arise not from spiritual intervention, but through the efforts of human beings themselves. Chinese philosophy was therefore more humanistic than religious.

The first and the greatest of the Chinese thinkers was a man known as Kong Fuzi ("Master Kong"), whose name was translated into Latin by the first Jesuit missionaries as **Confucius**. Born in 551 B.C., he lived an unspectacular life. He held minor government offices in his native state, and then travelled around visiting many of the lords of other states trying to convince them to adopt his principles. Failing in this task, he returned to his homeland where he taught until his death in 479 B.C. His words were recorded after his death by 72 close disciples, and these sayings exist today in a short collection of 497 verses called *The Analects*. This book became the "Bible" of Chinese civilization.

Confucius believed that the solution to the evils of his time was for all human beings to practise the virtue of *ren* (pronounced run), which we translate as "humanity," "benevolence" or a kind of "perfect virtue" that was a combination of courtesy, generosity, good faith, diligence, and kindness. "Love others," said Confucius, "and do not do unto others that which you would not have them do unto you!" His negative expression of the Golden Rule predated Christ's injunction by 500 years.

The idea of *ren* was probably not new in Chinese society, and Confucius always said that he was only a transmitter of the better ways of the past. What was new in his philosophy was that he offered a specific blueprint for the achievement of humanity. He believed that human beings were all equal and alike at birth, and went on to say that it was learning and practice that set them apart. In *The Analects* he defined precisely what learning and practice were all about.

Education, both formal and informal, was necessary to bring about a benevolent world. Education, he decreed, must be free of all class distinctions, open to all. Teachers must respect their students, but at the same time, students were responsible for their own education. "If I lift one corner of a square," said Confucius, "and if a student cannot come back to me with the other three corners, I will not bother to repeat the point." Confucius believed in a curriculum that included history, poetry, etiquette, music, and physical education. He said that we should never stop learning and he admitted that his own education was not complete until he reached the age of 70!

What did he mean by practice? It consisted of three major elements. The first was ***filial piety***. This meant that young people must respect and obey all those older than themselves. The reason Confucius placed so much emphasis on this virtue was that he believed that the family was a microcosm of society. If a person learned to live in harmony, co-operation, and obedience in the family, that person could help turn the whole world into a family. He also believed that all of us become more experienced and wiser as we get older. He saw that the wars that devastated his world were fought by passionate and ambitious young men. They needed the wisdom and contemplation of the elderly to convince them that peace and harmony were preferable to strife.

The second element of practice was a doctrine called the rectification of names. Confucius put it like this: "A father is a father, and a son is a son. A ruler is a ruler and a subject is a subject." He meant by this, that in any society there were universal definitions of what constituted good fathers and good sons, good rulers, and good subjects. He believed that as people progressed through each stage of life, they should simply strive to be good at what they were, and not try to usurp the position above them. This would lead to the end of overambition and envy, of covetousness and competition. He probably realized that it could also lead to a fairly static society, but he saw that as a good thing.

Finally, Confucius insisted on the practice of courtesy, of observing the rules of etiquette and propriety in all our dealings with other people. If we always behaved with courtesy, we would expand our sense of goodness each time we performed even a small polite act. This should do away with the need for laws and punishments in society.

If everyone followed these principles of learning and practice, the result would be a society governed by princely persons who had attained the state of true humanity. The ruler would be the most princely of them all. As Confucius said: "The virtue of the princely person may be compared to the wind, and that of the commoners below, to that of the weeds. Under the force of the wind, the weeds cannot but bend."

Eighty generations of Chinese have followed Confucius. All of them have honoured him as their greatest teacher. He was the thinker who defined the most distinctive hallmarks of Chinese civilization: filial piety, family-centred values, a thirst for education, a strong work ethic, and a belief in courtesy, not confrontation, to achieve a final harmony in the family of humanity.

Beliefs in the Zhou Dynasty

To a large extent, the other systems of thought of this period arose as a reaction to Confucius. Some disagreed with his philosophy, others followed him but tried to answer questions he had not raised.

His earliest opponent was a man called Mo Zi (pronounced mo-tzy) who lived from about 470–391 B.C. He criticized Confucian philosophy as too idealistic and too secular. Although Confucius asked human beings to change their behaviour, Mo Zi said, he offered no incentive to do so. His own belief was that humans were motivated by selfishness, and that they would change only if they could see benefit for themselves in it.

His solution for the ills of his time was the practice of universal love, rather than the hierarchical, family-centred love advocated by Confucius. "Be willing," he said, "to destroy yourself from head to foot for the sake of others." This will benefit everyone. To enforce this difficult behaviour, he promised that heaven would punish the wicked and reward the good not in the next world, but in this one. Ghosts and spirits were the agents of heaven and would harm the unloving. In the superstitious climate of the time, this threat had great force, and this philosophy, called Moism, was a popular one.

Mo Zi also advocated frugality, and a life of the barest essentials: no music, no elaborate weddings and funerals, and no accumulation of wealth. He condemned war as the most futile of all endeavours. No victory could ever be worth the inevitable loss of human life and human resources, and no victory was permanent. In fact, Mo Zi's pacifism, his simple, self-sacrificing lifestyle, and his emphasis on heaven led early Christian missionaries in China to compare him to Jesus Christ.

In spite of his initial popularity, however, Mo Zi's influence lasted only a few centuries, unlike that of Confucius's second rival, the philosopher known simply as "The Old Master," Lao Zi, the founder of **Daoist** philosophy (also written as Taoism).

Little is known of him, and some scholars even doubt his existence. His book, consisting of only 5000 Chinese characters and called *The Way and the Power* (*Daodejing*), has been very influential in Chinese history, and has been translated into English more than 40 times.

Lao Zi opposed Confucius's doctrines of social responsibility. He believed in individual freedom and spontaneity, a flight from the cares of the world into a oneness with *nature* or the *Way*. For him, disorder and violence arose when human beings tampered with nature or tried to overcome it. He was therefore opposed to education, taxation, law, war, and any kind of government interference in the lives of the people. The best government, according to him, was one that existed but did not act. The only function of the ruler was to "empty the minds and fill the bellies" of his people.

Finally, Lao Zi realized that to get people to change their behaviour, he would have to change or even reverse their usual perceptions. He therefore filled his book with startling insights that might make people think. He asked, "What is the most useful part of a cup? Not the handles or the bowl, but the empty space which can be filled." "Water is soft and rocks are hard," he observed. "Yet the water wears away the rock. Men are strong; yet not so strong as the newborn babe whom no-one would ever dare to harm. Men are powerful, yet women possess the greatest of powers—that of giving birth to new life." Lao Zi's most important advice to the world was his doctrine of *wu-wei* "do nothing and nothing will not be done."

In time, Confucianism and Daoism ceased to be rivals, and it is often said that the Chinese were "Confucian at the office and Daoist at home."

This is only a sampling of the variety of Chinese thought and the intellectual debate that permeated the age. Later Confucians like Mencius and Xun Zi (pronounced shun-tzy) argued about whether human beings were born good or evil, and whether they should be regulated by virtuous rule or harsh laws. Other philosophers studied the workings of the universe, trying to manipulate the complementary forces of *yin* and *yang* to bring about order. Still others became disillusioned with the whole search for order and devoted themselves to proving such propositions as "a fire is not hot" and "a white horse is not a horse."

At last there appeared a group of philosophers who called a halt to philosophical speculation. Enough was enough they said. It was action, not "vain talk" which solved problems. They were mostly hard-headed realists and practising politicians and were known as the Legalists. They put forth a set of principles that would bring about the unification of China.

The First Empire

Legalism was a philosophy that was not concerned with ethics, morality, or human values, but only with the power of the state and the elevation of its ruler. It had three guiding principles: anything done to strengthen the state was by definition good; the ruler must use devious methods to keep officials and other potential rivals from gaining any power; and the common people must be subjected to detailed, regular laws which embodied harsh punishments and lavish rewards. Furthermore, Legalism insisted that offensive war was a good thing, not only because it enriched the state with new territory, but also because it united the people against an external enemy and thus made them ready to obey the ruler without question. Finally, Legalism said that pro-

BELIEFS

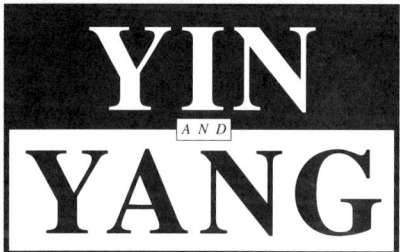
YIN AND YANG

Most westerners are familiar with the diagram that depicts the central feature of Chinese cosmology and the basis of East Asian philosophical and proto-scientific thought. We simply call it *yin-yang*, but to the Chinese, it is the *Taiji*, or Great Pivot, which explains the action of the universe. It was already an old idea in China by the time of Confucius.

The basic notion of the *Taiji* is that the universe functions through the constant interaction of two complementary (not opposite) forces, called yin and yang. Yang is bright and hard, yin is dark and soft; yang is dry, yin is moist; yang is heaven, yin is earth; yang is the father, yin is the son; yang is the male, yin is the female. Both of these elements are necessary to complete the circle, and neither one is necessarily superior to the other. At the same time, the diagram is a dynamic one; always in the process of change. Yin is always in the process of becoming yang. Dark turns to light and back to dark while soft turns to hard and back to soft. The diagram also contains a spot of white in the black section, and a spot of black in the white section. In every male, there is a little female and in every female, a little of the male. The eyes of an infant may be old, and the mind of the old person may be child-like.

This pattern of thought is one of the more profound expressions of the human mind. We are used to a dialectical pattern of thought; black is not white, yes is not no. The basic idea of yin-yang is that black-and-white situations are never quite that clear. In every yes there is a little bit of no.

The tomb of Shihuang was built either in 246 or 212 B.C. for the first emperor of China, Quin Shihuang. It took 700 000 men to build this tomb which replicated an underground city. The city and the tomb were protected by an army of more than 7000 horses and soldiers.

ductive agriculture was the only valid occupation. All commerce and intellectual enterprise must be discouraged. Nothing could be permitted to interfere with the creation of a strong, rich state.

The most famous of the Legalist philosophers was a prince called Han Fei Zi (pronounced hon fay tzy). Before his death in 233 B.C., he served as tutor to the young prince of one of the seven warring states and persuaded him that if he adopted his doctrines, he could make himself the First Emperor of China. The young prince learned his lessons well, and in 230 B.C. he began a series of massive and bloody military campaigns that destroyed the remaining six states. Although there were hundreds of thousands of casualties, his prime minister, Li Si (pronounced lee ssu), later wrote that it had been "as easy as sweeping dust from the kitchen stove."

China's First Emperor

In 221 B.C. the young prince created a new title for himself and proclaimed China's first real dynasty. He called himself **Shi Huangdi** (pronounced shih hwong dee), which means, "the first emperor." He called his dynasty the Qin (pronounced chin) which became the origin of our name for China. He then directed his vast energies to the transformation of his country. In ten short years he created a legacy that would endure until the twentieth century.

To begin with, and working closely with his prime minister Li Si, he seized all the land once held by the feudal nobility, and divided China into 42 prefectures under magistrates whom he appointed himself. This centralized the country and ended **feudalism** forever. He constructed a magnificent capital near present-day Xi'an (pronounced shee-on) and using the conscript labour of 700 000 persons, constructed a palace complex which covered about 70 km^2 and included 270 pavilions, meeting halls, and sleeping palaces where his many wives and concubines resided. Most of these structures were connected by covered walkways and secret passages so that he could conceal his movements from assassins.

Next, he acted swiftly to unify and standardize all the coinage, the weights and measures, and even the size of chariots in his new empire. He outlawed all local customs, local festivals, and folksongs as well as local religious practices. He ordered Li Si to produce China's first standard dictionary in 214 B.C., and he built a network of royal roads to distant regions of the country. Some of them even had express lanes! He built canals which are still in use today.

Acting on the principle that warfare enriched the state, he sent out great armies. First they fought against aboriginal peoples south of the Yangtze River, and began to incorporate them into China. Then he sent his troops into Central Asia where they battled a nomadic tribe called the Huns who had frequently raided and pillaged in North China. His expeditions were generally successful but they were also costly, and he determined to find a permanent solution to the problem of the northern border. Using hundreds of thousands of soldiers, merchants, conscripts, and both male and female prisoners, he began the most ambitious building project of the ancient world—the **Great Wall of China**.

The Great Wall was not a new idea, since several northern states had already built shorter ones. The Emperor joined and vastly extended these walls, so that the finished project reached perhaps 2000 km and crossed some of the most inhospitable terrain on earth; mountains, deserts, swamplands, and forests. The workers were often harassed by marauding barbarians, and the number who were killed by them or died of exhaustion, exposure, or hunger is unknown. Many workers were buried inside the wall, and thus, the Chinese sometimes refer to it as "the world's longest graveyard." Nonetheless, it was a fairly effective defence mechanism, and defined China's northern territorial boundaries for centuries to come.

The magnitude of the First Emperor's achievements should have assured him a glorious place in history. If he had been a European monarch, his name would probably have been followed by "the Great." Instead, Chinese historians have given him a black reputation, criticizing him for his ruthlessness, his massive conscription of labour, his wars, his harsh laws, and above all, for what they consider the worst of his acts—the burning of the books.

In 213 B.C., Li Si complained that people were using the words of the wise and ancient philosophers to criticize the Emperor. The Emperor wasted no time in putting an end to the situation. Decreeing that only practical works on such subjects as agriculture, medicine, pharmacy, and divination were worth preserving, the Emperor demanded that all other books be surrendered to his officials to be burned in public. People were given one month to comply, and when some scholars were slow to do so, he made an example of them: 460 protestors were buried alive in the palace courtyards. There was no more resistance.

This barbaric act ended the golden age of Chinese thought. Never again would there be such diversity in the Chinese intellectual world; and Chinese scholars were forced to spend the next 400 years, until A.D. 175, reconstructing their classical literature and philosophy. At that time, the lost works were engraved on stone tablets so that they would never again disappear.

The First Emperor died unexpectedly two years later, leaving a country seething with discontent. His heir, the youngest of his more than 20 sons, was inexperienced, incompetent, and cruel. Rebellions broke out everywhere. In 206 B.C., one of the rebels, a peasant, founded a new dynasty called the Han which would last for the next 400 years.

The Han Dynasty

China's First Empire might be divided into three periods. The Qin dynasty founded it, the Han consolidated it, and the so-called Age of Disunion from A.D. 220–589 destroyed it.

The **Han dynasty** was an important period in Chinese history. It was an almost exact parallel to the

The idea of linking a number of existing walls into one Great Wall of China was conceived in 221 B.C. to protect the Northern Empire from invasions by nomadic tribes. With an army of 300 000 men and thousands of convicts, the architect General Meng Tian took ten years to finish the most extensive defensive construction to date.

Roman Empire in the West, and the level of the two civilizations was about the same. The Romans knew of China and called it The Land of Silk. The Chinese called Rome Great Qin, in recognition of the fact that it too, was a great state, like their own first dynasty. The world's first intercontinental trade route, called the Silk Road, linked the two empires.

Han dynasty China was a vibrant land. The population was somewhere between 50–60 million, and the peasantry, who composed about 90 percent of the population, was generally prosperous. Internal trade was lively and the state was expansive. Under the remarkable Emperor Wudi (pronounced woo-dee), who reigned from 140–87 B.C., China conquered Vietnam, Korea, and much of Central Asia, and made its earliest contacts with Japan. These states and many others along the Silk Road began to send regular tribute to China to acknowledge its leadership. Chinese princesses were often married to foreign rulers. Their husbands thus became sons-in-law of the Chinese emperor and part of the Chinese world family. Chinese civilization gradually became dominant in East Asia.

Under Wudi, Confucianism was declared the state religion and China's first university, with a curriculum based on Confucian philosophy, was founded in 124 B.C. Officials were selected for public office by the world's first system of competitive examinations; a system brought to the West in the nineteenth century. A well-organized **bureaucracy** appeared with nine ministries who managed everything from tax collection to defense.

Government, Bureaucracy, and Law.

The supreme figure in the Chinese government was the emperor. He was seen as the father and mother of his people, as the Son of Heaven, and as the single person who kept the universe in balance. He made the laws (though he was above them himself), educated his people, and was responsible for their welfare. He alone could perform certain sacrifices like the great annual ritual which asked Heaven to bless the earth, and each year he plowed the first furrow to produce a bountiful harvest.

Unlike many western rulers, he was not a god nor did he rule by divine right. The source of his power was the political doctrine called the **Mandate of Heaven**. This doctrine said that heaven chose the

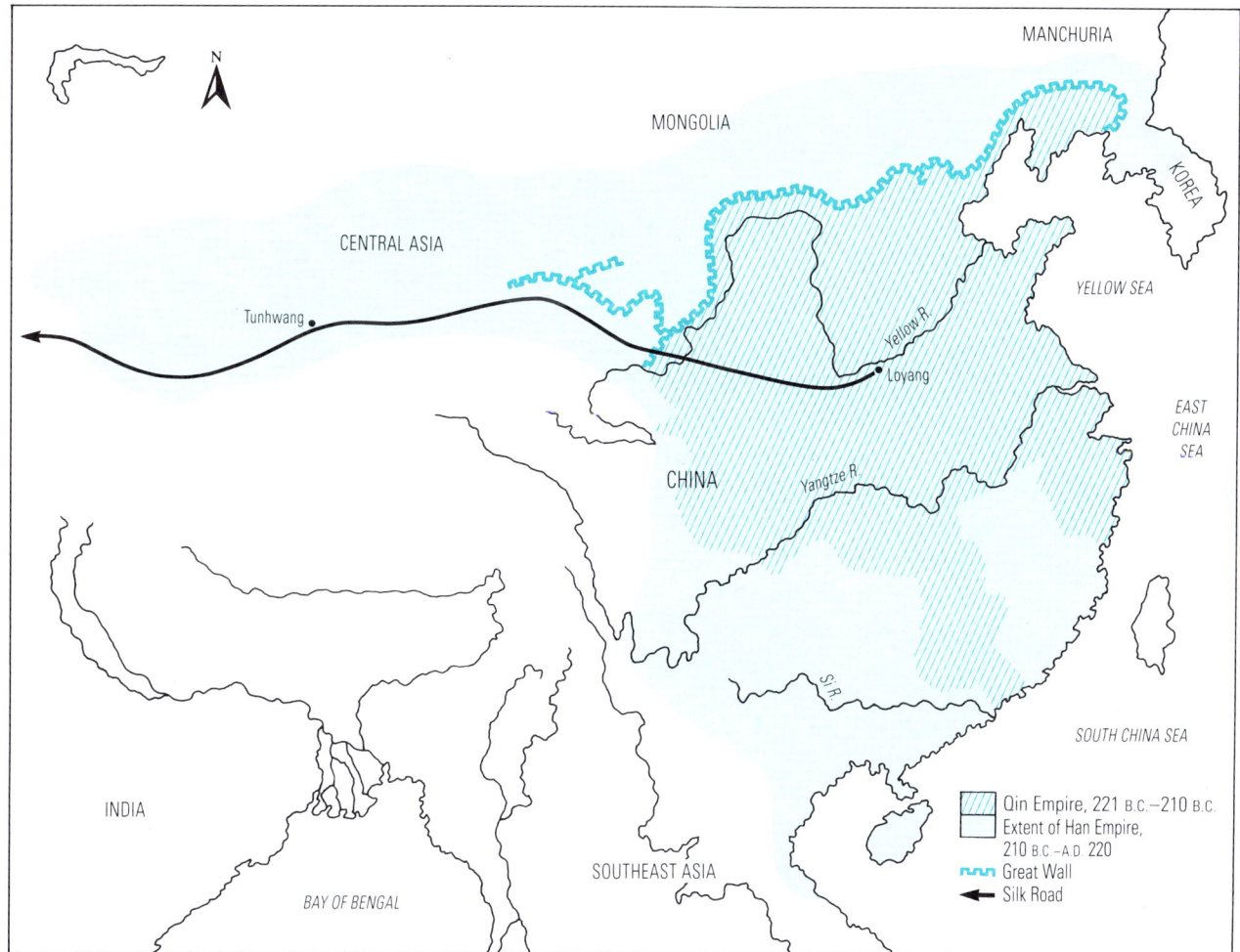

China: The Qin and Han Empires

ruler and heaven could get rid of a bad ruler. If a ruler failed to do his job, heaven would first warn him with omens and portents: floods, earthquakes, and strange phenomena like the birth of dragons or unicorns. If he failed to heed the warnings and change his behaviour, the people would rise up and depose him. The people of China thus had a right of rebellion that was not a part of other societies.

The emperor presided over both an *inner* and *outer* court. Both played a part in his rule. The inner court consisted of four elements. The first was his wife, the empress. She was responsible for the running of the palace and had few public functions. In fact, Chinese empresses were not to be seen in public though they often had great influence over their husbands and especially over their sons. A Chinese boy, even if he became emperor, always had to obey his mother! Second was the harem, a body of 121 women who served the emperor's personal needs. They entertained him, cooked his food, washed his clothes, and sometimes provided him with an heir. Third were the consort clans, the families of the palace women. The males of these families were often given high positions, and could help the emperor in his government. Finally, there were the **eunuchs**. These were males, castrated to prevent them from having relations with the women of the harem. Their job was to guard and care for the needs of the women, perform the heavy work of the palace, and sometimes even to advise the emperor. Eunuchs were originally criminals or captives of war, but later, they were often volunteers. In the seventeenth century, there were more than 100 000 eunuchs in Beijing.

The outer court consisted of the officials or bureaucrats, divided into nine ranks. They staffed all the civil and military positions in the government. They were chosen initially from noble or official families, but from the Han dynasty onwards, more and more were recruited through the examination system.

In its final form, the examination system consisted of three levels of examination, held each year in the prefecture, in the capital, and at the palace. Candidates were locked into cells for up to a week, and there they answered written questions on the Confucian classics and on matters of current affairs. To succeed, it was necessary to memorize approximately 400 000 words which made up the classics, and boys often began their preparation at the age of two or three. The system was closed to women and to persons of low professions, such as merchants. It remained in force until 1905, when protests that it had never tested scientific knowledge or other practical subjects brought about its abolition.

The organization of the Chinese government was very sophisticated. Below the emperor were a group of chief ministers, three Departments, six Boards, and nine Courts. The ministers discussed policy with the emperor and the Departments implemented it after reviewing its practicality. The Departments also kept records and corresponded with the local magistrates. The Boards were in charge of such matters as taxation, defence, public works, and the civil service. The Courts handled less important matters like foreign visitors and the regulation of clergy.

One of the Boards was in charge of justice, and law in traditional China differed greatly from that in the West. To begin with, Chinese law codes were very detailed and specific, often following the statement of a law with a series of "What if?" questions. The law treated people differently even if they had committed the same offence. For instance, officials and women were treated more leniently than ordinary men. Penalties for crime were much less severe than those in the West, using flogging, exile, and work camps to punish most offenses. The death penalty was applied only for murder and high treason.

Chinese law also reversed the western idea that a person was innocent until proven guilty. To them, the fact that a person was accused of anything was an upset in the cosmic balance, and that person was thrown into prison until innocence could be proven.

Chinese prisons were terrible places. They were small and filthy and only water was provided. Unless a prisoner's family brought food, the prisoner starved! Torture was used routinely to extract confessions.

On the other hand, the person who refused to confess had the right to a lawyer and to trial either by judge or jury. Moreover, throughout Chinese history, emperors issued frequent amnesties on auspicious occasions—the birth of their sons, or the occurrence of a bumper harvest—and the prisons were emptied of those who had committed minor offenses, and the punishments for serious crimes were lightened.

The Decline of the Han.

Wudi's capital of Chang'an (pronounced chong-on) rivalled Rome in size and population, but not in magnificence. The

Chinese built in wood rather than stone, and had no concept of public space like the colosseum or baths of Rome. The city, however, was a perfect grid, with the palace, or Forbidden City, at the north end, and the streets and avenues running in a north-south and east-west pattern. Great markets were built in the east and in the west. The government restricted the merchants, controlled the prices, and supervised the sale of everyday goods as well as exotic luxuries like glass, amber, spices, and slaves from foreign lands.

The energetic policies of Wudi, however, had their price. Before the end of his long reign, his military expeditions and the salaries of his expanded bureaucracy placed the government in a deficit position. Taxes were raised and the peasants suffered. One official complained that the farmers did not have enough land to use a single hoe, and that they were forced to live on the "food of dogs and pigs." The gap between rich and poor grew wider and wider, and many independent peasants were forced to sell their land and become tenants or serfs. Great landlord families arose and their power was so immense that they could corrupt the tax collectors and deny revenue to the impoverished government.

At the same time, a succession of weak emperors came to the throne, and although a few of them attempted reform, the decline could not be arrested. From about A.D. 75, most of the emperors succeeded to the throne as teenagers. They were dominated by their mothers and their mothers' families. Their policies were weakened by court intrigue and by power struggles between the educated officials and the palace eunuchs and harem. In A.D. 184, great rebellions broke out in the northeast and the southwest. Squeezed between these two forces, and betrayed by disloyal generals, the Han dynasty came crashing down. The last emperor abdicated in A.D. 220.

The Period of Disunion. The final stage of the First Empire was a bleak one. China was divided into three kingdoms, then briefly reunited, before hordes of nomads swept in from the north and the west and by A.D. 317 they had taken control of the whole country north of the Yangtze River.

These tribes, ancestors of the Mongols, the Manchus, and the Tibetans, held northern China in their grip for almost 300 years. In the south, at present-day Nanjing, a succession of weak, short-lived Chinese dynasties struggled to keep alive the culture of the Han. Some scholars regard these centuries as the Dark Ages of China.

The authority of the central government declined as great aristocratic clans set up independent domains. Peasants, who once worked their own land, fell into serfdom. The examination system disappeared, roads and canals fell into disrepair, barter replaced coinage. The Confucian arts, poetry, music, historical writing, and ethical studies declined. Talented men refused government service to become hermits or disillusioned beatniks. One philosopher described the only reaction possible to the times: "...to wander the country in the Beauties of Nature. A shovel and a jug of wine are all we need. Let us remain drunk; the shovel to bury us when we die." Warfare was frequent. North battled South, and again, the common people suffered.

But there were bright spots in this gloomy picture. Competition spurred technological advances in agriculture with new plowing, irrigation techniques, terracing, and double crops of rice. There were new medical techniques such as inoculation and cataract surgery, and a flourishing of alchemy, chemistry, and the martial arts. Figure painting and calligraphy surpassed the Han examples, and poetic expression became less Confucian and more free. The northern dynasties experimented with new administrative techniques like peasant militia and equal land grants to the farming population.

As time went on, they also tended to adopt the Chinese language, Chinese dress and food, and often intermarried with the native population. This has led to the common saying in Chinese history that

The appeal of Buddhism to the people of China is evident in the magnificent art created after the first century A.D. This art included massive images of Buddha in stone, such as the one depicted here.

"the Chinese have always absorbed their conquerors." Above all, this was a great Age of Faith.

Buddhism had been introduced into China from India in the first century A.D., and after some initial setbacks because of Confucian opposition and the difficulties of translating Buddhist concepts from an alphabetic to a non-alphabetic language, the foreign religion spread rapidly. Buddhism taught that human life was painful but that any person who became free of all human desire could escape the painful cycle of constant birth and re-birth, and reach a blissful state called *Nirvana*. Nirvana was like "the blending of a single drop of water in the limitless ocean."

In China at this time, because people believed that human life was indeed painful, the appeal of Buddhism was great. Buddhist temples, monasteries, and nunneries soon dotted the Chinese landscape. People flocked to hear sermons and many sought to be ordained. Pious Chinese made long pilgrimages to India to study, and returned to translate scriptures and to write accounts of their travels. Chinese Buddhists began to become more independent, and even changed some of the original Indian teachings to suit the Chinese environment. Their monasteries multiplied and because so many merchants stopped there overnight and asked the monks to guard their valuables these monasteries became the first banks and hotels in the country. Magnificent art was created—depictions of heaven and hell, and great images of the Buddha in bronze, gold, and stone. Some were so large that 12 people could stand on the Buddha's outstretched finger. From China, Buddhism spread to Korea and Japan, and by the sixth century, more than half the world's population was Buddhist! Buddhism also acted as a cohesive factor, keeping the Chinese people together in a time of disunion. Along with Confucian family and state ethics, a common language, and the memory of Han dynasty glory, it helped to ensure that the Chinese Empire, unlike that of Rome, would endure and rise to even greater heights.

The Second Empire

In A.D. 589, a remarkable general called Sui Wendi (pronounced sway won-dee) conquered the last of the southern dynasties, and re-united the country, founding the Sui dynasty. Like the First Emperor of

China, he was a vigorous ruler, restoring roads, canals, walls, and dikes, as well as the morale of the civil service. He rebuilt the schools and the examination system for choosing officials. He lowered taxes, and kept his government frugal and honest.

Like the First Emperor, he was also unfortunate in his successor. His son squandered not only the good-will created by his father, but also the entire state treasury. He demanded such luxuries as a harem of more than 3000 women, lavish canals where he sailed with his court on 24.4 m pleasure boats. Worst of all, he undertook three unsuccessful campaigns to reconquer Korea. These campaigns caused hundreds of thousands of casualties, brought China to bankruptcy, and so angered the people that rebellions broke out again. The emperor was killed by one of his own generals, and in A.D. 618, the Tang (pronounced tong) was established. It would last for almost 300 years.

China's Golden Age

The Tang is perhaps the brightest era in Chinese history. It was a confident and **cosmopolitan** period, a time when culture flourished as never before. Under the Tang, China reached its greatest territorial extent, and its capital, Chang'an, was the greatest city in the world. With a population of over a million at a time when Rome held only about 60 000, Chang'an was the cultural centre of Asia. Here there were thousands of Koreans, Indians, Syrians, and Arabians; foreign students, missionaries, entertainers, and merchants. Among the many Buddhist temples were churches of the Zoroastrians, Nestorian Christians, and Manicheans. There were floating restaurants, zoos, fairgrounds, frequent festivals, and sporting events. The women of the Tang, robed in low-cut, silken dresses, and their hair piled high and dressed with golden and bejewelled hair pins, competed in poetry contests, wine tastings, and even polo! They enjoyed a relatively high status during this period.

The second emperor, Taizong (627–649) is usually considered the best of all Chinese rulers. He is known not only for the great conquests he made in Central Asia, which extended China's power to the borders of Persia, but also for his contribution to the arts of peace. He restored the system of schools and universities, created a new law code, set up an office to compile the history of the preceding four centuries, redistributed land to the peasantry, consolidated a system of national defence, and put in place a system of taxation that was equitable to all. Above all, he listened to advice, consulting his ministers and through them, the common people, on all important issues. His wife was a source of support and wise advice. His son and successor was not a great ruler. He was, however, smart enough to place the fortunes of the dynasty in the hands of his wife, the Empress Wu; the only female in Chinese history to usurp the throne and rule in her own right as emperor. For almost 30 years, she ruled from "behind the screen," and in A.D. 690, after the death of her husband, she took the throne herself for 15 prosperous years. Capable, genuinely concerned about the common people, and at the same time astonishingly ruthless, she remains one of the most popular of China's historical rulers.

Her successor, Ming-huang (pronounced ming-hwong) was called the Brilliant Emperor because he presided over an era of glittering culture when literature, painting, architecture, textiles, and ceramics reached new heights. This emperor even composed and played music, which he taught his horses to dance to.

Poetry was the glory of his age, and China's most famous poet, Bo Juyi (pronounced bow jew-yee) wrote a poem after Ming-huang's death in which he told the story of the emperor's ill-fated love for the most famous beauty in China's long history. Her name is Yang Guifei (pronounced yong gwey-fey), and her unparalleled beauty as she danced in her "feathered-jacket and rainbow-skirt," led the Emperor to neglect the affairs of state and allow his government to fall into corruption and incompetence. This helped to bring about the rebellion of An Lu-shan (pronounced on lew-shon), which was the bloodiest rebellion in Chinese history.

It began in A.D. 752, and over the next decade, devastated the country and almost destroyed the Tang dynasty. The rebels, in fact, drove the unfortunate Emperor and the beauteous Yang Guifei from the capital. When Ming-huang's troops refused to march any further with the woman whom they blamed for their troubles, the Emperor was forced to put her to death.

Bo Juyi's poem tells of how Yang Guifei, in Heaven, sent back to her grieving lover a simple promise. One day they would be reunited, reborn as "two birds with the wings of one." Together, they would soar aloft, and never again be separated. The poem is called "The Song of Everlasting Remorse."

The Tang dynasty survived for more than a century after that, but its glory days were over. Later generations called the early period the Golden Age of Chinese civilization: high culture, stable government, expansive foreign relations, and a degree of prosperity that permeated all levels of society. During the first half of the dynasty, every peasant household was even granted a generous and equal amount of land. Nowhere else, and at no other time in history did a government show such concern for its humblest subjects.

Perhaps, expectations had been too high. After the great rebellion, China became regionalized, and local generals and warlords struggled for domination. The central government gradually lost control, and after 30 years of almost constant civil war beginning in A.D. 876, fell to one of its own generals in A.D. 907.

The Third Empire

The fall of the Tang was followed by a brief period of disunion in which five dynasties contended for power. In A.D. 960, the country was reunited, and the **Song dynasty** was founded.

Scholars often compare the Song with the Renaissance in Europe. It was a time when China's classical heritage was rediscovered and reinterpreted to become a vibrant and flourishing force. Song scholars began with the works of Confucius, blended them with the concepts of Taoism and Buddhism, and created a new ideology called **Neo-Confucianism**.

This ideology emphasized that "all under heaven" made up a family, and that in that family, the emperor was the ideal father, compassionate but fair, and entitled to obedience. His government was to be staffed by virtuous men whose goodness was best recognized by education and success in the examination system. All individuals, female as well as male, had a duty to transform themselves, and become the best they could possibly be. This was done by uniting knowledge and action. To use a modern example, a person who knows that cigarettes are bad but fails to quit smoking remains unenlightened.

The Neo-Confucians also developed the concept of *chi* (pronounced chee) (*ki* in Japanese). It refers to a vital life force or essence, and is central to all the East Asian martial arts like gong-fu, karate, and aikido. Even today, a Chinese athlete "concentrates the chi" before stepping up to the starting line.

The Song dynasty is notable for two other things: economic changes that were revolutionary, and artistic achievements that surpassed anything before or after in China. Industry, agriculture, and commerce formed the basis of the commercial revolution and of an economy that was the world's most advanced from the tenth to the eighteenth century.

INNOVATIONS

Chinese Writing

	DRAGON	HORSE	BIRD
SHANG DYNASTY ORACLE-BONE FORM, CA. 1500 B.C.	甬	𤕒	鳥
THIS FORM APPEARED IN THE WESTERN ZHOU DYNASTY CA. 1000 B.C.	尨	柔	鳥
THIS FORM WAS USED AS SIMPLIFIED CHARACTERS BEGAN TO APPEAR CA. 700–250 B.C.	龍	馬	鳥
THIS BECAME THE STANDARD FORM DECREED IN THE QIN DYNASTY IN CHINA'S FIRST DICTIONARY.	龍	馬	隹
BY THE HAN DYNASTY, THESE FORMS, WRITTEN BY A BRUSH, GRADUALLY BECAME UNIVERSAL AND ARE STILL USED TODAY.	龍	馬	隹

During the Song, important progress was made in shipbuilding, ceramics, and the production of coal and iron. The Chinese became the first people to use blast furnaces and fox-bellows to smelt and carbonize iron for the production of steel. They discovered, perhaps by accident, the explosive power of gunpowder and used it for the mining of coal and iron, as well as weapons. They refined papermaking, and with their invention of block printing, revolutionized education by making books more widely available. Some cities, like Kaifeng, became manufacturing centres. Guilds, like trade-unions, were formed for every profession from tea merchants to pickpockets!

To feed the population, which had now reached 100 million, agriculture progressed rapidly. Advances in fertilizers and water control were made, and in the south, the sound ecological practice of sowing one crop of rice followed by one crop of beans or wheat was developed. The fertility of the soil was increased.

In commerce, the Song dynasty made its greatest advances after the loss of most of north China to the so-called Golden (*Jin*) Tartars in 1127. The Song had never been militarily strong, and the move of their capital south to the beautiful city of Hangzhou (pronounced hong-joe), sometimes called China's Venice, was a wise one. By this time, perhaps two-thirds of the population and wealth of the Chinese Empire was found south of the Yangtze, and the loss of the rich agricultural north made the southern Song court turn to commerce for revenue. The so-called Southern Song dynasty became the "merchant" of the East Asian world. It was the first and last time that private **capitalism** was allowed to flourish without government interference. The medium of exchange for internal commerce was paper money, the flying cash first developed by the Chinese in the middle of the ninth century. For the maritime trade, barter was still the rule.

This period was one of the rare times that the Chinese encouraged foreign trade, and the government derived much revenue from customs and transit duties. China imported only luxury goods like textiles, spices, and some medicines, but exported silk, copper, and most particularly, porcelain, which only the Chinese knew how to make at this time.

Song porcelains—deep blue and green, translucent, eggshell-thin ceramics—have been found all along the coasts of Africa, India, and the Middle East, showing the vigour of sea trade in the twelfth century. Since the Chinese retained the secret of their kaolin clay for the next five centuries, the words porcelain and china became synonyms in most European languages.

The carriers of this trade were Chinese ships, called *junks*. Some carried crews of 500–600. The junks were guided by the world's first magnetic compasses, and featured such innovations as watertight bulkheads, buoyancy chambers, bamboo fenders at the waterline, axial rudders in place of oars, scoops for taking samples off the sea floor, sounding lines, cargo compartments, and even firecrackers to frighten off pirates. This ocean-going trade gave rise to foreign communities in such cities as Canton, where Middle Eastern merchants were subject to their own laws, could worship as they chose, and could even intermarry with the Chinese.

Finally, the Song represents the high point of the Chinese visual arts. Prior to the Song, paintings had been so formal that only the educated class could appreciate them and understand the symbolism. Scholars exchanged paintings only among themselves, and never signed their names since everyone in their circle knew the identity of the artist.

Now, artists became infused with a new more accessible vision of the world. They also wanted to profit from their art. Landscape painting, which everyone could appreciate, became the favourite medium. The typical Song artist would observe the landscape he intended to paint, sometimes for years. He (we have no female examples), would then meditate in his studio, and standing before a table, com-

The landscape paintings of the Song dynasty depicted the artist's reverence of nature with a new understanding of humanity's place within it. These paintings always had some sign of human life as does this one a "Temple in the Mountains on a Clear Day."

plete his painting in black and white, within the space of a few minutes. The artist painted not just one lake but all lakes, and in each of his paintings there was a sign of human beings. People were a part of nature and, unlike western practice, they were also a part of all landscapes. Sometimes the only sign of human life is a puff of smoke from a mountain cottage.

In the Song period, artists began to sign their works, especially when they painted for the newly-rich merchants, and connoisseurship became an art in itself. The red-ink seals that one sees on old Chinese paintings are the seals of the various owners. It would be like signing one's own name across the front of the Picasso hanging in the living room!

Daily Life in the Capital

In 1271, 85 percent of the population of China were subsistence farmers. Bad harvests often forced many of them to sell their daughters to tea-houses in nearby villages. Sons were rented out for six years at a time to wealthier neighbours as field hands. Some were luckier and were either sold into rich families or found employment with them in the city.

The city called Hangzhou was the Song capital. Marco Polo called it "the most noble city and the best that is in the world." Residences of the wealthy in Hangzhou were spacious, comfortable, and luxurious. Usually of a single storey, they were made of wood with brick floors, and had graceful, upswept, tile roofs. Each one was a walled compound and there were many side-buildings and pavilions for the cooks, artisans, musicians, dancers, acrobats, tutors, astrologers, and even matchmakers. Some pavilions were built for such esoteric purposes as viewing the moon or listening to crickets. Gardening was a fine art, and there were elaborate rules for the placement of ponds, rare flowers, gnarled trees, grottoes, and curious rocks. Formal Chinese gardens avoided the symmetry of European gardens, and instead tried to imitate nature with waterfalls and miniature hills.

Interior decor was simple, consisting of low tables and a few chairs. Chairs had appeared in China only in the ninth century. There were curtained beds with rush mattresses, and pillows made of pottery. Since only the emperor could use red lacquer, furniture was finished in black lacquer. Scrolls and landscape paintings hung on the walls, and the tables were decorated with antiques and flowers such as jasmine, peonies, chrysanthemums, and orchids. Incense and "mosquito smoke" freshened the air. Servants had lifetime employment and their masters often treated them like their own children, even arranging their marriages.

Outside the walls of each compound, the city was a colourful and bustling place, with men and women mingling freely in the streets. The women of the time wore their hair in a chignon with sometimes as many as a dozen metal and pearl hairpins arranged in the hair. They wore white make-up, rouged their cheeks, and painted their fingernails pink. Their clothing was colourful. Bright red, green, and yellow silk dresses reached to the ground, and were worn under knee-length blouses and sometimes a jacket of gold brocade. Poorer women had to be content with drab *pyjama suits* of hempen cloth.

The women seen on the streets of Hangzhou, moreover, were not the most "respectable" women of the city. Social custom confined women of the upper classes to the homes of their husbands, who were mostly government officials. They were further restricted by their physical lack of mobility due to **foot binding**. These were the women of the *golden lotus*, women whose feet had been tightly bound with bandages at the age of five or six, so that their feet always remained no more than 10 cm long. The toes were bent under the ball of the foot and the pain must have been excruciating. Sometimes the toes atrophied and fell off. It was a terrible price to pay for tiny feet, which in golden slippers, we are told, resembled the petals of a lotus.

To Chinese men, tiny feet were beautiful and desirable, and Chinese mothers saw small feet as a guarantee of a good marriage. Thus, in spite of frequent government prohibitions, the sad custom spread through all levels of society. By the beginning of the twentieth century, the majority of women had suffered this fate. The practice was not totally eradicated until 1949, and women whose feet were once bound can still be seen today.

The men of the Song added their own colour to the streets of Hangzhou. For them, clothing was a sign of social status. Men wore their hair long, bathed on every tenth day, and on their bath-day holiday, had their hair, face, and goatee oiled. Officials and wealthy men carried a parasol to shield their complexion from the sun, and wore black silk caps to distinguish them from the common people who wore a sort of turban. They wore long silk robes with flowing sleeves in which they carried fans and wallets. Sometimes trousers were worn underneath. The essential article of male clothing was a very wide sash, almost like a girdle, with a decorative plaque on the front. These plaques were ornamented with jade, ivory, or gold fashioned into the images of peacocks, fish, or mythological creatures. Some denoted the official rank of the wearer, and others were purely decorative. The dress of the people, along with the permanent fairgrounds which were filled with acrobats, trained animals, and fortune tellers made Hangzhou an exciting place to be.

*F*ood and Medicine

The rich and marvelous variety of food available in Hangzhou grew out of scarcity. Frequent famines in their history had taught the Chinese to use every edible foodstuff available in their cuisine, vegetables, roots, animals, fish, and even insects, and to waste nothing from the lips of a fish to the paws of a bear. The scarcity of wood and charcoal had led them to invent the wok; perhaps the most efficient use of heat in any of the world's cooking utensils. And the scarcity of any guaranteed recipe for long life had led them to experiment with unusual substances in their cuisine. The saliva of swallows, for instance, formed the basic ingredient of bird's nest soup, and the fins of sharks were thought to ward off colds and other illnesses.

Just as the various regions of Europe had their distinctive cuisines, so too, did the regions of China. In the markets of Hangzhou, the hungry stroller had a wide variety of choice. From the North, came more than 200 varieties of noodles and dumplings—thick, thin, light, and heavy, stuffed or covered with onions and mutton, shrimp and garlic, sweet beans and pork, or slices of crispy Peking duck.

From the Southwest came pungent chicken and river-fish, often marinated for many days in anise, coriander, fennel, and chili. It was then cooked with orange peel and cinnamon over a fire flavoured with camphor wood and tea-leaves. The southeast coastal cities like Canton, provided sweet and sour sauce served over pigeon, snails, and uncounted varieties of fish. Their many sauces contained such ingredients as seaweed, dried mushroom, ginger, sesame oil, cassia bark, peppercorns, and numerous varieties of wine and vinegar. All these foods were available 24 hours a day at the markets and at little shops like the fast-food restaurants of today and at a similar cost.

There exist several recipe books from the Song, but scholars have had a hard time deciphering them since the Chinese used poetic names for the ingredients used in their dishes. An entry on a typical menu might be called "Dragon Fights the Phoenix in the Clouds." This probably meant a dish made with snake (dragon), chicken (phoenix), and snow-cloud mushrooms. One contemporary source notes 200 dishes that might be served at a great banquet, and even tells us the correct order of service:

> There should be 41 dishes of shrimp, fish, snails, pork, goose, mutton and pigeon; all fried, sauteed, grilled, and spitted or roasted in the oven. There should be 42 dishes based on fruits and nuts, and 20 based on vegetables alone. There should be 9 rice dishes with different sauces, and 29 kinds of dried fish dishes, with 17 different types of drinks; pear nectar, litchee juice, ginger juice and uncounted types of wine.[1]

If the people of the time became ill because of their overindulgence in food or wine, or for any other reason, they could go to one of the branches of the School of Medicine which had been established in Hangzhou in 1076. The school admitted 200–300 male and female students each year and treated mostly patients from the upper classes. Ordinary people tended to go to private doctors, or more accurately, to doctor families since doctors trained all their children in the healing arts.

Medicine was specialized and divided into nine sections. The first two consisted of general medicine and theories of illness. Then, in order, came the specializations of rheumatism, ophthalmology, obstetrics, dentistry, abscesses, fractures, acupuncture, and finally, treatments by charms and amulets. Illness was diagnosed by taking the pulse for 5 or 10 minutes.

In general, most illnesses were treated by herbs and some prescriptions from the Song contain 25 different herbs. Massage and acupuncture, which had both been utilized for more than 2000 years, were frequently used. Moxibustion, a process where small stacks of medicinal herbs were placed on an acupuncture point and then burned, was common. Surgery was not. Some remedies, such as a cure for malaria, which consisted of swallowing a particular fly found on the body of frogs, may seem fanciful to us, but many Chinese herbs have found their way into the pills we take today. Acupuncture is still

---

[1] Jacques Gernet, *Daily Life in China on the Eve of the Mongol Invasion 1250-1276 (London: George Allen and Unwin Ltd., 1962), p. 138.*

ASPECTS OF DAILY LIFE

A BANQUET FROM THE SONG DYNASTY

In the first scene from *Night Revelry of Han Xizai* a lively scene of feasting to lute music is depicted. The guests, focusing their attention on the lute player, are gathered around low tables set with several dishes of food, containers of wine and wine cups. This painting is a valuable tool in the recreation of a banquet from the Song period as it clearly depicts the clothing, furnishings, and table settings of the time.

A Chinese meal has a few connections with western culture. Tea has long been the most important drink and is served both before and after a meal. Rice is also an essential part of any meal. It serves as a bland accompaniment to the food that is eaten with it and should never be sauced or seasoned.

Throughout the meal fresh fruits such as peaches, plums, cherries, melons, and litchees were available. Sweet dishes, such as preserves and small honey or sugar filled pastries were eaten early in the meal or between the dishes as it was thought to be healthier to eat sweets before the main dishes.

Following are a few recipes that may have been enjoyed at banquets such as the one shown here.

Quick Fried Shrimps

750 g shrimp or prawns, fresh (cooked and shelled) or frozen (defrosted, drained and dried), halve if large

5 mL salt

2 mL chili or cayenne pepper

20 mL cornstarch

15 mL sesame oil

50 mL vegetable oil

2–3 green onions, finely chopped

15 g fresh ginger root, peeled and finely chopped

10 mL sugar

25 mL light soya sauce

50 mL non-alcoholic wine

Mix the salt, cayenne, cornstarch, and sesame oil and toss the shrimp into this mixture. Heat the vegetable oil in a frying pan or a wok. When it is hot add shrimps and stir fry them quickly for one to two minutes. Add the onions, ginger, sugar, soya sauce and wine and continue to cook over a high heat for another thirty seconds. Serve at once.
Serves 6.
(From the British Museum Cookbook, by Michelle Berriedale-Johnson, © 1987. British Museum Publications.)

Ants Climb the Tree

250 g bean-thread noodles

250 g ground, uncooked chicken

50 mL vegetable oil

15 mL light (kikkoman) and 1 15 mL dark soya sauce

5 mL non-alcoholic wine

2 mL sugar

15 mL cornstarch

1 mL sesame oil

5–10 mL green onion

250 mL chicken broth

Soak the bean-thread noodles in cold water overnight. Marinate the chicken in a blend of 15 mL of oil, the soya sauces, sugar, wine, and cornstarch and sesame oil overnight in refrigerator. When ready to cook, heat 25 mL of oil in a wok and quickly fry the onions. Add chicken with marinade and stir for five minutes. Now add the drained noodles and chicken broth. Stir for one minute and serve. Sprinkle lightly with red pepper.
Serves 4.

Boiled Rice

Allow 50 g of dry white rice per person. Do not salt your cooking water; Chinese grains should be totally bland so as not to mask the flavours of the dishes which they accompany. Cook the rice in plenty of fast boiling water for seven to ten minutes or until it is soft without being mushy. Transfer it to the top of a steamer or a sieve over gently boiling water. Cover it with a cloth, foil or lid and keep it warm until you need to use it.

widely used in anaesthesia and addiction treatment, and the Chinese holistic view of wellness is finding much favour today.

Forensic medicine was advanced, and one text book for coroners outlines the way to identify possible means of death, whether from various poisons or by piercing the eardrum with a long needle. This textbook is the oldest work of its kind in history, and is also the first to outline various methods of artificial respiration. Doctors in the Song often advertised, placing signs in their windows guaranteeing fast recovery and distributing leaflets in their neighbourhoods to proclaim their specialties.

Beliefs

Religious life in Song China was so diversified that it is almost impossible to describe. The Chinese were not a monotheistic people, and individual Chinese seldom gave their sole allegiance to any particular religion. As a result, their history is almost wholly free of religious wars, persecutions, and inquisitions. They tended to believe that there were many paths to salvation and many deities to worship. It was prudent to respect all deities, both to avoid calamity in this life and to ensure happiness in the next.

The Chinese peasant, like most humans before the scientific revolution, lived in a world that we might call superstitious. Their beliefs changed little over 3000 years. The educated class in China was well aware of these folk beliefs and tended to be skeptical about them. However, even if they didn't believe fully in such things as ghosts, spirits, and the power of magical objects to bring rain, they still painted fearsome gods on their doors to ward off evil, and made sure that their graves faced the proper direction. Most of them saw no contradiction in attending services at the temples and shrines of both organized religions: Buddhism and Daoism. But the next day, they sacrificed a pig to the mischievous dragon who lived in the pool in their garden!

In China, however, there was one belief common to all classes: ancestor veneration. Any visitor to Hangzhou in the Song would be struck by the care taken of the dead. The Chinese believed that each human being possessed two souls. At death, one of these souls remained with the body until the proper mourning rituals had been performed. It then descended to the *Yellow Springs* and eventually dissolved. If the corpse was improperly buried, this soul remained on earth as a hungry ghost to terrify the living. The second soul left the body at death and ascended to a kind of heaven. From there, the ancestor watched over the family and affected its fortunes.

Throughout China, tablets inscribed with the name of the deceased were placed in each home. On special occasions, like birthdays, the Festival of the Dead, and the New Year, families visited the grave sites, swept them, bowed before them, and burned images of money, food, houses, servants, and anything else that might be needed in the other world. The smoke carried these objects to their destination.

Traditional families follow these practices of ancestor veneration right up to the present day. The New Year's Festival still remains the most important time in the Chinese calendar. Whether in Toronto or Beijing, you will see families doing what was done in thirteenth century Hangzhou. The house is swept clean of all the bad influences of the past year, new clothes are put on, a feast is prepared, and the food is then shared with the *stove-god* who will ascend to the ancestors to report on the conduct of the family.

Finally, if you visited Hangzhou, you would be struck by the number of religious festivals that dotted the Chinese calendar. Several times each month, there were festivals of flowers, lanterns, dragon-boats, the Buddha's birthday, mid-Autumn moon viewing, and many others.

One of the most charming, and one very popular festival among young people in East Asia today, falls on the seventh day of the seventh month. On that day, two constellations called the Divine Weaving-maiden and the Divine Shepherd meet on the bridge of the Milky Way. To celebrate the brief happiness of the heavenly lovers, young people write down the name of their own "valentine," and tie the colourful, folded paper to a tree branch in the hope that the Maiden and the Shepherd will see it and smile on their wishes.

The Mongol Conquest

Hangzhou in 1271 was a fine bustling city, but over it there lay a shadow. That same year, far to the north, the Emperor Khubilai Khan proclaimed a new dynasty and sent his hordes southward to destroy the Song. In A.D. 1279, Hangzhou fell. One Chinese poet of the time visited the former palace of Hangzhou after the conquest and wrote:

> The grass grows high round this old, old ruin,
> Gone the guards, the gatekeepers
> Fallen towers, crumbling pavilions,
> My soul destroyed.
> Beneath the eaves of ancient halls,
> Swallows dart.
> But within,
> Silence.
>
> Xie Ao, *On Visiting the Former Imperial Palace*

The Yuan dynasty was founded by the Mongols, a nomadic people whose disunity and internal quarrels had kept them from becoming a threat to their more civilized neighbours for many centuries. However, in the year A.D. 1206, a remarkable man called Temujin united the various tribes, proclaimed himself **Chingghis** (or "universal") **Khan**, and set out to conquer the known world. He very nearly succeeded.

At that time in history, many of the peoples of Eurasia were in a state of flux. Northern China and Tibet were in disorder. There were struggles in southern Russia and in the Turkish and Persian empires. Europe was gripped in the fervour of the Crusades and Constantinople had just fallen. This unsettled situation made the Mongol conquest easier, but it is doubtful that any of the surrounding peoples could have stood up to them anyway.

The Mongol armies were simply invincible. Each soldier, armoured in heavy leather, carried two bows, capable of killing a person at 180 m. Each had three horses, bred for speed and endurance, and changed mounts whenever one horse got tired. Mongol warriors could sleep on horseback, could survive by drinking horse blood and mare's milk. Therefore, they could cover great distances with incredible speed. In battle, they were utterly ruthless, taking prisoners only when they needed human shields for the next city they attacked! They poisoned wells, razed cities to the ground, and slaughtered even those who willingly surrendered to them.

When Chingghis died in A.D. 1227, most of Central Asia, Northern China, and all of Tibet were in his hands. His successors extended Mongol rule to Korea in A.D. 1231, Kiev, Moscow, and parts of Poland and Hungary in A.D. 1240, as well as Baghdad and the rest of the Middle East in 1251. Terrified Europeans had, for the most part, never seen an Asian person and they did not know who these warriors were. In their chronicles, they referred to them as demon-creatures unleashed by an angry God to scourge their sinful world.

When, at last in A.D. 1279, the Mongols conquered Southern China, they found themselves in control of the greatest land empire in all of human history! Originally, they divided all their land into four parts with the capital in Mongolia. In A.D. 1260, Khubilai Khan, Temujin's ablest grandson, realized that China was the richest part of his vast empire and moved the capital to Beijing.

China in the Yuan Dynasty.

The ordinary people of China felt very little impact from the con-

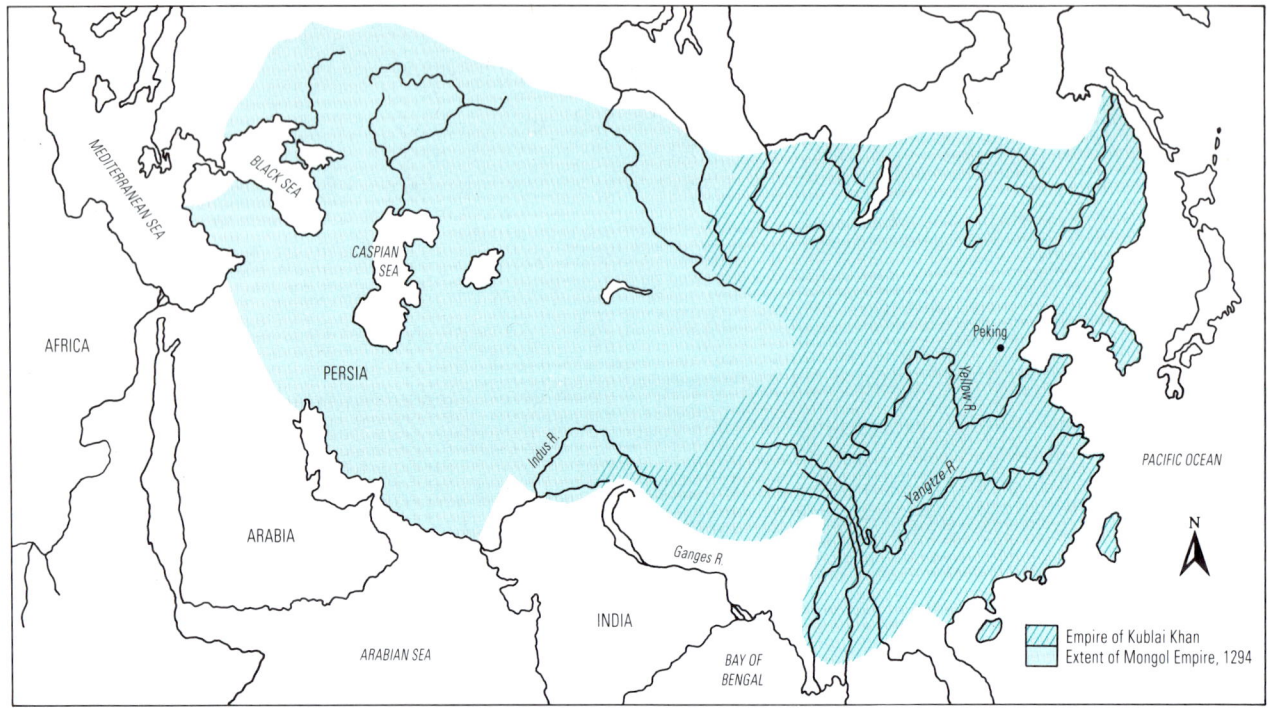

Mongol Empire Late Thirteenth Century

quest. After all, the Mongols never numbered more than 250 000 persons at a time when China's population had passed 100 million. The Mongols, moreover, left the local administration in place and the ordinary peasant probably never saw their conquerors.

The educated elite of society, on the other hand, were very much aware of their presence. Mongol rule was more harsh than that of the Song, and court officials, for instance were now subjected to cruel beatings. The taxes of officials and their families were raised and their salaries were eroded by inflation. The Mongol rulers made clumsy attempts to discourage Confucian practices like ancestor veneration, and to impose on China a crude form of Buddhism as the national religion. Worse than that, the Mongols blocked the road to official advancement by using Mongols and other foreigners in all the highest posts of government. As Marco Polo,

who served Khubilai from A.D. 1275–1292, said, "... the Great Khan rules Cathay not by hereditary right, but by conquest. Having no confidence in the native people, he has put all authority in the hands of Tartars, Saracens, and Christians..."

The Mongols set up a hierarchy of social classes with themselves at the top, applied different laws to the Chinese and to themselves, continued to wear leather and fur, to eat milk and cheese, to forbid intermarriage, and to allow their women far greater freedom than the Chinese thought proper. They even abolished the examination system. Resentment grew among all the educated Chinese.

One unintended result of the exclusion of Chinese from official life was that scholars were forced to turn to other pursuits and two new art forms appeared. The first was the novel, and second was the drama. In these works for the stage, plots were romantic or historical, costumes were lavish and

160 UNIT 1 *Civilizations of the Near and Far East*

female roles were played by males just as in Shakespearean England. Today, we call this drama Peking Opera.

A final feature of the Mongol Empire is that many Chinese innovations now made their way not to Europe, but to West Asia. Caravans travelled regularly between Baghdad and Beijing and ships sailed back and forth from the Persian Gulf to Canton. The trade had little impact on Europe, but Russia, Persia, and Mesopotamia were introduced to Chinese gunpowder, printing, paper money, textiles, and porcelains, as well as iodine and the technique of inoculation, and even playing cards. The Chinese assimilated some mathematics, astronomy, and map making from the Arab-Turkish culture, but in general showed little interest in the outside world. The Muslim religion, however, took permanent root in northwestern China.

The Last Empire

Mongol rule in China lasted less than a century, coming to an end in 1368 after a series of bloody rebellions. Mongol leadership had exhausted itself in court intrigue and in wars with Korea and other parts of its far-flung empire. Chinese resentment against their foreign overlords had remained strong, especially south of the Yangtze. There secret societies had been formed to expel foreign rule. It was the leader of one of these societies, a peasant later called Emperor Taizu, who emerged victorious among all of the rebel groups. He chose the name Ming (meaning "brilliant") for his new dynasty. It would last until 1644, and together with the Qing (pronounced ching) dynasty which ended in 1911, it would constitute China's last empire.

The 276 years of Ming rule are seen by scholars as a time of peace, prosperity, and stability. It was a time when the Chinese civilization seemed to have reached a balance or an equilibrium, and as a result, the pace of change slowed to a crawl.

Napoleon was later to say that "China slept" for several centuries, though that is not quite true. Some changes occurred. The village economy and internal-trade networks continued to develop. Confucian philosophy was further refined, the examination system reached its final form, and scholarship progressed rapidly. Traditional arts and crafts were perfected, a new elite class emerged, and the position of the emperor reached its final stage of development.

None of these changes, however, could match those that were taking place in Europe. Ming emperors were on the throne when the travels of European explorers took them to the Americas and round the Cape of Good Hope and they still ruled when Europe was transformed by the Renaissance and Reformation. Their successors, the Qing, remained oblivious to the European wars of religion, witch burnings, the formation of nation-states, and the various revolutions of the Western world; French, American, scientific, and industrial. If China did not sleep, it at least dozed.

How might we account for this? There were three major reasons. First, the Chinese ruling group had seen too often that in their own history, technological change had brought about social disruption in the form of urbanization, the weakening of the family, and even peasant uprisings. They preferred stability. Second, the Chinese of the Ming were proud of their victory over the Mongols. They now came to believe that since they had once again solved their own problems, they could continue to do so. They had used traditional ways to free themselves, not new solutions. Their own history held all the answers they needed, and they would change only within their own tradition.

Finally, their bitter experience with foreign rule led them to believe that they were better off without outside interference. What did they have to learn from anyone else? In the Ming and Qing, it seemed as if the Chinese had psychologically immunized themselves against foreign influence. There was no antagonism toward the rest of the world—only a growing sense of superiority. The Chinese became **xenophobic**.

On the Eve of Western Contact

The Ming dynasty has existed for almost 150 years before the first Europeans, Portuguese traders and pirates, made their presence felt on China's south coast in A.D. 1514. The objects of their desire, spices, silk, porcelain, and later tea, were high-profit items for them, but they had nothing of similar value to offer the Chinese. For that reason, they simply took what they wanted, behaving with violence and greed in the Canton area, and earning the name *yangguei* or "ocean-devils." They even bought kidnapped Chinese children as slaves. The Chinese, however, believed that they bought these children to eat them!

It was only when the Jesuits arrived in Peking in A.D. 1600 that educated Chinese began to have a more favourable impression of westerners. The Jesuits were well educated in Chinese literature and respectful of Chinese ways. Though they made few converts, they impressed the Chinese court with their mechanical clocks, their knowledge of astronomy, and their willingness to learn from a "superior" civilization.

The Jesuits were more impressed with China than the other way around and began to send back glowing reports to Europe. They had good reason to be impressed. The Ming was a prosperous, confident, and stable dynasty, and seemed to the Jesuits, an oasis of calm and wealth when compared to their own turbulent world. The first two Ming emperors, who between them ruled from A.D. 1368 to A.D. 1425, had firmly set the course of the dynasty.

In the first place, they had fostered strong leadership. Abolishing the office of chief minister as well as other ministries that had checked the emperor's power, they created alternate offices like the grand secretaries who served the emperor's whim, and could be dismissed at any time. They forced their ministers to kneel before them. They used eunuchs as a secret service to keep files on civil servants so that they could be arrested at any time. They manipulated the examination system to produce the kind of officials they wanted. Chinese historians deplore this emerging despotism, but cannot deny that it produced a unified command centre.

Secondly, the despotism was exercised on the officials, not on the people. The early Ming emperors fostered the rise of a new ruling class, the gentry, who moderated the effects of absolute rule at the local level. The gentry, wealthy families who produced officials and held land, became the real rulers of China. They acted as an unpaid civil service, building schools, recruiting militia, repairing dikes and roads, setting up orphanages and homes for the aged, and settling legal disputes. They made their own lives models of Confucian rectitude, lived in the public eye, and encouraged the peasantry to follow their example. They understood their people and their people understood them. Orders from the capital in Beijing were often modified to fit local custom and conditions.

Finally, the second emperor demonstrated what he saw as China's preeminence in the world. He began the series of seven great maritime expeditions which took place between A.D. 1405 and A.D. 1433. They made China, for a brief time, the greatest of the world's maritime powers.

These expeditions, which sometimes included more than 300 ships and a total crew of over 30 000, plied the seas of Southeast Asia and extended Chinese influence into the Indian Ocean, along the east coast of Africa and into Arabia. More than 20 states and kingdoms now began to trade and offer tribute to China, but China seemed to be little impressed. The expeditions were stopped in A.D. 1433 for reasons we do not fully understand, though it is clear that the expeditions were expensive, and the commercial returns negligible. The missions were led by a great explorer called Zheng He (pronounced jeng-huh) but he was a eunuch and jealous scholar-officials of the court were constantly undermining him. Finally, the Ming dynasty felt confident enough in its power that it seemed unimportant to announce it abroad. It became even more introverted. What would have happened had the Chinese maintained their interest in the sea is one of the great "what if's" of history.

As time went on, the Ming revelled in its wealth. In 1425, it is reported that the emperor employed more than 6000 chefs in the palace and became a great patron of the famous blue and white porcelains, which would later become all the rage in Europe. The population of China was now approaching 150 million, literacy was spreading, and the Yangtze delta with its manufactured goods of iron, ceramics, silk, cotton, indigo, sugar cane, and even wood-block prints was perhaps the wealthiest area in the world. Drama and the novel continued to develop. On the eve of its first contact with the West, China was a civilization that was self-contained, inexperienced with Europe, and complacent in its success.

The Chinese World View

The Chinese, even before Confucius, had seen themselves as the Middle Kingdom. Surrounding them, and positioned on a series of concentric circles, were all the other peoples known to them. The Chinese emperor was at the very centre, the father of the human family. As Confucius said, "Within the four seas, all are brother and sister."

This view of the world implied that like a father, the Chinese emperor would teach, educate, and when necessary, punish his children. In turn, his children had a duty to learn. Therefore, the position of another country on the circles was determined not by geography, but by culture. How closely did their civilizations resemble that of China? Korea, Vietnam, and Japan who adopted Chinese culture early, were on the inner circle, even though they were geographically more distant from the Chinese capital than some of the Central Asian nomads.

From the second century B.C. onwards, Chinese emperors had issued engraved seals or *chops* to neighbouring rulers. These seals confirmed the rulers as friends of China, and gave them permission to send delegations to the capital where they offered tribute to the emperor. The surrounding peoples valued this privilege since the return gifts from the emperor usually exceeded their own, and more importantly, because, if they did not offer tribute, they would not be permitted to trade with the Chinese. For more than 2000 years, tribute-envoys came regularly to China. Special officials conducted them to the capital by prescribed routes so they did not disturb the people. There they lodged in fine hotels and awaited the pleasure of the emperor. Ushered into his presence, they *kowtowed* before him, and presented their gifts. To kowtow, they had to kneel before the emperor, and bang their foreheads on the floor three times. The kowtow symbolized the submission of the envoys, along with their rulers and their countries, to the Chinese emperor.

The tribute from foreign lands was valued. From Japan came painted fans and decorated papers, sulphur for matches, and razor-sharp swords. From Korea came medicinal ginseng, rhubarb, and soft furs. From Central Asia and the oasis cities came spirited horses, beautifully embossed leathers, and musical instruments. From Indo-China and the island-kingdoms of Indonesia came pungent spices and rare woods. Exquisite jewelry, tiles, and perfumes came from the Arab world, and the first Portuguese traders offered mechanical clocks and muskets. Animals from around the world populated the Imperial Zoo, and Ming emperors, in particular, loved giraffes which they saw as unicorns. Entertainers of all sorts accompanied the tribute missions and enlivened the Chinese court. One Chinese emperor found the Russian ballet vulgar, and made a note in his diary that Russians should be taught about music! Under the Ming, more than 40 states called themselves tributaries of China.

At the ceremonial meeting, the emperor asked about affairs in the foreign kingdom. He often demanded that internal quarrels be stopped or that Chinese criminals who had fled there be returned. He offered advice on all manner of subjects, and insisted that local rulers curb pirates or border-raiders. He was father to "all under Heaven."

The tributary system was not imperialism as we usually define it, but simply an expression of cultural superiority. Its fatal flaw was that it refused to acknowledge equality in inter-state relations. Inevitably, there would be a clash with the West.

Suggested Sources for Further Research

Blunden, C., and M. Elvin, *A Cultural Atlas of China* (Oxford, 1983).

De Bary, W.T., *et. al.*, *Sources of Chinese Tradition* (Columbia University Press, 1968).

Gernet, J., *China and the Christian Impact: A Conflict of Cultures* (Cambridge University Press, 1982).

Guisso, R.W.L., and C. Pagani, *The First Emperor of China* (Stoddart, 1989).

Hucker, C.O., *China's Imperial Past* (Stanford University Press, 1975).

Loewe, M., *Everyday Life in Early Imperial China* (G.P. Putnam's Sons, 1968).

Michael, F., *China Through The Ages* (Westview Press, 1986).

Needham, J., *Science and Civilization in China* (Cambridge University Press, 1900).

Rossabi, M., *Khubilai Khan: His Life and Times* (University of California Press, 1987).

Schwarz, B., *The World of Thought in Ancient China* (Harvard University Press, 1985).

Sullivan, M., *The Arts of China* (Thames & Hudson, 1984).

Wright, A.F., *Buddhism in Chinese History* (Atheneum, 1959).

Focus Your Knowledge

1. The society of the Shang dynasty had clear class divisions. Describe the various levels.

2. What factors contributed to the decline of the Zhou dynasty?

3. What were the essential ideas which Confucius stressed in attempting to bring order from a disordered world?

4. Not all people accepted the teachings of Confucius. Two of the most famous dissenters were Mo Zi and Lao Zi. How did their ideas differ from Confucius?

5. What factors contributed to the decline of the Han dynasty and what happened to China in the years following its demise?

6. Describe the homes and clothing of the people of Hangzhou.

7. Which features of the Mongolian army allowed them to enjoy the success they achieved? What impact on China and the world did the Mongolian invasions have?

8. Why did China become conservative and attempt to close its borders to outside influences?

Apply Your Knowledge

1. The Chinese reckoned time differently from many western civilizations. How did their concept of time reflect a philosophical difference in the view of the rise and fall of dynasties and progress over time?

2. Briefly describe the methods used by Shi Huangdi to unify China and bring it under his control. Considering the methods used, would Shi Huangdi be described as a heroic figure or a villain?

3. Assess the strengths and weaknesses of the Chinese government by reflecting on the make-up and role of both the inner court and outer court. Compared to other monarchical systems, what were the merits of the Chinese system?

4. Various periods of Chinese history are remembered for the incredible achievements in science, art, and literature. Using an organizer clearly illustrate the reasons the Zhou, Tang, and Song dynasties are particularly remembered.

5. To what degree do Chinese advancements in medicine reflect a sound understanding of the nature and causes of illness and disease?

6. How did the social customs of the Chinese reflect their beliefs regarding the soul and the afterlife?

7. How did the Chinese world view help to shape their reactions to European contact?

Extension Activities

1. After carefully rereading the section on oracle bones attempt to recreate the process. Have fellow students make requests of questions they would like answered.

2. Prepare a report to be shared with the class on Confucianism or Daoism. You may wish to prepare a bulletin board to illustrate the concepts contained in each of the beliefs. In doing your research try to find out if there is a Daoist church in your community or neighbouring communities.

3. Based on further research build a model of one of the great architectural feats of China including the Great Wall of China, the tomb of Shi Huangdi or the Forbidden City.

4. Based on the information in the feature study on a Song Banquet and the text plus additional research prepare and host a banquet recreating as closely as possible the food, clothing, and setting of the Song period.

5. Based on further research recreate the persona of a famous character from Chinese history. The role playing could be done live for the class, on video-tape, or for a special audience such as a primary school group or members of the community invited in for the presentation. The following is a list of characters you may wish to choose from.

   Shi Huangdi   Chingghis Khan
   Confucius   Lao Zi
   Empress Wu   Emperor Wudi

6. Playing the role of a eunuch in the inner court record in a journal or diary your reactions to the first European traders and missionaries who began to arrive in China. Conversely you may wish to do research into the lives and experiences of people such as St. Francis Xavier and write your diary from the perspective of the Europeans and their first impressions of China and the Chinese court.

SKILLS FOCUS

Unit Overview

Students may wish to read "Developing An Organizer" before answering the following questions.

1. The civilizations studied in this unit are all river valley civilizations. Why did these civilizations arise in proximity to a river? What impact did the river have on the civilizations?

2. The role of women has long been neglected in the study of history, although more recently historians have taken it into account. Compare the role that women played in the various societies discussed in this unit. Based on what you've learned, which civilization would you feel most comfortable living in as a woman. Explain why.

3. For each of the civilizations covered in this unit religion played an important part in the development of their culture. Briefly summarize how religion helped shape the culture. Were there differences between the religion of the early civilizations of India and China and the later civilizations?

4. Briefly explain the law codes, government hierarchy, and how government officials were selected for each civilization. Based on your information, which was the most equitable society and which was the least equitable society? Explain your answer.

5. Determine the extent to which each civilization developed in isolation, its receptiveness to outside influences and the importance of these influences. Does a society progress more through contact with other societies or in isolation? What are the implications of this in terms of today's global village?

Art: A Window to Our Past

Refer to the colour-plate section for Unit 1.

1. Speculate as to why there are few humans in cave art and why the art of the early civilizations concentrates more on humans and human achievements.

2. Compare and contrast the art of the civilizations in this unit. You might consider the artistic style and conventions used as well as the influences of the environment, social organization, customs, and beliefs. To what extent is art truly "A Window to Our Past"?

3. Examine the different art forms in this unit. Which do you find more appealing? Select your favourite piece of art from this unit and state why this is your preference.

Effective Questions

Learning effective questioning skills is critical to success in completing a task. Good questions help

STEPS TO EFFECTIVE QUESTIONING	EXAMPLE
1. Clearly define your subject or topic.	1. *What are river valley civilizations? Around which river did each civilization settle?*
2. Based on the information on the topic you have been given identify the purpose of your study and the aspects needing to be covered.	2. *What is the impact of the river on each civilization? Why did these civilizations spring up here? What role did major rivers play in the development of civilizations?*
3. Brainstorm a set of questions that will lead to answers on the purpose of your study and particular aspects you need to find out about.	3. *What influences did the river have on lifetstyle, agriculture, transportation, religion, political divisions, government, settlement patterns, development of society, and culture for each civilization?*
4. Select those questions that are specific to your topic and to the resources available.	
You may find that some questions become less relevant as you work your way through your study. Do not hesitate to formulate new questions based on what you have learned.	

you define your task, limit your topic, and give you a sense of direction. Good questions operate at a variety of levels and formulating questions based on these steps will lead to effective questioning. These questions are based on "Unit Overview" question 1.

Developing an Organizer

The study of history can leave one overwhelmed by the amount of information available. Having too much information can be frustrating since it needs to be processed and you might not know where to begin. An effective way to handle a large amount of information is to prepare an organizer. An organizer helps to sort and classify information, thereby making it more manageable. A good organizer should not only classify content but also help you analyze information.

The above is a sample organizer set up for overview question number one, based on the focus questions that were created in "Effective Questions." The information can now be classified in a meaningful way.

TASK: *APPLYING EFFECTIVE QUESTIONS AND CREATING AN ORGANIZER*

Select one of the questions from the "Unit Overview." Follow the procedures outlined on page 169:

1. By using the four steps to effective questions set up a list of questions to direct your information gathering and to help you focus.

2. Set up an organizer that would help you organize and analyze your information. Using this information prepare a short report on one of the "Unit Overview" topics.

| | NATURE OF THE RIVERS | IMPACT OF THE RIVERS ON |||| OVERALL ASSESSMENT |
		Agriculture	Transportation	Political Divisions	Settlement Patterns	
Mesopotamia (*Tigris, Euphrates*)						
Egypt (*The Nile*)						
India (*The Indus*)						
China (*The Yellow*)						

SKILLS FOCUS

UNIT 2
Civilizations of Greece and Rome

CHAPTER 6
The Rise of the Greeks

CHAPTER 7
Classical Greece

CHAPTER 8
The Rise of Rome

CHAPTER 9
The Roman Empire

The western world owes much to the civilizations of Greece and Rome. By the early second millennium B.C. the Minoans had established an advanced civilization on the island of Crete. Over the next 2000 years the Mediterranean would be home to two of the world's great civilizations. This unit begins by tracing the rise of the Greek city-states. Throughout the history of Greece the triumph of the Greek spirit is evident in sport, art, architecture and philosophy. Despite their numerous cultural successes, politically the Greeks were unsuccessful at attempts to unite. The unity of Greece was to remain elusive until the time of Philip of Macedon.

In the concluding two chapters of this unit the rise and decline of the Roman Empire is traced from its humble beginnings on the banks of the Tiber River to its vast empire spanning much of Europe. While the Greek influence pervades Roman culture, Roman civilization was much more than an extension of *Hellenism*. The *grandeur* of the Roman Empire was reflected in their practical yet often monumental achievements such as roads, aqueducts, the Colosseum, and the Circus Maximus. Of course no study of the Roman Empire would be complete without an examination of the rise of Christianity and its role in the latter part of the Empire.

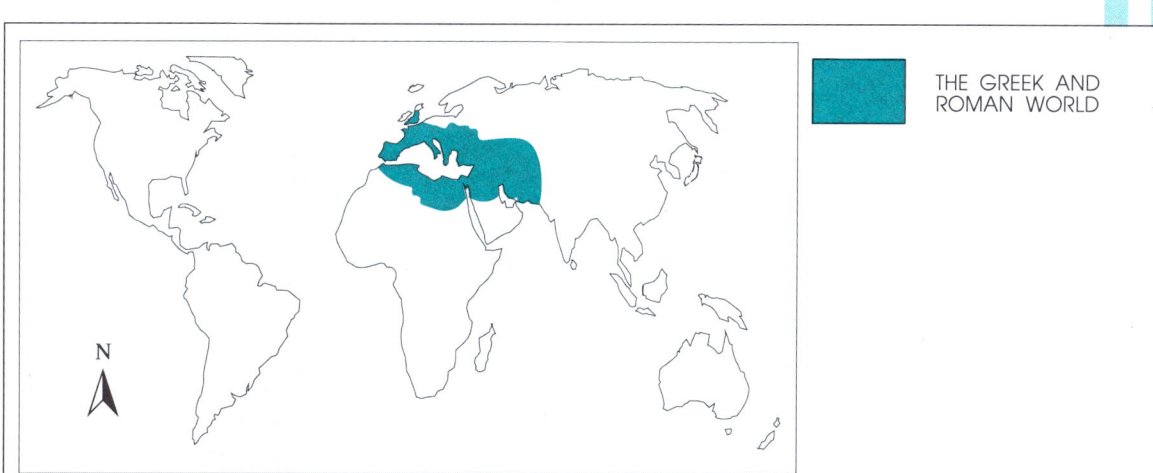

THE GREEK AND ROMAN WORLD

CHAPTER 6

The Rise of the Greeks

Chapter Highlights

- the legend of Theseus and the Minotaur

- the writings of Homer

- the beginning of the Olympic Games

- the first formal democracy

- the Marathon run

Herodotus is called the Father of History for his book describing the conflict between the Greeks and the Persian Empire (ca. 547–479 B.C.). The outcome of the conflict was crucial to the early development of European history and culture. Herodotus viewed the conflict as a struggle between West and East, between Europe and Asia, between the Greeks and those he called "barbarians," though he meant simply foreigners. He wrote:

> These are the Researches [Histories] of Herodotus of Halicarnassus set down to preserve the memory of the past, and to prevent the great and wonderful achievements of the Greeks and the "Barbarians" from losing their glory, and in particular to show how the two peoples came into conflict.
> Herodotus *Histories* I.i.

This chapter will look at the development of Greek civilization leading to the great Persian Wars. While Herodotus could only trace the legendary first disagreements between West and East in the lively myths of the Greeks, we now know that there were in fact two other civilizations in the area of Greece before the Classical Greeks. We call these two earlier civilizations **Minoan** and **Mycenaean** since we are still not sure what they called themselves.

Key Concepts

Minoans

Mycenaeans

Knossos

Theseus and the Minotaur

Heinrich Schliemann

Homer's Iliad *and* Odyssey

Olympic Games

democracy

ostracism

Xerxes

▼▼▼

The Minoans

A look at a map of the eastern Mediterranean shows that the island of Crete is the nearest significant European land mass to the old civilizations of Egypt and the Near East. Crete is a kind of stepping stone from the Near East to the European continent. It is, therefore, not surprising that given the agricultural wealth of the island, and the inhabitants' development of skills in navigating their ships, the people of Crete were the first Europeans to acquire the trappings of civilization. These trappings included a form of writing, a palace-based social organization, advanced metal working, and highly skilled forms of art. These appear about 2000 B.C., a thousand years later than in Egypt.

The island of Crete, about 200 km long and divided into segments by tall mountain ranges, enjoys a very pleasant, semi-tropical climate. When the first settlers sailed across to the island in the seventh millennium (7000–6000 B.C.), probably by island hopping from Asia Minor, they found a fertile, inviting home. They brought with them a rudimentary knowledge of farming, and over the centuries

City-States of Ancient Greece

they spread across the island, building their small villages, growing grain crops, pasturing sheep and goats, hunting and fishing to supplement their diet, and occasionally trading with their neighbours both on Crete and on the nearby islands. One important trade good was the volcanic glass called obsidian from the island of Melos, 135 km to the north. Obsidian could be used for knives, scrapers, and other tools to make life a little easier for these farmers.

After 3500 years of a Neolithic farming life on the island, a new element was introduced to the culture: the use of metal to make better tools and weapons. The metal of greatest importance was bronze, an alloy of nine parts copper to about one part tin. Its introduction had as profound an impact here as it did elsewhere in the ancient world, so that we mark its appearance by calling this early age of bronze on the island the Early Minoan period.

Early Minoan ca. 3200–2000 B.C.
Middle Minoan ca. 2000–1550 B.C.
Late Minoan ca. 1550–1100 B.C.

These chronological divisions were established by Sir Arthur Evans, and were meant to parallel the divisions of Egyptian history into Old, Middle, and New Kingdoms.

Copper was mined on Cyprus. Tin was rarer and more expensive, perhaps coming from as far as Afghanistan. Separately these metals were not much better than stone for tools, but combined they produced a tough, malleable metal with a reasonably low melting point. Bronze was ideal for producing sharp knives and spear points, tough saws, hard chisels, and many other implements.

Can you imagine the reaction of the Minoans to

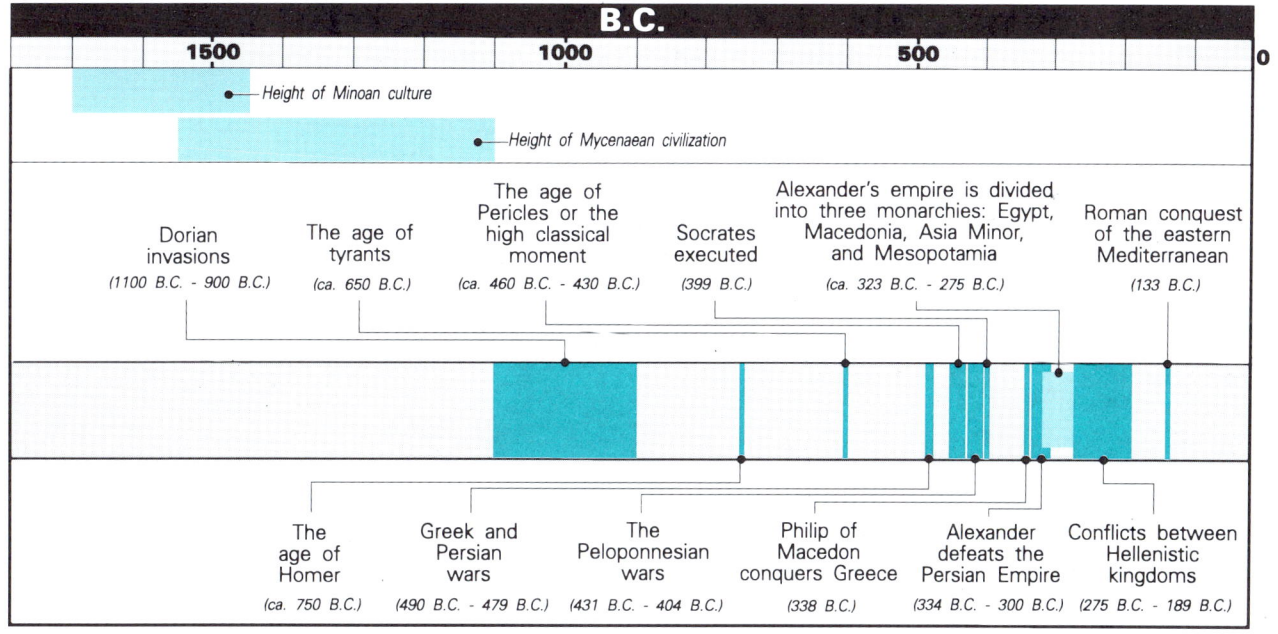

The Rise of the Greeks   CHAPTER 6

these new and expensive metal tools? Curiosity and skepticism as to their worth must have changed over the years to an acceptance and indeed a strong demand for them. But how did the Minoans pay for bronze since there was no such thing as money? They were farmers and Crete had no other valuable products to exchange for bronze except food. So began an economic cycle involving farmers who produced surplus food, traders, merchants, and metal workers. The economic cycle, and the resultant profits, would have stimulated the marketplace.

The process was quite a slow one, but over a thousand years the introduction of bronze brought about a much more complex society with greater class differentiation, more diverse skills and occupations, increased population, and the accumulation of wealth by a few people; perhaps ones already exerting political control over the masses. The archaeological evidence shows that wealthy people found ways to spend their wealth, building bigger and finer houses, which eventually became palaces. They had fine jewelry and clothing made for themselves, enjoyed works of art, and imported luxury products. To keep track of their wealth they developed first, a method to mark ownership of property using seals; second, a system of record keeping using hieroglyphic characters; and finally, a script that we call Linear A. Thus the first civilization appeared on the doorstep of Europe about 2000 B.C.

The Palaces

Knossos was always the site of the largest and most important palace on Crete. Together with the palaces of Phaestus and Mallia, it was also the oldest. Only three or four other buildings of a palace type have been found so far on the island. These palaces were certainly centres of political power and so Knossos must have been home to the most powerful monarch, king or queen, on the island. The palaces

The elaborate maze-like design of the Palace of Knossos may have inspired the labyrinth in the legend of Theseus and the Minotaur. Much of the palace was two or three storeys high, as shown above, and the downward tapering columns were a distinctive feature of Minoan architecture.

were also centres of exchange for the Minoan economy. The large storerooms for agricultural produce and other goods provide evidence of their role in the local economy.

The palaces are the most impressive buildings constructed by the Minoans. Dozens of interconnecting rectangular rooms on two, three, or more storeys are grouped around a large open courtyard in the centre of the palace. Various areas in the palace were used for different purposes: administrative, residential, religious, storage, and workshops. The finest rooms were decorated with colourful wall **frescoes** depicting processions of gift bearers, scenes of nature, lively ceremonies, or charging bulls. The builders' skill can be seen in the fine masonry, reinforcing wooden beams used to protect them from earthquakes, in the deep light wells (like elevator shafts) to bring air and light to the lower storeys, and in the advanced plumbing.

The earlier palaces were all destroyed at the same time, ca. 1625 B.C. It seems likely that a massive earthquake caused the catastrophe since all the palaces were rebuilt almost immediately, with no sign of any changes to their structure or decoration. Such earthquakes are still common in the Aegean area where the earth's **tectonic plates** collide: the African plate is pushed down by the European plate. It is at about this time that the volcanic eruption of Thera took place 120 km to the north of Crete. This eruption was sparked by a similar movement of the earth's plates.

The palaces were rebuilt as large and as fine as ever. The Minoan civilization continued for another 200 years with as much vigour as before. Then about 1450 B.C. the palaces were once again destroyed, all except Knossos. This time it was not a natural disaster but invaders, the Mycenaeans.

In 1939, Spyridon Marinatos first proposed the theory that there was a link between the Greek legend of the lost continent of Atlantis and the destruction of the Minoan palaces. Marinatos believed that Atlantis was in fact Crete, and that the Minoan palaces on Crete except for Knossos were destroyed in the eruption of the volcano on Thera. His excavations on Thera gave some support to the theory of the cataclysmic destruction of Minoan civilization. There was, however, always a troubling gap in time between the eruption, previously dated about 1500 B.C., and the fall of the Minoan palaces about 1450 B.C. Recent scholarly work suggests that the gap in time was more than 50 years, and the theory of a link between the eruption of Thera and the destruction of the palaces has been weakened.

The evidence is quite clear that new lords took over the rule at Knossos, the most convincing of which is that a new language was being written on the clay tablets keeping track of the palace goods. Linear B script, a form of writing derived from Linear A, was used to record the language of the

The centre of the island of Thera (modern day Santorini) blew out and then collapsed into the sea in an eruption which is now dated to 1628 B.C. In 1967, the ancient town of Akrotiri, which had been buried by volcanic ash, was remarkably well preserved. The excavations, shown here, continue to yield important information about Bronze Age Greece.

Greek-speaking Mycenaeans, not the non-Greek language of the Minoans. This brilliant discovery was made when a young Englishman, Michael Ventris, deciphered Linear B in 1952.

What form the invasion took, and what its initial purpose was, is impossible to say. The Minoans could not protect the shorelines of Crete with their navy, and their palaces lacked defensive walls, as they were not built with defense in mind. Knossos was captured and for a short time seems to have served as a kind of capital. Graves near Knossos contain the bodies and weapons of some of these lords. Then the palace at Knossos was destroyed by a great fire, on a day when the wind crossed the mountain from the south and whipped the flames into a frenzy. What caused the fire—an accident or attackers—is not known, but the Mycenaeans did not bother to rebuild Knossos since they could rule their Minoan subjects without palaces. Life on the island began reverting to its simpler past.

The Labyrinth

The art of the Minoans, particularly their wall paintings, has long suggested to us that the Minoans were a peaceful, nature-loving people. They delighted in flowers, birds, small animals, and marine scenes. There were no scenes of bloody battle, and few that showed violent action even in sport. The lack of weapons in their graves or fortifications around their palaces seems to confirm their peaceful nature. This view may still be correct, but there lurks a sinister element in the Minoan character.

The Classical Greeks preserved a myth about King Minos of Knossos. It told how the King's wife gave birth to a monster, half-man and half-bull, called the **Minotaur**. The dangerous Minotaur was imprisoned by the king in a maze-like structure built by Daedalus and called by the Greeks, the labyrinth. His food was young, unmarried men and women. King Minos forced the people of Athens to send seven young men and seven young women each year as a sacrifice for the Minotaur. This sad ritual continued annually until the young hero, **Theseus**, volunteered to go to Knossos as part of the sacrifice. With the help of King Minos's daughter, Ariadne, he killed the monster and found his way back out of the labyrinth following a string he had unwound on his way in.

Such a tale of human sacrifice seems out of character for the Minoans; however, in some Minoan art a very dangerous sport is depicted. In these scenes young men and women are shown leaping over the long, pointed horns of charging bulls. At times these acrobats are successful, at other times they are not. They are gored and severely injured. Perhaps there is an echo of the Minotaur myth in these scenes. This idea is strengthened by the palace of Knossos itself: its complex plan of rooms and corridors is comparable to a labyrinth. The word labyrinth may also be derived from *labrys* meaning a "double axe." It so happens that the double-axe symbol was found everywhere at Knossos carved into the blocks of the palace. Finally, as if to confirm the kernel of truth in the Minotaur myth, archaeologists in recent years have found the bones of two young boys in a basement room at Knossos dating ca. 1450 B.C. Marks on the boys' skeletons show that they were ritually sacrificed.

The Mycenaeans

Mainland Greece developed in the same way as Crete and at about the same pace until ca. 2200 B.C. Neolithic farming villages were scattered in the narrow valleys of Greece from ca. 6500 B.C. to 3000 B.C. Then as elsewhere around the Aegean, bronze appeared and slowly life changed. To mark the distinction of this culture from that on Crete, this era is called the Early Helladic period. Several large, carefully planned houses have been excavated by archaeologists showing the increased wealth of the period. They have found that people of this age were concerned about identifying personal property through the use of seals. But unlike Crete, this development was arrested by several waves of destruction, probably caused by invaders coming from the north into the Greek peninsula. By 2000 B.C., while the Minoans were building palaces for their monarchs, the peoples of the mainland had reverted to a poorer and simpler farming life.

Early Helladic ca. 3000–2000 B.C.
Middle Helladic ca. 2000–1550 B.C.
Mycenaean ca. 1550–1100 B.C.
Sub-mycenaean ca. 1100–1050 B.C.

There is no evidence as yet to show that the invaders from the north spoke Greek before they

Among the most famous entrance ways of antiquity are the Lion Gates of Mycenae. The two lions form the relieving triangle above the massive lintel of the main entrance to the ancient fortress. This gate must have been an inspiring welcome to the visitors of Mycenae.

came. Rather, the language may have developed after their arrival when the invaders and **indigenous** peoples began to integrate. What we do know is that the Mycenaeans, the descendants of these Middle Helladic peoples, spoke an early form of Greek.

During the sixteenth century B.C., a surprising change occurred in Greece, or so it seems from the evidence first revealed by **Heinrich Schliemann**. A very powerful and very wealthy civilization sprang out of the simple farming life of the previous few centuries. What caused this sudden transformation is still not well understood, but it is so noticeable and important that the new culture is called Mycenaean rather than Late Helladic. The name comes from the chief political centre of this culture, Mycenae.

Heinrich Schliemann did not know what he had found when he uncovered the fabulously wealthy shaft graves at Mycenae in the fall of 1876. He thought he had discovered the graves of King Agamemnon and his family, and so confirmed for the second time, after first digging at Troy, that **Homer's epics**, the **Iliad** and the **Odyssey**, were true stories. These two poems describe the adventures of Greek heroes who took part in the Trojan War about four hundred and fifty years before Homer's own time, that is, ca. 1200 B.C. The myth about Agamemnon of Mycenae, leader of the Greek army at Troy, is that after being victorious in war he returned home and was murdered by his wife. In those early days of Bronze Age archaeology, Schliemann could not know that the graves he found belonged to the royal family of Mycenae some 300 years before the Trojan War. Much more digging by other archaeologists, including the discovery of a second grave circle nearby, has put the shaft graves into their proper context. The wonderful gold funeral masks, inlaid bronze daggers, faience-style pottery and other exquisite objects of gold, silver, and ivory, are witnesses to a powerful civilization appearing in Greece ca. 1550 B.C.

Mycenaean kings lived like feudal lords, each governing his own wide area of Greece from a well fortified palace. All of them may have owed some allegiance to the king of Mycenae, since indications from the tombs and the walls of the city certainly point to Mycenae being the most powerful of the peninsula states. The wealth of these kings probably came from trade, particularly in metals, from piracy,

This painting of the Queen's Hall in the Palace of Knossos shows the elaborate and spacious interior design of a Minoan palace. The scroll and dolphin motifs were quite popular among the Minoans.

a noble profession in those days, and their own control over the subject peoples of their realms.

In their first two centuries the Mycenaeans were strongly influenced by the older Minoan civilization to the south. This is especially seen in Mycenaean arts and crafts. The Mycenaeans developed their script, Linear B, from the Minoans' Linear A as well as adopting the art of wall painting, styles of dress, types of vases, seal carving, and many other things. After Crete was invaded and the palaces destroyed, Minoan influence diminished.

Mycenae's buildings were impressive and later Greeks believed that only the one-eyed giants, the Cyclopes, could have lifted the stones of these great citadel walls into place. The later Mycenaean royal tombs are equally impressive. They had the shape of a bee-hive or of a stubby artillery shell standing on end. They attained a height of up to 13 m. To build these tombs, mammoth chambers were cut out of the hillside and encircled with fine masonry. Each ring of stone blocks was a little narrower than the one below till a single capping stone could close the opening. A great doorway was left with a roadway leading to it. To span the doorway, two or three huge blocks were moved into place. One of these blocks is 9 m long, 5 m wide, and 1.2 m high, and weighs about 120 t. Bronze doors were fixed on hinges to close the opening. The burial goods inside these round tombs have almost all been located by grave robbers since the tombs were so easy to find. The shaft graves, deep trenches cut into the ground, were well-hidden and relatively intact when excavated.

The Trojan War

> Sing of the building of the horse of wood, which Epeius made with Athena's help, the horse which once Odysseus led up into the citadel as a thing of guile, when he had filled it with the men who sacked Troy.
> Homer *Odyssey* VIII. 492–495.

The Trojan horse and the expression, "beware of Greeks bearing gifts," have come down to us today as a symbol of clever deceit. Despite the fame accorded to the Trojan horse in later western culture, little information about the horse is preserved in early Greek literature and only the brief reference cited above appears in Homer's *Odyssey*. The Trojan War itself, despite Homer's long epics about it, is still a vague event in Mycenaean history. According to the careful excavations of Carl Blegen, Level VIIa at Troy was destroyed in a battle ca. 1240 B.C. At that time the city was in reality just a fortified town; just over two hectares in size and rather poor in its standard of life. No wonder some scholars hypothesize the war was a dispute over fishing rights or control of the Hellespont's shipping, rather than the great conflict of West versus East which later Greeks considered it. Whatever the true nature of the Trojan War, the Mycenaean Greeks were soon to experience an equally grim fate. By about 1200 B.C. all of the citadels, with the exception of Mycenae itself, were captured and destroyed. Mycenae withstood attacks for almost a hundred years, but despite strong walls and special underground water supplies, Mycenae's fate was sealed.

The elaborate feudal bureaucracy, the fine Mycenaean building techniques and craftsmanship, and the complex system of record keeping by scribes quickly vanished. The glue binding the fabric of Mycenaean civilization together dissolved. What caused this unexpected calamity is not known. The Mycenaeans were near the height of their powers. However, similar disasters were occurring to the Hittites in Asia Minor and to peoples in the Near East, including the Egyptians, at this very time. Invaders from abroad, civil unrest, possibly drought, famine, and disease contributed to the events. Refugees with their salvaged belongings took to the roads and seaways. Many from the Peloponnesus, the southern peninsula of Greece, gathered in Athens before going on to new homes on islands in the Aegean and on the east coast of Asia Minor. It has been estimated that over a fifty-year period, ca. 1100–1050 B.C., the population in Greece declined by 75 percent or more. Many thousands of lives were lost; for the survivors, life reverted to subsistence levels, farming a few hectares, pasturing some sheep or goats, working to provide enough for one's family. The Mycenaean world ended as suddenly as it had begun, and a dark age descended on Greece.

Geography and Climate

> Our country is closed in, all mountains that have the low sky for a roof day and night…When we go down to the harbors on Sunday to breathe we see, lit in the sunset, the broken planks from voyages that never ended, bodies that no longer know how to love.[1]

It is time to pause a moment and consider in what kind of land the Greeks made their homes. Flying into Athens today, a summer visitor would be struck by three things: the tall-grey mountains, the clear-blue sky, and the deep-blue sea. The mountains are everywhere, rocky heights that isolate one valley from another and one small cultivated area from its neighbour. They act less as real barriers than they do as partitions. They trap the fall and winter rains,

---

[1] George Seferis, Collected Poems 1924–1955, trans. F. Keeley and P. Sherrard, (New Jersey: Princeton University Press, 1967).

LITERATURE

EARLY LITERATURE OF ANCIENT GREECE:
HOMER'S ODYSSEY AND AESOP'S FABLES

The earliest form of Greek literature was the epic poem. The epic was a narrative poem sung by bards who had to memorize thousands of lines. These narratives, which were of a lofty and serious nature, often revolved around the heroic exploits of a central figure whose actions determined the fate of entire cities, tribes, or nations. The epic poems, many of which were composed during the Dark Ages of Greece, were tales based on actual historical events which had been embellished to capture the glories of ages past. Not all of the early literature of Greece was so aristocratic and high-minded. A rich tradition of folk wisdom which was passed from generation to generation also made up a large body of early Greek literature. These stories were handed down in the form of fables and parables which contained both human and animal characters and usually contained a moral. The two men who best exemplify these two genres of early Greek literature were Homer and Aesop.

Homer was an Ionian Greek believed to be from the island of Chios. He is thought to have lived during the eighth century B.C. and was a professional bard who earned a living by composing poems which he recited on his travels. His most famous epic poems, the *Iliad* and the *Odyssey*, capture the essence of all Greeks not just those of a particular city. The excerpt below recounts the famous meeting of Odysseus and his men with the Cyclopes.

Aesop was a sixth-century slave from the Aegean island of Samos. Little is known of his life except for the fact that he was murdered by inhabitants of the holy city of Delphi. He is best remembered for his fables, which provided brief anecdotes of a single event and were designed to teach a moral. Unlike the language of the Homeric epics the Aesopic fables are simple and concise. The selections below illustrate Aesop's use of both humans and animals to convey his message.

Odysseus Meets the Cyclopes from Homer's *Odyssey*

We looked across at the land of the Cyclopes and they were near by, and we saw their smoke and heard sheep and goats bleating....when we had arrived at the place...we saw the cave, close to the water, high, and overgrown with laurels....Inside there lodged a monster of a man...he was a monstrous won-

provide pasturage for animals, yield highly-prized Greek marble, and keep apart a nation by dividing it into small units.

The sea provides a special blessing. While the mountains hinder communication and transportation between communities, the sea is a vast blue highway linking every part of the country and bringing it together. At no point in central or southern Greece is the sea more than 60 km away. This highway extends well beyond the bounds of the Greek nation, stretching hundreds of kilometres in all directions, and joins the Greeks with all the nations der made to behold, not like a man...but more like a wooded peak of the high mountains seen standing away from the others....Lightly we made our way to the cave, but we did not find him there, he was off herding on the range with his fat flocks. We went inside the cave and admired everything inside it....But after he had briskly done all his chores and finished, at last he lit the fire, and saw us, and asked us a question: "Strangers, who are you? From where do you come sailing over the watery ways?"...So I spoke, but he in pitiless spirit answered nothing, but sprang up and reached for my companions...There we built a fire and made sacrifice, and helping ourselves to the cheeses we ate and sat waiting for him inside, until he came home from his herding. He carried a heavy load of dried-out wood, to make a fire for his dinner, and threw it down inside the cave, making a terrible crash, so in fear we scuttled away into the cave's corners. But when the Cyclopes had filled his enormous stomach, feeding on human flesh and drinking down milk unmixed with water, he lay down to sleep in the cave sprawled out through his sheep.

Aesop's Fables

THE DOG AND THE REFLECTION

It happened that a Dog had got a piece of meat and was carrying it home in his mouth to eat it in peace. Now on his way home he had to cross a plank lying across a running brook. As he crossed, he looked down and saw his own reflection in the water beneath. Thinking it was another dog with another piece of meat, he made up his mind to have that also. So he made a snap at the image in the water, but as he opened his mouth the piece of meat fell out, dropped into the water and was never seen more.

Beware lest you lose the substance by grasping at the reflection.

THE OLD MAN AND DEATH

An old labourer, bent double with age and toil, was gathering sticks in a forest. At last he grew so tired and hopeless that he threw down the bundle of sticks, and cried out: "I cannot bear this life any longer. Ah, I wish Death would only come and take me!"

As he spoke, Death, a grisly skeleton, appeared and said to him: "What wouldst thou, Mortal? I heard thee call me."

Please sir," replied the woodcutter, "would you kindly help me to lift this bundle of sticks on to my shoulder?"

We would often be sorry if our wishes were gratified.

of the Mediterranean. The peoples of Greece have been forced by their geography to the sea and have been sailors since at least 7000 B.C. These sailors brought home with them ideas and wealth from abroad, giving their culture a special advantage.

The Dark Ages

One group of people who helped fill the vacuum left by the Mycenaean collapse, if not being one of the causes of the collapse, were the Dorians. These people, speaking a new dialect of Greek, came down from the northwest and settled in the Peloponnesus, defeating the local inhabitants, displacing them, or in some cases perhaps enslaving them. From the Peloponnesus, the Dorians sailed across the southern Aegean to take the islands of Melos, Thera, Crete, Rhodes, and Cos among others. A similar migration of Ionian Greeks occurred after the Mycenaean collapse. As refugees from Athens, they settled the central islands of the Aegean; Paros, Naxos, Samos, Chios, and others, as well as an important stretch of the Asia Minor coast from Clazomenae to Ephesus to Miletus. The third migration started in central Greece. The Aeolian Greeks sailed first to the island of Lesbos and after settling it, they moved across to the coast and began farming from Assos to Smyrna.

There was a period of recuperation lasting about three hundred and fifty years during which the various groups of Greeks settled into their new homes, established new sanctuaries for their gods, farmed their new land, and built secure communities. Beyond vague notions of what life was like or what political changes were occurring, we know very little about this period. Writing was entirely lost with the disappearance of Mycenaean civilization because there was no longer a flourishing trade to document. There are absolutely no written documents from this period, nor did the later Greeks preserve information about it in their collective memory. For this reason the period is called the Dark Age of Greece. The Greeks forgot the present, but they did remember their Mycenaean past as if it were an age of heroes, of supermen, like Heracles (Hercules), Hector, Jason, and Achilles.

Wandering minstrels moved from village to village. Finding the houses of the local nobles they would sing their tales of past glories and daring in exchange for a bed, meal, and small gift. After centuries of the oral repetition of these tales and of course the constant embroidering of them, the bard Homer finally came to compose in writing his great epic poems. These poems are now often dated ca. 750 B.C. for the *Iliad* and ca. 725 B.C. for the *Odyssey*.

Several very significant developments mark the end of the Dark Age in Greece and point to the blossoming of a great new culture. One is the appearance of a new national literature, epitomized by Homer's work. This literature not only provided the Greeks with a glorious past, whether real or imagined, but also gave them a common view of their gods, in a way like a national religion. A second development was that the Greeks began sailing beyond the Aegean Sea for purposes of trade. Their first destinations were in the eastern Mediterranean, probably exchanging food for finished products. More important than the objects they bought were the skills they learned: ship-building techniques; metal working, including the smelting of a new metal—iron; and not least, the alphabet. The alphabet we use today for English and many other languages came from the Greeks by way of the Romans. The Greeks in turn had learned it from the Phoenicians. The new script had only 27 letters, and for the first time was easy enough for almost anyone to learn.

Soon after their voyages to the east began, the Greeks also began sailing westward. Establishing contacts and settlements in Italy they gained access to the iron and other metals found to the north of Rome. This led to the third development. The trading expeditions exposed the Greeks to the rich agricultural lands available for settlement in Italy, Sicily, and other Mediterranean coastal areas. Pressure was building in Greece to find better land; the trickle of colonizing groups soon became a flood. Hundreds of Greek colonies were established over a 200-year period, making much of the coasts of the Mediterranean and Black Sea an extension of the Greek homeland.

A fourth development, the **Olympic Games**, though minor at first, became increasingly important in time. The first Olympic Games, in honour of the god Zeus, were established ca. 776 B.C. This is the first firm date we have in Greek history, the starting point from which later Greeks marked their own passing of time. The Olympic festival was one of four athletic Games that drew competitors and spectators from every corner of the Greek world and acted to unite a Greek nation which was otherwise divided by tall mountains and long expanses of sea. Since the prizes at these four prestigious festivals were crowns of branches, they were called Crown

SPORTS AND LEISURE

The Olympic Games
Past and Present

When the modern Olympic movement was started it was hoped that the spirit of the ancient Greek games could be revived. In ancient Greece the Panhellenic (all-Greek) Games were considered so important that they managed to unite for the duration of the events, the usually fragmented city-states. A sacred truce was declared whenever such competitions were held so as to protect travellers going to and from the games. Participation in the Games were limited to free-born Greeks and those who competed did so in the true spirit of competition, perhaps seeking fame and honour but certainly not fortune.

A Spartan woman of royal blood, named Kyniska, was the first woman to win an event at the ancient Olympic Games. Married women were banned from Olympia during the Games on pain of death, but she twice entered a 4-horse chariot team (ca. 396 and 392 B.C.) and won. Since she was the owner of the winning team, although not the driver, she was awarded the wreath and the right to erect a statue of herself at Olympia. But she was never able to see her team win, nor pick up the wreath.

The Modern Olympic Movement

Our own modern Olympic Games were established in 1896 by the work of a Frenchman, Baron Pierre de Coubertin. He wanted to revive international athletic competition under the same high ideals which he believed existed in the ancient Olympic Games. The Greek games at Olympia began in 776 B.C. and continued until A.D. 393 when the Roman emperor Theodosius I, a Christian, ordered all pagan sanctuaries closed. One of the events introduced to the new games by its founder Coubertin was the Marathon race. The story which was the inspiration for this race was of a messenger who ran all the way to Sparta and back before the Battle of Marathon. The same runner ran from Marathon to Athens after the battle to announce the victory. He is supposed to have arrived at the Council House, spoken the words, "We have won! Rejoice!" and to have died on the spot from exhaustion. The truth is that there was never an ancient marathon race.

To what degree has the modern Olympic movement managed to capture the spirit of the ancient Games? What problems have existed in today's Olympic Games? If you were a member of the International Olympic Committee (I.O.C.) what changes would you make?

PANHELLENIC GAMES

Games	Site	Held	God	Prize
Olympics	Olympia	Every 4 years	Zeus	Olive wreath
Pythia	Delphi	Every 4 years	Apollo	Laurel wreath
Isthmian	Isthmia	Every 2 years	Poseidon	Pine wreath
Nemean	Nemea	Every 2 years	Zeus	Wild celery

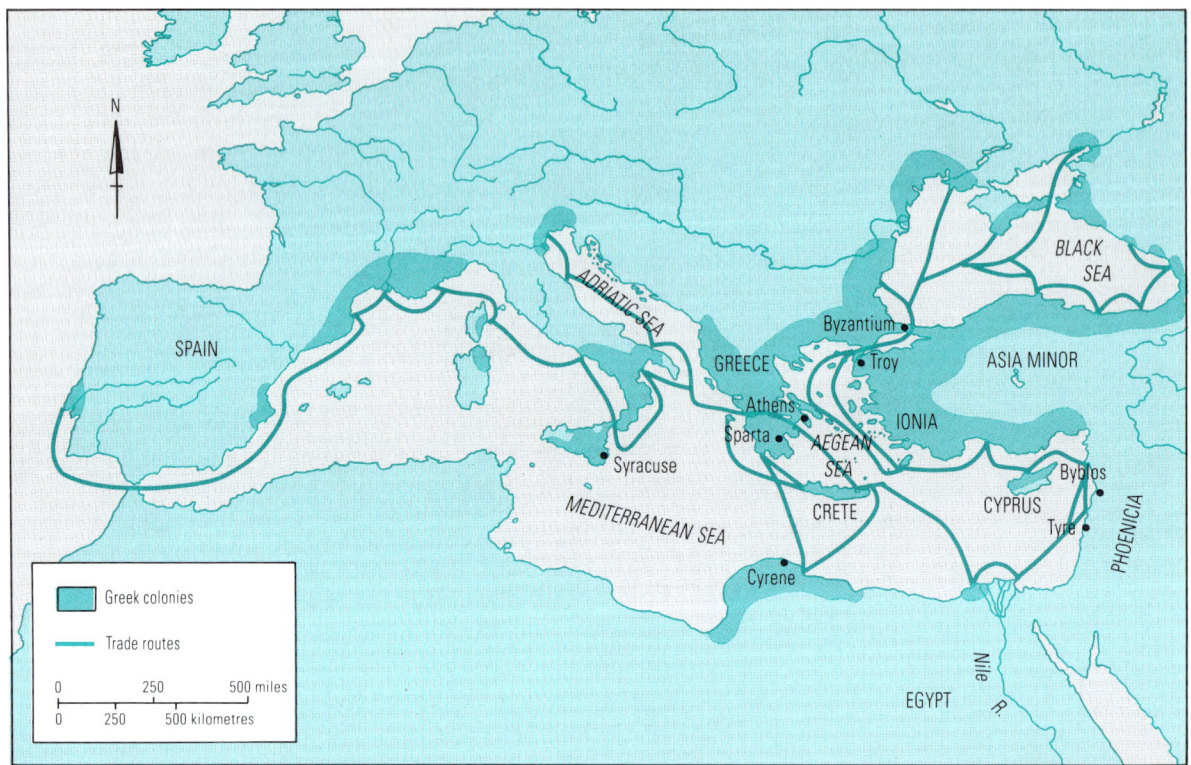

Greek Colonies 700–500 B.C.

From World History: Traditions and New Directions by Peter N. Stearns, Donald R. Schwartz, Barry K. Beyer, © 1989 by Addison-Wesley Publishing Company, Inc.

Games. There were some 300 other local athletic games around Greece where winners received very valuable rewards. These were called Prize Games.

Colonization

The problems suffered by the Greeks in their homeland included a lack of good land for new farms (especially as the population increased), fighting between aristocratic groups within the Greek states, and drought leading to famine. A ready solution for these problems was to send groups of settlers overseas to the new lands being explored by Greek ship captains on their trading voyages.

Towns in Greece wishing to establish independent colonies often consulted the **oracle** of Apollo at Delphi (an ancient temple) for information about the new lands. Then with the oracle's blessing, they organized a group of several hundred men, equipped them with ships, all the tools and equipment they would need—an expensive undertaking in itself—and with due religious rites and promises of further help, the excited, anxious colonists would sail away. We do not know whether women and children accompanied these expeditions or whether they came later. We do know that many Greek men took native wives, but there must have been many more who brought Greek wives to the new colony.

Once they had arrived at their destination, the

colonists chose the best location for their new town; usually a harbour site. Besides the countless tasks of dividing the land, planting the first crops, and building their homes, the colonists also had to contend with the native people whose land they were taking. The colonists of Cyrene, for example, were often helped by the native Libyans, but there were also bitter wars. According to Herodotus, 7000 Greeks were killed by the Libyans in one battle. The number of dead sounds unbelievably high but it points out the seriousness of the problem.

Greek Government

The Age of Tyrants. **Democracy** is just one of many political systems invented by humans in order to govern their communities. The Greeks were the first people to develop a formal democratic system by which the people governed themselves through voting procedures. The word democracy comes from two Greek words, *demos*, "the people" and *kratos*, "the rule" or "power". Democracy was not invented easily, it was arrived at after a long, painful process of adjustment after other systems of government were tried and found deficient.

The early Greek states were centred around a main town in a valley. The normal system of rule in these states was a monarchy, government by a king. Each king acted as the chief judge, chief priest, and chief general of his state. These kings, however, did not have absolute power—nor was their power passed on to their sons necessarily. A king's authority was limited by the rights and powers of a small, close-knit group of aristocrats who acted as councillors to the king. The kings regularly mingled with the people and so their habits and faults, not to mention those of their close relatives, were well known to everyone. The king would have been seen to be on the same level as his subjects.

During the Dark Age of Greece many of the kings of the small Greek states lost some, or all, of their powers to other members of the royal family, or even to members of the noble families around the king. Priesthoods, leadership positions in the army, even rights to hear court cases became the functions of the aristocrats. Rule by the aristocratic families replaced monarchy in some Greek states. This form of government is called an oligarchy, meaning rule by a few, and is derived from the Greek words *oligoi*, "the few" and *arch*, to "rule." This step, however, did nothing to satisfy the grumblings of other Greeks who were now just beginning to be heard. Hesiod, a poet who follows Homer, ca. 700 B.C., complained about the judicial system run by aristocrats in his home area:

> O Perses,...We split our property in half, but you
> Grabbed at the larger part and praised to heaven
> The lords who love to try a case like that,
> Eaters of bribes. The fools!
> Hesiod *Works and Days*, 27–42.

The arbitrary administration of unwritten laws was just one concern. The power held by certain aristocrats and not by others provoked dissent; as did the lack of a voice in government by wealthy men of non-aristocratic background. Poor Greeks suffered from the loss of land and property and even enslavement for debts owed to the wealthy nobles. The aristocrats maintained their power as long as they were the military backbone of the state. Down to the early seventh century, fighting depended on heavily-armed, individual warriors backed up by lightly-armed supporters. Only the wealthy aristocratic families could afford the necessary arms and armour for this style of warfare.

This all changed in the period ca. 675–650 B.C. A new style of warfare was introduced that depended on the unified movement of large numbers of warriors. This is called *hoplite* warfare. Hoplites were heavily-armed warriors carrying large round shields with shin protectors, helmets, and body armour.

They fought with heavy spears which they thrust, not threw. By standing shoulder to shoulder, eight lines deep, and maintaining their places in the lines, they found that they could easily defeat the old style of fighting. Numbers were crucial to prevent the hoplite lines from being rounded and attacked from behind. As there were not enough aristocrats to fill the new battle lines, any citizen who could afford the armour now stood shoulder to shoulder with the nobles. The strategic importance of these new fighters soon led them to demand more political power.

People in control of a government do not easily surrender their power. The force required to seize power often leads to violence. In the richer Greek states near the Isthmus of Corinth a method was found to overthrow the aristocrats, and Corinth led the way. A man of noble blood, Cypselus, was excluded from the ruling circle of nobles at Corinth despite his ability and great ambition. He gathered a military force composed of the other discontented citizens and in 657 B.C. defeated and forced the ruling clan of nobles into exile. He took control of the government and began to rule for the benefit of the middle class people that supported him. A person who seized power unconstitutionally, whether for good or bad reasons, was called by the Greeks *tyrannos*, or tyrant.

Solon and Peisistratus. Athens avoided tyranny for many years, first, by giving in to demands for a written code of law 620 B.C., and second, by appointing a special *archon* in 594 B.C. to try to solve the continuing problems between aristocrats and common citizens. The archon was Solon, one of the famed Seven Sages of Greece. Solon brought in economic reforms and changes to the code of law to help relieve the debt and land problems of the poor. One such reform was to abolish the practice of selling debtors into slavery. When poor farmers had one or two bad crops in a row, they needed to borrow seed grain from wealthier land owners to plant again. To obtain the seed they would put their bodies up as security for the loan. If the next crop failed they could be sold into slavery for nonpayment of the debt.

Solon's political reforms were an important step on the road to democracy. The most significant reform was that all wealthy men, whether aristocrats or not, could run for the highest government offices. This way birth into an aristocratic family was not the only qualification for holding office.

Solon created a new institution, the Council of Four Hundred, who were elected annually. This council was comprised of 100 citizens from each of the 4 traditional tribes of Athens. This body met

The Greek hoplite was a lightly-armoured foot soldier who wore body armour over a short skirt. Greaves armour tailored to the legs much like shin pads extended high enough to protect the knees. The Greeks wore a variety of helmets which were elaborate in design and carried beautiful swords which had both edges sharpened.

regularly to prepare legislation for voting by the entire citizen Assembly, and also probably acted as a court of appeal from the judgements of the archons.

Many adults living in Athens, or in any of the Greek city-states for that matter, still had no political power at all. Athenian citizenship was restricted to males over the age of 18, whose parents were both free-born Athenians. This excluded women; slaves, who had no personal rights; and foreigners, who rarely acquired citizenship.

The man who eventually became tyrant of Athens was Peisistratus. He was an ambitious nobleman, famous for his military career, and actually attempted three times to become tyrant. His first attempt occurred about 561 B.C., the second, in the mid-550s B.C., and the third in 546 B.C. On the second try, he brashly selected a very tall, handsome woman named Phye from a village outside Athens, dressed her in the guise of Athena with armour and spear, and rode through the streets of Athens in a chariot proclaiming that the goddess had come to restore him to power in the city. Incredibly it worked, though it was doubtless helped by some strong supporters. On his third attempt, he defeated his opponents in battle and took the city. He ruled wisely and generously till his death in 527 B.C., handing over power to his son, Hippias.

Athenian Democracy. Hippias, the son of Peisistratus, continued the tyranny in Athens after his father's death, but eventually lost support. In 510 B.C. the Spartan army besieged Athens and when Hippias tried to smuggle the Peisistratid children out of the city, they were captured and used as hostages. This forced Hippias and his family to surrender and to go into exile. Athens was once again free to find new political solutions to its problems.

The solution was one proposed by Cleisthenes, a member of the noble Alcmaeonid family. It was a novel approach as it set aside the ancient division of Athenian citizens into four tribes, based on family and clan relations. Cleisthenes suggested an equitable division of citizens into ten new tribes. Each of the new tribes was given a cross section of citizens; about one-third came from the coastal areas, one-third from the city of Athens, and one-third from inland. Members living in Athens could easily attend meetings of the Assembly and new Council (it was a two-day walk to Athens from the farthest parts of Attica), and so it was important that each new tribe have the same geographical distribution of members.

Cleisthenes' reforms replaced the old Council of Four Hundred with a new Council of Five Hundred, with fifty members elected from each tribe. Not only did these 50 members take part in meetings of the full Council, but for one-tenth of the year they acted as the executive committee of the Council. The executive met daily to prepare the business of the Council, receive foreign embassies, and oversee the day-to-day work of the government. Each tribe also elected a military general, *strategos*, who would sit on a board of ten generals and lead the city in all its military affairs including battle actions. By 487 B.C. it was recognized that only the generals needed to be highly qualified officials and therefore be selected by voting. In truly democratic fashion, the other offices came to be filled by drawing lots. Any fit citizen could now hold these high offices.

Another novel measure was introduced in Cleisthenes' reforms, the famous practice called **ostracism**. This measure was meant to rid Athens of any citizen who might again try for tyranny. Ostracism allowed the state to send any citizen, along with his family, into exile for a period of ten years. Every year about January (the middle of the Athenian calendar year), the Assembly voted whether or not an ostracism was needed that year. If the Assembly decided to use the ostracism procedure, then about a month later, the special vote was taken. If a minimum of 6000 votes were cast, the person whose name appeared most often on the *ostraka*

BELIEFS

THE GODS OF GREECE

For many, one of the most enjoyable aspects of the study of ancient Greece is the mythology. Today we equate the myths of the Greek gods with falsehood and accept only that which can be proven empirically. To the ancients the gods were an essential part of their lives representing an array of emotions. Arianna Stassinopoulos, in her book *The Gods of Greece*, argues that we can still respond in a very profound way to the gods. Below is an excerpt from *The Gods of Greece* in which Stassinopoulos sets out her modern Greek perspective of the myths of ancient Greece.

The gods may have gone underground for centuries at a time but, like an underground river flowing through western culture, they have continued to send up springs and fountains inspiring, shaping and fertilizing the western imagination, even when it was suffocating in the dross of exclusive materialism.

And we can still respond to the gods and goddesses, nymphs and heroes, of ancient Greece at some profound, obscure level of our imagination because they correspond to realities within ourselves and point to realities beyond themselves long before we have interpreted and understood them. When we look at the gods through the prism of the age of reason we miss their symbolic significance for our lives. We still have the magnificence of the stories, but we lose the living truth they spring from....

The whole of Greek mythology comes alive when we see the

(potsherds used as ballots) was sent into exile. The first ostracism occurred in 487 B.C.; the last was held 70 years later.

Sparta

The Spartans as warriors struck fear in the hearts of all other Greeks. It was a hard and fairly won reputation. Despite their relatively small numbers, perhaps 5000 full Spartan warriors in good times, this city-state enjoyed a position of leadership among the Greek states for about three centuries. But the price paid for this position was a high one.

When other city-states suffered from a lack of land in the eighth century and looked to sending the excess population overseas to settle, the Spartans took a different course. In a long war against the Messenians, neighbours to the west, Sparta was able to beat Messenia and win a large new piece of territory. The defeated people were made serfs, joining the previously conquered Helots of Laconia as virtual slaves to the land. To prevent an uprising of these Helots who far outnumbered them, the Spartans were forced to take special precautionary measures. This is one of the reasons for the very different development of Spartan society and life.

Family life for boys ended at the age of seven as harsh military training and rugged barracks life took over. A formal system of group training for all Spartan boys forced them to withstand pain without complaint, be unquestioningly obedient to their leaders, be cunning when called for, and above all never to admit defeat. Spartan athletes eventually had to withdraw entirely from the brutal, combat

> Greek gods and goddesses not as beings external to ourselves but as parts of our own inner pantheon. When we recognize the psychological forces personified in the gods, we see them for what they are: not self-conscious poetic fancies, but universal images that compel us to attune to the "mythic" unity—the pattern and wholeness underlying the fragmentary moments, decisions, and events of everyday life.
>
> The myths....'are no longer stories in an illustrated book. We are those stories, and we illustrate them with our lives'...It is through our conflicts, dilemmas and anxieties, as well as through our joys and accomplishments, that the gods enter our lives and become real. Being a wife, bearing a daughter, experiencing jealousy, aggression or sexual passion—these are all everyday mysteries that we take for granted but which the myths of Hera or Demeter, Aphrodite or Ares, help us enter more deeply and understand more fully, more consciously, and more symbolically.
>
> To test Stassinopoulos' theory regarding the relevance of the Greek myths to our lives research one of the gods listed below. When doing your research try to determine what universal theme is represented by the god studied and try to apply this theme to an aspect of modern life.
>
> | | | | | |
> |---|---|---|---|---|
> | **Zeus** | **Hera** | **Ares** | **Athena** | **Poseidon** |
> | **Aphrodite** | **Hades** | **Dionysos** | **Hermes** | **Hephaistos** |
> | **Artemis** | **Hestia** | **Demeter** | **Apollo** | |

sports at the Olympics since they could not admit defeat even when they were hopelessly beaten and faced serious injury.

By age 20 the young men were put in the front ranks of the army, though training continued for ten more years. By 30 years of age, Spartan men became full citizens, could vote in the Assembly and hold office, marry, have a house and be given an estate worked by Helots. Military service, however, continued for many more years.

There was a third group in Spartan society besides the Spartans and the Helots. The men of this group had much the same training as the Spartans, but they did not have citizen rights. These were the Perioikoi ("dwellers about"). The Perioikoi were free men with their own estates, or trades. They had no vote, but were loyal to the Spartans and when called upon, fought bravely on the battlefield with them.

The Spartan government was unusual in having two kings who ruled equally. This system provided a strong check on the powers of the monarchy since one king could oppose the power of the other. Advising the kings was a council of elders, 28 men over the age of 60 who belonged to the Spartan aristocracy. This body alone could present legislation to the Assembly for approval. The Assembly could not initiate legislation, nor could it even discuss the legislation. The Council of Elders would explain the legislation to the Assembly and even give opposing views, but then the Assembly had to vote in favour or against it. Its decision was final. As a kind of safety valve for the common citizens, a new institution, called the Ephorate, was created. This consisted of five men who were elected by the Assembly to hold office for one year. It soon took a leading role in running Spartan affairs.

The Spartan system was rigidly conservative in order to protect against a revolt of the Helots, as occasionally happened. At birth, babies were exposed to die if they were not healthy; as boys, they were sometimes brutally beaten and whipped; as young men, they were put in the front ranks of the army; at 30 the survivors could look forward to a simple family life with no luxuries or wealth. It is ironic that women in Sparta enjoyed more freedom and privileges than anywhere in Greece. As girls, they were encouraged to take part in sports to develop healthy bodies so they could have healthy children. They were given training in music and dance like the boys, and allowed great independence. When they reached adulthood, they had property rights and rights within the marriage.

The Persian Wars

Compared with the huge empires of the Near East, such as Egypt, Assyria, Babylonia, and Persia, the Greek city-states were tiny. Even a coalition that included every Greek town only equalled a fraction of the size of one of these eastern powers. The fact that the Greek states weakened themselves by fighting each other, and rarely agreed on anything long enough to act in unison, made defence against a mighty empire appear impossible. However, Greek soldiers were tough, their battle tactics and weapons better than anyone's, and they found good leaders among the Spartans and Athenians when they needed them. The rise of the greatest of all Near Eastern empires, the Persians, put Greek freedom in perilous danger. The development of civilization in Europe hung in the balance as Greeks faced their greatest trial—war with Persia.

The empire of the Medes and Persians had expanded northward toward the Greeks in the early sixth century, but was stopped by the wealthy power of the Lydians in central Asia Minor. The Lydians fought the Medes and Persians at the Halys River, but the battle was stopped by an eclipse of the sun. This eclipse (probably on May 28, 585 B.C.) was supposedly predicted by the first Greek scientist, Thales of Miletus.

In 559 B.C., a great king and general ascended to the throne of Persia: Cyrus the Great. He gained power over the Medes, and with his combined forces he continued to expand the Persian Empire. It already stretched from Afghanistan in the east to the shores of the Mediterranean in the west. A chance to expand further occurred when Croesus decided to attack Cyrus across the old boundary between the two empires in 546 B.C. An oracle from Delphi, we are told, predicted that "if Croesus crossed the Halys, he would destroy a mighty empire." Little did Croesus think that it would be his own.

The fall of Sardis, capital of Lydia, brought the eastern Greek states face to face with the barbarians (Persians). They tried to get favourable peace terms, but could not. Then they tried to fight, but were not able to unite against the invader. So they surrendered and accepted their fate, a loss of freedom and forced service in the Persian armed forces.

The Greek governor of Miletus, Aristagoras, finally stirred up a revolt among the eastern states in 499 B.C. These states called for help from the other Greeks across the Aegean but got only 20 warships from Athens and 5 from Eretria. They attacked and burned Sardis, the Persian governor's capital, but then they retreated and fought to defend their homeland. A naval battle off Miletus in 494 B.C. spelled the end of the Ionian revolt. The Persians soon destroyed Miletus, killed many of the men, and sent the rest of the Milesians into exile 2000 km away at the mouth of the Tigris River.

Marathon

The Ionian Revolt was the spark that brought the Persian king back to the Aegean. Many wealthy Greek cities already belonged to King Darius's Empire, but there were so many more just on the other side of the sea. The deposed tyrant of Athens, Hippias, had long begged the Persians to restore him to power and now Darius had cause for revenge

The Persian Invasions of Greece

against Athens and Eretria.

In 490 B.C. Darius sent a fleet with about 20 000 soldiers to punish these two cities. First Eretria, after a six-day siege, was betrayed to his army. The gates opened and his force burned and plundered the city. Then with old Hippias as their guide, the Persian fleet sailed south from Eretria to the eastern coast of Attica where a sheltered beach and small plain provided a perfect base for the Persian army. The plain was called Marathon.

The Athenians sent a professional messenger ("all-day runner") to Sparta 250 km away pleading for help. He returned about 4 days later saying that the Spartans could only come after the full moon, still a week or more away. So the Athenian citizen army of 9000 warriors went to Marathon alone to meet the Persians. Before long their only help arrived, about a thousand men from Plataea, their close neighbours to the north.

In their camp in the hills above Marathon, the ten Athenian commanders debated what to do. Democratically, they voted on how to proceed. It was close, but one of the generals, Miltiades, convinced them to attack. This was a dangerous decision because a loss would leave the road to Athens unprotected; however, it proved to be the right choice. It gained Miltiades and the Athenians everlasting glory.

The Greeks in their [heavy armour] charged the Persians on the run, catching them off guard. Despite the Persians' two-to-one advantage in infantry the Greeks defeated the two wings of the Persian army and surrounded the central part. Amidst the confusion, and as they fled to their ships, the Persians were cut down. Herodotus says 6400 Persians were killed; only 192 Athenians died. The burial mound of the Plataeans killed in the battle has yielded less than a dozen bodies, including a young boy, perhaps their piper. Thus the Persian threat was beaten back, but the empire was far from destroyed.

Thermopylae

The victory at Marathon provided the Mainland Greeks with a ten year period of grace from further Persian attacks. Finally in 480 B.C., the Persian king, **Xerxes**, who succeeded Darius, crossed the Hellespont on twin bridges of boats held together by cables as thick as a man's torso, made of linen and papyrus. Once in Europe he counted his troops. Herodotus says that the infantry alone numbered 1.7 million men, and that with the fleet, cavalry, other contingents, and camp attendants over 5 million people were with the expedition. The figure is grossly inflated, as is common with ancient accounts of war. A conservative estimate is 200 000 men in Xerxes'

PRIMARY DOCUMENT

HERODOTUS

Born about 484 B.C. in Halicarnassus, an East Greek city under Persian rule, Herodotus may have been a merchant, since it is obvious from his book on the Persian Wars that he travelled extensively to Persia, Egypt, probably Libya, and the Black Sea area. Wherever he went, he heard stories about the people, their history, and the local customs. He recorded these wonderful tales, retelling them with the grace of the best storyteller. Eventually he moved to Athens where he recorded all the details about the Persian Wars, and especially the Athenian part in them. The Athenians gave him a large reward for his work, but they could not give him citizenship since he was a foreigner there. When Athens sent out a colony to Thurii in South Italy in 443 B.C., Herodotus joined the settlement. We have very few details of his life after this, but he seems to have lived until the 420s B.C. when his book was completed.

The excerpt below taken from *The History of the Persian Wars* is Herodotus' account of Darius' resolve to attack Greece after the initial failure of the Persians at Marathon.

When the message about the battle of Marathon came to King Darius, son of Hystaspes, greatly enraged as he already was against the Athenians because of their attack on Sardis, he was now even more full of wrath and more resolved to march upon Greece. So he sent forthwith, throughout the cities, messengers, bidding them provide a much greater force than before, and ships, horses, corn, and vessels. With these demands Asia was all of a flutter for three years, the best men being enrolled for service against Greece and getting ready. In the fourth year the Egyptians, who had been enslaved by Cambyses, revolted from Persia. So then Darius was even more set on making war, on both them and the Athenians.

Herodotus wrote from the vantage point of a Greek patriot. How does this excerpt reflect his bias? How does this description of the Persians' preparation for war serve to enhance the glory of the Greek victory which is to follow?

army, which is still an immense force for the time.

The Greeks had done little to prepare themselves for the new invasion. Athens, at least, on the advice of the great leader Themistocles, had used the money from a rich new strike of silver at its mines near Laurion to build a strong fleet of 200 ships. Many other Greeks, however, had already symbolically surrendered "earth and water" to the Persians, intending to accept Persian domination without resistance. But Athens and especially Sparta with its League of Peloponnesian states gathered for a congress at Corinth to plan their defence. Finally, the decision was made to defend the narrow pass in central Greece called Thermopylae (the Hot Gates), through which the Persians had to pass.

A small force of 4000 men led by King Leonidas of Sparta with his bodyguard of 300 was sent to hold the pass till the full Greek army arrived. This small force was backed by the Greek fleet just offshore. Their stand was heroic, but a local Greek shepherd turned traitor and showed Xerxes' frustrated forces a mountain path around Thermopylae. The Spartan king, Leonidas, and about a thousand Spartans and men from Thespiae who refused to escape the Persian trap died fighting. The epitaph of the 300 Spartans at the site reads:

> Go tell at Sparta, thou that passest by,
> That here obedient to her word, we lie.

The Persian army poured southward through Boeotia and into Attica. Most Athenians took to their ships and abandoned the city to Persian destruction. A few held out behind the wooden walls on the Acropolis, but Athens' real defense was the wooden walls of her ships. The Persians took revenge on the city for their earlier defeat at Marathon.

Salamis and Plataea

In September 480 B.C. the combined Greek fleet of over 300 **triremes** remained at Salamis, a large island just off the coast of Attica to the west of Athens. After much delay, the Persians, with about 600 ships, were finally enticed into the straits by false information (from Themistocles) that the Greek fleet was going to escape by night. The Persians divided their fleet to block both ends of the straits around the island, but they lost some of their numerical superiority by doing this. Rowing into the eastern end of the strait, the Persians led by ships from Phoenicia and east Greece were attacked by the swift, well-manned Greek triremes. Lack of space in the strait caused crowding when the invading ships pushed forward from behind; there was mass confusion among the invaders. Xerxes could only watch in despair from his throne placed high on a hill above the straits.

Aeschylus, a Greek writer who probably fought at Salamis, puts these words into the mouth of a Persian messenger in one of his plays:

> First, the torrent of our Persian fleet bore up; but when the press of shipping jammed there in the strait, then none could help another, but our ships fouled each other with their rams, and sheared away each other's banks of oars. But the Greek ships, skilfully handled, kept the outer station, and struck in; till hulls rolled over, and the sea itself was hidden, strewn with their wreckage, dyed with blood of men. The dead lay thick on all the reefs and beaches, and flight broke out, all order lost; and all our eastern ships rowed hard to get away.
> Aeschylus *The Persians*, 412–423

The battle was a severe loss for the Persians. Not only did it mean that an invasion of the Peloponnese by sea was impossible, but it also meant that the Greek fleet might sail to the Hellespont and destroy the bridge of boats, leaving the Persian army trapped far from home. Xerxes realised his precarious position. He decided to retreat from Greece himself, but leave behind his army under Mardonius.

In the new year (479 B.C.), Mardonius took up a position on the southern edge of the Boeotian plain near the town of Plataea. Here finally the full Greek land army, led by the Spartans, ventured to meet the barbarian host in an all-out battle. The Greeks won a great victory. Mardonius himself was killed and the vast Persian camp with its amazing wealth and luxury was captured. The remnants of the great invasion force hastily retreated out of Greece. The Greek navy followed up this victory at Plataea by attacking the Persians in Asia Minor and freeing the East Greeks.

Greek Culture

The great wars against Persia highlight the differences between the civilization developing in Greece and the older civilizations of the East. The Greeks beat back the eastern threat to their freedom and thereby won the opportunity to develop their own culture unencumbered by eastern influence. This paid great dividends in the coming centuries as the greatest Greek artists, writers, philosophers, and scientists began to explore their world in new ways and to new heights. But the Greeks were only ready for this great leap forward after they had absorbed many important ideas and influences from the East in the eighth and seventh centuries. At this time, Greek art and culture was so far behind the East that it was forced to catch up by accepting many of these eastern ideas. This period in Greek art is even called orientalizing because of the numerous eastern influences.

For Greek art, the opening up of Egypt to Greek merchants and travellers was very important. Here the Greeks observed huge statues carved in fine, hard stone, which they soon imitated in the finest, white marble of their homeland. They learned how to build great temples in stone after viewing the marvels of Karnak, Luxor, and other sites in Egypt. They began to appreciate the fine skills of drawing and use of colour after seeing wall paintings adorning buildings and tombs all along the Nile. Likewise metal-work skills, faience making, glass making, and other important crafts were learned very quickly and brought back to Greece. In every case though, the Greeks were not slavish imitators. They were creative adapters of the skills they acquired so that they could be applied to their own needs and tastes. This is one of the secrets to the greatness of Greek civilization.

To give just a hint of the great strides made in Greek art from the Dark Ages of Greece to the Persian Wars, perhaps a comparison can be made. Temples changed from small wood and clay houses to grand marble showcases for Greek treasures, such as the temple of Artemis at Ephesus, one of the Seven Wonders of the Ancient World. Sculpture was transformed from rather abstract figurines in bronze or clay to natural looking lifesize statues in bronze, marble, or combinations of ivory and gold. Vase painting shows a similar change from little black stick figures to wonderfully fluid, idealized characters against a black or a white background.

Greek philosophy and science took its first tentative steps also. Men from Miletus were the first to ask, "What is the origin of the world," and not be satisfied with the answer, "The gods produced it." They wanted to know how and from what. So they proposed theories about the world's origin, suggesting that the world was formed from some basic element like moisture, air, or fire, through various fundamental processes, like condensation and vaporization. These ideas are no longer accepted by thinkers, but it is significant that the development of philosophy—Greek *philo* ("love") *sophia* ("wisdom")—and a systematic science began here in Greece.

Greek literature passed from the age of epic poems like the *Iliad* and *Odyssey* of Homer to an age of Lyric poetry in dozens of forms. Drinking and war songs, poems sung by choruses or by a single person, love poems, and poems in praise of athletic victories are just a few of the new themes. Besides this, the very first dramatic plays were written in Athens just before the Persian Wars. They were performed in honour of the god Dionysus, god of wine and fertility.

It must have been an exciting period of change and progress for the Greeks, but it was just the prelude to the high point of Greek history, the **Classical Age** of Greece.

Suggested Sources for Further Research

1. Please see page 228 for complete list for Chapters 6 and 7.

Focus Your Knowledge

1. What attracted people to the island of Crete?
2. Describe the royal palaces of the Minoans.
3. What evidence is there that the Myceneans were heavily influenced by the Minoans?
4. Who was Homer? What purpose did his stories of the Trojan War serve in the Dark Ages and later?
5. Why were Greek colonies established throughout the Mediterranean? Where were the main areas of colonization?
6. Using the organizer below compare the various forms of government used by the Athenians prior to the development of their democratic system.

    TYPE OF GOVERNMENT   POWER HELD BY   EFFECTIVENESS OF GOVERNMENT

7. How did the Persian invasions contribute to advances in Greek culture? Be sure to touch on art, architecture, literature, and philosophy.

Apply Your Knowledge

1. Our understanding of history is not static and unchanging but is ever evolving as new discoveries are made and new interpretations are put forward. Using the decline of the Minoans as an example show this to be true.

2. The myths and legends of the past are often seen as mere stories. How has the story of Theseus and the Minotaur shown that some legends, despite their seeming to be fanciful, might be based on historical truths?

3. How successful was Heinrich Schliemann in using the *Iliad* and the *Odyssey* in finding Troy and Mycenae? Do his finds convince you of the historical accuracy of Homer's writing?

4. Compare Athenian democracy to our system of government. Which system do you feel gives fairer government to the people? Which system do you think is more efficient and productive? Would you like to see Canada adopt any aspects of the Athenian system of democracy?

5. Describe life in ancient Sparta. Can you think of any twentieth century societies that are similar in their organization? What are the advantages of such a society? Given the choice would you have preferred to live in ancient Athens or Sparta?

6. What were the major causes of the Greek-Persian wars? In what ways were these wars typical of wars throughout history?

7. The strategy employed by the Greeks in the second Persian invasion (480–479 B.C.) was to fight in narrow places. Assess the effectiveness of this strategy by examining the battles of Thermopylae and Salamis.

Extension Activities

1. Using the medium of your choice (i.e. clay, cardboard, plasticene, papier-mâché) build a model of the Palace of Knossos or Phaistos, the Treasury of Atreus, the citadel, the Lion Gate, or the Royal Grave Circle at Mycenae.

2. Research various aspects of daily life among the Minoans and write a fictional account of a Day In The Life Of An Ancient Minoan. In writing your account assume the role of a character for whom you could describe daily routines and duties. In your description of Minoan culture include clothing, architecture, sports, and art.

3. Based on further research of Homer's epic poems the *Iliad* and the *Odyssey* prepare a skit that recreates one of the many adventures. The class may wish to coordinate the skits so that the story of the Trojan War or Odysseus' voyage home are retold. Alternatively, students may wish to video-tape their segment,

which would allow the class to produce a lengthy video-taped production based on the works of Homer.

4. Based on further research of one of the battles from the Greek-Persian wars, prepare a detailed and colourful overhead that would illustrate the events of the battle. Present the overhead to the class as part of an explanation of the battle.

5. Hold a class Olympics based on the original ancient Greek model. Groups of students should be responsible for researching, preparing, and hosting one of the events that would have been included in the games. Other students could be responsible for preparing and presenting the awards to the winners.

CHAPTER 7

Classical Greece

Chapter Highlights

- Sparta and Athens' rivalry

- the beauty of the Parthenon and the Elgin Marbles

- Socrates, Plato, and Aristotle

- the riddle of the Gordian knot and how it was solved

- Zeus and other Gods of Greece

- life and leisure in ancient Greece

The accomplishments of Greek civilization can usually be recalled simply by mentioning some of the famous men of the age; Socrates, Pericles, Sophocles, Plato, Aristotle, and Alexander the Great. The Seven Wonders of the Ancient World were mostly Greek monuments; the gold and ivory statue of Zeus at Olympia, the lighthouse at Alexandria, the bronze Colossus of Rhodes, the Mausoleum of Halicarnassus, or the Great Altar at Pergamum. The finest of all Greek buildings, the Parthenon, was built by the Athenians under Pericles' guidance as a showpiece of Athenian wealth and power. The development of art, medicine, biology, philosophy, drama, and **rhetoric** in this period is part of the foundation of western culture. The people and monuments mentioned belong to the cream of Greek civilization and the milk just below this cream was outstandingly rich. This chapter will look at the accomplishments of the Greeks but will also consider the troubled political events of the age.

Key Concepts

Delian League
Pericles
Peloponnesian War
Thucydides
Parthenon
Elgin Marbles
Philip the Great
Socrates
Aristotle
Hippocrates
Sappho

The Glory of Athens

The Growth of the Empire

The Persian invasion of 480–479 B.C. was repelled by the Greeks and a sliver of land along the coast of Asia Minor was shaved from Persia's great Empire. The Greeks fully expected the Persians to attack again in order to recover lost territory. A permanent alliance to continue fighting the Persians was needed. At this point Sparta had the chance to show leadership in diplomacy, rather than in war, but refused to be further involved in affairs outside the Peloponnese. Athens, with a strong fleet and great reputation after the wars, filled the breach. Aristeides, acting for Athens, helped organize the **Delian League** to defend Greek states in case of further aggression from Persia. Each Greek state signed a treaty of defense with Athens agreeing to pay an annual tribute toward a common fleet. Athens provided all the officials and commanders of the League, and swore not to interfere in the internal affairs of the allies. Aristeides carried out the first assessment of the tribute to be paid by each member of the League; his fairness earned him the name Aristeides the Just. The larger, wealthier states contributed ships to the fleet, while smaller states paid to support the ships, particularly Athenian ships. The treasury and meetings were held at the great sanctuary of Apollo on the island of Delos, thus the name—the Delian League.

This League, which was originally a voluntary association, soon became a forced union. Some states who did not want to join were compelled to

Classical Greece CHAPTER 7 201

enter the alliance while others, who wanted to drop out when the Persian threat receded, were forced to remain and pay their share. Cimon, the son of Miltiades, victor at Marathon, molded the league into an effective military instrument. As the fleet's military commander, Cimon beat the Persians decisively in 467 B.C. and kept them from further attacks in the Aegean. After this success, the League, led by a young Athenian commander named **Pericles**, felt strong enough to try to free the Greeks on the island of Cyprus and to help in a new revolt in Egypt against the Persians. The Egyptian expedition in the 450s ended in catastrophe when a Persian force trapped the Greek fleet in a branch of the Nile River and wiped it out. For fear of a Persian reprisal by sea, Pericles had the treasury of the League moved away from the island of Delos back to Athens in 454 B.C. This was final proof that the league had now become an Empire controlled by Athens.

Pericles and Democracy

The city of Athens enjoyed its greatest period of wealth and power under the thirty-year guidance of Pericles. To us the term democracy means an opportunity to voice opinions through the media and public meetings, and to vote for political representatives who will present our views in political bodies like parliament or municipal councils. In Pericles' day, it meant far more. Every citizen could speak and vote on every piece of legislation in the Assembly and had an equal chance to hold almost every public office, with few exceptions. So the law and government were firmly in the hands of the citizens. In lines reminiscent of President John F. Kennedy's famous speech, "Ask not what your country can do for you, ask what you can do for your country," Pericles proclaimed, "we judge the man who takes no part at all [in public affairs] a useless, not just a 'quiet' person."[1]

Pericles himself was annually elected to the Board of Generals and so maintained his leading position in the city. The other civic offices, even the archonships, were only one-year positions and people were selected by lottery from candidates proposed by the tribes. The lottery system itself weakened the power of the other offices since weak candidates often filled the positions. The introduction of wages for being a council member, jury duty, and various civic offices allowed even the poorest citizen to take time away from his work. Salaries for civil service was a radical departure from the earlier system of government.

In the funeral oration for the Athenian dead at the beginning of the **Peloponnesian War**, Pericles declared:

> Our constitution is called a democracy, because power is in the hands not of a minority but of the whole people. When it is a question of settling private disputes, everyone is equal before the law; when it is a question of putting one person before another in positions of public responsibility, what counts is not membership of a particular class, but the actual ability which a man possesses. No one, so long as he has it in him to be of service to the state, is kept in political obscurity because of poverty.
> Thucyides *History of Peloponnesian War*, Rex Warner, trans., p. 117.

The opportunities for citizens to participate in political affairs were far greater in Athens than in our modern democracies. There was, however, no pay for attending the Assembly until the fourth century B.C., so many poor people could not afford to attend. Also women, slaves, and foreign residents could not hold citizenship, and Pericles himself introduced a law which restricted citizenship only to those men

---

[1]MacKendrick and Howe, *Classics in Translation*, (Madison: University of Wisconsin Press, 1959), 1:2, p. 241.

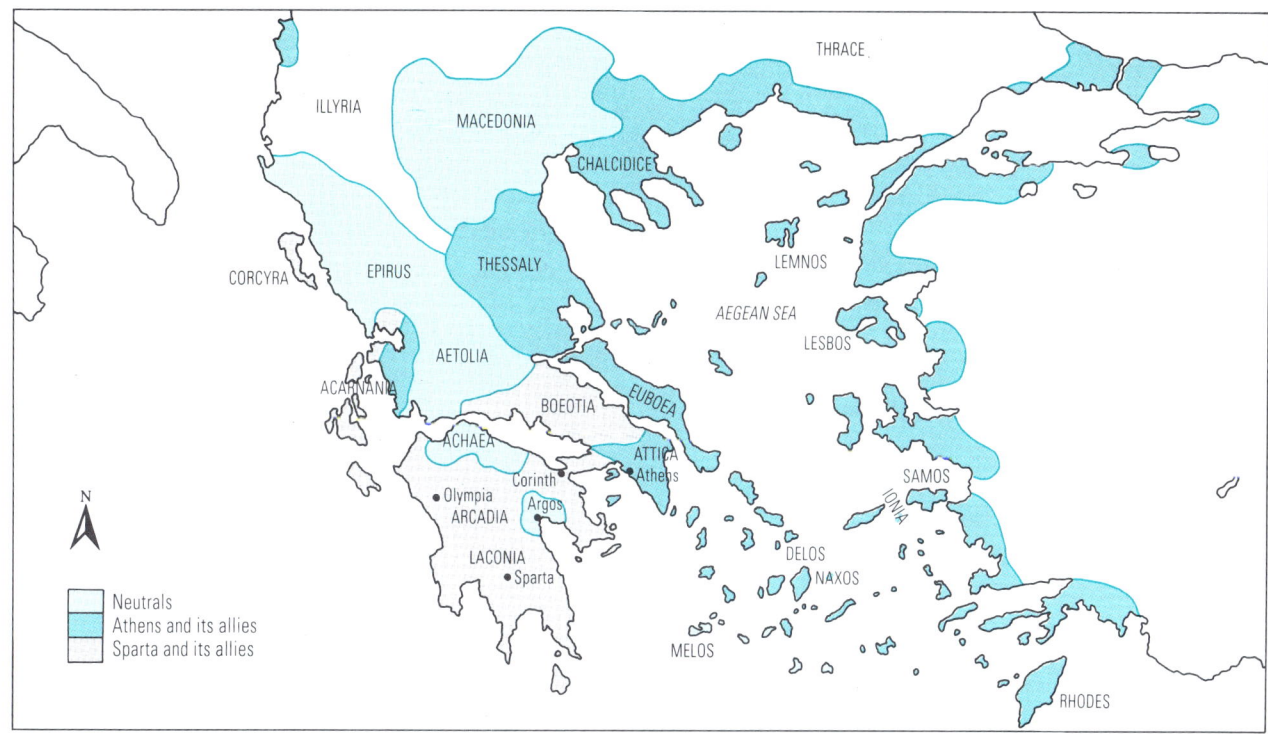

The Peloponnesian War

whose parents, both mother and father, had been born of citizen fathers.

Rivalry of Sparta and Athens

While holding the office of general, Cimon acted to defuse the natural rivalry between Sparta and Athens, the two main powers in Greece. Things changed when Sparta asked Athens for help during a dangerous Helot revolt in 462 B.C. Cimon convinced the Athenians to send soldiers to help suppress the revolt. When they arrived, Sparta refused their help and sent them home. This insult led to Cimon's ostracism the next year, and the quick rise of Pericles into political pre-eminence.

In the 450s Pericles attempted to increase the Athenian land empire in central Greece, a move which was a threat to Sparta's traditional power base. Although it did not last long, this attempt by Athens to gain land in central Greece increased tensions between the two states. To try to defuse the increasingly bitter rivalry, Athens and Sparta signed a peace treaty in 445 B.C., agreeing to stay out of the internal affairs of each other's federations. Sparta still led the Peloponnesian League, which included members or allies in central Greece. Athens held tight rein on the many coastal and island states of its empire in the Aegean. The peace treaty postponed, but did not prevent, the war to settle this rivalry.

There were basic differences between Sparta and Athens. Sparta was a land power, with a conservative, oligarchic government, backward in terms of trade, wealth, and recent advances in culture such as rhetoric, philosophy, and literature. It sought leadership among the Greek states in order to protect itself and its interests rather than for wealth, power, or expansion. Athens was the opposite. A sea power governed by a radical democracy, Athens was at the forefront of advances in culture; it was progressive, wealthy, and a trading nation. It maintained and tried to expand its empire for the sake of the power and income the expansion provided. These differences, in themselves, caused suspicion and dislike between the two states, but it was the other Greek states, especially Corinth, who finally pushed the two towards war.

The Peloponnesian War

Corinth was a rich trading city like Athens, but it belonged to Sparta's Peloponnesian League and so remained quite independent. Athens kept Corinth's merchants from the profitable trade of the Aegean and provoked Megara, another League state, by likewise excluding it from ports of the Athenian Empire. When Athens began to interfere with the affairs of Corinth's colonies, the peace treaty was broken and by 431 B.C. this caused the outbreak of the so-called Peloponnesian War. This was the longest, most bitter, and costly war that the Greeks ever fought. Almost every city-state was aligned with one side or the other. The outcome was surprising since Athens seemed far stronger and better prepared at the beginning.

Pericles knew that Attica could be invaded yearly by the more powerful land army of the Spartans. He arranged for food to be imported and the people to take refuge behind the Long Walls connecting the seaport of Piraeus and Athens whenever Attica was attacked. The Athenian fleet was strong and could raid the coast of the Peloponnese at will. There was a surplus in Athens' treasury, and prospects for victory looked good.

What Pericles could not foresee was the plague that struck Athens in the second year of the war, 430 B.C. The Athenians had sought refuge between the Long Walls when Sparta invaded that year. In the cramped, unsanitary conditions, the virulent disease ravaged the population. **Thucydides**, who wrote the history of this war, caught the plague himself but survived it. He left a detailed description of its terrible symptoms. In two years, perhaps one-third of the Athenians had died, including Athens' great leader, Pericles. The result was that the resources of the two opponents were now closely balanced.

The conflict lasted for 27 years. First one side would gain a strategic victory; then the other side. When 300 Spartans were trapped and captured alive off the coast of the Peloponnese, Sparta sued for peace. Then Sparta successfully attacked Athens' allies in the North Aegean and Athens wanted peace. Finally King Brasidas of Sparta, and the rabble-rousing leader of the radical democrats in Athens, Cleon, were killed in battle at Amphipolis in the north Aegean, provoking a brief peace in 421 B.C.

Athens found a new leader who pushed for further hostilities. He was Alcibiades, the nephew and ward of Pericles. Athens put together an alliance to fight Sparta on land in 418 B.C. which was not very successful. Then they attacked Melos in 416 B.C. and tried to bring this Dorian island into Athens' Empire. With these moves, Sparta was on the point of attacking Athens again.

At this critical juncture, Athens foolishly ventured an expedition of conquest against Syracuse, the most powerful city on the distant island of Sicily. This two-year campaign (415–413 B.C.) used huge quantities of ships, manpower, and money to launch, but it turned into a total disaster. Alcibiades had backed the expedition, and might have been able to save it, but he was charged for a schoolboy prank of revealing the Sacred Mysteries of Demeter at a drinking party and was forced to flee to Sparta for several years. When he finally returned to Athens to help its

The theatre of Epidaurus was one of the largest and the best of the ancient world. Someone sitting near the top of the theatre can easily hear a speech given from the orchestra. The size and quality of the theatre at Epidaurus stands as a testimony to the importance of drama and comedy to the culture of the ancient Greeks.

sinking cause in 411 B.C., he was able to turn around the war effort for a short time. When he went into exile again for losing a small naval engagement, Athens could find no other great general to take his place.

By 408 B.C., Persia, with its great wealth, had begun supporting the Peloponnesian side by providing ships to fight the Athenians. The Spartan general, Lysander, developed more effective ways to combat the Athenian fleet, and Athens became desperate as its money for new ships dwindled and losses at sea continued. After one victory at sea by Athens in 406 B.C., a storm suddenly blew up, preventing the Athenians from picking up 2000 men who were adrift, having abandoned their wrecked triremes. The Athenians recalled the ten naval commanders to stand trial for this added loss. Only six of them dared to return for the trial, one of whom was Pericles, the son of the great Athenian leader. The six were found guilty and executed.

The decisive final battle occurred in 405 B.C. at Aegospotami in the Hellespont area. Athens put one last fleet on the water depending on it for victory. After days of manoeuvring against the Peloponnesian fleet without a battle, the Athenian sailors beached their ships to collect food for their lunch as they had on previous days. The Peloponnesians caught them off guard, burned or captured the ships, and rounded up the sailors. The end had come. Since the Athenians had killed all the men of Melos in 416 B.C. and enslaved the women and children, they now expected the same treatment for themselves.

Sparta's allies, Thebes and Corinth, forcefully encouraged Sparta to do to Athens what the Athenians had done to Melos. What a tragic loss it would have been for Greece, despite Athens' great transgressions against other states. In the end Sparta spared Athens, but the city was supposed to tear down its Long Walls, surrender all but 12 of its ships, take back its political exiles, and acknowledge Spartan leadership in matters of peace and war.

Even after this loss of freedom, the Athenians had to endure more. Thirty men, soon to be called the Thirty Tyrants, were empowered to rule in Athens with the backing of a Spartan garrison. A reign of terror began with many people arbitrarily being declared outlaws and being executed. In eight months 1500 men died. Finally the city was taken over again by exiles favouring democracy. The bloodbath ended in 403 B.C. and Athens began a swift recovery; but it was never again a first-rate power.

The Classical Moment

Fifth-century Athens was the focal point of a brief age of brilliance sometimes called the Classical Moment. With Pericles as leader and people like Sophocles, the playwright, and Pheidias, the sculptor, expressing Greek ideals in artistic form, Athenian society reached a cultural pinnacle. It was a period of optimism, at least until the results of the Peloponnesian War became clear. Greeks believed that their world could be made better, and that the troubles they faced could be overcome. Sophocles in *Antigone* wrote this hymn to humankind:

> There are many wonders, but none more wondrous than man.
> Across the white-capped sea in the storms of winter this creature makes his way
> on through the billowing waves.
> And earth, the oldest of the gods,
> the undecaying and unwearied one, he wears away
> With constant ploughing, back and forth, year after year,
> turning the soil with horses he has bred...
>
> Language, thought swift as the wing, and the patterns
> of city life he has taught himself, and escape from the shafts of storms, and the shelter-piercing frosts of clear days.
> He can cope with everything, never unprepared whatever
> the future brings. Only from death does he fail to contrive escape.
> Even for diseases thought hopeless he has figured out cures.
>
> Clever, with ingenuity and skill beyond imagining,
> He veers now toward evil, now toward good...
> Sophocles *Antigone*, 332–68.

Other writers of comedy and tragedy were hoping to improve their world through their writing. Aeschylus and Euripides were examining serious issues like the basis of justice and the status of women in Greek society. The comic playwright Aristophanes aimed to change his world, but by poking fun at it. In his comedy *Lysistrata* he turns society on its head by having Greek women go out on strike in order to force men to end their destructive war:

> When the War began, like the prudent, dutiful wives that we are, we tolerated you men, and endured your actions in silence. (Small wonder—you wouldn't let us say boo.)
>   You were not precisely the answer to a matron's prayer—we knew you too well, and found out more.

The Parthenon, one of the greatest architectural achievements of the Greeks, was adorned with some of the greatest sculpture of antiquity. The frieze was decorated with relief sculpture, which depicted a procession at a festival called the Panathenaia; here horsemen are preparing to mount.

Too many times, as we sat in the house, we'd hear that you'd done it again—manhandled another affair of state with your usual staggering incompetence. Then, we'd ask you, brightly, "How was the Assembly today, dear? Anything
in the minutes about Peace?" And my husband would give his stock reply.
"What's that to you? Shut up!" and I did...
But this time was really too much:...
We women met in immediate convention and passed a unanimous resolution: To work in concert for safety and Peace in Greece. We have valuable advice to impart, and if you can possibly deign to emulate our silence, and take your turn as audience, we'll rectify you—
we'll straighten you out and set you right.
Aristophanes *Lysistrata*.

In the visual arts, by far the greatest achievement was the building of the **Parthenon**, which dominated all of Athens from its perch on the Acropolis. Designed by Pheidias and the architect Ictinus, it was a marvel of skill and beauty. Each block of this huge temple to Athena was carved with incredible accuracy. There was hardly a straight line in the entire building—the foundation bulged upward slightly, the columns swelled in the middle and were tilted inward, and the entablature above the columns likewise curved upwards from the corners and tilted outwards. These marvelous but difficult refinements may have been meant to compensate for the optical illusions produced by the lines of such a large building.

ARCHITECTURE
GREEK TEMPLES

One of the great legacies left by the ancient Greeks are the temples which reflect their love of order, balance, and logic. The temples were a product of the tremendous engineering and mathematical skills possessed by the Greeks. The nature of Greek religion required that only an altar was necessary for religious services. It should be remembered that the temples were built to house a statue of the god or goddess while the actual ceremonies took place outside.

The temples began as simple one-room structures (naos) with a porch (pronaos) added for appearance. As the Greeks liked things to look balanced they added a back porch. They also felt that temples looked best when all four sides were decorated the same way and so a ring of columns was built around the temple. This colonnade is called the peristyle. In some rich cities where grand temples were built a double peristyle surrounded the temple.

Doric and Ionic Orders

In the construction of Greek temples there were two basic designs: the Doric order and the Ionic order. Both orders used a basic post and lintel system in which upright posts or columns support lintels or beams. Where they differed was in the style and design of the columns and other architectural details.

The Doric order makes use of sturdy columns whose height is four to six times their diameter. The base rests directly on the step of the temple while the column is topped by a simple capital which resembles a cushion. The capital supports a plain horizontal band of stone called the architrave on top of which is another horizontal band called the frieze. The Doric frieze is divided into alternating triglyphs and metopes. Triglyphs are vertically grooved rectangles and appear over each column and between each pair of columns producing a pleasing visual effect. The metope is the rectangle appearing between triglyphs, and is decorated with painting or sculpture. There are 20 vertical grooves or flutes cut in the Doric columns which come to a sharp edge.

In the Ionic order slimmer columns whose height is eight to ten times their diameter are used. These columns rest on a base and are topped by a scroll-like capital. The architrave above the capital is divided into three horizontal steps. The frieze is an undivided horizontal band of stone and is often decorated with relief carvings. The columns contain 24 flutes which are separated by a smooth vertical band.

The pitched roof of a Greek temple leaves a triangular gable or pediment at the front and back. This space is filled with brightly painted sculptures.

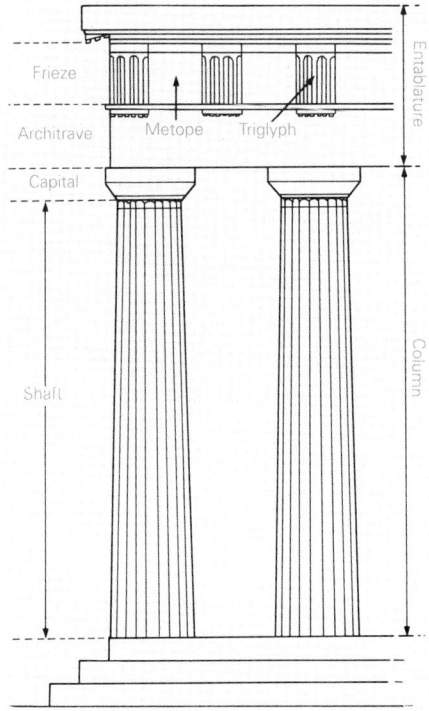

A corner of a temple in the Doric order

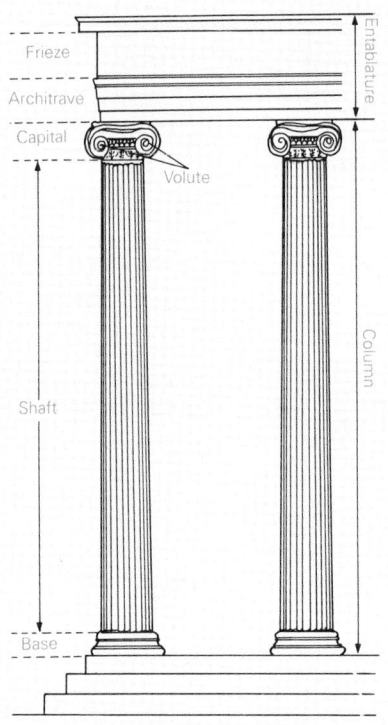

A corner of a temple in the Ionic order

The Parthenon is considered the perfect Doric temple. It was to be the centrepiece of Athens' plan to establish itself as the artistic centre of the Greek world. The Parthenon symbolized the logic, order, and sense of beauty in Greek architecture. Illustrated here is a reconstruction of the completed Parthenon as it looked in 432 B.C.

209

It is the sculpture, much of which is preserved as the **Elgin Marbles** in the British Museum, that drew the most attention. Each figure showed the ideal form of human beauty, serenely calm and unaffected by the transitory events of the world around it. Represented in the sculpture were myths such as the Battle of Gods and Giants, and the Fall of Troy, which reminded the Greeks of their great victory over the Persians. The Athenians refused to represent their victory over the Persians in 479 B.C. on the temples because they believed that such pride (*hubris*) in their own accomplishments would be surely punished by the gods.

In the triangular space above the columns at the two ends of the Parthenon were other marble sculptures: larger than life-size sculptures representing two events in the life of Athena. At the east end, which was the front of the temple, was depicted the birth of Athena. She was born fully armed and fully grown out of the head of Zeus. The other event, on the west end, was the contest between Athena and Poseidon for the patronage of the city of Athens. Athena gave the city her gift of the olive tree and so won the contest.

Housed in the great *cella* ("sanctuary") of the Parthenon was a towering statue of the warrior goddess, Athena, made by Pheidias himself. The statue was over 12 m high and made of ivory and gold plates set on a wooden frame. A reflecting pool sat in front of it. One can only imagine the awe that it inspired as worshippers entered the darkened cella and beheld this immense gleaming statue. It is also worth bearing in mind that it was the revenue from Athens' Empire, a forced federation, that paid for much of this beauty.

The Road to Persia

The end of the Peloponnesian War did not see the unification of the Greeks. Athenian imperialism was curbed, but Sparta tried to forcibly lead the Greek city-states as Athens had done. As a result, new alliances were made against Sparta. Corinth joined with its old rival, Athens, to fight against Sparta. For a brief time (371–362 B.C.), another city-state, Thebes, defeated the Spartans and took over Greek leadership. Its success was due to changes in military tactics. They had developed a deep formation of men (called a phalanx) with longer than normal spears to punch holes through the enemies' lines. Thebes' dominance ended with the death of its best general, Epaminondes. The careful balance of power between the leading Greek city-states was soon to be upset by a new force from the north, the kingdom of Macedonia.

Philip of Macedon

The broad plains and hilly country of the north Aegean were home to a people considered to be backward cousins of the Greeks. The Macedonians

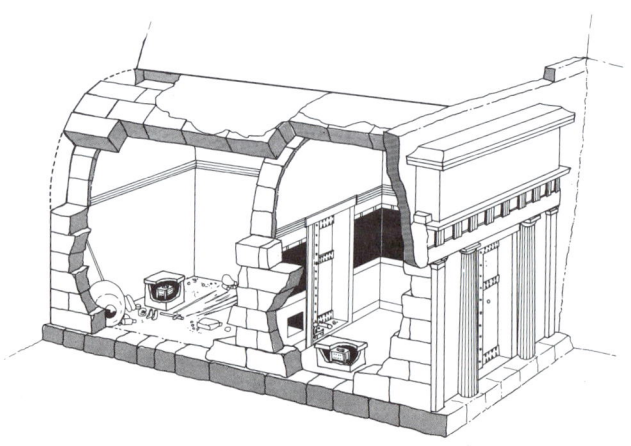

In one of the most exciting discoveries the tomb of Philip was excavated at Vergina in northern Greece. Inside a vaulted chamber were found silver drinking cups, bronze armour, and a heavy gold box containing a beautiful wreath of oak leaves and a purple cloth decorated with gold threads. Wrapped inside the cloth were the burnt bones of Philip himself.

spoke a dialect of Greek, but they were farmers and shepherds, not crafters and traders. They fell behind their southern cousins in wealth and culture. In the fourth century several kings rose to unite the Macedonians and bring them success in battle. The key figure in this success was **Philip the Great**. He had learned the new battle tactics of Thebes, when he was held hostage there for three years. By creating a professional army, with a strong cavalry and more flexible battlefield units, he not only united his country, but also defeated the southern Greeks at the Battle of Chaeronaea in 338 B.C. For the first time Greeks were joined together under the rule of a single man. It is likely that this ruthless, ambitious monarch planned to turn the combined Greek forces against their old enemy, Persia, but before he could launch such an expedition, he was assassinated at a wedding celebration by one of his own officers.

Alexander

The rule fell to Philip's 20-year old son, Alexander, one of the greatest generals the world has ever seen. He took his father's professional army and plans for conquest, his own genius for command and finding the weaknesses of his enemies, and set out against the Persians in 334 B.C. He never returned to Europe. Whether he intended to or not, he soon conquered the entire Near East.

How could such a young man with a relatively small army of 35 000 foot soldiers defeat the Persian Empire? The question boils down to strengths and weaknesses. The Macedonian army was the culmination of improvements in Greek warfare. It had been demonstrated long before that Persian soldiers were no match for the Greek hoplite. The Macedonians were led by great commanders and all were devoted to Alexander. The Persian army was larger, but made up of different subject peoples. The Persian king was a despot who ruled by force. Once Alexander defeated the Persian soldiers in the army, the rest of the non-Persian troops lost their eagerness to fight. The battle of Gaugamela, October 1, 331 B.C., was the final blow against the Persians. The victory was complete. All the land and wealth of Persia now fell into the hands of Alexander the Great.

Further conquests took Alexander all the way to India. He turned back only when his army, suffering from exhaustion, mutinied. He dreamed of conquering the entire world, but finally faced the fact that he had to govern what he had won. Alexander showed his brilliance here as well. He tried to make Greek culture and language a kind of common, uniting force among all peoples. At the same time he respected the customs and laws he found in place, and he encouraged the leaders of the conquered peoples to help him rule the various parts of his empire. Perhaps this great experiment would have worked, but Alexander died of an illness in 323 B.C. at the age of 33. The empire he created soon split apart as his best generals each seized large pieces.

Legends of Alexander

Legends often grow around famous people, which greatly embellish details of their lives, and so it is with Alexander. It is difficult to tell how much truth there is in any of them, but they give an idea of how Alexander became a larger than life figure to many people in the ancient world.

It was said that Alexander was born on the same night that the magnificent temple of Artemis, at Ephesus, was burnt down by an arsonist. It was said that Artemis was so preoccupied with the birth of Alexander that she could not return to put out the flames.

Alexander's father, King Philip, was foretold that three great events would happen on the same day; his general, Parmenio, won a great victory over the Illyrians, his horse won a race at the Olympic Games, and his wife gave birth to their first son, Alexander.

PERSONALITIES

The Secret to Alexander's Success

Alexander the Great is undoubtably one of history's most successful military leaders. In less than fifteen years and using a relatively small army, Alexander managed to establish a massive empire stretching from Greece to the Indus river. Had he not faced an untimely death from a fever likely contracted by drinking polluted water, the extent of his conquests would surely have been even more stupendous.

The key to Alexander's success lay in the strength of his army. Despite often being outnumbered the Macedonian army was able to emerge triumphant on repeated occasions. For example at the Battle of Guagamela the Persians outnumbered the Macedonians by five to one; and yet when the battle was over the Persians had lost upwards of 40 000 men while Alexander's army had lost only 500. Without question much of the success can be attributed to the brilliance of Alexander's leadership. Other factors also played an important role such as advances in Greek warfare. The cavalry carried straight stabbing swords and the xyston, a long cavalry spear that was longer than Persian weapons. The cavalry was supported by the highly trained Macedonian phalanx, or foot soldiers, who could readily adapt to various formations. For example on the defensive the phalanx drew close locking shields for protection.

Despite dying at the young age of 32 Alexander's influence on the history of the world was profound. He founded 70 cities, many of which bear his name,

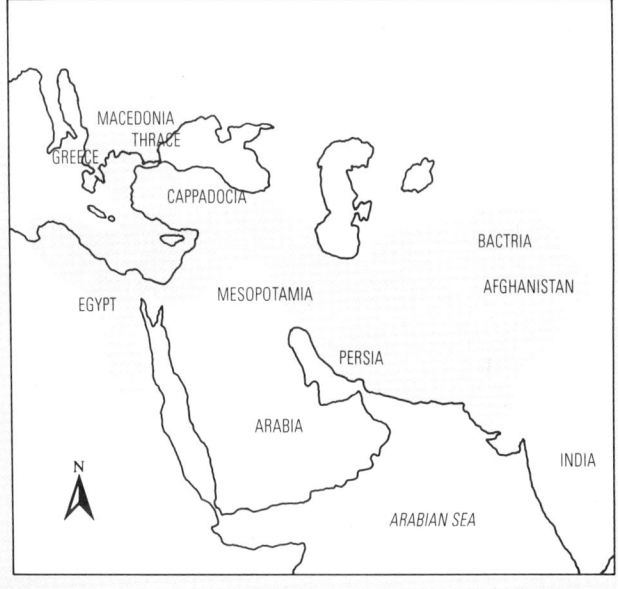

This map indicates the extent of Alexander's empire at the time of his death in 323 B.C.

212

and which were to become important cultural and trade centres. Alexander had an almost limitless passion for learning. Following his death many of the universities which he founded continued to teach subjects which had been of interest to him including warfare, medicine, botany, zoology, and astrology.

This diagram illustrating the military advancements includes the Boeotian helmet, a broad helmet which protected both face and shoulders, yet allowed for all-round vision; a horseman of the companion cavalry carrying a xyston. Also illustrated is the straight stabbing sword carried by the cavalry.

Companion cavalryman

Boeotian helmet

The prophets (seers) proclaimed "that the son whose birth coincided with three victories [events] would be always victorious."
Plutarch *Alexander*, bk. III, 11.5.

When he visited Corinth, Alexander drew a great crowd of people eager to congratulate him for his accomplishments. He learned that Diogenes, the famous Cynic philosopher who scorned worldly possessions, was staying nearby but was taking no notice of Alexander. So, Alexander went to visit him and found Diogenes lying in the sun. When Alexander asked him if there were anything that he wanted as a gift, Diogenes replied, "Stand a little out of my sun." Alexander so admired the grandeur and haughtiness of the man who had nothing and wanted nothing that he said to his followers, "Verily, if I were not Alexander, I would be Diogenes."

Alexander was not a one-sided character, interested only in armies and battles. Aristotle had been his tutor, instilling in him a love of literature and an interest in medicine. Plutarch tells us that Alexander slept with a dagger and a copy of Homer's *Iliad* under his pillow.

One of Alexander's most famous deeds was to solve the riddle of the Gordion knot. During his conquest of the Persian Empire, Alexander stopped at Gordion, the old capital of the Phrygian Empire, near modern Ankara in Turkey. There he was shown a wagon with a yoke pole attached to it by a carefully tied knot of cornel bark, where all the ends of the knot were tightly concealed inside the knot. Alexander was told that whoever was able to unravel the knot would become king of the world. Puzzled at first, Alexander drew out his sword and cut through the famous knot.

The Hellenistic Age

The death of Alexander in 323 B.C. marks the end of an era. It divides what historians call the Classical period (480–323 B.C.) from the Hellenistic period (323–31 B.C.). Greek culture burst out of the Aegean basin and through conquest became the common culture of all the Near East countries. Teachers, soldiers, crafters, artists, writers, and scientists flooded out of Greece into the newly conquered lands, taking advantage of the rich new opportunities for fame and fortune in the Near East. Greek culture was so dominant that it largely replaced or significantly changed the local cultures everywhere it went. Even when the Romans in turn conquered the Near East, these lands remained Greek in their traditions until the coming of the Arabs and Turks.

The history of the Hellenistic Age is like a complex dance with four or five participants. But, the dance is not a friendly one since the partners are always fighting. One of Alexander's generals, named Seleucus, took over the Asiatic part of his empire and established the Seleucid dynasty. Another general, named Ptolemy, established the Ptolemaic dynasty in the African portion of Alexander's empire. Another Macedonian general, Antigonus, was able to snatch the European portion, including Greece and Macedonia, and founded the Antigonid dynasty. Smaller powers like Pergamon and Rhodes became involved in the feuds between the Hellenistic kingdoms. The results of these wars belong with the history of Rome, since it was Rome that conquered them and incorporated them into the Roman Empire by 31 B.C. As for mainland Greece and Macedonia, they were incorporated as one province of the Roman world by 146 B.C.

Greek Culture

Philosophy

At the same time that Greek architects and sculptors were creating monumental statues and temples, philosophers were shaking the foundations of Greek society by questioning traditional beliefs. Men called sophists sold their services as teachers to wealthy youths, training them in public speaking (rhetoric) and logic. One such sophist, Protagoras of Abdera, tried to throw out all the previous standards for judging what is right and wrong, good or bad, ugly or beautiful. He argued that people are the measure of all things—meaning that humans themselves set all such standards for judgement. Greek philosophy was often concerned with scientific inquiry, such as the nature and origin of the universe. These philosophers questioned what humans can really know for certain, when all the information about the world comes to us through our easily deceived senses. One noteworthy idea to come from this inquiry was the theory that all matter is made up of tiny, indivisible particles called atoms.

Into such intellectual turmoil came **Socrates**: a man with a brilliant, questioning mind who had the ability to stand for hours in one spot concentrating on solving a philosophical problem. "Ugly in body, but magnetic in mind; convivial and erotic, yet Spartan in habits and of enormous physical endurance," is one scholar's description of him. Socrates left none of his philosophy in writing, but through the works of his disciple Plato, we learn that he believed it was the the duty of every person to care for one's inner being. The inner being, or soul, is the moral and intellectual personality of every human and must be nurtured in order to make it as good as possible. Socrates was very interested in the problem of what the right conduct for life was. His method of cross-examining people to show them errors in their beliefs made him many enemies. Socrates' impact on later philosophy has been profound, but in his own day he was often ridiculed, and was in the end tried and executed by his own city.

Socrates developed a group of devout followers. The most familiar is Plato, who set up his own school, called the Academy. The purpose of the school was to teach philosophy to advanced students. Plato wrote many books, called *Dialogues*, with Socrates as the main character, in which he sought to explain concepts such as love, beauty, justice and "the good." The concept of the good had a strong impact on later Christian thinking since it was similar to the Christian idea of God.

Aristotle was one student at Plato's Academy. After Plato's death, Aristotle started his own school, the Lyceum (from which the French word *lycee* is derived). He organized his students to carry out research in many fields of scientific learning. Aristotle himself made many important advances in biology, zoology, astronomy, meteorology, psychology, political science, ethics, and rhetoric. He also made great contributions to philosophy, opposing some of the main ideas of Plato concerning the nature of true knowledge and the relationship of the world of the intellect to the world of the senses.

Besides these schools there were dozens of others, including the Cynics, the Stoics, and the Epicureans, some of which influenced the Romans. The Roman practice of committing suicide when the chips were down, for example, was derived from ideas in Stoic philosophy. Stoics believed that virtue was the only good and that where virtue was not concerned, there were some external circumstances that were preferable to others: health was preferred to sickness, wealth was preferred to poverty, and so on. Some external circumstances were treated as indifferent to the Stoics, and these included life and death. Life was not to be preferred to death, they were indifferent.

Art and Architecture

Photography today allows us to capture on paper exactly what the eye sees. Or does it? People look through two eyes and then combine the two images in the mind to produce a true three-dimensional picture, like a stereoscope. The art of photography really is just selecting exactly what we want to take a

ASPECTS OF DAILY LIFE

Life and Leisure in ANCIENT GREECE

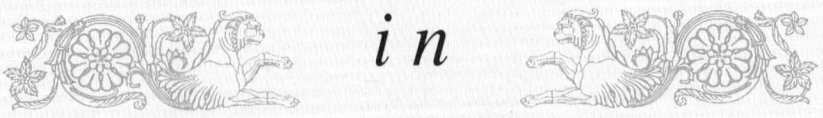

Clothing

Most Greek clothes were shaped like a rectangle and could be stored without creasing. The rectangular tunics, called chitons, had holes for the head and the arms with the sides sewn and the shoulders pinned. Younger people wore knee length tunics while the rest wore longer ones with a belt at the waist, and the width of the cloth determined the length of the sleeves. For more warmth another rectangle was worn over the tunic as a cloak. The colours of these tunics ranged from red to yellow, black, green, and purple. Patterns were woven into the material and were usually geometric. Footwear included sandals, boots, and slippers. Ornamentation included simple jewellery out of gold and silver, fashioned into bracelets, necklaces, and earrings. Women usually wore their hair up in a ponytail or bun with a hairpin. Since Greeks liked tall, pale women, cork-soled high heels would make them taller and a painted face would make them paler. Perfumes were essential since it was an effort to take a bath and the bathwater was always cold.

A Symposion

For pleasure a number of friends would be invited to an evening meal and drinking party, which they called a symposion. Only 7–8 guests would be invited so as not to have too many conversations going on at once. The rose hanging above the table symbolized silence, meaning the conversations at the table must go no further. The woman of the house

 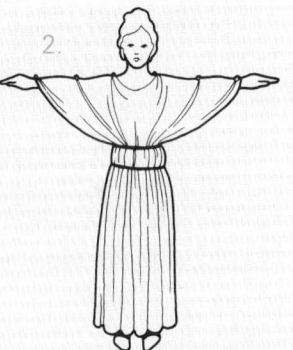 

For a long chiton: 1. Fold the cloth and pin along the shoulders and arms. 2. Tie at and below waist. 3. Pull the cloth out from belts.

was not invited although she was responsible for the decorations and garlands. The invitations sent would be little sculptures of clay showing people eating or walking. The professional cook would discuss the meal which would consist of three courses: the first course would be small items such as olives, onions, and radishes, the second course would be a meat dish, and the third course would be sweets, such as tarts, pastries and quinces. The meal was supplemented with watered-down wine and entertainment such as musicians and acrobats. For this type of festivity, lamb, which was the most important meat of the classical Greek diet, was served in abundance. As well as lamb, other dishes such as the ones following would be served.

On this Greek vase men and women are depicted at a symposion. While some relax on couches, others are playing musical instruments including a type of lyre and double-pipes. The woman seated on the left is looking at a drinking cup called a kylix.

Food

Braised Tuna Fish

125 mL	olive oil (if you are using tinned tuna include the oil from the tin)
8	leeks, finely sliced
8	sticks celery, finely chopped
4	sprigs each fresh rosemary and thyme, if fresh not available, teaspoon each of dried
	salt and pepper to taste
1/2	medium cucumber, thinly sliced
300 mL	each water and non-alcoholic wine
6	tuna steaks or 800 g tinned tuna fish

Heat the oil in a large pan and gently cook the leeks and celery till they start to soften. Add the herbs, seasoning, cucumber, wine, and water and mix well, then lay the tuna steaks on top of the vegetables. Cover the pan and simmer gently for 30-45 minutes, depending on the thickness of the steaks. Adjust the seasoning to taste and serve with plenty of rice and a good green salad. If you are using tinned tuna, break up the fish in large chunks into the vegetables and simmer for 15 minutes to heat the fish and amalgamate the flavours.

Honey and Sesame Balls

100 g sesame seeds
60 mL or more honey

Put the seeds with the honey in a pan and simmer them gently for between 10 and 20 minutes, stirring every now and then. The mixture should turn a rich gold. To test whether it is ready, drop a spoonful on a wet plate, leave it to cool for a minute or so, then squeeze it into a ball. If it holds its shape it is ready. Take the pan off the heat and allow it to cool, stirring it every few minutes. When the mixture is almost cold, wet your hands thoroughly in cold water and roll spoonfuls of the mixture into little balls; as long as your hands are cool and wet it will not stick to you. The sweet-meats should be stored in individual sweet wrappers to prevent them gradually running into each other. Alternatively, store them in a flat tin or container and cut them into small squares to serve, like Turkish delight.

(From *The British Museum Cookbook,* by Michelle Berriedale-Johnson, © 1987. British Museum Publications.)

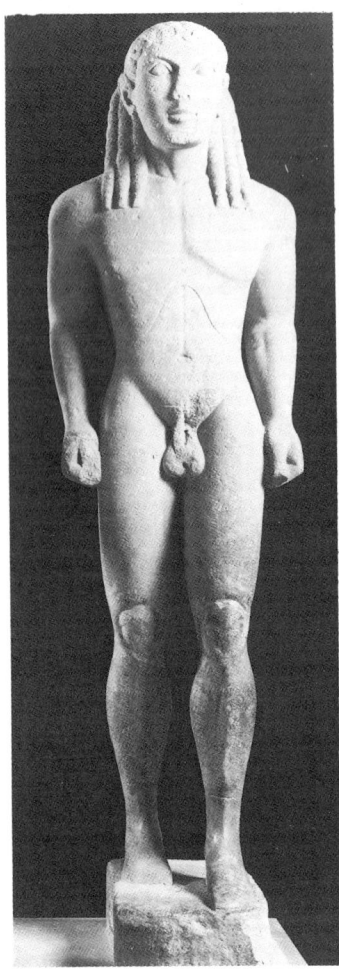 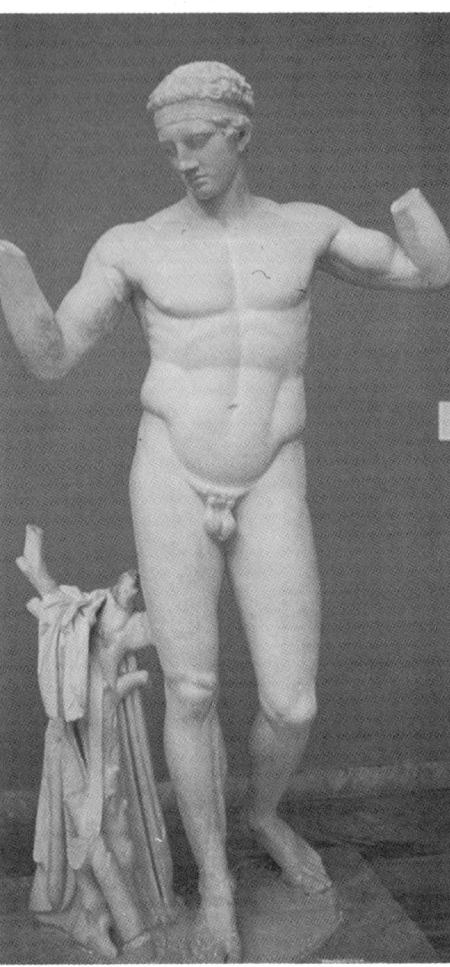

Greek sculpture evolved from the Kouros style of the Archaic period which reflected the heavy Egyptian influence, to sculpture of the Classical period, which is still unsurpassed in beauty and detail. Greek artists emphasized male nudes in which they strove to depict physical perfection. On the left is the "Cleobis" sculpted by Polymedes in the early sixth century B.C. Note the clenched fists, the left foot forward and the hair and face typical of Egyptian sculpture. The sculpture on the right, a Roman copy of Polyclitus, the "Diadoumenos" or reef binder captures a young man at rest with the weight of the body on the right leg and the muscles gently flexed. Note how the details of the face, the hair and the body achieve the sought after realism.

picture of and then mechanically producing it. The pictures that we see every day as colour photographs or posters can also be produced by hand, through the use of paint. This form of painting was first developed by the Greeks.

If you look at examples of Egyptian painting, you will see that these are really coloured drawings. A figure is drawn and then flat colours are added, like a child's colouring book. Greek artists learned how to depict depth on a flat surface by observing how light bounces off objects and produces many shades of the same colour. They imitated these shades of colour, and used foreshortening (near objects bigger than distant ones) to produce images that looked real. Unfortunately most Greek paintings have not been preserved, but we hear stories of how birds tried to eat grapes painted on a canvas, or how live horses neighed at painted ones. Greek painters aimed not only at producing real-looking pictures, but also ideal-looking representations. Their people were ideal ones, perfect in beauty, stature, and expression. When they depicted the gods, they showed them as ideal, human figures, though larger in size than humans.

The same was done by sculptors. It is remarkable that hundreds of artists in earlier civilizations had sculpted figurines and statues by the thousands trying to represent humans, animals, and objects. But none achieved a truly naturalistic representation. The Greeks concentrated on statues of young male figures, and over time observed each detail of the body, trying to render it in stone. This concentration on detail resulted in statues that were almost lifelike. Perhaps it was the young Greek athletes who always carried out their games and exercises in the nude that gave sculptors the chance to observe details of the body better. In the Classical period, the sculptors like the painters usually portrayed men and women in their most perfect state: in the prime of life and in their most beautiful or handsome aspect.

Greek architecture advanced in refinement from the Doric and Ionic styles, but not necessarily in new methods or principles. Many subtle curves were introduced to what were once the straight lines of temples; the foundations bowed slightly upwards, the columns bowed outward, but leaned slightly inward, and so on. These were done largely for optical reasons to make the temples appear more beautiful to the eye. The Greeks had learned how to build arches and vaults out of stone by the time of Alexander the Great, but it was the Romans who really took advantage of these new building principles for spanning open space in their architecture.

Daily Life

The majority of ancient Greeks were farmers. A small plot of land, perhaps five hectares or so, would yield a crop of olives for oil, a field of grain for bread and porridge, enough grapes for a year's supply of wine, and a couple fig trees, for fruit. Pasturage for sheep and goats gave the people a small supply of meat, usually eaten at festival times, and of cheese, another staple of their diet. Most people lived close enough to the sea that they could get fresh fish occasionally, though salted fish was common too. Meat could also be found by hunting game, especially hares. Cattle were only killed on very special occasions, such as the 100 bulls sacrificed at the Olympic Games festival. Sausage was a popular method of preserving meat. A few vegetables, like cabbage, beans, squash, and onions were also grown. Garlic was a common flavouring, and honey was used to sweeten foods.

Hesiod, in his poem *Works and Days*, advised people how they should farm successfully. Here is a small part of his advice:

When ploughing-time arrives, make haste to plough,
You and your slaves alike, on rainy days
And dry ones, while the season lasts. At dawn
Get to your fields, and one day they'll be full.
Plough, too, in springtime; if you turn the earth
In summer, too, you won't regret the work.
Sow fallow soil while it is still quite light;
Remember, fallow land defends us all,
And lulls our children with security.
Make prayers to Zeus the farmer's god and to
Holy Demeter, for her sacred grain,
To make it ripe and heavy, when you start
To plough, and hold the handles in your hand
And strike the oxen as they tug the straps.
A slave should follow after, with a stick
To hide the seeds and disappoint the birds.
Good habits are man's finest friend, and bad
Are his worst enemy.
Hesiod *Works and Days*, 458–72.

It was in Greek cities that the great contributions to western civilization were made, and it was here that daily life was diverse and bustling. A slice of this life can be seen from archaeological excavations in the Agora (marketplace) of Athens. It was the Agora, not the Acropolis, that was the centre of life.

A typical day for an Athenian citizen might have happened as follows. Early in the morning a citizen leaves his daughters and wife at home and takes his son to the gymnasium for his classes in music, literature (Homer), and wrestling or boxing. He stays for an hour to chat with friends and admire Kallias who is practising the pankration, a sport combining wrestling and boxing. Kallias won this event at the 77th Olympiad though three of his fingers were broken. Then he strolls past a city fountain where four women are filling their water pots and putting them on their heads to take home. He heads down to the Agora and directs a slave, who has accompanied him, to carry out the household errands. The slave buys some wool so the women at home may spin and weave cloth. The slave continues on, checking the vegetable sellers' tables, bargaining for a fresh fish at the stalls near the Great Drain, and arguing with the sandal-maker whose work fell apart, yet again. Everywhere vendors shout out their prices and bargains, and people carry baskets full of goods from place to place.

The father has his business to carry out. His farm, on the slopes of Mt. Hymettus, produced a good crop of olives this year, so he needs two dozen large vases made for shipping the olive oil. Near the shop selling transport *amphoras* are others with fine pottery. A new vase for mixing one-part wine with six-parts water is needed for an upcoming party with his drinking pals. The man chooses one with an exciting scene of Greeks fighting Trojans to remind his friends of the great victory over the Persians in recent years. He also buys a little white jug for perfumed olive oil. This he will place on the grave of his older son who died fighting last year near the island of Aegina.

A new graft law, just posted on the base of the heroes' statues, is being discussed outside the Council House and a fierce argument is raging inside. He listens intently and decides which way to vote when the law is presented to the Assembly. Nearby, one of the open-air courts is busy with a trial for slander, and a jury of 501 old men listen as the defendant with his crying wife beside him and his two ragged children pleads his innocence. The father knows the man is a scoundrel but he is good at pleading his case. It is early afternoon and the sun is hot. Time to return home for a cool drink and a light lunch brought to him by a slave. His wife and daughters have been taking turns spinning wool for a new cloak for his son, and washing their dresses for the upcoming festival to Demeter at Eleusis. His older daughter will begin the initiation into the mysteries of the Demeter sanctuary this year. Time for a long afternoon nap now before he rides out to his farm to check on the sausage being made from two goats killed the day before yesterday.

Medicine

Greek medical facilities, the equivalent of our hospitals, were located at sanctuaries of the healing god, Asclepius. In comparison to the other gods, the worship of Asclepius began very late in Greece, ca. 500 B.C. These sanctuaries were usually located well away from the noise and dust of the city, near a source of clean, cool spring water. As the architect Vitruvius recommends:

> the healthiest regions and suitable springs of water therein be chosen first for all temples and particularly for Asclepius, Hygeia and those gods by whose medical art very many of the sick seem to be cured. For when sick bodies are transferred from a pestilent to a healthy spot and are treated with water from wholesome fountains, they will recover more quickly.
> Vitruvius *On architecture*, 1.2.7.

The oldest Asclepius sanctuary was at Epidaurus, and from there the cult spread to Corinth, Athens, Cyrene in Libya, the island of Cos, and many other places. At these sanctuaries Greek doctors learned the use of potions, ointments, healthy regimens, and surgery. A device to remove barbed arrows, such as out of the eye of Philip the Great, was one of their surgical inventions. The usual cure for disease was to sleep in a special hall and wait for a dream of the god coming to work a cure; this was likely in conjunction with healthy medical practices.

The most famous Greek doctor was **Hippocrates**, whose oath to care for the sick is still repeated by graduating doctors today. Hippocrates worked at the Asclepius sanctuary at Cos at the same time Socrates lived in Athens. He was the first to study the working of the body and its parts in relation to the whole body.

There was a great deal of superstition and religion mixed with the practise of ancient medicine, but cleanliness, healthy food, rest, and a number of good, naturally occurring drugs, like silphium from Libya, helped the healing process. There are many records of cures left at these sanctuaries. Some of the cures seem nearly miraculous, but we have no reason to doubt the truth of the inscriptions or the hundreds of clay body parts dedicated to the god in thanks:

> Hermon the Thasian. (The god) healed this man who was blind but afterwards when he did not bring the thank-offering, the god made him blind again. When he came and again slept in the shrine, the god cured him.
> *Inscriptiones Graecorum*, IV2, 1.122.

One common complaint was solved in antiquity, at least in the case of Heraieus of Mytilene. His dedication inscription reads:

> He did not have hair on his head, but a great deal on his chin. Being ashamed because he was laughed at by others, he slept in the shrine. And the god, anointing his head with a drug, made him grow hair.
> *Inscriptiones Graecorum*, IV2, 1.121.

Homosexuality

While some societies have abhorred, ridiculed, or even attacked homosexuality, this was not the case among the Greeks. On the contrary, homosexuality was quite a conspicuous part of Greek life. The Greeks were ready to respond favourably to the open expression of homosexual affection whether in words and behaviour, or in literature and the visual arts. Many vase paintings, for example, depict homosexual courtship and love. For the most part, these represent relationships between older males and younger ones. This was particularly a feature of aristocratic circles. Homosexuality is also a common theme in Greek poetry, and Plato treats it on a philosophical level when examining the concepts of ideal beauty and love.

The finest unit of warriors in the Theban army during its period of dominance in the fourth century B.C. was called the Sacred Band. This Sacred Band was entirely made up of homosexual partners. It was believed, and indeed proved correct, that such warriors would fight most bravely if standing in battle beside their beloved partners. At the battle of Chaeronaea in 338 B.C., when Philip the Great crushed the Greek army opposing his rule over mainland Greece, the Sacred Band of Thebes died to a man fighting ferociously against him.

The exceptional example of female homosexuality is found in the poetry of **Sappho** (ca. 600 B.C.) who ran a finishing school for aristocratic girls on the island of Lesbos. Her poetry was regarded by the Greeks as among the most beautiful ever produced. The common theme in her poems is her deep love for certain students of her school. It is because of the poetry of Sappho that the island of Lesbos has given its name to female homosexuality.

Science and Technology

Greek mathematics reached very advanced levels, especially by the Hellenistic Age. Best known is the work of Pythagoras and Euclid in the area of geometry, but algebra and even trigonometry were also well developed. In the field of science only biology had advanced, most particularly due to the efforts of Aristotle. The Greeks had not yet learned the scientific method. They were able to observe natural phenomena carefully, but they were not able to carry out accurate experimentation to test their theories.

The Greeks did develop a number of more complicated machines based on simple devices such as the pulley, the lever, and the plane. Clock-like mechanisms with complex gears, perhaps to measure astronomical data, have been found. Large siege machines for hurling huge rocks against city-walls were built. The famous mathematician and inventor, Archimedes, developed a device, named the Archimedes screw, which is still used to bring water up out of streams to irrigate fields.

Archimedes lived in the Greek city of Syracuse in Sicily in the third century B.C. His preserved books show him to be one of the most imaginative mathematicians to have ever lived. As an inventor, he devised marvellous machines to repel the Romans' siege of Syracuse (214–212 B.C.), in which he himself was finally killed. He is remembered for having boasted, "give me a place to stand on and I will move the earth," no doubt thinking he could build a machine of pulleys and levers so that one person could lift the weight of the entire earth. Archimedes is probably best known for his shout of "Eureka!" meaning "I have found it!"

The king of Syracuse gave gold to a jeweller to make a crown, but when it was done, the king suspected that silver was used to replace some of the gold, even though the weight of the crown equalled the weight of the gold first given to the jeweller. He consulted Archimedes on how to prove this. Archimedes was puzzling over this when he went to the public baths and sat down in a full tub of water to relax. He watched the water pour over the tub rim as he lowered his body and suddenly realized he had the solution to his problem. He is said to have jumped out of the bath and run home naked, shouting, "Eureka!" He now knew that the volume of water displaced by the crown could be compared to the same volume of pure gold. The weight of this volume of gold could then be compared to the weight of the crown to see if it was indeed made of pure gold. More simply, the loss in weight of an object put into water is equal to the weight of the water displaced by the object. Archimedes discovered that the jeweller had indeed cheated the king.

Humans have always been ingenious at devising new weapons. For the siege of Rhodes in 305-304 B.C. Demetrius, nicknamed the Beseiger, constructed a nine-storey tower called the "Helepolis — the city destroyer" filled with catapults. It needed 3400 men to move and 200 to work the catapults.

The Role of Women

The question of women's roles in Greek society has received much scholarly attention in recent years. It is a topic, however, which depends on very spotty evidence since most of the archaeological and historical information was produced by Greek men. Governments were run by men, temples were built by men, writers and artists were men almost exclusively. One exception was the poet, Sappho, from Lesbos, who wrote in about 600 B.C., and was famous for her beautiful lyric verses.

Among the Greek city-states, the women of Sparta enjoyed more independence and rights than any other Greek women, as was mentioned earlier in Chapter 8. The militaristic orientation of Spartan society often meant that men were away from home, either at war or living together with other Spartan men in barracks-type conditions. This left a larger role for women to play in daily affairs. The women of Athens led very sheltered lives. They oversaw the running of their own households, but rarely ventured out in public, even to shop. Their skills in the production of textiles were admired, but cloth was woven just to fill household needs, not for commercial reasons.

Equality between men and women did not exist in any Greek city-state, yet it is curious to learn just how equal in power the male and female gods of the Greeks were. Part of the explanation is that female deities were commonly worshipped in Greece before the Greek tribes arrived, so the Greeks absorbed them into their religion. Their cults continued to be strong in the Classical period. Probably, there was also a strong perception that aspects of the divine world were closely associated with elements of the female personality.

In the area of religion women had a significant public part to play. In Athens more than 40 priesthoods were held by women, and some festivals and rituals were led by women, such as the Thesmophoria festival of Demeter, goddess of fertility and agriculture.

Another good example of a women's festival occurred at the sanctuary of Artemis at Brauron, located about 30 km outside Athens on the east coast of Attica. Here Artemis was worshipped as the goddess of childbirth, and especially of happy deliveries. She was linked to the bear, though the reason is no longer known, so that her young worshippers, girls not yet married, took the guise of little bears (arctoi) in the rites performed in Artemis' honour. Little girls as novices of the cult wore yellow dresses, reminiscent of the skin of the bear, in the ceremonies. It was a rite of initiation preceding puberty and was meant to guarantee a fertile marriage and safe childbirth. This was probably the single most important aspect of a Greek woman's life.

Women in Greek society fulfilled their role in life almost entirely as homemakers. It was mostly through the imagination of Greek men that they found a place in the literature and art of this civilization. Occasionally a woman played a part in public life, as wife or mother of a ruler, such as Demarete at Sparta, but otherwise they did not participate in political life, either to hold office or even to vote. In truth, women in most city-states could not even own property, and had to have a male guardian in legal matters. One exception to this was in Sparta. The guardian was usually a woman's father before she married, and her husband afterwards.

Women led a secluded life in their homes. Pericles summarized womanly virtue this way:

> Great is your good name…when you give men the least occasion to talk about you, whether it be by way of praise or blame.
> Thuc. G.F. Else, MacKendrick and Howe trans., II.46, p. 243.

There was a separate section in the home for men only called the *andron*. Here men would hold drinking parties often with cultured female non-citizen "companions." Pericles himself lived with one of these companions, a brilliant woman named Aspasia.

Some ancient authors leave the impression that Greek men were nervously fearful of women and that they regarded the female character as unpredictable and mysterious. Other authors regard women with a more liberal attitude, such as Herodotus who shows their influence in many historical events, or the Athenian playwrights, who have women in key roles in their dramas.

Attitudes towards women and their role in society began to change after 400 B.C. Women appear in Greek art in much less modest attire, many times naked. Women are allowed to participate in important athletic competitions, though the Olympics were never opened to them, and they began to acquire a stronger role in public life. Women like Cleopatra, ruler of Hellenistic Egypt, were still an exception in terms of political power.

Beliefs and Festivals

The Greeks did not set aside one day out of seven for religious observances as is common nowadays. Instead there were many special days to celebrate and honour the different gods. These days occurred at irregular intervals. On the other hand, Greeks also did not wait for a holy day to pay their respects to the gods. There were altars, shrines, temples, and statues of the gods everywhere in their towns and in the countryside. As one felt the need for help in a certain aspect of one's life, a person might give a small gift and say a little prayer at the appropriate god's shrine and then be on one's way. There were gods of birth, death, and the Underworld; gods for women, the weather and wine; gods of war, peace, victory, and healing; in short for all aspects and segments of society. There were, however, about a dozen more important gods, most of whom were thought to reside on Mt. Olympus. It is to these gods that the Greeks built their beautiful temples.

All the gods were thought to have human forms and characters, in other words they were anthropomorphic. This is an important idea to understand as it explains the Greek attitude towards the gods. Just as relationships between people are governed by the principle "something for something," so were the relationships between people and gods. People paid honour to the gods with festivals, offered sacrifices of honey-cakes, terracotta figurines, or animals, and in exchange they expected the god's blessings, or at least to avoid the god's punishments.

Priests were usually chosen from aristocratic families whose tradition it was to guard the sacred cults, but they had no special education or training in theology. Their duty was to organize and perform the sacred rituals on behalf of the communities. In order to explain the many unusual rites and choice of cult locations, myths grew up. These myths told about events in the lives of the different gods. This was as close as the Greeks came to a rational theology or statements of doctrine.

Temples were built as houses for the gods. The richer the city, the greater the temples which were built. The temples were symbols of the wealth and power of the community and of its protecting patron deity. The temples themselves were not places of worship; virtually all rituals in a cult revolved around altars that were outside the temples. In fact in most sanctuaries there was only an altar and no temple at all.

The Greeks strongly believed that the gods communicated with them; this might take place through the songs of birds, the rustling of leaves, the entrails of animals, or the voice of a special person like a prophet. So, for example, the sanctuary of Apollo at Delphi became famous because the oracle there was regarded as so reliable. Apollo spoke answers to peoples' inquiries through his priest, an old woman called the Pythia.

It was also possible for people to address their concerns to the gods. The normal way was through prayers accompanied by gifts, but in the popular area of black magic and sorcery, it was also possible to cast spells and put curses on people. A curse on an enemy might be invoked by scratching the enemy's name and the desired curse on a sheet of lead, often scrambling up the letters, then folding up the sheet and driving a bronze nail through it. The piece of lead was then buried in a grave or in a sanctuary to the goddess Persephone—who was supposed to dwell in the Underworld for six months of the year—so that the Underworld powers might carry out the curse.

Festivals were of many different types depending on the cult, its rites, and its importance. Fertility cults often had very wild, ribald festivals, in some cases with people dressing up in costumes and becoming drunk, or otherwise changing their personality, so that they took on a kind of animal nature. Festivals of Dionysus were like this, and the one in Athens eventually led to the development of drama; as part of a competition plays were performed there in honour of the god.

Most festivals included a procession of priests, worshippers, sacred objects, and animals for sacrifice. The more popular festivals often had competitions in poetry, music, dance, and athletics with valuable prizes to the winner. The Olympic Games, for example, were part of a five-day festival in honour of Zeus at Olympia, in the Peloponnese. Athletic contests were held on the second and fourth days of this festival as well as on the afternoon of the third day. The first, third, and fifth days were given over to processions, sacrifices, and prayers to Zeus. No music or poetry contest interfered with the athletic games here, and although the reward at Olympia was a simple wreath of sacred olive branches, the home city of a winner usually gave its victors prizes equivalent to tens of thousands of dollars.

The Greeks were generally quite tolerant of the religious beliefs of others, probably because Greek religion did not have a fixed theology, mother church, or rigid rules. For example, the sophists in fifth-century Athens could discuss their serious doubts about the existence or knowability of the gods, and the comedy writer, Aristophanes, could portray Dionysus as a cowardly fop in *The Frogs*. But the Greeks could also be deadly serious about religion, especially at times when they thought the gods may have been ill-disposed towards them. So Protagoras, the sophist, is said to have fled Athens after being convicted on a charge of atheism in 411 B.C., Socrates was executed in 399 B.C. on the twin charges of corrupting the youth of Athens and introducing new gods to Athens, and in 414 B.C. a number of wealthy young men of Athens were tried and executed on the charge of impiety.

Trade and Coinage

In Greece, trade over great distances or in any large quantities was carried out by ship since overland travel, by pack animal, was difficult and expensive. It seems probable that Phoenician ships first visited Greek shores during the Dark Ages for trading purposes. This stimulus may soon have encouraged Greeks to make voyages in their own ships, perhaps built especially for the purpose, though more likely ones used for fishing or island raiding. In any case they were small, as underwater archaeologists have shown from actual remains, with a crew of four or five and a capacity of several tonnes.

It was soon found that profits from a successful voyage could be high, as much as two or three times the cost of the cargo, but the risks from storms and pirates, as well as costs of a ship, were high. A normal venture began with a merchant borrowing money from a banker at a rate of 25 to 60 percent for the term of the voyage. The money would then be used to purchase a cargo. The merchant would make a contract with a shipowner for space on his ship to carry the cargo, for example copper ingots from

Cyprus back to Athens. The shipowner presumably would have a contract with another merchant to carry a cargo outbound to Cyprus from Athens, for example, olive oil and fine pottery. The merchant would accompany the ship in order to make the best deal possible for the copper. Returning to Piraeus, the merchant then had to find a buyer for his cargo, and pay off the shipowner and his banker with the necessary interest. If demand for copper were high, as in wartime when bronze armour was needed, the merchant may have made a considerable profit.

The most common trade goods included grain to Greece from south Russia, Sicily, or Egypt in exchange for olive oil and wine; luxury goods like glass, alabaster, perfumes, and ivory from Phoenicia and Egypt for Greek silver or white marble; timber and pitch for shipbuilding from the north Aegean in exchange for olive oil and finished goods like pottery, furniture, jewelry, or textiles.

For century upon century trade had depended on a system of bartering. Traders made deals to exchange a certain amount of one product for a certain amount of another—there was no money involved because money did not yet exist—200 kg of salt might be traded for 150 kg of grain, and so on. Countless days were no doubt spent arguing over amounts and types of compensation. Eventually traders recognized that small amounts of precious metals might be conveniently accepted almost anywhere in exchange for more usable products. The precious metals, copper, bronze, silver, electrum (an alloy of silver and gold), and even pure gold, could be carried in small chunks, weighed by the traders and used as a form of exchange. Chunks of different sizes always had to be weighed against different standards of weight which was awkward. Of course there were also widely varying standards of purity for metals, or different percentages of metals in alloys. The answer to these difficulties was to stamp the chunks of precious metal as a symbol of their weight and purity. This began in the eighth and seventh centuries. The stamp of certain traders came to be trusted more than others. An important step occurred when states began to do their own stamping of metal chunks, and so throw the reputation of the state or monarch behind the quality of the metal and its standard of weight. Thus was born the first coinage.

The first mints dating to the seventh century B.C., were in Lydia and the east Greek states, but it quickly spread to the trading cities of Athens, Corinth, Aegina, and Chalcis in the western Aegean. Silver became the most common metal. By the time of the Athenian Empire in the fifth century, the so-called owls of Athens, with an owl on one side and the head of Athena on the other, became the most common coinage in the Mediterranean area.

The Greatness of the Greeks

There is no use in trying to show that the Greeks as a people were in any way superior human beings. They were not; and even if they had some special characteristic, it could not be conclusively demonstrated now. Their accomplishments were great, but the explanation is not such a mystery. A very large portion of the male population had the freedom and encouragement to exercise their natural talents. If all Greeks, men and women, slaves, foreigners, and free people, had had the same opportunity, the accomplishments would likely have been proportionally greater.

The geography of the country produced a vibrant tension between communities, but also an opportunity for sharing of ideas and feelings. The sea provided a kind of defensive moat protecting the Greeks from more powerful neighbours, but also a ready vehicle for the exchange of goods, ideas, and information. The Greeks were very receptive towards the ideas offered by the Near East. On the other hand, their independent nature never allowed them to be slavish imitators. When it came time to build on the accomplishments of Near Eastern cultures, the Greeks used careful rational thought combined with their natural curiosity. This use of logical thought may be partly credited to their political system. In their small city-states, personal power was derived from being persuasive in public argument. Persuasion depended on being rational. In this way rationality was encouraged.

Their climate was comfortable and conducive to the outdoor life and mingling with neighbours. The system of farming with slaves and tenants, and the mercantile interests of many Greeks, produced both wealth and leisure time. This in turn gave freedom to many individuals to turn to other areas of human interest: literature, philosophy, music, art, and so on.

It is hard to imagine western civilization separately from its foundations in the Greek civilization. Trying to explain the lasting influences of Greek civilization is like trying to dissect the whole of western civilization itself in order to examine its skeleton. There are, for example, thousands of words used in English and other European languages that are derived from ancient Greek such as technology, history, geography, politics, philosophy, economy, democracy, and microscope. The study of all later philosophy is said to be merely footnotes to Plato. Of course this is an exaggeration, but it points clearly to the importance of Plato and to other Greek philosophers not only for initiating the field of philosophy, but also for introducing many of the greatest philosophical questions.

Classical art strongly influenced artists during the Renaissance in Europe, both sculptors and painters. Much modern art that is very abstract or non-representational is in fact a reaction against Classical art. Classical artists were so successful in their art that modern artists have felt no room to improve on it, so that it has been necessary to break away into entirely new types of art. In architecture, there was a

One of the great sculptures of antiquity, which profoundly influenced artists of the Renaissance, was the Laocoon group. This detailed composition depicts the priest Laocoon and his two sons engaged in a deadly struggle with snakes. It was discovered in Rome in 1506 and was of great inspiration to Michelangelo.

strong Neo-classical revival beginning in the eighteenth century, so that banks, art museums, train stations, and stately mansions imitate the Doric, Ionic, and Corinthian styles of Greece.

It is probably in the field of drama that Greek innovations had the greatest impact on our lives. Live theatre goes back to the staged productions at the festivals of Dionysus in Athens. But when you think about it, our movies and television shows are just another form of the comedies and tragedies performed by the Greeks.

Finally, it is the Greeks we must look to for the foundations of the discipline of history. Herodotus was dubbed the "Father of History" by the Roman writer Cicero. He might also be called the Father of Comparative Anthropology according to some. His immediate successor, Thucydides, set a standard for historical research that has lasted through the ages till the modern era. Greeks were the first to treat the writing of history not as the simple recording of events, but as the rational explanation of those events. This certainly is still one of the primary goals of historians.

Suggested Sources for Further Research

Biers, W.R., *The Archaeology of Greece, An Introduction*, rev. ed. (Cornell University Press, 1987).

Boardman, J., Griffin, and O.J. Murray eds. *The Oxford History of the Classical World* (Oxford University Press, 1986).

Boardman, J., *The Greeks Overseas: Their Early Colonies and Trade* (Thames and Hudson Ltd., 1980).

Bury, J.B., and R. Meiggs, *A History of Greece* (MacMillan Co., 1978).

Cadogan, G., *Palaces of Minoan Crete* (Barrie and Jenkins Ltd., 1976).

Chadwick, J., *The Mycenaean World* (Cambridge University Press, 1976).

Frost, Frank J., *Greek Society* (D.C. Heath and Co., 1987).

Grant, Michael, *The Classical Greeks* (Charles Scribner's Sons, 1989).

Hammond, N.G.L. and H.H. Scullard, eds. *The Oxford Classical Dictionary* (Oxford University Press, 1970).

Hooker, J.T., *The Ancient Spartans* (J.M. Dent & Sons, 1980).

McGregor, M.F., *The Athenians and their Empire* (University of British Columbia Press, 1987).

Meiggs, R., *The Athenian Empire* (Oxford University Press, 1972).

Warren, P., *The Aegean Civilizations* (Elsevier-Phaidon Press, 1975).

Focus Your Knowledge

1. How did Athens use the fear of further Persian invasions to its advantage?
2. What was the outcome of the Peloponnesian War? What proved to be the decisive factor in determining the eventual victor?
3. Briefly summarize the major advances made by Greek artists during the fifth century B.C.
4. What role did religion play in the daily lives of the ancient Greeks?
5. How did trade enrich life in ancient Greece? Explain why coinage was a by-product of the development of extensive and complex trading networks.

Apply Your Knowledge

1. Although the Persian Wars temporarily united the Greeks, in the long run they proved divisive. By examining the rise of the Athenian Empire and the causes of the Peloponnesian War show this to be true.
2. The fifth century B.C. is considered to be the Golden Age of Athens. By examining the major achievements of the Athenians in this century show why this period is seen as the cultural zenith of the Greeks.
3. Considering his talents and achievements, is Alexander deserving of the title "the Great"?
4. Was the wealth and prosperity of ancient Athens reserved for the elite or is there evidence of a reasonably equitable distribution of wealth? Did all Athenians benefit from the achievements in art, architecture, and government?
5. Compare and contrast the role of women in ancient Greek society to that of the role of women in our society.

Extension Activities

1. Carry out research on life in ancient Sparta focusing on areas such as child bearing, education, the role of men and women in society, and marriage. Based on your research write a lively and vivid description of daily life in ancient Sparta from the perspective of a visitor from the twentieth century.

2. Select a play from one of the Greek writers such as Sophocles, Aeschylus, and Euripides. From the play chosen select a segment that could be learned and performed for the class. You will need to provide a summary of the play to set the stage. You may wish to follow your performance with a discussion of the issue presented in the play.

3. Based on your own research build a replica of the Parthenon. Be sure to include a brief written description that explains the various features of the Parthenon such as the built-in curves and slants, the architectural sculpture and the statue of Athena.

4. Choose a famous philosopher of ancient Greece and write a summary of some of his main ideas. Select an issue from today that the philosopher being studied would like to have grappled with. Provide a speculative answer that he may have given had he been faced with the issue. You may wish to present your response to the issue through a written report or by recreating the persona of the philosopher and doing a live or video-taped presentation.

5. Do a feature interview for the evening news with the great politician Pericles. Ask him questions about the pros and cons of the Athenian system of government as well as his opinion on the state of democracy in Canada today. Pericles should respond with both the problems he sees as well as solutions he would suggest.

6. Using the feature study on "Life and Leisure in Ancient Greece" as a starting point carry out further research into ancient Greek food and entertainment in preparation for hosting your own symposium in class. Attempt to recreate the clothing, food, furniture, and entertainment as accurately as possible.

CHAPTER 8

The Rise of Rome

Chapter Highlights

- Italy from its beginnings

- the Roman Republican government and the Ladder of Leaders

- the great Carthaginian leader Hannibal

- the Appian Way, the first paved road from Rome

- Caesar's rise to power

- daily life among the Romans

Human experience is, in reality, a very recent thing. The civilizations of the Near East and Egypt evolved, flourished, and faded away. Having prospered for a few centuries or even millennia, these once powerful societies have left only puzzling remains, which archaeologists attempt to recover and explain. After these great, complex societies came the Greeks. The Greeks were the first people generally recognized to leave behind a documented history of their day. From them we have inherited concepts that have had a lasting influence on modern society.

The Romans and their civilization succeeded the Greeks as the dominant political and cultural force in the Mediterranean basin, centred initially in the heart of the Italian peninsula. From the ultimate transformation of western-Roman society to our own day, there is a period of only about one and a half thousand years. Approximately the same length of time, from a legendary foundation date of 21 April 753 B.C., the Roman civilization took to develop and expand to encompass the entire known world.

We study Roman civilization today for many reasons. The Roman Republican constitution, the essentials of which were fixed as early as 509 B.C., is a model for many democracies. Roman architecture, with the invention of concrete, and its ability to vault great spans, was unmatched until recent times. The Romans' talent of administering to a people through their own bureaucracy while allowing them to maintain a unique cultural identity is a marvel and should, perhaps, be a model to us. The practicalities of the thousand-year-long enterprise were continually addressed by Roman administrators and bureaucrats with a mix of idealism and pragmatism. Roman society was founded on principles of justice and fair treatment for themselves and foreigners (*gentiles*) alike. Indeed, Roman justice was based on the proper application of evidence, which was not something the earlier Greeks were ever noted for. Moreover, the Romans had at the core of their being an unassailable belief in their own destiny to rule the known world. According to Virgil their mission was "to spare the conquered and put down the proud."

We study Roman civilization in an attempt to discover something about ourselves and our societies. Will we fade away just as the Romans did? Will our own increasingly globalized community be transformed beyond our ability to imagine its future shape or recognize its roots?

Key Concepts

Etruscans

Etruscan League of Twelve Cities

Romulus and Remus

Roman Senate

consul

Punic Wars

Hannibal

Appian Way

Gracchus Brothers

Julius Caesar

First Triumvirate

Vestal Virgins

Cicero

epicureanism

Italy: The Republican Period

Geography

The Italian peninsula lies in the geographic centre of the Mediterranean basin, surrounded on three sides by what the Romans called *Mare Nostrum* or Our Sea. More east-west than north-south (modern-day Venice is, in fact, west of Rome), the land mass is separated from the rest of Europe by a rugged mountain chain, the Alps. These mountains form an escarpment which is more readily crossed from the north. It provides the people of northern Italy, however, with a formidable protective barrier. The peninsula is approximately 1000 km long and 200 km wide. It is itself divided for most of its length by the Apennine Mountains. This diagonal barrier, no higher than about 3000 m, is still not easily penetrated. In Roman times, it proved to be quite a hurdle for internal communications.

Water-borne transport was a favoured means of communication. However, there are few rivers that were naturally navigable for most of their length. The most important were the Po River, which for many centuries acted as a border between the civilized inhabitants of Italy proper and their wilder neighbours to the north, and the Tiber River in central Italy. The story of Rome is the story of the growing influence and expansionist policies of a small settlement in the Tiber Valley, about 20 km from the sea.

Although there were few good harbours and the Romans were notoriously unadventurous sailors, coastal trade was brisk. To the southeast were the ports of Brindisi and Taranto. To the northwest were the two ports of Genoa and La Specia; although they were hardly ever used in Roman times. The later Roman navies were stationed in the Bay of Naples south of Rome and in the north on the estuary of the Po, at Ravenna. An artificial, commercial port was built at Ostia at the mouth of the Tiber to supply the city of Rome. The word port, in fact, comes from the place's name, Portus.

Sources of metal ore were rare in ancient times. Those mineral deposits that were mined were chiefly in the northwest along the coast of Tuscany (copper) and on the island of Elba (iron). Tin, which when added to copper forms the alloy bronze, was imported to the peninsula from as far away as Cornwall in southwestern Britain. Building materials were plentiful. There was a porous, easily-worked, yellowish limestone called tufa found near Rome. There was also marble from Carrara (modern Luna), but this stone was expensive and hard to work. As a result, it was not exploited until the first century B.C. These were supplemented by a dust, pozzolana, originally identified near Vesuvius, a volcano extinct for most of recorded time. This dust had several desirable qualities, not the least of which was its ability when mixed up with aggregate to make a concrete that would set under water. Concrete came to be Rome's unique contribution to the art of building.

Vesuvius, as has been said, remained dormant for much of Rome's history. Overlooking the Bay of Naples, it is merely one in a series of volcanoes, active and inactive, that stretch down the Tyrrhenian coast of Italy to Stromboli in the Lipari Islands and Etna in Sicily. The presence of volcanic soil on the western side of the peninsula increased the fertility of Italy's cultivable land, already enriched by **fluvial deposits** brought down from the northern mountains by the river Po. While the Italian peninsula was generally fertile along the narrow coastal plains and in river valleys, an expanding urban population led to an increased reliance on grain imported from Sicily and Egypt. From the height of the Roman Empire to its ultimate collapse in the west in the sixth century A.D., the urban population of Rome was dependent on foreign imports of grain and, therefore, was vulnerable to external pressures.

The climate of the peninsula is Mediterranean, that is to say, relatively mild. Temperatures in winter and summer are moderated by the proximity of the

On August 24, A.D. 79 the towns of Pompeii and Herculaneum were frozen in time. Without warning, Mount Vesuvius (background) erupted blowing off the top of the mountain and burying Pompeii (foreground) in ash, and Herculaneum under 21 m of mud. The remarkable state of preservation of these two towns has provided a wealth of knowledge about daily life in ancient Rome.

sea, although greater extremes of cold (snow) and heat are felt in the hinterland. In the summer months, the heat is intensified by a dry, southerly breeze that rolls away the clouds to allow the sun's uninterrupted glare. In winter, from October to March, the wind's direction is reversed, bringing cold fronts in from the European continent and making the period unsuitable for sailing.

The relatively mild climate, general agricultural prosperity, seclusion from the rest of Europe, and a central position in the Mediterranean world, were all important factors in the development of Rome. Combined, these factors helped the peasants of Rome grow from their rustic beginnings to become the inhabitants of a great city and ultimately the guardians of a world power.

The Etruscans

Before Rome developed into a great urban centre on the banks of the Tiber, a sophisticated society held sway in Italy. This was the society of the **Etruscans**. They controlled territory roughly from the Po to Cumae on the northern edge of the Bay of Naples. To the northeast, Etruscan power—though not influence—was limited by the Apennine chain.

Rome itself, however, was not one of the **Etruscan League of Twelve Cities**, the first true European **confederacy**.

Even though the Etruscan language has never been convincingly deciphered, enough is known about these people today to form a relatively precise opinion of how they contributed to the rise of Rome and to distinctive aspects of Rome's psyche.

The Etruscans buried their dead in tombs hollowed out of the ground or under great mounds of earth (tumuli). Usually the interiors of the tombs were fitted out to resemble the houses of the living. Much can be learned about the Etruscans from the relief sculptures cut in the rock walls of the chambers. The Etruscans often decorated these tombs with frescoes (wall paintings) depicting banquets, gladiatorial combat, chariot races, and the like. It is known that several characteristic elements in Roman life (including numerals, human blood sports, a belief in Hades and the underground gods, auguries, and excessive superstition) were all inherited by the Romans from the Etruscans. Not only were elements of the Etruscan way of life preserved by Romans, so too were characteristics of Etruscan political affairs. The high magistrates of the Roman Republic took over the purple garb and ivory thrones of the Etruscan kings (lucumones) and their symbols of authority over life and death (fasces). The fasces (an axe in a bundle of rods, in this century the symbol of the Fascists) were carried in attendance by an escort of officials known as lictors.

The Etruscans may have been indigenous to Italy or an immigrant people from Asia Minor (the Middle East). They were skilled artisans and accomplished traders. There were only two other competing civilizations in the Mediterranean world in the heyday of the Etruscans: the Greek city-states, especially Sicily and Magna Graecia (southern Italy from Taranto up the west coast as far as Naples), and the Carthaginians in Tunisia. Various complex arrangements kept Greek commercial interests dominant in the south; while, in the north, the Etruscan and Carthaginian fleets co-operated to their mutual advantage.

In 524 B.C. the Greeks attempted to gain control of the islands of Sardinia and Corsica. The Etruscans

MAJOR EVENTS IN ROMAN HISTORY

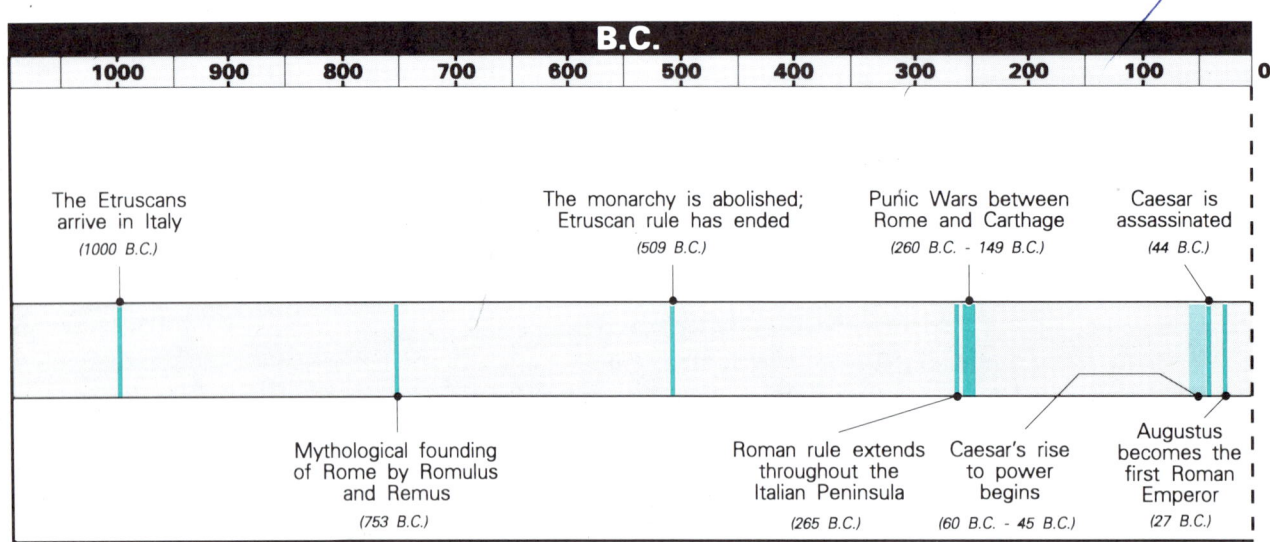

responded by trying to overpower the Greek colony of Cumae. Some 50 years later, in 474 B.C., the Greeks under Hiero of Syracuse engaged the Etruscans in a naval battle off Cumae. The Greek fleet was victorious and smashed forever the sea power of the Etruscans. Until the sack of Veii by the Romans in 396 B.C., the cities of the Etruscan League became essentially land-based powers.

The Monarchy

In the beginning kings ruled Rome, and as with other Etruscan cities, there was a rigid aristocracy. Inherited membership in the aristocracy was based almost exclusively on the ownership of land. The period of monarchical rule lasted from Rome's mythical founding 21 April 753 B.C. to 509 B.C., when the last Etruscan king, L. Tarquinius Superbus (Tarquin the Proud), was expelled in a popular uprising.

According to the historian Livy (Titus Livius, 59 B.C.–A.D. 12), there were seven kings of Rome. The first was **Romulus** (753–715 B.C.). Romulus was allegedly the son of the god of war, Mars, and a priestess, Rhea Silvia. The death of Romulus and his twin brother **Remus** had been ordered by a cruel uncle Amulius. Cast adrift on the Tiber by generous servants, they eventually came to shore near the Palatine, later recognized to be one of the Seven Hills of Rome and residence of the Emperors (hence palace). There, they were nurtured by a she-wolf. Eventually, the boys were discovered and raised by a shepherd. The essentials of several legends relate that once the boys had attained manhood there was a bitter falling out between the brothers over Romulus's authority to found a city. In response to a direct challenge, Remus was killed. So Rome, a city destined for greatness, had its origins cloaked in bloodshed and **fratricide**.

The second king, Numa Pompilius (715–673 B.C.) was supposedly a Sabine (another non-Etruscan tribe in Italy) and responsible for several religious innovations. He was followed by a more war-like king, Tullius Hostilius (673–641 B.C.). He is known for his expansion of Rome's influence and his attack on Alba Longa, Rome's mother city in Latium, from

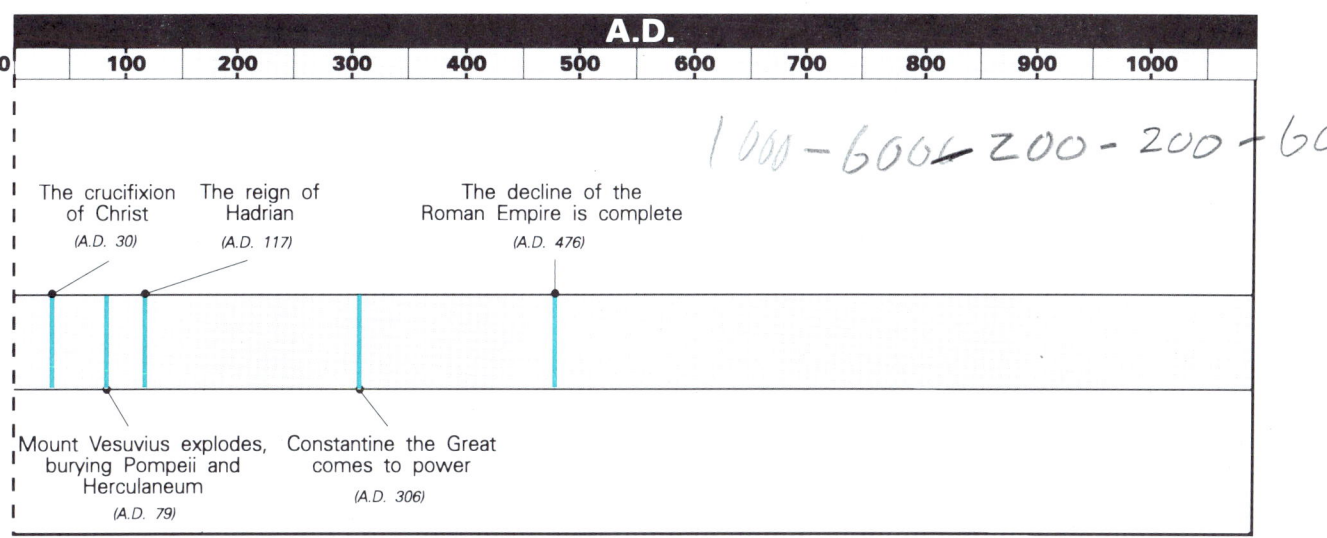

THE ARTS

THE ETRUSCAN LEAGUE OF TWELVE CITIES

The Etruscan League was a genuine confederacy of independent city-states whose populations spoke the same language and worshipped the same gods, two aspects of civilization that more or less define a society in the ancient world. The sacred headquarters, a sanctuary, was located at *Fanum Voltumnae* near *Volusii* (modern Bolsena). The cities of the League, as far as we know, were:

ANCIENT NAME	MODERN NAME
Arretium	Arezzo
Caere	Cerveteri
Clusium	Chiusi
Cortona or Faesulae	Cortona or Fiesole
Perusia	Perugia
Populonia	Porto Baratti
Rusellae	Roselle
Tarquinii	Poggio Colonna
Vetulonia	Volterra
Volsinii	Bolsena
Vulci	Ponte della Badia

The art of the Etruscans was influenced by the Greeks and later influenced the Romans. Their style is distinctive as is evident in this coffin from Cerveteri, dating from the sixth century B.C.

This famous statue is known as the Capitoline wolf, since it was found on the Capitol hill in Rome. The wolf is an early Etruscan sculpture, but the figures of Romulus, the legendary founder of Rome, and Remus, his twin brother, were a latter addition.

which Romulus had recruited the original colonists. His successor, Ancus Marcius (641–616 B.C.) was not so belligerent but still had to deal with the resentment of the Latins (hence the language) for the earlier attack on their city. Ancus Marcius became known for his statesmanship and for resettling the Latins in Rome and granting them security.

In time, the Etruscans expanded their power to the south and extended their dominion over the Romans. Their first king was L. Tarquinius Priscus (616–579 B.C.). He attempted to make Rome supreme and, to that end, constructed the great temple of Jupiter Optimus Maximus (Jupiter Best and Greatest) on another of Rome's seven hills, the Capitoline. In later years, one of the features of civilized living in a Roman town was the central focus provided by the town's capitolium, a temple dedicated to Jupiter, the Father of the Gods. Civilized living in Rome itself was also made possible by this king. It is said that the cloaca maxima (great sewer), whose outflow into the Tiber may still be seen today, was built on his command to drain the valley between the Palatine and Aventine hills. The second Etruscan king was Servius Tullius (579–534 B.C.). His great accomplishment is said to have been the completion of the program of urban renewal initiated by his predecessor.

A popular rebellion was the cause for L. Tarquinius Superbus's and the Etruscan overlords' expulsion from Rome. Tarquin the Proud, the last Etruscan king, gained a reputation for being overbearing and tyrannical as had his son, Sextus Tarquinius. In fact, it was the latter's rape of Lucretia that sparked the rebellion. Lucretia's virtuous behaviour, imaginatively described by Livy, became an example of model womanhood for later Romans. Lucretia disclosed the violation to her husband and father, and disregarding their impassioned entreaties she killed herself.

With the removal of the last king in 509 B.C., Rome had a clear way to form a relatively democratic Republic. It is interesting, however, to observe that the origins of Rome, in legend at least, are shrouded in violence and savagery; the murder of a brother and an assault on a woman.

The Republic

The Roman Republic (Res Publica, public matter) was a result of the people's discontent with the tyrannical, domineering attitudes of the kings. However, much of the subsequent, internal history of the state to 27 B.C. can be traced by following the relations between an over-bearing, land-owning aristocracy, the Patricians, and the often-times, landless poor, the Plebeians.

During the roughly five hundred years of the Roman Republic, the state faced several critical, external pressures. As with the Etruscans, the Roman state had to face the power of the Greeks and

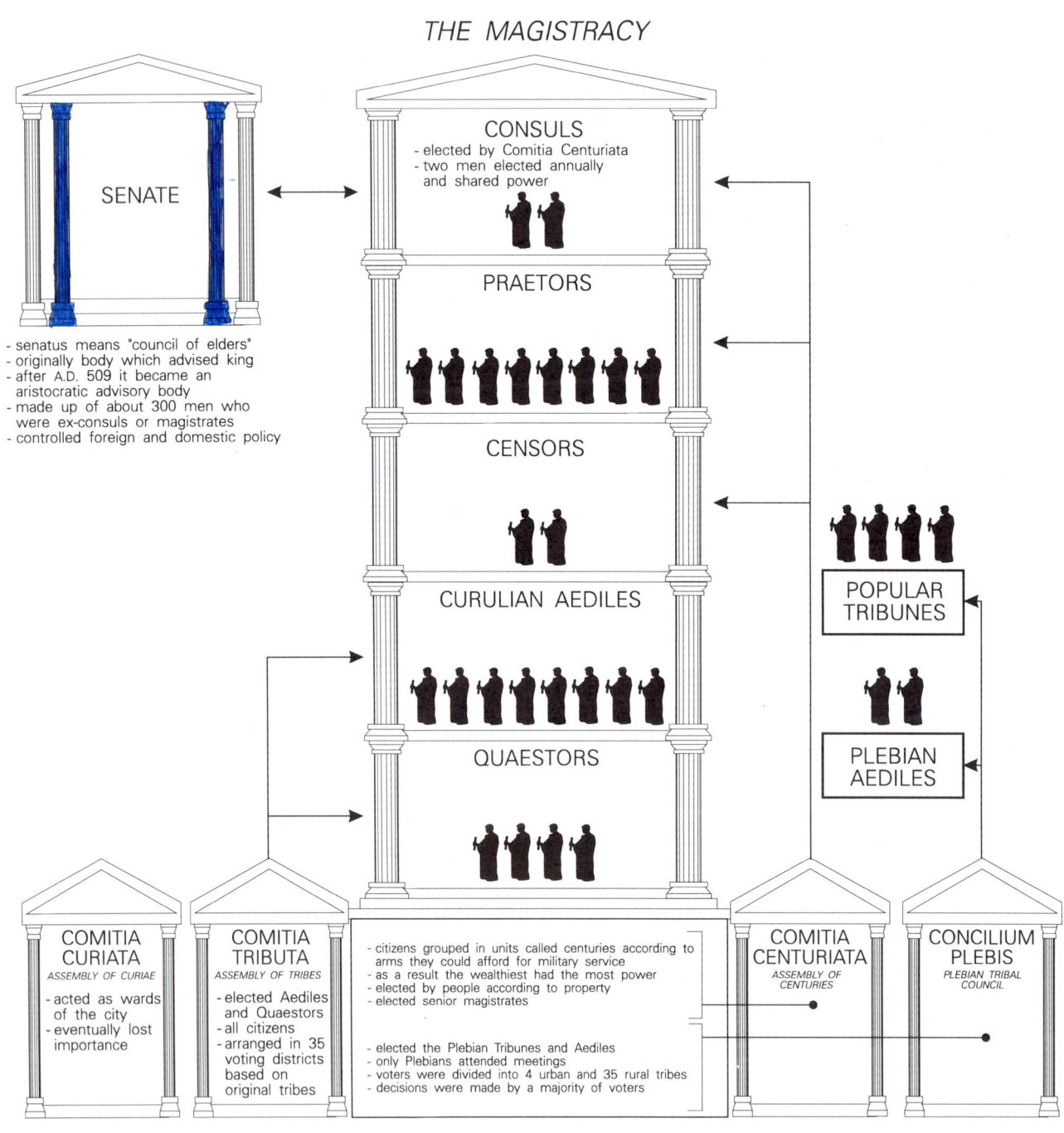

of the Carthaginians. In opposing and defeating such powerful enemies, Rome came to be a city-state whose influence and power constantly expanded. Ultimately, the city fathers of Rome became masters of most of the known world.

The Ladder of Leaders

The Roman Republic was known to its citizens significantly as the Senatus Populusque Romanus (SPQR, the Senate and People of Rome). As the name implies, there was constant tension between the Senatorial aristocracy and the people. Nowhere was this tension and the state's efforts to accommodate it more evident than in the means of government they developed as they reached political maturity. Today, the basic elements of the constitution of the United States of America are directly modelled on the Roman republican constitution, though they are slightly altered and the Roman constitution was never produced in a written form.

Assemblies. The Roman republican government was composed of several assemblies from which the magistrates were drawn. Before the expulsion of L. Tarquinius Superbus (Tarquin the Proud) in 509 B.C., the kings of Rome had been advised and supported by a council made up of the males who controlled the most land. This body was known as the **Senate** and continued to be important throughout the history of the Roman Republic.

The Comitia Centuriata was an important assembly of all land-owning male citizens, which was segregated according to wealth into five electoral classes (the wealthiest being the first to vote). The Comitia Centuriata passed laws presented to it by the annually elected senior magistrates.

In Rome's feudal state, the Comitia Curiata comprised the thirty divisions of the citizenry (curiae) from the three clans; Ramnes, Luceres, Tities. The main function of this assembly seems to have been attending the inauguration of the king and, later on, confirming a magistrate's right to exercise the authority already given by the Comitia Centuriata.

The Comitia Tributa was a shadowy assembly that consisted of all the **enfranchised** people in the city who belonged, nominally at least, to tribes. This assembly could pass laws on behalf of all the people; aristocrats who owned land and the mass of ordinary folk.

Finally, the Concilium Plebis was a tribal assembly much like the Comitia Tributa with the exception that aristocrats could not be members. It passed *plebiscita* (plebiscites) that had the force of law. (For more detail, see page 242, The People and their Tribunes.)

Magistrates. After Tarquin's removal, two men were elected from the Senate to become **consuls**, the chief magistrates of the Roman state. Consuls were elected annually; and, as we shall see with the other lesser magistrates, one colleague could veto (Latin for, I forbid) the decisions of the other, thereby acting as a check to the other person's possible abuse of power. This principle of collegiality lasted, off and on, throughout the whole history of the Roman world until its collapse in the sixth century A.D. in the west.

In addition to the regular, annual Ladder of Leaders, there was the extraordinary position of dictator. A dictator, who was appointed by the consuls, held the position for a specified period, usually six months. The appointment was made in relation to a specific crisis such as a war.

Elected annually, too, were the praetors. These officers were the next most powerful men in the state to the consuls. Originally, there was only one, a patrician responsible for the administration of justice in Rome itself. After a short while, however, another was added whose primary responsibility became relations between Roman citizens and non-Romans. As Rome took control of foreign territories, others were added. The number of praetors was increased to four in 227 B.C. on the conquest of Sicily and Sardinia, and to six in 197 B.C., with the tenuous acquisition of Spain. Eventually, the power of the patricians was eroded and not only was the number of praetors dramatically increased but plebeians won the right to stand for election.

Censors were established in the mid-fourth century B.C. Two would hold office together for five years. As former consuls, the major task facing these men was to draw up revised lists of citizens. As Rome became more powerful, so Roman citizenship became more attractive. The modern meaning of censor is derived from a secondary responsibility of the Roman officials, which was to oversee public morality.

Continuing the ladder of elected officialdom in the Roman republic were the aediles (originally two). At the beginning, their function was to assist the consuls. Later, however, their number was increased and they became responsible for such things as the maintenance of roads in the city, public executions, water, and official standards of measure.

Last on the rung of originally patrician officers were the quaestors. These annually elected officials were charged with administering financial matters, always considered a rather sordid business. At first, there were two quaestors, but as the area of Roman influence expanded, more were appointed.

The People and their Tribunes

For all the continuing attempts to control tensions and curb individual abuse of power, the division of patricians and plebeians remained a division between rich and poor, between those with power and influence and those without. Early in the fifth century (494 B.C.), in an attempt to redress that balance, a Council of Plebeians was set up and membership was restricted to non-Senatorial males. Two tribunes, who were given sacred immunity (like that of foreign diplomats today), were appointed and elected annually. They could even veto decisions made by the consuls. The tribunes, of which there were eventually ten, came to be very powerful interpreters of the people's wishes. This became especially true later in the century when decisions taken by the Council of Plebeians no longer needed the Senate's approval.

Growth and Maturity

For the next four hundred years the Roman Republic underwent incredible expansion and faced extreme danger. First, the wild Gauls of Europe, north of the Alps, crossed the mountains into Italy. Their leader Brennus is remembered at the Brenner Pass, one of the most important road and rail links between modern Italy and the rest of Europe. Although Rome was besieged and sacked by the Gauls, the city recovered and struck back, defeating and dispersing them.

Next, as the desire for increased trade grew, Rome's struggle for power over the sea intensified. Of necessity, this led to a clash with the Carthaginians who were at that time the greatest maritime power in the western Mediterranean. The Carthaginians were quite different to the Romans, racially and in outlook. Worshipping gods who demanded child sacrifice among other things, they came originally from what is now Lebanon and settled in North Africa. Above all, they were traders. Throughout much of their conflict with the Romans, from 264 B.C. till the time of the final destruction of Carthage in 146 B.C., they maintained a commercial empire, with links to Spain and southern Italy.

At the same time Rome was in conflict with Carthage, it was also expanding its dominion into the eastern Mediterranean, taking control of the eastern Greek cities. In Italy, they had already subdued

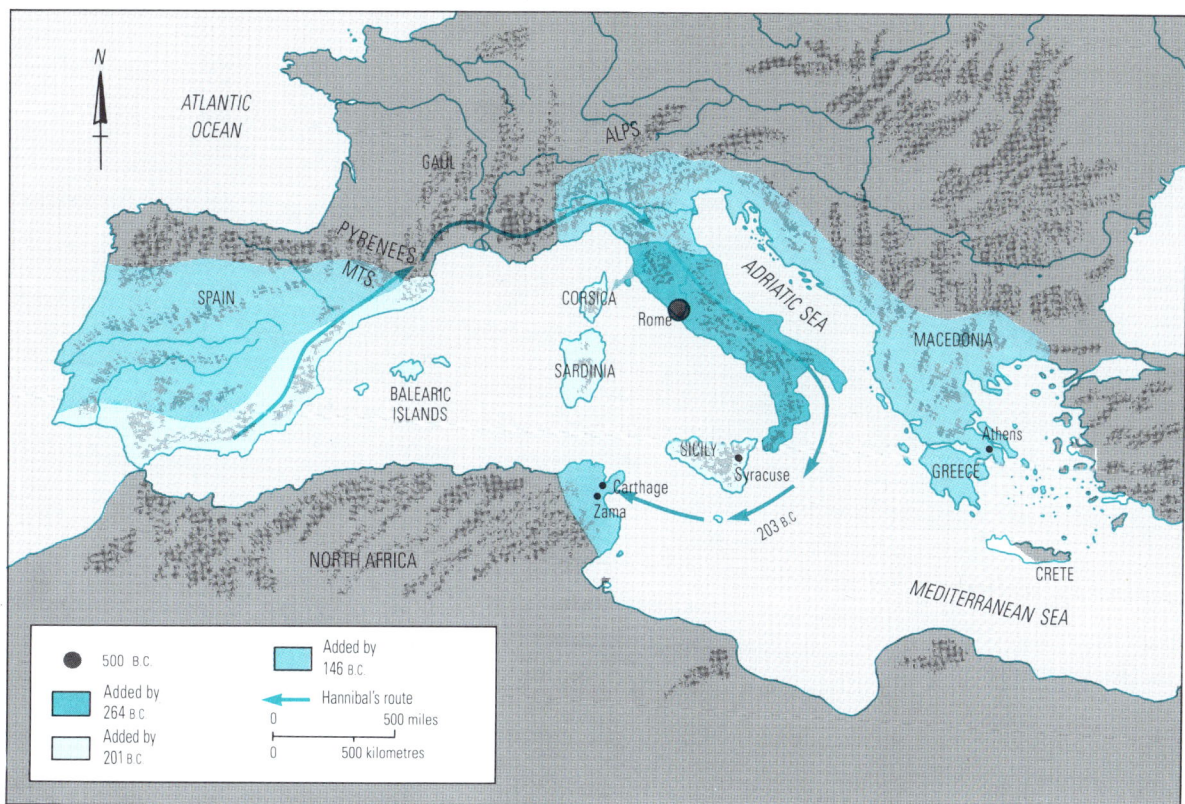

Roman Territory 500–146 B.C.

From World History: Traditions and New Directions by Peter N. Stearns, Donald R. Schwartz, Barry K. Beyer, © 1989 by Addison-Wesley Publishing Company, Inc.

many rival city-states and tribes and had planted, or encouraged to prosper, towns that would support their interests.

The Punic Wars

There were three fateful clashes with the Carthaginians: the **First Punic War**, 264–261 B.C.; the **Second Punic War**, 218–202 B.C.; and the **Third Punic War**, 149–146 B.C. (Punic is derived from the Latin word meaning Phoenician, referring to Carthaginian origins). Undoubtedly, the most dangerous time for Rome after the defeat of the invading Gauls, was the Second Punic War. The Carthaginian military leader at this time (218–202 B.C.) was **Hannibal**, stationed in Spain. Hannibal was the son of Hamilcar Barca, who had done much to help restore Carthage after its first defeat by the Romans. He now ruled the Iberian peninsula like a private kingdom.

In 218 B.C., Hannibal left Spain and led a land-based attack on the Romans by crossing the Alps, a feat which is still marvelled at today. Hannibal started from Spain with between 35 000–40 000

The Rise of Rome CHAPTER 8 243

troops and 37 elephants, but when he arrived in Northern Italy only about 26 000 soldiers and a single elephant had survived the crossing of the Alps. It is probable that Hannibal's military skill was poor and that the Alpine barrier was much more formidable than he had been led to believe. For all Hannibal's losses, he engaged in four great battles over the next two years. These battles were astounding for the magnitude of Roman losses. On 2 August 216 B.C., for example, at Cannae in southern Italy over 50 000 soldiers from a Roman army of 86 000 were annihilated in one day.

Hannibal managed to conquer most of the Italian peninsula. The Battle of Cannae, however, even though one of history's most resounding successes, did not lead to Hannibal's conquest of Rome itself; all that happened was that the Carthaginians gained a base in southern Italy. Fourteen years later, through patient guerilla warfare, the Romans eventually drove Hannibal out of Italy and finally defeated him in Tunisia, North Africa.

One question asked many times about Hannibal's invasion of the Italian peninsula is why did the city of Rome escape? Perhaps the answer is twofold. First, the Carthaginians saw no advantage in setting siege to a city that had been recently fortified. (The so-called Servian Wall was constructed after the Gallic invasions. A reconstructed part of that wall may be seen to the right when leaving the entrance of Rome's main railway station, Roma-Termini.) Second, Hannibal was fearful of a city that after so many disastrous engagements could continue to raise army after army.

Scipio Africanus

Publius Cornelius Scipio was born into an aristocratic, military family in 236 B.C. He is said to have saved his father's life in an early battle against Hannibal in 218 B.C. at Ticinus and to have rallied the survivors of the disaster at Cannae in 216 B.C.

Appointed by the people to command in Spain, he followed the aggressive strategies previously adopted by his father. In a brilliant series of manoeuvres, Scipio systematically rid Spain of the Carthaginians. Although complete Roman domination of the Iberian peninsula was years in the future, it was Scipio who established a permanent and undeniable Roman presence in Spain. The determination Scipio displayed in Spain continued through his consulship in 205 B.C. when, against Senatorial opposition, he took an army to Sicily and wrested parts of the island from Hannibal's control. In the year following his consulship, Scipio crossed with 35 000 men to Africa. Again, in a series of engagements reminiscent of the Spanish campaign, Scipio besieged the fortress at Utica (204 B.C.), defeated three Carthaginian armies, and captured Tunis (203 B.C.). The Carthaginians sued for peace.

While the terms for peace were being considered in Rome, Hannibal returned to Africa across the sea from southern Italy. Carthaginian morale was restored and the Punic state once more took up arms. Scipio, however, joined with a king from nearby Numidia, Masinissa, and together in a typical Scipio style defeated Hannibal at the Battle of Zama in 202 B.C. For that victory, Scipio was awarded the honorific name Africanus by the Roman state. This was, perhaps, Scipio Africanus's greatest moment, but not the end of his career. In 199 B.C., Scipio was elected censor and became the leading man in the Senate. A lover of Greek things, he argued during his second consulship (194 B.C.) that mainland Greece should not be totally abandoned, but to no avail.

Subject also to the jealousies often met by successful but humble people, Scipio Africanus was eventually humiliated in a series of trials. The trials were not merely politically motivated and directed against his family, but were also engendered by the Roman apprehension toward those enthusiastic about Greek culture. He retired from the city in 184–83 B.C. and died soon after. The great lesson for

Rome from Scipio Africanus's life was that the Roman state had the potential to be the preeminent power in the Mediterranean world, and not merely a powerful city in the Italian peninsula.

From the Carthaginians defeated at Zama in 202 B.C., the Romans exacted a heavy toll. The Carthaginians were obliged to pay huge war reparations, forfeit their commercial empire, and to dismantle their once-powerful navy. Within fifty years, however, their power was again on the rise. A neighbouring kingdom in North Africa, Numidia, became fearful of that increase in power and appealed to Rome.

The Romans, under the pretext of assisting Numidia, waged a war against Carthage. Remembering their incredible losses at Cannae and elsewhere, the Romans not only defeated the Carthaginians but entirely razed the city of Carthage itself. In one of the most savage acts the world has seen, the city was plundered, burned, and eventually ploughed under. Into the furrows left by the plough, ritual salt was poured. The reason? To symbolize the curse of eternal sterility the Romans had laid on the site of the once proud city.

Thanks to the record of a contemporary historian, Polybius, who was present at the destruction of Carthage, we have the actual words of the commanding Roman general, P. Scipio Aemilianus, grandson of Scipio Africanus: "We have made a desert and called it peace."

Eastern Expansion

The obliteration of Carthage was not the only result of Rome's expansionist policies. The Greek world in the eastern Mediterranean came to experience the power of Rome's armies. In the same year as Carthage was destroyed in North Africa, another ancient capital came subject to the Romans; Corinth, the last independent Greek city-state.

Always a turbulent independence, there had been conflict in the Greek world since the death of Alexander the Great in 323 B.C. These squabbles were among the inheritors of Alexander's Empire: the kingdoms of Antigonus in Macedonia and the Peloponnese, Seleucus in Asia Minor, and Ptolemy in Egypt. Added to this volatile mixture were the pirates in the Adriatic sea between the Italian and Balkan peninsulas. Roman trading and maritime commerce were not secure. Furthermore, the Romans became entangled in a series of complicated dealings with the rulers of the post-Alexander kingdoms. Rome, so it seems, had no particular desire to become embroiled in the politics of the Greek world. The state, after all, had its hands full with Carthage. Nevertheless, matters came to a head when a Senatorial deputation arrived in Corinth in 147 B.C. and was treated badly. No longer could Rome tolerate the insults of the Greeks.

In 146 B.C., an attack was mounted against Corinth. The city was razed and its treasures plundered. Later, Romans would equate the destruction of that wealthy city and the theft of its treasures, fine art, and opulent furnishings with the beginning of decadence in their own city. For many, the seizing of Corinth marked the loss of innocence and the passing of old-world virtue. That loss of innocence was affirmed by the further acquisition of luxury that came some thirteen years later in 133 B.C. when Attalus III, the last king of Pergamum in Asia Minor, died and bequeathed his entire, and very rich, state to the Romans.

Expansion and Colonization

To 133 B.C. the story of Rome has been told as one of external expansion and conflict, the deliberate wars against Carthage and the almost accidental acquisition of influence to the east. However, in Italy, too, the Roman state exercised increasing authority in the years following the foundation of the Republic.

The Romans used their remarkable engineering skills in building roads such as the Appian way. This illustration depicts a surveyor sighting the most direct course. Slaves, convicts, and soldiers cut and levelled the roadbed, pounded it smooth, and raised a wall. Huge volcanic paving blocks were fitted together with mortar.

From the earliest years when the Latins immediately to the south of Rome (in modern-day Lazio) had been granted security, the Romans had exhibited a flare for the management of neighbours. The Latins had been given a particular form of citizenship, not quite Roman but not quite foreign, by which they were protected. These were known as the Ius Latinum (Latin Rights) and they became prized by Rome's immediate neighbours. Soon, however, a new form of external citizenship was developed through which the non-Roman magistrates of a town were given full-citizenship rights, while the rest of the town's inhabitants received Latin Rights and were obliged to pay taxes. These were known as municipia. Further, an important step in the Romanization of the peninsula and a model for the subsequent domination of the rest of Europe, other coloniae (colonies) were created in strategic places where there was no pre-existing population. These coloniae were composed of full-Roman citizens who could be counted on to support the interests of the Roman regime. As often as not, the inhabitants of the colonies were recently discharged soldiers or members of the urban poor who had exchanged their impoverished occupation for a tract of land and the benefits of a rural existence.

After construction of the first paved road leaving Rome, the Via Appia or **Appian Way** which had been begun by the Censor Appius Claudius Caecus in 312 B.C., colonies were planted throughout the Italian peninsula south of the Po River during the third century B.C. Examples were Cosa in the northwest and Venusium (modern Venosa) in the wild interior of southern Italy. Situated on the Via Appia, which then extended to Tarentum (modern Taranto), the colony of Venusium became an important Roman presence in the conquest of southern Italy and the subsequent opposition to Hannibal.

Dissatisfaction within the Republic

In the same year as Attalus III died and left his kingdom of Pergamum in Asia Minor to the Romans (133 B.C.), tensions between the land-owning rich

ARCHITECTURE

CHARACTERISTICS OF ROMAN SETTLEMENTS IN THE THIRD CENTURY B.C.

A distinguishing characteristic of Roman colonies in the third century B.C. was their adoption and reflection of peculiarly Roman modes of government. This was reflected in the organization of their public buildings and public spaces. Every colony (and many *municipia*) were endowed with the following:

Basilica (Covered Hall): A later addition to the characteristic structures of a Romanized town. This was essentially a covered *forum* and had the same functions.

Curia (Senate House): Also called *Curia* in Rome. This was where the leaders of a *colonia* or *municipium* would meet to deliberate on important issues.

Comitium (Assembly Place): The centre of voting and place for the popular assembly to meet. It was normally circular in tiers. As was the case with the *capitolium*, this recalled an actual place, the function of which was similar, in the heart of Rome, in the northeast corner of the *Forum Romanum*.

Forum (Town Square): The less official heart of a town. This, like the *Forum Romanum* in Rome itself, would be the marketplace. Not only could goods be bought and sold here, business transactions would take place and legal matters settled.

Capitolium (Capitol): The centre of religious practice and dedicated to the chief god of the Roman state, Jupiter. This usually was in the form of a temple on a high *podium* fronting on to a *forum*.

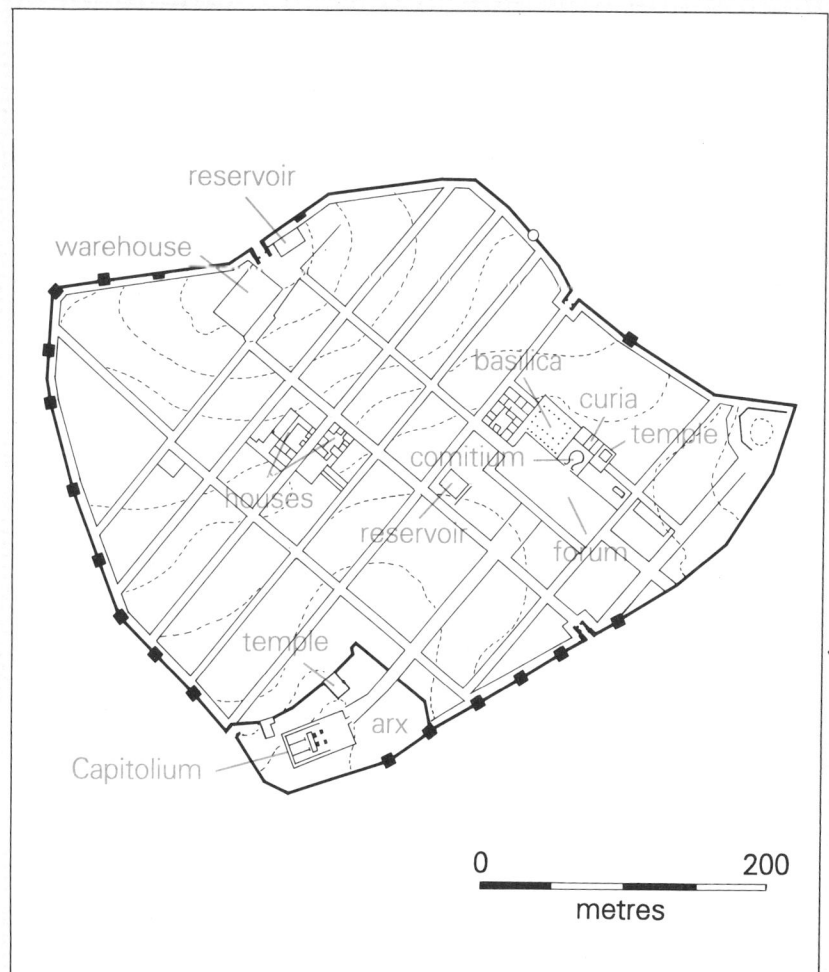

247

and the urban, landless poor came to a head. There had also developed two new aspects in Rome's growth to political maturity. A new class of **entrepreneur** grew among the more affluent of the non-Senatorial masses. The equites (knights: their income had originally allowed them to own and equip cavalry) discovered in earlier wars that wealth and influence did not derive solely from land ownership but could also come from commercial enterprise, considered a sordid business by the Senatorial aristocracy. There were also the non-Roman Italians. With the eventual defeat of the Carthaginians and the spread of Roman influence, the acquisition of Latin Rights or even full citizenship became an envied goal of many communities.

First and foremost, however, there was the widening gulf between the land-owning rich and the urban poor who had no means to support themselves. In 133 B.C. a reformer was elected as tribune of the People. Tiberius Gracchus knew how to solve the problems of the urban poor. He knew this, even though he himself belonged to the **gentry**, his mother being Cornelia, the daughter of Scipio Africanus. Tiberius set about redistributing land to the urban mob that had become depopulated during the long wars. Earlier much of the public land had been appropriated quite illegally by richer members of the Roman populace (no one was allowed to lease more than 145 ha of ager publicus and many wealthy Romans had exceeded that limit). A Land Commission was set up to distribute 10 ha plots.

Tiberius Gracchus, however, overstepped his authority. He announced that he would seek re-election as tribune, an unheard of action, and a riot, instigated by an aggrieved land-owning Senate, broke out in the heart of Rome. Some three hundred people were slain, among them Tiberius Gracchus himself. Nevertheless, the Land Commission continued to function and about 80 000 people from the city were resettled.

In 123 B.C., Tiberius's brother Gaius Gracchus was elected tribune. He was driven by the same reforming zeal that had impelled his brother. However, there were now three factions to deal with. First, there was the land-owning Senate, who did not support the successful workings of the Land Commission. Second, the urban poor wanted land but did not want more Italians to receive Roman citizenship or Latin Rights, fearing their own privileges would be diluted. Thirdly, there were the Italians themselves, who at the same time resented the Roman redistribution of Italian land and were envious of the privileges accorded to the urban mob. Gaius Gracchus, like his brother, believed he had the answer to these problems and could satisfy such conflicting desires. To satisfy the urban mob, he instituted a free, monthly supply of grain. Second, in an attempt to meet the needs of the landless poor while not irritating the Senate, he proposed new colonies at Capua, Taranto, and Carthage. Each city awaited settlement after their destruction in the Punic wars. To accommodate the ambitions of the new middle class of entrepreneurs, the equites, he transferred control of the jury courts to them and awarded them the lucrative business of extorting taxes from Rome's overseas subjects. Lastly, and fatally, he proposed a package of moderate compromises to give some rights to the Italians.

All Roman citizens were offended either on moral and religious grounds or because they feared the dilution of their privileges among the Italians. The reasons for religious scruples were clear: Carthage, after all, had been cursed with eternal sterility. Given almost unanimous opposition, Gaius Gracchus made no headway with his proposals but merely incurred wrath. As a result, in 121 B.C., he was declared a Public Enemy and, realizing at last that his was a lost cause, he killed himself.

The attempts made by the **Gracchus brothers**, ten years apart, at bringing a greater political harmony to the Roman state had come to nothing. Eventually, over the course of the next hundred years, the state's inability to bridge the gulf between rich and poor and to come to grips with the new-found wealth and increasing commercialism led to the Republic's demise. Out of the collapse of the Republic arose a new age of imperialism. First, however, the pressures on the state would increase and the people would seek salvation not in the Senatorial democracy, which had ultimately failed them, but in the abilities, sometimes more imaginary than real, of powerful individuals.

The Enfranchisement of Italy

In the aftermath of the failed attempt at reform, the free population of the Italian, non-Roman communities felt increasingly isolated from decisions affecting their welfare. Colonies and municipia, by now, had been founded all over the peninsula, especially to the south of the river Po and their resentment of Rome came to a boil. It was not that the Italians, as they called themselves, wished to replace Rome. Rather, they sought a share of the privileges which they observed in the market-places, the fora and comitia of the colonies and municipia.

A bitter "Social War" broke out in 90 B.C. and ended with the cruel suppression of the Italians in 89 B.C. The Romans, being pragmatic people, granted the citizenship the Italians had fought so hard to obtain. Now, all of Italy south of the Po gained Roman citizenship. North of the Po, the ordinary inhabitants were given Latin Rights, while several select cities were made full coloniae.

The Generals. The city-states in the Italian peninsula had become dependent to a greater degree on Rome. Though suppressed by force of arms, they had already chosen voluntarily to yield some part of their **autonomy**. Nevertheless, it would be wrong to stress their loss of autonomy. The Italian peninsula is difficult to traverse even today and it was only in the nineteenth century A.D. that Italy was truly unified as one country. In Roman antiquity, with poor land communications, communities were geographically and often spiritually and linguistically isolated.

Two generals figured prominently in the military suppression of the Italians. Gaius Marius (155–86 B.C.) was a veteran of foreign wars, particularly in Africa and northern Italy. A "soldier's soldier," he lacked the diplomatic skills needed to turn military prowess into personal gain. Although he had totally transformed the army and the way Romans fought, after the "Social War" he was passed over for a battle command; the battle was against Mithridates, a rich king near the Black Sea. In his place, a younger rival was chosen, L. Cornelius Sulla (138–78 B.C.).

Marius was furious. He formed a militia of armed supporters and seized power in Rome itself. Not to be thwarted, however, Sulla turned on Marius and drove him out of the city. Having expelled and, as he thought, dispensed with Marius, Sulla departed for the east and war with Mithridates. Marius, however, returned to Rome and until his timely death in 86 B.C., presided over a reign of terror in which he attempted to exterminate all his Senatorial opponents.

Sulla, his war won, came back to Rome in 83 B.C. Turning his armies on Romans themselves he emerged victorious in a particularly bloody battle against the Marians at the city's Colline Gate. In 81 B.C., he had himself appointed dictator for an indefinite period and continued to kill all his perceived or real opponents, mostly democrats.

These were the so-called proscriptions. The proscriptions were a nightmare in which the names of those people whom Sulla wanted dead were posted (proscribed) in public places. Once a name was published, the person was fair game. As often as not, opposition was imaginary. A person was killed so that Sulla could acquire his estate. At last, Senatorial

6000 legion
1
480 cohort
1
80 centuries
1
10 contubernia

This soldier from the Roman Republican legion is carrying a 4 m long spear and a large oval shield. His armour consists of a mail shirt and a helmet. He would have been between 17 and 46 years old and would have fought in a unit of 120 to 160 men.

aristocracy sufficiently restored, Sulla retired to private life and reputedly utter debauchery in 79 B.C. He died a year later.

[The Army]

The essential formation of the Roman citizen army may be attributed to Gaius Marius at the beginning of the last century of the Republic. Throughout the whole of previous history, soldiers had tilled their fields, sown their grain, and then gone off to war. The campaigning season ended in the fall, always in time for the same soldiers to return home to gather the harvest.

Seasonal campaigning had become a problem, however, in Marius's time. Now, there were not so many citizen soldiers left at Rome that owned land. Grain, therefore, was becoming scarcer. The scarcer the grain, the more essential it was for the soldiers who owned land to return in the fall. At the same time, there were many landless people normally resident in the city. These people had less reason to return in the fall.

Marius realized the dimensions of the problem and created a new, standing army. A standing army is a permanent force and is not only recruited to meet a particular need. Also Marius gave his legionaries a fixed term of service, sixteen years in the ranks and four years as a veteranus, with the possibility of being called up if needed. After this, the soldier retired with a pension, a gratuity, or a plot of land. Now, too, he was allowed to marry.

Reformed conditions of service including regular pay, the provision of food, and clothing allowances, were only part of the more sweeping rearrangements that affected "Marius's mules," so-called because each man had to carry a certain standard minimum of equipment when on the march. Soldiers now served in reformed legions and, with a new aquila (eagle, legionary standard), began to develop a fierce pride in belonging to a particular unit.

The legion, now a heavy infantry unit of about 6000 men, was broken into smaller subdivisions termed cohorts. There were ten cohorts to a legion with the first and most experienced cohort having a double complement of soldiers. Each cohort had approximately 480 men. These units were again divided into smaller and more manageable units termed centuries with 80 men to a century and reporting to a centurion who was essentially the equivalent of a sergeant. The ultimate division was the contubernium of eight men sharing one tent. There were ten contubernia to a century.

The result of these complicated arrangements was that a recruit would begin his service in the most junior century of the most junior cohort of a legion. As he gained experience, the soldier could work his way through the ranks to the Primus Pilus, the centurion commanding the first century of the first cohort, a sort of Regimental Sergeant Major. Another advantage from this arrangement was that the legion, with its smaller divisions, was easily deployed. The major drawback in this scheme was that ordinary soldiers looked to their generals for security and pensions rather than the state. By the first century B.C., there were Sulla's legions rather than Rome's legions.

From Pompey to Caesar

By now, the lesson had been learned. The man with a powerful army or who was backed by a band of ruthless and armed thugs could usurp the constitutional government. In quick succession, Gnaeus Pompeius (Pompey, 106–48 B.C.), M. Licinius Crassus (115–53 B.C.), and G. Iulius Caesar (**Julius Caesar**, 100–44 B.C.) came to power. Military adventurers to a man, they cared nothing for the Republican constitution from which they had prospered. In a cynical act, utterly devoid of constitutional precedent, they split the government of Rome between themselves and in 60 B.C., according to a private arrangement, formed the **First Triumvirate**, which means the Rule of Three Men.

Caesar had the armies of northern Italy. He set about gaining military glory by subjugating the entire population of what is now southern Germany, France, Switzerland, and parts of Austria. Crassus first did his part in Italy in a bloody crushing of the slave rebellion led by Spartacus; 6000 of the ex-gladiator's followers were crucified in a line flanking the Via Appia in 71 B.C. He then went off to campaign in modern-day Iran against the Parthians. Pompey, already covered in glory from his extermination of the pirates in the Mediterranean sea (67 B.C.) stayed at Rome and was gradually seduced by the flattery of the Senate.

Still, no private arrangement could outlive ambition. Crassus was defeated by the Parthians at Carrhae and killed in 53 B.C. Pompey, having become the fervent guardian of Senatorial privilege, came to oppose Caesar and agreed with a Senatorial demand in 50 B.C. that Caesar should discharge his army. Caesar realised that the disbanding of his army would leave him defenceless and would be tantamount to suicide. Therefore, he committed an illegal act, and in January 49 B.C. with his army crossed the little stream known as the Rubicon that marked the border between his area of control and Italy proper. Pompey hurried to the defence of the constitutional, Senatorial government. Repulsed essentially on all fronts, Pompey retreated to Alexandria in Egypt. Here his army was defeated and the Senate's champion decapitated. Pompey's sons, however, survived, only to suffer almost total defeat at Munda in Spain.

In 46 B.C., Caesar had himself appointed dictator

for ten years, in 45 B.C. the appointment became for life. In the latter year too, he became Pontifex Maximus (Chief Priest) and assumed virtually all responsibility for decision making. Now, Caesar was more a king than a guardian of the Republic. He was even offered a golden crown by a young supporter, Marcus Antonius (83–30 B.C.). Caesar's victory, however, was short-lived. On 15 March 44 B.C., the ides of March, self-proclaimed defenders of liberty could no longer tolerate the tyrant's growing **megalomania**. Brutus, Cassius, and other conspirators converged on the dictator beneath Pompey's statue in the theatre built by Pompey and stabbed him to death.

Gaius Iulius Caesar

G. Iulius Caesar (Julius Caesar, 100–44 B.C.) was a brilliant general, lucid writer, and arrogant politician.

As a young man, Caesar escaped the Sullan proscriptions by travelling to the east and undertaking minor diplomatic tasks. On his return, he was eager to prove himself a capable and successful military commander. After he had formed the First Triumvirate with Pompey and Crassus in 60 B.C., he needed some military command that would provide him with an opportunity to equal Pompey's exploits. This need led Caesar to persuade the Senate at Rome to give him control of northern Italy beyond the Po, Cisalpine Gaul, and southern Gaul outside Italy, Gallia Narbonensis. Caesar made the most of this command and, having taken the offensive against a variety of Gallic tribes, was brilliantly successful.

The Senate became very fearful of Caesar's military power. Caesar eventually won control of the entire Roman world and had himself appointed dictator for life, a quite unconstitutional and unprecedented act. His growing megalomania was perceived to be a real threat to the process of republican government. The result was that Brutus, Cassius, and other conspirators took on the role of Liberators and attempted to restore constitutional government by assassinating the dictator.

Apart from being a brilliant military strategist and superb tactician, Caesar was a lucid writer of Latin and an ardent reformer, although the reforms he initiated were not as momentous or as enduring as they might have been. He abolished the trade guilds that had become political, secret societies and settled his veteran soldiers in far-flung colonies. He attempted to soften the harshness of Rome's rule through generous grants of citizenship, especially in the west, and reduction of the tax burden, particularly in Asia Minor. In Rome in 59 B.C., he even made the Senate keep and publish daily records, thus becoming, as it were, the first daily newspaper publisher.

The most famous and lasting reform, however, was introduced on 1 January 45 B.C. On this day the Julian calendar was introduced by Julius Caesar, as Chief Priest, to bring the civil year into line with the solar year, which were approximately three months out of synchronicity. The calendar initiated by Caesar was in use for a long time until the reforms of Pope Gregory XII in February 1582. Even today, however, members of certain eastern European and Greek Christian faiths adhere to the Julian calendar in the celebration of their religious days.

Daily Life

During the five hundred years since the fall of the monarchy, the Roman people had developed superstitions, institutions, and modes of living. These practices and beliefs helped them, even in difficult times, to maintain a distinct identity and a cultural integrity. We will now consider aspects of those practices and institutions.

Beliefs

The Romans were among the most superstitious people the world had seen to that point. They adopted, essentially, the whole **pantheon** of the Olympian gods of Greece and added them to their own and Etruscan deities in a remarkable synthesis. In addition to the major gods, the Romans also believed in minor deities, werewolves, and all forms of magic. They inherited from the Etruscans the dark arts of laying curses, casting spells, and telling the future. From their contacts with the east, they absorbed astrology and a belief in the Signs of the Zodiac.

The official religions came under the supervision of the Pontifex Maximus. Naturally, he was also in charge of the Roman calendar, which originally was an ordering of the months and days when the various deities were to be honoured.

Do ut des, I give so that you might give, was an elementary principle in Roman religion. Thus, a common means of honouring gods and placating them or seeking their help in times of crisis was the sacrifice of animals. A particular favourite was known as a suovetaurilia, the simultaneous sacrifice of a pig, sheep, and ox. Other sacrifices included, for example, the slaughter of a red dog at the feast of Robigalia on 25 April each year at the fifth milestone from Rome on the Via Claudia to the spirit of mildew. Let not mildew attack this year's wheat crop!

Family Life and Morality

Unlike today, where personal behaviour is legislated by the state with codes of criminal and family law, the Roman Republic was based on the family unit as the elemental building block of society. The head of the household, the male Paterfamilias, originally held complete and utter power over his wife, offspring, and slaves. This included the legal right to abuse or even to kill. He was endowed, above all, with potestas, which was legally recognized and absolute power. He also maintained a public appearance marked by gravitas (conservatism) and dignitas (dignified status), and, usually, severitas (the ability not to shrink from harsh justice).

Ultimately, the passing on and inheritance of property was the most important fact in Republican life. The state, Senatus Populusque Romanus, in fact consisted of families that were all linked to each other in gentes (clans). Anything that endangered the integrity of the family was met with the harshest punishment.

Inheritance was through the male line. Thus adoption was a regular feature of society; younger men even adopted older men on occasion. Affection was personal; adoption was not. Men who kept on having daughters (it was believed to be the woman's fault) could divorce and remarry at will. Julius Caesar, who had several wives, was obliged to adopt in his last will and testament the young Octavian, the son of his niece Atia.

Even though marriage was a duty rather than a pleasure, often with neither partner having freedom of choice, marital harmony and developing affection for one another was the order of the day in the Roman world. Children, especially male children, were well cared for. Of course, as in any society where the inheritance of property is paramount, the legitimacy of offspring was the chief concern. A newly born infant had to be recognized by the father. The baby was laid on the floor before the paterfamilias, who then recognized the legitimacy of the infant by picking it up. Should the father not pick up the infant, it was exposed in a public place. Then a childless person could take the child for his own (as was the case with the Emperor Vespasian's wife) or it would be left to die.

Children of wealthy families in the Republic were brought up, male and female together until puberty, usually by a nurse and family tutor. Girls were taught, as boys were, to read and write. They were

BELIEFS

PRINCIPAL DEITIES OF THE ROMAN EMPIRE

Apollo: Jupiter's son who was the god of poetry and peace.
Aesculapius: Apollo's son and the deity to which medical doctors prayed.
Bacchus: The god of wine and ecstasy. Occasionally, his worship was banned and his followers expelled from Rome.
Diana: The goddess of hunting and fertility.
Fors Fortuna: This was the spirit of Good Fortune. The Republican Romans had countless deities related to luck and beneficial outcomes.
Janus: Not only a war god but also the god of beginnings. Hence it was that January became the first month of the year in 153 B.C. Previously, the Roman year had started with March. Janus had two faces; one looked backwards while the other peered forwards.
Jupiter: Father of the gods and chief deity of the pagan Roman state. He was worshipped in many guises along with his sister/wife **Juno**. Jupiter was responsible for the weather. Juno looked after marriage and was a woman's deity.
Lares: The worship of these protectors of the Roman household declined during the Republic, although altars to them were in nearly every Roman home. They were very personal deities.
Mars: *The* god of war. During the Roman Republic his worship had to take place outside the *pomoerium,* the city's ritual boundary. He was often paired with **Venus,** the goddess of love and female passion.
Mercury: The patron god of liars and thieves, he was also the messenger of the gods.
Minerva: The goddess of wisdom. She was the intellectual opposite to Diana.
Priapus: An erect (priapic) male god, symbol of procreativity. Quite often, he would appear as the scarecrow in a garden. The phallus was considered a powerful amulet for warding off the "Evil Eye."
Vesta: A female deity whose cult was restricted to women. She protected Rome's symbolic hearth. There were normally six "Vestals" (see here).

also instructed in the arts of singing and dancing and in the crafts of spinning and weaving. The latter two were thought to exemplify old Republican virtues. "Casta fuit; domum servavit; lanam fecit" (she was chaste; she kept the house; she worked the wool) are words taken from an old Republican gravestone.

Legitimate male children were given a liberal education in the arts of speaking and logical argument and in the later Roman Empire, there were even formal schools and universities. Under the Republic, students kept regular hours of instruction, had vacations, and homework. We know the names of some schoolteachers and among them one Orbilius stands out as the harsh taskmaster of the famous poet Horace. After a youth's introduction to public life, in which he was formally led to the Forum Romanum dressed in the toga of manhood, he was expected to pursue a career in the law courts or army. Whichever option was chosen, young men were expected to serve the state first and themselves last.

The Role of Women

Girls were educated in the home or sent to elementary school until they were married, when they gained an independence that their earlier Greek sisters would have envied. With marriage, apart from the duty of bearing children, came the ability to go out shopping, attend to business, and accompany one's husband to dinner. The normal age of marriage seems to have been about fifteen. There were two forms of marriage with different associated wedding rituals. The most ancient transferred the authority the father held to the husband. The woman remained a minor but now she was in the position of daughter in all matters concerning property and inheritance, as well as that of wife in her new family. This marriage in manum (into the power of) was conducted according to ancient rituals, of which the most common was a symbolic sale. In this, the father sold the daughter to the bridegroom.

The other form of marriage came to be the most popular by the end of the Republic. This was usus (cohabitation). A couple stated their intention to live together in a married state. As long as they lived together, they then remained married. Divorce was simple, though always regarded as an exceptional act. All one partner had to do was send a messenger to the other telling him or her to take their belongings away. Although apparently a preferable form of marriage, it should be stressed that such a union, sine manu (without power) meant that the woman remained legally subject to her father as a minor for the rest of her adult life.

Women could own property and engage in business activities. Occasionally, women even endowed public buildings and became important people in their own right. An example of such a woman is Eumachia, who sponsored the construction of a large portico at Pompeii near the Bay of Naples. During the Republic and much of the history of the Western Empire, though excluded from the male political sphere, women exercised great influence. It was basically due to an inherited eastern ambivalence that the woman's role was changed in the Roman world to one of less authority. The teachings of Paul of Tarsus reflect that loss of influence. These expressions do not, however, reflect the initial equal treatment that was accorded women by Christ himself:

> It is my desire that everywhere prayers should be said by the men of the congregation, who shall lift up their hands with a pure intention, excluding angry or quarrelsome thoughts. Women again must dress in becoming manner, modestly and soberly, not with elaborate hair-styles, not decked out with gold or pearls, or expensive clothes, but with good deeds as befits women who claim to be religious. A woman must be a learner, listening quietly and with due submission. I do not permit a woman to be a teacher, nor must woman domineer over man; she should be quiet. For Adam was created first, and Eve afterwards; and it was not Adam who was deceived; it was the woman who, yielding to deception, fell into sin.
> 1 Timothy 2.8-14.

Childbirth

Having offspring to continue the family's existence was the main purpose of being married, so a girl, about fifteen years of age, could expect a fairly rapid introduction to her responsibilities. Even children as young as twelve were sometimes subjected to the risks of bearing infants in immature bodies. Since male babies were most desired, a woman could expect multiple pregnancies until such offspring, and their survival, had been assured. Alarmed at a decreasing birthrate, Julius Caesar's adoptive son Octavian, who became the first Roman emperor with the name of Augustus in January 27 B.C., gave special privileges to those families in which the mothers had borne three children. The beneficial

ASPECTS OF DAILY LIFE

ROMAN CLOTHING: TUNICS, TOGAS, AND STOLAS

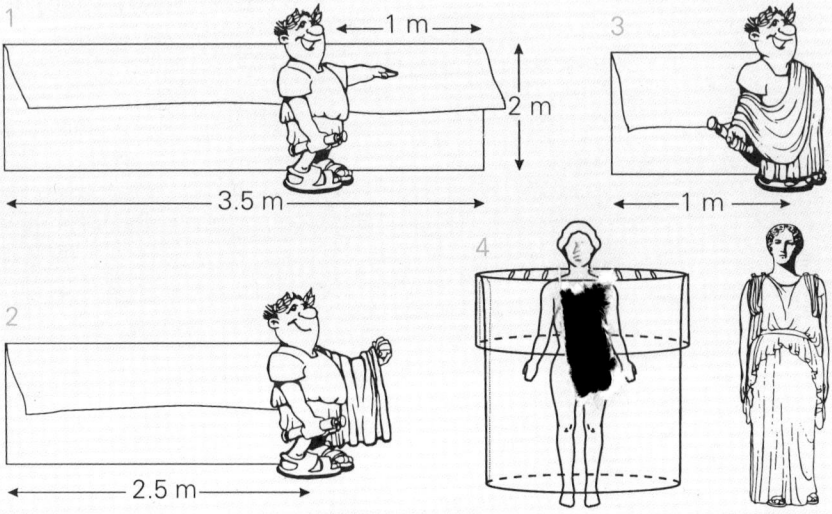

The clothing of the ancient Romans was relatively simple with variations of three different styles: the tunic, the toga, and the stola. The tunic, which is a simple piece of clothing, was worn by the commoners. It was made of two square pieces, a back and a front, sewn together with holes for the arms and the neck. It could be shortened by pulling it over the belt. It was worn as a sleeveless gown tied at the waist with the folds distributed evenly. The tunic of a knight had two narrow purple stripes over each shoulder.

The toga was worn only by Roman males. Senators and knights were distinguished by a narrow purple band running along the lower edge of the cloth. A toga was made from a piece of unbleached material measuring 2 by 3.5 m. It would be folded lengthwise with 0.5 m of the material on the inside. The Roman would stand about one metre from the left end and extend the left arm(1). The one metre of cloth would be hung over the left shoulder and arm, adjusted into pleats and draped until it reached the floor(2). The long right side is loosely wrapped around the body, under the right armpit and over the left shoulder with one metre remaining(3). This material was draped across the back of the shoulders over the right arm, across the chest, over the left shoulder with the end hanging down the back.

The stola, worn by Roman women, was made of fine wool or silk. Women of rank would wear a very long stola forming a train at the back. The size of the material depended on the wearer; for length it would measure from ankle to shoulder and back again to below the waist. The width would be double the measurement from wrist to wrist with arms extended. The fabric would be stitched together on one side to form a tube. Holding the material at ankle length, the extra would be draped over the outside. The top would be fastened at the neck with decorated pins and arms would be put through the two openings(4). Sleeves could be created by pinning material two or three more times on each side. The belt or cord would be tied underneath the breasts and the material would be bloused out to hang over the belt. A tunic was often worn underneath the toga or the stola.

Footwear included sandals, slippers, or military boots.

effect of the measure on the birthrate, however, was not readily noticeable.

Vestal Virgins

Vestal Virgins were six girls and women of high rank who were selected to tend the sacred fire of the goddess Vesta in the heart of Rome. They took a vow of virginity for 30 years. The first ten years, we are told, were spent in learning one's duties. The second decade was passed in performance of those duties, and the last ten years were occupied in instructing novices. After their 30 years of service, Vestals were released and allowed to be married. We are assured that few did, having become used to a life of chastity and holiness.

If a Vestal Virgin was found to have broken her vow of chastity, the consequences were terrible. The fallen priestess was entombed alive in a mound just outside the city wall. In the mound was a little room in which were placed bread, milk, and water; just enough sustenance to keep the priestess alive for a little while. There was also a little oil with which the Vestal could continue Vesta's sacred rites. It could not be charged that the person consecrated to her religious offices died of starvation.

The Toga

The toga was the distinctive dress of the free Roman. This was an elliptical piece of cloth about three and a half metres by about two metres at its widest point. The colour of the main body of the cloth differed according to the status of the wearer: a natural colour for ordinary use, pure white for candidates standing for election to high office, and dark for a person in mourning. In addition, there was a broad or a narrow purple stripe along one edge according to membership in the Senate (broad) or if a person were slightly inferior in rank (narrow).

The correct draping of the garment was all-important and absolutely essential if a man was to be considered civilized. The art, however, was difficult and often a slave trained in the proper procedures assisted the person. To begin, the long straight edge was draped over the left arm so that the stripe hung down the back. Next, the rest of the garment was draped across the shoulders and back, and underneath the right arm. The end was then tucked inside a fold of the cloth or grasped by the right hand.

Naturally, this was an awkward garment to wear and men began to avoid its use, to the chagrin of some traditionalist emperors who tried to legislate the toga's use. In the very late Empire, even in Rome itself, men took to wearing military dress to which they were not entitled. In A.D. 389, there was a decree ordering this practice to come to an end. In the same half-century, men were enjoined not to wear trousers in the city of Rome on the grounds that trousers were unmanly.[1]

Writing Materials

The favourite materials on which to write were papyrus, made originally from Egyptian reeds of the same name, and parchment.[2] The papyrus could either form long rolls of twenty pages, which were sundried then glued together, or be sold as individual pages. Since the fibres of the cut papyrus plant were glued and hammered together at right angles to each other, only one side of the page could normally be written on. This was the side with exposed transverse fibres. Occasionally, the other side was used in the last resort. The edges of the rolled scroll would be smoothed down with pumice stone before being stored for safety in a wooden chest or other container.

---

[1] J. Liversidge, Britain in the Roman Empire (London: Routledge, Kegan, Paul, 1968), p. 123.
[2] U.E. Paoli, Rome: Its People, Life and Customs, trans. R.D. Macnaghten (London: Longmans, 1963), p. 174–87.

INNOVATIONS

SILPHIUM—THE WONDER DRUG

From the seventh century to the first century B.C., a plant in Cyrenaica in North Africa had become the single most sought-after medical and food supplement known to the ancient world. With the Roman presence towards the end of that period, the plant (also known as laserpicium) became even more widely known. Eventually, worth more than its weight in gold, possession of silphium came to represent wealth. Bales of the plant were actually stored in Rome's treasury. Today the wild plant, over-harvested in Roman times, is extinct.

As an ingredient, the juice of the plant was most in demand, then the leaves (which looked a little like parsely), then the stalk and roots. The juice was used as a flavourful sauce for every kind of fish and meat dish. The leaves were good fresh or boiled. The stalk was used as a vegetable dish, braised like celery, or roasted. The roots were also good fresh. They could, however, be sliced and marinated in vinegar. The roots were kept in jars of flour.

Silphium was made famous for its medical properties, perhaps, by the fact that there was a well-known medical school at Cyrene in the fifth century B.C. Hippocrates (born about 460 B.C.) advocated the use of Silphium to treat many different maladies. The various parts of the plant could be eaten raw or mixed with honey, wine, or vinegar. Consumption could also aid in digestion or act as a medicine against, for example, pleurisy, migraines, jaundice, and a whole variety of fevers. Extractions of the plant, too, could be applied externally as an antidote to snake bites or scorpion stings.

In order to write, one needed ink. Made from several substances including soot, resin, and the excretion from squid or cuttlefish, care had to be taken when writing not to dilute the ink too much. Mistakes could be erased with a clean, wet sponge. Pens could be copper alloy (bronze) instruments with nibs or, more popularly, sharpened reeds or goose quills. Also, there were notepads or wax tablets. These were usually two or more rectangles of wood fastened together. The interior sides had raised borders around their outer edges and within this frame, there would be hardened wax the writer scratched with a sharpened point (stylus). The outer sides then protected the writing. These tablets were often used for sending letters. The recipient would read the message, take a stylus, which always had a blunt end, and scrape the message clear. The wax was then smooth and ready for a return message.

Art and Literature during the Republic

As the Roman world came into ever increasing contacts with the Greek communities of southern Italy and farther afield, it absorbed new ideas and modes of expression. By the end of the Republic, it was hard for contemporary observers to discern who was the victor and who were the conquered peoples.

In literature, of which very little survives intact from the earliest times, Ennius (239–169 B.C.)

stands out, if only because he not only wrote in verse but also attempted to provide a year-by-year account of Rome's developing power. This account, the *Annals*, were also in verse. In the primitive stages of development, when there is a heavier reliance on memory than on written record, verse is more commonly used than prose.

There are many people, mostly men, who are known to us today by name and by surviving scraps of their work. From the period before 133 B.C., two writers of comedy are known to us through whole plays; T. Maccius Plautus (?–184 B.C.) and P. Terentius Afer (Terence, 190–159 B.C.). There are 27 surviving plays, 21 by Plautus and 6 by Terence from this period. Filled with stock characters such as lovesick youths, cunning slaves, free-born prostitutes, and grasping old men, they have had a very great influence on the development of western drama and on the writings of such playwrights as Molière, *The Miser* and Shakespeare, *A Comedy of Errors*. Comedy, however, was not considered good for public morality. As a result, there was no permanent stone theatre in the city of Rome until one was built at the direction of Pompey in 55 B.C.

In the first century B.C., literacy in Greek and Latin became common among the upper classes. All sorts of people committed their thoughts to the written word. These were such men as the philosopher T. Lucretius Carus (Lucretius, 94–55 B.C.). He wrote *On the Nature of Things*, an epic poem describing his theories on existence and ethical behaviour.

A philosopher, but also known for his speeches in the law-courts, was M. Tullius **Cicero** (106–43 B.C.). Perhaps one of the most famous Romans, he was a prolific writer, one-time consul, and staunch defender of the Republic. As an orator, Cicero defended notable Romans and prosecuted several others. One of his most famous prosecutions was against a former governor of Sicily, G. Verres. As a defender of the idea of constitutional government, Cicero was ideologically and bitterly opposed to M. Antonius whom he attacked in his published speeches, the *Philippics*. Eventually, he was killed by M. Antonius on 7 December 43 B.C. for his outspokenness.

Julius Caesar, of course, was well acquainted with Cicero. Not only a brilliant general and ambitious statesman, Caesar was an avid recorder of his own military exploits. He was much admired for the clarity of expression that is to be found in his works, for example, the *Gallic Wars* (the record of his conquests in modern France).

Known to both Cicero and Julius Caesar was the poet C. Valerius Catullus (Catullus, ca. 84–47 B.C.). Catullus was known to Caesar, certainly, for his lampooning and abusive attacks. Although some of Catullus's poetry is such that it would even fall afoul of Canada's fairly liberal obscenity and libel laws today, on the whole it is refreshingly immediate and skillfully created.

> I hate and I love
> well, why do I, you probably ask
> I don't know, but I know it's happening
> and it hurts[3]

There were several other greats in Roman literature who wrote in the declining years of the Republic. We will meet these when we discuss the origins of the Empire and The Age of Augustus.

Epicureanism

Epicureanism was a system of philosophy popular during the last days of the Republic. Its most brilliant exponent was the above-mentioned Lucretius. Essentially, the teachings of the Greek philosopher Epicurus (341–270 B.C.), as they were adopted by

---

[3] F.O. Copley, *Catullus—The Complete Poetry* (Ann Arbor: University of Michigan, 1957), p. 104.

the Romans, were both ethical and physical. Their aim in particular was the reduction of a fear of death and of an unknowable afterlife.

The ethical objective had its base in the pursuit of happiness, pleasure, and the absence of pain. It was the belief that people generally strive for pleasure and individual gratification that has caused such a "bad press" for Epicureanism. A life free from pain, however, could not be realized by being selfish or by abandoning traditional virtues, such as temperance and moderation. What is more, the gods do not interfere with the activities of mortals and as a result, there is no good reason for fearing the supernatural.

The physical world is closely linked to Epicurean moral philosophy. For Lucretius, the universe is made up only of atoms. When one dies, therefore, these "seeds" (atoms) merely dissipate, thus one need not fear death. Atoms have different shapes, however, and move downwards as a general rule. Occasionally they deviate at random from this vertical direction. When the atoms swerve, they collide with one another. The different shapes of the atoms cause them to adhere to similar atoms and from these imperceptible collisions everything is created.

zenry was justifiable in a state without any social safety net. In Rome of the first century B.C., if you were poor and without personal means of livelihood, you starved, became a slave, or worse.

Under the Empire, the subject of the next chapter, things were only slightly better for most Romans, who were tired of bloody civil wars. Augustus, as we shall see, soon consolidated his stranglehold on political and military power and ingeniously claimed that he had "restored" the Republic. In reality, he was the first in a long succession of de facto emperors lasting in the west until at least 476 A.D. These were monarchs who relied on military power, moral authority, or spiritual ascendancy to make their control of the known world legitimate. Whether or not Augustus and his individual successors were good emperors, their rule was absolute.

*T*he Republic's Decline

The Roman Republic, a bold and innovative experiment in 509 B.C., eventually collapsed. At the outset, when the kings had been overthrown and Tarquin the Proud expelled, true democracy (rule of the people) had appeared possible. This possibility seemed to be strengthened by the fact that Rome's dealings with its neighbours had been generally fair, if harsh. Strong class divisions, and indirectly Marius's army reforms, led to factional strife and to the people supporting particular army chiefs, military leaders like Sulla, Pompey, or Caesar. In part, this self-interested support on the part of the citi-

Suggested Sources for Further Research

Please see page 293 for complete list for Chapters 8 and 9.

Focus Your Knowledge

1. What were the key features of Italian geography that influenced Rome as a power?
2. Who were the Etruscans?
3. What were the driving forces behind Rome's desire to expand?
4. To what degree was Rome a male-dominated society?

Apply Your Knowledge

1. Assess the effectiveness of Etruscan rule and account for their eventual expulsion in 509 B.C.
2. Today the United States of America prides itself on the high degree of individual freedom enjoyed by its citizens. Their constitution has several parallels to the Republican constitution of ancient Rome. Assess to what degree the Roman constitution provided its citizens with equality and effective government and what weaknesses existed in the system of government.
3. How did Rome's conflicts with Carthage contribute to their expansion abroad?
4. To what degree did the actions of the Gracchus brothers reflect the growing dissatisfaction of the Roman masses?
5. Describe the changes implemented by Gaius Marius to the Roman army and assess the strengths and weaknesses of the rise of the Roman army in power and prestige.

6. Considering Julius Caesar's actions and achievements do you feel that Brutus and his cohorts were justified in perceiving him as a threat to Republican government and in assassinating him? Justify your answer.

Extension Activities

1. Using the medium of your choice build a model of a typical Roman settlement. Be sure to include key features such as roads, the forum, the walls, a basilica, a temple, and a curia.

2. Reenact the story of the founding of Rome. Your rendition could be presented to the class live or could be video-taped. Try to incorporate as much reality as possible by using costumes and props.

3. Restage the murder scene from Shakespeare's play *Julius Caesar*. This may be done as Shakespeare intended or may take on a more humorous tone as was done by the comedy team of Wayne and Schuster. Again props and costumes will help make your production a success.

4. Based on further research of one of the following characters prepare an on the spot interview for the evening news. Be sure to display all the traits of a good journalist by asking probing questions. This interview should be video-taped and will require some costumes.

Tarquinius Superbus	Hannibal
Gaius Marius	Pompey
Spartacus	Cicero

CHAPTER 9

The Roman Empire

Chapter Highlights

- Antony, Cleopatra, and Julius Caesar

- a Roman bath

- the sights and sounds of ancient Rome

- gladiators and other forms of Roman entertainment

- the decline of the Western Roman Empire

- Constantine the Great

The rule of the generals continued, characterized in the late Republic by personal loyalties to army commanders such as Marius, Sulla, and Pompey. After Julius Caesar's assassination on 15 March 44 B.C., a great struggle for power ensued between Caesar's adopted son (G. Iulius Caesar Octavianus, the future Emperor **Augustus**, 63 B.C.–A.D. 14), M. Antonius (Antony), and a third powerful man M. Lepidus. To make matters more confusing, a son of Pompey the Great, Sextus Pompeius (Sextus Pompey), essentially ruled the waves of the western Mediterranean.

After Caesar had been cremated, Octavian went into battle against Antony and defeated him. Octavian then had himself appointed consul after the two consuls of the year (43 B.C.) had been killed in the Battle of Mutina. Although Antony had been defeated in battle, Octavian formed a three-way alliance between himself, Antony, and Lepidus (a Second Triumvirate to restore the Republic). They then went about avenging Caesar's murder by routing the so-called Liberators at the Battle of Philippi in 42 B.C.

In 40 B.C., the three men met at Brundisium (Brindisi) in southern Italy to shore up the tottering alliance. There, they divided the Roman world among themselves: Antony the east; Octavian the west; and Lepidus, Africa. The pact was sealed with the marriage of Octavian's sister to Antony. Within five years, the Second Triumvirate was renewed, but with Lepidus now pushed out of the Triumvirate and given the position of Pontifex Maximus (Chief Priest).

In 36 B.C., Octavian's admiral Marcus Agrippa defeated Sextus Pompey in a naval battle. In the same year, Antony had met, fallen in love with, and married the descendant of Ptolemy and female ruler of Egypt, Cleopatra VII.

Key Concepts

Augustus
gladiators
Colosseum
Jesus Christ
Pantheon
stoicism
aqueduct
Cult of Isis
Mithraism
Visigoths
Ostrogoths
Attila the Hun

Antony and Cleopatra

Antony and Cleopatra, by all accounts, were motivated by sheer, romantic love. Antony already had a Roman wife, Octavia, the sister of Octavian, and in marrying Cleopatra, he rejected Octavia. Octavia, however, never recognized the validity of the divorce.

Cleopatra, for her part, even though absolute ruler of an autonomous Egypt, was no stranger to Roman rulers. She had consorted with Julius Caesar and had borne him a child, whom they named Ptolemy Caesar (commonly known as Caesarion). By 34 B.C., Antony and Cleopatra had guardianship of Caesarion and they had three children of their own (two boys and a girl). Together, the infatuated and politically unrealistic pair divided the rule of the east between themselves and their children. This division, of course, was more theoretical than real; the children were very young and the inhabitants and kings of the eastern world were not consulted.

Their control of the east was soon opposed. On 23 September 31 B.C., Octavian with Agrippa as admiral put the combined forces of Antony and Cleopatra to flight at the Battle of Actium. Within a year, Antony and Cleopatra had committed suicide at Alexandria.

Caesarion, who posed a dynastic threat, was immediately killed. However, Cleopatra's children by Antony were allowed to survive. In fact, they were raised by none other than the long-suffering Octavia. In addition to her own three children by a previous husband, she also had two daughters by Antony, another two of Antony's sons by his previous wife Fulvia, and now she allowed into her household Antony and Cleopatra's three children. Octavia's loyalty to Antony was praised in antiquity. She died in 11 B.C.

The Growth of the Empire

All opposition crushed or thrust aside, Octavian was the master of the Roman world. Octavian, in an ingenious act, announced to the Senate in January 27 B.C., that he was returning the state formally to the Senate and the Roman people. For restoring the Republic, he was awarded the semi-divine name, Augustus. He also re-distributed all the territories (provinces) of the Roman world. Those provinces having large armies he kept for himself to be administered through deputies or legates and those provinces with a small or no military presence he gave to the Senate. Augustus maintained Egypt as a private **fiefdom**.

From now on, Augustus tightened his grip on the Roman world. In 23 B.C., he increased his powers by becoming Tribune of the People, thus bridging a gulf between respect for the rights of the ordinary Roman and the aristocratic, Senatorial control of the late Republic. Again in 12 B.C., Augustus expanded his powers. Lepidus had died and Augustus assumed the title of Pontifex Maximus, and with the title the ultimate decision-making power in all of Rome's religious matters. Now, Augustus perversely claimed that although he outdid no one in the holding of official magistracies, he exceeded all in authority. The Roman Empire was born and Augustus, in no uncertain terms, was the first Roman Emperor.

The Principate

From 30 B.C. until his death in August A.D. 14, the Emperor Augustus was sole and undisputed ruler of the Roman world. What is remarkable about the onset of the Empire, however, is the skill with which Augustus expanded his authority and the spheres of his influence and power. He took great pains not to cause disaffection. He did not, for example, gain the reputation for arrogance that marked the reigns of his immediate successors Tiberius (A.D. 14–37), Caligula (A.D. 37–41), or Nero (A.D. 54–66), a reputation that ultimately led to the murder of Caligula and Nero. The word Principate refers to the emperor's rule as *primus inter pares* (first among equals).

This careful management of the Roman world, perhaps initially caused by an instinct for survival, was all encompassing. The benefits of an Augustan peace were extolled in the fine arts and literature. Just to make sure that no one missed the message in Rome itself, Augustus, either by himself or through members of his family, rebuilt 82 temples and public places. He restored the Forum Romanum and built new fora still visible today.

In the arts of civil administration, Augustus made

LITERATURE

LIVY'S ACCOUNT OF THE STORY OF ROMULUS AND REMUS

Titus Livius (Livy) was one of the most notable and famous writers of ancient Rome. As a member of a wealthy family he was able to devote his life to the writing of his mammoth 142 volume *The History of Rome From its Foundation*. Throughout his writings Livy stresses the simple life and traditional moral discipline which he saw as lacking in the latter years of the Roman Republic. Livy's description of Rome's distant past is often mythical and is always idealized. It was Livy's hope that his history of the foundation of Rome would be a morally uplifting work that would inspire his fellow Romans to follow the simple and soldierly virtues of their forbears and avoid the self-indulgent luxuries and immorality that he saw as a threat to Rome's leadership in the world. In the excerpt which follows Livy retells the story of the founding of Rome.

...I shall find antiquity rewarding, if only because, while I'm absorbed in it, I shall be able to turn my eyes from the troubles which for so long have tormented the modern world...

The Vestal Virgin was raped and gave birth to twin boys. Mars, she declared, was their father.... The mother was bound and flung into prison; the boys, by the king's order, were condemned to be drowned in the river. Destiny, however, intervened; the Tiber had overflowed its banks: because of the flooded ground it was impossible to get to the actual river, and the men entrusted to do the deed thought that the flood water, sluggish though it was, would serve their purpose....In those days the country thereabouts was all wild and uncultivated, and the story goes that when the basket in which the infants had been exposed was left high and dry by the receding water, a she-wolf, coming down from the neighbouring hills to quench her thirst, heard the children crying and made her way to where they were. She offered them her teats to suck and treated them with such gentleness that Faustulus, the King's herdsman, found her licking them with her tongue. Faustulus took them to his hut and gave them to his wife Larentia to nurse.

Such, then, was the birth and upbringing of the twins. By the time they were grown boys, they employed themselves actively on the farm and with the flocks and began to go hunting in the woods...

Now Faustulus had suspected all along that the boys he was bringing up were of royal blood. He knew that two infants had been exposed by the king's orders, and the rescue of his own two fitted perfectly in point of time. Hitherto, however, he had been unwilling to declare what he knew, until either a suitable opportunity occurred or circumstances compelled him. Now the truth could no longer be concealed.

Romulus and Remus [after having been told of the events surrounding their birth], were suddenly seized by an urge to found a new settlement on the spot where they had been left to drown as infants and had been subsequently brought up.... Unhappily the brothers' plans for the future were marred by the

> same curse which had divided their grandfather and Amulius—jealousy and ambition. A disgraceful quarrel arose from a matter in itself trivial. As the brothers were twins and all question of seniority was thereby precluded, they determined to ask the tutelary [guardian] gods of the countryside to declare by augury which of them should govern the new town... Remus...was the first to receive a sign—six vultures; and no sooner was this made known to the people than double the number of birds appeared to Romulus....Angry words ensued, followed all too soon by blows, and in the course of the affray Remus was killed....
>
> This, then, was how Romulus obtained the sole power. The newly built city was called by its founder's name.

a career in provincial government or the army a desirable and patriotic calling. He created a professional civil service at Rome along with the vigiles, a police force *cum* squad of paid firefighters. Abroad and even in Italy, he linked the worship of Rome, Roma, as a spiritual entity with a concept of his own supernatural being. In Italy, Julius Caesar was deified. In the Greek world, Augustus was worshipped as the New Zeus. At Lugdunum (Lyon in modern France), in the newly formed Gallic provinces, an altar was set up to Rome and Augustus.

Finally, Augustus created a fine mix in which material prosperity, literature, and the arts, religiosity and a common sense of "Romanity" flourished. This was not mere propaganda although Augustus proved himself to be a consummate public relations person. Augustus really did find a city of brick and left it as one of marble, as he was said to boast.

Two factors above all contributed to the ultimate success of the Principate: the people's ardent desire for peace after years of brutal civil wars; and the fact that the supreme ruler of the Empire had a very long lifespan, outliving most of his projected heirs as well as all of his opponents.

Literature in the Age of Augustus

The Age of Augustus was a time in which all the arts, architecture, sculpture, and literature blossomed. This was especially true of literature while C. Maecenas was alive. Maecenas, who died in 8 B.C., was very much Augustus's unofficial Minister of Culture.

Three Masters. P. Vergilius Maro (Virgil, 70–19 B.C.) gave Rome its national foundation epic, the *Aeneid*. That epic poem details the escape from Troy of the Torjan hero Aeneas and his ultimate arrival and victory in Italy. The Julian family and Augustus's parentage through his adoptive father Julius Caesar are descended from Aeneas and his son Iulus. Although not part of the poem, the Trojan hero's son, Ascanius by another name, founded the city of Alba Longa in Latium, mother city of Rome itself. This curious mix of legends also relates that Romulus and Remus were directly descended from Aeneas.

Q. Horatius Flaccus (Horace, 65–8 B.C.) wrote in a variety of Greek metres. He used his gift to applaud the benefits of peace, Augustan rule, and Roman domination. Though an advocate for Augustus, Horace took pains never to appear enslaved to Augustan ideals. Originally, he was a soldier on the wrong side in the civil wars that were ended at Philippi.

P. Ovidius Naso (Ovid, ca. 43 B.C.–A.D. 19) was a poet who composed his works in only one metre. A wit, he wrote a well-crafted parody of an instructional booklet called *The Art of Love*. When that was not well-received by Augustus, he wrote another called *The Remedy for Love*. For these poems, and for an unspecified crime, which probably involved Augustus's daughter Julia, Ovid was banished from

Rome. He died in Tomi, at the mouth of the Danube on the shores of the Black Sea.

Buildings in the Empire

Some of the principal structures in Roman cities were discussed in the preceding chapter. These were the Senate house, place of assembly, temple to Jupiter, and temples to other gods and goddesses as well.

Basically, a people can be described as a coherent society when the majority of that community speak the same language, is subject to the same laws and principles of government, and worship the same gods. Further, to qualify as a civilization, the core of the society should be centred in a city or urban development. In Roman society, however, there were other communal activities, several of which developed relatively late and which were mostly related to entertainment. There were also certain features that were characteristic of private houses, although the ordinary Roman would probably have had difficulty in understanding the modern difference between the work-place and home. First, we shall examine public buildings and places for entertainment. Second, we shall review the basic plan of a Roman house from those preserved at Pompeii.

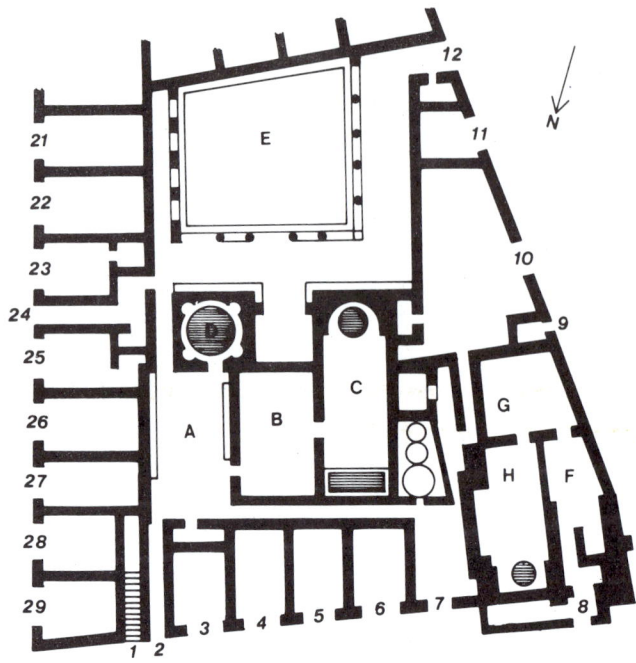

Bathing for those of ancient Rome was a far more complex ritual than it is for us today. The Baths of Caracalla (floorplan shown here), which could accommodate 3000 people, was typical of the more elaborate baths. The baths were alive with activity as servants and slaves ran about looking after their masters, gamblers calling out the odds, manicurists plying their trade, and jugglers entertaining.

Imagine yourself attending the Baths of Caracalla at the height of the Roman Empire. Writing from the perspective of either a patron or one of the many people serving the needs of the bathers write a diary entry in which tou vividly describe a day at the baths.

Thermae (Baths)

Heated bath suites were perhaps the greatest of all Roman contributions to the art of living. These, of course, were not the simple 1.5 m or so long containers of modern times; rather they were elaborately built structures for steaming (like a sauna), for gently relaxing, or for taking an ice-cold plunge. Above all, these large public establishments were for social interaction. This was a form of relaxation enjoyed by poor and rich alike.

The Forum Baths at Pompeii were divided into men's and women's sections. One entered this bathing establishment after paying a small fee and went directly to an *apodyterium* (A)(F) (changing room). There, the bather stripped and deposited her or his clothes in a niche. Next, the bather moved to the *frigidarium* (D), a room in which there was a tank of cold water. Having taken a cold plunge, one passed through a *tepidarium* (B)(G), used to lessen the shock of moving from the frigidarium to the caldarium (hot room). The *caldarium* (C)(H) was the main room in a bath suite and was equipped with basins. One could also take advantage of the *laconicum* (sweat room), a room with a dry heat, if there was one. A *palestra* (E) was a place where one could exercise and sun. There were also some shops (3–6) for the convenience of the patrons.

The baths were heated from beneath by a fire in the *hypocaust* (literally meaning being burned below). Hot air would circulate beneath the floor and up the walls through hollow flue tiles buried in them. For a pleasant diversion, one could splash with members of the opposite sex in the *piscina* (swimming pool) or exercise in the *gymnasium*. Bath suites were very luxurious in Rome and very popular. The early Christians considered them to be evil places where immoral behaviour was rampant.

Theatres

Permanent theatres were a late introduction into the Roman world, where *gravitas* (weightiness of manner) was prized as a personal attribute among the upper classes. In fact, as mentioned earlier, the first stone theatre in Rome was built as late as 55 B.C. by Pompey the Great.

The theatre was normally built on the Greek model, semicircular with a dancing-floor (orchestra), a stage, and a backdrop (skene). Behind the backdrop would be changing rooms and property storage. As the Greek concept of an independent chorus became less influential, the orchestra diminished in size and the stage became more prominent. The backdrop was often built in the provinces away from Rome as an architectural facade complete with columns and pediment. There were also covered, roofed theatres called Odeums.

Drama as a spoken art form became less popular during the age of Augustus. Pantomimes grew in popularity, no doubt due to the increasing decadence of the Roman taste, which demanded nudity and sexually-explicit performances. The theatre was also used for the presentation of wild beasts and armed combat between opposing pairs of **gladiators**.

Amphitheatres

The amphitheatre, which was devoted to public entertainment, came late to Rome. The first stone amphitheatre was constructed in Rome in 29 B.C., although Pompeii had one about 50 years earlier. The most famous amphitheatre, an oval arena surrounded by tiers of seats, is undoubtedly the Flavian Amphitheatre or **Colosseum** dedicated in Rome in A.D. 80 by the Emperor Titus (A.D. 79–81).

The Colosseum is so named because a colossal statue of the Emperor Nero (A.D. 54–68) stood nearby. It is perhaps the most massive surviving structure from the Roman era. There were 80 entrances of which 76 (not those on the long or short axis) were public. There were four seating areas, and tickets inscribed with the entrance numbers on them have been found. It is estimated that there was room for about 50 000 spectators. The Colosseum's inaugural games lasted 100 days and some 9000 animals were slaughtered in "wild hunts." An untold number of convicted criminals were also executed as part of the public displays at the inauguration of the Colosseum.

An elephant farm and an ostrich farm had been established near Naples since it was cheaper to raise exotic beasts in captivity than to pay for their capture in the wild and for their transport. Also, this farming made the supply more reliable.

Circus

A Roman circus was not a three-ringed show under a big top. It was a long race-track with starting gates at one end, a central wall (spina) around which chariots raced, and turning-posts at either end of the wall.

ARCHITECTURE
A VISITOR'S GUIDE TO ANCIENT ROME

Rome

Along the banks of the Tiber River, nestled among seven small hills which rise above a fertile plain grew a village which was to become one of the greatest cities of the western world. At the time of the Roman Empire Rome was the undisputed political and cultural centre of Europe. People from all over its vast empire flooded to this great city to revel in the wealth and opulence of Rome. Visitors from both the past and the present share a sense of awe at the grandeur of the city.

The models of Rome below depict the city as it was at its height including many of the buildings for which Rome is famous. Visitors to Rome can still experience the sense of awe that travellers have felt for ages by exploring the various sites which preserve the grandeur of the Roman Empire.

PANTHEON 1

One of the most impressive structures of ancient Rome is the Pantheon. The structure, built by the Emperor Hadrian after Agrippa's Pantheon burned down, remains one of Rome's most impressive sites. The Pantheon was designed as a temple to the gods and has survived because it was converted to a Christian church, thus remaining an important religious site.

THE MAUSOLEUM OF HADRIAN 2

Around A.D. 130 the Emperor Hadrian constructed for himself and his successors a mausoleum which exists today as Castel Sant' Angelo. It was completed in A.D. 139, a year after his death. Resting on a square base roughly 100 m long and 17 m high is a cylindrical body, divided inside by radiating walls. The roof was covered with earth and cypress trees and crowned by a statue. The interior was decorated with stucco and statues. The funerary chamber, reached by a spiral stairway, holds the bodies of Hadrian and his wife as well as various others.

THE COLOSSEUM   3

This is the most famous amphitheatre in the world. Its present name comes from a colossal statue of Emperor Nero which stood nearby. Built in the first century A.D., the seating capacity was close to modern day stadiums such as the Skydome. The Colosseum had 80 entrances and room for 50,000 spectators.

THE ROMAN FORUM   4

All Roman towns shared a common feature in the forum or town centre. The forum was a square with shops along three sides and a basilica (town hall) at one end. The most famous forum was the Forum Romanum which was situated near the Colosseum in Rome. Today one can wander through what is left of the Forum Romanum and see the remnants of great buildings such as the Temple of Venus and Roma.

SAN CLEMENTE   5

Situated just three hundred metres from the Colosseum is one of Rome's hidden treasures. The Basilica of San Clemente lies on top of 2000 years of religious worship. When visitors enter the Basilica they are in a structure built in the thirteenth century. By descending a flight of stairs you enter the remains of a fifth century Christian church which stood until about A.D. 1100. Descending another set of stairs leads one to a Roman street dating to the first century A.D. Here you can walk down a Roman street and peer into a Mithraic schoolhouse or one of the only remaining Mithraic temples.

PALACE OF DOMITIAN   6

The Emperor Domitian (A.D. 284–305) erected buildings throughout the city of Rome. On the south half of the Palatine he built a magnificent palace which towered over the Circus Maximus. The public wing consisted of a basilica, a reception hall, and a shrine. Throughout the palace were large rooms, pools, and elaborate fountains creating an atmosphere of opulence.

THE CIRCUS MAXIMUS   7

In the "Great Circus" 24 chariot races of 7 laps each took place daily entertaining some 250 000 spectators. The most exciting part of the race was the turns which were very sharp and crashes were frequent. The track was a long oval which measured 600 m by 200 m with a barrier of statues down the middle. The outlines of this structure can still be seen today.

REPUBLICAN WALL   8

Following the Gallic invasion in 390 B.C. the Romans decided to improve the defences of the city by building a wall made of large blocks of a hard and strong stone known as Grotta oscura. This wall, sometimes known as the "Servian Wall" helped protect Rome from Hannibal's threat of attack and served as the boundary of the city limits even after urban buildings and activities spilled outside the walls.

The Colosseum remains one of Rome's most impressive sites. From the inside, pictured here, visitors can still imagine the roar of 50 000 spectators witnessing a host of bloody sports events. Beneath the floor of the Colosseum, now gone, were numerous cells which held wild animals, gladiators, convicted criminals, and Christians.

Races were popular, in part because the circus seating was mixed; people of either sex could sit together here, something forbidden by law in the theatre. In every part of the Roman Empire, in any city of relative importance, there were circuses and chariot racing. The teams of charioteers, wherever they were, were divided into four competing factions: the Greens, Whites, Blues, and Reds. Fan support for these factions was intense and sometimes violent. The races themselves were limited to a fixed number of chariots racing counter-clockwise round the spina seven times. Charioteers, who were the subjects of individual adulation much like rock stars today, were not expected merely to race. They also had to perform tricks, like leaving the car to mount the back of the horses, all while galloping at full tilt. Hunts of wild animals and simultaneous pairings of gladiators were also exhibited in the circus.

The Circus Maximus at Rome was probably the most famous circus. Built of stone with tiers of seats on either long side, the circus was approximately 200 m wide by 600 long (6 by 2 football fields). It is estimated that it could hold some 200 000 spectators.

Naumachiae

The first of these artificial lakes for mock sea battles was built in Rome by Augustus at the foot of the Janiculan hill. Hardly pretend for the participants, the sea battles were real. In front of spectators, real ships and real marines (prisoners) rammed one another and fought in hand-to-hand combat. There is little reason to accept a widely-held belief that in later years the Colosseum was flooded to hold such games.

Gladiators

Pairs of gladiators fought each other for public amusement, wherever the sponsors of public games wished: in theatres, amphitheatres, the circus, even the Roman Forum. There were formal rules and there was, as in hockey or baseball games today, even musical accompaniment from organs. The Thracian, armed with a curved sword, was conventionally set against a Samnite, who had a crested helmet and was protected by a long shield. In other competitions, the retiarius, a fighter whose principal weapon was a net, was arrayed against a secutor armed with a short sword and small rectangular shield. Since the retiarius fought bare-headed while their opponents' heads were protected by helmets with face masks, the Emperor Claudius (A.D. 41–54) would invariably order their deaths *pollice verso* (thumbs down). This was because the Emperor took delight in watching and observing the fighters' facial contortions.

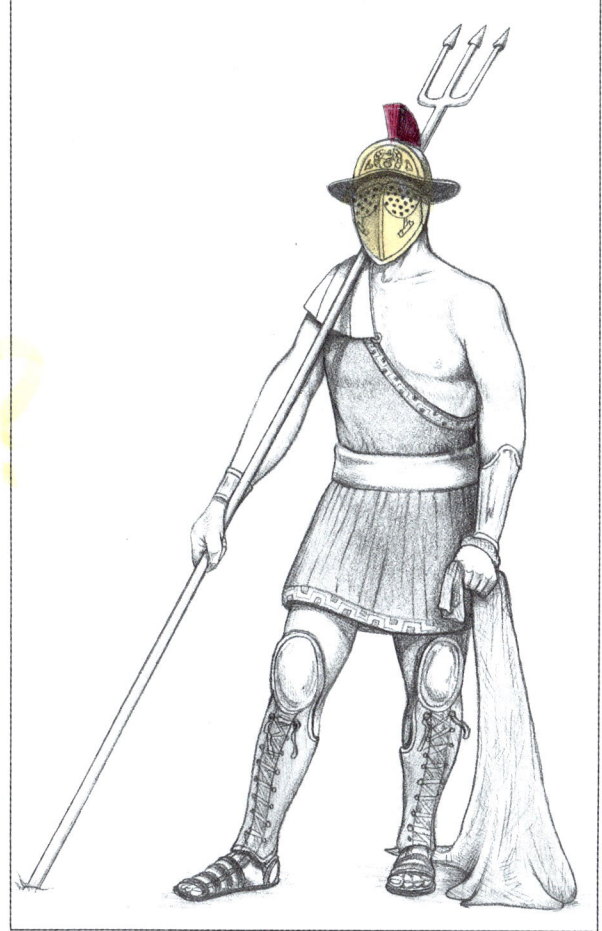

Gladiators were slaves trained to fight to the death. They wore different weapons to make the struggles more entertaining.

The Private House

The Roman house, though varying in parts of Europe and by the second century A.D. generally having bath suites, is best known to us from the houses buried at Pompeii. These plans are supplemented by the writings of the great Roman architect Vitruvius.

Although of widely varying dimensions, there seems invariably to have been a long and deep entrance. This opened into an atrium, a rectangular area open to the sky, with a sloping roof. Rain water

The Roman Empire CHAPTER 9 273

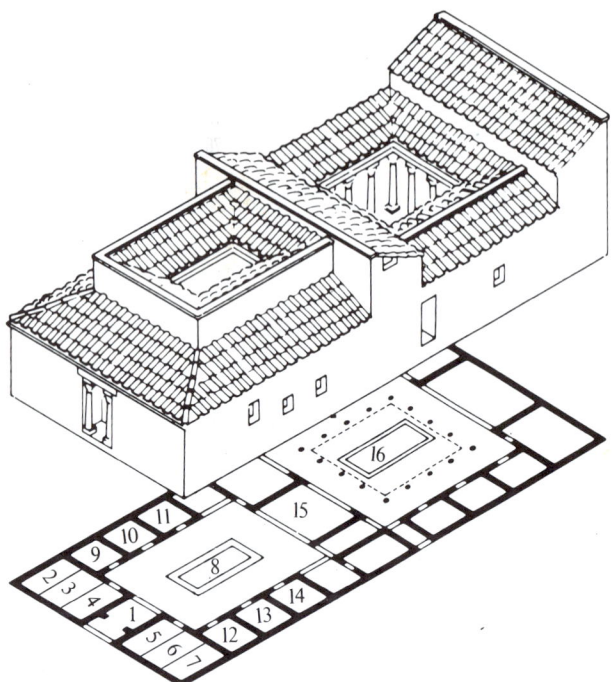

Diagram of a Pompeian House
The roofed and unroofed areas of this house are clearly visible as are the various other elements. One would enter the house by the entrance passage (1) which was flanked by six shops that opened up onto the street (2), (3), (4), (5), (6), and (7). Once through the entrance one would be in the atrium or front hall (8). The rooms surrounding this were cubicula or sleeping quarters (9-14) and the two larger rooms could have served as sitting areas. The tablinum or reception room (15) was open to the atrium and the colonnaded garden or peristyle (16) at the rear of the house. The servants' quarters were arranged behind the garden along the other side.

dripped from this roof into a waterproof, concrete tank set into the floor of the atrium. Generally, this water-trap system is known today as an impluvium. The water was piped away and saved in an underground cistern.

On either side of the atrium, there were usually small rooms, thought to be bedrooms. Opposite the entrance was the tablinum, often open to the atrium on one side and separated from a cloistered garden on the other by a moveable wooden screen. The cloistered garden, or peristyle, was a regular feature of a house and was obviously used for relaxation and recreation.

At Pompeii, the so-called House of the Vettii Brothers is remarkable for the fact that archaeologists and botanists have recently been able to reconstruct the formal cloistered garden. Shrubs have been planted there which, from their root systems, are known to resemble closely those of plants obliterated on 24 August A.D. 79.

Often around the peristyle there were other rooms, either bedrooms or triclinia (dining rooms). The little rooms used for storing scrolls or parchment "books" usually had an eastern exposure for reading in the early-morning sun and for the prevention of mildew.

The Rise of Christianity

Earlier we looked at the principal pagan gods of Rome and Greece. Now, we will consider the beginnings and growth of Christianity. Despite its various forms, there are certain essential elements that are common to all Christian religions.

Christianity has its basis in a form of Middle Eastern monotheism, Judaism, in which the record of the religion (the Torah) is believed to have been written under direct, Divine inspiration. The laws, which govern all aspects of Jewish life even today, are believed by the devout to have been written on two tablets of stone by God and handed to Moses on Mt. Sinai. This reverence for the immutable "Word of God" was unlike anything to be found in the pagan world. Essentially, all history, according to the tenets of the Jewish faith, is to be interpreted as the fulfilling of prophecies.

Around A.D. 30 in Palestine, a charismatic teacher made his way toward Jerusalem, the centre of the Jewish faith, teaching that the prophecies of the

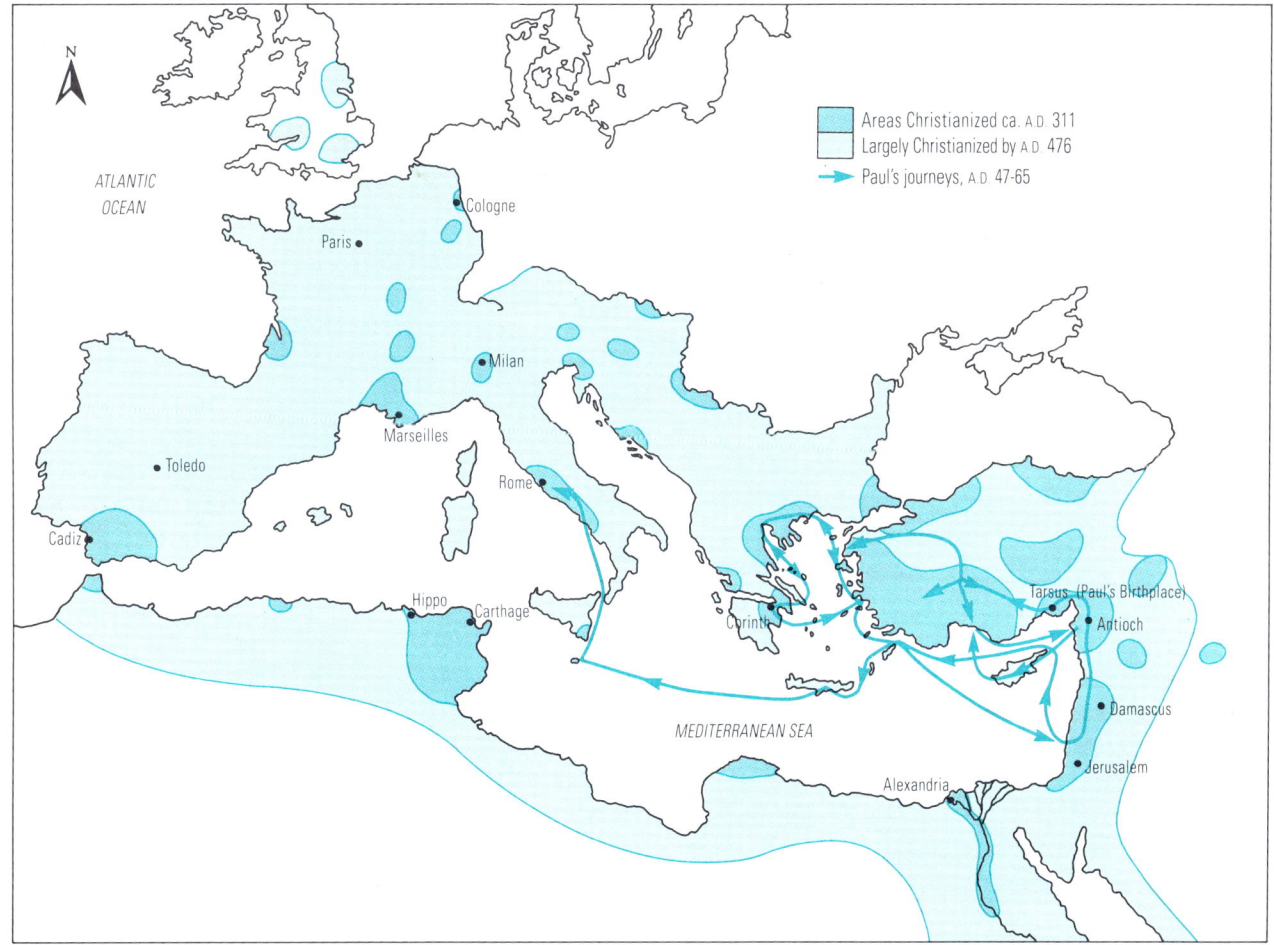

The Spread of Christianity

Torah were not to be fulfilled at some indefinite time in the future. This teacher was **Jesus Christ**, whose qualifications, like others of the time, were unofficial. He was believed by his followers to be the Son of God: and he taught that the Kingdom of God was present now. The miracles he performed were signs of this reality. Healing, too (another sign), was to be effected against a background of repentance and genuine contrition for sins. Jesus forgave sins; the repentance which he sought required not only contrition but a complete and unquestioning acceptance of Jesus as God's sole agent.

For the leaders of the formal Jewish religion, however, Jesus' actions were unacceptable; only the one God could forgive sins. While teachings of the Messianic tradition were not unfamiliar, they were completely transformed and made unacceptable to religious leaders by the "Good News" (Greek word Euangelion) that God's Kingdom had begun to arrive and that a belief in Jesus was the only criterion for admission. Arriving in Jerusalem with a band of followers (the 12 apostles) Jesus set about challenging the most powerful people in the Jewish hierarchy, the Sadducees who controlled the Temple itself. It must be noted here that there is little evidence to suggest that Jesus sought an earthly power and the ejection of the Romans from Palestine.

Betrayed by one of his close followers, Jesus was arrested by the Sadducees and accused of a variety of crimes. Unable to exact capital punishment themselves, the offended Sadducees thrust the responsibility for trying Jesus on the Roman administrator, the provincial prefect and procurator (financial officer) Pontius Pilate. He at first was unwilling to become involved in a religious matter, but eventually condemned Jesus to crucifixion on the grounds that he would not deny that he was "King of the Jews," a direct challenge to Roman imperial power. Three days after Jesus' death and burial, some of his followers maintained that they had seen him alive again.

After his resurrection and ascension to heaven, Jesus' surviving adherents started spreading the word about their master and, thus, came into direct conflict with the official Jewish religion. It was that conflict and the unexpected conversion of the main opponent of the dissidents, Paul, that led eventually to the demise of the old pagan gods and the growth of the new faith.

At first Paul, a Roman citizen and a very zealous Jew, went about applying sanctions against the followers of Jesus. Then, in A.D. 36, in an astounding realization of his own harshness in applying those sanctions, he converted to a belief in the Christian faith. The realization or conversion is said to have happened suddenly in a flash of light while travelling on a road to Damascus in modern Syria.

At first, Christianity, a belief in Jesus Christ as a personal saviour, was a relatively minor Jewish sect. The next step in its transformation into an independent religion took place some two decades after Jesus' crucifixion, when former worshippers of pagan gods were allowed admission into the faith without the accompanying rituals. Now the conversion of people other than Jews spread very quickly. The attraction of the religion lay in the essential equality it offered. No matter what one's station in life (slave or noble), an equal opportunity for salvation and a better life in the world to come was possible.

Generally the Roman state maintained a tolerant attitude to the new faith, with notable exceptions like the Emperor Nero who used Christians as scapegoats for a great fire in Rome. The newly-formed rituals of worship, the consumption of bread and wine, were also misinterpreted by the uninitiated pagan Romans as evidence of cannibalism and even infanticide. In addition, the Christians were made vulnerable by their supreme regard for a heavenly God rather than the terrestrial but equally divine emperor.

The main reason for the distinction today between Christian and Jew is perhaps grounded in the later history of the first and early second centuries A.D. The Jews twice rebelled against Rome and after a series of vain attempts to assert independence they were defeated in A.D. 70 and again in A.D. 135. The first time was at the hands of that same Titus who later inaugurated the Colosseum; the second defeat was engineered by the Emperor Hadrian. Now, the Jewish Christians suffered the hardships and disgrace felt by all Jews. The gentile Christians, for survival, distanced themselves from Judaism and from any apparent association with Jerusalem. In A.D. 70, Jerusalem was ransacked and the Temple destroyed by Titus's occupying army. The record of this pillage is visible to all in the relief carvings on the interior walls of the Arch of Titus in Rome; the Arch was erected posthumously in A.D. 81.

Explanations for Christianity's Spread

An attempt should be made to explain the spread of Christianity and its rise in popularity. The positive promise of life after death, the sense of equality the new faith espoused, and the sheer morality of converts to the religion provide only a partial (though compelling) answer. One of the biggest boosts the religion got, as we shall see later, was its official adoption by Constantine the Great in the early fourth century A.D. However, to reduce very complex matters to simple statements:

First, the Christian religion was practised by converts intent on behaving morally toward all people. They combined this conduct with a missionary zeal that often marks out converts to a new and persuasive faith. Christians had all the power of conviction on their side, as opposed to the pagans who believed in exhausted, worn deities who were disinterested in the human condition.

Second, the religion's adherents were, in a word, protective of their new faith. More importantly, they were organized as no other religion had been in the pagan world, with the obvious exceptions of Egypt and the quasi-religious cult of the Emperor. The Christian religion, whether accepted or not by contemporaries, had a defined bureaucratic structure with Church elders and bishops. Among these, there was a well understood hierarchical ranking; the bishops of metropolitan cities such as Rome, Antioch, and Carthage clearly had precedence over others from smaller, less cosmopolitan centres.

Third, the Christians had a coherent body of holy writings which they coupled with common rituals. No matter where you were from, as a Christian you could feel fellowship.

In short, while the pagan religious world was fragmented and offered no universally accepted rites, scriptures, or structure the Christian Church was an effectively organized bureaucracy. This bureaucracy had great influence and held, for example, more than one Empire-wide Council. So pervasive was the Church's influence, that its **temporal** power came to be immense and was felt to challenge the secular administration of later Roman emperors.

Perhaps, it was this very success in spreading its message as an organized entity that brought about (blindly and with much intolerance, to be sure) the great persecutions of the Christian Church in the third century A.D.

The Successors of Augustus

Augustus, the founder of the Roman Empire, died in August A.D. 14 having outlived almost all of his potential successors. The first person to inherit the "purple" was Augustus's adopted son Tiberius (A.D. 14–37). Purple was an imperial colour because of its expensive method of extraction from murex, a sea shell. Tiberius's reign became increasingly harsh and he eventually spent the later years of his life distanced from Rome on the pleasant island of Capri in the Bay of Naples.

Following him in A.D. 37 was the Emperor Gaius Caligula (A.D. 37–41). He took his nickname from the little boots (caligulae) he wore when in his father's army camp as a tiny infant. At first, his reign was beneficial. Soon, however, it came to be marked by all manner of cruelty and vice. It is said that he had so little respect for the Senate that he made his favourite horse, Incitatus, a member. At any rate, he cared little for the sanctity of marriage and engaged in several openly adulterous and incestuous affairs. Gaius was eventually murdered in January A.D. 41 by a group of Senatorial conspirators and Cassius Chaerea, a member of the Praetorian Guard whom Gaius constantly ridiculed for his homosexuality.

Next came Claudius (A.D. 41–54). This man, long considered by his family to be an imbecile, proved himself to be an able and just administrator. It was under his rule that the lasting conquest of Britain got underway (A.D. 43).

Claudius's successor was the strange, moody Nero (A.D. 54–68). Groomed for the purple by his ambitious mother Agrippina whom he caused to be murdered in A.D. 61, his volatile nature was at first restrained by the philosopher Seneca. He, however, became ever more unpopular. The great fire of Rome (A.D. 64) was even rumoured to have been set by him. This is probably based on a misunderstanding of the reason for stringent building codes instituted by him after the fire. Nero built a huge palace on the site of what is now the Colosseum. Using Christians as scape-goats for the fire, he tied several to the tops of poles in the grounds of that palace (the so-called Golden House), covered the unfortunate people with pitch and set fire to them. The ghastly spectacle thus provided an eerie light for a night-time party.

The assassination of Nero in A.D. 68 left a void which several people tried to fill. Eventually, after very brief periods of rule by Galba, Otho, and Vitellius, in A.D. 69 Titus Flavius Vespasianus (Vespasian, A.D. 69–79) came to power. Vespasian ruled wisely for ten years before his death and the accession of his son Titus (A.D. 79–81).

Titus's rule was brief, but was also considered beneficial. Titus himself gained a reputation for generosity. When Vesuvius erupted in August A.D. 79 obliterating the towns of the Bay of Naples, Titus lent much valuable assistance to the devastated residents.

Vespasian's younger son Domitian (A.D. 81–96) followed Titus to power in A.D. 81. A strict and autocratic man, he was infamous for his persecution of Christians and Jews. He was murdered in A.D. 96 with the connivance of his wife Domitia and probably his immediate successor Nerva.

Marcus Ulpius Traianus (Trajan, A.D. 98–117) was born in Spain and, before his accession in A.D. 98, spent several decades refining his abilities as a soldier and provincial administrator in the Iberian peninsula, the Rhineland, and what is now Hungary. In the early years of his reign Trajan embellished the city of Rome itself. One example of his generosity is the Forum with its famous column celebrating successive victories over the Dacians in a remarkable spiral relief (Dacia is now modern Romania north of the Danube). Another example is the multi-level Macellum (Market). As an emperor of provincial origins, however, he paid particular attention to the territories outside Italy. He expanded the borders of the Empire in every direction (to the north in modern Romania, to the east across the Arabian desert and in Mesopotamia, to the north and west in Britain). He also was so convinced that the health of the provinces was of fundamental importance to the well-being of Rome itself that 13 of the 21 years of his rule were passed beyond the borders of Italy. Trajan was an able administrator who set the scene for his ward, adopted son, and successor, Hadrian.

Publius Aelius Hadrianus (Hadrian, A.D. 117–138) was one of the truly great Roman emperors. Like his adoptive father, he was born in Spain and spent many years as a soldier and administrator in the provinces. He, more than any previous emperor and most of his successors, consolidated Roman rule throughout the known world. This was done by extensive travel and a personal interest in Rome's subjects.

Hadrian's first great journey was in A.D. 121–125, and it took him almost everywhere in the Empire from west to east and north to south. During the second journey from A.D. 128–134, Hadrian played the part of imperial benefactor, founding cities and restoring buildings. The Hadrianic colony at Jerusalem, however, was not well received by the Jews. Ultimately, they rebelled and after a brief but heady revolt from A.D. 132 were repressed in A.D. 135.

Hadrian was incurably inquisitive and a lover of all things Greek. The most famous and enduring monuments to his reign, apart from the sprawling but magnificent villa at Tivoli outside Rome, are Hadrian's Wall in northern England and the almost completely intact **Pantheon** in Rome itself.

Wishing to secure the Empire, Emperor Hadrian built a wall across northern England to prevent the Picts from raiding. The wall, pictured here, was wide enough for chariots to travel on and had a number of fortresses situated along its length.

The Pantheon

The Pantheon is a circular temple, built in 25–23 B.C. by Agrippa, and totally rebuilt in about A.D. 126–128. It stands out in history as one of the most architecturally influential buildings in the western world. It is certainly as important, if not more so, as its predecessor the Parthenon in Athens. It also is no less impressive than its successor in Constantinople, the church of Hagia Sophia. The Pantheon, with its impressive dome, has inspired modern architects of every generation, from Palladio to the present. In North America, its most famous successor is the Capitol building in Washington, D.C.

Today, the Pantheon stands in a little piazza in Rome with all of its original external facing gone. For most of its circumference, it presents a rather austere brick drum to the viewer. The entrance to the north, restored by Septimius Severus (A.D. 193–211) and Caracalla, is uncomfortably in the style of a traditional Greek or Roman temple. When one enters by the huge, antique bronze doors, however, one is faced with a space as high as it is round, 43.2 m, until fairly recently one of the largest enclosed spaces in the world. The ceiling, ornamented with sunken panels, is hemispherical and springs from the interior walls of the rotunda at exactly half its height, 21.6 m. The whole structure is illuminated by a single oculus (circular opening) 8.3 m across.

The construction of the Pantheon is deceptively simple. The drum is made of concrete with brick

The Roman Empire CHAPTER 9

facing and, at the lowest course above the foundations, is 6.15 m wide. The foundations are ring shaped, 7.3 m wide by 4.5 m deep. As the dome approaches the oculus, however, it is only 1.5 m thick. The concrete also is varied in composition: heavy, solid material at the foot of the drum; lighter, volcanic material in the dome. The rotunda, although it appears massive to the casual observer, is in reality a series of eight relief arches and the apparently tremendous weight of the whole is lessened considerably by the niches and voids built into the drum.

The survival of this amazing structure is due entirely to its conversion to use as a Christian church, Santa Maria ad Martyres, in A.D. 608, when it was given to Pope Boniface VIII by the Byzantine Emperor Phocas. Today, it is one of Rome's most important churches and the burial place for several notables including the painter Raphael.

Literature in the First Two Centuries A.D.

Although neither read nor studied as much as works of the late Republic or the age of Augustus, writings of the late first century after Christ and onwards are of equal sophistication and literary value. Among the famous historical writers of this period are Cornelius Tacitus (Tacitus, ca., A.D. 56–unknown) and C. Suetonius Tranquillus (Suetonius, ca. A.D. 69–140). Both these writers wrote about the early emperors. The first affected impartiality but really composed his *Histories* and *Annals* from a hostile senatorial viewpoint. The second, actually a secretary to the Emperor Hadrian at one time, in his *Lives of the Twelve Caesars* was unashamedly racy.

In this period also narrative fiction became more popular. Petronius Arbiter (first century A.D.) compiled a work of often scandalous tales (including *The Dinner of Trimalchio*) perhaps parodying the Emperor Nero himself; certainly he poked fun at the extravagance of the times. Apuleius (A.D. 123–unknown) wrote the only true novel surviving from antiquity. The *Metamorphoses* or *Golden Ass* is the story of one Lucius who is transformed into an ass. After several hair-raising and humorous adventures, he is returned to being a human by the most widely worshipped goddess of the day, Isis.

In the first century after Christ, there were also scholars like C. Plinius Secundus (Pliny the Elder, A.D. 23–79) who wrote many works including the 37-volume *Natural History* which still exists. He died while trying to rescue people fleeing the eruption of Vesuvius. His sense of curiosity led him to the coastal town of Stabiae in an attempt to observe the eruption. Overcome by the noxious gases, he suffocated on the shore. Pliny the Elder's last hours are recorded for posterity by his nephew and adopted son C. Plinius Caecilius Secundus (Pliny the Younger, A.D. 61–112). This man compiled a highly prized nine-volume set of letters.

Poets also loom large in the first and second centuries after Christ. In addition to the rather refined works of P. Papinius Statius (Statius, A.D. 45–96), there were the epigrams (short and witty poems) of M. Valerius Martialis (Martial, A.D. 40–104) and the biting satires of, among others, D. Iunius Iuvenalis (Juvenal, late first and early second centuries).

Stoicism

Stoicism was a moral and physical philosophy popular in the first two centuries A.D. This was a system of thought which gained its name from the Stoa (portico) in Athens where it first flourished. The essential message of the philosophy was "not to worry." The aim in life was to accept whatever comes along. All nature is, and whatever "is" is right.

Among the adherents of stoicism was L. Annaeus Seneca (Seneca, ca. 4 B.C.–A.D. 65). Born in southern Spain, he was a philosopher and teacher and did

Art: A Window to Our Past

▼▼▼▼▼▼▼▼▼▼▼▼▼▼▼▼▼▼▼

UNIT ONE: *COLOUR PLATES*

Much can be learned about a society through the art it produced. Artistic expression is often a mirror of the values and aspirations of a people. As well, much can be learned about how a society earned its living from the nature of the art produced. Agricultural societies tend to be more religious than urbanized industrial societies since so much of their livelihood is dependent on forces beyond their control. Throughout the ages humans have sought to express their innermost thoughts, desires, and values, and to record their triumphs and defeats through art. Such attempts at visually expressing significant aspects of a culture have provided us with a fascinating window to the past.

The art of the Paleolithic hunters clearly reflects the reverence for nature held by these societies. The earliest paintings and sculptures are often of a variety of animals, some of which are now extinct. As people began to settle along the banks of such mighty rivers as the Nile, the Tigris, the Euphrates, the Yellow, and the Indus the themes of art changed. Increasingly, humans became the focus of artistic expression although in some societies, such as Egypt, nature deities continued to play an important role. Chinese art was much more humanistic focusing on humans and their achievements. In both Chinese art and philosophy it is evident that they sought to live in a harmonious relationship with nature but were not preoccupied with its forces. The art of the Chinese is not dominated by nature deities but rather depicts human activities or uses colourful symbolism to illustrate the order of the world as they perceived it.

◀ *The paintings of the Lascaux caves, dating to 15 000 B.C. preserve the ingenuity and creativity of the Paleolithic artists while capturing the reverence paid to nature. Found deep within a cavern in southwestern France, the paintings are believed to be related to hunting-magic rituals. Depicted here is a section of the bull's room showing the first bull and several horses. This photo was taken in Lascaux II which is a reproduction of the original.*

Courtesy of D. Debaye, Directeur du Service Départemental du Tourisme de la Dordogne

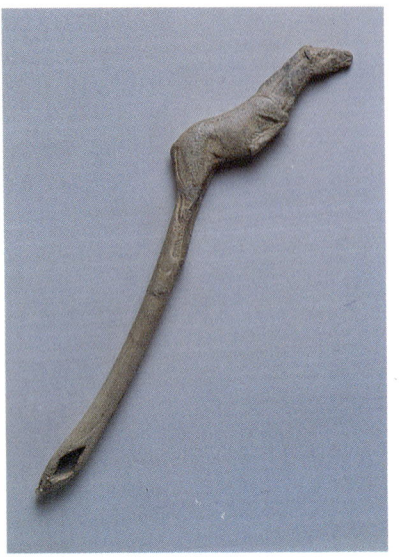

The Golden Throne, found in the tomb of Tutankhamon, is an elaborate armchair of wood overlaid with sheet gold and silver and decorated with glass, faience, and semi-precious stones. The scene depicts Queen Ankesenamun anointing her husband Tutankhamon with perfume in a floral pavilion which is bathed in the rays of the sun. The conventions in art, such as the use of colour to separate sexes and compositions of scenes, were relaxed to the degree that this scene could actually depict an informality and tenderness between husband and wife.
© 1980 Fred J. Maroon

During the period known as the Upper Paleolithic (16 000 to 9 000 B.C.) both artistic and hunting skills improved. The spear-thrower, pictured above, is an example of the objects made of bone or antler which were practical in nature yet of great beauty. Horses, such as the one sculpted on the end of this spear-thrower, were commonly used for decoration.
© Clichés Réunion des Musées Nationaux

The so-called Standard of Ur, dating from about 2500 B.C. was found at the Royal Cemetery at Ur which was, at the time, one of the most powerful cities in Mesopotamia. The three bands of inlaid shells on a background of lapis lazuli show aspects of Sumerian society in peace and at war. The side depicted shows a king and officials celebrating at a banquet (top row) while servants bring animals and goods, probably as gifts and tributes.

Reproduced by courtesy of the Trustees of the British Museum

◀ *This imperial dragon robe dating from the nineteenth century is made out of elaborately woven silk tapestry. The motifs of this robe are closely linked to nature with the waves at the bottom and four mountains indicating the four corners of the universe. Above the waves are creatures such as bats, symbolizing fertility and nine dragons, a number reserved for the emperor. The robe is designed so that when the emperor is wearing it he is placed at the top of the universal hierarchy.*
Courtesy of the Royal Ontario Museum, Toronto, Canada

Among the most widely recognized and highly valued ceramics in the world are the Ming vases. Their distinctive blue and white patterns have been imitated in Japan, Indochina, and Persia. The vases shown above, decorated with dragons are typical of the early period dating to the first half of the fifteenth century. By the early part of the seventeenth century the mass production of the vases had resulted in a general decline in quality.
The Nelson-Atkins Museum of Art, Kansas City, Missouri (Nelson Fund) 40-45/1,2 ▶

The Mughal emperor Akbar (1560-1606) was a great patron of miniature paintings and personally took the painters under his wing. The heads of painting schools were often Persians. This painting shows the court in session, and is alive with movements of people. The details of the dress and aristocrat lifestyle of the courtiers with their horses, citahs, hawks and above all their colourful costumes, are quite clear.

Courtesy of the Board of Trustees of the Victoria and Albert Museum

For centuries the wearing of turbans has been an important aspect of life in India. Prior to the twentieth century all males wore turbans. The turban, which varies in shape and material, identifies a person's class and profession as well as the region they were from. Turbans were often adorned with jewellery like the clasp shown here. Such elaborate adornments were generally worn for formal occasions such as weddings or when meeting guests at festival times and were a reflection of the individual's wealth. This turban clasp, dating to the eighteenth century, is made of gold and precious jewels.

Courtesy of the Royal Ontario Museum, Toronto, Canada

UNIT TWO: *COLOUR PLATES*

While the art of the ancient Mesopotamians or Egyptians still holds some fascination for us, it is the art of the Greeks that has dominated the western world. For over two thousand years classical imagery has been a part of western culture. Even today we identify more closely with the Greek effort to attain perfect beauty than with Egyptian art with its rigid conventions. For the Greeks, their subject matter was essentially humans and human achievement, and they strove to imitate and even improve on nature. The actions and aspirations of individuals were performed by gods or heroes of the past whose bodies were those of the perfect mortal athlete. The Greeks's desire to attain perfection was reflected also in the development of vase painting. Through years of experimentation Greek artists developed techniques that enabled them to create colourful and detailed scenes on pottery of everything from heroic deeds to events in daily life.

Rome's military conquest of Greece in the second century B.C. did not end the Greeks' dominance in the arts. In fact Greek art was so admired by the Romans that a century later Augustus imported the best Greek sculptures to create works that would reflect the civilizing effect of his rule. The key feature that distinguished the Romans from the Greeks was their blending of practicality and idealism. Whereas the Greeks were master sculptors, the Romans became master engineers, and while the Greeks studied humans and their relation to the world, the Romans studied how to organize the world and have it run smoothly and efficiently. Hence, among the most important achievements of the Romans are engineering marvels such as their roads, aqueducts, and buildings such as the Pantheon.

The palaces of the Minoans were richly decorated with fresco paintings which included geometric designs, dolphins, lions, and various sporting activities. Pictured above is one of the best known of the Minoan frescoes, depicting athletes somersaulting over the back of a charging bull. The narrow waists and broad shoulders of the figures, and the use of a reddish colour to distinguish men from women are common in Minoan art.

Courtesy of the Greek National Tourist Organization

The Vapheio cups found in a tholas tomb near Sparta, are among the most spectacular finds from the tombs of the Mycenaeans. These solid gold cups depict hunters attempting to capture wild bulls. The finely crafted images were typical of the gold objects recovered by Schliemann and attests to the wealth and power of the Mycenaeans.
National Archaeological Museum, Athens Prehistoric Collection

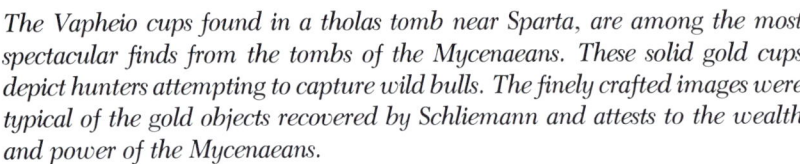

Among the ancient Greeks, pottery shared prominence with painting and sculpture among art forms. For the Greeks, pottery served a dual purpose being both functional and aesthetically pleasing. Red-figure pottery such as the Column-Krater decorated with a procession for Dionysos shown above, was a major advancement in pottery as it allowed for much finer and more detailed work.
Courtesy of the Royal Ontario Museum, Toronto, Canada

The Greek search for beauty and their centuries-long experimentation with the human form led them to achieve a high degree of perfection during the fifth century B.C. In 1972, two stunning bronze sculptures were pulled from the sea near the Italian town of Riace. The warrior pictured above reflects the Greek concept of the ideal male body where each part is correctly proportioned to be a harmonious part of the whole.
Reggio, Museo Nazionale

Roman temples reflect both their admiration for Greek architecture and their own expertise. Buildings such as the Pantheon blended Greek style with Roman features to create entirely new designs. Inside the Pantheon (pictured above) one's eyes are drawn upward to the dome which soars 42.5 m. The dome, truly a marvel of Roman engineering, creates a sense of grandeur typical of much Roman architecture.

The Interior of the Pantheon: Giovanni Paolo PANNINI; National Gallery of Art, Washington; Samuel H. Kress Collection

Surviving from the first century A.D. is the Portland Vase, *one of the finest examples of glass blowing and cameo-cutting. It was produced for the Court of Augustus and made by carving away the upper white glass layer to achieve a cameo effect. This vase blends Greek figures perhaps from mythology with Roman methods of glasswork.*

Reproduced by courtesy of the Trustees of the British Museum

The Villa of the Mysteries, located outside the walls of Pompeii, was built in the early second century B.C. The Hall of the Great Mural is renowned for its frescoes depicting a large composition of 29 figures who are believed to be involved in the initiation rites of the Dionysiac mysteries. The figures, which are life-size, are not painted in the conventional manner and seem to come to life in the mural. The combination of figures is pleasing and moves the eye from scene to scene, as does this example of a winged goddess, striking a woman whose head is buried in another's lap.

The Granger Collection, New York

▲
By the first century B.C. mosaics had become a common form of floor decoration in the homes of the wealthy. The technique, learned from the Greeks involved creating designs by carefully arranging small stone cubes to form a picture. One of the most famous mosaics of antiquity is the Alexander Mosaic found in the House of Faun at Pompeii. This partially deteriorated mosaic is a battle scene, which depicts Darius (at centre) fleeing from Alexander's forces at the Battle of Issus, and was made from over one and a half million tiny glass beads.
Courtesy of the Soprintendenza Archeologica delle Province di Napoli e Caserta

UNIT THREE: *COLOUR PLATES*

Throughout the world great civilizations have risen and declined. In some areas such as Central and South America, contact with other cultures has had devastating effects on the people and their society. For both the Maya and the Aztecs the arrival of the Spanish brought drastic change to their cultures. The condemnation by the Spanish of Maya and Aztec art and customs as pagan and the work of the devil, and the imposition of Christianity irrevocably altered these cultures. While some traditions were blended with Catholic customs, many died out. For these cultures art serves as a vital mirror of a past destroyed by the meeting of two worlds. The temples, pottery, murals, and stelae of the Maya and Aztecs all attest to the advanced and complex nature of the civilizations that flourished in Central America prior to the arrival of the Europeans.

Some areas of the world were able to not only withstand attempted incursions by Europeans but to in fact inflict significant defeats on European powers. For over seven centuries Muslims ruled Spain, and when the Crusader armies attempted to win back the Holy Land they met with stiff resistance and ultimate failure. Similarly, Europeans found their attempts at establishing Christianity and a trade network in Japan during the sixteenth and seventeenth centuries thwarted. The highly centralized and militaristic society of Japan took from the Europeans what they desired before closing the door on them. Both Japan and the Islamic world provided splendid examples of unique cultures which owed little to the western world. Although both drew inspiration from other cultures such as China, India, Persia, Egypt, and Byzantium they remained distinct societies. As with the Maya and Aztecs, art and architecture is the vital window to the rich and vibrant past of Japan and the Islamic world.

As the Islamic faith prohibits pictorial representations and religious decoration, painting never became a favourite art form in the Islamic world. Instead architecture, calligraphy, and arabesque were favoured. Paintings were generally exclusive to the upper class who could afford to pay artists to illustrate manuscripts. The finest examples of Islamic paintings are often found in secular manuscripts such as this fourteenth century painting of Arghan Khan with two of his wives and his son Ghasan which is from the illuminated manuscript of Rashid-Al-Din.
Bibliotheque Nationale de Paris/ Robert Harding Picture Library

The warrior culture in Japan was an interesting blend of militaristic values and a highly aesthetic appreciation. The samurai, while trained as warriors, were also taught to appreciate art and to sing and dance. Prints, such as the one depicted here, were reproduced in large numbers, helping to make the samurai image a romantic one and spreading samurai values to all classes.

Eastern Images Picture Library

The Arabic script was used to transcribe the Koranic text, and above is a page from a Spanish or North African Koran from the twelfth century written in a regional script. Since the Muslims had an aversion to images in religious art, their creative energies were focused on calligraphy. It became a major art form in the early centuries, ornamenting the Koran, as well as both the interiors and exteriors of mosques. Thus, some forms of Arabic script came to serve much the same purpose as stained glass in the Gothic cathedrals of Europe, communicating ideas from the holy text.

The Metropolitan Museum of Art, Rogers Fund, 1942. (42.63) Copyright © 1942 By the Metropolitan Museum of Art

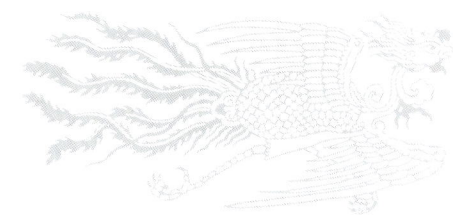

In stark contrast to the fierce-looking paintings of the samurai were the richly-painted screens that adorned castles and the homes of the wealthy. A splendid example of the richness of the screen painting from this period is evident from Kano Eitoku's Birds, Trees, and Flowers *depicted at right. This screen, done in ink, colour, and gold on paper, was considered quite innovative for its time. It is part of a pair of screens measuring 155.2 cm by 340 cm.*

The Cleveland Museum of Art, Gift of William G. Mather, 48.128

This painting, commonly referred to as "The Fishing Village Mural," was found at Chichen Itza and is a good representation of an oceanside village in northern Yucatan. The scene appears to be either a ceremonial one or the departure for a battle, as the figures are holding shields and various ornaments. On land a variety of village activities are depicted such as men carrying a heavy burden borne by a tump line and, to the right, what appears to be a temporary shelter for ceremonial purposes. Note the serpent rising up out of the roof.
Peabody Museum, Harvard University. Photograph by Hillel Burger

Nezahualpilli was the ruler of Texcoco and an ally of Montezuma. He was known as a philosopher and poet and is reputed to have been a great astrologer. At night he would go to the roof of his palace and from there he would observe and study the stars. Here he is dressed in an elaborately woven loincloth and cotton cloak, with a large jade bead necklace, all emblems of his high rank. While the costume is clearly Aztec the style of the painting is unmistakably European.
© Bibliotheque Nationale, Service Photographique

This colourful vase dating to the ninth century A.D. depicts a lively scene of considerable symbolic significance to the Maya. The humans shown on the vase are wearing costumes so as to impersonate deities and are stalking deer. The stalking and killing of the deer was symbolic of drought to the Maya. The woman seated on the rearing deer is "Ix Chel," an important Maya goddess associated with the moon.
Property of the Government of Belize; photograph courtesy of The Royal Ontario Museum, Toronto, Canada

UNIT FOUR: *COLOUR PLATES*

The collapse of the Roman Empire was accompanied by a drastic decline in the arts as many aspects of classical culture were lost during the barbaric invasions. It would take Europe centuries to recover from the destruction of these invasions. Europe's recovery from the chaos and brutality of the Dark Ages was accompanied by a revival in the arts which reflected the prominent role of the Catholic church. Throughout the High Middle Ages religious themes dominated the art of the western world. Soaring cathedrals constructed to the glory of God were adorned with numerous sculptures, all of which served to educate the largely illiterate populace of medieval Europe about Christ's message. The interior of these magnificent structures appeared light and airy thanks largely to the impressive stained-glass windows. Manuscript illumination was another art form that reflected the medieval preoccupation with religion. Illuminated manuscripts, richly decorated with a variety of themes and designs, are among the most beautiful pieces of art from the Middle Ages.

The revival of trade and the growth of cities brought to a close the medieval period and set the stage for the Renaissance. Many of the great works of the Greeks and Romans which had been lost to Europeans for centuries had been preserved in various libraries in Byzantium. The opening of trade routes allowed for classical ideas to be reintroduced to Europe, ushering in a rebirth of classicism. Throughout the fifteenth and sixteenth centuries art became increasingly humanistic as there was a renewed focus on humans and human actions. This renewal of classicism was often fused with religious themes, producing some of the most powerful works of art in the history of the western world.

Christ in Majesty *is from the Codex Aureus, a particularly luxurious and colourful manuscript produced during Carolingian times. The art of the Dark Ages was a direct contradiction to the Greek preoccupation with the human figure. In the Dark Ages, the focus changed and art became a means to depict and promote religious values and ideas. This manuscript is unusual in that it combines the human figure in a realistic fashion within a religious composition. Aesthetically the picture is pleasing, yet it contains much of the religious imagery common in this age.*

Bayer. Staatsbibliothek Munchen, CLm 14 F.6v

Advancements in Gothic architecture, such as the flying buttress, allowed for a roomier interior and for walls containing elaborate expanses of stained glass. In Chartres, the over 100 stained-glass windows carry a complex system of themes and imagery. Religious depictions include Christ, the Virgin, and scenes from the Old and New Testament, which would have served to educate the masses. This North rose window with its twelve sections lends itself to the more secular themes of the Labour of the Months, Virtue and Vices, and the depictions of tradesmen who would sponsor that particular section. These stained-glass windows contributed much to the overall feeling of lightness and grace within a Gothic church.

Courtesy of La Crypte Editions Houvet

In the twelfth and thirteenth centuries, manuscript illumination reached a high level of skill and refinement as is evident here by this illuminated page from the Winchester Bible. This page, on which two of St. Jerome's translations of the psalms appear, as two elaborately decorated letter "B"s. On the left, David is shown rescuing his sheep from a bear (top) and a lion (bottom). On the right, Christ is shown delivering one of his human flock from an evil spirit (top) and rescuing the spirits of the deceased from the devil (bottom).

The Dean and Chapter of Winchester

▼ *This illustration of the month of March is from the* Tres Riches Heures du Duc de Berry, *a calendar book produced about 1415. By choosing secular themes rather than religious ones the Limbourg brothers managed to capture the essence of medieval life. In this scene a real feeling for the people who worked the land is portrayed by the peasants toiling in the fields in the shadow of the castle. This arrangement visually depicts the essence of feudal society.*
Giraudon/Art Resource, NY PEC 4900, Tres Riches Heures du Duc de Berry, March. fol.3v Chantilly, Musee Conde

The Black Death, which wiped out one-third of Europe's population, profoundly affected society. These effects were gruesomely depicted in the art form known as "danse macabre" which depicted death and disease in all its horror. In The Three Ages of Woman and Death, *shown above, a grotesque figure representing death holds an hourglass above a woman depicted in three stages of life. The paintings served as a reminder to the viewer of the uncertainty of death's arrival.*
Kunsthistoriches Museum, Vienna ▶

One of the best examples of art's increasing secularization in the fifteenth century is Jan Van Eyck's Giovanni Arnolfini and his Bride. *This is believed to be a commissioned portrait of the wedding ceremony of Giovanni Arnolfini, an Italian financier. The realism of the scene aided by the use of oil paints, the detail and symbolism, as well as the use of light to illuminate the interior are all significant advances. The realism is especially evident when one examines the folds in the heavy clothing, the fur of the dog, the brass of the chandelier, or the reflection of the scene in the mirror. Other objects do not adorn the room but carry a specific symbolic meaning: the oranges symbolize fertility, the dog fidelity, and the mirror purity.*

Reproduced by courtesy of the Trustees, The National Gallery, London

Pieter Brueghel, a humanist painter, portrays the reality of human existence, which is in direct opposition to the artistic celebration of the human form by the masters of the Renaissance. His favourite subject was peasant and village life which he portrayed in all of its unadorned reality. The Peasant's Dance *is a lively "slice of life" composition, truly a window to the past. One catches a glimpse of peasants gaily carousing to the music of bagpipes in their village of thatched-roof cottages decorated with banners.*

Kunsthistoriches Museum, Vienna

▲
In his monumental painting of the Sistine Chapel, Michelangelo united classical ideas with religious themes. To cover the 3000 square metres of vaulted ceiling required over 300 figures and took Michelangelo four years. Using brightly painted scenes from Genesis, Michelangelo attempted to capture the Renaissance belief in the dignity of humans. The idea of the beauty and perfection of humans is best expressed in the Creation of Adam *(above) where God and Adam are both portrayed as perfect beings — one divine and the other human.*
Photo Vatican Museums

much to temper the harshness of Nero's early years as emperor. His influence declined, however, and eventually he was forced to commit suicide. There were other noted adherents. Principal among these were the slave-born Epictetus (A.D. 55–135) and the Emperor Marcus Aurelius (A.D. 121–180), whose principal claim to fame is the 12 books of his somewhat disorganized *Meditations*.

Trade and Commerce

Trading and commercial activity came into its own with the establishment of a peaceful order under the Empire. From the Far East, China, and the Indies came silk and all manner of spice. Negotiatores and mercatores (merchants) were exchanging all sorts of goods by the mid-third century. For example, they traded amber from the Baltic coast or woollen cloaks from Britain.

Probably the most widely traded goods, after grain which was bought by imperial agents and distributed free to the urban populace, were wine and olive oil. These were transported in amphorae. Amphorae are heavy pottery containers found all over the Roman world. Their shape is often characteristic of their date and place of origin. A Spanish amphora from a ship-wreck has even been found recently in the estuary of the River Thames in England. Thus it confirms that highly prized olive oil was exported from Spain in every direction.

Once the amphorae were emptied of their original contents, they could be put to any number of secondary uses. Often they were broken, either accidentally or on purpose. Today a veritable hill of shattered amphorae sherds, named Monte Testaccio, is to be found by the banks of the Tiber in Rome near to the site of ancient warehouses.

Coinage

Roman coinage has a long history that spans both the Republic and the Empire, but the beginnings of using coin as a substitute for barter are lost to us today. Before approximately 290 B.C., bronze coins had spread throughout the peninsula, and by 241 B.C., the stereotypical Republican bronze coin (the head of Janus on one side, the prow of a ship on the other) had become well established. The worth of the coins was their face value.

At the time of the Punic wars, the silver denarius was introduced, valued at 10 asses (1 *as* being the worth of the previous bronze coinage). Gold issues (aurei) were also produced, worth 20–60 asses. The denarial standard continued through to the end of the Republic. Money (so-called because coins at Rome were minted in the temple of Juno Moneta) was produced in the first century A.D. often under the supervision of magistrates, hence *ex s.c.* (by the authority of the Senate) which appears on many of the coins.

After several important reforms by the first Roman Emperor, Augustus, the value of Roman coinage, for a long time more nominal than real, was reduced even further. In A.D. 215, Caracalla issued the antoninianus which soon after replaced the denarius. The gold aureus became in the third century A.D. only a plated coin with a value that bore no relation to its weight in precious metal. This decline in value continued. In about A.D. 309, Constantine the Great introduced a lighter aureus. This was called the solidus and was, above all else, the coin of tax payment. The solidus marks essentially the last major coin of the Western Empire. After the Empire's fall, it was this coin that was imitated by successive Barbarian kings.

Slavery

It would be difficult indeed to gloss over the contribution made to the progress of the western world by omitting at least a reference to the use of slaves. In the Roman world, as in the earlier Greek world and almost to modern times, slavery as an institution may be defined as the enforcement of labour by the subjugation of one person to the domination of another. Another definition is that a slave is one who is unable, due to a variety of reasons, most often force, to withdraw his or her labour.

The Romans throughout the Republic and Empire employed slaves in almost every aspect of human activity. There were slaves who were trained as gladiators, as was Spartacus and his followers. There were slaves who were used to power the treadwheels of cranes and other construction machinery. There were educated slaves used for accounting or dictation, for teaching the free youth, or grooming the mistress's hair. In Rome, there were public slaves who would act the part of executioners or clear out the corpses of their dead brethren from the Colosseum. Even once the terrible ordeal of public auction had passed, the fate of slaves was often not as pleasant as ancient writers, such as Horace, make out. Torture of slaves was a standard way of finding out whether or not that slave's master had been up to no good.

The lowest order of private slaves were those men and women who worked their master's land outside of Rome. Next, there were those who worked indoors on the country estates. A higher caste of slaves were those who were employed at their masters' houses in Rome. These, also, could belong to an indoors and an outdoors caste. Youthful slaves were required to cater to their owner's every whim.

With the spread of *pax Romana* (Roman peace) by the late second century A.D. to all parts of the known world, there were few territories left to conquer and few readily accessible sources of slaves remaining. Human power, therefore, became expensive and slaves were better cared for. Slaves, of course, could never own property and, like women in early twentieth-century Canada, were not legally considered to be persons. A slave couple, however, could form a legally recognised contubernium (literally shacking up) which their owner could not dissolve by selling one of the partners independently of the other. Of course, even though the Emperor Hadrian forbade the private execution of slaves, in reality there was still the possibility of mistreatment of the sort that one slave suffered at the hands of Vedius Pollio. After the slave let slip a particularly expensive goblet and it crashed to the floor, Pollio ordered that the man be fed to the flesh-eating lampreys in his fish pond.

Often a slave could expect to achieve release from servitude by **manumission**. Manumission was when the slave bought his or her freedom at a mutually acceptable price having diligently saved a small peculium or was released by the terms of a deceased owner's will. There were formalities to be observed, however, and they almost all involved the presence of witnesses. Once freed, the slave was tied to his or her former owner for the rest of that person's life as a libertus(a) (freedman or freedwoman).

Aqueducts and Water Supplies

The advance of technology during the whole period of the Roman expansion from being a small cluster of huts by the Tiber to becoming a world power would be a story in itself. In many of the minor crafts (pottery production, glass blowing, metalworking) the Romans came to be particularly adept. In fact, so skillful were the Romans that their prowess was not surpassed to any measurable extent until the Industrial Revolution. Still, perhaps, the most spectacular and impressive remains attesting to Roman ingenuity are the ***aqueducts***. The provision of clean water is one of the most basic needs of any society and aqueducts were built by the Romans to fill this need.

These aqueducts are famous and are to be found in every part of the Roman world from Manchester in Northern Britain to Segovia in Spain, from Rome and the Aqua Claudia to Jordan. Indeed, the most famous fountain in the world, the Fontana di Trevi in

A functioning Roman aqueduct is found in Segovia, Spain. It still carries the city's water supply. Dating from the first century A.D. it combines elegance with utility.

Rome is at the outlet of an aqueduct (the Aqua Virgo) inaugurated by M. Agrippa in July, 19 B.C.

To begin with, a water source was located. Usually, this source was found on a hill-side where the flow was fairly constant and its height was such that the water could be fed some distance by gravity alone.

Then there were several fairly sophisticated elements to an aqueduct system. First, the source was normally pooled into a settling tank, where the flow of water could be regulated at the intake. Second, a channel lined with waterproof mortar and covered to prevent contamination or a sudden increase due to a rain storm was directed from the source to the outlet around the contours of a hill, over arches, or tunnelled through the hill; preferred because the aqueduct was less vulnerable. Shafts, in this case, were sunk approximately every 35.5 m. The apparently close spacing of the vertical shafts allowed for easy repair and the release of increased air pressure, again in case of a sudden cloud-burst near the source.

Aqueducts carrying water over a series of arches are among the most spectacular surviving remains from Roman times. These were generally a single series not more than 21 m high and never very long. The Aqua Claudia at Rome was 57 km long but only

ASPECTS OF DAILY LIFE

BANQUETING AMONG THE ROMANS

Banqueting for the ancient Romans was a ceremony of civility. They were occasions for people to relish in their achievements and to show off to their peers. Banqueting among the Romans was a true art during which people dined with friends of all ranks. Banqueting took place around a pedestal table which participants were assigned dining couches. Lounging at one's table was the typical fashion at a Roman banquet. People leaned on their left arm keeping the right hand free to eat with. The left hand was never used to eat with as the Romans believed it to be unclean as it was used for more discrete functions. In Latin, the word for left is *sinister*, which in our language has come to mean suspicious or evil.

The evening was divided into three parts. To begin with people ate without drinking; this was followed by a period of eating and drinking; the evening was concluded with a period of drinking without eating. Throughout the evening guests were expected to express their views on a variety of topics including politics and philosophy. Between the dishes professional entertainers including jugglers and musicians who were hired for the evening performed.

Roman table manners were much less elaborate and formal than ours are today. Forks had not yet been invented and thus knives and spoons were used for serving. Eating with the fingers was standard practice and belching was encouraged as a symbol of the enjoyment of the meal. It also should be remembered that overeating was not a concern to the ancient Romans. After each course servants would bring wash basins to each table so that hands could be cleansed.

The food served at the banquets was quite spicy and covered with an array of exotic sauces. Romans tended to prefer their meat boiled rather than braised or roasted and enjoyed food which was sweet-and-sour in taste. The standard drink of the Romans was of course wine. The recipes below were selected to give a sampling from the three courses served at a Roman banquet; the gustus (hors d'oeuvres); the cena (main course); and the secunda mensa (dessert). These recipes were taken from *The Roman Cookery of Apicius*, an actual cookbook from the third century A.D. Rome is the only ancient civilization for which such a treasure exists.

HORS D'OEUVRE

Sweet Apricot Hors d'oeuvres

500 g	apricots
Sauce:	
5 mL	mint
5 mL	cinnamon
15 mL	honey
125 mL	sweet raisin wine
125 mL	non-alcoholic wine
5 mL	white wine vinegar
15 mL	olive oil
	flour
	cinnamon or nutmeg

Take washed apricots, halve and pit them, and put them in a stew pot. For the sauce, first mix mint and cinnamon. Blend with honey, sweet wine, wine, and vinegar. Pour the sauce over the apricots, add olive oil, cover, and stew over very low heat for ½ hour or until done. When cooked, thicken liquid with flour. Sprinkle cinnamon or nutmeg over the apricot hors d'oeuvres, and serve.

MAIN COURSE

Apician Baked Ham

2 kg	ham
15	large dried figs
6	bay leaves
15 mL	honey
350 g	wholewheat flour
30 mL	olive oil

Put the ham with the figs and bay leaves in a large pot and cover with water. Bring to a boil and simmer for approximately 40 minutes per kilogram. While the meat is cooking make the pastry by stirring the oil into the flour then mixing to a soft dough with cold water; set aside. Remove the ham from the water and peel off the skin. Cut the skin into small squares. Soak the squares of skin in honey melted in 30 mL of the cooking liquid.

Allow the meat to cool slightly then roll out the pastry and cover the meat tucking the pastry in around its bottom. Transfer to a baking sheet and bake at 180°C for 30 minutes or till the pastry is cooked. Ten minutes before it is ready take the ham out of the oven and stick the pieces of skin all over it, holding them in place with cocktail sticks; return to the oven to finish.

Meanwhile, remove the figs from the cooking juices and reserve. Take 600 mL of the cooking liquid, add the honey mixture the skin was soaked in, and boil it fast to reduce it to 500 mL. The ham can be served hot or cold accompanied by the figs and the reduced cooking juices. If it is to be served cold the juices should be chilled so that any excess fat can be removed before serving.

(From The British Museum Cookbook, *by Michelle Berriedale-Johnson, © 1987. British Museum Publications.)*

DESSERT

Dates Alexandrine

20	whole dates, pitted
20	blanched almonds
5 mL	cinnamon
	butter
	salt
	liquid honey

Roll almonds in cinnamon and stuff one in each date. Place dates on a greased pan. Sprinkle salt over the dates, then coat each one with honey. Glaze in a 225°C oven for 10 minutes, then serve.

Mild Fish Pickle

A favourite relish used by the Romans was Garum or fish pickle. This delicacy was widely used much as we would use catsup or soya sauce. While the original recipe may not be appealing to our tastes the recipe given below has been adapted to the modern kitchen and is quite palatable.

125 g	drained and washed canned tuna or salmon, or unsalted sardines or unsalted anchovies
10 mL	non-alcoholic wine
15 mL	vinegar
2 mL	mustard seed
2 mL	oregano
2 mL	celery seed
15 mL	olive oil
2 mL	honey
	pinch of basil
1 mL	thyme
1	mint leaf, finely chopped

Combine ingredients in a mixing bowl thoroughly. If a stronger taste is desired, replace the herbs and spices with 1 clove of crushed garlic, some rosemary, parsley, pepper, and sage. This recipe can be stored in a glass container for up to two weeks.

a seventh of its distance was carried on arches. Occasionally aqueducts were very high; at Segovia the aqueduct is carried in a double series of arches 50 m high, and the Pont du Gard (Nîmes, France) was carried over a deep gorge in a triple series of superimposed arches 54.8 m high.

Aqueducts and pipes, of course, were not the only hydraulic features known to and used by the Romans. The shadouf or Archidemean screw pump was well known, and pressure pumps (of one or two cylinders with appropriate valves) were quite common. Faucets and water wheels also were regular elements of Roman hydraulic systems.

The Roman Cook

The Roman cook of the Empire was inventive and went in, it seems, for beauty of presentation as well as tastiness. Sauces were very contrived with ingenious combinations of herbs and spices. Various degrees of sweet and sour were concocted using various amounts of honey and vinegar. The opulence at Roman banquets of the Empire is almost legendary, and the following description by Petronius may be as much parody as exaggeration.

> Behind them a great dish and on it lay a wild boar of the largest possible size, and, what is more, wearing a freedman's cap on its head. From its tusks dangled two baskets woven from palm leaves, one full of fresh Syrian dates, the other of dried Theban dates. Little piglets made of cake were all around as though at its dugs, suggesting it was a brood sow now being served. These were actually gifts to take home. Surprisingly the man who took his place to cut up the boar was not our old friend Carver but a huge bearded fellow, wearing leggings and a damask hunting coat. He pulled out a hunting knife and made a great stab at the boar's side and as he struck, out flew a flock of thrushes.
>
> Petronius *Satyricon*, sec. 40, p. 54.

The Empire to Diocletian

During the latter half of the second century after Christ and for much of the early third century, the Roman world remained secure and free from threat. There was a succession of good and bad emperors, however, from Antoninus Pius (A.D. 138–161) and the **philanthropic** philosopher Marcus Aurelius (A.D. 161–180), who met his end on the Danube near Vienna. Next, there was the disquieting Commodus (A.D. 180–193) and then the first emperor from the province of Africa, Septimius Severus (A.D. 193–211). Septimius Severus's son, Caracalla (A.D. 188–217), gave all free residents of the Empire Roman citizenship in A.D. 212. Party strife and self interest on the part of the military gave rise to a further 11 "legitimate" rulers of varying competence before Gaius Aurelius Valerius Diocletianus. Diocletian (originally named Diocles) was promoted to the purple in A.D. 284 by fellow soldiers in the Praetorian Guard.

The seeds of the Western Empire's ultimate downfall had already sprouted by the time Diocletian became emperor. There was staggering inflation and poor people were abandoning marginal agricultural lands and thereby creating vast tracts of *agri deserti* (literally meaning deserted lands). In addition, although numerically strong, the military could not effectively resist the pressure placed on the frontiers of the Empire. Northern borders at the Rhine and Danube were being invaded by groups of Barbarians. Finally, the Empire had grown too large for the administrative abilities of one man.

Diocletian's Reforms of the Army and State

In A.D. 293, although as yet not having visited the city of Rome, Diocletian instituted the first and ultimately the most fateful of his reforms. He divided the rule of the Empire between east and west. Consequently, there were now two senior emperors, Augusti, and two junior assistants, Caesares. Although the two parts of the Empire at first interacted closely, the split was permanent and eventually the Western Empire would fade away, and the eastern portion would evolve into the glorious world of Byzantium. Diocletian also re-organized the imperial bureaucracy, re-ordered the administration of the provinces, and completed the military reforms begun by his predecessors.

From now on, there would be standing armies spread along the frontiers and mobile units distributed throughout the provinces ready to quell internal disturbances and lend support to those soldiers posted at the frontiers. Cavalry units now became as important as the infantry. Also, while always a Roman practice, there was an increase in the recruiting of Germanic immigrants.

Diocletian was never able to conquer the hardship caused by inflation, even though he came out with a famous Edict establishing maximum prices and wages in A.D. 301 and instituted a complex series of taxes. Diocletian suffered a stroke shortly after visiting Rome for the first time in A.D. 303. He abdicated on 1 May A.D. 305, along with his partner Maximian, the western Augustus, to spend the remaining nine years of his life peacefully at his palace in Split, Yugoslavia. As an emperor, Diocletian remained true to the old Roman gods and was opposed to the rise of Christianity.

Diocletian's Persecution of Christians

In A.D. 250, at a time when the Roman Empire was threatened by all sorts of catastrophe, Decius (A.D. 249–251) found a scapegoat in the spread of Christianity and the rejection of old pagan gods. He demanded that all citizens make sacrifice to these gods, and those that refused were executed.

In A.D. 284, when Diocletian was made emperor he started the last and most destructive persecution in an attempt to destroy the faith. Churches were dismantled and the holy writings (scriptures) burned. People were obliged to sacrifice to Diocletian or die. To some **martyrdom** (openly suffering torture and death and not repudiating their faith) was preferable. In Egypt, there were a hundred such martyrs in one day. Diocletian, however, suffered a stroke and retired in A.D. 305, and with his abdication the active persecution of Christians ceased.

Constantine the Great

A successor to Diocletian, Flavius Valerius Constantinus (Constantine the Great, A.D. 306–337), defeated his opponent Maxentius at the Battle of the Milvian Bridge outside Rome in A.D. 312. A contemporary account attributes the victory in part to the Christian God. Certainly that was Constantine's claim and after a confused process of conversion the first Christian emperor issued his famous edict of toleration in A.D. 313.

There can be no doubt, however, that Constantine the Great remained confused over the nature of the Christian religion. He himself had worshipped the Unconquered Sun, a mild form of monotheism that he evidently blended with the Jewish concept of One God. Sunday is the Christian day of worship, based on the belief in the resurrection of the Son of God on the day after the Jewish Sabbath, Saturday. Constantine in his edict of March, A.D. 321 apparently thought that Christians set apart this day for veneration of the Sun.

Constantinople

After his conversion, Constantine the Great showed great favour to Christian communities everywhere. By this favour and his establishment of Byzantium or Constantinople as the major seat of government, Constantine forever changed the course of western civilization. The idea of Rome was transformed subtly into a concept of nationhood under God. A witness to Constantine's perception is the official name of the revitalized city, New Rome. Eventually the city was given equal constitutional authority to the city of Rome in Italy in A.D. 359. Another equally telling witness to the vision of a new Christian and Roman Empire is the Christian church of Divine Wisdom (Santa Sophia or Hagia Sophia) dedicated in A.D. 360. Here, all Roman precedent put aside, was where he and his successors were buried.

The magnificent church surviving today, now a mosque, was built on the site of the earlier church and was consecrated by the Emperor Justinian in A.D. 537. In an act of notable irony, it was the Christian armies of the fourth crusade that broke in and desecrated the church on 13 April A.D. 1204.

Rome in the Fourth Century

Although Constantine the Great moved the centre of imperial administration to Constantinople, the ancient city of Rome was still very much the emotional centre of the world. Above all, for an Empire that had just adopted Christianity as its official religion, this venerable city remained the seat of the Bishop of Rome. The Pope or Pontiff was successor, in a way, to the Pontifex Maximus although that pagan office still existed. Rome was therefore a favourite haunt of tourists.

In the fourth century A.D., handbooks (the *Notitia*, A.D. 354, and the *Curiosum*, A.D. 375) were published as guides for tourists and the curious. What follows is a synopsis of their descriptions:

In the fourth century A.D., the city had 11 public and 856 private baths, 37 gates, 423 parishes (*vici*), 29 main roads from the centre to the outskirts, to which must be added an enormous number of minor streets, alleys and *areae*, small squares scattered among the network of streets; 25 suburban roads; 8 bridges, 2 Capitols, 190 granaries, 2 large markets (*macella*), 254 mills, 8 large parks (all the open land that was left), 11 forums, 10 basilicas, 37 marble arches, 1,352 fountains, 28 libraries, 2 circuses, 2 amphitheatres, 2 *naumachiae* for naval shows and 4 gladiatorial barracks (*ludi*).[1]

Two Cults

In addition to the pagan worship of the Unconquered Sun and the Christian and Jewish faiths, there were numerous other forms and modes of religious belief in the Roman West of the early fourth century including the **Cult of Isis** and **Mithraism**.

The Cult of Isis. Isis, according to Egyptian religion, was the wife of Osiris and the mother of the god Horus. The Cult of Isis became one of the great, and occasionally persecuted mystery religions of the Roman Empire. There were elaborate rituals in honour of the goddess at Rome. At Pompeii, for example, she had a temple complete with cistern for holding the sacred Nile water. Within the mysteries of her worship, Isis could have many guises and appear as any number of deities. In fact, so numerous were these different manifestations, that it is hard to tell what rituals were appropriate to her alone.

To judge merely from the archaeological evidence such as sculptural reliefs, gravestones, and gems, her worship was indeed widespread. There are many

---

[1] U. Paoli, Rome. Its People, Life and Customs, trans. R.D. Macnaghten (London: Longmans, 1963), p. 1.

The young warrior god Mithras slaying the bull is one of the central elements to Mithraism and often forms the centrepiece for the temples. He is wearing the cap and trousers characteristic to him and the scene is always the same; with Mithras, the bull, the snake, the dog, and the scorpion.

symbols known to be associated with her cult, particularly of the sistrum which was a form of hand-held tambourine. Her worship and that of Mithras were overwhelmed by Christianity, especially after the latter faith was adopted as the official religion of the Roman Empire by Constantine. For all that the worship of Isis and the parallel cult of Mithras competed, as it were, with Christianity. Several elements in all three religions appeared similar to one another, especially the insistence on purification toward a personal salvation.

Mithraism. The Persian, or Iranian, deity, Mithras, was especially popular among the soldiers and the merchants of the fourth century. They were converted to this faith as they travelled across the Empire, at first mostly in the far east. His titles included Lord of Light, God of Truth, Saviour from Death, and Giver of Bliss. The attraction that is evident in these titles, personal immortality, was very much a Christian belief as well. The similarity with the ultimately victorious faith is furthered by the mysterious rituals through which an initiate had to pass (7 grades), a form of baptism, and the consumption of a ceremonial meal. It must be observed, that whatever connection there was between the two faiths is nowadays opaque. It cannot be ascertained whether either belief derived its rituals from the other.

At the heart of the cult of Mithraism was a ritual bullslaying (tauroctony). This act signified a spiritual victory of life over death and of good over evil.

B.C. to A.D.

The common terms for the division of eras in most of today's world are based in the Christian religion. They are not favoured, for example, by adherents of Islam or by the followers of Judaism. The abbreviations mean Before Christ (B.C.) and *Anno Domini* or In the Year of Our Lord (A.D.).

Eras were based, however, on different events in the ancient world. One common base for the year in the Roman sphere was A.U.C. (*Ab urbe condita*, from the foundation of the city) calculated to have taken place by today's reckoning in 753 B.C.. Another base was the Olympiad, a period of four years reckoned from the first celebration of the games at Olympia, traditionally said to have been held in 776 B.C. Yet another base was reckoned from the mythical fall of Troy in 1183 B.C., according to Eratosthenes, a Greek scholar.

Years were handled differently and imprecisely. Often, Roman chronographers used consular years, that is, they named the years for the consuls who were elected annually. Another method was to refer to the number of years which a particular ruler had attained, such as in the sixth year of Augustus.

The Christian method of reckoning eras was introduced by the priest Dionysius Exiguus, who died around A.D. 540. The sixth century monk, how-

PRIMARY DOCUMENT

TACITUS' GERMANIA: A GEOGRAPHICAL AND SOCIO-CULTURAL STUDY OF THE ANCIENT GERMANS

The Roman historian Tacitus (ca. A.D. 56–118) was also a distinguished orator and public official. Success in his appointments furthered him to achieving the highest administrative post, that of the proconsulate of Asia. Believing that the Roman Empire was on its way to decay, he provides in his writing examples of better behaviour, morals, and customs. In the excerpt below a warning is clear in the contrasting of the rich and materialistic ways of the Romans to the simple and healthy lives of the Germanic tribesmen.

...They choose their kings by birth, their generals for merit. These kings have not unlimited or arbitrary power, and the generals do more by example than by authority. If they are energetic, if they are conspicuous, if they fight in the front, they lead because they are admired.

...About minor matters the chiefs deliberate, about the more important the whole tribe. Yet even when the final decision rests with the people, the affair is always thoroughly discussed by the chiefs....

...In their councils an accusation may be preferred or a capital crime prosecuted. Penalties are distinguished according to the offence. Traitors and deserters are hanged on trees; the coward, the unwarlike, the man stained with abominable vices, is plunged into the mire....Lighter offences, too, have penalties...he who is convicted, is fined in a certain number of horses or of cattle.

...They transact no public or private business without being armed. It is not, however, usual for anyone to wear arms till the state has recognised his power to use them.

...When they go into battle, it is a disgrace for the chief to be surpassed in valour, a disgrace for his followers not to equal the valour of the chief. And it is an infamy and a reproach for life to have survived the chief and returned from the field.

...Whenever they are not fighting, they pass much of their time in the chase, and still more in idleness, giving themselves up to sleep and to feasting, the bravest and the most warlike doing nothing, and surrendering the management of the household, of the home, and of the land, to the women, the old men, and all the weakest members of the family. They themselves lie buried in sloth, a strange combination in their nature that the same men should be so fond of idleness, so averse to peace.

...It is well known that the nations of Germany have no cities, and that they do not even tolerate closely contiguous dwellings. They live scattered and apart, just as a spring, meadow or a wood has attracted them.

...They all wrap themselves in a cloak which is fastened with a clasp....They also wear the skins of wild beasts....The women have the same dress as the men, except that they generally wrap themselves in linen garments, which they embroider with purple, and do not lengthen out the

> upper part of their clothing into sleeves. The upper and lower arm is thus bare, and the nearest part of the bosom is also exposed.
>
> ...Their marriage code, is strict, and indeed no part of their manners is more praiseworthy.
>
> ...Thus with their virtue protected they live uncorrupted by the allurements of public shows or the stimulant of feastings.
>
> ...No nation indulges more profusely in entertainments and hospitality. To exclude any human being from their roof is thought impious; every German, according to his means, receives his guest with a well-furnished table.

ever, was out by a few years. It is probable that Jesus was born shortly before Herod's death in 4 B.C. The reckoning is made more confused by the fact that a year 0 is not inserted between 1 B.C. and A.D. 1.

Literature

The fourth century was a time in which many of the finer arts flourished. In Roman North Africa, for example, there are many splendid examples of the mosaicist's craft dating to this century. In literature, also, this was a period of renewed activity. Ammianus Marcellinus (A.D. 330–395) was Rome's last great historian. A soldier and pagan, he wrote in particular about the exploits of his hero Julian. Julian, commonly known as the Apostate, was Rome's last pagan Emperor, and ruled briefly from A.D. 360 to A.D. 363. He was fatally wounded in battle.

Some other writers were Christian. In addition to the surviving and delightful seven books of Macrobius's Saturnalia (A.D. 400), there are the histories of Sulpicius Severus (A.D. 403), the varied poems of Ausonius (to A.D. 395) and, among several other poets and philosophers of the early fifth century, Claudius Claudianus (after A.D. 404).

The End of the West

The last phase of the Western Empire, the period of a transition between Romanity and the rise of a new medieval world, is marked by successive incursions of Barbarians from the north. In particular, there were the Goths (**Visigoths** and **Ostrogoths**), Alans, Franks, Suebi, Vandals, and Huns. Indeed, the tale of the last years of the Western Empire may be told by relating the movements of these Germanic peoples and the efforts of successive emperors in accommodating them.

The Barbarians

After Constantine the Great died in A.D. 337, the interior of the Empire went about its business in temporary prosperity and the imperial courts (east and west) were wracked by continual intrigue. Beyond the borders of the Empire there were great movements of peoples and a great disturbance among the nomadic and the more settled tribes. Visigoths and Ostrogoths took lands previously settled by the Alans and by the Romans (Dacia). Then by the middle of the century, sweeping over the Hungarian steppes came the Huns. These were a fierce horse-riding tribe that displaced the Alans and Goths, who consequently sought the security of the Empire across the Danube.

Gross mismanagement by the Romans led to confrontation, and in A.D. 378 the eastern Augustus, Valens (A.D. 364–78), suffered a disastrous defeat, Valens himself being killed at the Battle of Adrianople. In the aftermath, the western Augustus, Gratian (A.D. 367–383) invited Theodosius (A.D. 379–395) to take charge in the east.

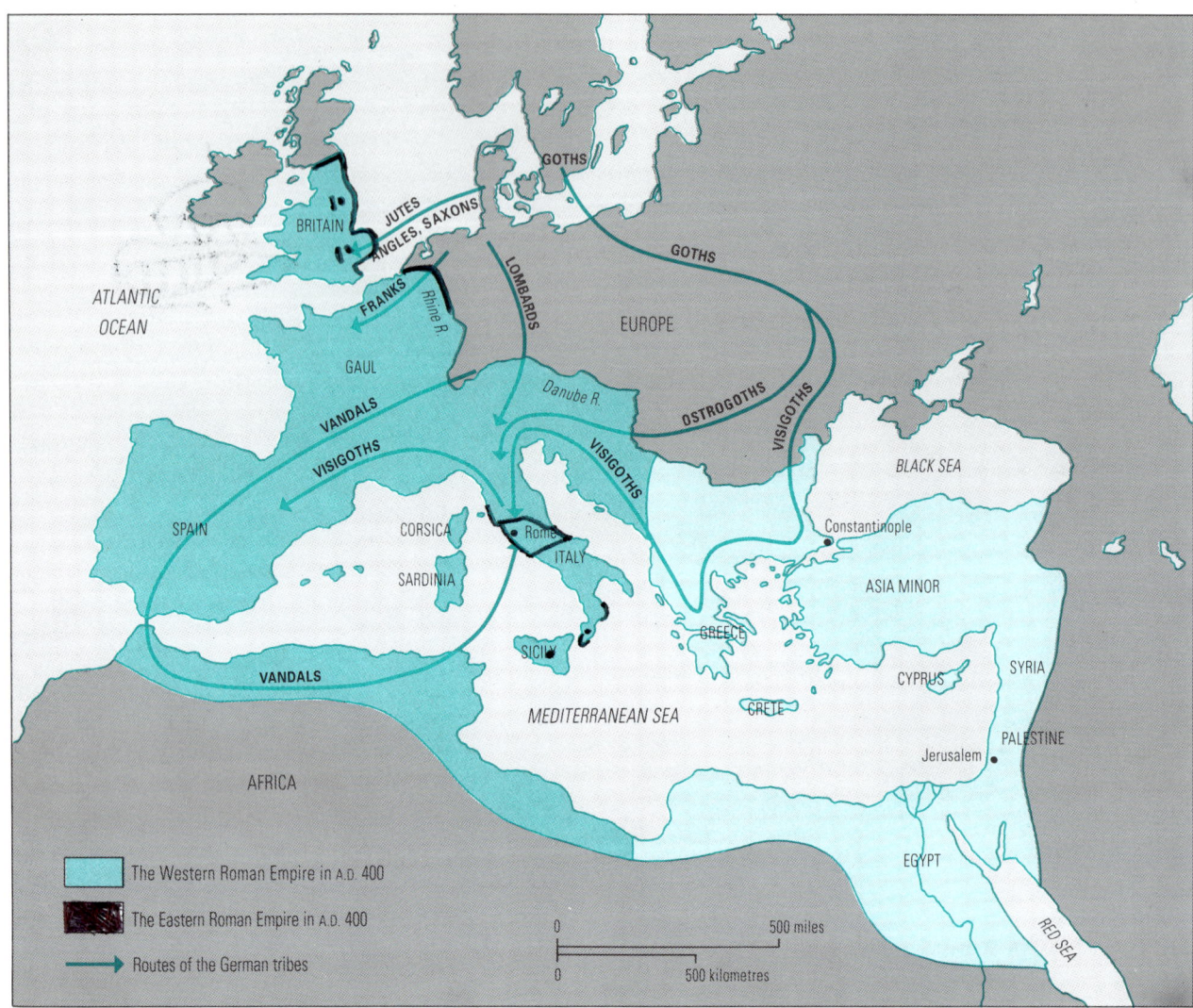

The End of the Roman Empire

Theodosius the Great

Theodosius ruled with restraint and wisdom. Coping with incessant court intrigue, he was nevertheless able to deal effectively with the Barbarian menace, even employing Visigoths as mercenary soldiers.

Theodosius was also a devout Christian and a zealous believer of the Nicene Creed. This Creed was a statement of Christian belief arrived at by a consensus of Bishops at Nicaea, now in Turkey, in A.D. 325. It is still proclaimed in Christian churches today. In A.D. 391, Theodosius put a ban on all pagan worship and ordered the temples closed. In A.D. 393, he abolished the Olympic Games as they were a pagan festival.

The Visigoths

When Theodosius died in A.D. 395, his sons took over the reins of government, Arcadius (to A.D. 408) in the east and Honorius (to A.D. 423) in the west. A new Visigothic leader had been elected and the restraint on the part of the Visigoths and their eastern masters was lost. The new leader, Alaric, was persuaded to attack the power of the west and its current de facto champion, Stilicho. Stilicho was a Vandal by birth, but had become thoroughly Romanized. Essentially, he ruled the west for the boy-Emperor Honorius.

Though Stilicho defeated the Visigoths in A.D. 401 with the help of the Alans, whom he allowed to settle to the north of Italy, he was soon courting Alaric to help stave off famine in the peninsula. Alaric agreed but demanded a huge payment. In the meantime Stilicho was branded an outlaw and beheaded in August A.D. 408.

When the Visigothic leader realized that payment was not forthcoming, he laid siege to Rome, captured the city and sacked it in August A.D. 410. It was a terrible moment and, although the western imperial court was protected by the marshes of the Po estuary in northeastern Italy at *Ravenna*, the emotional impact of the event resounded around the Mediterranean world.

Alaric having died in the meantime, the Visigoths moved through modern Spain and Portugal (where they destroyed the power of the Alans) to southern France. The Visigoths settled there in A.D. 418 with the blessing of the imperial western administration. With their capital at Toulouse, the Visigoths did not attempt to subjugate the Romans. Rather, they worked out an elaborate and effective way of sharing the land. Also, they established a code of law that allowed them to be judged according to their own standards while leaving the Romans to their own justice system.

The Huns

The Alans, defeated by the Visigoths, joined forces with the Vandals and settled around Carthage in modern Tunisia. The first half of the fifth century A.D. was a time of disintegration in Europe. To the north, the British provinces were overrun by the Saxons and Franks, and Alamanni had settled south of the Rhine. Other permanent incursions had been made by, among others, the Burgundians to Worms, and the Suebi. Next came the Huns. They made their first advance into Roman territory under **Attila the Hun** in A.D. 451 and were repulsed in what is today central France. The following year, in A.D. 452, they invaded Italy and were forced to withdraw, but not until after causing massive devastation. Attila died in A.D. 453.

The Last Years

The Western Roman Empire continued to survive, after a fashion, with its share of heroines and heroes. Galla Placidia, a formidable empress, had been obliged to marry the Visigoth, Athaulf. Restored in A.D. 416, she was able to keep the west tottering on until her death at Ravenna in A.D. 450. Flavius Aëtius, a Roman general with a Germanic wife, was the victor over the Burgundians at Worms and Attila in France. Although a man of great ability, he could do little against Attila's advance into Italy. He was assassinated in A.D. 454. The Western Empire finally gave out in A.D. 476, some 1200 years after Rome's supposed foundation. In that year, the ineffective Romulus Augustulus, an appropriately diminutive name, was deposed by his general Odoacer. Odoacer was short-lived and was replaced at Ravenna in A.D. 493 by Theoderic the Great. Theoderic ruled Italy, principally from Ravenna but also from Rome and Verona, as the peninsula's first Gothic king until his death in A.D. 526. Theoderic, who had been converted to a form of Christianity while outside the

Empire, fell out with the Catholic Boëthius towards the end of his rule and had him executed in A.D. 524. Boëthius was a former consul and one of the truly great philosophers of the day.

It may be said that Theoderic's reign marked the transition in western Europe between a Roman world and a medieval age. In the Germanic sagas he is known as Dietrich von Berne, Theoderic of Verona.

Students of Roman civilization are left with two questions: Why did the Empire in the west collapse? and What are the major legacies that we have inherited from the Romans?

First, the reasons for the downfall of the Western Roman Empire are many, apart from citing unprovable and quite subjective theories of moral decay. One can point to the overwhelming pressures placed on the frontiers by the movements of the Germanic people. Or one can point to crippling inflation in the later years when, for example, the price of gold itself skyrocketed some 600 percent. Diocletian's Edict on Prices was supposed to have stabilized a public economy. It had the opposite effect, however, and drove the economy underground.

The effect of establishing a new religion, Christianity, also should not be underestimated. The abolition of the old Roman gods (and along with them, the idea of an eternal Rome) lessened the people's belief in the supremacy of the Roman ideal. Also, the promise of a better life to come may have been taken very literally, resulting in a concurrent stagnation of personal initiative. Even Augustine of Hippo (A.D. 354–430) believed he was obliged to defend the Church from similar pagan accusations.

Constantinople and the Eastern Roman Empire, however, did not fall. Rather they changed into a courtly, splendid, and prosperous Byzantine society which would not be destroyed for another millenium, A.D. 1453. Also, under Byzantine rule the values of Roman law as exemplified in the Justinianic Code were reasserted. This was a work in Latin, though published in the Greek-speaking Eastern Empire in A.D. 534.

Perhaps, then, the complex root causes for the Western Empire's fall lay in events or influences only applicable in the west, for example, in the prolonged struggle against Barbarian invaders. The Empire was transformed into a series of Germanic kingdoms; the Empire in the west was never really a **monolithic** entity in any case. The viability of these kingdoms can be sensed in the independence of spirit that persists in Europe even today. The final event in the transformation of an ancient Roman west to an emergent modern one is seen in the success of the expansion of an Arab state from A.D. 634 over the former territories of Africa, southern Spain, Egypt, and Syria. The Western Roman Empire did not fall so much as it disappeared.

Rome's Legacy

What did the Romans leave for posterity? Again this is a question that is not easy to answer fully. The simple answer is that the Romans left their language. Latin is, after all, the root of French, Italian, Spanish, Portuguese, Romanian, and a dialect in Switzerland, Romanche. In addition, the English language in its vocabulary has been immeasurably enriched through the adoption of Latin-based words.

Also, the Romans ultimately left a faith to which many people subscribe. Although certainly a near eastern religion, it can be said that Christianity and the Catholic Church was so heavily influenced by Rome that it can be considered a Roman religion. The rituals, vestments or clothing of the priests and acolytes, who were assistants to the priests, and even the organization of **dioceses** and archdioceses represent a late Roman structure and recall late Roman court ritual.

Roman architecture has had an enduring influence, and not merely from its influence over later, neoclassical masters. The Roman invention of concrete, never totally lost, has been one of the truly great gifts to the world. More significant, however, is the arch. The art of spanning a great space was never forgotten. A glance at the great cathedrals of Europe and even certain railway stations in North America is ample evidence of that.

In the realm of government, too, the Roman state (here the Republic) left a lasting influence. This is especially true of most bicameral (two chambers) democracies in the world today.

However, the Roman world, which endured over 1000 years, has bequeathed something else, something almost indefinable: a sense of civilization. In every aspect of our lives, whether it be education, sport, religious belief, the economy, or even the family, we have been touched in our western heritage by Rome's influence.

Suggested Sources for Further Research

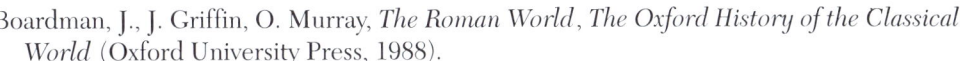

Boardman, J., J. Griffin, O. Murray, *The Roman World*, *The Oxford History of the Classical World* (Oxford University Press, 1988).

Cary, M. & Scullard, H.H., *A History of Rome Down to the Age of Constantine* (Macmillan, 1975).

Grant, M., *History of Rome*, (Charles Scribner's Sons, 1979).

Edwards, J., *Roman Cookery* (Hartley & Marks, 1986).

Hodges, H., *Technology in the Ancient World* (Penguin Books, 1971).

Landels, J.G., *Engineering in the Ancient World* (University of California Press, 1978).

Lefkowitz, M.R. & Fant, M.B., *Women's Life in Greece and Rome* (Johns Hopkins University Press, 1982).

Potter, T.W., *Roman Italy* (University of California Press, 1987).

Scullard, H.H., *From the Gracchi to Nero. A History of Rome from 133 B.C. to A.D. 68* (Methuen, 1982).

Sear, F., *Roman Architecture* (Cornell University Press, 1982).

Toynbee, J.M.C., Eds. N.G.L., *Oxford Classical Dictionary* (Hammond H.H. Scullard, 1970).

Veyne, P. (trs. A. Goldhammer), *A History of Private Life I, From Pagan Rome to Byzantium* (Harvard University Press, 1987).

Ward-Perkins, W.P., *Roman Art and Architecture* (Oxford University Press, 1981).

Webster, G., *The Roman Imperial Army* (A. & C. Black Limited, 1969).

Focus Your Knowledge

1. What happened to the Roman Republic following the death of Caesar?
2. Explain why Christ was crucified and why, after his resurrection, Christianity became a popular sect in the Roman Empire.
3. How extensive a role did slavery play in the Roman Empire and how were the enslaved people treated?
4. How were Christians treated during the reign of Diocletian?
5. Explain the difference between B.C. and A.D.
6. For what is Constantine the Great best remembered?

Apply Your Knowledge

1. To what degree can Augustus be credited with restoring peace and prosperity to Rome?
2. It has been said that architecture is an accurate reflection of the society which produced it. The pyramids of Egypt showed their devotion to their pharaohs and the degree to which they prepared for death. The Parthenon in Athens shows the mathematical precision of the ancient Greeks and their attention to perfect beauty. By examining some of the major buildings of ancient Rome what can we learn about its people?
3. Differentiate between Judaism and Christianity and identify the point in time at which Christianity ceased to be a Jewish sect.
4. Despite writing nearly half a century apart Livy and Tacitus shared a common concern. Identify this concern and explain how each, in their writings, attempted to provide a guide for how Romans should live their lives.
5. What signs of decline were evident during the time of Diocletian and how successful were his attempts to prevent further decline?

Extension Activities

1. Using the feature study on Roman clothing choose a position in Roman society for whom to make a costume. These costumes could be used for further activities such as banquets, plays, or video-taped skits.

2. Using the feature study on "Banqueting Among the Romans" prepare a Roman dinner party. This activity should be done as a class project in which students take responsibility for preparing various dishes, recreating the setting, providing entertainment, music, and so on. Students should select a position in society to represent such as a slave, a gladiator, an entertainer, a nobleman, or noblewomen. Further research will be required. For a guide to where to begin see the list of selected readings at the end of the chapter.

3. Do further research on one of the emperors discussed in this chapter. Based on your research recreate the persona of the emperor selected in a "Witness to Yesterday" style interview in which one student plays the role of a host/interviewer while another student role-plays as the emperor. To produce an effective interview you will need to ask background questions as well as probing questions into the emperor's life and activities.

4. Using a medium of your choice build a model of one of the following structures of ancient Rome.

A Roman Bath	An Amphitheatre
A Circus	A Private House
An Aqueduct	A Theatre

5. It has been said that the Greeks are best remembered for their brains while the Romans are best remembered for their drains. What is meant by this statement? From your study of the Greeks and the Romans what evidence can you find to support or refute this claim?

SKILLS FOCUS

Unit Overview

1. Some historians argue that Roman civilization is simply an extension of Hellenism (Greek civilization). Examine the impact of Hellenism on Roman history and the achievements of Rome. Is this a valid statement, or does Rome deserve its own place in history?

2. The Greeks tended to operate in the realm of the ideal: the ideal society, the human ideal, the ideal form of government. The Romans were more practical in nature turning their energies to developing effective institutions and the construction of roads, aqueducts, and buildings. Considering this, can it be argued that the Greeks developed the ideas that the Romans built on and disseminated? Which civilization was more instrumental in shaping the western world?

3. Which factors in Greek history limited their expansion as a power in the Mediterranean and which factors in Roman history allowed for expansion in the Mediterranean basin? Be sure to consider geographical features, political divisions, and other factors.

4. Athens has been called the birthplace of democracy and the Roman constitution was so respected that the Americans modelled their constitution on it. Consider the relative freedom enjoyed by the Greeks and Romans. Was it enjoyed by all people, or only by some? Was one society more advanced and open than the other? Is it fair to credit the Greeks and Romans with creating equitable civilizations? What lessons can we learn from these civilizations' experiences, successes, and failures? Would you feel comfortable living in either Greece or Rome? Why or why not?

Art: A Window to Our Past

Refer to colour-plate section for Unit 2.

1. By examining the art and architecture of both Greece and Rome, what can we learn about the people, their values, and the society?

2. The Greeks and Romans strove to depict their ideals of perfect beauty based on a concept of perfect proportions. Do these ideals fit yours? Why? What do you like? Do your ideals differ from the Greek and Romans? What would you change?

3. The Greeks and Romans are often referred to as classical civilizations because of their stunning achievements in art and architecture. Select one piece of art and architecture from each civilization which you feel best reflects the magnitude of Graeco–Roman achievements. Justify your selection.

4. The art of the Greeks and Romans has had a profound influence on western culture. What examples can you find in your home or community of Graeco–Roman artisitic or architectural influences?

Locating Information

To locate information, you first need to know what you are looking for. Begin with a list of questions (as outlined in the previous unit) that define your topic, identify the aspects needing to be researched, and narrow and specify your focus. When locating information go from the general to the specific; begin with your textbook and go to the suggested readings at the end of the chapter; use the encyclopedia to get general information, which can become specific subtopics. Start with broad sources and move into the more topic specific ones. Don't forget to use the index at the back of book to locate a topic. Resources should include:

1. The library card catalogue to find resources.
2. The library periodicals.
3. The librarian who can help in locating information both in the library and through interlibrary loans.
4. Other sources such as the media; documentaries, films, newspapers; radio; the community or specific contact people; or agencies such as travel agents and museums.

Effective Recording of Information

When the focus of your study has been determined, and your resources have been found and gathered you must effectively and efficiently record the information. When making notes:

- Use point form.
- It is helpful to develop your own system of abbreviations and symbols.
- Differentiate between vital and redundant information.
- Keep your research questions and the focus of the task in mind. Maintain your direction.
- Good research questions can become your major subheadings, which will help you organize as you record and develop your topic.
- Organize as you research by keeping separate pages for each subtopic, leave space between points so they stand apart and can be added to.
- Use a variety of sources, one or two are not enough. Check your information with other sources. Don't assume that everything in print is correct.

Please note that this is not a guide to effective notebooks. The skills presented are solely to obtain maximum benefits from resources by effectively recording information. Remember, in order to analyze and interpret information effectively, you need to know: where to look; what you are looking for; and how to gather and record it.

TASK: *LOCATING AND RECORDING INFORMATION*

Using the skills on focusing and organizing your topic developed in the last unit, and by using this unit's information on locating and recording information, research and take notes on one of the following topics.

1. Choose a topic that interests you from either the Greek or Roman civilization. From your notes prepare a short videotaped documentary of this topic. Use this as an opportunity to make use of any visuals, such as models, that have been prepared in this unit.

2. Select your favourite character from this unit and bring her/him back from the past. Using your notes, hold a mock interview either on video or in front of the class.

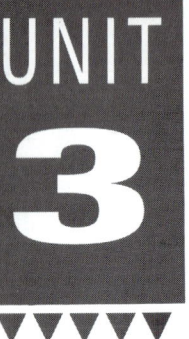

UNIT 3

Civilizations of the Non-Western World

CHAPTER 10
The Islamic Middle East

CHAPTER 11
Japan: Land of the Rising Sun

CHAPTER 12
The Ancient Maya

CHAPTER 13
The Ancient Aztecs

No study of the civilizations of the past is complete without an examination of societies that lie outside the European sphere of influence. For much of the history of the western world these areas were either unknown or viewed as barbaric, uncivilized or inhabited by infidels. As a result these cultures have too often been studied in relation to European events rather than as complex civilizations in their own right. Throughout this unit four separate and independent civilizations are studied: the Islamic world, the Japanese, the Maya, and the Aztecs.

The study of any or all of these civilizations reveals that neither a major river valley nor interaction with the western world is required for the development of a complex and highly civilized society. The focus of each of these chapters is primarily the history and cultures of the areas studied with little emphasis on contact with the Europeans. Throughout each chapter the artistic and cultural achievements of the societies studied will both enrich and enliven the study of the past.

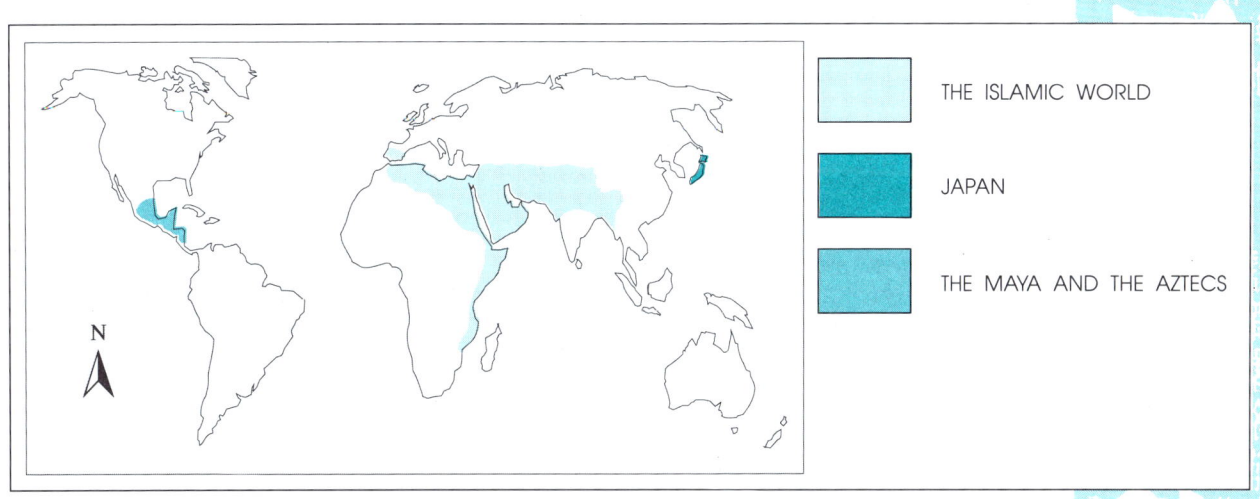

THE ISLAMIC WORLD

JAPAN

THE MAYA AND THE AZTECS

CHAPTER 10

The Islamic Middle East

Chapter Highlights

- the world's second-largest and fastest growing religion

- the Crusades from the Islamic point of view

- Sufi literature and the Arabic script

- Saladin, the ''defender of the Islamic faith''

- the One Thousand and One Arabian Nights

- the Dome of the Rock

The Middle East from the seventh to sixteenth centuries can rightfully be called Islamic. In those 900 years Islam was born and spread to become the majority religion of the area. Political organization and high culture were developed with reference to Islam. Classical forms of Islamic philosophy, law, art, and architecture date from this time. Although today Islam is a world religion and the majority of Muslims live outside the Middle East, the Middle Eastern legacy remains important for Muslims everywhere. In describing the rise and development of Islam, this chapter will demonstrate that Islam has neither been static nor uniform. Indeed, its potential for dynamism and growth remain unabated on the eve of the twenty-first century.

▼▼▼

Key Concepts

Mecca
Islam
Muslims
Koran
Sunni
Shi'i
sunna
Sufi
Umayyad caliphate
Abbasid caliphate
Fatimid dynasty
Saladin
mosque
Ottoman Empire
Safavids
Arabian Nights
Dome of the Rock
caravanserai

Geography

Geography and climate have strongly conditioned the history of the Middle East. It is a semi-arid area extending from Morocco in the west to Pakistan in the east, and from Soviet Central Asia in the north to the Sudan in the south. Historically, styles of life and forms of political organization have been conditioned by the availability of water in the region's four main physical environments: river basins, mountains, steppes, and deserts.

River basins such as those of the Nile (Egypt) and the Tigris-Euphrates (Mesopotamia and Iraq) possess reliable water supplies. They have been able to support large populations of settled, peasant farmers. In pre-Islamic and Islamic times, settled peasantries produced large food surpluses that Egyptian and Mesopotamian rulers appropriated through taxation. With this income Egyptian and Mesopotamian rulers built states, raised armies, paid theologians, and patronized artists. The continued prosperity of river-basin states depended on the rulers' protection of the peasantry and river irrigation systems from attacks of hostile armies or pastoral nomads.

Mountains, such as those along the Mediterranean coast or on the Iranian plateau, absorb seasonal rains that re-emerge at lower altitudes as perennial springs and streams. Village communities grew up around these water sources. Because of the ruggedness of the terrain, mountain villages' agricultural surpluses were smaller than those of river-basin villages. Also mountain villagers, unlike river-basin peasants, often were able to resist central authority. Mountain areas tended to be economically self-sufficient and were removed from central, political authority. The weakness of central authority in mountain regions meant that local clan and tribal affiliations acquired political significance.

Steppes are vast areas of the Middle East where irregular seasonal rainfall makes grain cultivation possible in some years but not in others. Due to the unreliability of their rainfall, steppes were lightly populated compared to the intensively cultivated river basins and spring-fed mountains. People living in the steppes could not depend solely on agriculture, so they adopted a way of life called **pastoral nomadism**. Pastoral nomads raised livestock (sheep, goats, camels, and horses) which were moved across the landscape according to the seasonal availability of vegetation for fodder. Due to their mobility, pastoral nomads were generally independent of state authority, and organized into kinship units and tribes. Until the twentieth century, pastoralists' mobility and weaponry made them more than a match for state armies. Pastoralists usually resisted state attempts to extend settled agriculture at the expense of pastoralism, and when states were weak pastoralists tried to appropriate village surpluses to themselves. States based in river basins and other areas of settled agriculture had either to absorb the pastoralists or fight them to defend the states' claims to the produce of agricultural villages. The line separating pastoralism and settled agriculture (the desert and the sown) has constantly shifted back and forth on the steppes of the Middle East depending on the balance of power between states and pastoralists. Only in the twentieth century have states won seemingly definitive victories over pastoralists.

Deserts are those areas where water is so scarce that even intermittent cultivation is impossible except around permanent water sources called oases. Deserts proper were and are virtually uninhabited, although merchant caravans crossed them using oases as stopping-places along their way, much as seafaring ships make ports of call. The two greatest Middle Eastern deserts are the Sahara in North Africa and the Arabian in Arabia. Most oases are small and of only local importance, but some (such as Damascus in Syria) are vast and fertile enough to support urban life. Damascus's water resources are so abundant that it is believed to be the oldest continuously inhabited city on earth.

Given the variations in water between river basins, mountains, steppes, and deserts, populations of the Middle East were not evenly distributed. Instead they were concentrated where water made agriculture possible. A population map of the Middle East would show a large concentration of people in the river basins, the fertile mountains, and the fertile plateaux (Turkey, Iran), separated by vast arid regions where population density was low. On the face of it, one would expect that the populations of these distinct and separate areas would have little in common with each other, linguistically or culturally. But in fact, the Middle East historically has been marked by a paradoxical mixture of unity and diversity. The rural areas in particular tended to be diverse and particularistic, reflected in their distinctive clothing, dialects and languages, and religious beliefs. But the urban Middle East has been the home of a remarkable cultural unity, expressed in the religion and high culture of Islam. The material basis of this cultural unity was provided by trade and commerce.

Trade and Commerce

A clue to understanding the region's commercial role is given in the phrase Middle East. It is a Eurocentric term coined to indicate that part of the

East lying between the Near East and the Far East. Ironically, Middle East is now used even by Middle Easterners themselves. Despite its Eurocentrism, there is some justification for the adjective "middle" if not the noun "East." The region is a kind of middle world, lying at the junction of three continents: Africa, Asia, and Europe. This central location has made the Middle East a major crossroads of international trade. Middle Eastern merchants travelled far and wide carrying the luxury goods of different regions to markets elsewhere. (Before modern communications, only luxury goods were valuable enough to justify the high costs of transport.) The Middle East was a link between the two trading worlds of the Mediterranean Sea and the Indian Ocean, as well as a link between the Mediterranean world and sub-Saharan Africa. The legendary Middle Eastern cities of Fez, Istanbul, Cairo, Damascus, Aleppo, Baghdad, Shiraz, and Samarkand were great mercantile cities. Although Italian city-states dominated the Mediterranean trade in the Middle Ages, Middle Eastern and Muslim sailors monopolized the Indian Ocean trade until the early modern period. The legends of Sindbad the sailor attest to this seafaring legacy.

The centres of Middle Eastern civilization were in constant communication with one another due to trade and commercial links. These links underlay the cosmopolitan world of Islam in the Middle Ages, and formed the material foundation of Islamic civilization. Although Islam is often regarded in the West as a "religion of the desert," this view is incorrect despite the original spread of Islamic rule by desert-dwelling pastoral nomads. The Middle East in the formative period of Islamic civilization was a markedly urban and mercantile region. Islamic law, philosophy, architecture, literature, science—the elements of medieval Islamic civilization—were developed in an urban framework. The rustic Islam of the peasants and pastoral nomads was quite distinct from the high Islam of the cities.

Beliefs

Muhammad and Islam

The arid Arabian Peninsula was a political and cultural periphery in ancient times compared to the established states and civilizations of Byzantium (the Eastern Roman Empire), Persia (Iran), and Abyssinia (Ethiopia). Each of these empires subjected the fringes of Arabia to pressures and influences, but Arabian lands and peoples did not play a major role in imperial calculations. Therefore it is remarkable that a new religion that changed world history came out of Arabia in the seventh century.

The religion was Islam and Muhammad was its prophet. Muhammad was a merchant of **Mecca**, a town in western Arabia that benefited in the sixth century due to the diversion of East-West trade from the overland Fertile Crescent route. The Fertile Crescent lands of Iraq and Syria had been wracked by a series of Byzantine-Persian wars that left both empires exhausted. Because of their trading links the people of Mecca were aware of events and ideas in Byzantium, Persia, and Abyssinia. In his early career as a merchant, Muhammad is said to have travelled to Byzantine Syria and had conversations with Christian monks. Though most inhabitants of Arabia were **animists** (believers that natural objects have souls) or polytheists, Jewish and Christian communities were found in the more settled regions of the Peninsula.

Muhammad's life was radically altered in A.D. 610 when he is said to have received the first of a series of divine revelations. After a period of self-doubt and introspection, Muhammad accepted his role as a prophet of God and began to build a community of followers. His message was **Islam** (submission to God) and those who accepted it were **Muslims** (those who submit to God). Muhammad and his followers believed that these divine messages were identical to the prophecies that God had earlier sent

Abraham (Ibrahim), Moses (Musa), and Jesus (Issa). But because Jews and Christians had misunderstood or corrupted these messages, God was now retransmitting them through a final prophet, Muhammad.

Doctrinally Islam was strictly monotheistic. Therefore Muhammad's message contradicted the animism and polytheism widespread among Arabians. Islam stressed the unity and transcendence of God, and on these points was critical of Christianity. According to the Islamic message, Christian belief in the Trinity (three persons in one God) denied the unity of God. The Christian doctrine of incarnation (that God became human in Jesus Christ) denied the transcendence of God.

The early revelations transmitted by Muhammad emphasized principles of faith and conduct. As the community of Muslims grew, the later revelations spelled out rules for believers to follow. After Muhammad's death in A.D. 632, the revelations he had transmitted were compiled into Islam's holy book, the **Koran**. Muslims believe that the Koran is the literal Word of God, rather than (as in Judaism and Christianity) scripture inspired by God. Muhammad did not interpret God's Word, he transmitted it.

Muhammad was opposed by the wealthy mercantile establishment of Mecca, who resented Islam's sympathy for the poor and the powerless. This establishment also feared that Islamic monotheism would threaten Mecca's position as a polytheistic regional pilgrimage centre. So in 622, due to the persecution they faced, Muhammad and his followers elected to emigrate from Mecca to the town of Medina, a religiously and tribally-mixed town, whose citizens asked Muhammad to arbitrate their internal disputes. This emigration is the event from which the Muslim calendar is dated. At Medina Muhammad established an Islamic city-state. Now with a political base, the community of Muslims continued to grow. By the time of his death, Muhammad had brought into the fold of Islam not only his former adversaries at Mecca but also most of the pastoral nomadic tribes of Arabia. Muhammad's success is attributable to the power of his message, to his personal charisma, and to his remarkable qualities of leadership and integrity. Later generations of Muslims would seek to model their lives on his.

Islam makes five basic demands on believers. First, Muslims are required to recite a short creed: "I witness that there is only one God and Muhammad is his messenger." Second, they are required to pray facing Mecca five times a day. Third, they are required to fast during daylight hours in the lunar month of Ramadan. Fourth, they are required to give **alms**. Fifth, each Muslim should try to make the pilgrimage to Mecca at least once in his or her lifetime. Sometimes a sixth duty is added: the obligation to wage holy struggle, *jihad*, to defend the interests of the Muslim community.

Islam is both a personal and a social religion. On the one hand Muslims are expected to have personal faith in God and to express this faith through prayer, fasting, alms-giving, and pilgrimage. On the other hand Muslims believe that through the Koran God has laid down rules and principles for community life. The Islamic **polity** at Medina established in the lifetime of Muhammad is regarded as a norm for imitation. Muslims must implement Islamic ideals not in personal isolation but in a community organized in accordance with God's laws. These laws, eventually codified by Muslim legal scholars, seek to implement Islamic principles of fairness, social responsibility, and justice.

Diversity and Dissension

After Muhammad's death no successor had his personal religious authority. Moreover, as the Muslim community grew and became geographically and culturally diverse it was natural that disagreements should emerge over how properly to understand and to implement the principles enunciated in the

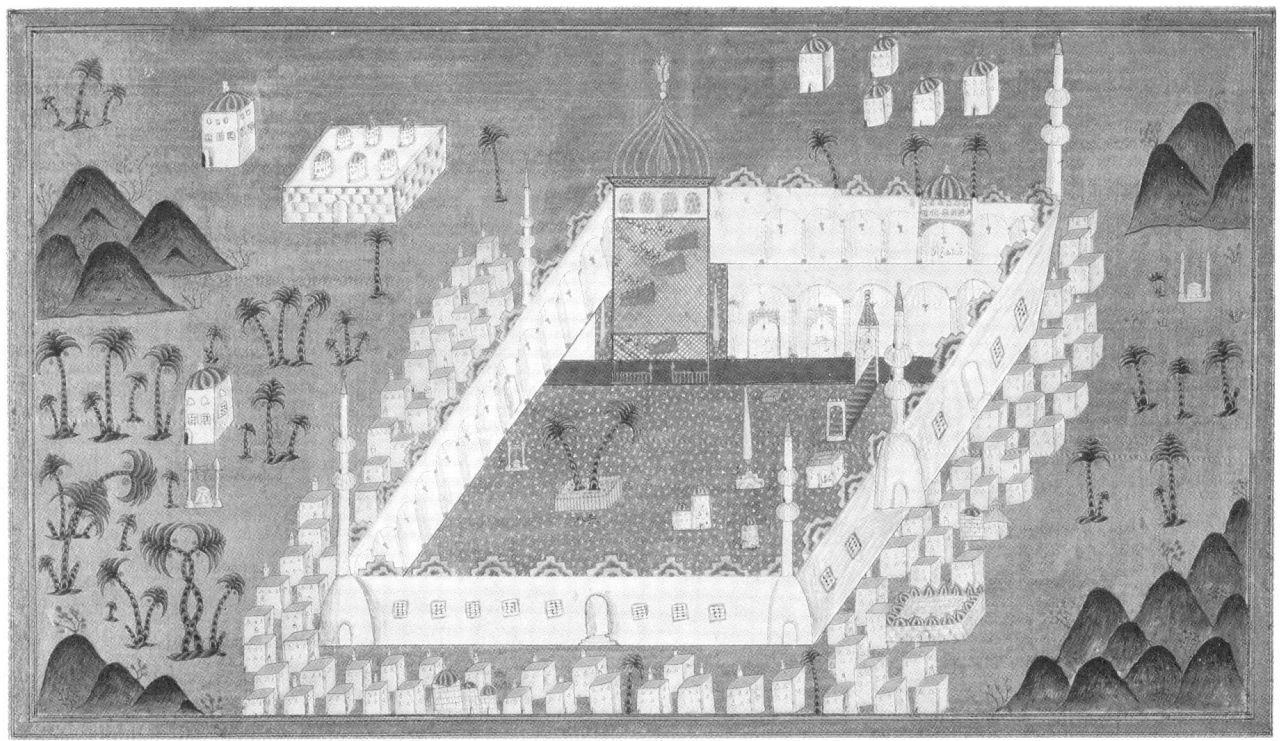

Muhammad, forced to flee from Mecca, was welcomed in Yathrid, a city later called Medina. In this town, divided by quarrels between Arabs and Jews, his message was well received. After amassing a large following, he became the town's leader. This painting depicts Medina as it looked during Muhammad's lifetime.

Koran. Islam came to reflect the diversity of its following.

Another aspect of Islamic diversity is the distinction between **Sunni** Islam and **Shi'i** Islam. The origin of the Sunni and Shi'i division was a political quarrel over who should succeed Muhammad as leader of the Muslim community. The majority favoured an elective principle for choosing Muhammad's successor. The minority, called Shi'is, believed leadership of the community rightfully belonged to the prophet's family, beginning with his cousin and son-in-law Ali.

The Muslim majority argued that the rules for proper individual and social behaviour were to be found in the Koran and in the precedent of Muhammad's own behaviour: in Arabic his **sunna**. Therefore, in order to establish guidelines for a good Muslim life, one should study the Koran and the sunna, and from these sources deduce religious law. In time the Islamic community will reach a consensus on the proper implementation of principles derived from the Koran and the sunna. Adherents of this methodology were called Sunnis. The scope of their inquiry was narrowed as successive generations of Sunni scholars established a consensus on a code of conduct derived from the Koran and the sunna.

While Shi'is agreed that the Koran and the sunna were the bases of Islamic law, they disagreed with Sunnis as to the content of the sunna, i.e., what Muhammad really said and did. For instance, Shi'is believed that Muhammad designated Ali as his successor, a contention that Sunnis reject. Shi'is also argued that Muhammad's legitimate successors—namely Ali and his descendants—had special insights into the faith that allowed them great latitude in interpretation of Islamic law. So ultimate authority in interpreting the faith resided not with the community as a whole, but with Ali and his successors, called imams. According to Shi'i belief, the rightful imam remains present in the world but has been hidden from humanity since the ninth century. Therefore, learned scholars acting in the imam's absence could interpret Islamic doctrine for the faithful until the imam's reappearance at the end of time. Shi'i religious scholars allowed themselves more flexibility in the interpretation of religious law and doctrine than their Sunni counterparts.

Both Sunnis and Shi'is emphasized the importance of religious law to govern personal and collective behavior. Sunni and Shi'i codifications of religious law were completed in the Middle Ages. These codifications spelled out Muslim laws for marriage, divorce, inheritance, economic life, and criminal penalties. In fact, religious law was rarely used for criminal cases, which instead were handled through state courts that ruled according to customary or common law; but personal status (marriage, divorce, inheritance, property) was usually regulated by religious law. Muslim religious scholars argued that the criterion for judging a government Islamic was the ruler's enforcement of religious law where applicable. Today, Muslim religious law is a basis of civil law in most Muslim countries, and in some countries it is imposed in criminal cases as well.

Sufi Mysticism

As far as the medieval religious scholars were concerned, religious law was the practical expression of Islam. Obedience to religious law was the mark of a good Muslim. But the legal-minded scholars were challenged by the **Sufi** mystics, who argued that direct inner experience of God was more important than outward conformance to religious law.

Sufis were important in both Sunnism and Shi'ism, and tended to regard Sunni-Shi'i theological quarrels as unimportant. The dry, scholastic religion of theologians and scholars held little appeal for ordinary Muslims. In the pre-modern period most people were illiterate and had little interest in the finer points of theology and law. The Sufi mystics humanized and personalized religion, making it accessible and meaningful to people in their daily lives. Sufis favoured trance-inducing ceremonies culminating in the direct experience of God; they promoted deep respect of saints; they also enjoyed reputations as living saints and miracle workers. Sufism enjoyed popular followings in both Sunni and Shi'i populations. Religious scholars frowned on Sufi populism, but Sufism was essential to the spread of Islam. The conversion of Christian Anatolia to Islam after the Turkish conquests can be attributed to Sufis, who Islamized many pre-existing popular religious traditions. Sufis played a similar role in the spread of Islam in Africa and India.

Islamic Philosophy

Alongside the religious scholars and the mystics were the Muslim philosophers. The first centuries of Islam saw a flowering of Islamic philosophy. Islam became a cosmopolitan and universal civilization. This civilization did not displace but absorbed and transformed existing, pre-Islamic traditions and cultures. The Hellenistic Greek legacy, particularly the works of Aristotle and Plato, were important in Islamic philosophical thought. Like medieval Christian philosophers, Muslims sought to demonstrate their faith through philosophy. Their challenge was to demonstrate the compatibility of faith and reason, to demonstrate that philosophical categories could explain rationally what religion taught through faith (the existence of God). Philosophers such as the famous Averroes (d. 1198) of Muslim Spain believed

LITERATURE

SUFISM AND POPULAR RELIGION

As in many societies, the formal religion of the church theologians was complicated and unappealing to ordinary people. The success of Islam owed a great deal to the mysticism of the Sufis. The term Sufi was probably derived from the Arabic word "suf" meaning wool, as the early mystics wore robes of rough white wool as a symbol of their piety and rejection of the material world. The ultimate end sought by the Sufi mystics was to attain union with God, which was achieved through the extinction of the individual. According to al-Hujwiri "The Sufi is he who has nothing in his possession nor is he possessed by anything." Sufi literature, which is highly entertaining and consequently of great appeal to the general populace, reflected the emphasis placed on saints who often had special if not supernatural powers. Yet the appeal of the Sufis is not just popular religion but philosophy for the masses, such as "On Being a Dervish," and entertaining verse dealing with such familiar topics as love in "Looking for Leyla."

On Being a Dervish

Ten dervishes will sleep under a blanket, while two rulers cannot be accommodated in one continent.

Looking for Leyla

One day Majnun was sifting dirt in the middle of a road.
An ascetic asked him: "What is it you are seeking here, Majnun?"
"I seek my beloved Leyla," Majnun replied.
The ascetic said: "How can you expect to find a pearl in the midst of rubbish?"
"Well," Majnun answered, "I look for Love everywhere; I am apt to find her somewhere."

that philosophic truth was highly refined and therefore inaccessible to most people. Therefore the allegorical truths of religion and prophecy were necessary so that the masses would not be left in moral ignorance. This glorification of philosophy at religion's expense did not sit well with religious scholars. In the defensive mood of the late-medieval Islamic world provoked in part by the Crusades and the ongoing Christian reconquest of Spain, royal patronage for philosophers dried up and religious scholars tightened their grip on intellectual life. By the time of the Mongol conquests in the thirteenth century the philosophical tradition had fallen out of favour in most Muslim centres of learning. Nevertheless, by this time Arabic philosophical treatises had been translated into Latin and helped to fuel the revival of philosophical studies in the Latin West, including the work of Thomas Aquinas. In the Muslim world philosophy continued to be taught in Shi'i schools, and its legacy lived on in dissident Iranian religious thought of the early modern period.

The Growth of Empire

The Islamic Conquests

Since Muhammad was the last of the prophets he could have no successor in that capacity, but the succession question did arise with regard to leadership of the Islamic community. Muhammad's successors were called caliphs, from the Arabic word meaning successor. The first four caliphs were chosen on an elective principle by Muslim community elders. But within a short period of time the **caliphate** succumbed to the dynastic principle under the dynasties of **Umayyads** (661–750) and **Abbasids** (750–1258).

At Muhammad's death, Islam prevailed in most of the Arabian Peninsula. Under the caliphs the Islamic polity expanded. Arabian tribes, forbidden by Islam from internal raiding, turned their energies outward against the weakened and debilitated Persian and Byzantine Empires. Within 20 years of Muhammad's death Egypt, the Fertile Crescent, and the Iranian plateau had been brought under the rule of Arab Muslims. Later the Islamic conquests were extended westward into North Africa and Spain, and eastward into Central Asia and India.

The Umayyad Caliphate

The Umayyad dynasty of caliphs was established in 661. The Umayyads were a prominent aristocratic family of Mecca who had opposed Muhammad through most of his prophetic career. But once the Meccans had agreed to accept Islam, the talented Umayyads emerged as important leaders of the Islamic conquests. In 661 the Umayyad governor of Syria obtained majority Muslim recognition for his claim to the caliphate. The Umayyads established

MAJOR EVENTS IN THE HISTORY OF ISLAM

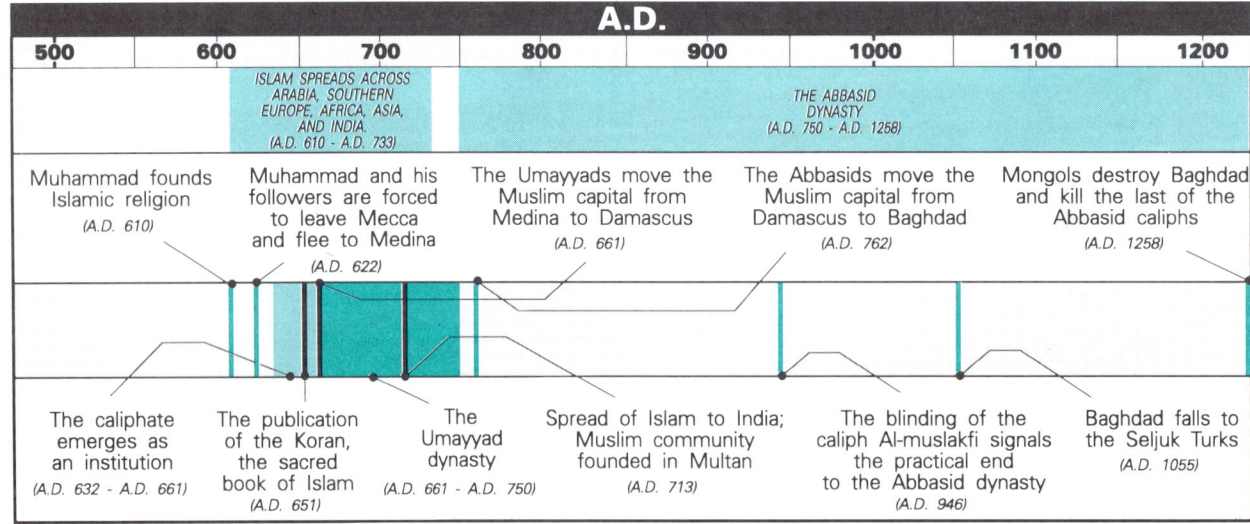

310 UNIT 3 *Civilizations of the Non-Western World*

themselves at the city of Damascus, which became their capital. Under the Umayyad caliphs (661–750), the Islamic political system, or polity, was a kind of Arab kingdom. Muslim Arabs were the privileged rulers, and their old tribal ties and affiliations continued to determine alliances and shape conflicts. Under Umayyad rule Muslim Arabs were governors of the various provinces, were exempt from taxes, and shared the income of taxation among themselves. Initially the Umayyads retained many of the state structures inherited from the Byzantines and Persians, including bureaucratic structures and personnel. Later Umayyad caliphs consciously "Arabized" the administrative system by requiring that official business be conducted and recorded in Arabic. The Arabs could act as a privileged elite under the Umayyads because in these early days of Islamic rule most Muslims were Arabs. The subject populations of Egypt, the Fertile Crescent, and Iran at first retained their former religions, and only gradually converted to Islam.

Although the Umayyads established the Arab kingdom on a firm institutional footing, their policies gave rise to increasing opposition within the Muslim community itself. Some Arab Muslims believed that the Umayyads had usurped the caliphal title from the family of Muhammad, represented by his son-in-law Ali (d. 661) and grandson Husayn (d. 680). This party of Ali (*shi'at Ali*) were known as Shi'is. The Muslim majority (the Sunnis) honoured Muhammad's family, but unlike the Shi'is they did not believe that Ali and his descendants had a rightful, hereditary claim to the caliphate.

Another kind of opposition to the Umayyads grew out of the changing nature of the Muslim community. As increasing numbers of non-Arabs converted to Islam, they resented the special privileges that Arab Muslims enjoyed under Umayyad rule. The new Muslims believed that the Islamic message was universal, and that special privileges for Arabs contradicted Islam.

Dissident groups including Shi'i partisans of Ali and his descendants, non-Arab Muslims, and Arab tribal opponents of the Umayyads, rallied behind an opposition movement led by the Abbasid family, descended from one of Muhammad's uncles. The Abbasid-led movement overthrew the Umayyads in 750 and established the Abbasid caliphate at Baghdad in Iraq, near the old Persian capital of Ctesiphon. Once in power the Abbasids expelled their uncompromising Shi'i followers and claimed legitimacy as the upholders of the true Islam, which the Umayyads had allegedly betrayed.

The Abbasid Caliphate

The Abbasid caliphate (750–1258) marked the zenith of the Islamic Empire. The Abbasids consciously strove to eliminate discrimination against non-Arab Muslims. In the Abbasids' view all Muslims, whatever their linguistic or ethnic background, should be able to identify with the Abbasid caliphate. To bolster their religious credentials, the Abbasids lavishly patronized the emerging Islamic religious establishment. The Abbasids also adopted Persian imperial forms of government and administration, and hearkening back to pre-Islamic Persian kings the Abbasid caliph claimed to be the shadow of God on earth. Arab tribesmen ceased to be the backbone of the caliph's military, and were replaced by standing armies of mercenaries and Turkish slave-soldiers recruited from Central Asia.

If the Umayyad caliphate had superimposed Arab rule on older Byzantine and Persian traditions, the Abbasids assimilated older traditions into a new Islamic synthesis. The Abbasid Empire was characterized by a religiously legitimated ruling establishment who appropriated the agricultural wealth of Mesopotamia. The rulers used this wealth to support a vast bureaucracy and military establishment, to patronize the arts, to construct public works, and to indulge in a lavish lifestyle. An example of Abbasid

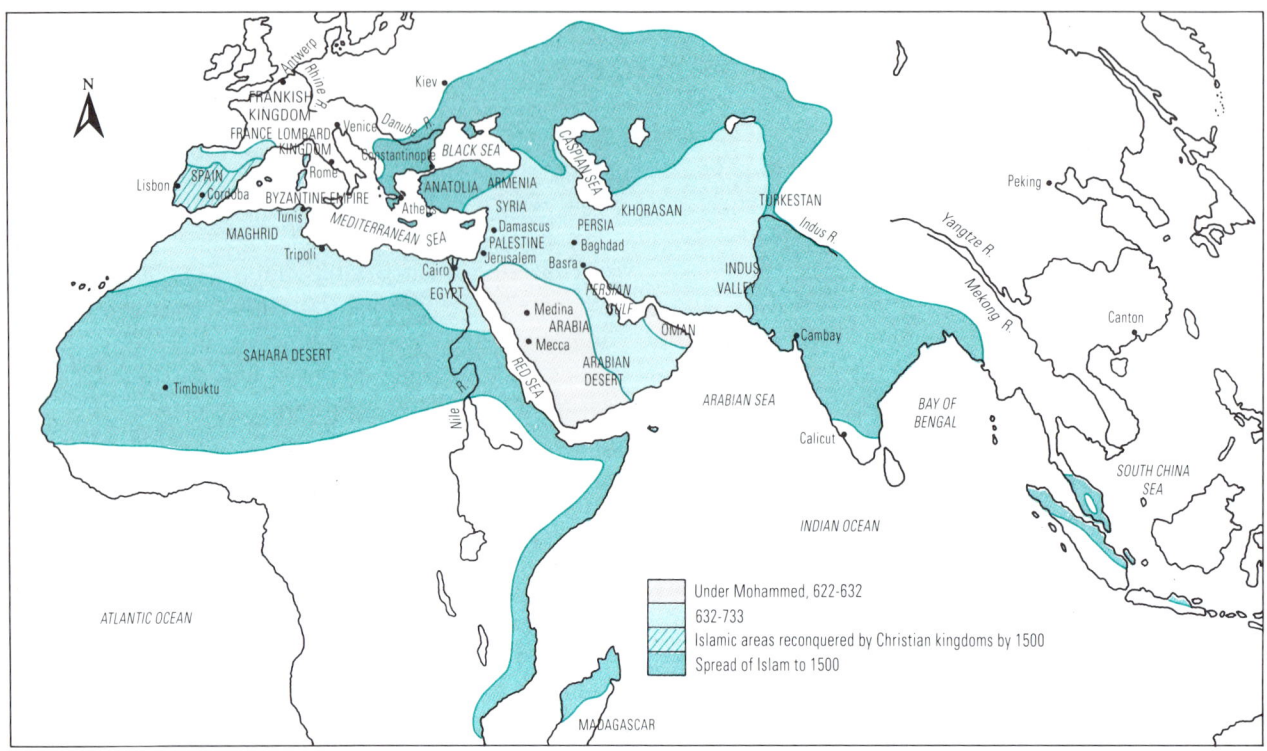

Islamic Expansion to A.D. 1500

extravagance is one caliph's tenth-century palace whose Hall of the Tree "housed a large pond in which stood an artificial tree of gold and silver with eighteen branches and multiple twigs on which silver or gilt sparrows and other birds chirped by means of mechanical devices. On both sides of the pond there were statues of fifteen mounted horsemen moving in one direction as if chasing each other."[1]

During the first century of their rule the Abbasid caliphs centrally governed their far-flung empire, which extended from North Africa in the west to Central Asia and parts of India in the east. But the political authority of the Abbasid caliphs began to decline in the last half of the ninth century. Political power and taxation revenue increasingly were taken by provincial governors who established their autonomy of Baghdad. Eventually the caliphs' effective authority was reduced to a small area around Baghdad itself. Indeed, during some periods the caliphs were little more than tools of transient local dynasties. This devolution of power is not surprising given the uneven population distribution in the Middle East, and the frequent difficulties of communication between one region and another. From an Islamic Empire, the Abbasid caliphate became a kind of Islamic commonwealth.[2]

---

[1] George Dimitri Sawa, Music Performance and Practice in the Early Abbasid Era (Toronto: Pontifical Institute of Medieval Studies, 1989), p. 2.
[2] Hugh Kennedy, The Prophet and the Age of Caliphates: The Islamic Near East from the Sixth to the Eleventh Century, (New York: Longman, 1986), p. 203.

As Abbasid power waned, most of the Islamic dynasties, states, and principalities continued to recognize the caliphs as theoretical leaders of the Islamic world. The major exception was the **Fatimid dynasty** of Egypt (969–1171), which established a Shi'i counter-caliphate with universal pretentions. The Fatimid caliphs maintained that the Abbasids were illegitimate. The economic and demographic base of Egypt sustained the Fatimids and permitted them to build an empire encompassing Syria and much of North Africa; but their universalist claims notwithstanding, the Fatimids were unable permanently to extend their rule to other parts of the Islamic world. Eventually the Fatimid dynasty collapsed and Egypt reverted to Sunni rule. Nevertheless the dynasty's legacy was considerable. The Fatimids founded the city of Cairo in 969 plus the mosque-university of al-Azhar. One-thousand years old, al-Azhar today is the oldest institution of higher learning in the world.

Crusader and Mongol Threats

The struggle between the Fatimids on the one hand and the Sunni dynasties who recognized the Abbasids of Baghdad on the other hand was typical of the political fragmentation of the Islamic world on the eve of the Crusades. The Crusades were launched in 1096 by relatively small numbers of Frankish knights in a papal-inspired bid to regain the holy land (Palestine) for Christendom. The explanation for the Crusades lies less in the Middle East than in Europe from whence they came. European Christendom was emerging from the Dark Ages and the popes of Rome saw the issue of Christian holy places as a way to galvanize support for the papacy. Only the internal divisions of the Islamic world at the time made a Frankish conquest of coastal Syria including Palestine feasible. Although they conquered Jerusalem, the Crusaders' political control of the Syrian and Palestinian coast was always tenuous.

Once Egypt and Syria had been reunited after 1171 under the Sunni Muslim warrior **Saladin**, the Crusaders lost Jerusalem and were subsequently destroyed in the thirteenth century. The Crusades loom large in the Western imagination, but were a relatively small episode in the sweep of Islamic history. With the exception of Jerusalem no major towns were lost to the Crusaders. The net effect of the Crusades was to accelerate the conversion of Middle Eastern Christians to Islam. The Crusaders' atrocities (such as their massacre of Muslims and Jews in conquered Jerusalem) cast Christianity in a bad light and intensified militancy among Muslims who previously had no particular axe to grind with local Christians. The Crusader period also confirmed the importance to the Islamic world of Turkish soldiers, who were critical to the success of Saladin (himself a Kurd) and subsequent rulers. Turkish dynasties of rulers called sultans were established in the shadow of the Abbasid caliphate from the eleventh century onward.

A more successful crusade was the Christian reconquest of Spain. Muslim rule of Spain was firmly established by the eighth century, when a fugitive Umayyad prince fleeing the Abbasids' wrath established an Umayyad dynasty at Cordoba. Spain subsequently became an important centre of Islamic-Arab civilization, in contrast to the Frankish barbarism that prevailed north of the Pyrenees. But by the eleventh century Muslim rule in Spain was weakening, and Christian rulers began their long reconquest of the peninsula in 1085. The last Muslim principality in Spain, Granada, fell in 1492. Christian rule was characterized by religious intolerance, symbolized by the Spanish Inquisition, and conquered Muslim and Jewish communities were subject to fierce persecution. Muslims and Jews who refused conversion to Catholicism were finally expelled from Spain in the sixteenth century and took refuge in the various lands of the Islamic Middle East.

PERSONALITIES

Saladin: Defender of the Islamic Faith

Among the great heroes of Islamic history is Salah ad-Din, or Saladin, who was the most successful defender of Islam against the onslaught of the Christian Crusaders. Saladin has been described as a great and charismatic leader both cultured and chivalrous who devoutly believed that he had been chosen by God to lead the resistance against the infidel Crusaders. As vizier to the Fatimid Caliph of Egypt, Saladin was well positioned to seize power. When the Fatimid Caliph died in 1171, Saladin proclaimed himself Sultan of Egypt and went on to conquer Syria. During his rule Egypt emerged as the leader of the Islamic world and began a renewed golden age; but it was his leadership against the Christian Crusaders that earned Saladin lasting fame.

At a critical battle at Hittin in northern Palestine on July 4, 1187 Saladin used his knowledge of the terrain to win a decisive victory. By controlling all the wells and starting brush fires which sent smoke into the Christian armies he was able to invoke confusion and despair amongst his enemies. The Christians, having marched across the hot desert in their oppressive armour were left gasping with thirst. They soon became confused and discouraged and were easily slain or captured. Following the battle, Saladin displayed both his mercy and his vengeance, freeing Guy of Lusignan but beheading Reynauld of Chatillon who had for years been a belligerent and treacherous foe to all of Islam. He showed no mercy to the Templars and Hospitallers who were also executed on his command.

The Third Crusade, 1189–1192, pitted the honourable Saladin against England's chivalrous Richard I, also known as the Lion Heart. These two men grew to share a mutual respect and admiration for each other's military abilities. Once, seeing Richard unmounted, Saladin is reputed to have sent him a charger, feeling that so gallant a warrior should not have to fight on foot. On another occasion, gripped by fever Richard cried out for fruit and a cold drink; Saladin responded by sending him pears, peaches, snow, and his personal physician. When a three year peace treaty was signed in 1192 Richard declared that he would return to conquer Jerusalem; to which Saladin replied that should he lose his land he would prefer to lose it to Richard rather than to any other man.

Saladin's achievements on and off the battlefield earned him the reputation of being a great individual. He was a deeply pious and honourable man who was gentle to the weak and merciful to the vanquished. He treated his servants with kindness and cared little for material wealth. Prior to his death he said to his son; "If I have become great it is because I have won men's hearts by kindness and gentleness." The great Saladin, who had devoted his life to the Islamic faith died in 1193 at the age of 55.

The loss of Spain to Islamic rule, however painful to Muslims, affected only a geographic periphery of the medieval Islamic world. The Crusades touched the Islamic heartlands, but were eventually repelled. But a third and very ominous threat to medieval Islam came not from the West but from the East, the steppes of Mongolia. There the Mongols, horse-mounted warriors and pastoralists, were united under the leadership of Chingghis Khan in the late twelfth century. Within a short time they conquered Central Asia, and after a breathing spell they continued their westward advance into Iran and Iraq. The Mongols were **shamanists** and Buddhists who had no particular respect for or interest in Islam or the urban civilization Islam represented. The Mongols sought to terrify settled populations into surrendering without resistance. Chingghis Khan and his lieutenants were merciless toward populations that resisted them, and left smoking ruins and towers of skulls in their wake. The message was: "If you resist you will all be killed." Many local rulers wisely declared their allegiance to the Mongols and became loyal vassals, sparing their lands from destruction.

The last Abbasid caliph, however, chose to make a heroic stand with predictable results. Mongol warriors captured and sacked Baghdad in 1258 and ended the Abbasid dynasty. Legend has it that the Mongols were superstitious enough not to lay hands on the caliph directly, so they wrapped him in a rug and beat him to death instead. Little was left of the legendary Abbasid capital, its libraries and its cultural riches, once the Mongols were finished robbing, looting, and burning. Mongol warriors continued to move westward, but were stopped in Palestine in 1260 by an Egyptian-based dynasty of Turkish slave-soldiers called Mamluks (1250–1517). This victory saved medieval Cairo from Baghdad's fate.

The destruction of Baghdad and the Abbasid caliphate symbolized the Mongol conquest of the Eastern Islamic world, particularly Iraq, the Iranian plateau, and Central Asia. As pastoral-nomadic warriors the Mongols were hostile to urban civilization generally, medieval Islam included. Apart from the physical destruction of towns, the Mongol conquests led to a rapid decline in the irrigation networks that

This Muslim warrior is drawn from a Turkish miniature of the Battle of Badr. Fighting for their religion these Muslim horsemen posed a formidable threat to enemies and due to their order and discipline they were usually victorious.

had once made intensive cultivation in Mesopotamia possible. Although Mesopotamian agriculture had been slowly declining anyway due to inadequate drainage and the resulting salinization of the soil, the Mongol conquests delivered a grave blow to the irrigated cultivation that remained. In fact, Mesopotamia (Iraq) did not fully recover from this thirteenth-century disaster until the twentieth century. With the destruction of the Abbasid caliphate, Cairo by default became the major centre of Islamic civilization and learning for nearly two centuries. In the Arabic-speaking Muslim lands, Cairo has retained its pre-eminence to the present day.

Nevertheless it is important to note that, Iraq excepted, those Muslim countries conquered by the Mongols eventually recovered, particularly Iran. Moreover, the Mongol rulers of Iran (known as the

The Dome of the Rock, or Omar Mosque, is in Jerusalem. This early example of Islamic architecture dates to the seventh century, the first wave of Arab expansion. Its name comes from the rock, underneath the mosque, which is believed to have been the site for two major events — the ascension of Muhammad and the sacrificing of Isaac by Abraham.

Il-Khans) eventually converted to Islam and embraced the high culture and civilization that their predecessors had tried to destroy. The conversion of the Il-Khans and the resurrection of urban civilization in Iran is a testament to the strength of Islamic urbanism. The Il-Khans patronized a revival of Islamic arts and learning before their own dynasty passed away in 1350. They adopted Persian as their language of administration and built **mosques** and mausoleums, some of which still stand. They also tried to revive agriculture, which staged a modest recovery without, however, attaining pre-Mongol levels.

Bureaucratic-Patrimonial States

From the Il-Khans onward, Muslim rulers and the political thinkers they patronized developed the theory and practice of the bureaucratic-**patrimonial** state. According to this theory, the entire state apparatus, including soldiers and bureaucrats, was the patrimony or personal property of the ruler (sultan, shah, padishah). In fact, servants of the state were legally slaves of the ruler, but this was a slavery of high status. The ruler and his slaves were a ruling class, legally separated from the rest of society, the ruled. The role of the ruled was to pay taxes to and obey the rulers. The rulers were to collect and spend taxes, and offer in return the administration of justice.

Therefore under the Il-Khans and later Muslim dynasties the principle of stratification was no longer (as under the Umayyads) Arabs–non-Arabs; or (as under the Abbasids) Muslims–non-Muslims; rather it was rulers–ruled. The ruling class was Muslim by definition, but the majority of the subject population were usually Muslims as well. This organization of society was not ideologically questioned in the Islamic Middle East until the nineteenth century, when liberal and nationalist movements challenged the bureaucratic-patrimonial states.

The political resilience of the Islamic Middle East is demonstrated by the emergence in the early sixteenth century of two powerful bureaucratic-patrimonial states, one based in the old Byzantine lands of southeastern Europe and Anatolia, and the other based in the Iranian plateau.

Beginning in the eleventh century, Byzantine Anatolia was conquered by Muslim Turkish dynasties, whose language and religion were eventually adopted by most of the formerly Christian and Greek-speaking population. In the thirteenth century one Turkish dynasty, the **Ottomans**, became especially prominent. Eventually the Ottomans conquered Anatolia from their Turkish rivals and southeastern Europe from Christian rulers, incorporating the Byzantine capital of Constantinople (Istanbul) into their empire in 1453. By the sixteenth century the Ottomans had extended their conquests to include the Fertile Crescent, Egypt, and North Africa. They possessed the most powerful land army in Europe. As a European power, the Ottoman Empire became enmeshed in the web of intra-European intrigue. Religious ideology was subordinated to power politics as the Muslim Ottomans allied with the Catholic French against their common adversaries, the Catholic Hapsburgs of Austria. The Ottoman Empire remained a great European power until the eighteenth century.

Ottoman society was multi-ethnic, multi-lingual, and multi-religious. The bureaucratic-patrimonial political formula of rulers and ruled worked well for a time. The Ottomans permitted the various religious, ethnic, and tribal communities internal self-government as long as these communities recognized Ottoman authority and paid taxes. Religious and linguistic conformity were neither demanded nor expected. The nineteenth-century breakdown of this Ottoman system led to the emergence of the Balkan, Arab, and Turkish nation-states of the present day.

Along with the Ottomans' consolidation of their power in Anatolia and southeastern Europe, the Iranian plateau was reunified under a single, Iranian-based dynasty for the first time since the Muslim conquest. In 1501 the ***Safavids***, leaders of a messianic religious and political movement, claimed the kingship of Iran. The Safavids proclaimed Shi'i Islam to be the state religion, to distinguish themselves from their rivals and adversaries the Sunni Ottomans. Thus Shi'i Islam became the official religion of Iran, which up until then had been a predominantly Sunni country. It took some time for Shi'ism to implant itself among the Iranian population, but by the seventeenth century Shi'ism had triumphed at the grass-roots level and Sunnis were a minority.

The Safavids turned Iran into a powerful bureaucratic-patrimonial state. Like the Ottomans at Istanbul, the Safavids embellished their capital of Isfahan with architectural monuments that still delight the eye. Although the Safavid dynasty collapsed in the eighteenth century, Iran remained politically unified after a period of confusion. Both in terms of establishing the unity of the Iranian plateau under one political unit, and of establishing Shi'ism as the distinctive, state religion, the Safavid dynasty was a harbinger of modern Iran.

To sum up, the relatively united Islamic Middle East became politically fragmented after the first 200 years of the caliphate. Thus it became vulnerable to Crusader and Mongol incursions. But the resilience of the Islamic Middle East was demonstrated by the Muslims' repulsion of the Crusaders from the Middle East, and the assimilation into Islam of the Mongol conquerors. Only in Spain did Islamic civilization lose ground where it had sunk deep roots. At the beginning of the modern era in the sixteenth century, the Islamic Middle East was poised for a new era of cultural achievement and political power under the Ottoman and Safavid dynasties.

Social History

Social Structure

The social structure of the Islamic Middle East varied depending on the four physical environments discussed previously.

River basins were peasant societies where the principal elements in the social structure were peasants and landlords. The landlords of Egypt and Mesopotamia, unlike their feudal European counterparts, were usually agents of the state and not absolute owners of their domains. Peasants lived in villages and paid tribute to the landlords, as representatives of the state. These areas were the most productive of the Islamic Middle East, and their populations were heavily exploited by states and landlords. At one point in the eighth century, slaves of African origin laboured on Mesopotamian plantations, but agricultural slavery was not the norm. The resources of river-basin agriculture allowed Egypt and Mesopotamia to be distinct and often rival bases of state power, both before and during the Islamic period.

Mountain Regions. Mountains offered refuge from exploitation by states and attacks from pastoral nomads. Mountain peasants (such as those in North Africa and the lands of modern Turkey, Syria, Lebanon, the Palestinian West Bank, and parts of Iran) were politically organized in clan and kinship groups. Because mountain agriculture yielded less than river-basin agriculture, central governments were often content to accept tribute from mountain peasants rather than mount costly military expeditions to subjugate them directly. Therefore in the mountain regions the principal classes were clan chieftains on the one hand and peasant cultivators on the other. Mountain peasants engaged in livestock-rearing as well, moving their flocks up and down the slopes with the changing seasons. Mountain chieftains were not as rich as the river-basin landlords, and the peasants were not as miserable and exploited as their counterparts in the river-basins. Because of their relative autonomy from central control and exploitation, the mountain areas became redoubts of linguistic and sectarian particularities. The Christian Maronites and the tenuously Shi'i Druze and Alawis of present-day Lebanon and Syria are historically mountain-peasant communities. The Berbers of North Africa and the Kurds of modern Iraq, Iran, and Turkey are other examples of mountain peoples who remained aloof from the great empires of the cities and plains, co-operating with these empires when it suited their interests and opposing them at other times.

Steppes. Steppes were the domain of peasants and landlords, when states were strong, and of pastoral nomads, when states were weak. Compared to river-basin land, steppe land is marginal for agricultural purposes. Nevertheless, under stable conditions steppe land could be productive through good rainfall or the construction of irrigation canals from elevated springs. Settled peasants in steppes were by definition exploited, either by state-supported landlords or by pastoral nomads demanding tribute. Oftentimes pastoral nomads would drive steppe peasants away by raiding or by making excessive tribute demands, after which the land reverted to pasture. The internal structure of pastoral nomadic society tended to be more **egalitarian** than settled society. Noble lineages existed and they often possessed more wealth than their fellow tribespeople, but such notables were expected to spread the wealth around through gestures of hospitality and generosity. Clan and kinship solidarity were necessary for the survival and well-being of pastoral nomads, and so checked the development of extremes of wealth and poverty. Although pastoral nomads often entered into relationships with state authorities and urban merchants (regarding protection of overland trade, for instance), these relationships were between equals since urban interests prior to the twentieth century had no way of forcing the highly mobile and warlike pastoral nomads to submit to urban interests. Today, Middle Eastern states have either suppressed and impoverished former pastoral nomads (Syria, Iran), or built state structures in alliance with them (Jordan, Saudi Arabia).

Desert Regions. Deserts are incapable of supporting large populations. Their importance was derived from scattered oases where settled cultivation was possible (typically date-palms), and which also served as stopping points on caravan trade routes. In the desert the pastoral nomads reigned supreme. They controlled caravan transport trade (from which they profited), and taxed those oases within their respective tribal domains. Oasis cultivators were in this sense subject to the pastoral nomads. Relations of exploitation were often softened, however, by real or fictitious kinship ties to their nomadic overlords.

Urban Regions. Cities must also be considered in any discussion of social structure. They were usually located in areas of river-basin agriculture (Cairo, Baghdad) or well-watered regions surrounded by steppe or desert trade routes (Damascus, Aleppo, Samarkand). The major cities of the Islamic Middle East were dependent on a combination of the following for their existence: location, administration, manufacturing, trade. Most of them in fact combined these functions. The populations of major cities were grouped into a hierarchy of power and wealth, typically in the following order from top to bottom: soldiers and bureaucrats; merchants, landowners, and religious scholars; artisans and manufacturers; and simple labourers. In the middle and later Abbasid period (tenth to thirteenth centuries) soldiers were increasingly drawn from geographically peripheral populations (Berbers, Turks, Kurds) distinct from the Arabic- and Persian-speaking town populations. Therefore merchants, landowners, and religious scholars often acted as mediators between non-Arab and non-Persian military rulers and the Arabic and Persian-speaking civil populations. Artisans and manufacturers were numerous in most cities. They served local and regional markets, and their skillfully-made products brought fame to their cities: Damascus for distinctive types of cloth and steel, both called damask; Mosul (Iraq) for its muslin cloth; and fustian cloth from Fustat (Old Cairo).[3] Of the simple labourers little trace remains in the written records of the time. They were probably a plurality (if not a majority) of most cities' populations, and were engaged in various menial and unskilled trades.

Role of Women[4]

The role and status of women in the Islamic Middle East combined two contradictory traditions: Arabian and Koranic practices, on the one hand, and the customs of Byzantine and Persian agrarian-urban society, on the other. Under Abbasid patronage these traditions were codified into Islamic religious law.

In the predominantly pastoral nomadic society of Arabia, women were considered subordinate to men but nevertheless played important public roles. Their advice and counsel was sought in political matters, they were respected for their composition of and recital of poetry (the major cultural pastime of pre-Islamic Arabia), and they could assume positions of religious leadership (the name of a local

---

[3]G. M. Wickens. "What the West Borrowed from the Middle East" in Introduction to Islamic Civilizations ed. R. M. Savoury. (Cambridge: Cambridge University Press, 1976), p. 122.
[4]The discussion in this section is drawn largely from Guity Mashat, "Women in the Middle East 8000 B.C.–1800 A.D." in Restoring Women to History: Middle East, eds. Cheryl Johnson-Odim and Margaret Strobel (Bloomington: Organization of American Historians, 1988), p. 22–51.

prophetess is recorded in the chronicles). They were neither segregated from men nor veiled. In some tribes, **polyandry** (marriage to more than one husband at a time) was permitted. However, the overall subordination of women to men was deeply ingrained; women could counsel tribal leaders but were not themselves leaders, and in times of extreme difficulty tribes practiced female infanticide.

Koranic revelation transmitted by Muhammad corrected abuses and made adjustments without radically altering the pre-existing situation. The Koran outlawed female infanticide and guaranteed women and girls a share in the inheritance of deceased husbands and fathers. The Koran also outlawed practices such as polyandry that would create doubts about paternity. In most other respects the Koran left the status quo alone. Consequently, women played important public roles in the early decades of the Islamic community.

The first convert to Islam was Muhammad's wealthy and respected first wife, Khadija. She gave him critical support during the early years of his prophetic career in hostile Mecca. Islam's first martyr was Sumayya bint Khubbat, a slave woman who was killed for her beliefs. Two of the first four caliphs were converted to Islam by their female relatives. Women also took part in the political and military battles of the early Islamic community. For instance, Muhammad's youngest wife, Ayisha, was a leader of the opposition to Ali when he claimed leadership of the Islamic community after Muhammad's death. Another woman, Hind bint Utba, was prominent in the Meccan opposition to Muhammad, but like other Meccans she eventually embraced Islam. There are numerous other examples of women who played visible roles in the public life of early Islam.

The Muslim conquests of the agrarian-urban Middle East (Egypt, the Fertile Crescent, Iran) gradually led to a change in Islamic customs. For many centuries women in the agrarian-urban societies of Byzantium and Persia had been limited to household and child-rearing duties, with emphasis on sexual segregation and veiling where practical (especially among the urban upper classes). As the Arab Muslim conquerors of Damascus and Baghdad began to assimilate the culture of the agrarian-urban Middle East, they introduced these restrictive practices into their own society. When Islamic law was codified under the Abbasids, it incorporated this pre-Islamic heritage. With regard to women, Islamic law downplayed Arabian practices (suitable for a pastoral-nomadic society) in favour of agrarian-urban traditions which now became sanctified by Islam. On the other hand, specific Koranic guarantees of women's property and material rights were retained in the codifications of Islamic law. So in the synthesis that this law represented, women's status was lower than it had been in Arabia at the time of Muhammad, but better than it had been in the pre-Islamic agrarian-urban Middle East.

After the first Islamic century, the public role of women in Islamic life largely ceased. Politics, war, and intellectual and cultural life were virtually monopolized by men, with a few remarkable exceptions that prove the rule. Two contrasting examples are the mystic Rabi'a al-Adawiyya of Iraq (d. 801), who wrote religious verse, and Shajar al-Durr (d. 1257), who briefly ruled Egypt in her own right. Among her exploits was the assassination of her Mamluk husband. This deed outraged her mother-in-law, whose slave girls subsequently murdered Shajar al-Durr. In recognition of Shajar al-Durr's singularity, there is today a street named after her in Cairo.

The general absence of women from public life belies their importance in society. Apart from their role as bearers and nurturers of children, women were critical in economic life as well. Among the elite and wealthy classes, Koranically guaranteed property rights gave ambitious women opportunities to manage their property from behind the scenes through trusted male kinsmen or agents. Peasant women laboured in the fields alongside men, and pastoral nomadic women cared for the livestock on which their communities' survival depended. Preparation and processing of foodstuffs and animal products for home use and for sale typically were women's responsibilities. Sexual segregation allowed the development of specialized trades among women who served other women as peddlers, healers, and prayer-leaders. Moreover, in Middle Eastern societies where the extended family or clan was an important economic, social, and even political unit, women had considerable influence in determining the shape of relationships within and between clans through their women's networks. The difficulty for the historian is that these kinds of networks are not recorded in the medieval chronicles and biographical dictionaries, all written by men.

On the whole, the Islamic Middle East was a male-dominated society in which patriarchy was legitimized by male religious scholars' interpretations of Islam. For instance, while Muslim women of Muhammad's day did not veil, religious scholars subsequently interpreted Koranic injunctions for female modesty as mandating head-to-toe veiling. Patriarchy was built into the Middle Eastern social structure, and not until this structure began to change radically in the nineteenth and twentieth centuries did reformists challenge patriarchy in the Muslim world (the same is true of the West). Nowadays, although some Middle Eastern women have broken with Islam entirely, Muslim feminists more commonly appeal to the Koran and early Islamic practices in their campaigns for women's rights.

Customs and Festivals

Festivals in the Islamic Middle East included those which were strictly religious and followed the Muslim lunar calendar (determined by the phases of the moon), and local festivals of pre-Islamic origin which followed the solar calendar (determined by the position of the Earth around the sun).

The greatest Islamic feasts were (and are) those marking the end of the fasting month of Ramadan, and the end of the annual pilgrimage to Mecca. The importance of these feasts (but not their religious meanings) is comparable to Christmas and Easter in Christianity. The end of the Ramadan fast was a joyous occasion. People who had endured a month of rigorous daytime fasting were now free to eat, drink, and celebrate in the company of family and friends. The religious purpose of fasting in Islam, as in Christianity, was to bring believers close to God and to remind them of the sacrifices faith demands. In many localities people looked forward to Ramadan despite its rigors. Special meals were prepared for Ramadan nights, and night-time festivals were held in cities such as Cairo (where the tradition is continued today). The second major Muslim holiday, the Feast of the Sacrifice, marked the end of the annual Mecca pilgrimage. Traditionally families sacrificed sheep to mark the occasion, and wealthy people were obliged to distribute the meat of their animals to the poor. Like the feast marking the end of Ramadan, the Feast of the Sacrifice was the occasion for community and family celebrations and gatherings.

The ceremony of the pilgrimage itself was and remains extremely important for fostering a sense of shared Muslim community. Pilgrimage to the sacred enclosure in Mecca predates Islam. Muslims believe that God's first prophet, Abraham, founded the sacred enclosure, and that by destroying polytheism Muhammad returned the enclosure to its original purpose. The pilgrimage ceremony itself lasts for a number of days and involves an ordered sequence of rituals and ceremonies. Every devout Muslim aspired to make the pilgrimage in his or her lifetime. In the days before modern communication this trip could involve considerable hardship and danger. At pilgrimage time Mecca became a microcosm of the

Islamic world, as pilgrims from all over met there for the ceremonies. Additionally, religious scholars from various Islamic lands settled in Mecca and Medina to study and to teach at its religious schools.

Among Shi'is who supported the claim of Ali and his descendants to the leadership of the Muslim community, the anniversary of the martyrdom of Ali's son Husayn in 680 acquired special significance. Husayn was killed by the army of the Umayyad caliph whose legitimacy he contested. Among Shi'is this anniversary, called Ashura, was a time for recollection and mourning. Beginning in the later Middle Ages, and more systematically after the establishment of Shi'ism as Iran's state religion by the Safavid dynasty in 1501, popular dramatizations of Husayn's martyrdom took place on Ashura. These developed into religious passion plays comparable to those that arose in medieval Christianity around the Passion of Christ. Nowadays Ashura is the emotional high point of the Shi'i religious calendar, and is commemorated on a large scale in countries with substantial Shi'i populations including India, Iran, Iraq, and Lebanon. Ashura was and is a solemn anniversary, like Good Friday in the Christian tradition.

Local secular feasts are also important in the Middle East. The best known are in Egypt and Iran, two countries with ancient civilizations that assimilated Islam at least as much as Islam assimilated them. Both Egyptians and Iranians celebrate spring festivals around the time of the vernal equinox. The vernal equinox is the new year according to the traditional Iranian solar calendar. Iranians also mark the winter solstice, customarily by staying up well into the long night reading and reciting poetry. An interesting point of contrast between Christianity and Islam is that Christianity assimilated pagan winter and spring festivals into Christmas and Easter, respectively, whereas formal Islam did not. The fact that seasonal festivals are regulated by the solar calendar, while Islam is regulated by a lunar calendar, may explain why such assimilation did not generally occur in the Middle East.

Cross-Cultural Influences

The high culture of medieval Islam was cosmopolitan, and reflected many cultural influences: Byzantine, Egyptian, Persian, and Indian. Nevertheless, the Arab conquerors of Egypt, Iran, and the Fertile Crescent were not culturally absorbed by pre-existing high-cultural patterns. Although Arabia was materially impoverished, the Arabic language by Muhammad's time was a highly developed literary and literate language. Their language, combined with the Islamic revelation, gave the Arabs the tools they needed to put an Arabic and Islamic stamp on the new Middle Eastern cultural synthesis that emerged following the conquests. In the Islamic Middle East up till the Mongol conquests, Arabic was the principal language of literate culture serving much the same role as Latin in medieval Europe. Literary Persian, for its part, was temporarily submerged by the Arab conquests, but re-emerged as a medium of poetry, literature, and government administration beginning in the ninth century. From that point on, however, Persian was written in Arabic script and borrowed heavily from Arabic vocabulary. Somewhat later, with the establishment of the Ottoman and other Turkish-speaking dynasties, literary Turkish adopted the Arabic alphabet and numerous Arabic and Persian loan-words.

By and large medieval Muslims had little to learn from their Western contemporaries. In Umayyad and Abbasid times Europe was in the throes of the Dark Ages. Even when European high civilization began to revive in the eleventh century, it lagged far behind that of the Islamic world in most respects. Cross-cultural borrowing between Muslims and Christians in the Middle Ages flowed from the Middle East to Europe, not the other way around. The

THE ARTS

THE KORAN'S IMPACT ON THE DEVELOPMENT OF ARABIC SCRIPT

The Muslim aversion to images created an art form in the ornamental calligraphy of Arabic script. The script was first developed to translate the Koranic text as accurately as possible and because of the importance of this manuscript the writing itself became more embellished with each edition. The Arabic script is based on the earliest known alphabet, the North Semitic, which had developed around 1700 B.C. in Palestine and Syria. The Dome of the Rock in Jerusalem carries a 240 metre-long inscription which declares the purpose of the building. Even in this early monument the principles of decorative writing are evident. The Islamic script used today contains 28 characters and is a consonantal alphabet.

ARABIC

Form	Name	Form	Name
ا	alif	ض	dad
ب	ba	ط	ta
ت	ta	ظ	za
ث	tha	ع	ayn
ج	jim	غ	ghayn
ح	ha	ف	fa
خ	kha	ق	qaf
د	dai	ك	kaf
ذ	dhai	ل	lam
ر	ra	م	mim
ز	zay	ن	nun
س	sin	ه	ha
ش	shin	و	waw
ص	sad	ي	ya

role of Islamic philosophy in stimulating a revival of Western philosophical thought has already been mentioned. The West's debt to Middle Eastern intellectual achievements did not stop there. Algebra, a word of Arabic derivation, was a Middle Eastern invention. Arabic numerals using zeros, invented in India, were passed to the West via the Middle East, supplanting clumsy Roman numerals. The origin of words like sofa, ottoman, mattress, and admiral, arsenal, and barbican, indicate the West's debt to the Middle East for both creature comforts and warfare. Likewise, words such as sherbet, orange, yogurt, and coffee reveal the culinary aspects of the West borrowing from the Middle East. Checkmate, from Persian *shah-mat* "the king is at a loss," discloses yet another Western import.[5]

Islamic civilization was itself a synthesis of many cultural traditions. The self-confidence of Muslims in this period encouraged an attitude of openness to other cultures, in the knowledge that they could be assimilated and Islamized. Self-confidence and openness combined to create a flourishing culture in the ninth to eleventh centuries that has been compared to the subsequent Italian Renaissance.

The Arts

Literature

Literary expression in the Islamic Middle East took many forms. One of the most prominent was poetry. Arabic poetry predates the Islamic era, and the Arabs had a well established tradition of poetry. In the cosmopolitan civilization that developed after the Islamic conquests, Arabic remained the principal literary language.

Other literary forms were chronicles recounting the exploits of kings and leaders, biographical dictionaries, humorous stories, folk tales, and epics. The chronicles and biographical dictionaries form the main source of raw material for writing about Islamic history. The most famous collection of folk tales are the *One Thousand and One Nights* or **Arabian Nights**. These were orally transmitted tales from many different lands and peoples, taken over by the Arabs who set them in Abbasid Baghdad, and finally written down in the late medieval period. Characters such as Schehrezade, Sindbad, Ali Baba, and Aladdin come from the *Arabian Nights*. Stories were also transmitted in poetry. One of the best known genres is that of impossible or unrequited love, such as that of *Majnun Layla*.

The tremendous literary output of the Islamic Middle East (and its scientific achievements as well) were made possible through royal patronage. The decentralization of the Abbasid caliphate from the tenth century onward—sometimes called the decline of the caliphate—worked to the advantage of literary production. "This cultural efflorescence was in some ways a product of the political fragmentation of the time, which provided new sources of patronage for authors....[T]he patronage of the caliphal court was replaced by support from many different sources which allowed a great variety of writing to emerge...."[6] Each ruler in the Islamic commonwealth vied to surround himself with poets, writers, and scientists to enhance his prestige. The Abbasid cultural environment reminds one of the Italian Renaissance, where the very fragmentation of Italy into prosperous city-states and principalities provided a multiplicity of opportunities for artists to find patrons.

---

[5]Wickens, "What the West Borrowed from the Middle East" pp. 121–23.

[6]Kennedy, *The Prophet and the Age of the Caliphates*, (New York: Longman, 1986), p. 201.

Architecture

Architecture is one of the most distinctive features of Islamic high culture. The characteristic building was the mosque, which required a basic floor plan allowing worshippers to fulfill the various rituals of ablution and prayer; but atop this floor plan a variety of architectural styles flourished. Usually mosques were surmounted by domes, and had a colonnaded courtyard plus distinctive minarets. In mosque decoration pictorial representations were usually avoided in favour of abstract geometric patterns (arabesque) and Koranic calligraphy. The earliest example of monumental Islamic architecture is the **Dome of the Rock** in Jerusalem, built by the Umayyad caliphs in the early eighth century. The Umayyad Mosque in Damascus also dates from this time. Both it and the Dome of the Rock illustrate how Romano-Byzantine forms were being assimilated into Muslim architecture. The mosaic work on both buildings is derived from Byzantine art, and the layout of the Umayyad Mosque in Damascus echoes the basilica pattern of Byzantine churches. Interestingly too, the mosaic-work in Damascus includes exceptional pictorial representations of Paradise, complete with cities, flowing rivers, trees, and gardens, but is devoid of animal or human representations. Their locations are also significant. The Dome of the Rock was built on the site of the former Jewish temple, destroyed by Rome in A.D. 70. Subsequently a Christian church was there. In Roman times the site of the Umayyad Mosque in Damascus had housed a pagan temple, then a church dedicated to St. John the Baptist. Inside the mosque today is a shrine venerated by Muslims that is believed to contain the head of St. John. Another notable early mosque is that of the Abbasid governor Ibn Tulun (d. 884) in Cairo. It is the best preserved specimen of monumental Abbasid architecture, since hardly a trace remains of the Abbasid era in Baghdad itself due to its conquest by the Mongols. The layout and design of the Ibn

The Court of the Lions, from the Alhambra Palace in Granada, Spain, dates to the thirteenth-fifteenth centuries. This magnificent palace, built by the Nasrid dynasty (1232-1492), is one of the best preserved examples of Muslim palace architecture.

Tulun mosque clearly shows the influence of pre-Islamic Mesopotamian architecture, especially the ziggurat-style minaret reminiscent of ancient Assyrian and Babylonian temple-towers. Later, the Ottomans embellished their capital Istanbul with beautiful mosques whose characteristic domes owe a debt to imperial Byzantine architecture. On a visit to Turkey, one can compare Emperor Justinian's sixth-century cathedral of Hagia Sofia with Sultan Ahmet's

LITERATURE

Tales of the Arabian Nights
Sindbad the Sailor

The tales of the Arabian Nights are of wide ranging appeal as they both preserve the heritage of the Middle East and provide Western cultures with a window to Middle Eastern cultures and customs. This rich body of literature weaves together a colourful tapestry of adventures, characters, and exotic settings while teaching important moral lessons. These tales, which have been handed down for centuries, cover a broad range of themes from whimsical to brutal and from sinister to mysterious and include such famous names as Ali Baba, Aladdin, and Sindbad. For those raised in a Western culture the tales hold a special fascination as they bring to life the sagas of far away lands in which genies replace witches, scimitars replace swords, deserts replace forests and viziers replace knights. According to legend the 1001 tales of the Arabian nights were the product of a queen's desperate attempt to avoid being executed by her vengeful husband who had sworn to take a new wife each day. Scheherazade, a particularly cunning and wise young woman resolved to end the king's bloody tirade by marrying him. After their wedding she began a series of tales, none of which she would complete until the following night; hence the origin of the tales of the 1001 nights.

Among the best loved and best known of these tales are the voyages of Sindbad the Sailor. The following extract is from the first voyage of Sindbad.

In the reign of Caliph Haroun al Raschid there dwelt in Bagdad, a poor porter named Hindbad....One very hot day he was labouring along a strange street, and overcome by fatigue he sat down near a great house to rest. Wondering who lived in so fine a house, he inquired of one of the servants. What, said the man, do you not know that Sindbad the Sailor, the famous circumnavigator of the world lives here? Alas, replied Hindbad...what greater merits does he possess that he should prosper and I starve? Now Sindbad happened to overhear this remark, and anxious to see a man who expressed such strange views he sent for Hindbad...and seating him at his right hand, served him himself, and gave him excellent wine....

...that you may know that my wealth has not been acquired without labour, I recite the history of travels for your benefit....

When still a very young man I inherited a large fortune from my father, and at once set about amusing myself....I soon wearied of the idle, luxurious life I led, and therefore I undertook another voyage. Overtaken by a dreadful tempest in the main ocean, we were driven upon an island which, the captain told us, was inhabited by hairy savages....We advanced into the island on which we were, and came to a palace....We entered the court, where we saw before us a large apartment, with a porch, having on one side a heap of human bones, and on the other a vast number of roasting spits....the gate of the apartment opened with a loud crash, and there came out the horrible figure of a black man, as tall as a lofty palm-tree. He had but one eye, and that in the middle of his forehead, where it looked as red as burning coal. His foreteeth were very long and sharp, and stood out of his mouth, which was as deep as that of a horse. His upper lip hung down upon his breast. His ears resembled those of an elephant, and covered his shoulders; and his nails were as long and crooked as the talons of the greatest birds. At the sight of so frightful a giant, we became insensible, and lay like dead men....After having examined me, and perceiving me to be so lean that I had nothing but skin and bone, he let me go. The captain, being the fattest, he held him with one hand,...and ate him in his apartment for supper.

...the next day, after the giant had gone out, we devised a means of vengeance. And so, when he had again made a supper off one of our number, and lay down to sleep, we prepared to execute the daring design....when we heard him snore, each armed with a spit, the points of which we had made red hot, approached the monster and thrust the spits into his eye at the same time, so that he was blind....

We lost no time in fleeing from the palace, and soon reached the shore, where we contrived to construct some rafts upon which to sail...Day had scarcely dawned, however, when we saw

our enemy coming towards us, led by two others...

We immediately took to our rafts; whereupon the giants... took up great stones, and,... threw so exactly that they sunk all the rafts but that I was upon; and all my companions, except the two with me, were drowned. We rowed with all our might and got out of reach of the giants...

Having thus finished the account of his third voyage, Sindbad sent Hindbad on his way, after he had given him another hundred sequins, and invited him to dinner the next day to hear the continuation of his adventures.

nearby Blue Mosque of 1000 years later.

These examples of Islamic architecture demonstrate the point that Islam was an heir of earlier Middle Eastern traditions, creating out of them a new cultural synthesis. The monuments of Islamic religious architecture today include some of the most famous buildings in the world, including the Great Mosque (now a Catholic cathedral) in Granada, Spain and the Taj Mahal of Agra, India.

The Caravanserai. Along with mosques, another characteristic Middle Eastern building was the **caravanserai**. This building combined the functions of a wholesale market and hotel for visiting merchants. Caravanserais were built in the major cities so that visiting merchants would have a place to stay and to do business. Particular caravanserais often were identified with distinct trades or nationalities, such as the silk caravanserai or the Venetian caravanserai. Characteristically a caravanserai was a two-story structure surrounding a central square or rectangular courtyard. Pack animals and goods would be kept on the ground level, and travelers' quarters were in the upper level. In addition to these urban establishments, modest, rudimentarily-equipped caravanserais were located at intervals of about one day's journey on major trade routes to accommodate merchants, their animals, and their cargos. The medieval equivalent of motels, caravanserais were usually owned by religious endowments who let them out to leaseholders. These leaseholders in turn charged patrons fees for use of the caravanserais. Caravanserais are numerous in the old quarters of many Middle Eastern cities. In countries such as Turkey and Syria caravanserais are being restored and preserved as museums. Others are still in use as warehouses, especially in cities, but most rural caravanserais have fallen into disuse with the spread of motorized transport in the twentieth century.

Urban caravanserais were usually part of a large central market complex, called souk in Arabic and bazaar in Persian and Turkish. The central markets were often covered to provide protection from the elements (anticipating modern malls). Characteristically they were organized according to craft or trade. Different streets of the bazaar would be identified with gold shops, copper shops, spice shops, woodworking shops, and fabric shops. A town's major mosque would usually be located near the central market area as well. In addition to these central markets, smaller neighbourhood markets would be located in residential quarters. Today the bazaars and souks of Istanbul, Tehran, Fez, Cairo, and Aleppo are among the busiest and best known in the Middle East.

Domestic architecture varied from place to place depending on climate and available building materials. Generally speaking houses were oriented inward around a courtyard, in contrast to the European and North American practice of orienting houses outward. One- and two-storey dwellings were arranged around a paved courtyard. This inward orientation allowed extended families to retain their privacy, while at the same time giving them a large pleasant interior domain to go about their daily business. Architectural and artistic embellishments were located inside around the courtyards, rather than outside facing the streets. This pattern prevailed until the twentieth century, giving Middle Eastern domestic architecture a bland and bleak appearance to Western travellers who never went into the houses. The arrangement of houses was such that the head of the household could receive visitors without the visitors violating the privacy of the family quarters.

The majority of houses in any city sheltered the poor, so were built and decorated in rudimentary fashion. But the middle and upper classes went to considerable lengths to embellish their homes and a few examples of these are today restored and open to the public in cities such as Cairo, Damascus, and

Aleppo. The most luxurious houses had elaborate stone and inlay work around their courtyards, decorated ceilings and running fountains in the rooms, and fountains and fruit trees in the open courtyards. Second-storey rooms overlooking the street often had elaborate wood lattice-work on the windows. Apart from promoting good ventilation, this lattice-work permitted people inside, particularly women, to look outside onto the street without themselves being clearly visible.

Painting

The characteristic paintings of the Islamic world are miniatures in illuminated manuscripts. On the face of it, this statement may be surprising. But "in spite of a common misapprehension that Islam prohibits the representation of human figures, figural motifs occur in Islamic painting from the very beginning."[7] The art of manuscript illumination can be traced at least as far back as the Abbasid period, although relatively few examples of these manuscripts survive. Much more numerous are the manuscripts from the post-Mongol period. These were produced as a result of court patronage in Iran and India (where Persian prevailed as the language of literature and learning among Muslim rulers), and in Ottoman Istanbul. The illuminations illustrated epic poems (including the popular *Book of Kings*), historical chronicles and scientific treatises. Subtle but distinctive differences can be seen in the art of miniature decoration in the different regions of the Islamic world. Ottoman-patronized miniatures tended to be simpler and less sophisticated than the elaborate miniatures produced under the auspices of Iranian rulers. By the same token, however, Ottoman painting was more realistic than the dream-like atmosphere evoked by Persian miniatures. Miniatures produced in India under the Persian-speaking Moghul dynasty were similar to, yet distinguished from, Iranian miniatures. "The strong, deep colours, very different in texture from the colours found in Persian [Iranian] paintings, are inherited from the Hindu tradition."[8]

With the exception of the Umayyad period, however, pictorial representation in the Islamic Middle East remained largely confined to manuscript illumination. Religious buildings were decorated by arabesque abstracts and calligraphy. The bias against pictorial representation in Muslim religious art and architecture in favour of abstracts probably explains why a tradition of painting figures on wood or canvas did not develop in the Middle East.

Science and Technology

The accomplishments of the medieval Islamic world in science and technology were considerable. Building on the legacy of Hellenistic and Indian learning, Muslim scientists added to the fund of general human knowledge. The secret of their achievements, apart from having wealthy royal patrons willing to support scientific work, was their use of the scientific method. Generalizations require testing and experimentation before they are accepted, and are always subject to change should new evidence come to light. Rather than blindly accept the conclusions of earlier authorities, no matter how eminent, Muslim scientists tested these conclusions and discarded them if they were found to be unsound. For instance the scientist known to the West as Alhazen, who studied optics in Cairo during the Fatimid period, "refused to accept Euclid and Ptolemy's

---

[7] R. Sandler, "Islamic Art: Variations on Themes of Arabesque" in Introduction to Islamic Civilizations. ed. R. M. Savoury (Cambridge: Cambridge University Press, 1976), p. 98.
[8] Ibid. p. 106.

theory that the eye emits visual rays; instead he advanced the theory that vision is due to the impact of light rays. Experimenting with reflection and optic illusions, he studied refraction through spherical segments filled with water."[9] Algebra, trigonometry, and geometry were invented or developed by Muslim mathematicians. Chemistry (or alchemy, a word of Arabic derivation) was likewise an invention of Muslim scientists. Muslim astronomers made exact measurements of celestial movements, developed astronomical tables and calendars and (inaccurately) estimated the circumference of the earth, which they (accurately) assumed was round. Astronomical tables developed under Il-Khanid patronage in Iran "were long regarded as the most exact of astronomical tables."[10]

Increasing political insecurity in the Islamic world, combined with a decline in its material fortunes after the Mongol conquests, brought original scientific inquiry to an abrupt halt. Muslim rulers were no longer willing or able as before to lavish sums on experimental research with no direct military applications. Therefore, while the sixteenth-century Ottoman Empire kept abreast of the latest developments in military technology, the spirit of scientific inquiry was not encouraged. The body of scientific knowledge inherited from medieval times was preserved, but not its inquisitive spirit. The Muslim scientific legacy was transmitted to Europeans via translations of Arabic scientific treatises from Spain. Islamic/Arabic knowledge remained the standard until the seventeenth century, and it formed an important basis on which European thinkers built the Scientific Revolution whose results soon surpassed the medieval scientific legacy.

Economy

Trade and agriculture were critically important to the maintenance of the high civilization of the Islamic Middle East. The patronage of science, the arts, and architecture on a lavish scale required large sums. Until the European voyages of discovery in the fifteenth and sixteenth centuries, the Middle East was the privileged trade route between the Far East and Europe, and between sub-Saharan Africa and the Mediterranean. This privileged geographic position gave Middle Eastern merchants a valuable role in East-West trade that enriched them and their societies. The late Middle Ages was marked by a partnership between Muslim governments and merchants, on the one hand, and Italian merchants on the other as the Italian city-states including Venice and Genoa dominated the Mediterranean leg of the East-West trade.

In times of security the Middle East's agricultural resources were more than sufficient due to the cultivation of steppe lands and maintenance of irrigation systems. In the aftermath of the Arab conquest of the Fertile Crescent from the Byzantine and Persian empires, "the Muslim conquerors began massive resettlement and reclamation of irrigable land. Immediately following the Arab conquests we hear of the introduction and/or expansion of important food and commercial crops from end to end of the Islamic world. Examples of agricultural diversification were the introduction of citrus crops, probably from India, and sugar cane from [Persian] territories into Egypt."[11]

But a disruption or interruption of trade could lead to impoverishment and throw the Middle East

---

[9]Sydney Nettleton Fisher and William Ochsenwald, *The Middle East: A History* 4th ed. (New York: McGraw-Hill, 1990), p. 105.
[10]*Ibid*, p. 104.

[11]Gladys Frantz-Murphy, "Teaching Pre-Modern Middle Eastern History" in *The World History Bulletin* (Philadelphia: World History Association Drexel University, Spring/Summer Edition 1990), p. 28.

back onto its own agricultural resources. In times of insecurity, the steppe lands reverted to pasture and irrigation systems were destroyed or allowed to deteriorate. Subsistence agriculture left little surplus for urban ruling circles to appropriate. Therefore the prosperity of the Middle East was fragile. The Mongol invasion of 1258 climaxed a period of increasing insecurity, which dealt a major blow to the region's agriculture. The opening of the sea route between the Atlantic and Indian Oceans by Portuguese sailors marked the beginning of the end of the Middle East's trading monopoly between West and East. Both Middle Eastern and Italian merchants found themselves operating in what was increasingly a commercial backwater in global economic terms. In this context it is not surprising that the Islamic Middle East, as well as Italy, declined in relation to the seafaring countries of Western Europe in the early modern period.

Although luxury trade criss-crossed the medieval Middle East, these lands were not an integrated market any more than medieval Europe was. Transport costs were too high to allow regional specialization in staples and essentials. Each region within the Middle East usually had to produce its own food, cloth, and tools. Peasants, townspeople, pastoral nomads were linked together in regional economies centred around major towns and cities. An example of a regional economy is offered by Damascus in Syria. Located on the edge of the desert, the oasis of Damascus is vast. The city's hinterland embraced over 100 villages, from which it obtained food plus raw materials for its craft industries. The products of these industries were in turn sold to the villagers. Pastoral nomads for their part traded wool and dairy products to townspeople and peasants for manufactured goods and food, respectively. Merchants based in Damascus often acted as go-betweens in these transactions, and they organized long-distance trade in luxury items as well. This pattern of interrelationships between peasants, townspeople, and pastoralists was duplicated across the Middle East wherever large towns and cities were found.

Islam Today

Islam today is the world's second-largest religion (after Christianity), and the fastest-growing one. This growth is due not only to population increases in countries with Muslim majorities (extending in an arc from west Africa to southeast Asia), but also to continuing conversions as well. The basic Islamic message is very simple: there is one God and Muhammad is His messenger. Moreover, the high culture of Islam, developed in the Middle East through the medium of Arabic, Persian, and Turkish, is a source of inspiration and pride for Muslims, whether born into the faith or converted to it. The high-cultural legacy of the Islamic Middle East is a powerful cultural tool for Third World peoples seeking to establish independence of, and equality with, the West that has dominated them for the last 400 years.

This is particularly true of the Middle East, where political nationalism has taken root in the last century. Arab, Persian, and Turkish cultural consciousness has acquired political significance. Arab, Iranian, and Turkish nationalists, as well as other predominantly Muslim Middle Eastern peoples such as the Kurds, have sought to construct national identities based on shared language, history, territory, and culture. The historical memory of the Islamic Middle East has been an important factor in the ideologies of nationalism. For nationalists, this historical memory is mainly cultural and linguistic. For Islamic revivalists, the religious significance of history is uppermost. Nationalists and revivalists alike look to the history of the Islamic Middle East for lessons, inspiration, and guidance as they confront the many challenges facing Muslim peoples on the eve of the twenty-first century. Events of a millennium ago are still on people's minds today.

Suggested Sources for Further Research

Ahsan, Muhammad Manazir, *Social Life under the Abbasids* (Longman, 1979).

al-Faruqi, Isma'il R. and Lois al-Faruqi, *The Cultural Atlas of Islam* (Macmillan, 1986).

al-Hasan, Ahmad Y. and Donald R. Hill, *Islamic Technology: An Illustrated History* (Cambridge University Press, 1986).

Arberry, A.J., *Sufism: An Account of the Mystics of Islam* (Harper and Row, 1970).

Denny, Frederick M., *An Introduction to Islam* (Macmillan, 1985).

Johnson-Odim, Cheryl and Margaret Strobel (ed), *Restoring Women to History: Middle East*. (Organization of American Historians, 1988).

Kennedy, Hugh, *The Prophet and the Age of the Caliphates: The Islamic Near East from the Sixth to the Eleventh Century* (Longman, 1986).

Khatibi, Abdelkebir and Mohammed Sijelmassi, *The Splendor of Islamic Calligraphy* (Thames and Hudson, 1976).

Nettleton Fisher, Sydney and William Ochsenwald, *The Middle East: A History* (McGraw-Hill, 1990).

Sandler, R., "Islamic Art: Variations on Themes of Arabesque," *Introduction to Islamic Civilization*, R.M. Savory (ed) (Cambridge University Press, 1976).

Watson, Andrew M., *Agricultural Innovation in the Early Islamic World: The Diffusion of Crops and Farming Techniques* (Cambridge University Press, 1988).

Wickens, G.M. "What the West Borrowed from the Middle East," *Introduction to Islamic Civilization*, R.M. Savory (ed.) (Cambridge University Press, 1976).

Focus Your Knowledge

1. What do the terms Islam and Muslim mean?
2. Prepare an organizer which clearly shows the similarities and differences between the Islamic faith and Christianity.

3. What are the five basic demands of Islam? How do the Shi'i beliefs differ from the Sunni beliefs?

4. Explain the decline of the Abbasid caliphate with reference to the impact of the Mongol invasions.

5. Describe the nature and importance of the major Islamic customs and festivals.

6. How were Islamic scientists able to further develop ideas expounded by the Greeks?

Apply Your Knowledge
▼▼▼

1. The Islamic Middle East is comprised of a diversity of cultures living in a wide variety of environments. Assess the impact of the environment on the various societies, including both the pastoralists and the city dwellers.

2. How did the Sufi mystics popularize and contribute to the spread of Islam? Can you think of any other examples from the past or present whereby populist appeal has assisted the spread of religion?

3. The Abbasid caliphate is considered the Golden Age of the Islamic Empire. What evidence is there to support such a view?

4. For both the Islamic world and Christian Europe the Crusades were to have profound effects. Assess the impact of the spread of Islam on the Europeans' decision to launch a holy war. How did the Muslims view the invading Christians? What impact did the Crusades have on Islamic history?

5. Account for the power and resilience of the Ottoman Empire.

6. Explain the apparent contradictions in the role and status of women in Islamic societies. On the whole, which of these two sides seems to have prevailed?

7. Throughout the chapter several references to the importance of the geographic location of the Middle East have been made. The cultural, economic, and social vitality of the Middle East owes much to its favoured location. Explain this statement with specific references to trade, architecture, science, and technology and other cross-cultural influences.

Extension Activities

1. Using the descriptions and floor plan from this chapter as well as further research build a model mosque, caravanserai, or piece of domestic architecture.

2. Select a position in Islamic society. Research clothing, social status, and daily life for your character. Choose from the following: a caliph, a sufi mystic, an Islamic warrior, a scientist or astronomer, a wealthy merchant, a servant, a beggar, a prominent woman, or a wife of any of the above. This research could be used as the basis for the class to stage A Day in Islamic Society.

3. Based on the reading of one of the works listed in the section on Islamic literature prepare a report or a visual display.

4. Based on further research into the scientific advances made by Islamic scientists recreate an experiment they may have carried out. As an alternative you may wish to prepare a map of the heavens or the earth based on the beliefs of the times. These projects could be added to the Day in Islamic Society.

5. Using the examples of Arabic calligraphy found in the book as a guide prepare an illuminated invitation for honoured guests to attend a special event such as the Day in Islamic Society.

CHAPTER 11

Japan: Land of the Rising Sun

Chapter Highlights

- *Tale of Genji* the world's first novel

- the sharpest swords in world history

- Nara, site of the oldest wooden buildings in the world

- writing haiku poetry

- *Bushido*—The Way of the Warrior

- the ''tea ceremony''

The Japanese people have always considered themselves uniquely blessed. According to legend, the gods or kami (pronounced kah-mee), who created their land had many children. These children became the rivers and mountains, the lakes, waterfalls, and boulders, the tiny islands, and the massive trees among whom they would spend their lives. Thus, from the earliest times, they spent their days surrounded by objects of worship. Over the centuries, they built shrines around them and at each one, they marked the space for the gods by erecting a red gate called a tori-i. Today, there are hundreds of thousands of these shrines in Japan and the people worship at these holy places just as they have done from time immemorial. Their land is known as the Land of the Divine!

The Japanese call their country Nihon (pronounced nee-hawn), which means Land of the Rising Sun. Their civilization is not particularly ancient, but it is distinctive from all the others in Asia. To this day, no one knows whether or not the Japanese have a single, distinct origin. No one knows the source of the Japanese language. No one can explain the root of such Japanese customs as the daily bath, the use of straw mats for beds, and rice paper for windows. No one can account for the exquisite courtesy that marks everyday human relations. Westerners have always seen East Asia as exotic, but from the time of the earliest explorers, Japan has been the "most exotic of the exotic."

No one would disagree that certain features of their civilization seem to make the Japanese unique. They are among the most homogeneous of peoples. Their country was never successfully invaded and never conquered, until their defeat in the Second World War. Therefore, unlike other island-nations such as England, and unlike entire continents like the Americas, Japan and its people were isolated from the rest of the world for much of their history and were never forced to mingle their blood or their customs with outsiders until very recent times.

The Japanese claim the longest unbroken line of rulers in human history. The present emperor, Akihito (pronounced ah-kee-hee-toh), is numbered as 125th in a line which originated with the Goddess of the Sun and extends from her descendent, Jimmu the first emperor, in 660 B.C., until the present day. Most scholars believe that Jimmu was a legendary figure and that the first genuine emperors did not appear until about a thousand years later, but the fact remains that throughout Japanese history only one family has ever occupied the Chrysanthemum Throne.

Key Concepts

Sun-line

Shinto

Heian

Tale of Genji

Minamoto Yorimoto

shogun

samurai

zazen/Zen

Bushido Code

Tomoe

ikebana

haiku

St. Francis Xavier

daiymo

Christian Century

Geography

Japan consists of more than 400 islands, but only the four largest are of historical importance. These are, from north to south, Hokkaido, Honshu (where one finds the major centres of population like Tokyo, Osaka, Nagoya, and Kyoto), Shikoku, and Kyushu. The islands were formed originally by violent volcanic activity on the sea bottom and Japan, as a result, is a mountainous land with numerous small rivers flowing directly to the sea.

In total land-area, Japan is approximately 380 000 km² (smaller than the size of Baffin Island), though today it supports a population of 125 million, about five times that of Canada. Only about one-fifth of the land is level enough to be cultivated, and as a result, Japanese agriculture is among the most intensive in the world. Japan has few natural resources and must import almost all of its energy requirements like oil, most of its minerals, and a good deal of its food.

At the same time, Japan's major islands have a temperate climate and abundant rainfall, with several climatic zones. If they were imposed latitudinally on the eastern coast of North America, their northernmost point would touch Montreal and their southernmost point would touch New Orleans. Located in the sea, the Japanese islands have few extremes of temperature and they have access to abundant fish and to a wide range of vegetable crops. This gives them one of the world's healthiest diets and the life span of the average Japanese is today the highest in the world. The climate is not only conducive to an energetic way of life but produces a variety of trees and flowers which makes Japan a land of astonishing natural beauty. The love of nature is a central feature of Japanese civilization.

Finally, the Japanese islands lie at the extreme edge of the Eurasian land mass and are, at their closest point, about 240 km from the Asian continent. People can swim the English Channel, but no one has ever been able to swim across the Sea of Japan. Ships which attempted the crossing, particularly before the invention of the compass, found it to be a dangerous and difficult undertaking, and shipwrecks cost many lives. The meaning of this simple geographical fact is that although Japan was deeply influenced by Chinese and Korean civilization, the historical interaction was sometimes close but never continuous. Japan was able to borrow from these higher civilizations but was always able to adapt the borrowings to its own needs in a distinctive way.

Japanese History

The history of Japan is divided into several periods:

The Formative Period (Jomon, Yayoi and the Yamato State)—ca. 10 000 B.C.–A.D. 710
The Nara Period—A.D. 710–794
The Heian Period—A.D. 794–1185
The Kamakura Shogunate—A.D. 1185–1333
The Ashikaga (Muromachi) Shogunate—A.D. 1336–1573
The Tokugawa Shogunate—A.D. 1600–1867

In 1867, and largely as a result of foreign influence, the Japanese shoguns were driven from power, and control of the government was restored to the emperors. Japan's modern era therefore begins at the same time as does that of Canada. The four emperors who have ruled Japan since 1867 have chosen to name the periods of their own rule, selecting names which indicate the goals for their reigns. These periods are therefore called:

Meiji (pronounced may-jee) or Enlightened Government—1867–1912

Taisho (pronounced tie-show) or Great Righteousness—1912–1926

Showa (pronounced show-wah) or Manifest Harmony—1926–1989

Heisei (pronounced hay-say) or Achieving Peace—1989 onwards.

The Growth of the Empire

The Formative Age

During the last ice age, which ended about 11 000 years ago, the Japanese islands were joined to the Asian mainland by a land bridge. Across this bridge came peoples from Korea and northeast Asia, and since Japan was geographically the end of the line, they settled there permanently. The earliest archaeological remains in Japan, consisting mostly of pottery, date from about 9500 years ago.

Over time, the first settlers were joined by peoples from South China or perhaps even from some of the Polynesian Islands, and in the space of thousands of years, they all blended together, creating a distinct culture, called the Jomon. This culture endured until about 300 B.C.

During this same period, another people came to Japan's northernmost island of Hokkaido. They were called the Ainu, and their racial characteristics were **Caucasoid** rather than **Mongoloid**: tall stature, fair skin, and facial hair. For many centuries they remained distinct from the rest of the Japanese, but today their ranks have been thinned to less than 20 000 through intermarriage, and they are on the point of disappearance. Their origin will always be a mystery. The Japanese are therefore a people of mixed origin, but for most of their history, they have ignored this fact. They have instead emphasized their mythological beginnings, their divine descent,

MAJOR EVENTS IN THE HISTORY OF JAPAN

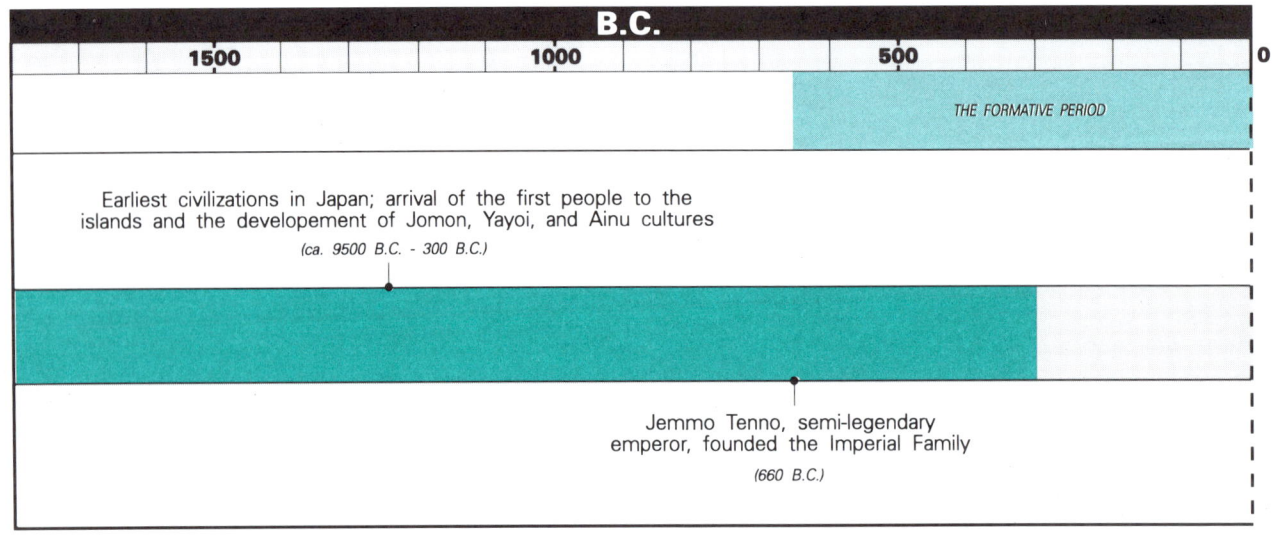

and their special place in the world.

Their earliest work of history is called the *Kojiki* (Record of Ancient Matters) and it was completed in A.D. 712. It relates the legend that Japan was created when two deities, male and female, stirred up the sea with a "heavenly lance" and created the many islands of Japan. The children of these deities became the gods or *kami* mentioned earlier, and their eldest daughter, Amaterasu (pronounced ah-mah teh-rah-soo) became the Goddess of the Sun. Because her great-great grandson, Jimmu, became the first emperor, the Japanese historically saw themselves as a people whose rulers were descended from a goddess. They also saw themselves as a single, unmixed people forever under her protection and guidance.

The Earliest Civilizations

The first culture to develop in Japan, the Jomon, was composed of people who were basically hunters, fishers, and gatherers. They took their name from a particular type of pottery which was decorated by pressing rope into wet clay, and which later came to include human figures with huge eyes which some scholars regard as an attempt to depict "windows to the soul." The female figures are usually larger than the male, and this may indicate some form of female dominance in society. In any case, the first Chinese accounts of Japan call it a Queen's Country.

Around the beginnings of the third century B.C., Jomon culture began to blend with that of a new people called the Yayoi who brought to Japan a knowledge of irrigated rice cultivation, bronze and iron, glass, and mirrors. Most scholars believe that the Yayoi culture came to Japan from Korea, and when China conquered the Korean peninsula in 108 B.C., Korea became a bridge civilization joining China and Japan.

About A.D. 300, the Japanese islands began to join together to form a distinctive state. The Japanese at this time still had no written language and historians are forced to rely on archaeological evidence and on Chinese accounts to gain knowledge of this early period.

The first Chinese account of Japan dates from

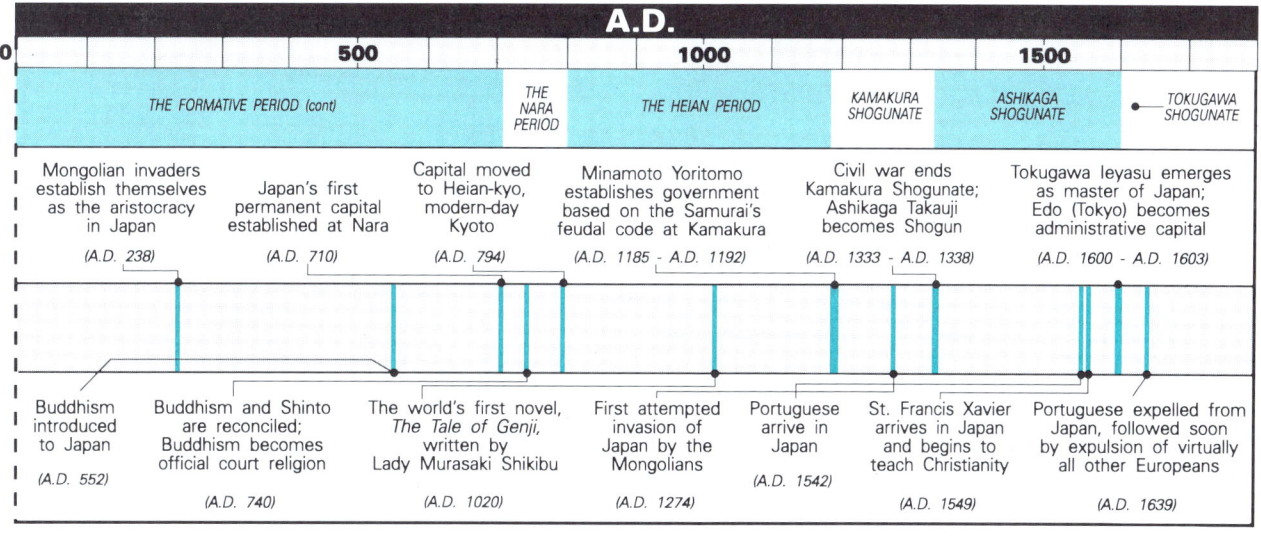

Japan: Land of the Rising Sun CHAPTER 11 339

A.D. 297 and tells of a land where the people went barefoot and ate raw vegetables. The most intriguing part of the Chinese account, however, concerns Japanese politics. Japan was ruled not by a king, but by a queen. For some 70 or 80 years, says the account, male rule had led to wars and disturbances, so that the people chose a woman called Pimiko as their ruler. She is said to have bewitched her people, to have lived in a great fortified palace with 1000 women and only one man as servants, and to have had a prosperous rule. On her death, the succession passed to a male, but more violence followed, and as a result, the people chose a female relative of Pimiko to rule them.

Japanese historians have always been skeptical of this account since the idea of female rule has been uncomfortable for them. However, early in 1990, archaeologists discovered what seems to have been the fortress of Pimiko at a small town called Yoshino-gari in western Japan.

Beliefs and Rulers

Archaeology has also revealed a great deal about other aspects of life in early Japan. The royal tombs, great mounds laid out in the shape of keyholes, contain artifacts which suggest that in the Yamato period, the Japanese were a warlike people who fought on horseback. These tombs are often surrounded by clay-baked figures, called baniwa, which show the clothing, armour, and other paraphernalia of daily life in the period. Interestingly, the baniwa do not suggest that death is a sad thing. Some of them seem to be dancing and singing, others are drinking sake, and still others seem to be contentedly tending their fields.

In the Yamato period, there were two other developments of great importance. The first of these was the rise of the Yamato clan or the **Sun-line** to political primacy. The second was the development of **Shinto** as Japan's native religion.

Early Japan was an aristocratic society. Each region was dominated by a certain family, called an uji, which worshipped a particular kami as their ancestor. Each owned a number of peasant retainers and slaves who farmed its land. In the warlike climate of the early Yamato period, and in a process which is not yet entirely understood, one of these clans was able to assert its supremacy over all the others by diplomacy, marriage relationships, and above all, by establishing the fact that its ancestor, the Sun Goddess, was the greatest of all deities. This was the origin of the imperial Sun-line of Japan which still rules today. The spiritual and temporal power of the Sun-line arose out of the second major development of the formative period, the coalescence of diverse religious beliefs into Japan's native religion called Shinto.

Shinto means the "Way of the Deities," and is a unique Japanese blend of earlier cults of animism, shamanism, fertility rites, and nature worship. The deities of Shinto are called kami, not gods in the Western sense. They are simply objects or personalities that are more highly-placed or which inspire awe. Kami could be mountains or lakes, caves or boulders, mythological figures, clan ancestors, and the emperor, even while he was still alive. The kami were responsible for the good and bad fortune of human beings, but there was no guarantee that they would answer human prayers. People could only placate the kami by offerings of rice, cloth, cakes, and horses and after they had done so, could do no more than hope for the best. In the Yamato period, the Sun Goddess, probably because of her influence on agriculture, came to be seen as the greatest of the kami. Her descendants therefore became the most important clan on earth. It is important to note that the Sun Goddess was never depicted in art, nor were images made of her. Shinto shrines are empty and the presence of the deity is made more awesome by

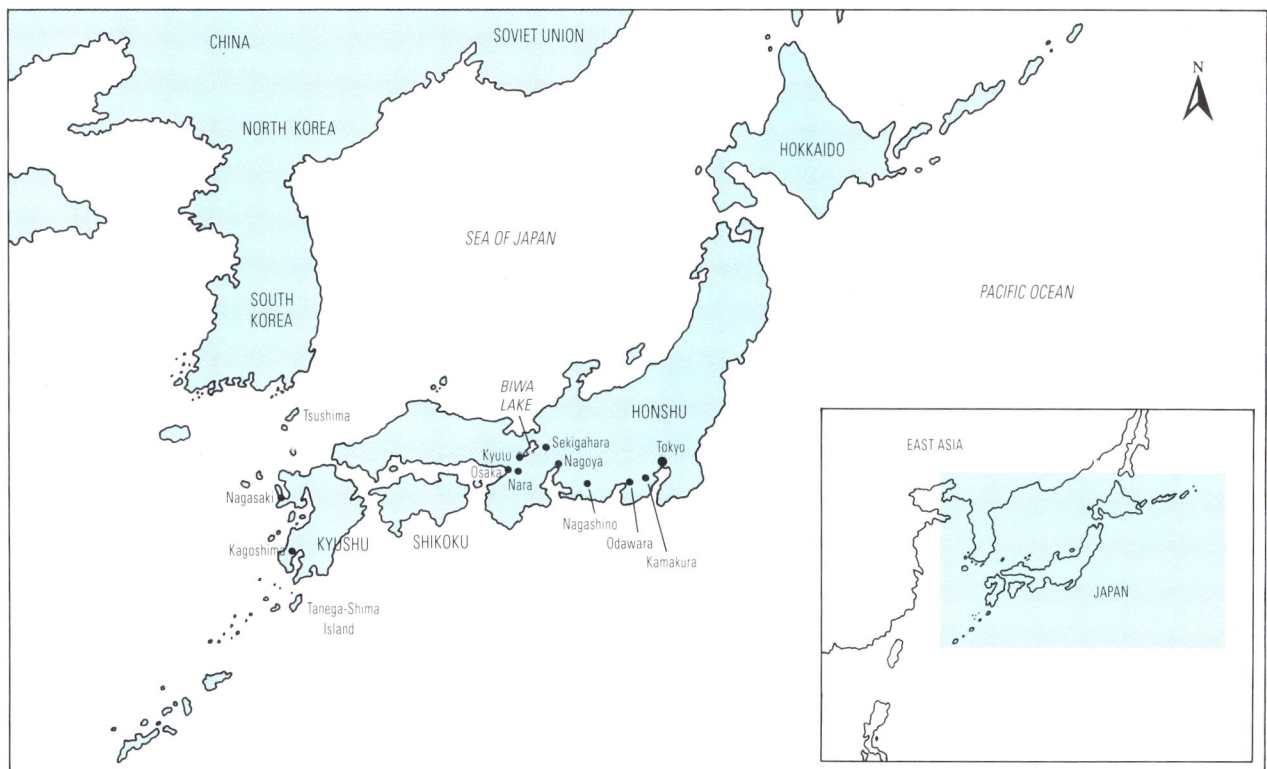

Japan

that very emptiness.

If the kami became unhappy, human beings suffered curses or pollution (tsumi). Pollution occurred for any number of reasons: wounding or being wounded, sickness, incest, snakebite, or any occurrence involving blood. Because human beings therefore had no real control over their fate, Shinto is called a pre-moral religion. Good actions did not result in reward, and bad actions were not necessarily punished. Pollution was cured by a period of isolation accompanied by purifying rituals, which usually involved water. This may be the origin of the daily bath in Japan today.

Early Shinto ideas about death and the afterlife are difficult to know, because it was also a preliterate religion with no written scriptures or laws. At death, it seems that everyone, regardless of his or her moral conduct, went to the same place: a gloomy and shadowy underworld called yomi. There, one lived on, in very much the same state as on earth, except that the body decayed and was eaten by worms. Shinto offered no comfort or consolation in regard to death, and no promise of paradise for those who had lived good lives. It might therefore be called a life-affirming religion, since it urged people to enjoy this world, and to make the best of present existence. Shinto encouraged joy, but its failure to promise any happiness after death meant that when Buddhism came to Japan and offered the consolation of salvation, it rapidly made many converts.

Shinto, however, could never disappear. Its greatest strength, its love, respect, and veneration of

The Horyuji Temple at Nara was founded by Prince Shotoku in A.D. 607. It has remained virtually unchanged throughout the centuries and today is the oldest wooden building in the world.

nature in a country of great natural beauty, could not be challenged. Where else would people erect a shrine to a single wave, a perfect maple tree, or to an entire island, like Miyajima near Hiroshima, simply because their beauty stunned the senses?

In time, all the natural beauty-spots of Japan became shrines. Each one had its own festival, and pilgrims flocked to each holy place in a steady stream. Worship was the same everywhere: believers first rinsed their hands and mouths for purification; clapped their hands to let the kami know of their presence, said a silent prayer, and then made an offering, usually of money. Major shrines had priests and priestesses who carried out rituals of prayer, song, and dance on special occasions. The great shrine at Ise (pronounced ee-seh) dedicated to the Goddess of the Sun, became the holiest such site in Japan, and even today is a popular place of pilgrimage.

During the late Yamato period, which begins with the introduction of Buddhism in A.D. 552, Shinto suffered a temporary eclipse. Some of its beliefs blended with those of the Buddhists, and it did not re-emerge as a distinct faith until the eighteenth and nineteenth centuries when patriotic scholars portrayed it as the deepest expression of the Japanese soul. Its contention of the divine descent of Japanese rulers and of the special favour bestowed by the Sun Goddess upon all Japanese, led to claims of superiority over the rest of the world. The revival of Shinto therefore played a large part in Japanese imperialism in the twentieth century and in Japan's entry into the Second World War.

The Late Yamato and Nara Periods

The year 552, which saw the introduction of Buddhism, is one of the most important dates in Japanese history. Prior to that time, Japan was a primitive civilization. It possessed no unified identity, no system of writing, no distinct forms of artistic expression, no law code, and nothing but the most rudimentary forms of political control. There was no capital city. Individual clan loyalties were strong, and although most Japanese accepted the need for societal hierarchy and for hereditary authority in politics, there still remained a good deal of opposition to the growing authority of the Sun-line.

Even before 552, a few Japanese were becoming aware of the continental civilization of China and Korea. Some had learned to write in Chinese and others had even begun to study the Confucian classics. In 552, however, the king of Paekche, one of the three Korean kingdoms of the period, sent to Japan a gift of some Buddhist images and scriptures. This event marks the formal introduction of a new religion to Japan, and it threw the Japanese ruling class into turmoil. The Sun-line and their chief ally, the Soga clan, immediately championed the new faith and made the Buddha the chief kami of the Soga clan. Their more conservative enemies rejected the Buddha, but when the Soga defeated all their rivals in war, the power of the new kami was proven. Cleverly asserting that only the Sun Goddess was superior to the Buddha, the Soga family then forged tight marriage alliances with the Sun-line and set out to reform Japan.

The architect of Japan's transformation was a man known as Prince Shotoku (574–622), whose face still appears on Japan's most common banknote. He never became emperor, but ruled as regent for his aunt, the Empress Suiko (pronounced soo-ee-koh), who probably played a role as great as his own in the reforms. Under Suiko and Shotoku, Chinese culture was imported with astonishing enthusiasm and swept in a great wave across the land.

Numerous seaborne missions, sometimes as large as 500 persons, braved the dangerous crossing to China. Some Japanese remained for up to 30 years studying in China, but others returned swiftly with knowledge of Chinese science and technology, Chinese books and writing, Chinese clothing and customs, and above all, Chinese methods of government. In 604, Shotoku proclaimed his famous Constitution of 17 articles, which offered no specific laws or details of a new governmental structure, but proclaimed instead Japan's commitment to such Chinese ideas as a single supreme ruler, a civil service chosen by merit, centralized government, and a role both for Confucianism and Buddhism in Japanese state and society.

Shotoku died in 622, but not before achieving many other things, among which was the foundation of the exquisite Horyuji Temple near Nara—the oldest remaining wooden building in the world. A power struggle followed his death, but the reformers retained the upper hand and from 645, embarked on a second wave of reform called the Taika or the Great Change. Over the next few decades, the supreme authority of the emperor or tenno was universally acknowledged, private land-holding was abolished, and central authority was extended to the provinces. The first census was undertaken and Chinese systems of taxation and law were introduced. Court ranks were reorganized, schools were founded, more Buddhist temples were set up, and finally, these and other reforms were made law in the Taiho Code of 702. Several of the reforms existed more on paper than in reality, but they provided Japan with the foundations for its future rapid development.

In 710, Empress Gemmyo established Japan's first city, which was also its first permanent capital. Prior to this time, the capital had consisted of little more than a palace which was moved on each ruler's death to avoid lingering pollution. Now a whole new city called Nara (pronounced nah-rah), was constructed and was laid out as an exact, small-scale replica of the Chinese capital. Its streets and avenues formed a rectangular checkerboard and the palace was in the north. Numerous Buddhist temples and Shinto shrines, markets, and parks all imitated Chinese styles, and today, the only remaining examples of eighth-century Chinese architecture are to be found in Nara rather than in China. This is because the

Japanese always reconstructed exact replicas of buildings when they were burned or otherwise destroyed.

Nara was not a fortunate capital. The Chinese and Korean immigrants who flocked to the new city brought with them smallpox and measles to which the Japanese had no immunity. From 735 onward, successive epidemics spread out from Nara and killed perhaps 30% of the entire Japanese population. Fires often swept through large quarters of the city, razing the wooden buildings and causing great loss of life. The fragile tax base could not support reconstruction, and increasingly, could not even pay for the basic services of the city. Arrogant and unruly monks interfered in politics, and even though this period saw such cultural achievements as Japan's first literary works—the *Kojiki* and a collection of 4500 poems called the *Manyoshu*—life in Nara remained unstable.

One important reason for this was that throughout the Nara period, the Buddhist establishment was becoming even more wealthy and powerful. Devout emperors and empresses decreed that Buddhist monasteries, nunneries, and pagodas be set up in every province. They levied heavy taxes on the people to construct such images as the great 16 m statue of the Buddha at the Todaiji temple which used a reputed million pounds of metal! The Buddhists also built for themselves a fabulous treasure house, the famous Shosoin (pronounced show-soh-een), which contained a collection of over 10 000 objects from the eighth-century world: books and textiles; exquisite objects of gold, lacquer, and pearl; weapons; screens; glass; and fine jewelry from such far-off places as Persia, India, Greece, Rome, and other outposts of the Silk Route. A curious accident of construction somehow provided this wooden building with climate control, and the collection can be seen there today in a perfect state of preservation.

Buddhism, finally, provided the catalyst which brought the Nara period to a close. The formidable Empress Koken, it is said, fell in love with a Buddhist monk. She abdicated the throne in 758 to be with him, but became unhappy with her successor and in 764, changed her name to Shotoku and again made herself empress. As she gave the monk more and more power and ever-higher titles, the court nobles and high officials feared that she might make him emperor and thus break the sacred line of Sun-line descent. However, she died before realizing her plans, and the monk was immediately banished. Because of this incident, no woman would again rule Japan until the seventeenth century. The new emperor, moreover, determined that he could no longer remain in a city where Buddhist clerics could become such a threat.

The court left Nara, and for the next decade, resided in temporary quarters until deciding to build a new capital. In 794, they designated a new site called Heian-kyo (pronounced hey-on-kyoh), or City of Peace, and began once more to construct a model of the Chinese capital. The city of Heian-kyo is known today as Kyoto, and was the capital of Japan from 794 until 1868.

The Heian Period

The **Heian** period and its aristocratic lifestyle is probably the most fascinating era in Japanese history. Scholars are generally agreed that it did little or nothing to advance the social, intellectual, or political history of Japan, but that it produced a glittering and elegant culture, and it defined the various emotions and aesthetic ideals which would leave a permanent imprint on Japan and its people.

Heian culture was initially an eclectic one. In 894, the Japanese court took the decision to ignore their former teacher, China, and for the rest of the period, sent no further missions. Instead, they integrated into their own civilization the ancient myths, folklore, and philosophy of China. They adopted its rich heritage of religion, literature, and historical writing, along with its most up-to-date techniques in architecture, textiles, ceramics, and engineering. To each of these borrowings they gave a distinctive twist, and once they had severed the continental contact, they developed all the things they had learned with an ever-greater degree of independence. By the end of the Heian period, Japan's resemblance to China was no more than superficial.

The population of Japan at this time was about 5 million people, and of these about 100 000 lived in the capital. The city of Heian-kyo (Kyoto) was thus as large or larger than any contemporary European city and was laid out as a perfect rectangle about 4 by 5.5 km in area. It was surrounded by a low 1.8 m wall and there were 16 majestic gates for entry and exit. The wide streets ran from north to south, and the tree-lined avenues, running east to west, were often 45 m wide. The city was surrounded by hills on three sides, hundreds of Buddhist temples and Shinto shrines were built, most of them in the northeast, to protect the city from evil spirits who always came from that direction. Rivers and canals criss-crossed the city, and the fragrance of plum and cherry blossom permeated the air. It made a charming capital, and by international agreement, it was the only major urban centre in Japan to be spared the bombs of World War II. It remains today as perhaps the most beautiful of all Japan's cities.

The emperors who ruled from this capital are not well-known, since throughout the period, they had little influence on policy and their power tended to become weaker and weaker. There are three principal reasons for this. First, their duties became increasingly remote from politics, as they found themselves the head of two religions, forced to preside over a dizzying round of both Buddhist and Shinto ceremonies. The rituals themselves and the purifications before and afterwards took up several days each month. Second, they were expected to be the cultural leaders of the country. Not only were they forced to spend endless hours practicing Chinese poetry, calligraphy, and painting, but frequently they had to sponsor such peculiarly Japanese festivals as poetic debates on which was the most beautiful of the four seasons, or the seasonal viewing of the flowers in the palace gardens. Many emperors became so exhausted by this routine that they retired to a quieter life in monasteries, even while they were still in their teens or twenties!

Finally, the emperors of the period were almost all dominated by their wives, and all of their wives came from one or another branch of a single aristocratic clan, called the Fujiwara (pronounced foo-jee-wah-rah). As the predominant clan of the country, second only to the Sun-line, they had early asserted their right to provide royal brides, often marrying their mature daughters to boys who had not yet reached their teens. Because the emperors were so young, the fathers or uncles of these empresses then created new offices for themselves—Regents and Chancellors—and issued their own orders in the name of the young emperor. Whenever an emperor showed signs of independence, he was encouraged to abdicate, and the cycle began anew. Sometimes an emperor who had been forced to retire to a monastery formed a cloistered government and issued his own decrees. Thus, during the Heian period, government policies originated from at least three or four sources, and since no one knew which ones to obey, politics became little more than an irrelevant annoyance to the courtiers and aristocrats in the capital. In the provinces, however, the lack of direction was to have severe consequences.

Whatever power there was rested with the Fujiwara. They were a clan typical of many great families which had gradually evolved over the preceding centuries. They had initially risen to power through a combination of military strength and the possession of large tracts of land, and had used these to secure for themselves court rank and

INNOVATIONS

JAPANESE WRITING

One reason the Japanese language is considered to be the most difficult in the world is that the same thing may be written in three different ways. Shown here is the term *"Genji Monoqatari,"* or *The Tale of Genji* written in all three ways. On the left, the title of this book is written in kanji or Chinese characters, which was the form that Japanese males of the Heian period were forced to write. It was very difficult to learn and unsuitable for the expression of the Japanese language. Today, the Japanese still use about 1200 kanji in their everyday publications, and all students are expected to memorize them. The middle example gives the same book title in a native Japanese alphabet called hiragana, a graceful, cursive script used by the women of the Heian period. It has become the most common way of writing Japanese today. This efficient alphabet has 50 sounds based on the "a-e-i-o-u" vowel system. Thus, the alphabet begins with the "a" sounds in the following form—"a-ka-sa-ta-na-ha-ma-ya-ra-wa" and follows this with the "e" "i" "o" "u" sounds in the same order. The same order is repeated for the other vowels. The third sample is called katakana, and is used to express the many foreign words which are part of the daily vocabulary used in Japan today. The Japanese would use this katakana alphabet, instead of hiragana, on envelopes used to send a letter to "Ka-na-da", or even if they were making a reservation at a "ho-te-ru" (hotel).

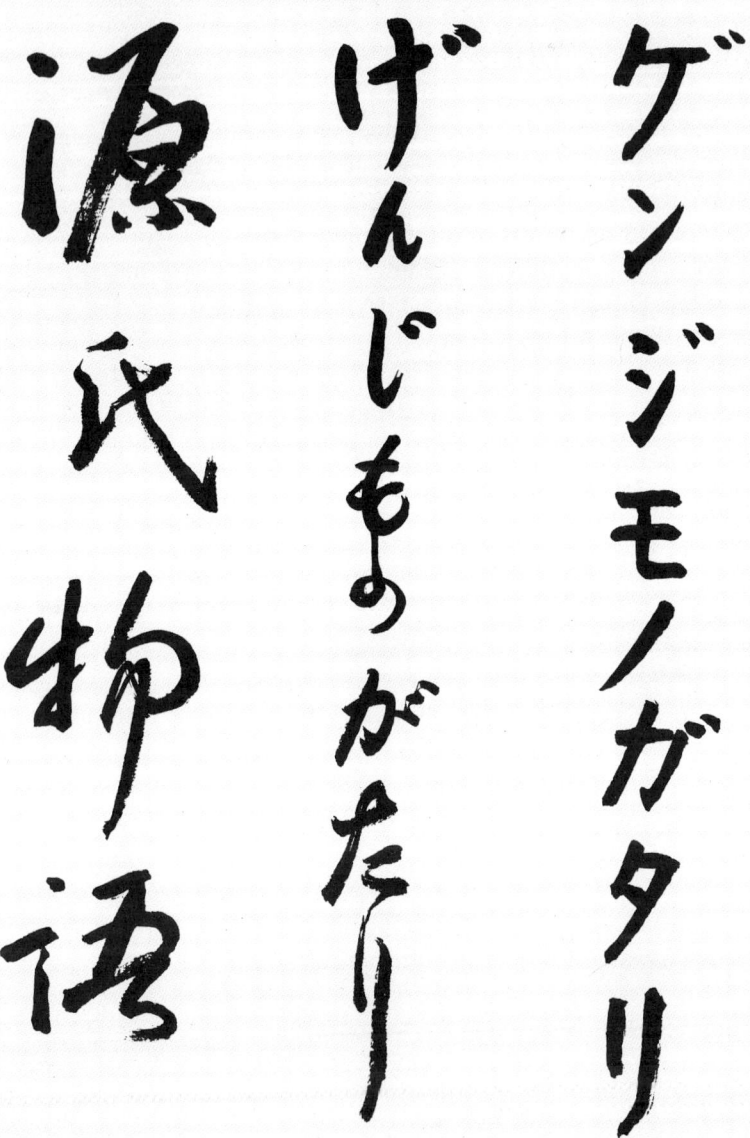

titles. By the Heian period, any clan which had rank and title had come to be included in the kuge (pronounced koo-geh), or aristocracy. The kuge was a totally closed class. Its members married only other kuge, monopolized all government posts, and supported themselves by official salaries and revenues from their provincial estates. They made up less than 1 percent of Japan's total population, and without exception, lived in the lofty isolation of the capital. The very thought of venturing outside its walls filled them with horror, and their lives became increasingly remote from those of the common people. Some scholars refer to them as "Dwellers Among the Clouds."

Daily Life in Heian-kyo

The capital aristocrats lived in a world of their own, insulated from strife, and largely free from worry of any kind. Both economically and politically, they felt secure, and the occasional quarrels or peasant uprisings in the provinces scarcely touched their consciousness. They devoted their time to leisure and to play; to such things as gossip, poetry, religion, and the gentle art of cultivating beauty in all its forms.

Our picture of life in the capital is derived from the voluminous literature remaining from the period; literature produced mostly by women. All the aristocratic males of the period engaged in a constant struggle to master classical Chinese, the only language of respectable literature. Few of them ever succeeded. Since Chinese was unsuitable for the expression of both the grammar and the nuances of Japanese, the results were stilted, artificial, and unclear. Women, on the other hand, were free to write in kana (pronounced kah-nah), a phonetic alphabet developed by the Japanese for the expression of their own language. The aristocratic women of Heian Japan wrote a good deal, and today we possess their poems, diaries, and pillow books: a form of literature in which they recorded at night their observations about the day's experiences. It was one of these literate women, Lady Murasaki Shikibu (pronounced moo-rah-sah-kee shee-kee-boo), who became the author of the world's first novel.

This brilliant work, called the **Tale of Genji**, or the *Tale of the Shining Prince*, was written over the space of twenty years (1000–1020). In over 50 chapters, filled with profound psychological insight and lively dialogue, it weaves a rich tapestry whose every thread is coloured with the lifeblood of the Heian aristocracy. From the lofty corridors of the imperial palaces and universities, the tranquil gardens of aristocratic estates and Buddhist temples, the novel sweeps its readers across the whole landscape of Heian life. What to wear today? What to eat? And is this a lucky day to cut one's fingernails? The *Genji* is one of the longest novels in world's history, containing over 360 000 words and running to over 1200 pages of small type in the best-known English translation by A. Waley. Its astonishing detail makes it an indispensable historical source, and today, educated Japanese know the *Genji* just as well as educated Westerners know the *Bible*.

What does the *Genji* tell us about Heian Japan? To begin with, it tells us about the appearance of the people. The typical aristocrat of the period would appear strange to us today. Both men and women wore heavy, light-coloured makeup, and it was often only a small goatee which distinguished the male from the female face. For both sexes, makeup covered part of the lips since small mouths (and small eyes) were considered a sign of beauty. Men powdered their faces frequently. The women plucked their eyebrows and painted new ones higher up. They used rouge on their cheeks and on their tiny mouths. They dyed their teeth black, and in another of the historical fashion-trends which harmed the health of women, they used a tooth-dye composed of a mixture of powdered iron, tea, vine-

This painting from the world's first novel The Tale of the Genji *depicts an early spring evening and a gathering seated on a veranda playing a game. The whole arrangement of house and its occupants is aesthetically pleasing, right down to the old cherry tree blossoming in the centre of the house. These delicate images provide a taste of the polished manners and elegant life of the Heian court.*

gar, and gallnut. A woman with white teeth, or "peeled caterpillars," as they are called in the *Genji*, was an object of scorn. A woman's hair was considered by all to be her "crowning glory." Parted in the middle, and left unadorned, it flowed to the ground, sometimes reaching 2 m in length.

The costume of Heian men, compared to that of women, was drab. Men wore a stiff black cap, a patterned, waist-length robe with voluminous sleeves over billowing trousers, the whole outfit dyed in shades of white, brown, or black. Women, on the other hand, wore long silken robes of gorgeous colours and intricate pattern. Sometimes, they wore as many as twelve of these robes, one on top of the other! The special feature of this costume was that each robe was slightly shorter in the sleeve than the one beneath, so that a rainbow of many colours flashed when the arm was moved. Matching the colours which showed at the sleeve was a serious business, and Lady Murasaki describes in her diary the embarrassment of one of her friends who was crushed when everyone ridiculed her costume. "It was not such a serious lapse of taste," remarked Murasaki, "just that the colour of one of her robes was a single shade too pale at the opening."

The Cult of Beauty

This preoccupation with the tiniest details of beauty and good taste extended into every area of life. Sending a letter was an art. The writer had to select the perfect paper, ink, and calligraphic style to create the proper mood. The paper had to be perfumed with the appropriate scent. The blossom attached to the letter had to be carefully chosen and the pageboy who delivered the letter had to be both good looking and perfectly dressed. Often, the pageboy was instructed to place a single, sparkling drop of water on the blossom just before delivering the message. This symbolized that the feelings of the writer were as pure and clear as the morning dew!

The ability to appreciate beauty also determined the divisions or gradations within the aristocracy. Rank and wealth played a part, but far more important were aesthetic sensibility and emotional depth. In the *Genji*, a princess with bad handwriting is scorned as a potential bride. A high Court Minister who was a clumsy dancer or wore an offensive cologne is rejected as a suitor. Any person, male or female, who could not compose a poem at the drop of a hat, or who could not speak eloquently in the frequent contests to compare the relative beauty of fans, birds, or blends of incense became a social outcast. One was either a ryo-min, a good-person, or one was not. Social pressure to be considered good was enormous, and the literature of the period is filled with stories of aristocrats driven to monasteries or nunneries because of their social failures.

Religion in the period was also influenced by the cult of beauty. Buddhist and Shinto sites were forced to compete in the elaborate embellishment of their architecture and their gardens. They found it necessary to make their festivals more lavish and gaudy. The aristocrats flocked to these festivals in their covered ox carts, dressed in all their finery, and according to contemporary accounts, flirted discreetly with each other or compared their dress and make-up during the religious services. Most of them could not read the long and difficult Buddhist scriptures and so they simply sat there, prayerbook in hand. The general belief was that a person gained grace by reciting the first and last sentence of each scripture and needed only to mumble a little while flipping the many pages in between. One aristocratic lady of the period insisted in her pillow-book that there should be one unalterable rule for all religions. The preacher should be handsome. In order to absorb any sermon, she said, the congregation must look at the preacher, and who, after all, can bear to look at an ugly man? An ugly preacher could therefore not convey his message, and so, she concluded disgustedly, the preacher himself becomes "a certain occasion of sin."

Homes in the Heian period were beautifully designed, but not very comfortable. They were generally built of wood, and most were raised about 30 cm off the ground to avoid dampness and humidity. Most had a small garden, with streams, moss-covered rocks, and dwarf trees, laid out usually to mimic, in miniature, a famous landscape from one of the beauty spots of Japan. Inside each building, furniture was almost nonexistent. One might find perhaps a chest or a low table, a decorative screen, or a charcoal heater, but people generally lived on the floor and kept such things as clothing and bedding in cupboards built into the walls. Moveable partitions created a bedroom, and people slept on straw mats or tatami (pronounced tah-tah-mee), just as they frequently do today. There were, of course, no glass windows. Bamboo shutters or screens of opaque paper offered some privacy, but they provided little protection from the cold or heat. Indoors and outdoors were hardly separated and in Japan, space included both. At night, light came from oil lamps, and because fish oil was expensive, it was used sparingly. Most people spent their evenings in a kind of perpetual twilight. To the best of our knowledge, there were no clocks of any kind in Heian Japan, and this, no doubt, contributed to a freer and more leisurely existence.

Food is seldom mentioned in the literature of the Heian period since the necessity to eat was regarded as rather vulgar. Rice was the dietary staple and it was served in the form of cakes, or along with such vegetables as carrots, eggplant, and onion. Meat was rare because of the Buddhist prohibition against taking life of any kind, but even devout Buddhists ate fish on the theory that a fish, once taken from the sea, willingly offered up its life for people to eat! A type of butter came to Japan in the Heian period, but was soon abandoned since it seemed to create body odour. Even today, Japanese seem sensitive to what they call *bata-kusai*, or the smell of butter, which they detect among westerners in Japan.

Relations between men and women in Heian Japan suggest that women enjoyed a mixed sort of freedom. Custom forbade them to be seen by any male except their husbands or members of their immediate families, and their clothing and long hair restricted their physical mobility. At the same time, however, the law guaranteed inheritance rights equal to those of the male, prohibited any kind of physical abuse, and allowed them a certain degree of sexual freedom. Many women, married and unmarried, took lovers of their choice. Women were active in politics, often managed large estates, and above all, were the arbiters of taste. Compared to their sisters in China or in Europe, the Japanese women of this period were more liberated in law, economics, and in their relations with the opposite sex. Men were permitted more than one wife, but wives could find their own diversions.

All in all, the Dwellers Among the Clouds enjoyed an idyllic existence. Through the cold and the heat, they saw beauty everywhere, even in the smallest things. But at the same time, their lives were tinged with a certain sense of melancholy.

While the aristocrats of the capital savoured their cherry blossoms, the provinces were showing signs of restlessness. For a long time, the aristocrats of the capital had paid little attention to the administration of their provincial estates and had failed to realize that in a land-poor country, possession of property was everything. Their vassals had been fighting for many years to protect the land of their aristocratic lords, and in the process, had developed unique fighting skills. It was out of this provincial strife that there arose the Age of the Samurai. From the twelfth century onward, a new class, the warrior or bushi (pronounced boo-shee), would dominate the history of Japan.

The Kamakura Shogunate

The Fujiwara clan had succeeded in dominating the imperial family for almost three centuries, but finally they ran out of daughters suitable for marriage and as a result, their power began to decline. At the same time, their provincial estates, or shoen (pronounced show-en), which had provided them and the other aristocrats with their revenue, were under constant threat from ambitious and greedy rivals. Provincial families were becoming ever more powerful and ever more independent as they honed their fighting skills in frequent battles to protect the land of their aristocratic masters. Many of them began to wonder why they should endanger themselves for the sake of some far-off overlord, and their ties of loyalty became very weak. In the capital, the aristocrats saw previous friends become enemies because of the scarcity of tax revenue and they began to fight among themselves. The frightened emperor called in the leader of the most powerful of the provincial clans to restore order, but he too, was ambitious, and in 1180, tried to make his two-year-old nephew into the emperor. This sacrilege resulted in the outbreak of a bloody five-year war and the foundation of the Kamakura Shogunate.

The victor in this war was a man called **Minamoto Yoritomo** (pronounced mee-nah-moh-toh yoh-ree-toh-moh. Japanese practice always puts the surname first). He was a relative of the emperor, a feared warrior and a skilled administrator. After his victory, he came to the realization that the capital administration was both decadent and incompetent, and that if he moved there, he and his followers might also become corrupt. At the same time, he was determined to become the real ruler of the country, and so he demanded from the emperor a special title. In 1192, he was made **shogun**, a title which simply means "general," but is better translated as generalissimo. Since his power base had always been in the east, at the small town of Kamakura, near Tokyo, he set up a national administration there, calling it a tent-government, or bakufu (pronounced bah-koo-foo). This is the term we translate as shogunate.

For the next century-and-a-half, until 1333, the bakufu governed Japan. It began as a small, streamlined and efficient structure, based on the absolute loyalty of Yoritomo's family and friends and their armed retainers, who were called **samaurai**, a term which means literally, one who serves. After subduing all his rivals, Yoritomo set up three government organs directly under himself: an Administrative Council in which he used experienced bureaucrats chosen from among the old aristocrats of the capital; an Office of Courts and Public Order; and the all-important Samurai-dokoro or Samurai Office. This office managed all the affairs of the fighting men: their appointments and dismissals, their salaries and promotions, the award of their ranks and privileges, and even the conduct of their families and their own personal behaviour. To govern the provinces, Yoritomo placed the most loyal of his followers in positions of civil and military governors (Jito and Shugo), constables, and land stewards. The administration was a feudal pyramid, with officials at each level responsible to a lord one level above; and the shogun was at the apex of the pyramid. Formally, orders came from the powerless emperors in Kyoto, but they acted only on the instructions of the shogunate. Their prestige, however, gave the shogunate legitimacy.

Yoritomo died in 1199, leaving two incompetent sons. His remarkable wife, Masako, however, held the regime together until 1203 when she finally lost patience with these two young men and decided to declare her father Shikken or Regent, to rule for them. Henceforth, the real power would reside in her family, the Hojo. The office of shogun now became like that of the emperor—a symbol. Succeeding shoguns in the Kamakura period were all young boys, usually chosen from the imperial family, and the structure of authority became very complex. Japan was nominally ruled by the emperor in Kyoto, but most of them were dominated by their fathers, who had the title of Retired Emperor. They, in turn, were dominated by the Shogun, who was, of course, dominated by the Regent!

A new law code was proclaimed in 1232, and it confirmed the whole chain-of-command, clarifying rights and duties at all levels of the administration. Interestingly, this Code also gave women more rights than they enjoyed elsewhere in the world at that time. They retained their equal inheritance rights, they could divorce their husbands, and the penalty for adultery was milder than anywhere else, and was applied equally to both genders. Elsewhere, the female was more harshly punished than the male.

Kamakura Buddhism

In spite of its somewhat confusing command structure, the Kamakura administration remained small and efficient. The Hojo regents presided over an era that was generally prosperous though there was a good deal of localized violence. This was, in fact, a good thing for the shogunate, since it allowed them to confiscate the land of defeated rivals and bestow it on their own supporters. The population grew, more cities appeared, internal trade expanded and contacts were renewed with China bringing to Japan new technology and new ideas.

Buddhism flourished. Monasteries extended their holdings of land, and often had to arm their monks to protect their property. New schools or sects of

BELIEFS

ZEN MEDITATION

In the practice of zazen, the disciple first assumes a quiet, comfortable sitting position. Ideally, the room is quiet and overlooks a tranquil garden. The setting, however, is less important than the state of mind, and a disciple who faces a blank wall will be just as successful. The master clears, opens, or empties the mind of the disciple with a koan (pronounced koh-on). This is a riddle, a nonsensical saying, or a question for which there is no answer. Some examples are:

"What is the sound of one hand clapping?"

"How can silence be expressed?"

"There is no place to start."

When the disciple asked the Master why he would not cure his fatal disease, the Master said, "So that you neither live nor die."

"Are the eyebrows acquainted with each other?"

"No."

"Why?"

"They are both in the same place."

"What is true?"

The Master lifted a tea-tray.

"What is the meaning of the Buddha's Law?"

"Filling the streams, filling the valleys."

The disciple, realizing that there is no answer, lets her mind go blank; the mind becomes open; empty but aware. The Master wanders quietly among the rows of disciples. Suddenly, he strikes just the right person with a bamboo pole.
Enlightenment.

Buddhism appeared and what distinguished them from earlier Buddhist forms was that their doctrines were easy to understand and were much more appealing to the common people. Their teachings were suited to the Japanese, rather than to the Chinese environment. In Japan's violent and militaristic society, they all emphasized the achievement of personal salvation.

The first of the new schools was called Pure Land or Amidist, and it taught that the individual could achieve enlightenment by faith alone. Simply by reciting over and over again the name of Amida Buddha, one could achieve rebirth in the Pure Land of Heaven. The second, called the Nichiren School, was founded by a monk of that name in 1253. He claimed that his was the only true form of Buddhism, that salvation was to be achieved by veneration of the Lotus Scripture, and that those who rejected his teachings would be damned.

The third, and ultimately the most important of the Kamakura schools was called **Zen**, or the School of Meditation. It emphasized self-discipline, the idea that emotion was the source of action, and the practice of *zazen* or sitting in empty-minded meditation until a sudden flash of intuition brought enlightenment. Zen became the favoured school of the samurai class since their world was filled with violence and sudden death, and Zen provided both a technique for tranquility and composing the mind, and also a rationale for the sudden, spontaneous act of killing an enemy in battle. All schools of Buddhism forbade the taking of life, but through Zen, the belief gradually spread that it was the sword, not the person holding it, who was the killer!

The Mongol Invasions

The fall of the Kamakura shogunate was caused more by external than by internal factors. Early in the thirteenth century, the fearsome Mongols had burst forth from their Central Asian homeland, and had rapidly conquered much of the known world including Japan's two closest neighbours, China and Korea. In 1268, Khubilai Khan, now the Emperor of China, sent a mission to Japan, and in a letter addressed to "the ruler of an insignificant country," ordered the Hojo Regents to offer formal submission to him. They refused. in 1274, Khubilai responded by sending an armada of 450 Korean ships carrying 15 000 of his finest troops, to Japan's southern island of Kyushu.

The Japanese, though not entirely unprepared, were initially outmatched. The Mongols were master tacticians, fighting in coordinated formations. Their powerful crossbows made the Japanese bows look like toys, and they used catapults which hurled flaming explosives. The samurai had no defense but their swords and their courage. Nonetheless, the battles were inconclusive, and when fierce storms destroyed many of the Mongol ships, the invasion was aborted.

Khubilai, however, was not a man accustomed to defeat, and he immediately sent more envoys to demand Japan's submission. The shogunate responded with the ultimate act of defiance. First they beheaded the envoys, and then they began to prepare for war. Using all that they had learned from the first invasion, they built walls and fortifications along the coast and developed small, fast-moving warships which could harass the clumsier Mongol vessels. They stockpiled weapons, conscripted soldiers, forbade luxuries in daily life, and trained the samurai in defensive tactics and group manoeuvres. Never before had the country been so united in a single cause!

In the summer of 1281, Khubilai struck. He sent against Japan an armada of over a thousand ships carrying about 140 000 troops. This was the largest seaborne invasion force in human history before the twentieth century. The Japanese were hopelessly outnumbered, and once the invaders had successfully landed their troops, the samurai seemed doomed to defeat. For almost two months battles raged every day. The shogunate desperately tried to reinforce its diminishing troops as every monastery in the country mounted round-the-clock prayer services. Back and forth the advantage swayed, and accounts of the battle are so confused that no one will ever know who might have won and had it not been for the intervention of nature, or perhaps Japan's guardian kami.

At the end of August, 1281, a great typhoon with hurricane-force winds arose out of nowhere. For two days, it battered the Mongol fleet as it lay at anchor. Most of the ships were sunk and the soldiers who fought to save them were drowned. The remnants of the invading force, marooned on land, were slaughtered by the jubilant samurai. Victory was complete, and the good news swept the land. The typhoon was christened the divine wind, or kamikaze, and was considered proof for all time that Japan was a Divine Land, protected by the gods.

Even as the country rejoiced, and as the shogunate basked in its victory, there began to appear ominous signs of discontent. The samurai, who had fought so bravely, received no rewards for their valour since there was no land to be confiscated and no booty to be seized. Thousands and thousands of widows and orphans found themselves destitute, grieving their lost husbands and fathers who had left them without support and protection. Buddhist and Shinto clerics insisted that it was their prayers which

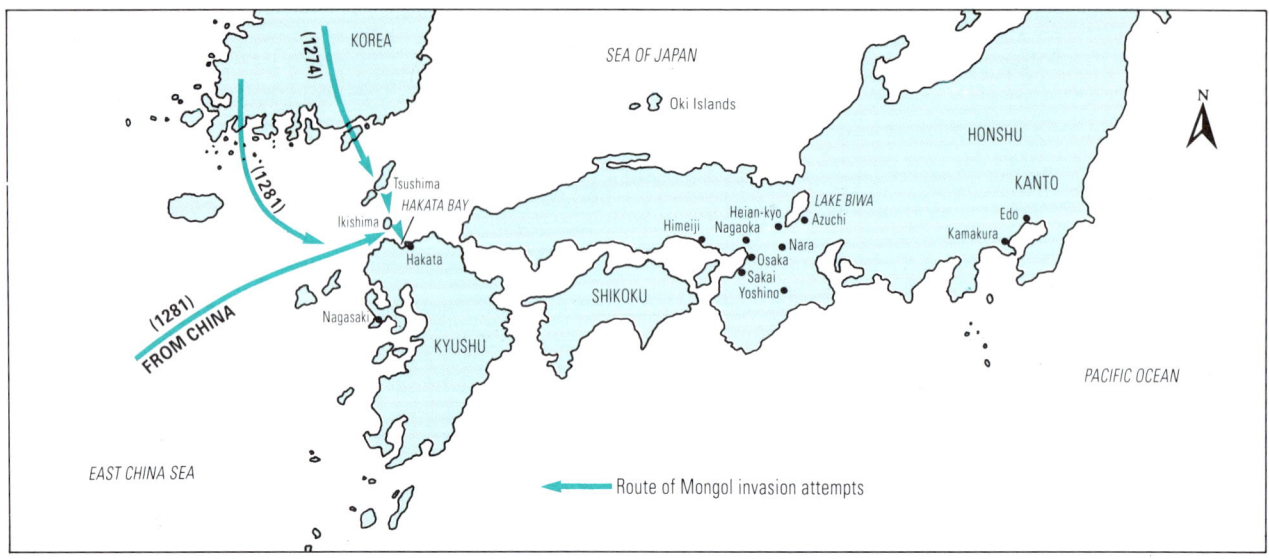

Attempted Mongol Invasions

had saved the country, and they too demanded compensation. But the shogunate had bankrupted itself in the preparations for war, and was forced to turn away all those who came to them for compensation. As these loyal subjects departed, empty-handed from Kamakura, they took their loyalty with them. The shogunate could no longer depend on its most loyal supporters.

The problems of the shogunate came to a head in 1318 when an unusually vigorous and ambitious emperor came to the throne in Kyoto. This man, Go-Daigo, felt humiliated by the loss of imperial power, and immediately after his enthronement, took a number of steps designed to reassert the influence of the emperors over the shogunate. Kamakura responded by demanding that he abdicate. When he refused to do so, they attacked him with a huge army commanded by one of their last loyal vassals, Ashikaga Takauji (pronounced ah-shee-kah-gah tah-kah-oo-ji). Takauji, however, switched sides. He turned his army around, and gathering support along the way, attacked Kamakura, burning the city to the ground.

Long and complicated negotiations with Go-Daigo convinced him, however, that his own interests would not be served under an imperial regime, and once again, war broke out. By 1338, he had forced Go-Daigo into a final exile and he proclaimed himself the new shogun, inaugurating a new era in Japanese feudalism. In this new shogunate, the old cult of beauty would blend and fuse with the brutality and sudden death of constant warfare, and with the profound peace of Zen Buddhism. Japan would become truly, a land of contrast.

The Ashikaga Shogunate

The Ashikaga shogunate began bloodily, ended bloodily, and witnessed almost three centuries of bloodshed in-between. This statement may be something of an exaggeration, but it is not far from the truth. The Ashikaga shoguns, with little support from the emperors, lacked the legitimacy of their predecessors, and were forced to depend on raw

Among the many castles built by daimos of the sixteenth century, Himeji stands out as the finest remaining example. These castles were so large they could house the daimo's entire army.

force to govern the country. The emperors, who had generally co-operated with the Kamakura, were impoverished and ignored. By the end of the period, one was selling his calligraphy in the streets of Kyoto in order to survive, and another lay unburied for fully six weeks after his death, since the court could not afford his funeral expenses. The Ashikaga shoguns saw no need to have the Sun-line sanction their actions. And under them, Japan came to resemble an armed camp.

The problem of the Ashikaga, from beginning to end, was rooted in the fact that their authority was not universally recognized as legitimate. Powerful local clans constantly intrigued against them and against their own neighbours, seeking the slightest weakness so that they might annex their estates. The most successful of the warriors in this long struggle became daimyo (pronounced die-mee-oh), and as they gained ever-greater revenues, they asserted their independence from the shogun's administration. Great castles, more like fortresses, began to appear, many of them protected by moats, clever booby-traps, and nightingale floors which would squeak at the approach of a ninja (invisible) assassin.

Forced to preserve at least a semblance of order, the shogunate began its reign by reorganizing the administration, allowing the office of Military Governor in the provinces to become hereditary, but placing the Governors under the authority of one of the three greatest clans in the country. These clans became the Sankan or the first line of defense for the shogunate. Four other clans were designated as the Shishiki, with responsibility for public order, samurai discipline, and the several subordinate offices which took care of the financial and secretarial functions of the government. This alliance, the so-called inner and outer lines of defense, was a re-affirmation of the principle of personal loyalty rather than pro-

The elaborate armour was the mark of the Samurai. Ornate suits were not usually worn to fight because the decorations seriously weakened the metal and the suit itself. This warrior crouches, heavily laden with weapons. The ornate helmet or kabuto adds to the overall ferocity of his appearance.

fessional expertise as the basis of government. It preserved the precarious power of the shogunate for almost three centuries.

The Ashikaga shoguns took up residence in the old capital of Kyoto. They built their magnificent residences in a section of the city called Muromachi, so that this period is often called the Muromachi period. Outside the capital, violence was constant, but during the reigns of such early shoguns as Yoshimitsu (pronounced yoh-shee-mit-soo), who reigned from 1368 to 1408, and Yoshinori, who ruled from 1428 until his assassination in 1441, all seemed well. These early shoguns presided over an era which saw a second great flowering of culture, a growing realization of nationhood among the Japanese, and most immediately, an understanding of what it meant to be a warrior.

Bushido

The class structure of the Ashikaga shogunate divided the people of Japan into four groups. On top was the warrior and then in order, the farmer, the artisan, and the merchant. It was not until the seventeenth century that this division was formalized in law, but throughout the Kamakura and Ashikaga shogunates, class divisions were hardening, and the ethos of the warrior was becoming more clearly defined. In time, it became a Way.

The creed of the samurai, or the **Bushido Code**, was composed of several elements. The first was the conviction that "death weighs no heavier than a feather," and that the mark of the true warrior was that he would never retreat and never surrender no matter how great the odds against him. The samurai seemed almost to welcome death, and the most admired figures in Japanese history are those who went down trying. One scholar has called this a love for the "nobility of failure," and has suggested that it lies at the heart of all Japanese literature.

The second tenet of faith was the necessity of absolute, unconditional loyalty to one's superior. Nothing took precedence over this. Nothing. The best illustration of this principle is also the most famous incident in Japanese military history: the story of the Forty-seven Ronin. The term ronin (literally meaning warriors riding a wave), was applied to those samurai whose lord had been killed in battle, leaving them directionless and without a master. In 1703, the famous Forty-seven lost their lord and decided that their honour demanded that his death be avenged. They killed the man responsible. Then, knowing that they had broken the law, they joined together in ritual suicide. Even today, the Japanese people so admire their courage and loyalty that they have made their grave a popular site of pilgrimage.

A third element of the creed was the importance of "face," a kind of pride which included a horror of bringing shame upon oneself or one's family. In the Ashikaga period, battles usually began with warriors facing each other to recite their pedigrees, dwelling on the brave exploits of their ancestors. Then, after an exchange of arrows, they charged on horseback into the fray, dismounting only to engage in hand-to-hand combat with a worthy opponent. If, in the confusion, they happened to kill an unworthy opponent, perhaps a groom or servant of their enemy, they were obliged to cut off one finger from their right hand after the battle. This usually meant that they would fight no more. They counted their victories by collecting the severed heads of the enemy, and with exquisite courtesy, they burned incense in their own helmets before a battle. If their own head became a trophy, at least it would be a fragrant one!

This sense of face sometimes led to death. A young samurai, only sixteen-years-old when he died, became the embodiment of this on the Japanese stage. His name was Yoshimasa, and he was struck in the eye by an arrow as he engaged in battle. A close companion tried to remove the arrow by placing his foot on his chest to get a grip on the shaft, but Yoshimasa struck at him with his sword. A samurai, he shouted, would rather die than suffer the indignity of anyone's foot on his chest!

The ultimate expression of face was, of course, ritual suicide. The Japanese call this act seppuku or more commonly, hara-kiri (pronounced hah-rah kee-ree), which means slitting the belly. It was undertaken to express shame, to show loyalty to one's lord, and sometimes even to admonish a lord to change his behaviour. It was a very painful way to die.

The Way of the Warrior had many facets. A samurai was physically hardened from youth, forced to stand for hours under a freezing waterfall, to run miles barefoot in the snow, and sometimes to go for days without food. No hardship whatsoever could make him complain. He was forced to be alert at all times by tutors who would otherwise sneak up on him and hit him with a heavy stick. He was taught to appreciate art, to dance and sing, to arrange flowers, and to paint. He was warned constantly to avoid a luxurious or soft life. And he was taught that his wife and children were expected to behave in the same way.

At the beginning of the feudal period in the twelfth century, there were also female samurai. The best-known of them was **Tomoe** (pronounced toh-moh-eh) of the Minamoto clan:

> She was a woman fair of feature with long black hair and a light complexion. She was a rider without fear, and neither the wildest horse nor the roughest terrain could dismay her. So skillfully did she handle her bow and her sword that she was a match for a thousand warriors, and she could vanquish both gods and demons. Many times she took the field, faced her heavily-armed foes, and won unparalleled fame as she fought the bravest of captains.... And so, in this last battle, when all the others had been killed or had run away, she was one of the last seven. Into the fray rode Tomoe![1]

As time went on, however, women like Tomoe became more rare and the general status of the female declined. Women came to be seen as too weak to defend property, and inheritance laws changed accordingly. Warriors spent more and more time fighting away from their homes, and their wives were confined to the tasks of child-raising, housekeeping, and managing the estate. Women of the

---

[1] A.L. Fadler, trans., Ten Foot Square Hut and Tales of the Heikē (Sydney: Angus and Robertson, 1928), p. 154.

ASPECTS OF DAILY LIFE

THE SAMURAI AND THE SWORD

The samurai class, which represented about 3-5% of Japan's population at any given time, was easy to distinguish from all other Japanese. Samurai alone were permitted to carry two swords, and to wear silk clothing. Their manner of walking was a swagger, and they all wore a kataginu—a special type of jacket with protruding, stiffened shoulders over a skirt and trousers. On the kataginu was a family crest. Warriors shaved the top of their heads, then gathered together the long hair from the back and sides, oiled it, and doubled it back over the crown, tying it tightly so that not a hair was out of place.

In battle, they wore several layers of undergarments and fitted over them an armour made of tiny scales of lacquered iron, which was strong, light, and flexible. It was considerably tougher than European chain-mail and weighed less than 12 kg. Unlike his European counterpart, the samurai needed no help in mounting or dismounting from his horse! The samurai helmet, with a riveted iron neck-guard and a fiercely-painted face-mask, was designed to prevent decapitation and to intimidate the enemy.

The most prized possession of the samurai was his sword: many were given names, while others came to be venerated as kami. Swords had lives and spirits of their own, and warrior literature is filled with stories of them and their masters.

The Japanese blade is probably the finest in world history, and its closest rivals, the blades of Damascus and Toledo, did not appear until much later. As early as the thirteenth century, each Japanese sword was tested by the maker before delivery to the buyer. Sometimes, he placed the sword upright in a stream. If it failed to slice cleanly through a floating leaf, it was rejected. The samurai tested other swords on the bodies of beheaded criminals, and occasionally on persons condemned to death. One famous incident tells of a prisoner who swallowed large stones to ruin the sword of his executioner. His plan didn't work!

Sword-makers in Japan were greatly honoured and took their craft seriously. They fasted and purified themselves before beginning work on any blade. They wore priestly white robes. They spent days melding together metals of varying hardness and softness, heating them to white-hot temperatures, hammering them out, and folding each layer over and over again onto the next. The completed sword consisted of thousands, sometimes a million, laminations of hard and soft metals. It would never break and would never become dull.

samurai class came to be used as pawns, hostages, or spies in the shifting alliances of the time, and so came increasingly to be seen as commodities. The Japanese never developed an ideal of courtly love as did the knights of Europe, and women were never placed on a pedestal. Instead, the warrior class became imbued with the masculine and militaristic spirit of the time. Women were compelled to practise the strictest chastity before and after marriage, lest samurai bloodlines be polluted or illegitimate sons make claims on the estate. In this warrior society, only the priestesses and shamans, the courtesans, and those female entertainers who would later become the famous geisha (pronounced gay-sha), were able to enjoy any freedom at all. The Japanese female, once equal or superior to the male was forced into a subordinate station.

Warrior Culture

The Way of the Warrior was symbolized not only by the sword, but also by the cherry blossom. The life of the blossom, like that of the samurai, was short, and when it fluttered to the ground, it was still in its full beauty. This metaphor is an apt one for the Ashikaga Shogunate since it enjoyed only a brief flowering under the first few shoguns before it allowed the whole country to dissolve into anarchy.

The accession of the third shogun, Yoshimitsu, in 1368, marked the beginning of a flash of glory in warrior culture which would survive his 40 year reign. Under his watchful and discerning eye, a whole new set of aesthetic principles began to evolve.

Warrior culture in Japan was composed of three elements: the superb taste of the old Heian aristocrats, the vigour and power of the samurai, and the spirituality of Zen Buddhism. It had three major characteristics, and these are seen in all the arts, whether major or minor. The first of these was called yugen, and it refers to a sense of sublime restraint, of symbolism, and of the mystery which lies behind appearances. The new theatre which developed at this time, called Noh, epitomized yugen with its lack of sets, its gorgeous costumes, hidden orchestra, and the masks of the performers. The masks hid the emotions of the performers, but a simple tilt of the head to catch the light in a different way, could alter the whole mood of a scene. Noh actors, all male, were trained from earliest childhood, in just how to tilt their heads.

The second characteristic was called wabi (pronounced wah-bee). It, too, was a mysterious quality, and referred to the beauty found in that which was lonely, or different, or unique; whether it was a rusted bucket lying on the roadside, or Yoshimitsu's magnificent Golden Pavilion which was set on a platform in the middle of a lonely lake. Wabi was seen in the superb ink and water (suiboku, pronounced sway-boh-koo) paintings of the time which often consisted of little more than a perfect circle representing Zen nothingness. An inscription in beautiful calligraphy might say, "Taste this."

Even more representative were the stark gardens of the period. A single weathered rock, surrounded by carefully-raked sand, a little moss, a stream, and a few tiny, twisted trees created a whole world no less awe inspiring than the sweeping expanses of the manicured gardens of Versailles. One special feature of Japanese gardens at this time was a simple length of hollow bamboo placed in the stream in such a way that when it filled with water, it tipped against a rock with a sound like a gunshot. The sudden, startling sound was an aid to enlightenment.

The final characteristic of Muromachi culture was sabi, (pronounced sah-bee), the mystery of change and ageing. The best example, perhaps, is the art of flower arranging, **ikebana** (pronounced ee-keh-bah-nah), which means the art of "making flowers live." Seasonal flowers were arranged in a classic

Ikebana "the art of making flowers live" demonstrates the deep appreciation of beauty held by Japanese society. Such appreciation extended even to the Samurai, who had ikebana as part of their training. The Rikka, the arrangement depicted here, was popular among the warrior classes because of its severe form and dignity.

fashion, each stem in perfect proportion to the others and to the bowl which held the arrangement. Blossoms were matched as to tint and size, and the symbolism of the various colours and lengths was matched to notions of "Heaven, Earth, and Humanity" or to "Body, Heart, and Soul." Sabi entered the arrangement as the flowers withered and faded. The person who knew sabi understood that the arrangement was as beautiful on its last day as on its first. For the same reason, women and men in the warrior period did not try to disguise their true age with cosmetics and hair dyes.

The Tea Ceremony

All these features of aesthetics were combined in the so-called tea-ceremony. Tea had been introduced to Japan by the earliest Zen monks, probably as a drink designed to keep them awake during long hours of meditation. Gradually, tea came to be cultivated in amazing variety all over Japan, and the drinking of tea became a ritual, providing the warrior a temporary respite, a small pause, in the serious business of killing. In the Muromachi period, tea-halls began to appear; small but elegant buildings situated in the most beautiful corner of a quiet garden. The building was made of rare and costly woods, rustic and humble in appearance, and the path leading up to it was made of stones so carefully selected that the true connoisseur of tea often searched the country for twenty-odd years to find one stone of just the right texture and shape to complete his perfect walk! Outside the teahouse was a basin where guests purified their hands and mouths before moving inside through a door so low that everyone had to bend to enter. This was a sign that all were equal in the tearoom.

The interior of the tearoom was the essence of simplicity; open space, a single flower, and a scroll often depicting just a single Chinese character hanging on the wall. The host made tea, and the guests paid careful attention to the rustic paraphernalia; the charcoal brazier, a simple old iron kettle, a bamboo whisk to mix the green tea, and the purity of the bubbles in the boiling water. Everyone spoke in hushed tones about the tranquillity of the setting and the beauty of each object in the room as the teamaster offered them a bowl of tea. Each one then turned the bowl in a clock-wise direction three times, sipped three times, wiped the bowl, and passed it to his neighbour. Tiny cakes were eaten, and conversation often turned to the tea-bowl. Prized bowls were bought and sold for a king's ransom, and their owners often cracked them deliberately and then repaired them with gold lacquer, on the theory that no beautiful object should be perfect. Some of these cracked bowls are designated today as national treasures of Japan.

Refined and restrained, quietly magnificent, simple and unique, filled with the spirit of that which changed and was consumed, the tea ceremony epitomized Muromachi culture.

The Warrior World on the Brink of Change

We should not think that the reality of these centuries was found only on the blood-soaked battlefields or in the rich glaze of an artfully-cracked tea-bowl. In the countryside, diligent peasants perfected the art of growing rice; pre-sprouting the kernel, creating special nursery-beds, and later transplanting the seedlings so that rice production grew enormously. They developed new means of pest control, for instance, the spraying of seedlings with a mixture of whale oil and vinegar heated together, and intercropped their rice fields with wheat and barley. Plums, persimmons, oranges and pears, radishes, lotus, and indigo became commercial crops, and both hemp and silk for clothing were produced. Certain regions began to specialize in the manufacture of such products as sake or rice-wine, tea, and paper. The life of the peasant was not an easy one, but the growth of internal trade brought some improvement in spite of frequent disorder.

Lively commercial towns began to appear, especially where the harbours were good, as overseas trade began once more to flourish. Early in the period, the Chinese had severed all commercial relations because of the depredations of Japanese pirates, but in 1402, Yoshimitsu had solved the problem by rounding up thousands of pirates and killing them. Now the Japanese began to import large quantities of copper coins, porcelains and paintings, books and medicine, in exchange for their swords, folding fans, painted screens, and sulphur from their volcanoes which the Chinese needed for gunpowder. Cities like Osaka and Sakai, Hakata and Nagasaki, were soon filled with merchants and tradespersons, and with great trading and manufacturing guilds (za), which are the distant ancestors of today's multi-national corporations.

Here, too, new forms of popular culture began to emerge, most of them less elevated than the culture of the samurai. The action-packed, sometimes vulgar, excitement of the kabuki and puppet theatres seemed more to the town dweller's taste than the sombre tones of Noh drama, and special amusement quarters, called ukiyoe or the floating world, began to be seen in the cities. Poetry became more accessible as the literacy rate rose, and the poems were far less refined than that favoured by the samurai class. One well-known example of the verse forms of the time was the **haiku.**

LITERATURE

WRITE A HAIKU

The earliest haiku appeared among the townspeople of sixteenth-century Japan as a reaction against the increasingly strict and rigid rules of court poetry. It reached its pinnacle and achieved recognition as a distinct poetic form in the next century, particularly in the work of Basho (pronounced bah-show) who lived from 1644–94, and wrote only a thousand poems, though each one was a masterpiece.

A haiku is a short poem, unrhymed, consisting of seventeen syllables in the pattern 5/7/5. Its purpose is to make the reader see, really see, the world that surrounds us every day, the world of which we are a part. Basho believed that each haiku should combine two elements—the eternal and the momentary. A good illustration might be:

Shi-zu-ka sa ya
I-wa ni shi-mi-i-ru
Se-mi no ko-e

How tranquil it is
But piercing into the rocks
Voice of the locust

In this poem the tranquility is eternal, and the cry of the locust is so sharp, so sudden and momentary, that it seems to stab the rocks. The reader also knows that it is a summer evening since that is the only time that locusts make sounds. The rocks suggest a craggy landscape and the many "i" sounds in the Japanese even suggest the chirp of the insects. A haiku should not just describe a scene or make a statement, but use the tension between the eternal and the momentary to illuminate a whole world.

Typical subjects of haiku were the seasons, the elements, natural landscape, gods and Buddhas, birds, beasts, flowers, and trees. The most common scene could become a haiku; if you looked around your own room, you might be inspired to write something like this:

On my soft silk shirt,
Sleeping, sunlit, my fat cat,
Extends her sharp claws.

It is the eternal nature of cats to sleep where they want and the warm, afternoon scene is a peaceful one. Then the claws rake the silk.

Try writing your own haiku.

The Coming of the Europeans

Soon all pleasure disappeared from Japan. In 1467, the so-called Onin (pronounced oh-neen) War broke out. Its immediate cause was a succession dispute in the shogunate, but other factors, too numerous to mention here, had been at work for a long time. The war lasted ten years: ten years of fierce, bloody, and unremitting strife. As severed heads piled up, the country was torn apart. When the war ended, almost sixty separate principalities had claimed independence and as each one strove to conquer the others, the fighting began in earnest. The next century in Japanese history is called the Sengoku Period, or the Period of A Country At War, and it was in this chaotic world that the first Western explorers and missionaries made their appearance.

The first Europeans to reach Japan were the Portuguese. To them, Japan was a welcome contrast to the "barbaric" peoples of Africa, Goa, and Indonesia whom they had previously encountered, and to the Chinese who had, in turn, treated them as contemptible barbarians. They found the Japanese friendly, civilized, and eager to acquire European knowledge of firearms and ships. The Japanese paid generously, in silver, to acquire Portuguese clothes and guns, as well as the silks and other luxury goods which the explorers had acquired in China. One sea-captain, Jorge Alvares, who visited Kagoshima in southern Kyushu in 1547, wrote with enthusiasm about all things Japanese, describing the beauty of the country and the abundance of exotic fruits and flowers, which he believed were not to be found elsewhere in the world. He commented with pleasure on the beauty of the women, was shocked by the habit of mixed bathing in public, and was astounded by the politeness of the people. "They speak softly," he said, "and look down upon our rough speech. Their etiquette demands that when receiving guests, they kneel with their hands upon the floor until their guests have been seated. . . . In the streets, when they meet others, they remove their shoes, and bow very low with their hands between their thighs." Alvares took some Japanese to Goa to meet **St. Francis Xavier**, and there, they became the first converts to Christianity.

Xavier, intrigued by the accounts of Japan, travelled there in 1549 and in his first year, succeeded in baptizing 150 converts. One special attraction of Christianity for the Japanese, aside from its association with European technology, was the fact that the life of Jesus Christ had ended in his courageous, self-sacrificing crucifixion. To the Japanese, this was an echo of their admiration for the nobility of failure!

In spite of his initial success, Xavier soon realized that guns, rather than theology, were the main spurs to evangelism. Everywhere he went, he encountered proud ***daimyo*** (pronounced die-mee-oh), the supreme samurai lords of each principality, who were much more interested in having Portuguese ships protect their valuable cargoes from the China trade, than in hearing about God or Deus, as the missionaries called him. Regrettably for them, the term Deus in Japanese, was rendered as dai-uso which also meant Great Lie!

Needless to say, the so-called **Christian Century** in Japan ended in failure. By about 1580, Japan was at a turning point. A few major daimyo had consolidated their power, and ruled domains as large and as populous as some European countries. A sense of nationhood was developing. The Japanese spoke the same language, practised the same customs, communicated freely with each other, held many of the same religious values, and in their powerless emperors and shoguns possessed symbols of unity. Above all, through all the horrors of daily life, the Goddess of the Sun shone upon them.

In 1573, the War of Unification began. Three great *daimyo*, each building upon the work of his predecessor, brought the country together, and in 1600, after the crucial Battle of Sekigahara, the ultimate victor, Tokugawa Ieyasu (pronounced toh-koo-gah-wah ee-ei-yah-soo), moved the capital to Edo (present-day Tokyo), and established the final Japanese shogunate, that of the Tokugawa. It would endure until 1867.

It is well, perhaps, to leave Japan here. Ieyasu and his successors brought to the country an era of total peace and order. They soon expelled all foreigners from the land, and crucified thousands of native Christian converts who had rebelled in 1638. Thereafter, no foreigner, not even shipwrecked sailors, would be allowed to live on Japanese soil. This was the beginning of Japan's Seclusion Policy. The feudal system was frozen and samurai rule was confirmed both in law and in custom.

Japan would remain isolated from the rest of the world for the next 250 years. Only when Commodore Matthew Perry's black ships appeared in Tokyo Bay in July 1853, would the Land of the Divine be catapulted into the modern world.

Suggested Sources for Further Research

▼▼▼

Cooper, M., *They Came to Japan: An Anthology of European Reports on Japan* (University of California Press, 1965).

Earhart, H. Byron, *Japanese Religion: Unity and Diversity* (Farleigh Dikinson University Press, 1974).

Elison, G., and B. Smith, *Warlords, Artists and Commoners: Japan in the Sixteenth Century* (University of Hawaii Press, 1981).

Hall, J.W., *Japan in the Muromachi Age* (University of California Press, 1976).

Leonard, J.N., *Early Japan* (Time-Life Books, 1968).

Morris, I., *The World of the Shining Prince* (Knopf, 1964).

Reischauer, E.O., *Japan: The Story of a Nation* (Knopf, 1970).

Sansom, Sir George B., *Japan: A Short Cultural History* (Appleton, 1943).

Swan, P.C., *The Art of Japan* (Crown, 1966).

Totman, C., *Japan Before Perry* (University of California Press, 1981).

Tsunoda, R. (*et.al*), *Sources of Japanese Tradition* (Columbia University Press, 1958).

Focus Your Knowledge

▼▼▼

1. Describe the physical geography and climate of Japan and comment on how it helped influence the nature of Japanese culture.

2. When and where did the earliest people come from? Provide a brief description of the Jomon and Yamato cultures.

3. In A.D. 552, Buddhism was introduced to Japan. Why is this a critical juncture in Japanese history?

4. In Japanese history there have been four capitals. List and describe each of these capitals including time periods and at least one significant fact or feature of the city or time period.

5. What can be learned about life in Heian Japan from the *Tale of Genji*.

6. How did government under the Kamakura shogunate differ from its predecessor?

7. What prevented the Mongols from succeeding in the attempted invasions of Japan?

8. What advancements in Japanese culture made during the Ashikaga shogunate suggest that Japan was more than just a warrior society?

Apply Your Knowledge

1. Review the essence of Shintoism and comment on what degree the scholars of the eighteenth and nineteenth century were correct in portraying it as "the deepest expression of the Japanese soul."

2. The influence of the Chinese on Japanese culture is extensive, yet Japan is a unique civilization. Review the key elements of a civilization (Chapter 2) and using these as headings prepare an organizer that assesses the impact of Chinese civilization on Japan. Also assess the degree to which elements of Chinese culture have been adapted making them uniquely Japanese.

3. Define the cult of beauty and discuss to what extent it pervaded Japanese culture. Have you encountered similar emphasis on aesthetics in other cultures you have studied or does this appear to be a trait unique to Japan?

4. The essence of Japanese culture during the shogunate periods is captured by the samurai who were a blend of the cult of beauty and the warrior society prevalent at this time. Comment.

5. Assess the role of men and women in Japanese society. Does Japan appear to have been a male dominated society or an open and equitable society as regards both sexes?

6. How did the Europeans first react to the Japanese? What caused the missionaries to send increasingly less favourable reports back to Europe? What does this tell you of both the value and dangers of using primary documents in the study of history?

Extension Activities

1. As a class project prepare a display which captures the essence of samurai culture. The display should include weaponry, samurai armour, clothing, art, ikebana, and samples of haiku.

2. Re-enact the Tea Ceremony taking care to establish the correct setting and rituals.

3. Using the recipes found in the feature study on Japanese foods prepare a Japanese meal and serve it in typical Japanese fashion.

4. Using the medium of your choice build a model of a famous piece of Japanese architecture such as Himeji Castle, a Buddhist temple from Nara, a tea house, or a shrine.

5. Based on further research of the samurai and knights from medieval Europe speculate in a piece of historical fiction what would have happened had the samurai confronted a medieval knight. What would they have thought of each other? How would they have reacted? What would the outcome of the battle have been?

6. Do further research into the life of the samurai. Based on your research prepare a video or presentation for the class which highlights elements of the samurai culture such as training and discipline, the Bushido Code, the weapons and armour, the appreciation of beauty and high culture.

CHAPTER 12

The Ancient Maya

Chapter Highlights

- the development of a jungle civilization

- Maya pyramids and other forms of architecture

- Maya mathematics and time

- the causes of the collapse of Classic Maya society

- Maya sport and entertainment

In most people's minds the word Maya creates a picture of gleaming white temples that stand abandoned in the Central American jungle, the remains of a remote and mysterious civilization that disappeared a thousand years ago. The exotic nature of the Maya land seems paralleled by the distance between the ancient people and ourselves, a gulf unimaginably broad, not just in time, but in almost every aspect of culture as well. Because of that gulf most people see the Maya of many centuries ago as no more than a small side branch on the great tree of ancient civilizations. In this chapter, by blending what archaeology can tell us with information from early Spanish records and from the modern Maya themselves, we shall come to see the Maya as a very real and very vibrant part of the story of human achievements through the ages.

Key Concepts

Maya highlands and lowlands

cenote

Palenque

Copan

Chichen Itza

stelae

Teotihuacan

Spanish Conquest

tortilla

Altun Ha

jade

obsidian

▼▼▼

Geography

Most people's picture of the Maya world is partly correct. Many of the ancient cities of the Maya are indeed enveloped in dense tropical forest, but the land where the ancient Maya achieved so much, and where their descendants dwell today, is not all hot, green, and wet. The land's diverse forms and resources shaped many different courses in ancient Maya life.

The territory of the Maya can be divided into two general zones. The first, and less well known, is the **highlands**, the great granite and volcanic spine of the Sierra Madre that runs down the western side of the Mexican state of Chiapas and through Guatemala into Honduras. In its plateaux, basins, and plains the ancient Maya found rich land and abundant water, as well as many other natural resources. It was in such places that they concentrated their settlements, but they made use of every part of the rugged land in one way or another.

The second zone, the **lowlands**, is made up of two parts. On the west, bordering the Pacific Ocean, lies a plain made fertile by erosion of the volcanic mountains behind it. The ancient population was high throughout the plain, an area that is still not well known archaeologically. The rest of the lowland zone, east of the mountains, is the most familiar part of the Maya land. The vast Caribbean topical lowlands of the Yucatan Peninsula (the modern Mexican states of Campeche, Yucatan, and Quintana Roo, and the country of Belize) and the Guatemalan Peten hold most of the famous ancient Maya cities, and have become a centre for tourism. Here more than anywhere else in the territory of the Maya the land, its forest cover, and its resources differ tremen-

Maya Civilization
A selection of important sites in the Maya area.

dously. To the great surprise of first-time visitors, one of the highly variable resources in this tropic setting is water.

Perhaps more than anything else, water supply dictated the locations of most Maya lowland communities. In the Guatemalan and southern Yucatan Peninsula rain forests, the river valleys were naturally attractive as sources of water and good agricultural soil in a region where most of the earth is thin and poor. The Maya made settlement throughout the forests possible by modifying natural sinkholes and building reservoirs where there was no surface water, as well as by many ingenious methods of irrigation and soil improvement. The situation was much more critical in the north, which has extremely poor soils and neither rivers nor the high rainfall of the south. Though its barrenness today is partly the result of eighteenth and nineteenth century cultivation, it was always a less than attractive place. In its eastern part the use of natural and excavated caverns (**cenotes**) as access to a shallow water table made life bearable, but in the hilly west no such solution was possible. Nevertheless, the Maya found ways to live here as well as to develop as rich a culture as they enjoyed elsewhere.

Maya History

Though the Maya had a complex writing system, they seem not to have recorded their history or the daily events in their lives. Furthermore, their civilization had changed a great deal before the first Europeans arrived in their land and most of what remained disappeared quickly under Spanish rule. Hence for every part of ancient Maya life we have to depend on two sources of information: archaeological evidence and early Colonial (sixteenth and seventeenth century) documents. Neither kind of evidence is enough by itself to give us a clear picture of how the Maya lived, and often the two do not agree. Besides, there are many things in the life of any society that are very unlikely to be recorded by a conquering people and just as many that leave no traces in the ground. As a result there are holes in our knowledge about every feature of Maya life and they are almost always large enough to be very frustrating. Nevertheless, there are many things in the Maya past that we do know and many more about which we can make intelligent guesses, despite the years and the cultural differences which separate that time from ours.

Archaeological work in the Maya world could be said to have begun a bit more than century ago, when scholars set out to explore, record, and sometimes excavate sites in Mexico and Guatemala. In a way though, the beginnings were in 1839, when two expeditions—the better known one by John L. Stephens and Frederick Catherwood, and the once almost unknown one by Patrick Walker and John Caddy—set off for Maya sites. The two journeys began as a sort of race to the site of **Palenque**, in Chiapas, but Stephens and Catherwood decided to head for **Copan**, in Honduras, first.

After the period of early exploration, which lasted until early in this century, came the first scientific excavations in the 1920s. Like the explorations before them they concentrated on large and famous sites such as **Chichen Itza** in northern Yucatan, Uaxactun in the Guatemalan Peten, and to a lesser extent the sites of Palenque and Copan themselves. The number of sites examined and of areas investigated increased until World War II brought such work to a halt. The modern era of Maya archaeology began in the 1950s and the number of archaeologists at work today on the story of the ancient Maya is greater than at any time in the past.

The Growth of Empire

Government and Law

Because we use one name for all the people who lived in the Maya area, one might think that they were a single nation under a single system of government and law. But the Maya surely never recognized themselves as one people, though there were many things besides related dialects of one language, Mayan, that bound them together. If you could ask an ancient Maya to identify the group to which he or she belonged, the answer would have been the name of a city and the territory it controlled. Each major Maya settlement was a city-state with its own ruler who controlled many towns and villages and

MAJOR EVENTS IN THE HISTORY OF THE MAYA

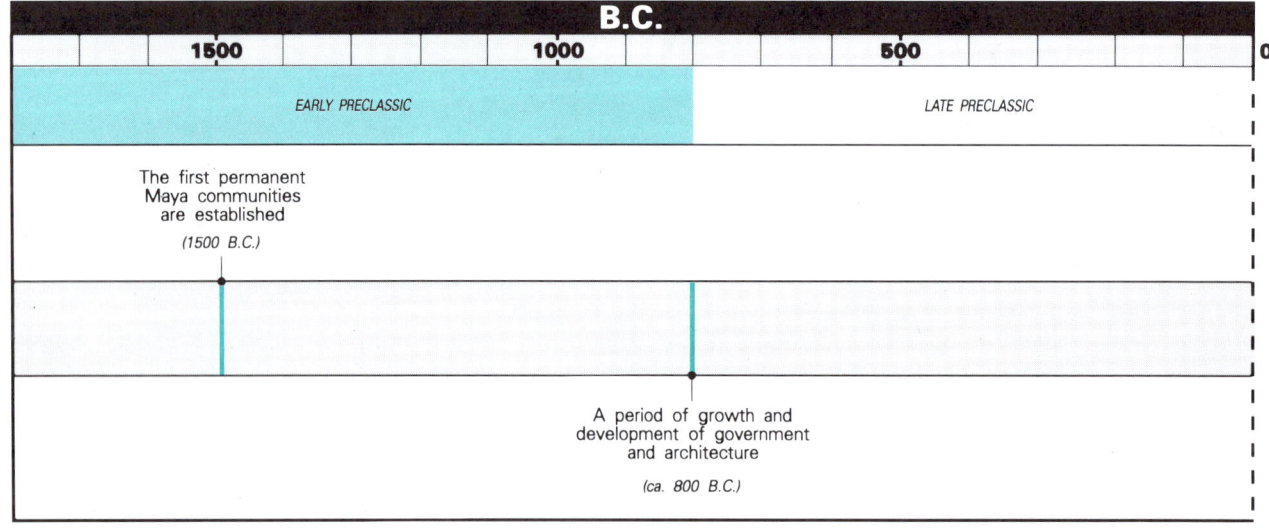

acknowledged no higher, central authority.

Even though the Maya had no king or emperor, our own experience leads us to expect that there would have been cities that were regional capitals of sorts. In fact at any given moment there certainly were some cities that were more powerful than others and there were alliances between communities that also increased the focus of power. Except for a brief period not long before the Spanish arrived, there was no time in which a single city dominated the Maya world. The importance of cities grew and shrank as circumstances changed, and some places that were early great centres were abandoned just as others were coming to prominence. So a list of important cities can be drawn up, and such places can be shown on a map, but the importance is at least partly the product of archaeologists' interests and of the history of exploration and excavation. Many of the most important discoveries about ancient Maya life have come from small, seemingly insignificant communities, sometimes from spots on the fringes of the Maya land.

The sharing of language and religious belief, as well as a great many aspects of technology, gave all Maya city-states some degree of similarity. It is very likely that the importance of religion in government made the political organization generally similar as well, but we do not know much about the rules of life in Maya communities. A large part of the energy of every group went into communal work, especially building, which was controlled by the ruler, his courtiers, and other members of the elite. How far did such control extend? Was a worker able to offer services to a private citizen, or even to someone from another city-state, without government approval? Was each individual under orders to perform certain tasks, or could some take on the work so that others could remain at home? We have yet to find answers to such questions. One thing, though, is very clear: the rulers of the city-states had far more power over their subjects than we would find bearable.

The Rise to Dominance

The beginnings of Maya civilization lie hidden deep beneath the great ruined cities, and in tiny villages

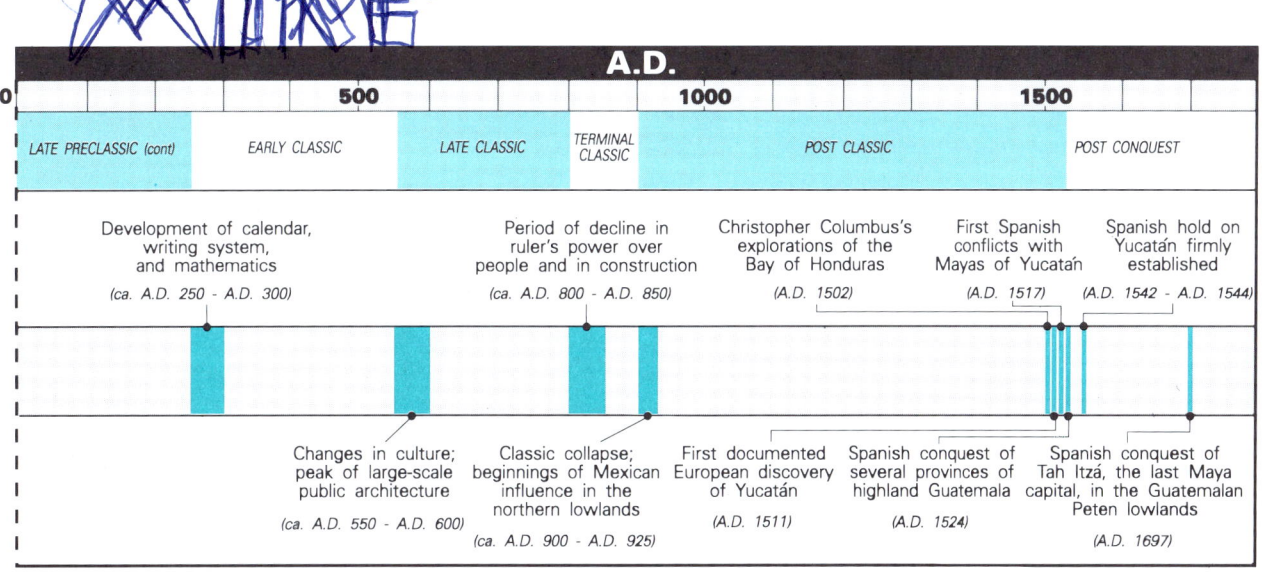

A stela is a vertical slab of stone which shows elaborate carvings of rulers and lists their accomplishments and information about their lineage. Many stelae have deteriorated over the years although some, like this one, have survived intact and provide valuable information about Maya society.

concealed by the forest. We do not know what led the first people to enter the area, probably long before the first recognizable Maya culture emerged about 1500 B.C. We also do not know where they came from or what language they spoke. We can be sure, however, that the earliest settlers lived simply, probably mixing farming with hunting and gathering. At this stage they probably had none of the things that their descendants welded into the greatest of the many high cultures in the ancient Americas.

As farming abilities increased and population grew the Maya spread throughout the land, not as conquerors displacing earlier inhabitants but rather as the first to make use of a difficult and rather forbidding part of the world. With the spread, in what archaeologists call the Preclassic period, came growth in community size: villages became towns, then cities, and finally city-states. The developments did not proceed at the same rate everywhere, but by about A.D. 1 most features of Maya society had made their appearance in city-states throughout the region. By A.D. 250–300 the time of greatest city growth, which archaeologists term the Classic, had begun.

At the heart of the development of Maya communities lay religion, the driving force behind every aspect of life. It was especially important in the growth of cities because as religious belief and practice became more and more complex the demand for temples and related buildings grew as well. In small villages, whether at the beginning of Maya prehistory or in later times, temporary or household shrines might have served the gods perfectly well. As the population swelled and wealth was accumulated, the building of temples—first in wood and thatch and then in stone—became something of a preoccupation. Out of this preoccupation came cities with many dozens of great stone buildings at their cores, and an ever greater demand on the populace for the labour required for the buildings' construction and maintenance.

Together with the physical development of cities came many changes in technology, including production of elaborate carved stone monuments (***stelae***) that showed rulers in elaborate costume, accompanied by texts that told of their lineage and their accomplishments. Like the construction of civic buildings and the many other tasks that were central to Classic Maya life, the making of stelae

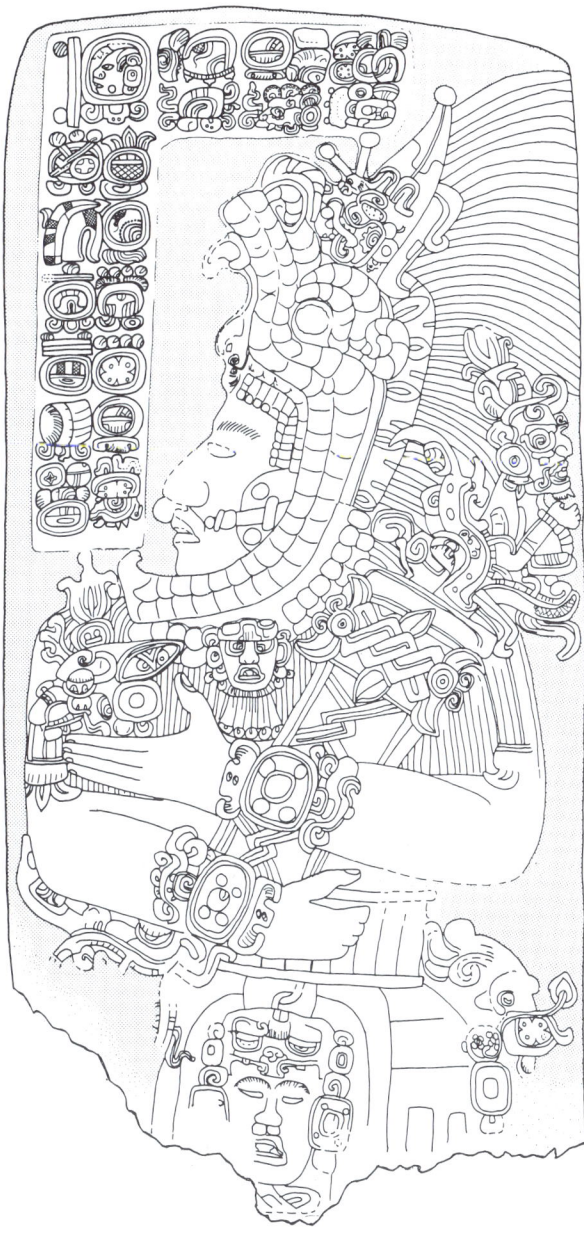

Monuments such as this stela are an important source of information about Maya rulers. The glyphs identify the name, titles, and lineage of the lord while the sculpting gives a vivid idea of the full regalia worn by the rulers. Here "smoking shell," wearing a serpent headdress adorned with the faces of gods, carries a ceremonial bar.

required a great deal of time and effort. All such labour tax on the people grew heavier as community size, temple size, and the general complexity of life increased during the Classic period. It may be, in fact, that it was this tax as much as anything else that brought the Classic period to an end in the southern lowlands of Guatemala and Belize about A.D. 900–925.

What is usually called the "Collapse" of the Classic period is probably the best known part of the Maya story. Foreign invasion, soil exhaustion, sickness, and famine have all been suggested as causes, but most authorities now believe that although each of these may have contributed to the collapse in some places, the primary causes lay within Maya society itself. Top-heavy government, increasingly unbearable burdens on commoners, and the growing isolation of rulers from the people they governed are very likely to have weakened Maya communities and made them vulnerable to decay. Because there was no central government there was no single course in the collapse, and no one time when all city-states died. The process was gradual, having started in some communities before A.D. 800, and the particulars of decline and abandonment were very probably different in each case. The ultimate result was, however, a general upheaval in politics and economy throughout the southern lowlands.

The fall of the great political and economic capital of **Teotihuacan** in central Mexico early in the eighth century probably helped set the stage for the Maya collapse. The event made life unstable over a very large region, and its shockwaves undoubtedly swept into the Maya area as well. At its strongest, Maya society, with a conservatism borne of very deep commitment to religious values, might well have survived the unrest that swirled around it. In their weakened condition, however, many—apparently most—of the southern city-states fell into decline and were gradually abandoned.

The decline and fall did not occur in every Maya

The Ancient Maya CHAPTER 12 373

community. Life in the highlands and on the Pacific coast had followed different paths throughout the Classic period, and continued to do so in the tenth century and afterward. In the northern part of the Yucatan Peninsula and, we now know, in a few centres in the southern lowlands life went on through all of what archaeologists call the Postclassic period. Society was changed in many ways and technology, including the kinds and sizes of civil buildings that were constructed, changed as well. Yet the Maya kept their religious beliefs and many of the other important aspects of their culture largely intact.

The southern lowland communities that survived somehow succeeded in staying alive as islands of relative calm in a sea of trouble as most of the great Classic centres fell into decay. The Classic period is often presented as a peak reached after many centuries of rise, and its end as a descent into the ash-heap of history. But the archaeological record of life in southern lowlands survivor communities, like that from city-states farther to the north, shows otherwise. The Postclassic period was in fact not a time of decline and decadence but rather a rich and vibrant period with its own identity. People clung to the old while moving towards the new, and probably enjoyed greater freedom and lower labour taxes as they did so. The catastrophes of the tenth century altered people's lives everywhere in the Maya area, but in many cases the changes are very likely to have been for the better rather than for the worse.

The Classic collapse and the events of the following centuries meant that the Spaniards who arrived in the Maya area in the 1520s and afterwards had no opportunity to see the culture in its most elaborate form. So the early Colonial documents tell us more about life in the Postclassic period—and even here only through the eyes of Europeans whose aim was to impose their rule on the natives—than they can tell us about what went before. Still, they show that the Maya culture encountered by the Spanish, though not as complex in some ways as in earlier times, was still as alive, changing, and exciting as it had been centuries before.

Beliefs

Mythology

Although the Maya built a vast and complex environment around themselves, they remained very conscious of the natural world that lay beyond the one they had constructed. As a result much of their mythology focused on forces in the natural world, both positive and negative. Very few tales that illustrate mythological beliefs have survived intact from ancient times, but a great many modern Mayas continue to believe in the power of natural elements to help or harm and are able to recite stories that are evidence of that power. Animals with human abilities appear in such stories, sometimes mingled with gods and bits of real history from the early years of the **Spanish Conquest**. Today the tales lie outside formal religion, which is Christian due to the Spanish influence. In times past, however, such stories were part of a formal religion which taught that the environment, whether on earth, in the sea, or in the heavens, was the home of deities whose favour had to be sought constantly if communities were to survive. The Guatemalan highland Quiche relate the following creation myth:

> And the creation of all the four-footed animals and the birds being finished, they were told by the Creator and the Maker and the Forefathers: "Speak, cry, warble, call, speak each one according to your variety, each according to your kind." So was it said to the deer, the birds, pumas, jaguars, and serpents.... But they could not make them speak like men; they only hissed and screamed and cack-

led; they were unable to make words, and each screamed in a different way. When the Creator and the Maker saw that it was impossible for them to talk to each other, they said: "It is impossible for them to say our names, the names of us, their Creators and Makers. This is not well," said the Forefathers to each other. Then they said to them: "Because it has not been possible for you to talk, you shall be changed. We have changed our minds: Your food, your pasture, your homes, and your nests you shall have; they shall be in the ravines and the woods, because it has not been possible for you to adore us or invoke us. There shall be those who adore us, we shall make other beings who shall be obedient."[1]

This unusual pottery drum was hung at an angle across the chest. The length of the tubes and the different diametres created different sounds. In Maya society the bat was associated with caves and the underworld. This particular bat was stuccoed and painted, most likely blue since traces of blue paint still exist.

Organized Religion

Religion was the main engine that drove Maya culture. It determined most of the form of city centres and laid down the rules for much of what went on there. It lay behind the organization and control of labour for communal construction, and dictated smaller-scale alterations of houses as well. In the countryside, religion established the schedule for agricultural activities and rituals that were performed both in the villages and in the fields. In every setting, religion spoke of a great variety of gods who needed appeasing.

The gods ranged from Kinich Ahau, the Sun God, one of the principal deities, to other heavenly figures such as Ix Chel (Venus), and on to natural forces such as Chac, the Rain God, and to creatures of nature such as Balam the jaguar and Zotz the bat. Each had special powers and had special periods in which those powers became all-important. All of the gods were presumably recognized throughout the Maya world, and some were worshipped everywhere, though probably not in quite the same fashion in all communities. Other gods were of limited importance overall, but might serve as the patron deity for a specific city-state, as the crocodile did for Lamanai (Lama'an/ayin, meaning submerged crocodile) in Belize. The power of such deities may have risen and fallen as the fortunes of their special cities shifted, whereas that of the major gods remained perpetually great. Hence Maya religion spoke in different ways to the people in different times and places; but it always spoke of the gods in an elaborate framework of time.

The Maya method of reckoning time, which we shall learn more about later, was so complex that, like many aspects of the religion with which it was linked, it was understood by only a few people in any community. The existence of a calendar allowed priests, led by the ruler, to predict eclipses and other celestial events. In this way it lent very real authority to priests' warnings of doom and to their orders for offerings of food and other things to stave off disaster. Because the Maya concept of time revolved

[1] Adrian Recinos, Delia Goetz, and Sylvanus Morley, *Popol Vuh: The Sacred Book of the Ancient Quiché Maya* (Norman: University of Oklahoma Press, 1950), p. 85.

around cycles, the calendar had the additional value of making it possible to fix appropriate times for the temple rebuilding that was the greatest undertaking in Maya cities, and at the very core of religious belief and practice.

Besides all its other functions, the calendar also set the times when the priests and the ruler offered up their own blood to the gods. Because the Sacred Well or Cenote of Sacrifice at the northern Yucatan site of Chichen Itza is so famous most people believe that human sacrifice was a major part of Maya religion. In fact, however, the offering of blood was the most important activity throughout most of Maya prehistory. Human sacrifice was rare or nonexistent in most communities throughout the Classic period, and only became common once the northern Yucatan Maya had come under Mexican influence in the Postclassic period. Then people—old and young, men and women—were cast into the cenote, supposedly to act as messengers to the gods. Had the Maya of earlier times been able to witness such sacrifices, they would probably have found them as horrific as we do.

In addition to blood sacrifice, continual reconstruction of temples was a mainstay of Maya religion. To the Maya, temples (and perhaps other civic buildings as well) seem to have been living things, with life cycles like those of human beings. The temples were avenues of communication with the gods, and if they were to serve this purpose they had to be kept alive. This meant periodic changes or complete rebuilding. Because the midline of each temple was the main lifeline to the gods, rebuilding could not mean a shift to a new spot, and generally could not involve complete destruction of the aging building. So Maya temples had to grow on the same spots over time, both upward and outward. Each change made possible the ceremonies that permitted priests to hear the voices of the gods. To hear those voices was to receive guidance that would keep the community alive; to be deaf to the voices was to invite disaster.

Temples served as great theatre settings for processions and ceremonies, and plazas in front of the buildings were places where commoners could witness such activities. The ceremonies were, like the buildings themselves, designed to be remote from the average person and to inspire awe and dread. Few if any viewers have failed to be convinced by the great show before them that the gods were all-powerful, all-seeing, and highly likely to stamp out the entire community unless kept well fed and happy. The ability of the priests to speak to the gods and transmit their messages was obvious and their knowledge of time and its measurement must have been awe-inspiring in itself.

Morals and Values

The importance of religion in Maya life created very strong systems of morals and values. The Spanish priests and others who wrote about Maya life judged things in European terms, and were almost entirely concerned with recording "**pagan**" practices so that they could be understood and overcome in the spread of Christianity. Nevertheless, a bit of the Mayas' morality and some of their values emerge from the Spanish documents.

In our eyes, and probably for the ancient Maya as well, the most important element in their moral and value systems was their view of their role in the world around them. This view seems to have been at the heart of Maya philosophy. It certainly set the tone of much religious activity, and probably of daily life as well. The Maya quite rightly saw themselves as simply one part of a unified world, what we would call a single **ecosystem** today. This meant that they did not have dominion over nature, but rather had to deal with the environment respectfully and atone for wrongs committed. Respect and atonement were given formal expression in religious rituals of sorts that are still carried out in many parts of the Maya area. This philosophical viewpoint did not produce

ASPECTS OF DAILY LIFE

RAISING A DAUGHTER IN SIXTEENTH-CENTURY YUCATAN

They [the women] teach their daughters whatever they know themselves, and bring them up very well in their own way, for they scold them and teach them and make them work, and if they commit any fault, they punish them by giving them pinches on their ears and arms. If they see them raise their eyes, they scold them well, and rub their eyes with their pepper, which causes them great pain.

---

the sort of conservationist attitude that is on the rise in our world, because if one sinned against nature it was possible to wipe away the sin through prayer and offering. Still, it does appear that the Mayas' values often made them better caretakers of their world than we have been of ours.

Social History

The Roles of Men and Women

Most Maya archaeological work in the past was done by men, and male domination of writing about Maya history and prehistory has been nearly complete until recently. Because of this it is even harder than it should be to sort out information about men's and women's roles in Maya society. It would be very difficult in any case, because most objects excavated by archaeologists tell us little enough about how they were used, let alone whether they were used by men or women. As a result we depend on studies of the modern Maya, and to a much lesser extent on early Colonial records, for our understanding of gender roles.

Whenever we speak about a culture as a whole we must talk about norms—what is done by most people most of the time—rather than about individual activity. If we accept that most household tasks were performed by women, we do not rule out the possibility that Maya men occasionally used a stone *mano* (roller) and *metate* (slab, with or without legs) to grind corn. Such deviations from the norm are, in fact, almost a certainty in any situation; they are brought on by emergencies such as illness or absence from the home, and in some societies including our own (and perhaps even that of the Maya) sometimes by an individual's free choice.

Male writers of Maya prehistory once saw only kings among the rulers, but we now know that there were city-state queens as well. It is unfortunate that below the ruler's level there are no portraits on stelae or carved texts to provide the information we have for the kings and queens. Were most architects male, or female, or did neither sex predominate in the profession? Did merchants include both men and women among their number, and if so did women travel as widely as men in hawking their wares to distant buyers? Were featherworkers female and jadecarvers male, or the other way round? Perhaps answers to such questions about gender roles in the

Social Structure

Maya society was organized into a very tightly knit multilayered structure. Parts of the organization seem to have been what we would call castes, which is to say that membership in them was hereditary and movement out of them was difficult if not impossible. For others there appears to have been more freedom, including the ability to improve one's lot in life and to move from one community to another.

At the top of the society was a large and complex elite that included the ruler, the royal family and retainers, courtiers, priests, and anyone else who by heritage or by association could claim a link with the community's leader. Some professional people such as architects formed part of the elite, as did higher-level merchants and others whose skills were used in the service of the ruler or in ways that earned them high status in the community. Beneath them lay a variety of other specialists, artisans, craftspeople, and probably managers and bureaucrats, especially in the late centuries of the Classic period. There must have been many such groups and they were surely ranked in importance, perhaps in different ways in different communities. Where movement from one group to another was allowed, it may have been made possible by talent, by contacts, or just by plain hard work. It is easiest to see this assemblage of groups as a middle class because in some ways it resembles the middle class in our own society. Its divisions, however, were much more rigidly defined than ours and movement upward, either within or beyond a group, was a great deal more difficult than it is in today's world.

Finally, below the middle class, there was within the cities themselves a lower class made up of all the providers of services needed to make cities run. The situation was made more complicated by the fact that labourers were brought in from surrounding communities to work on temples and other civic

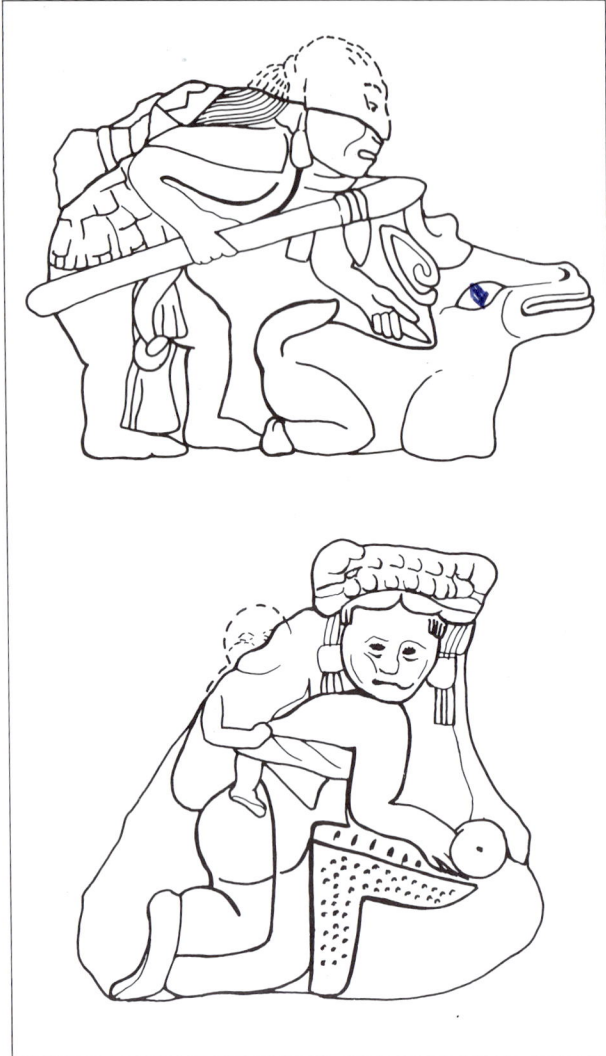

These line drawings of pottery whistle figurines dating to the eighth century are representative of the usual roles of men and women in Maya society. The hunter, carrying a backpack is apparently about to slaughter a deer. The woman is grinding something using a roller while carrying her baby on her back.

intellectual and high-technology areas of Maya life will eventually come from study of hieroglyphic texts.

buildings. As country people they might have been near the bottom of the lower class, but many must have been of fairly high status in their towns and villages. Such people are almost hidden in the archaeological record because very few lower-class houses, and no labourers' quarters, have been identified in Maya sites.

Customs and Festivals

Try to remember the last festival you attended, what archaeological evidence would there be of the event? There are a few scenes painted on Maya pottery vessels that have the look of festivals about them, but all are clearly religious or political. Apart from these there are no paintings of the Maya on festive occasions, though such things may once have existed on the walls of temples and elite residences. As to customs, such as the methods used in asking for a person's hand in marriage—indeed the very nature of marriage itself—we cannot hope to dig them up, or to detect them in Maya art.

The Maya are often portrayed as so bound up in religion that all customs were dictated by religious belief, all festivals were entirely religious in nature, all sports were dedicated to the gods, and all entertainment was either to be found in the festivals and sports or was somehow made to be part of religious activity anyway. Surely the Maya were more human than this. Excavations yield small pottery whistles, often in the shape of birds or other animals; such objects could have been used in religious activities, but it is hard to believe that none was ever blown for the sheer fun of it. Other musical instruments exist (including rasps, rattles, ocarinas, flutes, and conchshell trumpets), and except for conchshell trumpets—the shells were blown to summon the gods—all seem just as likely to have been chosen for everyday entertainment as for ceremonies. It is undeniable that religious thinking was present everywhere in Maya life, but surely it could not have stifled all natural human impulses to lighten life with music, dance, song, and other activities that forgot the gods, if only for a few moments.

Food and Drink

Accidents of preservation and studies of ancient pollen have given us some evidence of Maya vegetable foods, but we depend for the most part on animal bones from garbage heaps as our main source of dietary information. We are still a long way from being able to describe or prepare a typical sixth century Maya meal, though we know a bit more about food habits at the time of the Spanish Conquest. Except for items introduced by the Spanish or brought to the Maya area in more recent times, it is probably reasonable to take the food of the area today as a sample of what was enjoyed centuries ago. If you have had a chance to try Maya cooking, you know that it is nothing like the spicy cuisine of northern Mexico; it is, in fact, remarkably bland.

The agricultural staples in the Maya diet were corn, beans of several varieties, and squashes that were probably eaten when very young but otherwise were raised for their seeds. Chiles gave flavour to the meal, and modern Maya cookery suggests that a number of natural forest products spiced up the cook's work as well. Well over 150 foodstuffs can be collected in the forests of the southern lowlands, and a smaller but still interesting list comes from the highland forests. They were probably always used to supplement agricultural produce, and in times of crop failure they may have been of great importance. It is sad that many are no longer used in most of the Maya area, so the techniques required for their preparation are becoming a thing of the past.

Corn preparation seems to have omitted the great Latin American food, the **tortilla**, until late in the Classic period. It is hard to imagine Maya cuisine

SPORTS AND LEISURE

POK-A-TUK: A MAYA BALL GAME

This game was played with a rubber ball in a walled court about the size of two tennis courts. This area had sloping sides, stone rings, and a flat I-shaped surface. The spectators sat on stone bleachers above the walls. Two opposing teams or two contestants played, but the rules of the game are not known for certain and have been interpreted from stone and vase paintings. The object of the game was to keep the ball from the ground and a player could only do this by touching the ball with hips, knees, and elbows. The ball could bounce from the playing surface and the walls. The players wore a wide heavy belt of wood and leather, hip and knee pads, gloves, and helmets. The carving depicted here illustrates this protection and one is struck by the resemblance to a goaltender in a modern hockey game. There seems to have been a fair amount of gambling and betting going on and if a player drove the ball through the ring, he was allowed to take clothing and jewellery from the spectators.

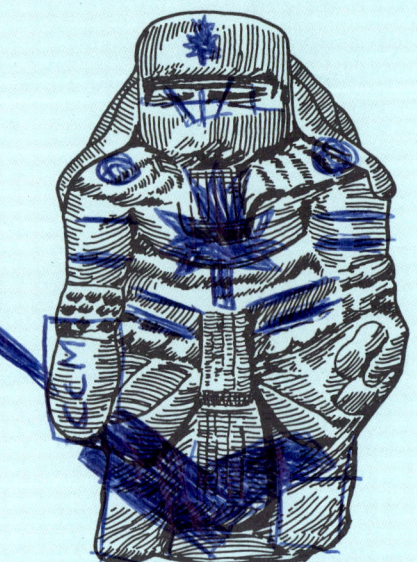

The ball court at Copan

Animals figure prominently in both codices and Maya pottery. The representations above depict animals as they were drawn by the Maya. The deer (left) was an important source of food as well as symbolic. The monkey (right) drawn as it was observed, probably as a tame animal and was defied—as was the jaguar (bottom left), god of the night sun that rests in the underworld. The mythological animal (bottom right) appears to be a combination of various animals.

without the tortilla, but it is certainly true that corn can be made into many other nourishing dishes. The importance of the tortilla (for which the archaeological evidence is the *comal*, the clay pan on which the flat cakes were cooked) goes beyond its value as a breadstuff. Treatment of the corn kernels with lime to permit production of a coarse flour makes the mixture of corn and beans an excellent source of a complete protein, vital to health. In addition, the tortilla probably served in the past as it does today as a container and a sort of spoon for many other foods.

The Maya had only the turkey as a domesticated food source; though dogs were present, there is no evidence that the kind eaten in parts of Mexico was ever among Maya delicacies. Some of the forest animals that could have been eaten seem to have been generally avoided, presumably for religious reasons. Even the jaguar, highly important in religious belief, may have seen service as a food animal on rare occasions. Deer were among the prized game, as were peccaries and armadillos. The guinea pig-like agouti and paca, much favoured today, are not as evident in the ancient bone collections as one would expect, but wherever possible the Maya made as much use of fish and turtles as they do at present. Lakes and rivers also yielded snails that were con-

ASPECTS OF DAILY LIFE

FOOD OF THE MAYA

Our knowledge of the ancient Maya is limited to archaeological remains and a few primary documents. Among the most important accounts of Maya culture is Bishop Landa's *Relacion De Las Cosas De Yucatan*. Landa was one of the first Spanish missionaries to arrive in the Yucatan following the conquistador's invasion. His memoirs form an important body of information concerning ancient Maya culture. The excerpt below is a description of the important foods in the diet of the Maya. Following Landa's description are a few recipes adapted from the ancient Maya. Try your hand at these and sample the cuisine of the Maya.

Bishop Landa's Description of the Food of the Maya

Their principal subsistence is maize of which they make various foods and drinks, and even drinking it as they do, it serves them both as food and drink. The Indian women put the maize to soak one night before in lime and water, and in the morning it is soft and half cooked, and thus the husk and the stock are separated from it; and they grind it upon stones, and they give to the workmen and travellers and sailors large balls and loads of the half ground maize, and this lasts for several months merely becoming sour. And of that they take a lump which they mix in a vase made of the shell of the fruit, which grows on a tree by which God provided them with vessels. And they drink this nutriment and eat the rest, and it is a savoury food and of great sustaining power. From the maize which is the finest ground they extract the milk and they thicken it on the fire, and make a sort of porridge for the morning. And they drink it hot and over that which remains from the morning's meal they throw water so as to drink it during the day; for they are not accustomed to drink water alone. They also parch the maize and grind it, and mix it with water, thus making a very refreshing drink, throwing in it a little Indian pepper or cacao.

They make a ground maize and cacao a kind of foaming drink which is very savoury, and with which they celebrate their feasts. And they get from the cacao a grease which resembles butter, and from this and maize they make another beverage which is very savoury and highly thought of; and they make another drink from the substance of the maize both ground and raw which is very refreshing and savoury.

They make good and healthful bread of different kinds, except that it is bad to eat when it is cold, and so the Indian women take a great deal of trouble making it twice a day. They have not yet been able to succeed in making a flour which they can knead like wheat flour, and if at times they make it like wheat bread, it is good for nothing.

They prepare stews of vegetables and flesh of deer and wild and tame birds, of which there are great numbers, and of fish of which there are large number. And thus they have very good provisions for eating, especially since they have begun to raise the pigs and poultry of Castile.

Maya Chicken and Pork Pie

2	large onions, roughly chopped
6	tomatoes, roughly chopped
6	large cloves garlic, roughly chopped
30 mL	ground annatto or 15 mL tandoori mix
2 mL	salt
350 g	pork, trimmed and cubed
2 kg	chicken pieces
300 mL	chicken stock
6	large tortillas

Puree the onion, tomato, garlic, annatto, and salt in a food processor. Lay the pork and chicken out in a pan and cover with puree. Pour on the chicken stock, bring to a boil, cover and simmer gently, for 45 minutes or until the meat is cooked. Cool it slightly, bone the chicken and return it to mixture.

Lay out 3 tortillas in a shallow dish large enough to hold the mixture. Transfer the meat with some sauce onto the tortillas. Cover the meat with the remaining tortillas and reheat the mixture in a moderately warm oven until the tortillas are lightly crisped. Reheat the remaining sauce and serve it with the pie.

(*From* The British Museum Cookbook, *by Michelle Berriedale-Johnson,* © 1987. *British Museum Publications.*)

Champurrado (Chocolate-flavoured atole)

375 mL	water
125 mL	masa harina (corn flour)
250 mL	water
45 g	semi-sweet chocolate
1	cinnamon stick
	brown sugar to taste

Bring the 375 mL of water to a boil.

Mix the masa harina with the 250 mL water and strain into the boiling water, stirring it well so that it is completely smooth.

Add the chocolate, cinnamon, and brown sugar. Keep stirring the mixture until it thickens and is well flavoured—about five minutes.

Maya Fish Steaks In Pepper and Garlic Sauce

1 kg	any firm white fish, cut into four steaks
4	cloves garlic, crushed
1 mL	cumin
2 mL	ground oregano
5 mL	ground annatto
	salt and fresh ground pepper
90 mL	fresh orange juice
60 mL	fresh lime or lemon juice
1	fresh chili, green or red, seeded and chopped
150 mL	olive or corn oil
1	large onion, thinly sliced
2	cloves garlic, minced
2	tomatoes, sliced
2	medium red peppers, seeded and thinly sliced
30 mL	chopped parsley

(*From* The British Museum Cookbook, *by Michelle Berriedale-Johnson,* © 1987. *British Museum Publications.*)

Place fish steaks on a dish. Prepare mixture of garlic, spices, pepper, salt, and fruit juice. Coat the steaks on both sides and set aside for 30 minutes.

Coat a shallow baking dish with oil. Place fish steaks and any spare marinade in the baking dish. Top steaks with chili, onion, minced garlic, tomatoes, and sliced peppers. Pour the rest of the oil over the fish and cover the dish tightly. Cook on a low heat for 15-20 minutes or until the fish looses its translucent look. Sprinkle fish with fresh parsley and serve at once.

▼ ▼ ▼

sumed in great quantities; dwellers near bodies of water thus had several food advantages, and probably strengthened their economies by trading dried fish, turtle meat, and snails to less fortunately located communities. All in all, the range of meat and vegetables available to the Maya was considerable, and its food value was quite high.

Drinks almost never leave traces, even if their containers are not well washed. Various concoctions of ground corn sweetened with honey were probably used by the ancient Maya, and *balche*, a fermented drink made from honey and tree sap, was available for religious use if not for everyday consumption. The Maya grew cacao, from which they produced chocolate in a form that we would recognize but might not be able to stomach. Cacao was, in fact, used primarily as an addition to other foods and not thought of as the basis of the kind of rich, sweet drink we enjoy today. The Maya surely enjoyed sweet drinks and foods, but their sweet tooth was undoubtedly far less than our own.

Although the range of ancient foods was great, it would be wrong to think of all the foodstuffs appearing on every individual's plate. In Maya society those who were highest got the largest share of the most desirable items. In some sites, refuse piles near rulers' and other elite residences contain almost all the deer bone, all of the large turtle, and much of the other favoured game. It has been suggested that the taller stature of most rulers is partly a reflection of better diet; whether this is true or not, it is clear that people with power lived better than those beneath them. One wonders, however, whether every hunter who bagged a deer immediately brought all the best parts to his leader, or if on occasion a lapse (followed by appropriate prayer and offerings) might not have placed some prime cuts of venison on his own table.

Cross-cultural Influences

We have had no opportunity here to look at the other cultures of ancient Mexico and Central America, so we cannot trace the many ties that linked the Maya to both near and distant neighbours. It is highly probable that the Maya were borrowers from the beginning and obtained their knowledge of the calendar, and at least part of their writing system, from earlier peoples on Mexico's gulf coast. Throughout their history they remained in contact with other peoples both to the north and to the south, exchanging ideas just as they traded material goods. It would be a mistake to think of the Maya as isolated by their environment, forbidding though the jungle and mountains may seem. Their trading networks were information networks as well, whether officially or simply because every traveller picked up gossip wherever it was available.

When Teotihuacan, which had influenced highland Maya life for many centuries and the lowland Maya for a briefer period, fell in the eighth century the rulers of Maya city-states had surely already heard about the troubles and anticipated the great centre's collapse. When the Aztec rose to power far to the north five hundred years later, the news must have reached what remained of Maya society long before any Aztec. Finally, when the Spaniards arrived, not only did news of their coming spread rapidly but ancient trade and information networks continued to serve native purposes long after Spanish rule was implanted in the Maya land.

The Arts

Literature

As the western world understands the term, no literature is known to have existed in ancient Maya culture. The Maya produced many books, but the three and a half accordion-fold bark paper specimens that have survived are all religious in nature and have to do with celestial events, deities, and predictions of the future. We do know, however, that books or documents of other forms and materials were used by the Maya. There is also indirect evidence that both bark paper and a kind of parchment were used for other purposes. Hence the possibility exists that someone might have set thoughts down on paper in a form that we would identify as literary. What a tale such a volume would be!

Architecture

Of all the objects created by the Maya, the largest and in many senses the most striking are their buildings. Though damaged or reduced to ruins by the effects of tropical rains and forest growth, Maya buildings remain testaments to the ability of the ancient people to design, build, and maintain structures as complex as any in the ancient world. The buildings differ from site to site; the Temple of the Inscriptions at Palenque seems almost totally unlike Temple I at Tikal, which in turn is very different from Temple B-4 at **Altun Ha**. Regional and community differences of these sorts are what one would expect in a city-state system, and almost every site contains unique buildings as well. Yet no matter how different from one another the temples, palaces, and other buildings may be, they all share a good many basic features. It is this sharing, like that in other parts of material culture, that gives meaning to the idea of the Maya as one people.

Maya buildings seem curious to some because they do not reflect the jungle environment by copying natural forms in stone. With a few exceptions they are tall, angular structures that seem almost to have been built in defiance of the realities of their setting. In fact there are few places in the world in which the architecture mirrors the environment. What is more important is the question of whether the buildings are a sensible response to the environment. For the Maya, the answer is partly yes and partly no.

This temple at Tikal is typical of the type built from the sixth to the eighth century. It is built of limestone and consists of a series of platforms with a chambered building on top. The interior may have held places for ceremonies to take place or for the priests to don their garments.

Maya architecture began with houses that were built of poles and thatch, and set atop very low platforms. These buildings, which were fairly standardized quite early, were excellent responses to the environment in two important ways. First, they made use of renewable resources that occurred naturally in the vicinity of most communities. Second, they were cool, weatherproof (as long as the roof had the proper pitch), and if not shaded by nearby trees they lasted many years with very little maintenance. All of these characteristics can be found in most

This reconstruction of Tipu in Belize depicts what villages all throughout Maya history may have looked like. Most buildings were made of perishable materials, though some stone may have been used. The buildings, other than the Spanish church in the left foreground, are all residential.

Maya houses to this day. Problems arose in the ancient cities only when builders moved from poles and thatch to stone and mortar, a move that began sometime after communal architecture had first made its appearance.

Excavations have not produced direct evidence of the shift from thatch to stone, but we can envision the move as an attempt to make important buildings more permanent. The new stone temples sometimes held the graves of rulers, but their main purpose was to provide settings for ceremonies. In use, in form, and in construction Maya temples and their platforms, though they were partly pyramidal, were very different from the great pyramids of Egypt. To create the new buildings the Maya used the soft limestone that was found in many parts of their land and was easy to quarry and shape. Where such material was unavailable they made use of granite, slate, or even river cobbles, but still kept the ideas of shape and size that marked work in limestone. The permanent architecture grew to be a highly important part of Maya religious life and a highly visible part of city centres. As it did, more and more material and more and more workers were required to meet community needs. This was just one of the ways in which stone architecture was a dangerous departure from the simpler style, it meant increasingly heavier labour tax on the populace.

The stone buildings retained many of the ideas that went into the thatched structures. Their rooms had ceilings that resembled the undersides of thatched roofs; the doorways in both types of structures were about the same width, and in both were generally placed in the long walls; and the building sat atop a platform, though much higher in stone than it had been in the simpler thatched structures. The main environmental problem was that stone buildings used a non-renewable resource. Limestone not only made up the facings, but was also burned to produce mortar and the plaster that coated building surfaces. The platforms were, on the other hand, a partial solution to an environmental problem. Because in many cases they were built of stone mixed with refuse collected around the city, they served the Maya as a kind of aboveground sanitary landfill.

Almost from the first the architects who designed civic buildings and the builders who created them must have recognized some of the problems they faced. The civic buildings were waterproof as far as room interiors were concerned, but were subject to damage from heavy rains that frequently made stairs and other parts of the structures unusable. The soil in platforms worked like a sponge, taking up water during the rainy season and losing it at other times, so that plaster surfaces cracked and once-level surfaces tilted dangerously. Though the rooms were cool shelters from the tropic sun, they were much harder to close against the wind and rain, and exteriors were impossible to protect against the effects of tropical weather. As a result, much more human time and energy were required to keep the buildings in reasonable condition so that they could continue to serve as scenes for religious ceremonies.

Frequent rebuilding solved some of the building maintenance problems, but it also created over time huge layer cakes of stone and earth that because of their great weight were very likely to spread down and outward just as real cakes may do in a hot room.

This jade object, probably the figure of a ruler, was carved from rich, deep green jade, a material very important to the Maya. This is a scale drawing of the figure, dating from around A.D. 650, which was found at Altunlta in Belize.

In a number of cities the supply of limestone for rebuilding eventually ran out; reuse of old stones became common, and the size of building additions decreased. It is a wonder that the buildings have survived as well as they have done in spite of the fact that they are not the best response to a tropical environment.

Sculpture

Because they are so awesome in both size and carving, stelae are the best known examples of Maya sculpture. Other large-scale sculptural work, both in stone and in plaster, adorns many buildings, especially in the northern Yucatan, at Palenque in Chiapas, and at Copan in Honduras. The most numerous sculptures are, however, small portable works in stone, primarily **jade**. Jade was especially significant to the Maya because its green colour was associated with water and living plants and hence with fertility. Pendants, beads, and other ornaments of the precious material were part of rulers' and priests' raiment, and were often buried with them. Most large sculptures and almost all the small work depicts rulers (as on the stelae), deities, or individuals who are probably rulers costumed as gods. Yet among the small works in stone are such things as a simple carving of a porter bearing a burden with a tumpline (headband) and numerous representations of animals. The uses of stelae are clear: they commemorate rulers, as do carvings on the faces of buildings. Many of the small carvings were also linked with royalty, but some, even those of jade on rare occasions, are found in middle class graves, where their uses and meanings are much less clear. Out of all such pieces, though, shines the Maya artistic ability, technical skill, and love of material that made their civilization so great.

Painting

The image of Maya buildings as gleaming white is wrong; most were brightly painted, sometimes entirely in red but frequently (and increasingly in later centuries) in a great many colours. Sadly, most of the painting has disappeared with time, as have murals that once adorned building interiors. Only the most fortunate circumstances, often the result of the covering of one building by a later one, have preserved paintings partly intact. The best known murals, from Bonampak in Chiapas, were saved for us to admire by an even rarer event, the growth of a thin mineral coating over their surfaces. Elsewhere we have only traces to show what once was present and thus the greatest body of Maya painting is preserved on pottery vessels.

Out of a tradition of monochrome (single-colour) pottery the Maya evolved two- and then three-colour vessel painting, with rare use of additional colours. The basic palette of red and black on an orange ground was employed to depict rulers, gods, nobles, priests, and animals both fanciful and real, almost always in scenes that lack perspective. Though limited in colour, the paintings are our largest source of information on Maya clothing, of which only the tiniest fragments have survived. Pottery figures, often made as whistles when small or as incense burners at larger sizes, also show costumes. They were usually painted as well, generally on a stucco ground. Although the painting of standard bowls and other vessels can at times be less than beautiful, Maya vase painting at its finest displays a handling of body proportion and a delicacy of line that rival the best products of any ancient culture.

Science and Technology

Medicine

It is highly probable that the folk remedies used by the Maya today come down from ancient times, but in most cases knowledge of medicinal plants and their uses cannot be traced back securely even to the early Colonial period. As in any society, illness and injury were commonplace among the Maya, and evidence of healing of broken bones is not uncommon. The healing may tell us that the Maya middle class, or perhaps the elite, included medical practitioners, but no doctor's home or kit of instruments has yet been found. We do know, however, that the Maya possessed surgical skills and good knowledge of human anatomy and we can be sure that, like information on plant remedies, such knowledge was put to good use.

INNOVATIONS

DOING HOMEWORK IN MAYA MATHEMATICS

Maya arithmetic was probably written in various ways depending on the kind of calculation involved. We will use only one way here, which sets the numbers down vertically and has the lowest unit at the bottom. In the Maya vigesimal system (based on multiples of 20), each "level" above the bottom one in the vertical line is a count of units of 20 or multiples of that number. To read numbers one can start at either top or bottom, but it is usually easier to begin at the top.

= zero
= one
= five

Because there are only two symbols for numerals that function directly in computations, Maya arithmetic involves remembering that five dots (5 × 1) in any position convert to a bar (5) in that same position, and four bars (4 × 5) convert to a dot in the next higher position.

1 2 3
4 5

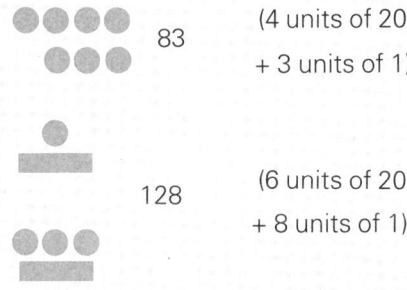

83 (4 units of 20 + 3 units of 1)

128 (6 units of 20 + 8 units of 1)

To add these two numbers, simply determine how many units of 20 there are in the total. Unless the total moves into the next higher category in the vigesimal system, units of 400 (20 × 20), the notation will remain in the same "levels" you have been using, thus:

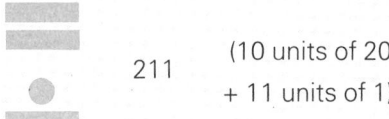

211 (10 units of 20 + 11 units of 1)

If the first numbers had been 183 and 228, making a total of 411, the notation would look like this:

(1 unit of 400)
(0 units of 20)
(11 units of 1)

This may seem a cumbersome system at first, but with a little practice you should be able to add and subtract. With some guidance you could learn to multiply and divide, but use of counters to represent the various elements in the system would be necessary at first unless you are a real whiz at maths. Most Maya merchants and others who used the system probably used counters, so if you set out to master Maya mathematics you need not feel inferior if you need visual reminders of where you are and what you are doing. The best guide to Maya mathematics is *Arithmetic in Maya,* by George I. Sánchez (c) 1961.

Discoveries and Inventions

Though clearly adept at use of many simple aids to human muscle power such as levers, inclined planes, rollers, and wedges, the Maya are not known to have invented any major technological devices. Their contributions in the area of technology lay in the application of immense patience to the production of objects large and small from materials that were often extremely difficult to work. The principal inventions produced by the Maya lay instead in the intellectual sphere: a calendric system, mathematics, and writing.

We have seen how the calendar affected so much of Maya life, and how important cycles were to its workings. The existence of the system, which was based as all calendars must be on very long periods of astronomical observation, remains one of the enigmas of Maya prehistory. The tropical lowlands are not well suited to astronomical work, and even the possibility that the calendar was introduced in its basic form from the Mexican gulf coast does not get round this problem. Beyond this there is the question of how anyone, having observed the moon's short cycle and concluded that other cycles might exist in the heavens, could have persuaded others to work for the tremendously long time needed to prove the existence of cycles, and then use the information to create a calendar. That this happened is beyond question, but how it happened will forever remain a mystery.

Maya mathematics involved discovery of something unknown elsewhere in the New World at the time, the principle of zero. In addition to the symbol for zero, the system, which was vigesimal (based on multiples of 20), used bars for five and dots for one. This would have been an impossibly cumbersome arrangement had the system not also used positions in the recording of unit counts (such as those in the calendar). Without this positional feature a Maya scribe could scarcely have found a writing surface large enough to hold a number above 1000. Besides their appearance in the calendar, number notations were presumably applied to measurements for building plans and many of the other uses numbers have in any society. So a good many people who knew nothing of the calendar were probably able to use the written numbers that were one of its principal elements. No everyday mathematical calculations have yet been identified, though bar-and-dot numbers appear in carvings on stone and bone and on quite a few pottery vessels.

The Writing System

To write their language, Mayan, the Maya created a complex hieroglyphic system that for many years could not be deciphered. Over the past twenty years, however, we have come to understand the basic elements of the system even though many hieroglyphs cannot yet be read and new ones are still being discovered. The hieroglyphs, which include day and month names, number in the hundreds, so it is clear that the system cannot be alphabetic. It is in fact both ideographic, which is to say that hieroglyphs can stand for complete ideas, and phonetic, which means that the symbols have sound values. Some of the ideas are known, but it is the phonetic aspect of the system that makes decipherment possible. Although texts, which occur on stelae, buildings, pottery vessels, and sculptures, as well as in the few remaining books, may not be entirely readable, the general meaning can usually be determined with reasonable certainty.

Ability to read the texts has told us much about relations among city-states, has changed our understanding of the information content of stelae as well as the reason for erecting such monuments, and has given us a picture of the workings of dynastic succession among the Maya. Perhaps most important, though, is the realization that not all texts are religious or political in nature. Before the hieroglyphs could be read archaeologists assumed, as they usually do when the meaning or use of something is not clear, that Maya writing was purely ceremonial in nature, but we now know otherwise.

Economy

Trade Routes and Contacts

Resources varied greatly in the Maya area and because of this internal trade was the lifeblood of the society. Commodities such as dried fish and shellfish, shell for the manufacture of ornaments and tools, and stingray spines and coral for ceremonial use made their way from coastal communities through the forest or up rivers to inland centres. Down those same routes may have come hardwoods, pottery clays, **obsidian** obtained by inland communities through long-distance trade, and all manner of other things unavailable on the coast. Often, because similar materials may have existed in several spots, we cannot be sure of either the source or the direction from which an import has come. Sometimes, however, as in the case of the marine goods, the source can be pinpointed and a specific route to inland centres can be suggested.

Obsidian, volcanic glass, from the Guatemalan highlands can be traced to its source wherever it occurs in the lowlands, often hundreds of miles from the quarry. Similarly, granite from the low mountains of Belize can be found over a wide area where it was prized for the making of manos and metates. When such materials come from mountain sources the existence of valleys and passes may permit a fairly precise detailing of a trade route, just as is often possible when we are tracing finished goods from maker to distant user. When we find central Mexican obsidian in a Caribbean coastal Maya site, however, no amount of detective work will reveal the route it took in travelling more than 1000 miles to its destination.

Countless examples exist of trade ties between Maya sites that involved very distinctive kinds of pottery, specific styles of jadecarving, or even—at the level of ideas—architectural styles. Such evidence makes it clear that the land of the Maya must have hummed with activity not only in each city-state but also along endless trails trod by porters (for the Maya had no beasts of burden) and their merchant masters. To fuel this exchange each community had to develop its own resources, both natural and human, to the fullest in order to provide materials and goods to pay for those things that could not be obtained locally. Though the output of pottery at some sites reached very high levels, neither in this nor in other areas did the Maya ever adopt mass production techniques. Their economy was based from beginning to end on cottage industry, organized and controlled at the first level by merchant-traders and ultimately by royalty.

Much of the force behind trade was, as we have seen, scarcity or absence of resources in one spot and relative abundance somewhere else. It is very likely, though, that human interest in exotic goods played a role in exchange as well. This is the hardest sort of trade to document because it involves materials or even finished goods that we cannot tell from the local products, though an ancient Maya could have told the difference in an instant. Such trade probably also was at work in foodstuffs, for the belief that the fish or the fruit from elsewhere are tastier than one's own products seems to be present in every society.

The matter of trade in staple food supplies cannot be studied from the archaeological evidence, for nowhere do we have an entire community's foodstuffs preserved and nowhere have we found a way to identify imported as opposed to local corn, beans, or squash seeds. The possibility exists that some areas, notably the Belize River valley and some of the lowlying northern parts of the country, may have been "breadbaskets" that supplied both nearby and distant communities. Exploitation of most such areas depended on elaborate irrigation systems that required fairly frequent maintenance. Distribution of the products of intensive agriculture on a large scale and over long distances would have forced inter-city organization and regulation, which must have been disrupted by the Classic collapse. This makes the survival of some communities in the midst of chaos all the more remarkable.

The ancient Maya emerge as an outstanding example of the ability of a people to build a great, complex, and long-lived civilization in surroundings that scarcely seem suited to the task. If we make the mistake of looking at the Maya in our society's terms we will see their civilization as a failure. This is because we emphasize growth as the only measure of success and many of the Mayas' grandest cities were swallowed up by the jungle a thousand years ago. We forget that before the collapse during the Classic period, the Maya had held sway over a very large territory for more than 2400 years. Even if we take the beginning of the Christian era as the starting point of modern western life (and it hardly seems realistic to do so), we have half a millennium to go before we can match the Maya record just up to the end of the Classic. And Maya society survived that upheaval and lived on until it was brought to heel by the Spanish over 3000 years after its first appearance on the human stage.

This collapse tells us much about the fragility of what seem to be enduring systems, but the centuries thereafter tell us just as much about survival in the face of radical change. The lessons of Maya prehistory, though they do not surround us in today's world, are there to be learnt, and they are worth learning because they show us more about ourselves as members of the human race.

Suggested Sources for Further Research

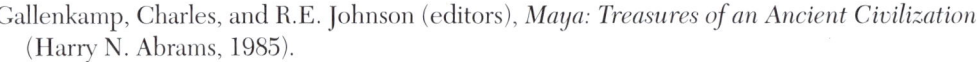

Gallenkamp, Charles, and R.E. Johnson (editors), *Maya: Treasures of an Ancient Civilization* (Harry N. Abrams, 1985).

Hammond, Norman, *Ancient Maya Civilization* (Rutgers University Press, 1982).

Henderson, John, *The World of the Ancient Maya* (Cornell University Press, 1981).

Kelley, David H., *Deciphering the Maya Script* (University of Texas Press, 1976).

Morley, Sylvanus, George Brainerd, and Robert Sharer, *The Ancient Maya*, 4th edition (Stanford University Press, 1983).

Sabloff, Jeremy A., *The New Archaeology and the Ancient Maya* (Scientific American Library, 1990).

Focus Your Knowledge

1. Describe the various geographical regions and how the Maya adapted to them.
2. What are the main sources of information regarding the Maya? Describe how these sources combine to create a picture of Maya life.
3. What role did religion play in Maya civilization?
4. What were the causes of the collapse of Classic Maya society?
5. Of what significance were the Maya temples?
6. Compare and contrast the role played by men and women in everyday Maya society.
7. Create a visual depiction of the class system of Maya society. Be sure to include all levels and aspects of society.
8. What do we know about Maya sport and entertainment?
9. Describe the nature of Maya food. What were the main ingredients? How was the type and preparation of the food indicative of the level of society in which it was consumed?

Apply Your Knowledge

1. How does the growth of Maya civilization challenge the concept that civilizations begin in river valleys?
2. In what ways were the Maya culturally similar? Why should they not be referred to as one people?
3. What evidence is there that Maya religion was more than just a set of beliefs and a moral guide and that religion, in fact, pervaded every aspect of their life?
4. Despite the fact that Maya architecture does not reflect the jungle environment, it is an accurate depiction of the society that produced it. Discuss this statement.

5. Which elements of Maya culture demonstrate that they were an advanced and highly literate society?

6. How did trade contribute to the standard of living in Maya cities? Of what importance to Maya life was the extensive trade network which existed?

7. Review the key elements of a civilization. Compare Maya civilization to other civilizations studied. Prepare an argument showing that the Maya were on par with the civilizations you have studied.

Extension Activities

1. Some people have attempted to suggest that Egyptians and Maya are linked, on the basis of pyramid and temple construction. Research the Maya temples in terms of construction, layout, and purpose and compare to the Egyptian pyramids to prove or disprove the above statement. This information can be presented in the form of a bulletin board, a video, a news special or a newspaper article.

2. Using the feature study on Maya food prepare a sample dish and serve it to the class.

3. Create a stela of your own out of plasticene, play dough, or on paper. Be sure it represents an appropriate subject and is set up according to the stelae created by the Maya. This would include using Maya hieroglyphics and numbers.

4. Based on further research create a model of a Maya town. Be sure to include temples and other significant features.

5. Using the *National Geographic* article "La Ruta Maya" from the October 1989 issue and further research, create a tourist guide to ancient Maya sites. Your information can be presented in the form of a bulletin board, a slide package, a tourist brochure, or an accurate model.

6. Based on further research, plan and hold a ball court game. Improvise rules where necessary.

7. Using a combination of the above suggestions your class may wish to host a Maya day. The ball court games could take place in the gym, food could be served in a Family Studies room, and the library could be the place for a tour of the models of ancient Maya sites and a place to view the stelae.

8a. Examine Spanish accounts of the early contact with the Maya with regard to religious practices, culture, food and clothing, government, homes, art and architecture. To what degree were these accounts accurate and to what degree did they reflect the ethnocentric biases? Report on the accuracies and inaccuracies of these accounts.

8b. Undoubtedly, the Maya too would have been guilty of an ethnocentric bias but unfortunately records of their reaction to the Spanish have not been preserved. Based on what you know of the Maya and European culture write a diary entry which captures the Mayas' reactions to their first contact with the Spanish culture and their customs.

9. Often, when one examines the decline of a civilization, it is seen as being negative, yet the Maya Postclassic period is not a decline. What evidence is there to support the idea that in the Postclassic period a vibrant society and culture remained?

CHAPTER 13

The Ancient Aztecs

Chapter Highlights

- Aztec diet and dress

- concepts of time and religion

- the splendour of Tenochtitlan

- how a man and a woman toppled the Empire of the Aztecs

- sport and leisure among the Aztecs

- the decimation of the Aztec population

There can be few chapters in history that record events as tragic, inevitable, and enigmatic as the Spanish Conquest of Aztec Mexico. Aztec legend had promised the return of an old and beloved god-king, **Quetzalcoatl**, to Mexico. The arrival from the east, the direction in which Quetzalcoatl had fled, of the bearded Spaniards with their strange beasts and advanced technology thereby perplexed the Aztec ruler, **Montezuma**, and undermined his determination to act quickly to protect his people. The captain of the conquest, **Hernán Cortés**, not only instilled fear through superior European war technology, but far more important, he succeeded in making allies of Montezuma's enemies. This diplomacy and communication was made possible through his translator and companion, an Indian woman known to the Spaniards as Doña Marina. Doña Marina originally joined the Spaniards when they passed through the province of Tabasco in 1519. This was indeed a fateful meeting, for Doña Marina rarely left Cortés's side. In fact, according to one of the chroniclers of the conquest, Bernal Díaz, a man who had been a soldier in Cortés's army, Cortés himself was known to most of the Indians as *Malinche*, which translates as "Marina's captain," because Marina and Cortés were always seen together.

The Conquest of Mexico on November 8, 1519, is a story that deserves its own chapter. What we will be concerned with here is a description of the Aztec civilization before it was shattered and forever altered by the Spaniards and priests of the Conquest. At the same time that the Aztecs became Christianized and adopted aspects of European culture, the Spaniards in Mexico also absorbed Aztec culture, married into Aztec families, adopted and adapted foods and cooking techniques, child-rearing practices, crops and customs, and often merged Christian saints and holidays with local celebrations. What resulted is the culture of modern Mexico, a true and vibrant blend of Old and New World traditions.

Although archaeology contributes a great deal to our knowledge of ancient Mexico, it is largely through the eyes and pens of the conquering Spaniards and the conquered Mexica (the name the Aztecs called themselves) that the civilization of ancient Mexico is known to us.

Key Concepts

Quetzalcoatl

Montezuma

Hernán Cortés

Tenochtitlan

chinampas

tribute

Toltec

Huitzilopochtli

Tlacaelel

patolli

Geography

The Valley of Mexico

Aztec civilization flourished in what is known as the Valley of Mexico, the home of modern-day Mexico City. The valley is one of a number of natural basins that are found in the mountainous region of central Mexico, a land now, as then, of volcanoes and earthquakes. Approximately 7800 km² in area, the valley floor is actually almost 2500 m above sea level. Some of the mountains surrounding the valley rise to over 5000 m. In Precolumbian times the valley floor was covered by a shallow system of lakes, and the Aztec capital of **Tenochtitlan** was situated on an island in one of the lakes, called Lake Texcoco. The city had an organized system of canals, and lake-bottom sediments were scraped up along shorelines to form rectangular plots of cultivable land that rose above the level of the water in the lake, which at its deepest was only 2.2 m. These plots were called ***chinampas*** by the Aztecs, and appeared to some of the Spanish conquerors to be floating gardens. Chinampas were extremely productive: as much as seven crops a year could be grown with the use of seed beds and crop rotation. The canals that drained the chinampas also served as access routes for canoe traffic. Today, Tenochtitlan, its canals and chinampas are buried by modern-day Mexico City.

As one sixteenth-century Spanish friar stated, "There are very beautiful hills which surround the city like a wall." This "wall" of mountains ringing the Valley of Mexico had no natural outlet. When it rained, mountainside runoff and overflowing spring water would collect in the lake; in fact, any changes in the pattern of rainfall in the past resulted in great fluctuations in the size of the lake. Excessive water flow would occasionally raise the level of the lake to cover one-storey buildings in Tenochtitlan. During the winter dry period, however, rain seldom if ever fell. Total rainfall, was, and is, less than half of that of the Maya lowlands. Conditions could be quite arid, creating problems for Aztec farmers in spite of the fact that the soils were fertile. Although two maize crops a year were possible at lower elevations, only one crop per year was normal in the Valley of Mexico. Loss of the yearly crop to arid conditions was devastating. In addition, if the rains did not come when they were supposed to, in May or June, but later, the maize would be planted late and might not mature before the onset of the frosts in November or October.

The frosts in the Valley of Mexico, according to the Spaniards, were not as severe as they were in Castille, but they were apparently unpredictable, at least as far as post-Conquest Spanish farmers were concerned. Indeed, one of the advantages of chinampas is that the high water table protected the Aztecs' crops against frost. Frosts damaged many of the crops the Spaniards brought to the Valley of Mexico—grapevines, fig trees, melons, eggplants—crops which the Spaniards thought they could grow with ease in the valley's temperate climate.

Central Mexico

There were zones outside the Valley of Mexico, particularly to the south and east, that were more temperate and more tropical and where threats of drought or frosts were minimal. The Aztec conquests of areas outside the valley were initially motivated in part by the need to control supplies of food such as maize. A devastating famine spread throughout central Mexico beginning in the year known in the Aztec calendar as 1 Rabbit, or 1450. Frosts destroyed crops in the valley, and this was followed by two years of severe drought. Temporary abandonment of the city occurred in 1454–1455. Some families were so desperate that they sold their children to people who lived in areas outside the valley where maize was still successfully grown. The childrens'

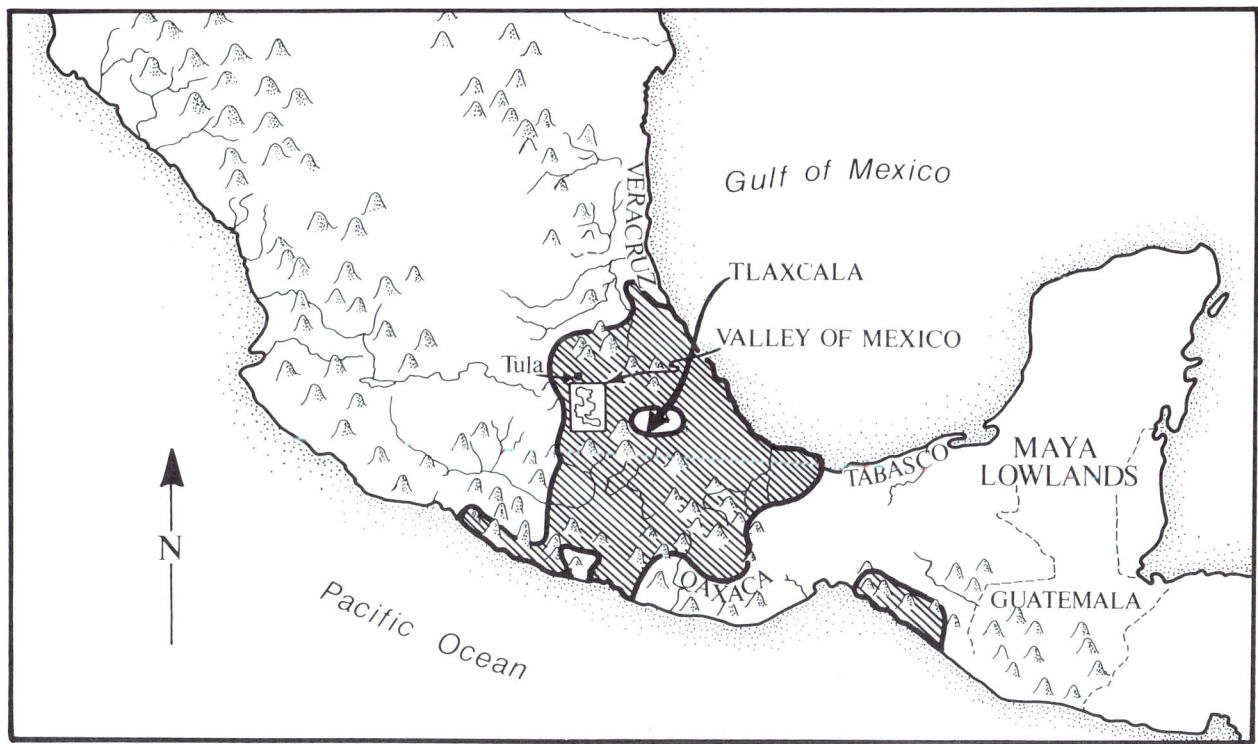

Mesoamerica
The extent of the Aztec Empire in Mesoamerica.

new keepers would maintain them while the famine lasted.

It is easy to see why the Aztecs would want to take action to avoid such tragedies in the future, and one of the things they did was to conquer people in fertile areas outside the Valley of Mexico who could provide them with **tribute** in the form of food. ("Tribute" was a form of payment, either in food, raw materials or manufactured goods, made to the Aztecs by the people they conquered. Most of the tribute paid to the Aztecs by conquered peoples was in the form of luxury goods, such as feathers and jade, or raw and manufactured materials, such as gold dust and cotton clothing.) By 1519, the Aztecs and their allies had gained control of areas outside the valley in which environmental conditions varied.

This meant that the timing of maize harvesting also varied, and in some areas more than one crop was produced. The conquered towns not too distant from the Valley of Mexico could then send tribute in the form of food to Tenochtitlan at different times of the year, and the Aztecs could store maize over a longer period. In this way the effects of local agricultural disasters for the Aztecs and their allies would be minimized and the famine of 1 Rabbit would not be repeated.

Adapting to a Dry Environment

Arid and cool conditions challenged Aztec ingenuity. Coupled with the high elevation and the physical constraints brought about by the ring of mountains

INNOVATIONS

NAHUATL: THE LANGUAGE OF THE AZTECS

The language spoken by the Aztecs is called Nahuatl (nah-wattle), and it is still spoken today in many parts of Mexico. Its pronunciation is none too easy for us—the proper names in particular seem long, and tangle the tongue.

The practice of writing Nahuatl using the letters of our alphabet was introduced by Spanish missionaries. Generally speaking, the letters in the Nahuatl names given in this chapter have the same phonetic value as in Spanish. The one exception is **x**, which is pronounced like the English **sh**. For example, the name "Mexica" is pronounced "Mesheeca"; and, Montezuma's second name, "Xocoyotzin," is pronounced "Sho-co-yo-tzin." The reason for this is that when the Spanish came to the New World in the sixteenth century, the "x" in their alphabet at that time stood for a "sh" sound. (This has since changed, and now an "x" in Spanish usually stands for the sound of an "h".)

When you try to pronounce Nahuatl words, remember that Nahuatl speakers normally put stress on the next-to-last syllable, as in Monte**zu**ma, or Quetzal**coa**tl (ketzal-**ko**-attle), with the "a" pronounced "ah" as in Spanish. Some Nahuatl words have worked their way into English: chocolate (from Nahuatl word "chocolatl"), chili (chilli), coyote (coyotl), tomato (tomatl), avocado (ahuacatl), ocelot (ocelotl).

The Aztecs of Mexico, like earlier Mesoamerican peoples, kept written records. They kept track of tribute payments, they wrote histories, and they recorded the passage of time. We call the writing symbols they used "hieroglyphs," or simply "glyphs" for short. The Aztecs had no alphabet, and they did not use signs to stand for sounds as extensively as the Maya did. Instead they put pictures of objects together to communicate an idea. For example, to represent the city of Tenochtitlan in writing they would draw a picture of a stone (tena in the Nahuatl language) with a picture of a cactus (nochtli). Another example is the glyph for the city of Coatepec, which consists of a picture of a serpent or snake (coatl) on a hill (tepec). A path or journey was indicated by a row of footprints and speech was indicated by drawing scroll-like symbols near people's mouths. Song was represented by speech scrolls with flowers. In the tribute lists, drawings of objects such as cotton cloaks simply represented the objects themselves. The Aztecs were concerned with recording exactly how many objects were to be paid in tribute, and they used a numbering system as well. A dot was used for each unit through 19; a flag represented the number 20; a feather represented 400; and a bag of incense represented 8000. As noted in the text, Aztec books were folded like an accordion, and the paper was made from the bark of trees. We call the books codices—the singular form is codex. As we learned in the previous chapter, only three pre-Conquest Maya codices have survived, but many more are known from the Valley of Mexico. Most deal with calendrical matters. Other codices were written by the Aztecs after the Spanish Conquest and these often show a mixture of Aztec and Spanish styles.

SYMBOL	MEANING
	Coatepec
	a path or journey
	speech
	one unit
	twenty units
	four hundred units
	eight thousand units

surrounding the valley, the dry, cool climate required management techniques that were different from what was suitable for the high temperatures and humidity of the Maya lowland forests. No two areas seem less alike than the Valley of Mexico and the Maya lowlands. Though the Aztecs and the Maya shared staple crops such as maize, beans, and squash, the varieties that were grown were different and there were crops and animals distinctive to the two areas. When we think of the Maya lowlands, we think of the source of cacao (chocolate), vanilla, water lilies, chicle (a tree sap made into chewing gum), rubber trees, crocodiles, cashews, quetzal birds, macaws, and monkeys. When we think of the Aztecs, we think more of desert-adapted plants and animals, as well as lake-dwelling species: cacti, rattlesnakes, coyotes, eagles, rabbits, herons, frogs, salamanders, turtles, and reeds. Of the cacti, two called nopal and maguey were important to the Aztecs for several reasons. The nopal yields a tasty fruit called prickly pear. Maguey fibers were used to make cord and clothing, the thorns were used as needles, and the plants themselves formed ideal field boundaries. The leaves were roasted and eaten, and the juice of maguey, when fermented, produces the alcoholic drink called *pulque*. More familiar to Canadians is the distilled and refined form of pulque known as "tequila."

Texcoco, the name of the lake surrounding the Aztec capital, produced a food called tecuitlatl. A Franciscan friar, known as Motolinia, left this account of tecuitlatl:

> There breeds upon the water of the Lake of Mexico a sort of very fine slime, and at a certain time of the year when it is the thickest, the Indians gather them with very fine nets until their acales or boats are full. On shore they make a very smooth plot two or three brazas [3.4–5.1 m] long and a little less wide on the earth or on very fine sand. They throw it [the tecuitlatl] down to dry until it makes a loaf two dedos [3.6 cm] thick. A few days later, it dries to the thickness of a used ducat [a coin]. The Indians cut this loaf in two wide bricks and eat a lot of it and think it good. This merchandise is carried by all the merchants of the land as cheese is among us. Those of us who share the tastes of the Indians find it very tasty. It has a salty flavor...[1]

Thus, with this taste of salt from Lake Texcoco, cheeks tingling from the high, dry atmosphere of the Valley of Mexico, and eyes turned towards the mountains cradling the Aztec capital, we journey back in time to the twelfth century and the misty origins of the Mexica.

The Origins of the Aztecs

The Aztecs called themselves *Mexica*, and gave their name to modern Mexico. We shall, however, persist in using the term Aztec because it is the better known, if less accurate, name. The Aztecs were newcomers to the Valley of Mexico. Numerous communities, such as Culhuacan and Azcapotzalco (and others with even longer, more tongue-twisting names!) already dotted the area. The people in these communities had a long and civilized history: they built monumental temples and public buildings, planned their cities, irrigated their fields, had state-administered tax and tribute systems, and had extensive markets and traded goods over long distances. They claimed that their traditions harked back to the days of Teotihuacan, and they viewed the Aztecs unequivocally as uncultured savages. It was not long, however, before the Aztecs became cultured enough

---

[1] *Fray Toribio de Benavente o Motolonía, "Memoriales o Libro de las Cosas de la Neuva España y de los Naturales de Ella," ed. Edmund O'Gorman in Bernard Ortiz de Montellano,* Aztec Medicine, Health, and Nutrition *(New Jersey: Rutgers University Press, 1990), p. 104.*

to view Teotihuacan as a model for their own particular destiny, so we shall digress long enough to describe two civilizations, at Teotihuacan and Tula, whose heritage was to influence the Aztecs so greatly.

Teotihuacan and Tula

Teotihuacan, on the northeast side of Lake Texcoco, was the centre of one of the greatest civilizations in the Americas. Its roots stretched back to 200 B.C., but it was at the height of its power between about A.D. 250 to 750. Teotihuacan had a population of about 150 000 people and covered more than 20 km^2. We do not know who these people were; we do not know what they called themselves, or what language they spoke. All this information is obscured by the mists of time. We do know that Teotihuacan was a thriving city, and that its markets attracted merchants and their goods from all over Mesoamerica, including the Maya lowlands.

Despite its sudden demise in the eighth century (A.D. 750), Teotihuacan provided a model of culture and behavior that later peoples who lived around the lakes in the Valley of Mexico would claim to remember. Although Teotihuacan was in ruins when the Aztecs came to power, the city of the dead contained the spirit of a glorious past that the Aztecs sought to capture.

Another past civilization which the Aztecs sought to emulate was that of Tula, which flourished from A.D. 900 to 1150. Although we do not know who built Teotihuacan, we do know that people called the **Toltecs** ruled Tula, which lies to the north of the Valley of Mexico. The area around Tula is arid and characterized by the growth of mesquite, a scrubby bush that is well adapted to semi-desert conditions. Recent research in environmental history has shown us that before the Spanish Conquest, the area around Tula was a settlers' paradise: wooded hills, bubbling springs, fields coloured green with crops nourished by an extensive system of irrigation canals. What happened? The Spanish introduced sheep and other grazing animals, but even these alone were not responsible for the extreme environmental degradation that took place. It was the extent of mismanagement and the huge numbers of sheep that were eventually let loose on the land, that caused irreversible processes to be set in motion. The vegetation was cropped to the ground, soils

MAJOR EVENTS IN AZTEC HISTORY

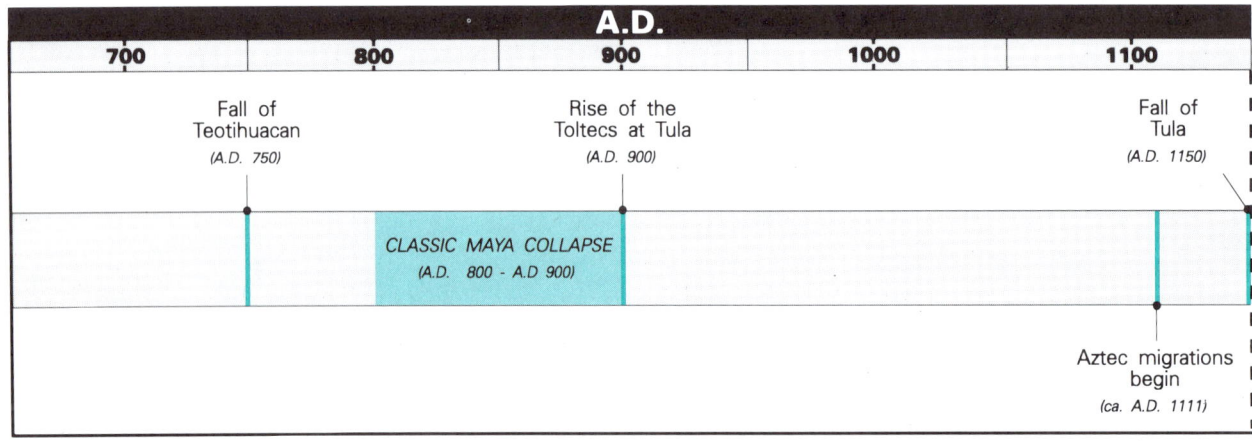

began to erode, nutrients washed away, and after a time, only hardy species like mesquite could take root in the dry, thin soil.

The Aztecs saw the Toltecs as rulers of a Golden Age. Aztec children would be told that the Toltecs had been the wisest of people, their houses were the most beautiful, their craftspeople the most skilled, their works were the ultimate in perfection. Although Tula had fallen before the Aztecs rose to power, the memory of the Toltec Empire was far fresher than the memory of Teotihuacan, and Aztec nobles would come to claim descent from Toltec heroes. But we have jumped far ahead of ourselves here, for the "civilizing" of the Aztecs did not happen overnight, and when they first reached the Valley of Mexico as wanderers from the north, they were seen by those people with deep roots in the Valley of Mexico as barbarians of little note.

*T*he Arrival of the Aztecs

According to Aztec legends, their home was a place called Aztlan, the "Place of the Herons." No one knows exactly where Aztlan was located. Some say it was in the southwestern part of the United States, others that it was only 100 km northwest of Tenochtitlan. Since the journey from Aztlan to the Aztec's final home in Lake Texcoco was supposed to have taken 200 years, it is easier to imagine Aztlan lying at least as far as the northwestern part of Mexico. Wherever it was, the journey from Aztlan was an arduous one. According to Aztec histories, the journey began, in our calendar, in the year 1111. From their homeland the Aztecs moved southward slowly, stopping in places for periods of time, building temples and ball courts, and then moving on. They spent time in the northern reaches of the Valley of Mexico, and are supposed to have visited the ruins of Tula. They celebrated an important new year's ceremony near Tula in 1163, and then proceeded to move southward. They arrived in the Valley of Mexico proper in the thirteenth century (probably by around 1250), but when they tried to settle among established peoples, they were driven away. One of the towns, called Culhuacan, finally accepted them, but with conditions.

The people of Culhuacan, the Culhua, saw themselves as direct inheritors of the high culture of the

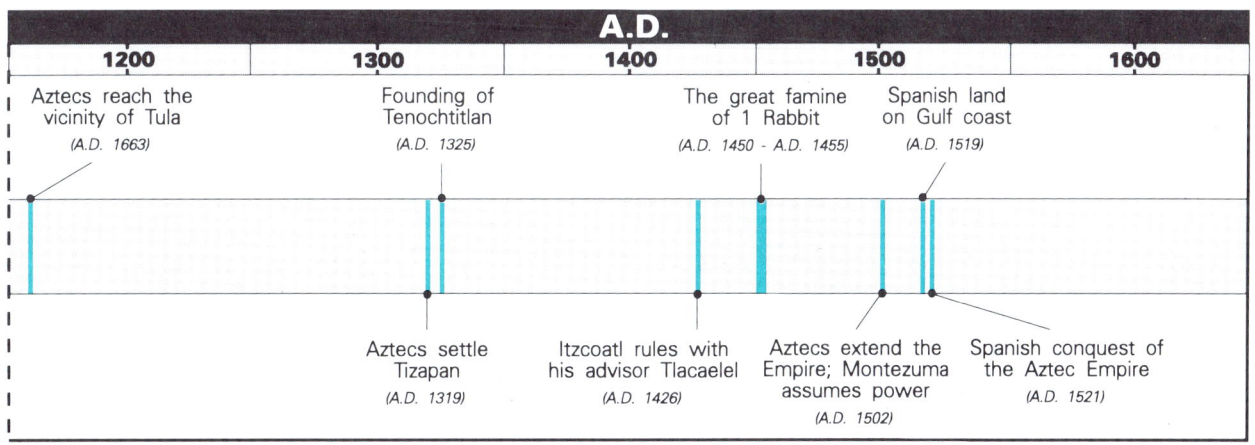

The Valley of Mexico

Toltecs at Tula. Tula fell because it was destroyed by Chichimec groups (predecessors of the Aztecs) who were migrating southward from the northern desert to escape conditions of drought and scarce game. The refugees in and around Tula fled southward to the Valley of Mexico and established towns around the lakes. Culhuacan was one of these towns.

Therefore the Culhua saw themselves as being in a position to set conditions for the Aztecs. They allowed the Aztecs to remain in the vicinity of Culhuacan if they would work the lands of their Culhua masters and live in a place no one wanted: a dreary, snake-infested place just west of Culhuacan, called Tizapan. To the surprise of the Culhua, the Aztecs thrived in this environment! Grudgingly, the Culhua came to accept the Aztec presence, and soon the Aztecs were serving as mercenaries for their Culhua lords. The Aztecs were fierce warriors and struck terror in the hearts of their enemies. All might have been well but for a horrible incident in which the Aztecs struck terror in the hearts of their allies too.

The story, much abbreviated, goes something like this. There came a time when the Aztecs went to the king of the Culhua and asked for his daughter—in some accounts, a ruler in her own right—to be mistress of the Aztec god, **Huitzilopochtli**. The young woman was brought to the Aztec camp and promptly sacrificed, apparently with the intent of provoking war. The Culhua king was invited by the Aztecs to attend the ceremony dedicating his daughter as a goddess, but when he found that his daughter had been killed, not wedded, fighting broke out immediately and the Aztecs were defeated and forced to flee into the marshes around Lake Texcoco.

The Aztec chronicles recount that their god, Huitzilopochtli, told them to settle where they saw an eagle perched on a prickly pear cactus. They wandered among the marshes until such a sign is supposed to have appeared to them, on an island in the lake. They named this island, their new home, Tenochtitlan. Another island, Tlatelolco, just north of Tenochtitlan, was also settled. Eventually, as swamps were drained and the land built up, the two islands became one. The founding of Tenochtitlan took place in 1325.

For a time the Aztecs served as mercenaries for mightier powers on the mainland: the Tepanecs of Azcapotzalco. Gradually the Tepanecs, with Aztec help, began to conquer other cities in the Valley of Mexico; in the process the Aztecs evolved from mercenaries of the Tepanecs to become their allies.

As could probably be predicted, the Aztecs became more and more powerful. Itzcoatl became the Aztec ruler in 1426. Under his leadership, the Aztecs turned against the Tepanecs, and two years later, with the help of new allies, brutally crushed Azcapotzalco. In the following years the Aztecs cemented relationships with their two most powerful allies and formed what is known as the Triple Alliance. From this point on, the Aztec Empire was established, and for the next 90 years, until the arrival of the Spaniards, the Aztecs and their allies embarked on a program of military expansion that had never before been seen in Mesoamerica.

Of the city-states around the lake, the Aztecs conquered Coyoacan, Cuitlahuac, Xochimilco, and Chalco. They signed a treaty with the Tlahuicas in Morelos, but failed to subdue the Tarascans, the Tlaxcalans, the Mixtecs, and the Zapotecs. They marched to the Gulf Coast and exacted tribute from the Cempoalans, and dominated peoples in Oaxaca, Chiapas, and even parts of Guatemala. By 1519 they ruled an empire of several million people who spoke a variety of languages, and their territory stretched from the Pacific Ocean to the Gulf of Mexico, and from central Mexico to Guatemala.

Beliefs

Human Sacrifice

The Aztecs were a people of contradiction. Their empire rested on war and human sacrifice, yet they sought to capture in song and poetry the beauty of the world around them. As they saw it, the continual offering of blood through human sacrifice ensured the perpetuation of the universe. It is this aspect of their culture and tradition that we find hardest to understand, yet it absorbs us in trying to explain it. Spanish observers, even those most sympathetic to the Aztecs, found the practice of human sacrifice revolting:

> ...the men or women who were to be sacrificed to their gods were thrown on their backs and of their own accord remained perfectly still. A priest then came out with a stone knife...and with this knife he opened the part where the heart is and took out the heart, without the person who was being sacrificed uttering a word....[2]

The Aztecs were unusual even among Mesoamerican cultures for the extent to which human sacrifice was carried out. Along with warfare, mass sacrifice was institutionalized as political policy. No one knows for certain how many humans met their deaths on the sacrificial block. Cortés estimated that 50 people were killed at each temple every year. This would put the yearly estimate at about 20 000 people. Tenochtitlan was certainly the site for the greatest numbers of sacrifices; as many as 800 victims were supposed to have been killed for one festival alone. One of the Spanish friars wrote that thousands of warriors were sacrificed at the consecration of the great temple of Huitzilopochtli. The skulls of victims were often displayed on what is called a skull rack. The largest skull rack stood in the plaza at the foot of the Templo Mayor, the major temple in Tenochtitlan. Here, the skulls were defleshed and displayed in rows. It is interesting that two of Cortés's soldiers estimated that at least 136 000 skulls were displayed on this particular device; however, there is little doubt that this was an extreme exaggeration. The major temple at Tlatelolco, near Tenochtitlan, has been excavated and only 170 skulls perforated for skull rack display have been recovered. Why the discrepancy? One answer

---

[2]Francicso de Aguilar, "Historia de la Neuva España," The Conquistadors: First Person Accounts of the Conquest of Mexico, ed. Patricia de Fuentes (New York: Orion Press, 1963), pp. 163-64.

PERSONALITIES

THE GREAT MONTEZUMA

The most familiar figure in Aztec history for many people is Montezuma, the great leader of the Aztecs at the time of the Spanish conquest. Much of the fame accorded Montezuma no doubt is derived from the Spanish records which have left a vivid picture of the Aztecs and their leader. The most complete account of the Aztecs and their capital city of Tenochtitlan was compiled by Bernal Diaz del Castillio in *The Conquest of New Spain*. Diaz wrote his famous account of the conquest of Mexico when he was over seventy years old. He was a participant in Cortés's expedition in 1519 and by the time he wrote *The Conquest of New Spain* he was the sole survivor of the conquerors of Mexico. The excerpt below is Diaz's description of the Aztec leader Montezuma. As you read the account, consider what this description says about Diaz's attitude towards the Aztec leader.

When we came near to Mexico, at a place where there were some other small towers, the great Montezuma descended from his litter, and these other great Caciques support him beneath a marvelously rich canopy of green feathers, decorated with gold work, silver, pearls, and chalchihuites, which hung from a sort of border. It was a marvellous sight. The great Montezuma was magnificently clad, in their fashion, and wore sandals of a kid for which their name is cactli, the soles of which are of gold and the upper parts ornamented with precious stones. And the four other lords who supported him were richly clad also in garments that seem to have been kept ready for them on the road so that they would accompany their master. For they had not worn clothes like this when they came out to receive us. There were four other great Caciques who carried the canopy above their heads, and many more lords who walked before the great Montezuma, sweeping the ground on which he was to tread, and laying down cloaks so that his feet should not touch the earth. Not one of these chieftains dared to look him in the face. All kept their eyes lowered most reverently except those four lords, his nephews, who were supporting him.

may be that many Spaniards exaggerated Aztec behaviour to provide justification for the often harsh treatment meted out to the Indians.

Even 170 sacrifices seems grossly out of proportion to us, although if one lived in Tenochtitlan one could draw some comfort from the fact that it was not the Aztecs but their enemies, conquered in battle, who provided most of the sacrificial victims. Even so, how did the Aztecs come to terms with such practices when they produced not only warriors, but poets and philosophers who wrote of matters such as the attainment of truth, the beauty of flowers, the transitory nature of earthly things? There is no answer we can give with security, but there is some explanation in the Aztec concept of the universe, in the history of Aztec consolidation of power, and possibly, too, in the extent to which individuals influence the course of human history, as in the case of the Aztec counsellor, Tlacaelel, whose policies we will describe later.

One Aztec legend relates that the Fifth Sun, the world in which the Aztecs lived, was created at

Teotihuacan (the Classic civilization in the Valley of Mexico) by the sacrifice of creator-gods. In order to create the sun and the moon and set them in motion in the sky, these gods cast themselves into a Divine Fire. Thus they set an example of sacrifice which humans were expected to follow. Another myth relates that Quetzalcoatl shed some of his blood to help restore life on earth. The Aztecs saw the shedding of blood as the ultimate gift to sustain life for the community. Aztec men and women could attain immortality in two ways, both associated with bloodshed: for women, death in childbirth; for men, death on the battlefield.

Tlacaelel's Reforms

Why this apparent obsession with the shedding of blood? The theme certainly is a thread running through all of Mesoamerican life, but at the end of the Classic period (ca. A.D. 800) militaristic groups and their warrior gods overshadowed and ultimately pushed aside the intellectual hierarchy of the older cultures and their nature gods. War and the taking of captives became all-important throughout the Postclassic period, but it was only the Aztecs who dedicated their lives and their empire to such pursuits.

It may be that a single individual had much to do with encouraging the frequency of human sacrifice among the Aztecs. This individual, **Tlacaelel**, was the royal counsellor to Itzcoatl, whom you may remember was the Aztec king who led the conquest of the Tepanecs in 1430. Tlacaelel was said to have persuaded the Aztec kings whom he served that they must make it their mission to extend the domain of their principal god, Huitzilopochtli, so that there would always be captives to sacrifice to him. Tlacaelel's advice was heeded and Tenochtitlan became the setting for the sacrifice of large numbers of captives from places as far away as Oaxaca, Chiapas, and Guatemala.

Tlacaelel is remembered for more than his ritual reforms. He revamped the Aztec judicial system, the army, and the organization of travelling merchants, the pochtecas, who often served the Aztec state as gatherers of information—literally an Aztec CIA—and of whom we shall speak later. Perhaps the most astounding reform was that Tlacaelel and Itzcoatl made the decision to change recorded Aztec history. The Aztecs, like the Maya, had a written language and recorded aspects of their history in books made of bark paper that were folded, accordion-fashion, rather than bound at the edges as ours are. Tlacaelel decided that the history that had so far been recorded did not serve the Aztec state, and he had the relevant books burned. In the new version of history the Aztecs became descendants of the famous Toltecs. Their god, Huitzilopochtli, was described as equal to older gods such as Quetzalcoatl, but perhaps most important, warfare was exalted to new heights and the Aztecs, the "people of the sun," were said to be destined to conquer all other nations. How revealing to find that the Aztecs, like other groups in history bent on conquest, sought extraordinary means to justify their ends! They destroyed records carefully kept for decades by their historians and scribes in order to create a past that better suited the goal of the Empire and the quest for captives for sacrifice.

As for Tlacaelel, he counselled the kings who succeeded Itzcoatl and died just before 1481. Little did he know that in less than 40 years the empire he had helped to create would be destroyed by an alien force that was beyond his power to foresee.

Aztec Deities

What were the gods like who demanded human sacrifice? There were too many to describe here. When the Aztecs conquered other people they assimilated their gods; thus, as the Empire grew, so did the pantheon. Basically, the gods can be divided into three groups. There are those associated with creation; those associated with rain and agricultural fertility; and those whom the Aztecs fought for in war.

In the first category are the Lord and Lady of Duality, often represented by a single deity with both male and female aspects. There was also Tezcatlipoca, the "Smoking Mirror." He was all powerful and could see everything that happened in the world as reflected in his mirror. He was associated with the night, the jaguar, and sorcery, and was the source of all natural forces, human strength and weakness, wealth, happiness and sorrow. He is usually shown with two mirrors, one at his head and the other in the place of a foot bitten off by an earth monster. His body was black and his face yellow with black bands. He was a warrior and carried a shield, an *atlatl* (dart thrower) and darts.

Huehueteotl, the fire god, was also associated with creation. Every 52 years the Aztecs celebrated a fire ceremony. All fires were extinguished and all household articles, such as statues and cooking implements, were discarded. When night fell people would climb to the housetops. In the darkness the priests would hold a ceremony at a nearby mountain peak in which a captive would be sacrificed, and a new fire kindled in the chest cavity of the victim. If the fire were successfully flamed, all would be well and the world and its people would exist for another 52 years. If perchance the flame died (as it never seemed to), the world, called the Fifth Sun by the Aztecs, would finally end, darkness would come over the earth and the celestial monsters would descend and devour all human beings.

Of the rain gods, Tlaloc is the best known. He is always portrayed with a distinctive mask which makes him look as if he had a large curled moustache and wore goggles. Tlaloc caused the rain to fall and the crops to grow. There were also a number of goddesses associated with fertility. One of these, Tonantzin, merged after the Conquest with the

This picture of Tlaloc, redrawn from an Aztec codex, shows him holding a corn plant. As the ancient god of rain he was crucial to agriculture. He is wearing the kilt typical of Aztec men and his distinctive mask, which has rings around the eyes and gives the impression that he is wearing eyeglasses.

image of the Virgin Mary. There was also Xipe Totec, the fertility god who heralded the arrival of spring.

Of the warrior gods, there was Tonatiuh, a sun god well known to many peoples in central Mexico. And of course there was Huitzilopochtli, the patron god of the Aztecs who was also associated with the sun. All Aztec warriors were dedicated to the service of the sun, and supplied the sun with the blood of their captives.

Outside of the three groups described above was Quetzalcoatl, the plumed or feathered serpent. Quetzalcoatl is a very old and revered Mesoamerican god. He is often shown as bearded, a sign that he was an ancient deity. He was worshipped in one form or another by the Maya and the Toltecs and is believed to have been a creator god who provided sustenance for humanity. He was also associated with the rain and the wind. Tezcatlipoca, the Smoking Mirror, was a capricious god who demanded warfare and human sacrifice, whereas Quetzalcoatl was said to be a benevolent god who brought maize to humanity, as well as learning and the arts, and who demanded of his people only the peaceful sacrifice of jade, snakes, and butterflies.

Social History

Social Structure

The fundamental division of Aztec life was that between nobles and commoners. Basically, there were, in descending order, rulers, chiefs, and nobles in the highest class. Intermediate positions were occupied by merchants and luxury artisans. The commoners were divided into free commoners, those in rural areas who worked the land of the nobles, and slaves.

All nobles considered themselves to be descended from Quetzalcoatl. The ruler wore the most intricately decorated cotton cloaks and nobles beneath him wore cloaks suitable for their rank. Commoners could not wear cloaks woven of cotton fibers but were restricted to cloaks made of maguey or palm fibers. Commoners could not wear cloaks that reached below their knees, unless as warriors they had received wounds on the legs. Neither could commoners wear luxury ornaments. Only nobles wore gold headbands with feathers, gold armbands, lip plugs, ear or nose plugs, and ornaments set with precious stones. Only certain nobles had the right to wear sandals, and only the king and his second-in-command could wear sandals in the palace at Tenochtitlan. In addition to clothing distinctions, only nobles could build two-storey houses. Even without this restriction it is doubtful whether commoners could afford to build such houses. What these status symbols make clear is that the nobles controlled most of the important economic resources of the empire, and it was through this economic power that they were able to acquire gold armbands and afford the labor it took to build large houses.

There were strict legal codes governing behaviour, and punishments were more severe for the nobles. For example, drunkenness in public was considered a serious offense for all but the elderly. Commoners found inebriated had their heads shaven; nobles, however, were put to death (at least this was the law; how often it happened is not known). Judges who accepted bribes or who favoured nobles over commoners in court or who used their offices for personal gain were severely punished.

Rulers (tlatoque). These individuals controlled cities, towns, and subject communities. In addition to the supreme ruler in Tenochtitlan there were others who held sway over cities and towns throughout the empire. Montezuma, for example, was the supreme Aztec ruler in Tenochtitlan at the time of the Spanish Conquest, but there were other lesser rulers of towns such as Texcoco who made their mark in Aztec history. Rulers controlled their own lands, managed labour and tribute, adjudicated disputes not resolved in lower courts, organized military activities, and sponsored certain religious celebrations.

They lived the lifestyles of the rich and famous, which in ancient Mexico meant elegant dress, a pleasant and large house, and lots of servants and slaves. There were jugglers and acrobats to keep the household amused. Rulers gambled as well, both at the ball game, a spectator sport, and at the playing of board games such as ***patolli***. Rulers ate well: tortillas and tamales of all kinds, sauces of many colors and flavours, turkeys, quail, venison, rabbit, lobster, fish and fruits. They drank chocolate, the most

ASPECTS OF DAILY LIFE

AN AZTEC FEAST

According to an account by Bernal Diaz the feasting at Montezuma's palace was as resplendent as any European court. The excerpt from Diaz's *The Conquest of New Spain* gives a vivid description of the elaborate meals served to the Aztec leader. Following Diaz's description are a couple of recipes adapted from recipes of the ancient Aztecs. Perhaps you could try to partially re-create the splendor of a feast at the palace of Montezuma.

For each meal his servants prepared him more than thirty dishes cooked in their native style, which they put over small earthenware braziers to prevent them from getting cold. They cooked more than three hundred plates of the food the great Montezuma was going to eat, and more than a thousand more for the guard.... every day they cooked fowls, turkeys, pheasants, local partridges, quail, tame and wild duck, venison, wild boar, marsh birds, pigeons, hares and rabbits, also many other kinds of birds and beasts native to their country, so numerous that I cannot quickly name them all....

Let us now turn to the way his meals were served, which was like this. If it was cold, they built a large fire of live coals made by burning the bark of a tree which gave off no smoke. The smell of the bark from which they made these coals was very sweet. In order that he should get no more heat than he wanted, they placed a sort of screen in front of it adorned with the figures of idols worked in gold. He would sit on a soft low stool, which was richly worked. His table, which was also low and decorated in the same way, was covered in white tablecloths and rather long napkins of the same material. The four very clean and beautiful girls brought water for his hands in one of those deep basins that they call xicales. They held others like plates beneath it to catch the water and brought him towels. Two other women brought him maize-cakes.

When he began his meal they placed in front of him a sort of wooden screen, richly decorated with gold, so that no one could see him eat. Then the four women retired, and four great chieftains, all old men stood beside him. He talked with them every now and then and asked them questions, and as a great favour he would sometimes offer one of them a dish of whatever tasted best. They say that these were his closest relations and advisors and judges of law suits and if he gave them anything to eat they ate it standing, with deep reverence and without looking in his face.

Montezuma's food was served in Cholula ware, some red and some black. While he was dining, the guards in the adjoining rooms did not dare to speak or make a noise above a whisper. His servants brought him some of every kind of fruit that grew in the country, but he ate very little of it. Some times they brought him in cups of pure gold a drink made from the cocoa plant, which they said he took before visiting his wives. We did not take much notice of this at the time, though I saw them bring in a good fifty large jugs of this chocolate, all frothed up, of which he would drink a little. They always served it with great reverence. Sometimes some little humped backed dwarves would be present at his meals, whose bodies seemed almost to be broken in the middle. These were his jesters. There were other Indians who told him jokes and must have been his clowns, and others who sang and danced, for Montezuma was very fond of music and entertainment and would reward his entertainers with the leavings of the food and chocolate. The same four women removed the tablecloths and again most reverently brought him water for his hands. Then Montezuma would talk to these four old chieftains about matters that interested him, and they would take their leave with great ceremony. He stayed behind to rest.

Mole De Poblano

3 kg	chicken pieces
2	onions
3	cloves garlic
15 mL	lard
50 g	mulato chilis
50 g	ancho chilis
25 g	pasilla chilis

(If the above chilis are not available use 50-100 g of any chili you can find. Remember that the shorter, thinner and greener they are the hotter their flavour.)

2	medium onions
2	cloves garlic
6	tomatoes, chopped
50 g	blanched almonds
50 g	dry roasted peanuts
50 g	toasted sesame seeds
2 mL	coriander
2 mL	aniseed
5 mL	ground cinnamon
50 g	dark chocolate
	salt and pepper
5 mL	sugar (optional)

Put the chicken pieces in a pan with the onion and garlic, cover with water, bring to a boil and simmer for 30 minutes or until the chicken is almost cooked. Drain and reserve the stock. Dry chicken pieces. Melt lard in a pan and gently fry the chicken until it is lightly browned.

Meanwhile, remove stems and seeds from the chilis, tear them up and soak the pieces in 300 mL of boiling water for 30 minutes. Then, puree the chilis with their water, the onion, garlic, tomatoes, nuts, and seeds (reserve a few for decoration), spices, seasoning, and chocolate. Remove the chicken pieces from the pan and pour off any excess fat. Fry the puree in the remaining lard for a few minutes then add the meat with enough of the chicken stock to just cover the meat. Simmer gently for 30 minutes or until the chicken is cooked. Let stand for 24 hours to allow flavours to develop. When ready to serve, reheat, adjust seasoning to taste. Serve with plenty of tortillas, beans, guacamole.

Serves 6

Zucchini With Green Pepper Sauce

4	medium green peppers, chopped coarsely
1	large onion, peeled and chopped
2	cloves garlic, chopped
50 mL	corn or sunflower oil
750 g	zucchini, washed and cut into thick slices
	salt and fresh ground black pepper
75 mL	heavy cream

Puree the peppers in a blender with onion and garlic. Heat the oil in a pan and sautee the puree stirring continually for 3-4 minutes. Add the sliced zucchini with salt and pepper and simmer 15 minutes or until tender. Stir in the cream, adjust seasoning to taste and serve at once.

Serves 6

(*Recipes from* The British Museum Cookbook, *by Michelle Berriedale-Johnson,* © 1987. British Museum Publications.)

highly valued beverage among the Aztecs, as it was among the Maya, and they smoked the most beautifully decorated cigars after meals. According to the Aztec nobles, tobacco was good for the digestion, and a meal without tobacco was not a real feast. Tobacco was accorded a degree of respect and had its place in Aztec custom; it was not smoked all day long, even by the nobles who had easiest access to it.

Chiefs (tetecutin). These formed the next lower rank of nobility. They controlled more restricted areas and sets of activities than the rulers and got their titles through success in war. They could hold a political, military, or judicial office, owned and controlled agricultural lands, and were heads of houses to which lesser nobles were attached, as well as commoners. Tlacaelel, the counsellor to Itzcoatl, for example, would have had the status of chief.

Nobles (pipiltin). These were the children of rulers and chiefs. They were attached to the chiefly house into which they were born and had rights to lands and to the people who worked the land. They could and did succeed to the ranks of rulers or chiefs when positions were available. Otherwise, they often became tribute collectors.

Luxury Artisans (toltecca). Metalworkers, engravers, painters of codices (books) and featherworkers formed, along with the merchants, a middle class in Aztec society. The creations of these luxury artisans were highly esteemed, and the products of their work were reserved for nobility. The artisans were organized into groups that were similar to the craft guilds of medieval Europe. They lived in their own residential sections of the city, known as *calpulli*, they controlled education within their ranks, they had their own deities and ceremonies and maintained special relations with the state structure. Artists and craftsworkers enjoyed positions of honour and respect.

Merchants (pochteca). Trade in central Mexico at certain levels could be carried out by anyone, but professional merchants (pochteca) were the only ones who dealt in large quantities of goods, who traded the luxury commodities destined for the noble class, and who carried out business in marketplaces and in neutral ports-of-trade that lay beyond the bounds of the empire. Identified by the carrying of a staff and a fan, merchants also wore distinctive clothing and were bound by law to a minimum of ostentation. Like the luxury artisans, the merchants enjoyed special privileges and status. Merchants also had their own guilds, residential areas, and were the only people allowed to create and enforce their own laws and codes. They had supreme authority over the greatest and most extensive market at Tlatelolco (just north of Tenochtitlan) where they enforced fair prices and ensured proper conduct in market dealings. Merchants travelled extensively to trade and to find new sources of raw materials or products that were valued by the Aztec nobility. Because their occupation took them outside central Mexico so often, they served as spies for the empire, particularly in areas that had not yet been brought under Aztec control, and they could actually declare wars and conquer communities. Both men and women were merchants, and at the top of the merchant hierarchy were principal merchants called "fathers" and "mothers." Below the principal merchants were the slave dealers, the merchants who acted as spies and state agents, and the ordinary merchants.

Commoners (macehualtin). These were the bulk of the Aztec population. They worked the soil, fished the seas and rivers, and specialized in certain crafts. They also served as soldiers in the Aztec armies of conquest. They were certainly poorer than nobles, but resources varied among them. Their homes were not luxurious, they had few garments, and their meals consisted chiefly of vegetables with chili and tortillas and no meat. They worked the lands of others but also had rights to work land for themselves. They were grouped into different wards or neighbourhoods based on family ties within a town or a city; each ward was called a calpulli. The calpulli was also a territorial and land-holding unit through which land was given out to members for their use. Usually the individual could not sell the plot he worked, but it would be passed on to his children. In some instances, though, the lands did seem to be possessed by the owner and could be sold.

Some calpulli included farmers, craftspeople, and traders. Others contained only those who worked specific tasks, such as the featherworkers or lapidaries (those who cut and polish precious stones) who were organized into their own calpulli. Each calpulli had a temple where members worshipped. Calpulli members were also expected to work land set aside especially for support of the temple.

Rural Tenants (mayeque). Often described as serfs, the mayeque were attached to the private lands of the nobles, and they could not leave these lands. Therefore unlike the commoners, or macehualtin, they were attached to individuals rather than to units such as calpulli. The macehualtin could leave the calpulli, in theory at least, but the mayeque could not leave the land of their lords.

Slaves (tlacotin). Commoners could become slaves for a variety of reasons. These include punishment for theft, gambling, or inability to pay off debts or tribute. On the whole, slaves were more common in urban areas rather than in the countryside. In fact, the greatest numbers of slaves were attached to households of nobles. The status of slave was acquired and not inherited. Children of slaves were born free. Slaves who were unco-operative were given public warnings before witnesses, and if this did not work, they were fitted with a wooden collar and sold in the marketplace. If they did not improve and were sold three times, they could then be sacrificed. Generally speaking, however, this was not common, and sacrificial slaves were supplied through tribute from the provinces and warfare.

Daily Life and Customs

Raising a Family

As in all societies, the prospect of the birth of children brought great joy, and banquets were held when conception had taken place, the expectant mother had a number of rules to follow to keep her healthy and to maximize the chances of a successful birth. Some advice has meaning for us, such as the fact that pregnant women were not to lift heavy objects. Other advice seems strange, such as that women were not to look at an eclipse of the sun or moon, not to sleep in the daytime, not to chew chicle, not to look at anything red. As men were seen to gain honour on the battlefield, women gained honour in bearing and raising children. If men lost their lives in battle, they were rewarded in the afterlife by following the sun in its rise to the zenith. Women who died in childbirth were revered as goddesses and were believed to accompany the sun as it descended from its zenith and set in the west.

After a successful birth, the midwife cut the umbilical cord and buried the afterbirth in a corner of the house. The cord of a baby girl was buried near the hearth; a boy's umbilical cord was dried and later left on a field of battle so as to dedicate him to service in war. The midwife bathed and swaddled the infant, and sung a song praising the baby, welcoming it but also warning that life was not a good place but a place of weeping, sorrow, and suffering. Despite the melancholy tones with which the infant was greeted, Aztec parents believed that young children should be healthy, strong, and happy.

From the age of three, children were supervised

INNOVATIONS

THE ORIGINS OF CHOCOLATE

Chocolate was a favourite drink of the Aztec nobles. It was not long after the Spanish made contact with the Aztecs that chocolate was passed to the upper classes in Spain. The chocolate drink was made from the entire cacao bean and therefore had quite a bit of fat (that is, what is now called cocoa butter) in it. The Aztecs flavoured the chocolate with vanilla beans and chili. Cocoa, as we know it, did not come along until years later in Europe, when the Dutch invented a way to separate the fat (cocoa butter) from the other components of the cacao bean (what we call cocoa powder) by using alkali. When we buy cocoa powder, it has had the fat removed. The fat or cocoa butter is used widely in the cosmetics industry. In the cheaper candy bars you buy, the cocoa butter has been replaced by some sort of vegetable shortening which is listed with the other ingredients on the wrapper. More expensive chocolate bars will list chocolate liquor, cocoa butter, etc. Chocolate liquor is the fermented substance from cacao beans that is the basis for all chocolate. The beans are removed from the cacao pods, pilled up and allowed to ferment. The fermentation produces theobromine, the stimulant in chocolate or cocoa. The beans are then processed and the chocolate liquor extracted.

---

by fathers in the case of boys, or mothers in the case of girls. When boys were ten or twelve they went to school. Sons of commoners, merchants, and artisans attended the telpochcallie or House of Youth. Here they received religious training and were taught the arts of war. They were also expected to work on the lands set aside for the support of the school, and to collect fuel (wood) for the temple fires. They also spent some time at home learning their father's craft. There was another school called the calmecac or priests' house. This was a school of higher learning for the nobility, but some children of merchants and commoners were admitted. Here, in addition to basic education, the students were prepared for careers as priests, public officials, and military leaders. Religious and philosophical doctrines were studied as were calendrics, timekeeping, astrology, and history.

There were also schools for girls which taught temple maintenance, ritual duties, weaving and other tasks, preparation for household maintenance and marriage, and music, which was considered important in the education of all children. From the age of fourteen or so, boys and girls attended the House of Song to learn singing, dancing, and the playing of musical instruments. Instruction here was not simply for training in religious ritual and ceremony. The songs and poetic texts were ways in which knowledge and beliefs were transmitted from one generation to another, and a great deal of cultural information was bound up in them.

Men usually completed their education at the age of twenty or twenty-two, women at sixteen or seventeen, at which time marriage was arranged by the parents. Matchmakers played a role in helping the families of the eligible girl and boy to reach an agreement on consent to the marriage. Soothsayers were consulted to help decide on a proper day for the ceremony, and the elaborate preparations took several days: cacao beans were ground, flowers were gathered, tobacco and smoking tubes were procured, pottery cups and baskets were bought, maize, tamales, and sauces were prepared. The bride was decorated with red feathers and dyes and was carried, after listening to advice from the elders, to the groom's house. The bride and groom were married on a mat in front of the hearth. Various rituals took place, such as tying the couple together by their garments. The bride and groom were then led to a private room where they remained for four days, at the end of which their marriage was to be consummated. The private room was guarded by the matchmakers, who apparently drunk pulque in quantity to pass the time. On the fifth day more festivities took place.

The Aztec Household

Once the household was established, the couple assumed the duties of life. The woman managed the household, developed her skills in food preparation and weaving, maintained household hygiene and health, and was responsible for the early education of her daughters. Men administered the household's property, advised and taught their sons, but were also required to fight on the battlefield and participate in community and temple activities. Commoner women could also participate in the market and buy and sell goods there. Noblewomen had servants to do the provisioning and were encouraged to develop arts such as weaving.

Noblemen were the only individuals permitted to have more than one wife. Divorce was possible for anyone but could be expensive as gifts had to be returned. Disputes from divorces or any other matters were settled according to an elaborate legal code, and a hierarchy of courts existed where cases were settled. Punishments were generally severe. Death was the penalty for murder, rebellion, wearing the clothes of the other sex, and adultery. Thieves were made slaves after one offense; anything further and the guilty were hanged.

This illustration redrawn from a codex illustrates an Aztec game called patolli. Using four beans as die, the stones would then be moved appropriate spaces on the board. Often treasured items such as necklaces or feathers would be bet on the game.

The Aztecs enjoyed games and gambling. The principal spectator sport was the ball game, the outcome of which was wagered on. The walls of the ball court were built of stone, and the playing field was shaped like an upper case letter "I". The object was to drive a rubber ball through a stone ring mounted vertically in the middle of the walls of the court. The ball could be hit with the hips, buttocks, or elbows but not with the hands. The knees and hips of the players were protected by leather guards. Professional ball players toured the country exhibiting their skills; rulers and nobles maintained their own teams. Gambling was fairly intense, and nobles wagered jewellery, cloaks, slaves, lands, and even houses.

A popular board game of the time was patolli. The board, similar to the modern game of parchesi, had a criss-cross pattern along which pieces were moved. As with the ball game, betting could be fierce. Conquest accounts say that some people were addicted to the game. These individuals would walk around with mats under their arms and their own dice tied up in small cloths, ready to sit, play, and gamble at a moment's notice.

Clothing

Most Aztec clothing was draped and not fitted. There were loincloths worn by men of all classes; these were cotton or maguey fabric and were wrapped around the lower torso, passed between the legs and tied in a large knot at the waist. Loincloths of the nobles were elaborately ornamented with dyes, embroidery, feathered disks, or ocelot or coyote fur.

The hip-cloth was another sort of garment worn around the waist but tied on one side and folded in such a way that a corner hung down at the sides or at back. The most important status item for men was the cloak or mantle, tied at one shoulder. Nobles could wear cotton cloaks, elaborately decorated, that hung below their knees. Commoners' cloaks were of maguey or other crude fibre, were plain and could not hang below the knees unless the individual had leg wounds received in battle.

Warriors wore padded cotton armor, a sleeveless garment that was pulled over the head, hugged the body, and reached to the top of the thigh. The padded cotton was very effective and was adopted by the Spanish soldiers in preference to their heavy, hot, metal armour. Nobles in battle wore special tunics with short skirts decorated with feathers. There was even a sort of body-suit that was used as a warrior costume. It had fitted sleeves and trouser legs and was constructed of cloth covered with feathers and made in a variety of colours and styles.

Women wore a mid-calf-length skirt secured at the waist. As with the men, it was the noble women who had the most magnificently embroidered and decorated clothing. In ritual contexts only, women wore a triangular slip-on garment, a bit like a poncho in shape, that hung on the shoulders and came down only as far as the chest. An example of similar special-purpose ritual clothing for men was a short, fringed sleeveless jacket that tied in front, which Aztec priests sometimes wore.

The basic upper-body garment for women, worn over the skirt described above, was a kind of long tunic or shift that hung to just below the hips or top of the thighs. It is still worn today by women throughout Mesoamerica, and is generally known as a huipil. The Aztec women embroidered the huipil borders with many colours, and worked feathers into decorative designs on the front in the area over the chest. Thread made from rabbit's fur was often used, which had a silk-like sheen and was supposed to hold dyes well.

Overall, Aztec clothing reflected the sharp stratification of Aztec society. Though the general garment styles were the same for different classes, the fabrics, specific lengths and especially the ornamentation were different for each level of society. Although not strictly speaking part of the clothing, but certainly part of the costume, was face and body paint. Though servingwomen could rub their feet with a mixture of burned copal incense (copal is a kind of resin) and dye, wearing elaborate face and body paint was a privilege for the nobility only.

Though nobles were permitted to indulge in greater clothing ostentation than merchants or commoners, the most elaborately decorated costumes were associated with rituals of religion and war. Clothing depicted on images of gods and worn by priests who impersonated these gods was very ornate and was sewn or decorated with the specific symbolism of the god. Among the nobility, it was those who had distinguished themselves in war who

ASPECTS OF DAILY LIFE

AZTEC CLOTHING

The interesting examples of clothing illustrated here are drawn from codices and illustrate a variety of items worn by the Aztecs. The figure at top left is a priest who appears to be wearing a skirt typical of Aztec women. At top right is a warrior dressed in a short sleeveless jacket with ties which are clearly visible. His costume suggests that he is either dressed for battle or for ceremonial purposes as he is carrying a shield and a club made of wood and inset with obsidian or chert. A weapon such as this was effective enough to cut the head off a horse in one swing. The woman weaving (bottom left) is wearing a huipilli (pronounced we-peel), a pyjama-like outfit that was common among Aztec women. The final figure (bottom right) is wearing a type of body suit made out of animal skins. Such a costume was worn for ceremonial purposes.

417

displayed huge feather headdresses and elaborate costumes with ocelot skins or eagle feathers. A rather touching addition to this is that these same nobility where the only ones who were accorded the privilege of walking about the city carrying bunches of flowers.

The Arts and Sciences

Literature and Music

Literature of the Aztecs was preserved in both written and oral forms. Literary forms and rules were learned in childhood in both the calmecac, the schools where noble children were trained, and in the "House of Song." Standardized songs and histories had to be memorized, as did religious songs and dances. People from all walks of life learned what they needed to know to participate in the various public ceremonies. There were also professional singers, who had to have clear voices and excellent oratory skills. These singers were employed by Aztec rulers to create songs and poems about the successes of their reigns. There were also singers who were attached to temples who wrote songs to the gods.

The Aztecs valued oratory skills, and the good narrator was said to be a speaker of joyful words, and to have flowers on his lips. Lyric poetry was also highly valued. Through this form of expression, Aztec intellectuals contemplated the significance of human and godly actions, and expressed doubts and fears about the course of life and the world around them. The meaning of life was not entirely clarified for them by their religion, and poetry and song provided an outlet, as it does for us today, for emotional outpourings of both doubt and joy about the human condition.

The Aztecs also recorded the history of their people through written chronicles. They focused on the adventures of heroes, the founding of cities, the lives of rulers, warfare, migration, and empire building. You will remember that the Aztec chronicles recorded an instance of manipulation of history, when Tlacaelel burned some of the Aztec records in order to create a more glorious heritage for his people. Written records were important to the Aztecs not only in preserving their past, but in passing on this information to future generations. The Aztecs used pictorial representations, and not an alphabet. Therefore their manuscripts had symbols that were recognizable to many people on the basis of the imagery alone. The Spanish missionaries borrowed this Aztec imagery and used Aztec symbols and the Aztec pictorial manuscript style to spread Christianity.

Architecture

Whatever remains of the great temples, palaces, houses, bridges, and streets of Tenochtitlan are today buried beneath the urban sprawl of Mexico City. Unfortunately, the Spaniards were not interested enough in indigenous architectural styles to provide us with detailed and accurate architectural descriptions. Most of the monumental buildings were temples, and the Spaniards' abhorrence of Aztec ritual prevented them from seeing or recording information of any but the most general historical or architectural interest.

There are similarities with the architecture of the Maya in that the temples were built of masonry (stone) and stood on the tops of terraced stone platforms, often called pyramids, with wide stairways leading from the base of the platform to the temple on top. The Aztec variation on this theme was the presence of double stairways leading to two temples on top of a single platform. Palaces and other houses were built on very low platforms and their rooms were spread out over one, or at the most two storeys, and did not tower skyward as did the temples. As in the Maya area, poorer people lived in houses built of poles with thatched roofs.

Though the Spanish conquerors did not leave us with accounts describing Aztec buildings in the sort of detail archaeologists would like, they did describe their impressions of the Aztec capital when they gazed on the magnificent and orderly city for the first time. Bernal Díaz, the soldier, has left us a description of the approach to the Aztec capital, when the Spaniards were walking along a wide road or "causeway" just outside the lakes area, and from which they could see Lake Texcoco and the cities built in its midst:

> Next morning, we came to a broad causeway, and continued our march...And when we saw all those cities and villages built in the water, and other great towns on dry land, and that straight and level causeway leading to Mexico, we were astounded. These great towns and temples and buildings rising from the water, all made of stone, seemed like an enchanted vision...Indeed, some of our soldiers asked whether it was not all a dream.
>
> Early next day we...followed the causeway, which is eight yards wide and goes so straight to the city of Mexico that I do not think it curves at all...
>
> With such wonderful sights to gaze on we did not know what to say, or if this was real that we saw before our eyes. On the land side there were great cities, and on the lake many more. The lake was crowded with canoes. At intervals along the causeway there were many bridges, and before us was the great city of Mexico.[3]

To many people, this description makes the Aztec capital seem like the city of Venice, with people bustling along in watercraft, and with picturesque bridges over the canals. Bernal Díaz was describing his march along one of the main causeways leading to Tenochtitlan. In the centre of the city he found a great plaza containing the major temple, markets, and other religious and political buildings. The four major causeways of the city radiated from this central location, but other minor causeways ran from city to city. The causeways were roads that saw a great deal of traffic as people travelled between cities or brought trade goods in and out of the capital.

Unlike Venice, however, Tenochtitlan was laid out in a systematic pattern. Its rectangular gridding made it practical for chinampa construction, and the orderly canals made it possible to ensure a smooth flow of traffic since literally thousands of canoes entered the city every day. Therefore Aztec urban planning accounted not only for population growth, but for traffic flow. As we will see later when we learn about tribute, the city depended on a massive influx of foodstuffs and other products in order to survive; therefore a free flow of canoe traffic, as well as travel by land over the causeways, was essential. Remember, however, that the Aztecs did not have domesticated beasts of burden, nor did they use the wheel, so that the roads leading into and out of Tenochtitlan would not have been worn down by horses, oxen, or carts, only people.

How did the Aztecs themselves describe their city? Not in terms that permitted architectural interpretation, yet in language that perhaps gives us more in that it conveys the beauty symbolized for the Aztecs by Tenochtitlan:

> The city is spread out in circles of jade,
> radiating flashes of light like quetzal plumes,
> Beside it the lords are borne in boats:
> over them extends a flowery mist.[4]

---

[3]Bernal Díaz, The Conquest of New Spain, J.M. Cohen, trans. (England: Penguin Books, 1972), pp. 214, 216.

[4]Miguel León Portilla, Los Antiguos Mexicanos (México: Fondo de Cultura Económica, 1961), p. 63.

This reconstruction of the city of Tenochtitlan shows in the midst of other temples and buildings, the Great Temple of Mexico (left). It was to this temple that all Tenochtitlan's causeways, canals, and roads led.

Sculpture

Aztec stoneworkers surpassed those of previous central Mexican civilizations in the quantity, quality, and range of production of stone sculpture. However, when the Aztecs praised their best sculptors they likened them to the earlier Toltec artists of Tula. Though the most famous Aztec sculptures, such as the Aztec calendar stone, are colossal in size, the Aztec repertoire also included miniature figures only two or three centimeters high. Deities were frequently represented in stone, as were various architectural elements such as serpent heads that were placed at the bases of temples near stairways.

At the other end of the spectrum, the Aztecs also carved, in smaller scale, dogs, turtles, jaguars, monkeys, rabbits, eagles, grasshoppers, and occasionally even plants such as squashes. Skulls were also a popular sculptural image. Skull carvings usually appeared as relief images on temples, but they were sometimes carved in the round.

Human figures, usually standing images of commoners or warriors, were carved in stone and placed at the entrances of temples to serve as standard bearers. Montezuma apparently commissioned 14 sculptors to carve a monumental statue in his likeness. The fact that sculptors often worked together suggests that they received a similar basic training, although it is not known whether they were organized into guilds in the way that the luxury artisans (such as featherworkers or lapidaries) were. We do know that they tended to concentrate in cities and it is in the cities that we see the most monumental sculptures.

The most awe inspiring Aztec sculpture is the one of Coatlicue, the goddess of the earth and the mother of gods and men, rising over 2.5 m high. The head has been severed from the body and two serpents rising from the neck meet to form a face.

Writing and Painting

Aztec libraries housed a number of different kinds of books and manuscripts. There were ritual and astrological records, calendrical records, tribute accounts, histories and genealogies of rulers, maps, and legal records. These books were written on paper made from the bark of a fig tree. The bark was soaked in water, the fibers were beaten to separate and smooth them, and various materials were then used to create a workable writing surface. For books or codices, as they are usually called, the sheets were folded in accordion fashion. For maps and tribute records, often large single sheets were used without folding.

The symbols or hieroglyphs that the Aztec scribes used were painted in a variety of colours, usually red, yellow, green, and blue, and were outlined in black. The Aztecs did not use symbols to represent the sounds of vowels or consonants in the way that we do. Most of their symbols were pictographic or ideographic. That is, a picture of a house would mean "house," or a picture of a flower would mean just that. They also used shorthand symbols: footprints to represent travel; a sort of squiggly line near people's mouths to represent speech; or a burning temple to mean conquest. There were some glyphs that were phonetic, they stood for sounds and not whole words or concepts. In these cases more than one hieroglyph would be used to form the names of cities or individuals.

In addition to the symbols and their meanings, the size of elements depicted was also important. Where people were drawn, the larger representations stood for more important people. Colours, too, were varied and transmitted critical information about the objects represented. For example, the cardinal directions were symbolized by different colours: south by white or blue; east by yellow or red; north by red or black; west by blue-green or white.

Science and Technology

Medicine

The Aztecs were actively involved in finding medical cures for a variety of illnesses and injuries. Physi-

These two figures are involved in making a medical prognosis and choosing a cure with corn. They would toss the corn onto a mat. If the corn fell in orderly rows, the patient would do well, if they scattered or fell in a circle the patient would die. Further examination of the patterns would also indicate the nature of the ailment and the type of medicine necessary.

cians were expected to be good diagnosticians, to be familiar with remedies, to restore people to health, to set broken bones, and to administer purges and potions. There were a number of herbal derivatives; herbs were used for poultices as well as internally, and different curers had different remedies, though there were some herbs that were generally associated with certain cures. Sweatbaths were popular and were recommended for various cures, and were particularly important in problems of childbirth. Sweatbaths were seen to be important in relaxing and soothing an individual during any sort of recovery.

When illnesses were believed to have a supernatural cause, shamans would be employed for a cure that would include more than medicinal herbs, but also some sort of ritual procedure and/or divinatory practices. For example, a diviner would, perhaps by scattering maize kernels on a cotton cloak, be able to determine the cause of a person's illness. The cure might then involve the administration of herbs and potions as well as a ritual, such as retrieving the patient's soul. Mirrors (of polished obsidian or hematite) were used to determine the extent of soul loss in a child: a blurred image meant that the case was severe, a clear image that recovery would take place soon. Thus, Aztec medicine was a mixture of cultural and pragmatic practices.

Calendrics and Time

The Aztecs were like us in that time was something they sought to control by measuring it in various ways. They did not all wear wrist watches, but they probably would have if given the choice. Unlike us they viewed time more cyclically and believed that events would recur. For example, they believed that the universe had already undergone four time cycles in which a sun had been born in each. Their existence was part of the Fifth Sun; at the end of this sun they believed that the human race would perish.

In a sense, the belief in recurring cycles made it even more important to keep track of time in order to be able to predict the future based on what had occurred in the past. To keep track of time, calendars were developed.

The Solar Calendar

The solar year of 365.25 days (the time it takes the earth to revolve around the sun) was divided into 18 months of 20 days each. The year was rounded out at the end with five days that were viewed as unlucky. Each month had a name and particular deities were worshipped during these days. What is important is that keeping track of the solar calendar would have involved observation of heavenly bodies in order to make sure that the Aztec year correlated with the earth's revolution around the sun. We "catch up" by adding a day onto February during Leap Year. We know that the Aztecs were aware of slippage and apparently accounted for it, but we are not sure how.

The Ritual Calendar

This calendar was not keyed into a solar year but was simply a different time cycle. They had a series of 20 day-names, such as *Cipactli* (alligator) or *Tochtli* (rabbit). So once the cycle of 1 to 13 days with coordinated day-names was completed, and day-1 came up again, it would have a different name than it had the "week" before. This would go on for 260 days (13 × 20) until the cycle would repeat itself. That is, the day 1 Alligator would recur once every 260 days.

It is important to note that each solar year was named after the number and day-name combination that fell at the end of the previous year. This explains why the great famine was said by the Aztecs to occur in the year known as 1 Rabbit.

When the solar calendar and the ritual calendar were combined, the cycle would repeat itself every 52 years. For example, the ninth day of the month Quecholli in the solar calendar, also Eight Wind in the ritual calendar, would not recur in this combination for 52 years.

Economy

Agriculture

Agriculture was the foundation of the Aztec Empire, and non-fluctuating food supplies were essential in maintaining the Aztec state. Essentially, there were crops that were grown throughout the empire, such as maize, beans, chia, amaranth, chiles, and squashes. For the Aztecs, then, it remained to coordinate tribute with the times these crops ripened in each area in order to maximize stability. There were other crops that were grown only in tropical areas, such as cacao, vanilla, cotton, and varieties of fruits. These were accessible predominantly through tribute. Cacao and cotton (often manufactured as cloaks) appear repeatedly on tribute lists.

Cultivation of crops involved what is called slash-and-burn farming, or fallowing. In this case a field was cleared of vegetation and cultivated for two or three years, then allowed to rest so that the soils would recover lost fertility. More intensive cultivation took the form of irrigation agriculture, and chinampa construction. Chinampas in Tenochtitlan ranged from 100 to 850 square metres and were cultivated by 2–3 to 25–30 people. They produced

The Aztec calendar stone is a 20 tonne black stone shaped like a disk. Buried by the Spanish in the fifteenth century, it was rediscovered in the late eighteenth century. Originally it was painted with many bright colours and was probably used as a calendar as well as an account of the history of the world.

maize, beans, chiles, amaranth, tomatoes, and flowers. Some archaeologists believe that their most important role was in producing fresh vegetables and flowers for the city of Tenochtitlan. Flowers were used in all religious festivals and political ceremonies and were always in great demand.

In addition to vegetable products, many animals were hunted to supplement the Aztec diet: deer, rabbits, hares, opposum, armadillos, pocket gophers, wild pigs, and tapirs. Bows and arrows as well as snares and traps were used. Many lake-dwelling creatures were also food for the table: turtles, salamanders, frogs, tadpoles, shellfish, and waterfowl. The Aztecs domesticated only five animals: the turkey, the Muscovy duck, the dog, the bee, and the cochineal insect. (The cochineal beetle was used to produce a dye.) The dogs raised for food were a hairless variety, probably very much like the modern breed known as Mexican hairless.

Aside from the major groups of foods already listed, there were others used by the Aztecs that seem strange and exotic to us: locusts, grubs, fish eggs, lizards, and tecuitlatl, the last of which, the lake slime, was described earlier in the chapter. Honey was used as a sweetener, and salt as a taste-enhancer, but chili of all kinds was the universal seasoning. Overall, one of the things that amazed the Spaniards was that the Aztecs could survive on so little food. The Aztecs imposed this regimen on themselves, and when children were quite young they were encouraged not to be greedy and to eat sparingly.

Tribute and Trade

No mention of Aztec economics is complete without a discussion of Aztec tribute and trade. Exchange in the Aztec Empire took three forms: tribute and taxation, state-sponsored foreign trade, and exchange in the marketplace.

The term "tribute" refers specifically to revenue

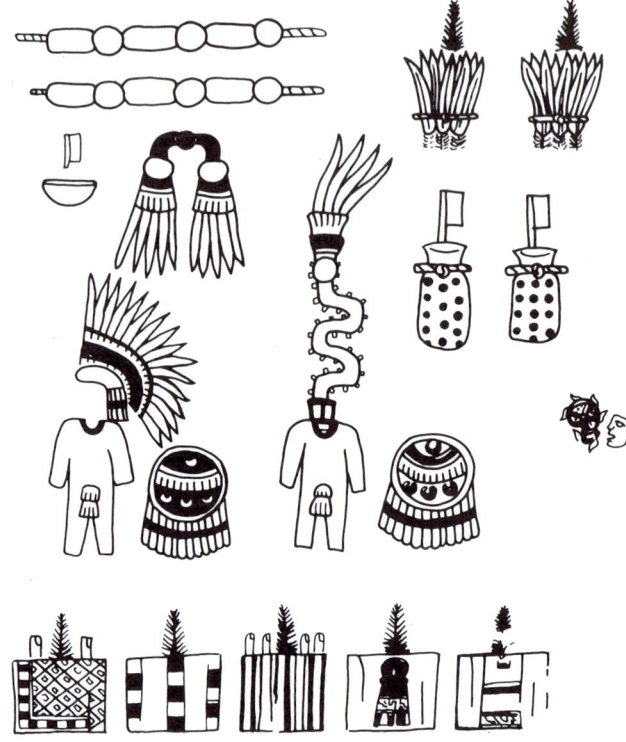

This page from the tribute roll of Montezuma records items received in tribute from a conquered town. These items include: strings of jade beads, dishes of gold dust, a royal headdress, bunches of feathers, bags of dye, warriors' costumes, and cotton blankets.

demanded and collected by the dominant Aztec state from the regions it conquered. State-sponsored trade involved specific transactions desired by the ruling powers in Tenochtitlan who would send out merchants to neutral trade areas to acquire specific goods, and usually luxury goods of some sort. Market exchange obviously involved people at all levels who came to centralized markets to sell or buy goods and services. Markets served to integrate surplus production at local, regional, and state levels.

Each conquered province of the Aztec Empire was required to pay tribute. People who lived close to the cities of Lake Texcoco gave foodstuffs and other supplies as tribute. For example, one province in a tropical area distant from the capital sent products not available in central Mexico:

> 9600 decorated cloaks
> 1600 women's tunics
> 1 warrior's costume and shield
> 1 gold shield
> 1 feather standard
> 1 gold diadem
> 1 gold headband
> 2 strings of gold beads
> 3 large jades
> 100 pots of liquidambar
> 7 strings of jades
> 40 lip plugs
> 16 000 rubber balls
> 80 handfuls of quetzal feathers
> 4 bunches of green and yellow feathers
> 24 little bunches of feathers
> 200 loads of cacao[5]

Tribute assigned to these provinces and cities were recorded in documents known as imperial tribute lists. These lists contained pictographs showing the nature and quantity of the sorts of tribute that the conquered territory was to provide to the Aztec capital. In this way there was little that was arbitrary concerning what was paid, and any changes had first to be recorded on the lists.

Of course it was the commoners who assumed the heaviest burdens regarding tribute, since they tilled the fields in which the food products were cultivated. Artisans, too, had to give part of their production in tribute payment. The nature of tribute was often indirect. For example, cotton was grown in lowland tropical areas and travelling merchants purchased the raw product and carried it to highland areas, where no cotton was grown. Here, however, the raw cotton was turned into finished cotton textiles, which in turn were given in imperial tribute. Therefore whatever demands the Aztec state made on the highland manufacturers in turn affected the lowland producers.

Once the tribute goods were carried to Tenochtitlan, there was an elaborate distribution system for the goods. In addition, each smaller capital had its own subject communities and tribute and distribution system that paralleled that of the state. Provisioning the royal palaces was certainly a major function of this sort of local tribute as was supporting the army and the urban population.

Markets

The markets of central Mexico were an important part of the economy. The largest and most famous market, and that which immediately impressed the Spaniards upon their arrival in the Aztec capital, was the market at Tlatelolco just north of Tenochtitlan. Cortés, in one of his letters to King Charles, estimated that 60 000 people traded at this market. Cortés recounts that every sort of merchandise in the land was found here: ornaments of gold and silver, brass, copper, tin stones, shells, bones, and feathers. He also saw building materials such as lime, cut and uncut stone, mud bricks, tiles, and woods. One street was devoted solely to the sale of live game and birds of all sorts, but the skins of birds of prey were also sold. Rabbits, hares, stags, and small gelded dogs were displayed on another street.

Cortés described streets of herbalists and the presence of apothecary shops where medicines were sold, as well as ointments and plasters. In other zones of the market were barber shops, and shops where people could stop for food and drink. There were porters available to carry loads. There was firewood and charcoal for sale, as well as earthen-

---

[5]*Frances Berdan*, The Aztecs of Central Mexico: An Imperial Society (*Toronto: Holt, Rinehart, Winston, 1982*), p. 36.

Cortés and Marina are depicted here with the lords and ladies of Tlaxcala. The Tlaxcalans, one of the few groups who successfully resisted Aztec domination, are shown allying themselves with Cortés and speaking to him through Doña Marina. This picture, drawn by Aztecs, clearly demonstrates that Aztec artists quickly adapted European artistic styles.

ware braziers, bedding and seats made of woven mats. All sorts of vegetables were sold, as well as syrups, and various alcoholic beverages. Spun cotton in a great variety of colours was displayed, as were colour pigments for painters, deerskins dyed and undyed, pottery of all shapes and sizes, maize, chicken, salted fish, eggs. At this stage in the list Cortés seems to falter, and ends this part of his letter by saying that he cannot possibly name everything because the variety was so great. He does, however, note how well run the markets were because they were strictly regulated by judges. These judges were, of course, the powerful merchants or pochteca.

The markets were indeed laid out in a planned manner and similar products were sold together in specific sections. Aztec officials would patrol the market to monitor business and trade transactions, and there was a court composed of senior merchants that would settle disputes. All goods were sold by count and volume but not by weight. Though there was no monetary system, there were items that had standardized values and were generally accepted in trade as a kind of "money." The most famous of these items were cacao beans, (the money that grew on trees), but cloaks, quills filled with gold dust, and small copper axes were also used.

With the arrival of the Spaniards, the world of the Aztecs—the people of the sun—came to an end. In the beginning, during the first encounters, the Europeans held Aztec achievements in awe. The conquistadors married native women, the priests were pleased by the Indians' reception of Christianity, and there was optimism about the creation of a New World culture that would surpass the Old. But it did not take long for prejudice to set in, and for greed to reign as Spaniards poured into Mexico bent on making fortunes by exploiting Indian labour, and by taking Indian land. The most devastating consequence of the Conquest was the radical depopulation that took place as the result of introduced diseases, forced labour, slavery, and certainly demoralization.

Estimates vary as to what the population of central Mexico was before the Spaniards arrived, but one source places it at 25 million just before the Conquest, with a decline of 95 percent by the end of the sixteenth century. The New World was not free of disease prior to the Conquest, but it was free of major epidemics and chronic endemic ailments. How tragic and unbelievable it must have been when the first waves of disease washed over the native Americans! People died by the hundreds and then thousands, and neither the native Americans nor the Europeans understood why. Eventually, after many died, some gained immunity and populations recovered, but it has taken until modern times in some areas to do so.

On this sad note, we leave the Aztecs, but close with a statement made by Hernán Cortés in one of his letters to the Spanish king that demonstrates the conflicting emotions the conquerors experienced about the people they were to overcome and the culture they were to destroy:

> Yet so as not to tire Your Highness with the description of the things of this city...I will say only that these people live almost like those in Spain, and in as much harmony and order as there, and considering that they are barbarous and so far from the knowledge of God and cut off from all civilized nations, it is truly remarkable to see what they have achieved in all things.[6]

---

[6]Anthony Pagden, Hernán Cortés: Letters from Mexico (New Haven: Yale University Press, 1986) p. 108.

Suggested Sources for Further Research

Anawalt, Patricia Rieff, *Indian Clothing before Cortes: Mesoamerican Costumes from the Codices* (University of Oklahoma Press, 1981).

Berdan, Frances, *The Aztecs of Central Mexico: An Imperial Society* (Holt, Rinehart, 1982).

Coe, Michael D., *Mexico* (Frederick A. Praeger, 1966).

Coe, Sophie, "Aztec Cuisine, Parts I, II, III" *Petits Propos Culinaires: Essays and notes on food, cookery and cookery books*: 19, 20, 21, (Prospect Books, Ltd., 1985).

Díaz, Bernal, *The Conquest of New Spain* Translated by J.M. Cohen, (Penguin Books, 1972).

Fagan, Brian, *The Aztecs* (Little, Brown, 1984).

León Portilla, Miguel (editor), *The Broken Spears: The Aztec Account of the Conquest of Mexico* (Beacon Press and Saunders, 1962).

Focus Your Knowledge

1. How did the Indian woman known as Doña Marina assist in the Spanish Conquest of the Aztecs?
2. Explain why humans were sacrificed by the Aztecs and comment on the significance of human sacrifice to their religion.

3. Using the following chart summarize the information for each of the Aztec classes in society.

	Clothing	Homes	Economic Resources	Function in Society
Ruler				
Chiefs				
Nobles				
Merchants				
Artisans				
Free Commoners				
Slaves				

4. What customs of the Aztecs reflect the importance of childbirth?

5. Explain how the education and upbringing of Aztec boys and girls differed.

6. How was the history and culture of the Aztecs preserved and passed on?

7. Comment on the accuracy of the Aztec's solar calendar and explain the differences between the ritual calendars and the solar calendar.

8. List and describe the various foods which were important in the diet of the Aztecs.

9. Describe the markets of central Mexico.

Apply Your Knowledge

1. Describe the climate and geography of the Valley of Mexico. Explain how it held great agricultural promise despite environmental challenges and explain what the Aztecs did to make the land productive.

2. What made areas outside the Valley of Mexico prime targets for Aztec expansion and conquest.

3. What does the story of the Aztec migrations and their eventual conquest of central Mexico tell us about these people?

4. The Aztecs are said to be a people of contradiction. Explain why by briefly commenting on their beliefs and view of the world.

5. The apparent bloodthirsty nature of the Aztecs was largely the work of one man. Respond to this statement.

6. Describe Tenochtitlan. After rereading Cortés' description of Tenochtitlan consider how you would have reacted to the people of this city and write a journal entry which could have been presented to the King of Spain.

7. Art is often a reflection of the society which produced it. What does Aztec art (sculpture, painting, writing) tell us about Aztec life?

8. How does the Aztec concept of time differ from both the Maya's and ours?

9. How important was the tribute system to the Aztec Empire and how were the goods distributed?

10. Throughout the chapter there are numerous quotations taken from Spanish reports. Is there an obvious sense that the Spanish perceived the Aztecs as different? Inferior? Civilized or uncivilized? Provide specific examples.

Extension Activities
▼▼▼

1. Based on the information about the gods write a myth about one or several of the gods. Include an illustration depicting what the god(s) would have looked like in your opinion.

2. Build a model of Tenochtitlan and situate it on an artificial lake.

3. Do further research on Aztec weapons and art forms. Based on your research create replicas which could be used in a seminar or to create an effective visual display.

4. Have your class host an Aztec day during which games such as patolli and the ballcourt game could be recreated, favourite foods of the Aztec could be served (be sure to include the chocolate recipe included in the Feature Study on Aztec Foods!), clothing from the period could be worn, a model of Tenochtitlan set on an artificial lake could be displayed and various religious ceremonies could be staged. Be sure that all classes of society are represented and try to recreate some of the art and weapons of the Aztecs.

5. Prepare a report for the King of Spain describing the Aztec people from the perspective of Hernán Cortés. Your report should include a description of their religious practices, their appearance, clothing, foods, customs, housing, and temples. Remember you are writing from the perspective of a sixteenth century explorer. In his eyes would these people have been civilized? On par with the Europeans?

SKILLS FOCUS

Unit Overview

1. Review the role that geography played in the development of the four civilizations discussed in this unit. To what degree is the concept that a river valley is necessary to the development of a civilization challenged?

2. Compare and contrast either the civilizations of the Maya and the Aztecs or Islam and Japan. Consider religion, beliefs, government, social hierarchy, clothing and appearance, geographical setting, food, agriculture, science, technology, medicine, writing, and housing and community.

3. The four civilizations in this unit are unique in that they developed almost in isolation to the western world. Develop an organizer to determine which features are unique in religion, technology, philosophy, arts, and literature. Then, based on your information, decide on the factor or factors most important to the development of a unique culture. Do this for all four civilizations: Islam, Japan, the Aztecs, and the Maya.

Art: A Window to Our Past

Refer to the colour-plates section for Unit 3.

1. How does the art preserve for us the history and the culture of the Maya and the Aztecs. Choose specific works of art and analyze them.

2. Which elements of Japanese and Islamic art demonstrate the uniqueness of each of these cultures? Choose specific works of art to explain your answer.

3. Identify the cross-cultural influences in Islamic or Japanese art. Are there similar cross-cultural influences in Maya and Aztec art? Illustrate your response with particular examples.

4. By examining the art of each of the four civilizations, decide if there is evidence of a strong religious influence, a hierarchical society, a strong reverence of nature, or humanistic attitudes. Justify your answer by referencing specific works of art and their themes, approaches, symbolism, and subject matter.

Analyzing Information

In compiling this text a variety of types of sources were used to draw on for the information. The writing of history, especially for past civilizations requires not only the use of a variety of sources, but also an understanding of the nature of these sources. The following questions are designed to help you identify the types of sources, to help you assess their value, to identify their pitfalls and to strengthen your skills in analyzing the information you have gathered. Data itself is raw and unprocessed information which is of little value. For information to be useful it needs to be analyzed, then it can be called evidence and will be of use to you during your research.

Define the following terms:

primary sources

secondary sources

ethnographic data

archaeological data

anthropological data

The following are different types of primary documents:

diaries	literature
journals	eye witness accounts
ships' logs	
legal documents	archaeological data
company records	anthropological studies
government records	

Prepare a chart which lists the various types of primary sources, and provide examples of as many of these as you can find in the four unit chapters. For any categories that you cannot find examples for, give an example of a document our civilization might leave behind for future civilizations to uncover.

IDENTIFYING BIAS

Primary documents are indispensable to the study of history because they provide the factual evidence from which we draw our conclusions. Primary documents also have their problems and we must be aware of them before we draw our conclusions. It is critical in using primary documents that one take into account the writer's bias. (Review Chapter 1.)

Review the various Spanish accounts found throughout the chapters on the Maya and the Aztecs. Can you detect in these documents a distinct bias by the author? Is there evidence of these accounts being biased by ethnocentric views? Can you account for the author's bias other than it coming from an ethnocentric view? Why is an obviously biased account still of significant value?

USING SECONDARY SOURCES

Most of the sources you will use at this level will be secondary sources. Secondary sources have the advantage of providing an analysis of primary material in a manageable form.

Compare the account of the Crusades in Chapter 10 with the account in Chapter 15. What similarities and differences can you detect?

Reading a variety of secondary documents can provide you with insights into the topic. The various chapters in this text are examples of secondary documents being created by researching a variety of primary documents. As you read you may find that there is a variety of information collected here that you did not know about, or that your conceptions about some civilizations were inaccurate or false.

Reflect on your understanding and views of Japan prior to reading this chapter. How were your views challenged? What misconceptions did you have?

UNIT 4

The Resurgence of Western Civilization

CHAPTER 14
Europe in the Dark Ages

CHAPTER 15
The High Middle Ages

CHAPTER 16
The Late Middle Ages

CHAPTER 17
The Foundations of Early Modern Europe

The barbaric invasions which contributed to the demise of the Roman Empire left Europe in disarray. Civilization, say some, was nearly extinguished in the era commonly referred to as the Dark Ages. The chapters in this unit examine the collapse of order during the Dark Ages and the triumphant resurgence of European civilization during the High Middle Ages. As the Dark Ages were not all shrouded in despair so was the period of the Middle Ages not entirely an age of cultural vitality. Incessant warfare, divisions in the Catholic church, famine and plagues made the late Middle Ages a turbulent age.

The first three chapters of this unit provide a detailed look at life in the Dark Ages, an examination of the major achievements of the High Middle Ages concluding with a study of the changes in culture and society which brought the medieval period to a close. Throughout these chapters two overriding themes are ever present: the central role of the Catholic church, and the rigid stratification of a society led by a warrior class.

The concluding chapter examines the resurgence of Italy as a leading cultural force during the Renaissance. Artistic giants such as Michelangelo, Leonardo da Vinci, and Raphael are studied. The focus then shifts to northern Europe where divisions within the church erupt. Led by men such as Martin Luther and John Calvin, Christianity is irrevocably altered by the birth of Protestantism.

MEDIEVAL EUROPE

CHAPTER 14

Europe in the Dark Ages

Chapter Highlights

- daily life in the Dark Ages
- the central role of the church
- the intellectual revival under Charlemagne
- Viking raids
- Clovis, King of the Franks
- the beginning of feudalism

By the end of the fifth century A.D. the classical civilizations of the Mediterranean had faded. As you will recall from Chapter 9, the barbarian invasions were the culmination of a number of factors which brought about the collapse of the Western Roman Empire. This collapse was a process rather than a single event, allowing the peoples of the Empire time to adapt. The most dramatic sign of Roman decline was the seizure of political power by the barbarian invaders. Throughout this unit we shall trace the decline and eventual resurgence of western European civilization from the Dark Ages to the Renaissance and Reformation periods of the fifteenth and sixteenth centuries.

There are three main stages in the journey from the fall of Rome to the discovery of the Americas: the Dark Ages (A.D. 500–A.D. 1000); the High Middle Ages (A.D. 1000–A.D. 1300); and the late Middle Ages (A.D. 1300–A.D. 1500). The Dark Ages began with the decay of the Roman Empire and the beginning of the relocation of political dominance from Rome to northern Europe. If Rome represented the past, the "barbarian" invaders who helped to bring Rome down represented the medieval present. The church looked for ways to explain and justify the collapse of familiar order and to preserve what it valued. Eventually the church reconciled Rome and its invaders, pointing the way to a different and constructive future.

Each of the three elements that forged medieval culture will be focused upon in this chapter. As was seen in Chapter 9, the decline of the Roman Empire was gradual and was much more apparent in the west than in the east. In the east, Byzantium continued Roman tradition with an increasingly oriental aspect and an increasingly Greek flavour. While the political structure in the west was eliminated, much else was preserved. Language, law, and culture retained distinctively Latin features despite the influx of the barbarians.

This chapter will focus on the history of two contrasting kingdoms: the **Ostrogoths**, who settled in Italy; and the **Franks**, who occupied Gaul. To understand the Dark Ages it is also necessary to examine the continuation of Rome in the form of the Byzantine Empire under Justinian. Understanding Justinian's policies brings out the values of the age and shows the complexity of the relationship of barbarians with the inheritance from Christian Rome. Finally, tracing developments in the church will take us to that wholly medieval world whose centre lay in new lands outside the Mediterranean basin.

Key Concepts

Ostrogoths

Franks

Vandals

Visigoths

Justinian Code

Hagia Sophia

Theodoric

Benedictine Rule

Pepin

Song of Roland

Vikings

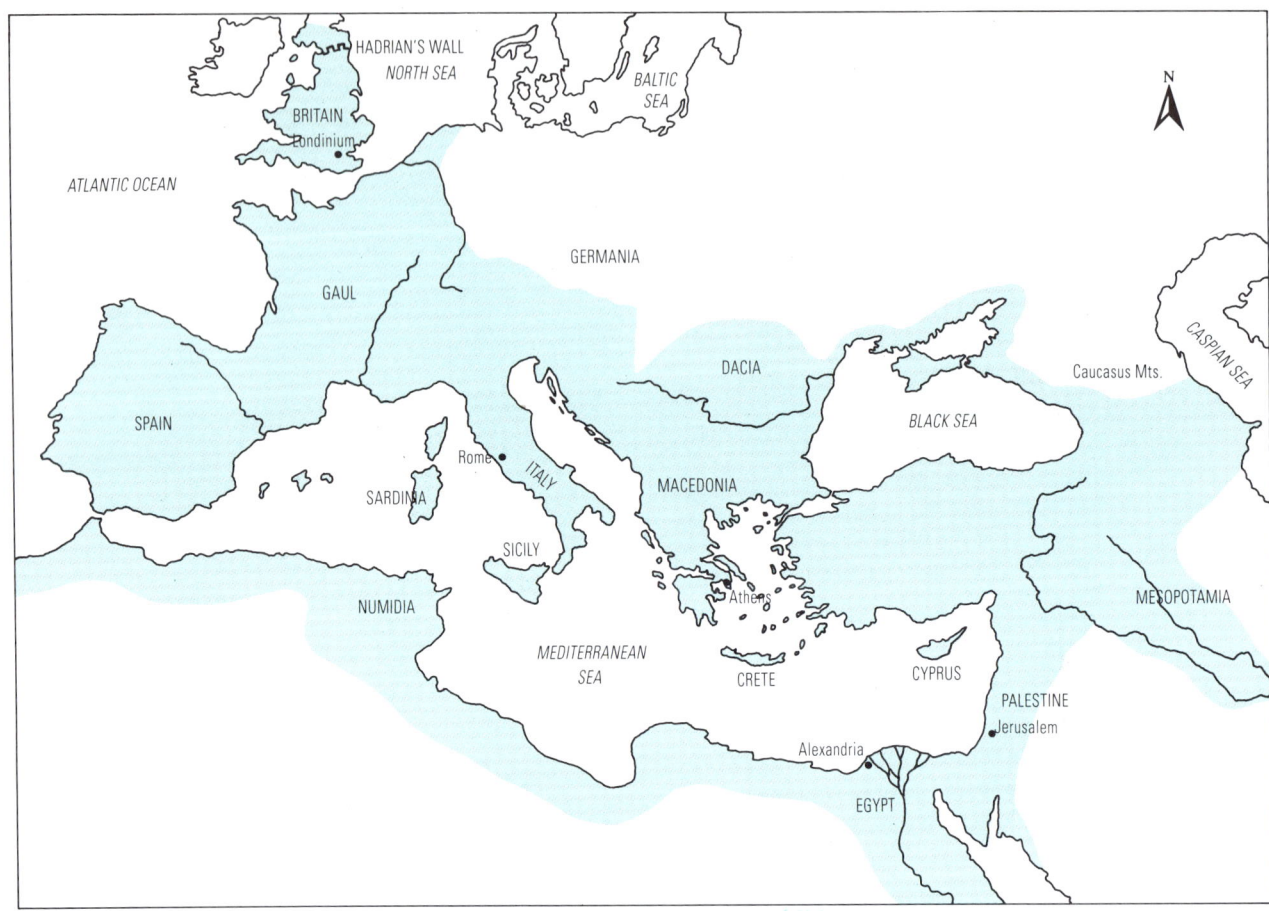

The Roman Empire in A.D. 200

Geography

If you have to travel somewhere unknown, it is sensible to look at a map. A map can also be useful in finding your way quickly through an unfamiliar period of history. If you look at a map of the Roman Empire and at another map of medieval Europe a thousand years after the fall of Rome, you will notice a striking difference. The map of the Roman Empire highlights the basin of the Mediterranean. It includes Gaul and Spain on the Atlantic and Britain to the north; but beyond the Rhine and Danube rivers, through what is now Germany and central and eastern Europe, the map is blank. On the other hand, Asia Minor, Syria and the Near East, Egypt, and the northern shore of Africa as far as Gibraltar, all have a large place in the Roman world. In the millennium following the fall of Rome, the empty lands beyond the Roman Empire took on as prominent a part in the politics of Europe as the Mediterranean basin.

Before the fall of Rome the idea of Europe hardly existed. This peninsula on the landmass of Asia had

The Nations of Europe in A.D. 1360

been home to people the Romans referred to as barbarians; in other words, non-Hellenic, non-oriental, non-citizens from beyond the borders of the Roman Empire. Barbarian Europe was densely forested and had high mountain ranges more extensive than any in the Mediterranean basin. The land had great rivers and extensive plains that allowed its inhabitants to be wasteful of its extensive resources. Unlike the Mediterranean, where the countryside was cultivated intensively and culture was founded on the life of cities, medieval Europe was largely rural. The only cities or towns that did exist were those left by colonizing Romans. Thus, there were significant differences between the map of the Roman world and the world of the Middle Ages in terms of the location of powers and the types of livelihood.

The Barbarian Invasions

It was pointed out in Chapter 9 that there was no unity among the invading "barbarians." The Goths tumbled out of the southern steppe of Asia following the Alans, **Vandals**, and Sueves who had preceded them; and they, in turn, were quickly followed by the Huns. At a later date the Avars, Magyars, Bulgars, and finally Turks erupted onto eastern and central Europe. Equally disruptive on the southern shore of the Mediterranean were the Arabs from the Arabian peninsula and the Berbers from the desert fringes of the Sahara. There was a more northerly, and slower moving, tide of Franks, Thuringians, Alemans, and Bavarians, not to mention the Angles, Saxons, and Jutes who crossed the North Sea to Britain. In the sixth century the Lombards made their home in northern Italy, and from the end of the eighth century the seaborne Vikings ranged down the northern and western coasts and rivers of Europe. To reconstruct the past of most of these peoples is difficult and confusing, as they only entered the historical record once they came into contact with Rome. There was considerable variety in their origins, in their traditions, and in the degree to which they assimilated Roman ways. Alans, Huns, and Magyars were from the steppe and their habits were nomadic, while the invaders of Britain, the Vandals in their march to Africa and later the Vikings, moved their institutions as well as their families to their new destination by sea. This was bound to alter familiar relationships and customs. The one factor common to all these people was that they engaged in conquest; and conquest favoured the warrior over the farmer thus laying the foundation for a military ruling class.

The Church

The church was an important element of the new order and having grown from the ruins of imperial Rome was deeply influenced by Roman tradition. From the pope in Rome to its bishops in provincial centres it mirrored the organization of the Empire. Church officials were frequently drawn from the traditional Roman landowners and were based in cities. The church, therefore, offered a continuation of Roman structure and character.

St. Augustine

During the latter part of the fourth century A.D. and the early part of the fifth century A.D., the bishop of

MAJOR EVENTS IN THE MIDDLE AGES

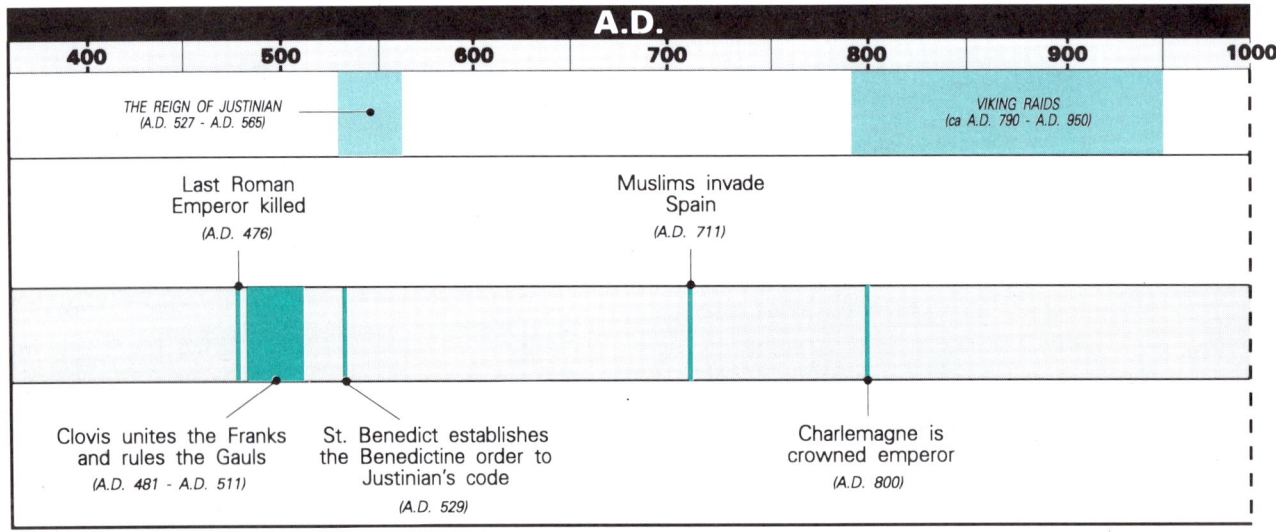

Hippo in North Africa issued two fundamental statements of faith. Augustine had been struggling with the implications of the collapsing Western Empire for the now officially supported church. He wrote *The City of God* to tell his readers that the collapse of the familiar order was not important by comparison with the assured mission of the Christian church. Roman power, he commented, would pass but the church was eternal. In other writings he affirmed the difficult doctrine of predestination which states that the will of God prevails over the wills of humans. He also wrote a personal testament that was unique at the time in its self-accusation and submission to divine providence. Augustine's *Confessions* expressed deep distrust of the sensual and particularly of the sexual drives of men and women. All his experience had led him to reject the values of the material world in favour of spiritual virtues which, in his view, lasted forever. While his outlook denied typical Roman values, Augustine's works were influential. This influence was partly due to his expert use of Latin style and language and by the exemplary piety in which Augustine, a formerly selfish man, lived his life.

Justinian's Byzantium

Justinian succeeded to the imperial throne in A.D. 527, a year after Theodoric, king of the Ostrogoths, died. He was the second emperor in a family, which a few years earlier had been farming near the imperial Roman frontier. He proposed as his goal the recovery of the lost territories of the Roman Empire but reconquest was to be more than the recovery of provinces taken by the barbarians; it meant the recovery of Roman traditions and imperial domination.

Three kingdoms were the targets of this single policy: the Vandals in Africa, the Ostrogoths in Italy, and the **Visigoths** in Spain. In each of them the invaders had been in place long enough for cracks in their unity to appear. In each of the kingdoms competition between ambitious warriors and differences over relations with the Romans created internal strife. Justinian took advantage of these quarrels by using skillful diplomacy to act as arbiter in some disputes and by taking sides in others. As a result his

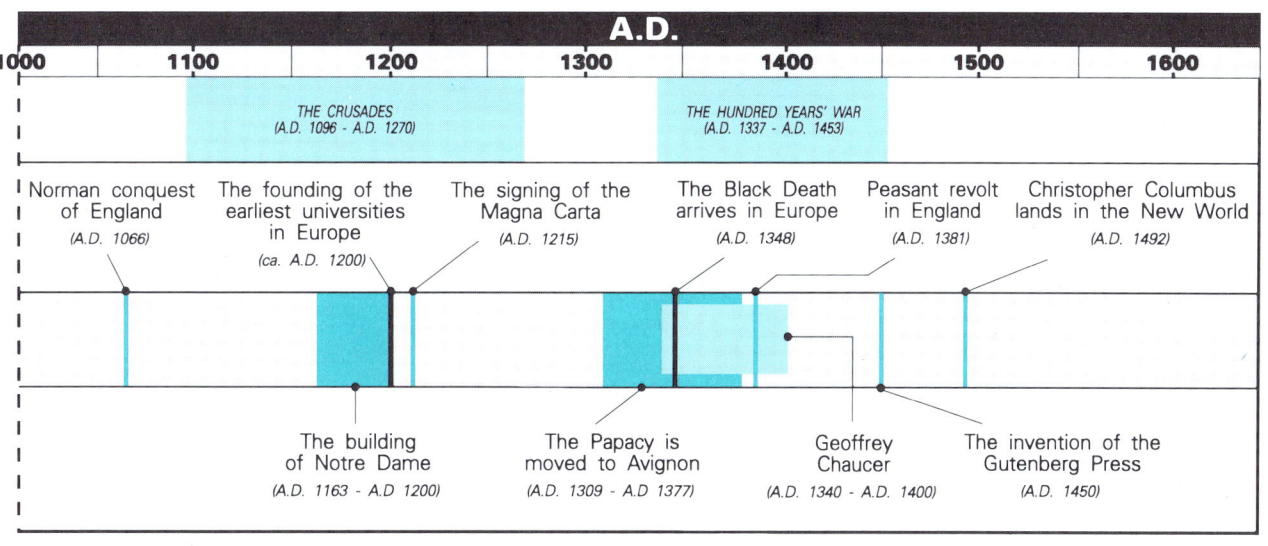

Europe in the Dark Ages CHAPTER 14

BELIEFS

THE ORGANIZATION OF THE CATHOLIC CHURCH

Despite the disappearance of the Roman Empire by the late fifth century A.D., its organization was preserved by the Roman Catholic Church. As the Roman emperors had ruled their vast empire from Rome, so the pope, the head of the church, made Rome the centre of Christianity.

The church also adopted the geographical units of the Roman Empire called "diocese." These dioceses, formerly ruled by governors were now the domain of the bishops. The impressive cathedrals (cathedra meaning chair) became their seat of power.

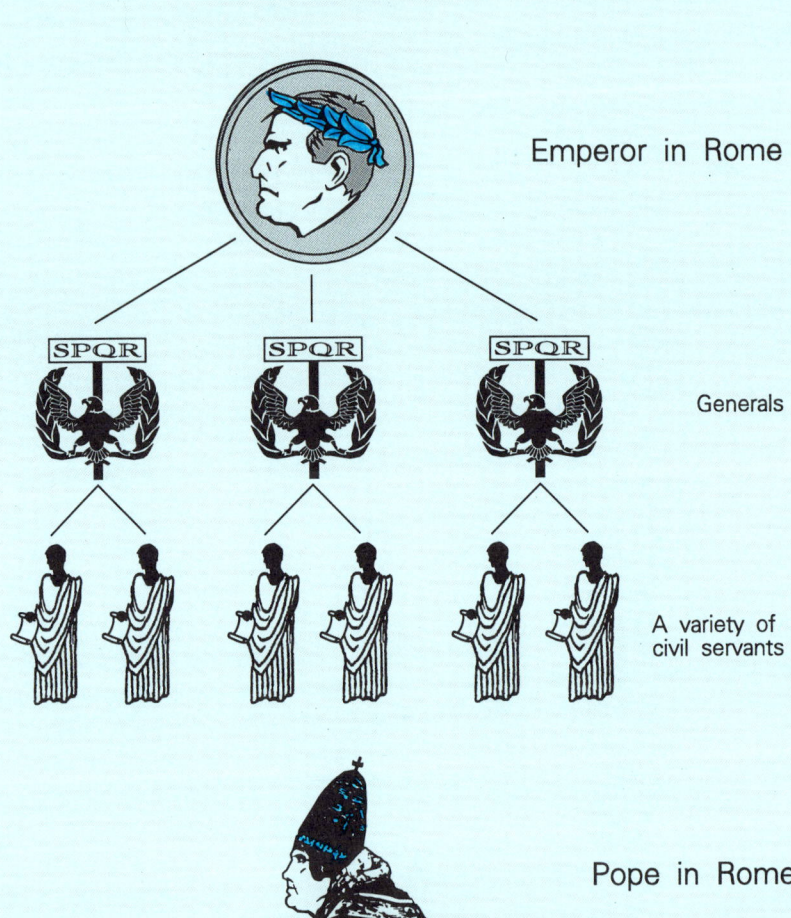

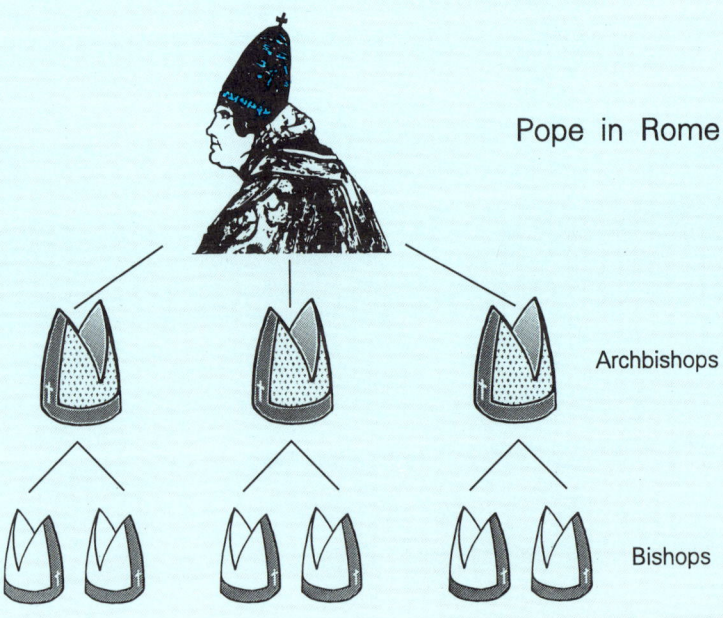

armies were able to take Africa from the Vandals (A.D. 533) and to recover parts of Spain from the Visigoths (A.D. 550). The cost of reconquest was high for Justinian. His armies, if limited in size, were almost entirely Germans or other **mercenaries** who had to be paid, and the fleets needed to transport and supply the troops cost a great deal. By the time of Justinian's death the Mediterranean may once more have been a sea dominated by Rome, but the cost to his treasury had been heavy. Justinian's conquest of Italy in 540 and the expedition in 552–554 to subdue the Ostrogoths were particularly destructive. The kingdom of the Ostrogoths was destroyed, and the people themselves were absorbed into the fractured fabric of what was left of Italy. Cities and the countryside were devastated, leaving the Italian peninsula in ruins.

The Justinian Code

An equally characteristic but more benign achievement of Justinian's reign (527–565) was the codification of Roman law. There were several parts to this activity, including a text for students of law and a technical commentary on principles and conflicts for the use of the expert and the *Code* itself. All of this was the work of a commission of lawyers and teachers, appointed by Justinian, who completed their enormous task between 528 and A.D. 533. When we consider that they had to review, reconcile, and codify for practical daily use in the imperial courts the whole contradictory mass of more than eight hundred years of legislation and volumes of learned discussion about those laws, their accomplishment must be seen as truly remarkable. Long after the empire had vanished, **Justinian's Code** continued to set the standard in the law of the church, and continues to do so to this day in the law of many states.

This kind of civilized, sophisticated review of a tradition of government shows how different Justinian's Empire was from the kingdoms which had followed the Roman Empire in the west. Efficient and effective government was disappearing in the west but the tradition of the state as an agent of philanthropy survived in Justinian's time in the east. In the sixth century A.D. philanthropy was expressed in publicly funded building, legislative reform, and the recovery of lost territory. Justinian financed a building program for public baths, court-houses, fortifications, and above all, churches and hospitals. The crowning glory amongst his buildings was the rebuilt basilica in Constantinople (now Istanbul) the church of **Hagia Sophia** (Holy Wisdom). The Hagia Sophia, now known as the Great Mosque, still amazes the spectator for its size, proportion, and grace.

Following the death of Justinian, Byzantium no longer had the strength to resist the political changes that were taking place in the eastern Mediterranean. An exhausting struggle between the Byzantine and Persian empires was to benefit Islam. Within a single generation the Arabs were able to establish themselves as the dominant force in the Near East. The result of Justinian's efforts was to take what remained of the Roman Empire out of what as now Europe:

> Justinian's heroic attempt to re-unite the Roman world into one Empire and one Church simply served to show that the Roman world had disappeared.[1]

Two Settlement Kingdoms

The difference in the fortunes of the Ostrogoths and Franks is seen most clearly in the reputations they would earn as distinct peoples. The descendants of

---

[1]R.H.C. Davis, *A History of Medieval Europe*, 2nd ed. (London: Longman, 1988), p. 60.

The church of Hagia Sophia (Holy Wisdom) is the greatest monument of the Byzantine Empire. It was begun in 532 during the reign of Emperor Justinian in Istanbul. After the church became a mosque (after the Turkish conquest), the four distinctive minarets were added.

the Franks are today inhabitants of France. If any trace of the Ostrogoths remains, it is in the word "Gothic," which is a term used later as the synonym for barbarian and non-classical. The Ostrogoths settled in Italy, in the very centre of the Mediterranean world, at the end of the fifth century. About that same time the Franks took advantage of the upheavals in Gaul, caused by other invaders, to establish a foothold in the northeast of the province. There, acting as nominal allies of Rome, they protected a remote frontier. From this base the Franks expanded slowly through the inhospitable wetlands at the mouth of the Rhine eventually reaching the more central parts of Gaul. Throughout their migrations the Franks seldom were in contact with any civilizing force until their leaders came into contact with provincial Romans in central Gaul. The Goths, meanwhile, had made their way from their home north of the Crimea into Italy, arriving towards the end of the fifth century. During their travels the Goths had been heavily influenced by Rome, unlike the more remote Franks.

The Ostrogoths

By the time the Ostrogoths began to move into Italy in A.D. 488 they had been a factor in imperial politics for more than a century. Emperors had tried to use them as a barrier against further barbarian intrusions, and at the end of the fifth century the emperor, Zeno, decided to use them to destroy the German commander who had recently deposed the last emperor in the west (A.D. 476).

At this time the king of the Ostrogoths was **Theodoric**. When his father, of the same name, had been ruler, young Theodoric had lived for some time at the imperial court in Constantinople as a hostage to ensure the good behaviour of his restless people. During that time he had come to know the emperor, his family and advisers, and to have a healthy respect for Roman abilities and culture. Once in Italy, he readily adopted a policy of live and let live towards his Roman hosts. His warriors provided security, and so long as the taxes which paid them came in, they kept to their camps and allotted settlements. For the Roman aristocrats, life on their large estates among their families, clients, and slaves went on much as before, dedicated to the cultivation of literary and humane taste in an atmosphere of good living. A number of these senatorial aristocrats, including the pope and his circle, worked for Theodoric in the tasks of government for which the barbarians were not suited. Government was correspondingly more Roman because of their involvement. Theodoric's aim was to keep Roman civilization intact behind a ring of Gothic spears, while being careful not to offend imperial Roman feelings. For example, he dated his official documents by the years of the consuls chosen by his Roman subjects, just as any Roman did.

Theodoric's efforts at maintaining harmony could not last. Many of his tribal followers were disgruntled at the amount of riches won from their conquest of Italy. The stability of Theodoric's position was undermined when the death of his only son left a daughter and her husband as his only heir. This served to weaken the military leadership among the Goths, whose position rested on their military superiority. As Theodoric became increasingly alarmed at the erosion of his power, he began to reverse the policies that had brought distinction and prosperity for most of his rule.

Visigoths and Vandals

The Visigoths, who had been the western neighbours of the Ostrogoths before the period of invasion, entered Italy at the start of the fifth century. After sacking Rome in A.D. 410 they realized that they did not have the numbers to consolidate their position in Italy where the Roman Empire still preserved some authority. The Visigoths moved along the Mediterranean coast, through Gaul, and eventually settled in Roman Spain. The Vandals had advanced through Gaul earlier, coming down the Rhone Valley in 406–407. From there the Vandals crossed the Pyrenees and, after a brief halt in Spain, passed over the Straits of Gibraltar to plunder the rich province of Africa. Augustine of Hippo was one of the many victims of a conquest that made the Vandals' name synonymous with destruction and cruelty.

The Franks

In the fifth century, when the Visigoths were occupying Gaul as far north as the Loire, the Franks were pressing against the northern boundary of the province. When they finally broke the Gallo-Roman resistance at the end of the fifth century, the central government in Constantinople was in no position to make a military response. Gaul's distance from the centre of the empire was critical to the development of the Frankish kingdom for reasons other than

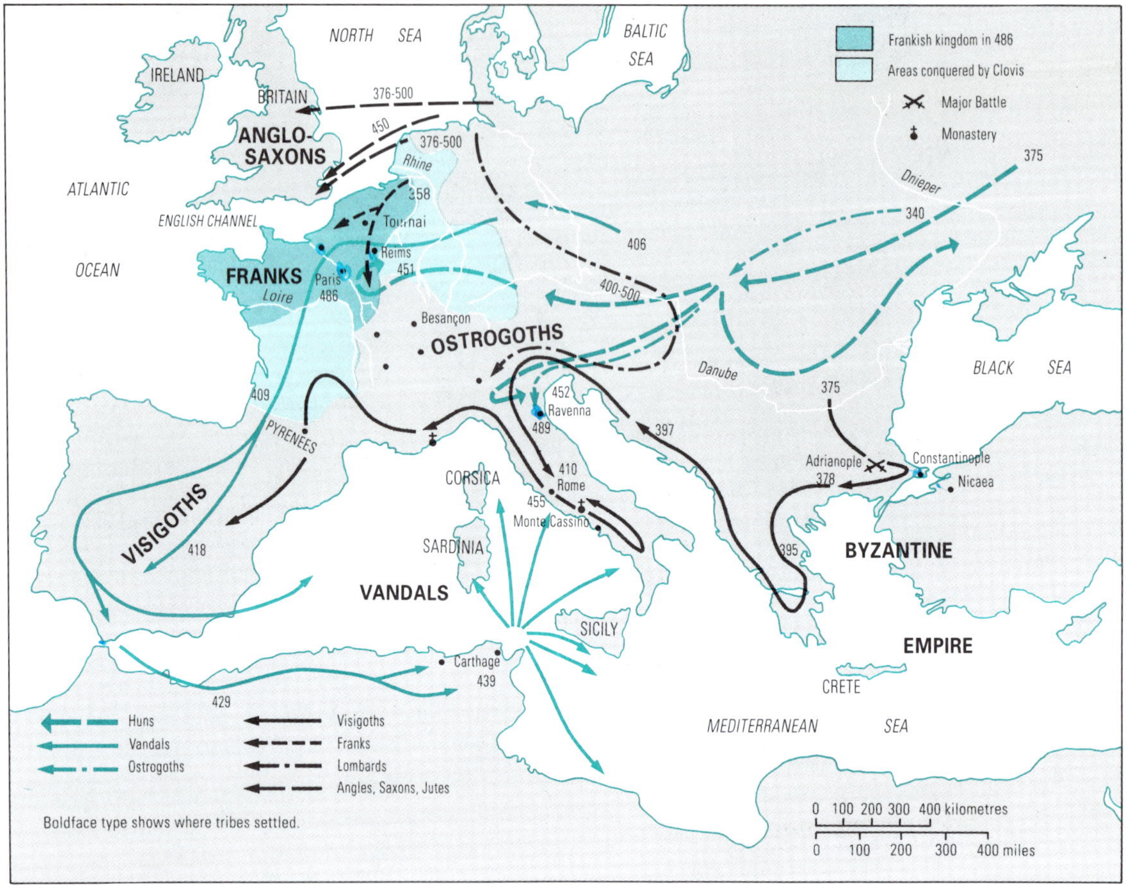

The Germanic Migrations

defence. Unlike the Goths, who were eventually absorbed by the Romans, or the Anglo-Saxons, who destroyed virtually all traces of Roman influence, the Franks were able to establish a balance in the process of assimilating what the Gallo-Romans had to teach them without losing their own character. This they were able to do because they settled Gaul in stages adapting to the least Romanised northern regions before encountering the more urbanized and populous south.

The Reign of Clovis. The foundation for the success of the Franks was laid in the reign of Clovis (ca. A.D. 481–511). Clovis exemplified the role of conqueror, essential to the reputation of a barbarian leader. He was the first ruler to consolidate the different groups of Franks and he created a powerful new kingdom. Beginning as ruler of a local division of the Franks, Clovis first subdued neighbouring Frankish regions and then defeated the independent provincial Roman administration. After that he coerced his eastern neighbours beyond the Rhine into submitting to his authority. Clovis mastered almost the whole of Gaul in his own lifetime. At the end of his reign, in A.D. 507, his warriors defeated the Visigoths at the battle of Vouillé and drove them

444 UNIT 4 *The Resurgence of Western Civilization*

out of central Gaul.

At some point in his career, although precisely [when is unclear, owing] to the sparse [sources, Clovis was] persuaded to [convert to Christianity, despite] the fact [that his wife was a Bur]gundian who [was already Catholic.] As a result of [his conversion, the Frank]s, who were [settled in the area]s south of the [Loire, supported the Cath]olic rather [than the Arians, who receiv]ed support of [the Visigoths. His] people to [victory at the battle of] Vouillé was [acknowledged by the Ro]man emperor, [who granted him the title] of consul. This [confirmed Clovis's ach]ievements in the eyes [of all.]

[Clovis's career was rem]arkable and [his legacy established] them as the [dominant force, but it wa]s not consoli[dated into a single fa]mily empire, [and after his death in 511], his territo[ries were divided in]to four more [or less equal parts. The o]ld Frankish [heartland and a n]ew southern [territory were each rul]ed by one of [his four sons. After t]he death of [Clovis, competition] among the [Frankish nobles was acute] and admitted. For [this reason Chilperic (561-5]) decided to [... while] was summoned [to the palace] watching an [acrobat perform with a p]ack of dogs. [In the middle of the specta]cle, [an assassin came up behind] him and the [...]

[Gregory of T]ours was a [member of an] aristocratic provincial family. His aim was to reproach Clovis's heirs for the political risks to which their rivalries exposed the kingdom of the Franks. He asserted that moral decline was the inevitable result of the loss of unity. Gregory of Tours believed that when properly led the Franks had swept all before them, winning important victories for the Catholic church. The purpose, therefore, of his stories was to shame his readers into recovering the traditions of Clovis.

When Gregory wrote his *History of the Franks* at the end of the sixth century, Frankish and Gallo-Roman nobles were steadily becoming assimilated with each other. Wars between rival kings had led to large tracts of land, and the political power that went with land, being given to the warrior nobility of the Franks to secure their loyalty. The Gallo-Roman nobility already had large tracts of land and a tradition of political power and so the two aristocracies came to share common interests. These similarities of interest and situation, their common Catholic faith, and their association at royal courts in pursuit of generous favours led to the integration of the Frank and Roman nobility, which Gregory promoted.

Living Conditions

Where did the common people fit into the violent and disjointed society of the Dark Ages? They were exposed in a world where raw power was the source of security. The Franks were not numerous, in fact they numbered only in the thousands. Those who could support the status of a free Frank (who were the majority of the people and were neither slaves nor members of the nobility) were summoned annually at the start of the campaigning season to increase the size of the army. The free Frank was also responsible for contributing to the royal treasury by payment or by some form of service.

Europe in the Dark Ages CHAPTER 14

The legends of King Arthur, which were greatly embellished by medieval writers such as Sir Thomas Malory, describe the knights of the Round Table as chivalrous warriors clad in full body armour. In fact, the dress of an Arthurian knight would have been much lighter as depicted here.

implements were light, made mainly of wood and generally only scratched the soil rather than turning it over. As there was only a basic understanding of the need to fertilize and rotate crops, the soil became exhausted and unproductive. When this happened more trees were cut down and the cultivated area was moved. For the most part, surplus production or produce that exceeded the basic needs of a family depended on animals such as cattle, pigs, and sheep. Unfenced animals habitually strayed, grazing on a neighbour's land. That was considered trespassing, and the Germanic codes of law gave a great deal of attention to the compensation awarded for damage done by straying beasts. This was but one aspect of the developing sense of individual property that was replacing the tribal communalism which had been typical of German societies in earlier times.

Law

In a world of political strife and economic disasters, beset by unknown forces in nature, the common Franks were vulnerable. Their chief security lay in ties of family consisting of a wide connection of siblings, cousins, and older relatives offering some of the material and moral support that the ordinary people needed. The importance of the family is one reason why the majority of the Franks took longer than their rulers to abandon their pagan beliefs and accept the faith of the church. The extended family was the guarantee that the individual had some legal protection. The Salic law of the Franks, like other codes among the German peoples, was a tariff of the compensation to be paid for offences to individuals or property. While the fact that these codes were written down by the clergy was a sign of civilization, they remain barbaric in nature as they were conceived in terms of particular remedies rather than of particular principles. For example, the laws preserved under the name of Ethelbert of Kent (England), set a different rate of compensation for

The daily routine of the common people was dominated by their work on the land. The techniques used in farming were primitive, with oxen as the animal commonly used to pull a plough or cart. As oxen were expensive it was common for communities to own a communal ox. Ploughs and other the loss of each finger: 20 shillings for a thumb, 9 shillings for a forefinger, but only 4 shillings for a middle finger. Restitution was set not only according to the offence, but also to the rank of the victim. It cost more to injure a noble or bishop than an ordinary free person. The blood of the royal house carried the highest price of all.

The means of establishing responsibility for a crime were primitive. The oaths of the accused and accuser were weighed against each other; the testimony of a noble was considered more valuable than that of a commoner. If the oaths on each side balanced, the court called for the ordeal in which God gave the judgement, either by fire or by water. For each ordeal there were special prayers to invoke the divine judgement. In the ordeal by fire the hand of the accused, after being forced into red-hot coals, had to heal within a prescribed time or the person was pronounced guilty. According to ordeal by water the guilt of the accused was established by the suspects being bound and thrown into a river or pond; if they floated to the surface they were pronounced guilty.

Daily Life

The common Frank obviously lived an uncertain and often violent life. Yet in many cases they had little to lose as crops were subject to the weather and the chances of wars or raids. Their stock, at least, was mobile. Animals shared the huts with their owner's family, which were built of a lattice of light timber daubed with mud and grass. The human occupants lived at one end, with minimal furnishings, and the animals at the other. Richer families could afford storage sheds, which were constructed near the house.

Living conditions for the nobles in the Dark Ages were not much better after the disappearance of Roman villas. Few rulers could afford the expense of building in stone as Charlemagne did in his model

The feudal system rigidly organized medieval society. Lords and their vassals had interconnected obligations, however there is no doubt which class was favoured.

palace at Aachen. Other rulers built with wood and crowded their followers and servants as well as their families into the one structure. The same hall served as the centre for business, entertainment, and relaxation as well as for all the different activities of daily life such as cooking, eating, drinking, and sleeping. Fires were needed for cooking even in seasons when they were not necessary for heat and as there were no chimneys or other forms of ventilation, people indoors lived in a haze of wood smoke. There was no privacy for anyone except for a raised dais for the master of the hall, his immediate family, and closest companions. With weapons at hand, too little to do, and values based on tales of heroes who had won their reputations in fights of the past, it is not surprising that this was a society dominated by physical strength and the ability to give and take punishment.

Early Signs of Feudalism

Some two centuries after the last Roman emperor in the west had been deposed, invaders and invaded in Europe had assimilated with each other to some degree. How that result was reached differed from place to place. In Italy and Spain the Roman legacy was least affected. In Africa and in what came to be England, the Roman population was destroyed or driven to the margins of the territory. The Franks in Gaul achieved the most balanced relations with their one-time "hosts." Yet everywhere that assimilation took place, the process was similar.

The settlement kingdoms that followed the barbarian invasions did not have the typical features of the classical feudal society of the eleventh and twelfth centuries: the castle, the armed knight, the feof which was the economic foundation for knight service, nor the feudal epics. Yet the conditions that produced the feudal society existed long before the typical forms and mental outlook of feudalism developed.

The conditions that encouraged lordship and led eventually to feudalism can be summarized in two words: insecurity and localism. The military environment of invasion and conquest left the average citizen in a vulnerable position. As the demands made by the governments on its free citizens became increasingly oppressive and repeated wars took their toll, people were compelled to consider the advantages of subordinating themselves to a powerful lord. Free citizens would then receive protection in return for the loss of independence and the legal status of being free. Because the independent farmers could not protect themselves and sustain the necessary level of production to fulfill their obligations, many surrendered their independence to a wealthy and powerful noble.

Localisation was the result of the breakdown of the economy. Cities and towns had flourished during the period of Roman rule, providing centres of government throughout the Empire. The disorder caused by the invasions added to the destruction of both towns and trade. Smaller populations abandoned whole quarters of established cities. When Islam gained control of North Africa and Spain in the seventh century and denied control of the Mediterranean to any other power, distant trade shrank to a trickle. The entrepreneurial Greeks, Syrians, and Jews who had been the merchants of the Roman Empire, almost disappeared; and with them disappeared the techniques for raising credit, which international trade required. The insecurity of trade overland in barbarian kingdoms, and the primitive level of aristocratic taste, led to what has been aptly called "an economy without outlets." Barter in goods replaced money, markets became restricted to largely local goods that could be carried short distances from the surrounding countryside, and stalls took the place of permanent shops as the process of buying and selling became sporadic.

The clergy, who provided what intellectual framework was needed in this impoverished society of the Dark Ages, identified three groups in society: those who fought, those who prayed, and those who laboured on the land to provide for the first two. There was no place for the merchant or the townspeople in the social hierarchy of the Dark Ages and feudal Europe.

The Catholic Church

The few who travelled long distances in the Dark Ages were more likely to be church officials than merchants. They were often bishops on their way to visit the king's court, the **papal see** in Rome, or to attend a regional or national council or synod. Missionaries and pilgrims were also more likely to travel great distances than most others. Despite the inherent violence and disunity of the Dark Ages, the church, whose authority rested on spiritual values, managed to play a leading role in the development of Europe and its culture. The central role played by the church would continue for nearly one and a half **millenniums**.

From the beginnings of the church, even before the conversion of the Roman Empire, bishops had been its chief executives. They worked out of the main city of their dioceses. Rome, as the chief city of the empire and the burial place of Saints Peter and Paul, became the dominant centre of Christendom; with its bishop given the title of pope and leadership of all bishops. The decay of cities, however, lessened the dominance of bishops in the church. The establishment of monasticism in the west provided a new role model for the church.

Monasticism

The calling of the monk had initially been to a life of separation and deprivation in the desert. They were to lead a life of prayer, reinforced by severe self-discipline. This practice in the Egyptian desert, where it first flourished in the fourth century A.D., became so popular that the original purpose of isolation was defeated. In fact, so many fled the worldly life that it was necessary to form communities in the desert. These communities became the early monasteries. Their essential task continued to be prayer, but increasingly they prayed together. In Italy during the fifth century, Saint Benedict placed his followers in a monastery to work together as monks. They lived a common life and followed a common timetable: they went to work in the fields around the monastery and in the writing workshop together; they ate sparingly, avoiding meat; and they slept in a common dormitory in the clothes which they wore in the daytime. *The Rule* written by Saint Benedict for his monks moderated the degree of self-denial and the individualism of the Egyptian desert; yet the central duty of the Benedictine monk continued to be prayer. They rose in the night to go together to the abbey's church to pray and they prayed together through the day at three-hour intervals from dawn to sundown. Benedict's monks, like all monks since that time, took solemn vows. They swore to embrace poverty and chastity as their way of life, and they promised obedience to their abbot who was the final authority for his monks, apart from *The Rule* itself. The abbey was a community dedicated to regular worship and prayer for the salvation of the world but because monks were ordinary men, many of them simple peasants, Benedict did not ask more than what an ordinary man might accomplish with the support of his brothers. While the abbot's authority was final, *The Rule* urged him to preside over his monks like a wise father of a family.

The Benedictine abbey proved itself to be an appropriate Christian response to the sea of disorder and uncertainty that then prevailed in Italy. Benedict, like so many prominent figures in the church of his time, came from an established landowning family. He had the same respect for order, authority, and stability as other members of his class, but the violence of the 540s made this period the opposite of these. So he abandoned the public career that was expected of him and left for a lonely existence in the Appenine mountains of Italy. His reputation soon attracted followers and, despite his original intention, he was forced to provide for a community. *The Rule of Saint Benedict* was a code by which those who had joined him could lead the religious life.

Gregory I

Although the poor communications of the Dark Ages meant that most popes of the period are forgotten there were a few outstanding popes from this period. The leadership of such men developed, over

PRIMARY DOCUMENT

THE RULE OF ST. BENEDICT

The monastic movement, which became a central feature of the Middle Ages, owed a great deal to St. Benedict of Nursia. As a young man, St. Benedict fled the corrupt secular society of sixth-century Rome and lived alone in a hillside cave. Word spread of his life of contemplation and devotion to God and soon he was approached by a religious community to be their leader. The monastery he founded at Monte Cassino was based on a set of guidelines called *The Rule of St. Benedict*. As you read the excerpts from *The Rule* reflect on the discipline and devotion such a life would require. Do you think you could have lived among the monks at Monte Cassino? Do you think such a life of austerity is necessary to express your faith?

Obedience: The first grade of humility is obedience without delay, which is becoming to those who hold nothing dearer than Christ. So, when one of the monks receives a command from a superior, he should obey it immediately, as if it came from God himself, being impelled thereto by the holy service he has professed and by the fear of hell and the desire of eternal life. . . .

Humility: Now the first step of humility is this, to escape destruction by keeping ever before one's eyes the fear of the Lord, to remember always the commands of the Lord, for they who scorn him are in danger of hell-fire, and to think of the eternal life that is prepared for them that fear him. So a man should keep himself in every hour from

---

time, an administrative nucleus capable of promoting a continuing vision.

Gregory I (A.D. 590-604) was perhaps the most outstanding example of a pope contributing to the process of moral refinement and administrative reform during the Dark Ages. He made a notable contribution with his writings: *Pastoral Care*, for the guidance of priests and bishops, and the *Dialogues* and *Moralia*, designed to exemplify in vivid stories the power of sin and the remedies that the church could supply. However, the monastic chant that bears his name, and is still sung in religious communities, was not historically connected to him. The tradition, nevertheless, is a tribute to the multifaceted activity of this remarkable man. He was the Prefect of Rome, the city's mayor as we might say, when he was elected pope, and he applied his political and organizing ability to rescue from ruin and seizure the papal properties which then stretched across Italy. He popularized the lofty theology of Saint Augustine of Hippo and promoted the influence of the **Benedictine Rule**. In A.D. 597, *The Rule of Saint Benedict* was brought to Canterbury, England by a monk called Augustine and a few companions. They had been sent from Rome by Pope Gregory I who had lived by *The Rule* before being chosen pope. Gregory was aware of the distant Angles and Saxons because of an earlier encounter in Rome with slave boys about whom he is said to have remarked "Not Angles, but angels." Thus the work of Pope Gregory I was to leave a lasting impression both on the papacy and on the wider church.

the sins of the heart, of the tongue, of the eyes, of the hands, and of the feet. He should cast aside his own will and the desires of the flesh; he should think that God is looking down on him from heaven all the time, and that his acts are seen by God and reported to him hourly by his angels....

The sixth step of humility is this, that the monk should be contented with any lowly or hard condition in which he may be placed, and should always look upon himself as an unworthy laborer, not fitted to do what is intrusted to him....

The seventh step of humility is this, that he should not only say, but should really believe in his heart that he is the lowest and most worthless of all men, humbling himself and saying with the prophet: "I am a worm and no man; a reproach of men, and despised of all people...."

The Daily Labor of the Monks: Idleness is the great enemy of the soul, therefore the monks should always be occupied, either in manual labor or in holy reading. The hours for these occupations should be arranged according to the seasons, as follows: From Easter to the first of October, the monks shall go to work at the first hour and labor until the fourth hour, and the time from the fourth to the sixth hour, they shall be spent in reading. After dinner, which comes at the sixth hour, they shall lie down and rest in silence; but anyone who wishes may read, if he does it so as not to disturb anyone else....

Monks Should Not Have Personal Property: The sin of owning private property should be entirely eradicated from the monastery. No one shall presume to give or receive anything except by the order of the abbot; no one shall possess anything of his own, books, paper, pens, or anything else....

Silence is to be Kept After Contemplation: The monks should observe the rule of silence at all times but especially during the hours of the night.

The Donation of Constantine

In an age when religion was power, the papacy could not avoid the politics of religion. Popes were concerned with the religious consequences of political attitudes in Byzantium. Pope Gelasius I (A.D. 492–496) had sought to insulate the church from the swings of imperial policy by claiming that, as pope, he wielded the spiritual sword, while the emperor held the sword by which worldly affairs were ruled. This doctrine of the two swords had little immediate effect, but it was revived later in the Middle Ages as an influential statement of relations between church and state.

Gregory II (A.D. 715-731) was the first Italian pope after a long period of Greek supremacy at the papal court. Rome and southern Italy remained part of the Byzantine Empire, and supported by Italian resentment against Byzantium's ineffective protection, Gregory II was the first pope to fail to report his election to the Byzantine emperor in order to receive his confirmation. At this time a document called the Donation of Constantine appeared as a weapon against the emperor in Byzantium, who was no better than a heretic in the papacy's point of view. The Donation, which was supposed to have been issued by Constantine I the first Christian emperor of the Roman Empire, claimed to provide the papacy with a title to political superiority over all the Western Empire. Although the document was found to be a forgery in the fifteenth century A.D., this was not known in the Dark Ages when it lent considerable support to claims made by the papacy. The promotion of **iconoclasm** in the east from A.D. 726

onwards broke the alliance of the pope in Rome to Byzantium and prepared the way for the transfer of imperial authority in the west to the Carolingian family at the end of the century. The papacy cultivated the kingdoms of western Europe as a counterweight to Byzantium and its claims to the control of Italy. The churches of the Anglo-Saxons, the Visigoths, and of the Franks especially, looked to Rome as the standard of worship and of legal order in the church. In the eighth century the popes regularly sent advice and direction to the bishops and abbots of these kingdoms and encouragement to their rulers.

Carolingian House

After the transformation of the Western Roman Empire by the barbarian kingdoms, the Carolingians began the formation of a very different kind of empire. The man who did most to create that empire was the Frankish ruler Charles the Great, or Charlemagne.

The ruling house of the Franks had been the Merovingians, but after Clovis no ruler had been able to hold on to authority over all the warring peoples. Unity was hard to come by because of the tradition of dividing the inheritance equally among the dead king's sons rather than passing the kingdom on intact to the eldest son. Before Charlemagne, the military hero of the Carolingians and of the Franks, was Charles Martel. He led the Franks in the bitter fight that turned back Islam at Poitiers in A.D. 735. To accomplish and consolidate this victory Martel took back, without compensation, lands given by earlier kings and nobles to the church. The wealth from this land he used to equip more heavily armed fighting men whom he put on horseback and used as cavalry. This was a radical change from the tradition of the footsoldiers who had won all earlier Frankish victories.

The Carolingians and the Church

Although the Carolingians had become the leading Frankish family, the Merovingian kings remained the rulers of the Frankish Empire, at least in theory. They spent their usually short lives in pleasure-seeking and self-indulgence. In principle they had immense powers, combining the **autocracy** of Roman imperial rule with the traditional powers of a barbarian leader. In fact they were powerless against the different regional interests led by the mayors of the palace. These officials, drawn from the leading noble family of each region of the Frankish Kingdom, were more than just palace managers as their titles suggest. They were in fact viceroys who exercised the King's power. For legal royal authority to pass to the real masters of the Franks, the Carolingian family, required an external sanction. This came from the papacy. First, one pope approved the claim of Martel's son, **Pepin**, to be the legitimate as well as the effective king. Shortly after, in A.D. 754 another pope left Italy and crowned Pepin on Frankish soil in the presence of a great assembly. The alliance between the Carolingians and the papacy was based on earlier partnerships. Pepin had collaborated closely with Saint Boniface, the Anglo-Saxon missionary who went to the pagan and independent lands east of the Rhine River. Boniface had approval from Rome for every new advance and kept the popes informed of his successes. Pepin also took Boniface's advice to encourage reforms in the Frankish church. As a result of this partnership the papacy had good reason to look to the Franks as political protectors. They needed this, for in A.D. 751 the Lombards had captured Ravenna, the seat of the Byzantine governor in Italy and their next stop was to be Rome. The Lombards, even though they were now Catholics, were rough neighbours. Not only had Byzantium failed to repulse them, the emperors in the east had, in fact, promoted the iconoclastic heresy. After his consecration as king of the Franks by a pope, Pepin was called upon to live up to his side of the implied agreement. He invaded Italy, seized the Lombard crown and, for the pope, secured the territory that came to be known as the Papal States. The forged Donation of Constantine provided a justification for his actions.

Martel, his son Pepin, and Pepin's son Charlemagne provided successive generations of outstanding leadership. Their personalities, however, were just one of an unusual conjunction of factors at work in Byzantium, Italy, and in Francia and its neighbouring territories, that led to the restoration of the empire in the west.

Charlemagne

Charlemagne has been justly seen as a patron of scholarship and the arts, an active lawgiver and reformer, and an attentive administrator. Yet he must also be seen as a great conqueror and barbarian warrior in the mould of traditional legendary heroes such as Beowulf who fought the dragon Grendel. As ruler or warrior, what was remarkable about the man was his energy. In the epics of the feudal age, legendary accounts of the events of Charles' time tell of his conquests, which reached from Apulia to Ireland. In one he is portrayed in old age as a snowy-bearded patriarch, worn out by his activity. Called on by the archangel Gabriel for yet another campaign to defend Christendom from the pagan threat Charlemagne remarked, "God, my life is hard indeed."

Although **Song of Roland** records a disaster for Frankish arms, Charlemagne's armies usually were victorious. They needed to be, since the Franks did not have the administrative means to control the lands they conquered. There were three directions to Charlemagne's constant campaigns. In the southwest he acted as an early crusader by actively engaging Islam in order to support the surviving Christian kingdoms in the southern foothills of the Pyrenees. In the southeast he had to repeat his father's intervention to keep the Lombards in order, and he was called upon to keep the peace in Rome itself. Nevertheless, his main preoccupation was with the independent pagan tribes on his eastern border. For 30 years he campaigned there on an almost annual basis. The Saxons on the Elbe were his most persistent opponents and warfare against them was savage. He also defeated the Frisians, Thuringians, and Bavarians who had all been partly subordinated by earlier campaigns. Finally, he destroyed the raiding empire of the Asiatic Avars who were based in the central Danube plain, thereby carrying German domination back towards their traditional homelands in eastern Europe.

Conquest was coupled with the conversion of pagans to Christianity. This compounded the bitterness of the Saxon wars, since conversion was forced on the conquered. The link between conquest and Christendom was forged by the clerks who held a prominent place at Charlemagne's court. They were indispensable because they were virtually the only literate people. Although Charlemagne struggled honourably to learn to read and write, and established a palace school for the instruction of his kinsmen and the sons of nobles, Latin, the language of written communication, remained a clerical monopoly.

An Era of Intellectual Revival

Charlemagne was served by a remarkable group of intellectuals. As well as Franks they included scholars from Spain, Italy, and England. The leading figures had all been influenced by monasticism and thus their outlook was traditional and conservative. Their goals were practical, limited, and directed in the first place to the needs of monks, such as more accurate transcriptions of the Bible and service

THE ARTS

CANADA'S SAXON HERITAGE

During the latter half of the fifth century A.D., the Saxons (along with the Jutes and Angles) moved into England, filling the void created by the Roman withdrawal. Over the following few centuries, the Saxons (under the capable leadership of men such as Woden, Ine, Aethelwulf, and Alfred) would emerge as the leading political power in southern England. The conversion of the Saxons to Christianity began with the arrival of Augustine in 597 A.D. Throughout much of the Dark Ages, complexes such as the bishop's palace, pictured here, would have served as the household for the bishop—and a centre of Christianity. The bishop's palace, as with the homes of the nobility, was a great barn-like structure of wattle and dub construction.

Canada's Saxon heritage is still evident in the names of many of our cities and counties. *Minster*, a Saxon word for "a religious centre," appears in names such as New Westminster, British Columbia. Other names also reflecting Saxon roots include Essex county in southwestern Ontario; and Sussex, New Brunswick. *Essex* and *Sussex* are both Saxon words meaning "east Saxons" and "south Saxons" respectively. Can you think of other cities or counties that take their names from places or terms brought to Canada from other countries?

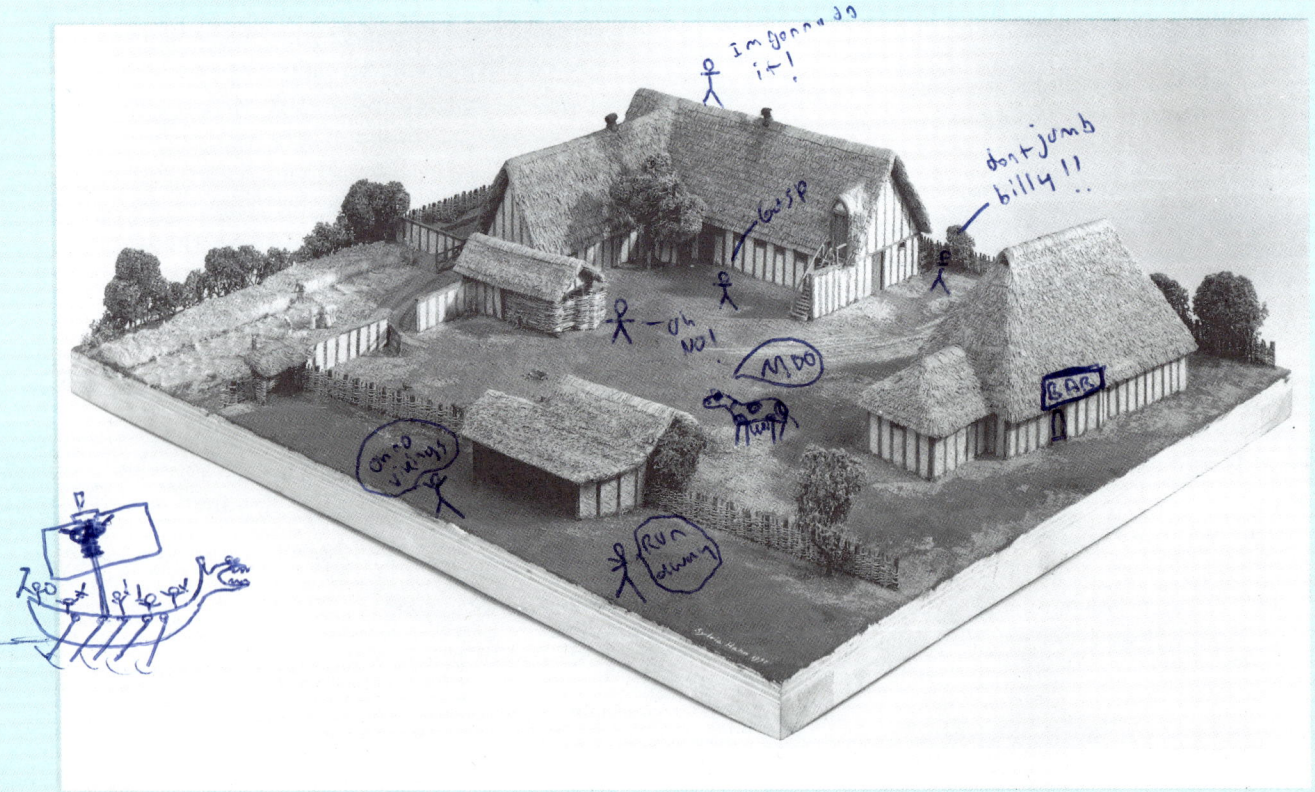

books used in worship and in improved handwriting to save corrected texts from corruption.

Alcuin was typical of this group as well as being the most influential adviser at court on cultural matters. He had been educated in York, England, and left when his family's traditional position in the school there was threatened. He later became the abbot of Tours from where he advised Charlemagne by letter and frequently attended the court as it moved round the kingdom. The ideology of Christendom and the purpose of restoring a Latin empire based on Christian values and character originated in these circles. Coming from York, the birthplace of Constantine I, the first Christian emperor of the Roman Empire, Alcuin was imbued with English loyalty to Rome.

The occasion for putting these ideas into practical shape was probably an accident. Pope Leo III (A.D. 795–817) managed to get himself into political trouble in Rome, and although tradition made the pope the leading citizen of Rome, Leo was discredited and driven out. Like his predecessors he came to the Franks for help. Since Pepin's time the king of the Franks had been protector of the Papal States. So, Charlemagne restored Leo to his see and happened to be in Rome for the Christmas ceremonies of A.D. 800. In a calculated gesture, but one of which Charles had probably not been told of in advance, the pope crowned the king of the Franks during the Christmas mass, and the shouts of the congregation acknowledged him as emperor. Thus was born what came to be known as the Holy Roman Empire, an empire Catholic and universal in inspiration and German in its ruler, which lasted until the nineteenth century.

After his coronation in Rome, Charlemagne built a permanent residence at Aachen, in northern Germany, to serve as a capital. As a sign of its importance, it was built in stone while its plan and architecture imitated examples from Constantinople through Ravenna. The palace at Aachen had no parallel north of the Alps, yet it was a poor copy of the models it was based on and only in old age did Charlemagne spend most of his time there.

Charlemagne's Successors

Before his death in A.D. 814 Charlemagne had shown that he remained more Frank than Roman by dividing his empire amongst his sons rather than passing the empire on intact. Two of the sons died before Charlemagne, however, and as a result the empire was passed on to a sole heir. Louis the Pious (A.D. 814–840) was crowned by his father in A.D. 811 to demonstrate that his rule over the Franks was not a gift of the pope or the church. Nevertheless, the new ruler's by-name, the Pious, shows how deeply Louis was influenced by the church and its values. In A.D. 817 the clergy tried to have Louis' eldest son designated as sole successor. Louis, however, did not have the energy of Charlemagne and failed to impose this or any other policy against the wishes of his sons or the traditions of his people. A second marriage brought him a further son, and Louis' favour to this child created jealousy among the stepbrothers. In the last decade of Louis' reign the brothers were continually at war with each other and plans for the division of territory on Louis' death often changed.

In A.D. 843 the three brothers who survived agreed on a plan for the partitioning of the empire, which proved to have lasting consequences. The western portion became the medieval kingdom of France; the eastern portion beyond the Rhine formed the core of Germany; and between these two lay the Middle Kingdom, which stretched from the Low Countries to Sicily. The Middle Kingdom was the eldest brother's share, and it included Aachen and Rome, the symbolic centres of secular and religious government in the Carolingian Empire. Thus the title of emperor stayed with Lothair, the ruler of the Middle Kingdom. This was now the realm of the

ASPECTS OF DAILY LIFE

VIKING RAIDS

The Vikings (Danes) were renowned for their seafaring ability and were feared for the brutality of their attacks. Generally a Viking raid would occur in one of two ways; i) small groups would make lightning quick raids on wealthy settlements or monasteries, escaping before help could arrive; or ii) larger raiding parties would establish a base from which to carry out extensive raids in a wide area.

How Successful Viking raids were Conducted

The swiftness of their ships and the dexterity with which they handled them allowed the Vikings to strike quickly. Before their opponent realized they were going to be attacked and could organize a defence the Vikings would be bearing down on them. While these raids often occurred along coastlines, the Vikings were also able to manoeuvre their ships up large rivers attacking cities such as London or York.

On larger raids the Vikings would moor their ships and quickly build a fortified base camp. This camp would be a wooden palisade surrounded by a ditch and rampart.

From their base camps, the Vikings would set out to plunder, stealing horses to aid in their raids. The pillaging would happen far and wide.

If the Vikings were faced with an organized defensive force they would dismount and form a shield wall. Many such battles were won by the battle-hardened Vikings, as their opponents were often peasants who did not have their training.

senior ruler in Christendom, but Lothair in turn left three sons of his own, which led to the further partitioning of the Middle Kingdom.

The Second Dark Ages

The empire of the Franks, therefore, was in no position to defend Europe against a new wave of invasions from outside its boundaries. The second wave of invasions did not transfer whole populations, as had happened in the fifth century A.D., but their cumulative effect was perhaps more destructive. They came from three directions: the **Vikings** came by sea from Scandinavia; the Magyars rode out of the Hungarian plains and marched slaves and pack-trains of loot back to their base near the Danube River; and the Saracens came out of North Africa, terrorizing and plundering at will on the Mediterranean coasts. This was the Second Dark Ages, which lasted through the ninth and into the tenth century. As a result of this new wave of invasions, central control, central response, and often hope itself, vanished. This proved to be a darker time than the earlier period of barbarian invasions. When hardly any place could feel secure from attack, there was a greater need for local defence and social protection. Thus trends that had already begun in the earlier emergencies were further consolidated.

The Carolingian achievement was remarkable and it has been called a renaissance, but it was shortlived. Its effect was greater on ideals for Christian order than for their application. Even when it was most effective under Charlemagne, the restored empire in the west was a crude affair compared with Byzantium or the Arab Caliphates in Baghdad or Spain. At the same time, the Carolingian Empire, as an expression of the aspirations of western or Latin Christendom, showed that the centre of political, social, and ideological gravity had moved from the imperial Roman sphere of the Mediterranean to the plateaux between Paris and the Rhine, where great feudal estates and patrimonies were being assembled. These were the units that would be the driving forces of the next stage of European history.

Suggested Sources for Further Research

▼▼▼

Please see pages 514 and 515 for complete list for Chapters 14, 15, and 16.

Focus Your Knowledge

▼▼▼

1. How did the Roman Catholic church preserve the organization of the Roman Empire?
2. What were Justinian's primary goals and how did he set out to achieve them?
3. Describe living conditions in Dark Age Europe by commenting on: farming, the importance of family, law, and homes.
4. Despite their withdrawal from society the monasteries came to play a very important role. Explain this role.
5. Describe the characteristics of Charlemagne.
6. What factors contributed to the collapse of Charlemagne's Empire?

Apply Your Knowledge

1. Compare and contrast the society of the Dark Ages to the society of the Roman Empire. Be sure to include social, political, and economic factors.
2. Looking at the map of the barbarian migrations prepare an organizer under the following headings: where they came from, where they settled, present day location.
3. What factors prevented Justinian's success and ultimately led to the separation of what was left of the Roman Empire?
4. How did Clovis establish the Franks as the dominant power in Europe?
5. Define feudalism and explain how it was a response to the changing conditions in Europe.
6. In what way was the rise of monasticism a response to the disorder and uncertainty of the times?
7. Charlemagne's accomplishments went far beyond the conquering of western Europe. He also led a time of spiritual and intellectual revival. By examining the achievements of Charlemagne himself as well as others such as Alcuin, assess to what degree this period was truly a renaissance.

Extension Activities

1. Research and build a model of a Germanic village of the Dark Ages.
2. Research a local monastery and ask about their daily routines and customs. Prepare a report comparing and contrasting medieval monasteries to the monasteries of today. If there is no local monastery, contact a local Catholic priest and inquire about how church doctrine and practices have changed since Medieval times. Prepare a report.
3. Do further research on Viking raids and write a fictional account of the day your village was struck by a Viking attack.

4. Research and role play one of the following personalities:

   Alcuin   Bede
   Benedict   Charlemagne
   Clovis   Justinian

   Working in pairs, develop a meeting between two of these individuals.

CHAPTER 15

The High Middle Ages

Chapter Highlights

- art and architecture

- student life at a medieval university

- popular beliefs and heresy

- knights and the chivalric code

- the development of castles

- the Crusades

While the foundations of the medieval period lay in the Dark Ages, the height of the achievements built on these foundations did not come until the period between 1150 and 1250. The first step toward the High Middle Ages was to reverse the disruption caused by the Viking, Magyar and Saracens invasions, which completed the downfall of the Carolingian Empire. This was accomplished by the spread of feudal order, which in turn made economic growth possible. The return of order to Europe and a revitalized economy led to reforms in the church, crusades against Islam, and an intellectual revival. This period was also characterized by a revolution in artistic style and taste. The increasing centralization in power that resulted from greater wealth and a more sophisticated system of government laid the foundations for modern European nation-states. All of this was the product of the era historians refer to as the High Middle Ages.

It was in the twelfth and thirteenth centuries that Europe witnessed a resurgence of cultural and intellectual vitality. This chapter will begin by examining the nature and importance of feudalism to medieval Europe. A complete picture of feudal Europe will require some insights into both the governing aristocracy and the **peasantry** who were governed. To complete the picture of life during the High Middle Ages some attention will be paid to the revival of towns and the emergence of a new, urban middle class. The High Middle Ages have often been referred to as the Age of Faith since the role of the church was central to the lives of the people and the politics of the nation. The reforms of the church in the High Middle Ages were particularly significant as they led not only to the Crusades but to repeated attempts by the church at suppressing heresy. This chapter will conclude by outlining the major artistic and intellectual achievements that earned this period the title the "High Middle Ages."

Key Concepts

feudalism

feoff

Bayeux Tapestry

manor

demesne

serf

guilds

Abbey of Cluny

War of Investitures

heresy

Albigensians

Crusades

Gothic architecture

▼▼▼

The Restoration of Order

The second wave of invasions led by the Vikings, Saracens, and Magyars was the final blow for the Carolingian Empire. The task of defence and of rebuilding an ordered society fell to feudal lords and throughout England and Europe. In much of Europe, rulers established fortified bases as strongholds, bought off attacks that they could not contain militarily, and waited for an opportunity to induce

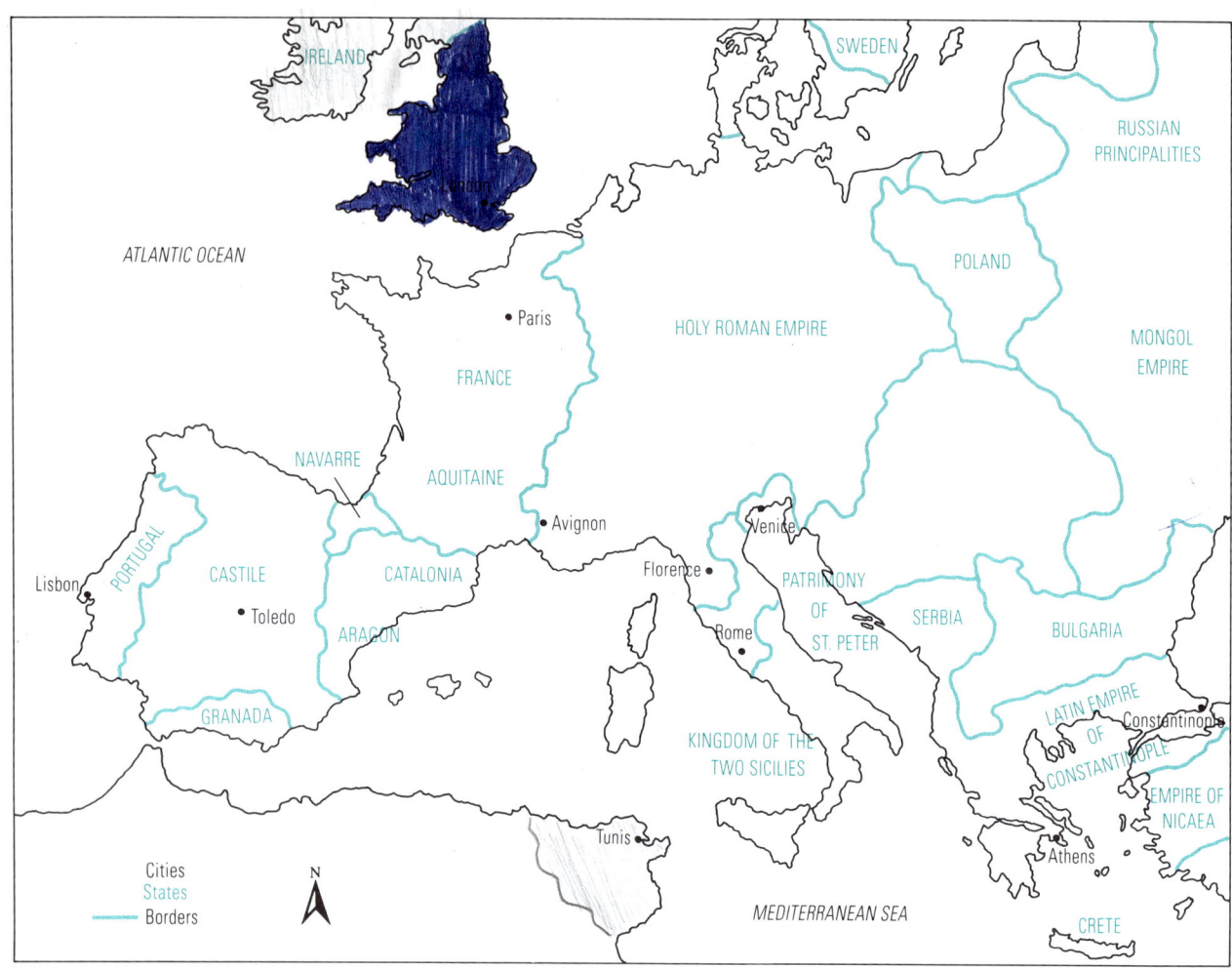

Europe: The High Middle Ages

their attackers to settle permanently or to defeat them. Even though England had never been part of the Carolingian dominions, its experience can serve as a model for western Europe as a whole. Alfred (871–899), a dominant figure of the ninth century, was a hereditary king of the West Saxons, which was the most western of the several small tribal kingdoms into which England had been divided before the Viking onslaught.

The West Saxons were driven by the invading Vikings to isolated strongholds in the Somerset marshes. Yet, by consolidating the military resources of his people, Alfred made complete success too costly for the invaders. His innovations included building earthwork fortresses (*burhs*), which the Vikings could not overrun, and dividing the Saxon obligation to military service: while part of his people were at war, the other part was left on the land to sow and harvest crops. In A.D. 886 the Vikings called off their attacks and settled in eastern and northern

England. By promising to pay an annual tribute, Alfred was able to preserve the integrity of his kingdom. In the next century and a half his successors reabsorbed the Vikings and united England into a single monarchy. Since England was a kingdom of manageable size, these kings with their families and immediate followers provided an effective centre of authority, which was linked by royal assent and local representatives to the provinces. When Duke William of Normandy in A.D. 1066 became the legitimate heir to the Anglo-Saxon throne, the firm direction that he gave to royal authority was readily transmitted to the shires (counties) because the channels had been previously developed.

Feudalism

Feudalism, which is the system of land holding that came to dominate north-western Europe, was an essential part of the response to the renewed chaos brought by the collapse of the Carolingian Empire and the repeated invasions of the ninth and tenth centuries. Feudal society did not develop overnight: it had many aspects, and some had been functioning for many centuries. Feudalism was a form of dependence that took on particular qualities.

The term "feudal" was an invention of seventeenth-century lawyers who took the adjective from the tenth-century Latin word feodum (**feoff**) which indicates the central role of land in the feudal relationship. Handing over a clod of earth often registered the beginning of a relationship concerning land between two persons or between a donor and an ecclesiastical body, such as a **bishopric** or abbey. At first the relationship bound only the contracting parties, but it quickly became hereditary. The fortunes of two families, rather than the two persons who began the agreement, were bound to each other by the feoff. The relation was a mutual one as both parties expected to benefit. The weaker party expected protection and support while the stronger party expected support and service. An older term, used in the later Roman Empire when the transfer of rights over land took place between a patron and a dependent, was **beneficium**, which suggested that the arrangement was to benefit both parties.

Another feature of feudal relationships was the personal bond between the two parties. Those with greater military strength expected personal service from the less advantaged peasantry who in return were ensured protection. Like the tie in land, this personal tie was much older than the tenth century. Its roots, however, lay more on the German side of Europe's inheritance than on the Roman side, for it sprang from war-band loyalties. The fighting unit among barbarian peoples like the Goths, Franks, and Anglo-Saxons was most effective when it combined leadership with mutual loyalty and respect among all members, who were initially of similar social rank. Where there was no formal military organization, a warrior needed true comrades at his side.

Feudal Knights

A new feature of feudalism that developed in the later tenth and eleventh centuries was the knight as a central figure in society. The coming of the second Dark Ages had heightened the military nature of society. The knight, who was a specialist in war with no other responsibilities, had been developed by the Franks, whom Charles Martel had mounted and armed. Thus, feudal society formed the categories of those who fought, those who prayed, and those who laboured.

Feudal society was an aggressively violent male society where the strong benefited. It was also largely a young man's society. The old, the immature, and the disabled had little power and played a limited role. In the early days of feudalism, a successful lord was surrounded by a household of young knights who had not yet acquired a fortune or had not yet married. The atmosphere was much like that of the earlier war-bands: competitive, boastful, often erupting into violence. Given this explosive mixture, a wise lord chose to get these ruffians out of his castle and to settle them on feoffs of their own.

Feudal society often combined a strange mixture of horrible violence and intense remorse, even in the same person. Evidence of this can be seen in the character of Fulk the Black, Count of Anjou (987–1040). Fulk built and captured castles; fought and won wars; and yet, out of a sense of wrongdoing, he built two abbeys and went on pilgrimages to Jerusalem three times. Mighty lords and knights always believed that there was a power stronger than they could ever be and who ruled for eternity.

The Feudal Agreement

The feoff, the lord who granted it, and the vassal who received it and delivered service in return for it are the central features of feudalism of the tenth to twelfth centuries. The feudal relationship was sealed in a public ceremony of homage, whereby the vassal knelt before his lord, placed his hands between the hands of the lord, and swore fealty or faith. He was thereafter the *homme*, or man of that lord, unless he renounced his homage with equal ceremony. The typical service that the vassal owed was that of one or more knights, depending on the size of the feoff. This pattern evolved most completely in northern France and appeared there first.

In its truest form feudal society was a pyramid with the king at the top as **suzerain**, from whom the greatest nobles held their land directly as tenants in chief. They in turn leased land to lesser nobles who had vassals below them, owing service both military and non-military. These rear vassals, as the lesser nobles were called, could easily be lords of other vassals while they owed service to their own lord. At times service could be replaced with a payment, and in fact from the thirteenth century onwards the feoff came increasingly to be seen as an asset to be exploited for economic profit.

Feudal Values

The Medieval Latin word for knight was *miles*, the word that the Romans had used for the simple soldier. Feudal virtues were, therefore, a soldier's virtues raised to an aristocratic level. While Roman soldiers had fought on foot, the medieval knight fought from the back of a horse. The rider and horse combined to form a missile. The impact of their charge was so great that stirrups and a saddle, with a bow in front and a cantle behind, were invented to keep the rider in their seat at the time of impact. The lance or sword, battle-axe, ball and chain, or mace were all weapons used in battle. For their own protection, knights wore a conical helmet to deflect a sword cut; a surcoat of mail, which was light chains linked together; a long leather jerkin; and a long shield to protect his flank on the side opposite to the held weapon.

In time veteran knights evolved, at least in idea, to the more refined knight of **chivalry**. The knight of the chivalric romance was a member of a court like King Arthur's. Most late twelfth and thirteenth century stories featured individual quests or acts of gallantry and faith, where the virtues of courtesy (*courtois*) and prowess (*preux*) added to the knight's reputation.

Besides knightly epics two other literary genres reflect the world of feudalism, but both approach it from the outside. The fabliaux were stories that satirized conventional society and transposed the criticism into a fable about animals, borrowing in many cases from Aesop's collection. They were anonymous, but it is a fair assumption that they were the creation of disenchanted clerks (members of the clergy) with urban rather than noble roots. The

The Bayeux Tapestry is a full pictorial account of the Norman Conquest done in eight colours of wool. The embroidery is done on a band of linen 69.3 m long and contains 72 scenes. In this scene, Harold is crowned king of England. Shortly thereafter, he is shown a comet (Haley's comet) overhead and is alarmed at the bad omen. Later, in the conflict with the Normans, Harold is killed when struck in the eye with an arrow.

(Tapisserie de Bayeux - XI siecle, avec autorisation spéciale de la Ville de Bayeux)

troubadours, who were courtly minstrels, were more closely associated with the values that their songs enshrined. Their ballads promoted rather than criticized feudal society. They depicted women in noble society as employing the stylized tricks and wiles of courtly love, which often conflicted with vows taken in marriage. These ideals of love came from the south, the least feudalized part of Europe, and the charms of the East, relayed through Islamic Spain, appeared in the songs of the troubadours. These two literary modes remind us that women and clergy did not fit easily into the feudal world of violence.

Feudalism and the Church

Some of the difficulties that the church had with feudalism arose from the fact that feudal society was governed by, and for, those who fought. Many of the church's leaders were born and grew up in noble families, and all members of the clergy were the product of a feudal society. The church acquired huge lands before and during the feudal age, and these lands carried feudal obligations of public service. More than half the army that Emperor Otto II led to disaster in Italy in A.D. 982 is said to have been made up of knights from church feoffs. Bishops and abbots held their lands as tenants-in-chiefs, similar to great nobles, although they were often a more reliable source of military forces than their **secular** counterparts. **The Bayeux Tapestry** illustrated here, was commissioned by the bishop of Bayeux, a half brother of William the Conqueror. This bishop had led his own knights on the field at the Battle of Hastings in 1066. In a few cases the church held its lands by what was known as *frankalmoign*, or free alms as an alternative to knight-service. In this case the clergy, rather than providing a fighting force for the lord, agreed to present the prescribed numbers of prayers for the welfare of the lord.

While the church could not avoid being immersed in feudalism, it had an equal obligation to moderate its worst abuses. It tried to contain the violence in two ways. Bishops and abbots preached the Peace of God and the Truce of God throughout the eleventh and into the twelfth century. These were efforts to ban armed violence in certain places, against certain classes including the clergy, and on certain days. It seems now a little naive to suppose that what was acceptable on an ordinary day was condemned on a holy day, and, in fact, this peacemaking effort was not very successful.

Castles in Medieval Europe

Castles are perhaps the most visible remains of the feudal age. While they were a product of the violence and disunity that characterized medieval Europe, today they serve as a reminder of the wealth and power enjoyed by a select few. Castles served both offensive and defensive needs. Many were built by powerful lords as a strong central fortification where his subjects could take refuge during an invasion. Others, however, were built to aid in conquest. William the Conqueror, following his victory over Harold Godwinson at the Battle of Hastings in 1066, set about consolidating his hold over England. In a thirty-five year period he had nearly 500 castles built. Similarly, when King Edward I set about subduing the Welsh in the late thirteenth century, he established a series of castles throughout Wales. These fortifications served as military strongholds from which the invading English forces could strike. Many of these castles, such as Harlech, Beaumaris, and Caernarvon, remain remarkably intact and are a visible reminder of England's medieval past.

Daily Life in a Castle

Accompanying the advances made in the defensive features of castles during the High Middle Ages were advances made in their comfort and privacy. Increasingly castles were coming to be seen as homes as well as fortifications. By the fourteenth century the living quarters had been moved to the upper floor of the keep and had become much more comfortable. Timber floors had replaced the earthen floors of earlier castles, and carpets were being used to cover walls, tables and benches, and eventually floors. Another significant change in the castle was the fireplace replacing the central hearth. Fireplaces provided better and safer heat distribution throughout the hall. In the bailey, near the kitchen, castle gardens were kept containing fruit trees, vines, herbs, and flowers. Sometimes a fishpond stocked with trout and pike was also maintained.

In the castles of the High Middle Ages water for washing and drinking was available at a central place on each floor. The water was carried to each floor by lead pipes. The latrine or *garderobe* was usually placed as close to the lord's bedchamber as possible. Often the garderobe was positioned so as to extend out past the castle wall, allowing waste to drop to the moat below or to be carried by a long shaft to a cesspit in the ground. Baths were taken in a wooden tub covered by a canopy and padded with cloth. In warm weather the tub was often placed in the garden while in the winter it was placed near the fireplace. It was common for a lord, when travelling, to take his bathtub along with him as well as a bathman who would prepare his bath.

A typical day in a medieval castle began early with the servants rising at daybreak and the knights and men-at-arms relieving the night watch. The lord and lady were shortly thereafter awakened from their sleep within their curtained bed. After washing in a

ASPECTS OF DAILY LIFE

THOSE WHO FOUGHT

The Role of the Medieval Knight

Violence and war was endemic to life in medieval Europe. It was a time when might made right and those with power ruled. Thus it follows that the aristocracy of the Middle Ages was a military class, trained from early youth in the art of mounted combat. Initially the aristocracy was divided into two levels, the first being the nobles or great land holders, and the second being their followers the knights. In time this distinction became blurred and the term "knight" acquired high prestige. The essential role of the knight in medieval Europe was to protect the church and the realm. As knights were trained warriors they were often brutal and callous; a far cry from the ideal knight embodied in the literature of the time.

Chivalry and Medieval Tournaments

Throughout the Middle Ages it was common to hear people lament that chivalry was dead. The chivalric conduct they were referring to was that contained in the Arthurian legends. According to the code of chivalry, knights were to be the embodiment of justice, the defender of the Christian faith, the king, and the weak and oppressed. The ideal knight was to be a brave warrior, pious and pure in heart, generous in charity, and willing to defend a woman's honour.

To keep their combat skills sharp knights often partook in tournaments during peacetime. These tournaments involved day-long mock battles as well as up to one hundred knights. During the course of the day's events it was not unusual for a participant to be maimed or killed or even taken and held for ransom.

Medieval Armour

By the end of the twelfth century the protective armour worn by knights was so extensive that he could scarcely be recognized. To solve the problem of not being recognized knights began to wear personal insignia or arms on their shields, hence the origin of a family's "coat of arms." The first layer of protection was the shirt of chain mail which was made of tiny linked rings of iron. Some knights wore a leather tunic under the shirt of mail. To protect their legs, knights wore leg coverings called chausses which were also made of chain mail. The knight's head was protected by a metal helmet. The suits of armour which covered knights in plates and tubes of metal and are often associated with medieval armour only replaced chain mail at the end of the fourteenth century.

A Medieval Castle

Castles built by Edward I represent medieval castles at their most advanced and were the last such structures used extensively in a feudal war. Beaumaris (floor plan pictured here) is located on Anglesy Island.

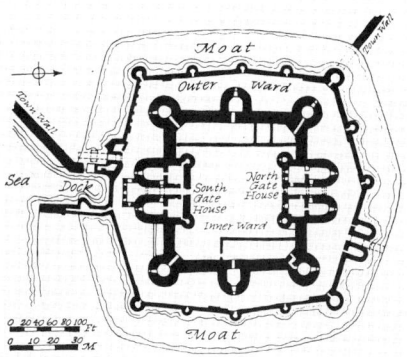

467

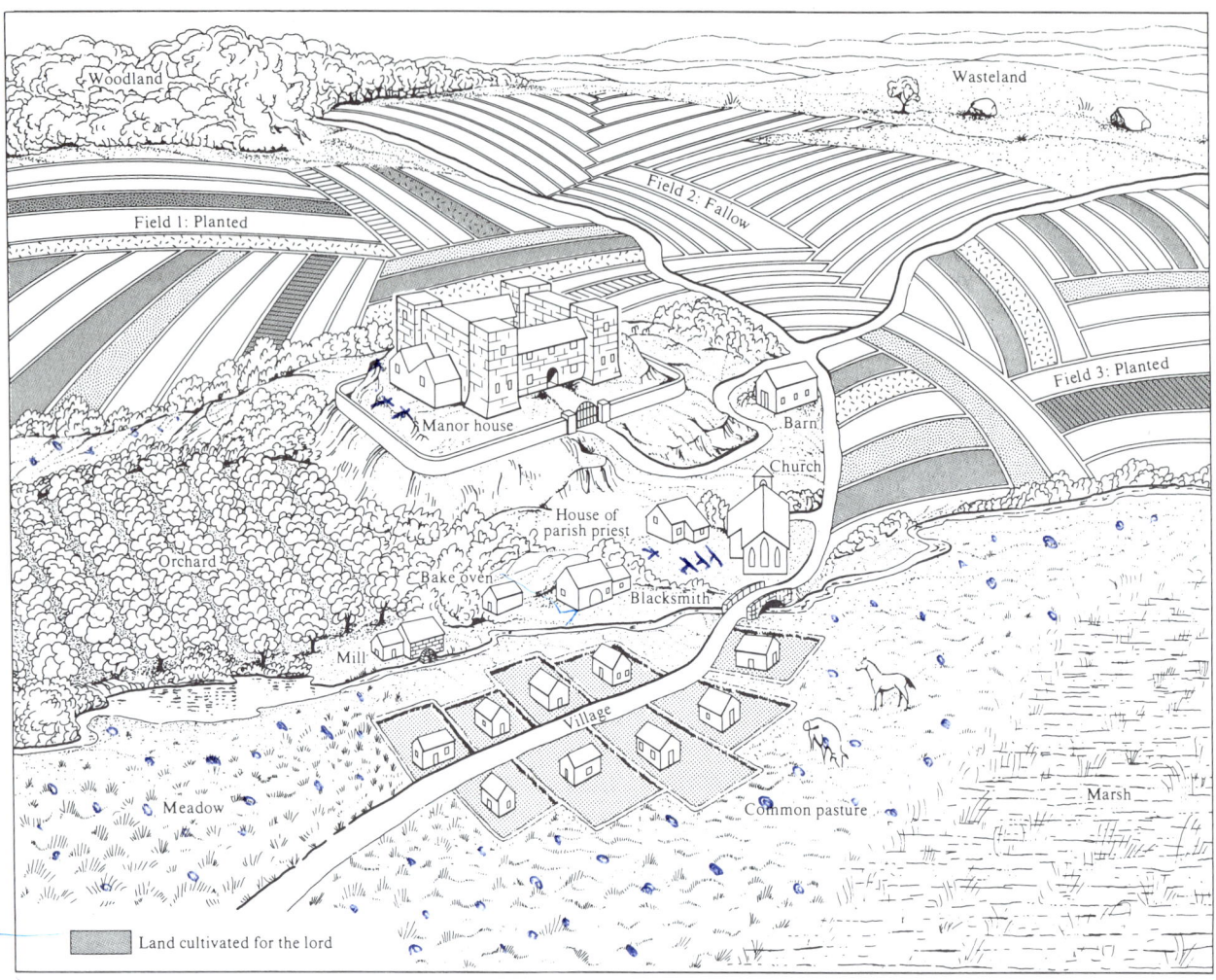

The basic unit of rural organization and the centre for medieval life was the self sufficient manor. The peasants' life of toil revolved around the manor. Here, the peasants farmed their meagre lot, had their grains milled by the manor mill, had their bread baked by the manor bake house; and when necessary, turned to the manor for protection.

basin of cold water and getting dressed, the lady of the castle would fix her hair in front of a mirror made of polished steel or glass over a metal surface and apply make-up that tinted her face pink and white. Mass was held in the chapel prior to breakfast, which usually consisted of bread washed down with either wine or ale. Following breakfast, the people in the castle went about their daily business. For the lord this usually meant meeting with various officials of the castle while the lady might oversee the domestic affairs of the castle. Others were also kept busy with the affairs of the castle including the smith who made nails, horseshoes, and other such items; the domestic servants who carried out such tasks as emptying chamber pots and bringing in fresh straw or rushes to cover the floors; the laundress who soaked sheets, tablecloths, and towels in a wooden tub before hanging them to dry; and the kitchen staff who turned meat such as beef, mutton, pork, poultry, and game near the fire on a spit.

The preparation and serving of dinner, which was a midday meal, followed very prescribed rules. Everything had a correct way of being done, from the laying of the tablecloths to the carving of the meat. In fact, part of the squire's training included how to properly serve the lord his meal. The conventions related to meals extended to the order in which dishes were to be served, where they were to be placed, and even how many fingers were to be used in holding a joint of meat for the lord to carve. Dining was often a lively affair with various forms of entertainment, including music, jokes, and storytelling. The activity around the castle generally subsided in the early evening as most people went to bed shortly after dark.

The Manor

As the feudal system was the product of a warlike aristocracy, those who laboured had a secondary place in society, at least in theory. In practice, however, it was the work of the labouring class that produced the resources by which the feudal nobles and clergy lived. In terms of the distribution of power, whether military or political, the rural peasantry had virtually no part of it. The exploitation of the vast majority of society by the powerful aristocracy was seemingly of little concern to anyone of the literate class. The productivity of the peasants was taken for granted, much as the weather on which the fortune of their crops depended.

Across Europe the vast majority of people lived in villages which were organized primarily for the support of a feudal lord. That lord may have been the king, a simple knight, or a member of the clergy. The term used in England for that organization was the **manor**. While the name differed throughout Europe the organization was quite similar. In each village the lord retained some land for his own use, called the **demesne**. In some places it might be a compact area of the best land while in other places the demesne lay in strips in the open fields, alongside the strips of the lord's tenants. Meadow for pasture was often the lord's preserve and it was his choice as to how it was used. The forest or park, which was used for hunting, was a jealously guarded enclosure. To provide rough grazing for the tenant's livestock and wood for fuel and light construction there was common land set aside. The rest of the manorial land was rented by the lord to the tenants.

Superficially, the peasants seemed to hold their tenement, or plot of land, in much the same way as a feoff was held, except for the smaller size of the tenement. This, however, was not the case. The feoff was held by an honourable tenure in which the lord and vassal were both members of the noble class and both expected a mutual benefit. The manorial tenement, on the other hand, was granted in the lord's name to someone considered a social inferior, who usually was not even a free person in the eyes of the law. By the eleventh century, free tenants were a small minority, particularly in England after the Norman Conquest. The typical manorial tenant was a **serf**, whose family was, and would always be, legally bound to the lord of the land. They became a commodity for production like the land to which they were tied by law. Landholdings were calculated so as to be large enough to support a family at a subsistence level in a normal season. The principal obligation of the tenant was to provide the labour services required to make the lord's landholdings profitable. That obligation consumed most of their time, and only when that obligation, which was particularly heavy in the crucial seasons of ploughing and harvesting, had been met was the tenant and their family free to work the scattered strips that they rented from the lord. Their freedoms were curtailed in many other ways as well. Tenants had to use the lord's mill, attend the manorial court, and serve in various manorial offices if called on. If their actions, the actions of their family, or the actions of their livestock infringed on life in the manor, the tenant faced a fine. This was the nature of serfdom: better than slavery, but still a lifetime of continual, year-round labour. Holy days offered some relief, but the only real escape was the exceptional gift of freedom from the lord (manumission), or escaping to a chartered town. If a serf escaped to a town and lived there for one year plus a day they were granted their legal freedom. A serf might also be offered more attractive terms of tenure by a lord hoping to attract tenants to areas of new settlement.

The chief protection of serfs against arbitrary decisions by the lord or his agents lay in the traditions of the manor. Villages were closely knit communities and highly conservative. The same families lived at close quarters over long periods, and the sense of community that this fostered was enforced in the manorial court. It was further reinforced by the practice of agriculture in open fields where no one had a fenced-off property. All the tenants and the lord had to act together in cultivating, fallowing, or letting their livestock graze. While the free tenants who owned their land (as opposed to renting it) might be poorer than the neighbouring serf, they could look to the king's court for protection of personal rights against the lord; whereas the serf could not. In addition to all these restrictions of serfdom, rural labour provided minimal rewards. Diet, housing, and dress were no better than in the Dark Ages because the lord claimed any surplus production; and, after the tenth century, the church could also claim a portion of the serf's produce through the **tithe**.

As a form of social organization feudalism did not offer many attractions, except to swashbuckling knights, and at times it provided very inhospitable conditions. When the Norman monarchy of England faltered because there was no direct male heir, in A.D. 1135 a civil war broke out, during which feudal lords helped themselves to lands, castles, and rights belonging to opponents or neighbours. A monk who recorded these two decades described them as the time when God and his angels slept. Whether feudalism provided anarchy or order depended on the effectiveness of the control imposed by the king, who was at the top of the feudal hierarchy. Henry I, who preceded the period of civil war in England, and Henry II, who followed it, both exerted firm control over their feudal lords; to the extent that both kings had rebellions on their hands, as their subjects believed that their rights had been overridden. Feudal justice was often rough and unpredictable but still was better than no justice at all. Rudimentary as they may seem by twentieth century standards, feudal resources proved adequate for the circumstances of the tenth and eleventh centuries. By the start of the twelfth century the decay that marked the decline of Carolingian authority had been reversed, and everywhere were signs of a new prosperity.

Life in a Medieval Village

Today a village refers simply to a small town, often a suburb of a larger, urban centre. In medieval times this was not the case. The village in medieval Europe was a collection of the homes, barns, and sheds of the peasantry and included the fields, meadows, pastures, and woods that surrounded the cluster of buildings. When permanent villages began to develop around the tenth century, they were typically situated near a spring or stream and were centred around the church and manor house. From the village centre, houses randomly sprang up in all directions. The people who lived in the medieval village formed a complete and permanent community organized around agricultural production. By the High Middle Ages over 90 percent of Europe's population lived in villages. These villages did not merely contain the homes of the peasants but were where the vast majority of people lived, worked, socialized, loved, married, gave birth, died, and were buried.

Birth, Marriage, and Death

In all levels of society, babies were born at home assisted by midwives. The dangers inherent in childbirth led to the custom of immediately baptising newborn children in case they died. If the newborn infant survived childbirth it was often swaddled. Swaddling entails wrapping strips of cloth tightly around the child's arms, legs, and entire body until it is immobile. This procedure causes the child's bodily functions to be depressed, the heartbeat to slow, and the child to sleep more and cry less. Often swaddled children were hung on a board that could then be set out of the way. While swaddling may have been convenient for the parents it quite likely contributed to increases in rashes, diseases, and death among infants.

In the High Middle Ages **primogeniture**, whereby the first-born son inherited the entire landholding of the parents, was widely practised. Although this effectively kept landholdings intact, it forced younger sons to leave the family estate to earn a living either in war or in the church. Younger sons of wealthy peasants may have been given a small landholding, which the father purchased for them, but the sons of the poor peasantry were not so fortunate. They were forced to choose between staying at home with their parents, accepting a celibate life as a member of the clergy, or attempting to earn a living as a soldier or day labourer. Left with limited options many slipped into a life of crime or vagabondage.

When a peasant couple decided to marry they usually spoke their vows at the church door, which was the most central place in the village. During the ceremony the priest asked the couple if any barriers to marriage existed, usually referring to the couple being closely related. If no barriers were known to exist the groom named the dower he would provide the bride and placed a ring on her finger. Clandestine marriages remained a problem for the church throughout the Middle Ages. These were marriages in which peasants chose to exchange their vows outside of the church. Such marriages, which were considered valid so long as both husband and wife gave their consent, were known to happen in the woods, in taverns, and usually took place without witnesses.

If a peasant survived childhood they could not expect to live much beyond the age of 45. Aside from deaths caused through violence and accidents, diseases such as tuberculosis, pneumonia, typhoid, and heart attacks took their toll. Leprosy was also widespread in medieval Europe. Victims of leprosy were isolated from society either individually or in colonies. They were permitted to be seen in public if covered by a sheet and clacking a pair of castanets as a warning. When peasants died they were given a simple funeral. The body was sewn into a shroud and carried to the church on a bier draped with a black pall. Following a mass, the deceased was buried in a plain wooden casket or simply in a shroud in the churchyard.

Colonial Expansion

The economic revival Europe experienced at the beginning of the twelfth century was accompanied by a rapid growth in population. Feudal order meant that harvests could be gathered; and so the food supply improved at a time when a warming climatic

ASPECTS OF DAILY LIFE

*T*HOSE WHO WORKED

A Medieval Village

This artist's impression is typical of an early twelfth-century village in England. The scene depicted is a busy autumn morning. In front of the lord's stone hall, an oxen is drawing hay. A market of livestock, local produce and cloth has been set up outside the fenced enclosure of the manor. Ale is being sold and barrels of wine are being transported to the hall. The market has drawn a crowd, but others are going about their daily routines. A boy is leaving the dovecote after having fed the pigeons while a woman is taking scraps to her goat. A farmer has a team of oxen out, plowing one of the common fields.

Life in the Countryside

Country people lived in villages like this one which was often surrounded by tracts of arable land and forests. The fields were divided into uneven parcels which made the medieval countryside look like a patchwork quilt. The peasantry which included both serfs and freemen was responsible for the agriculture in medieval Europe. Whereas freemen could own their own land and had rights under the law, serfs rented land from a lord and were bound by feudal obligations.

The peasantry sometimes did not own the land, and it was rare for a peasant to own a team of oxen, so planting and harvesting was a co-operative effort. The forested tracts were reserved for the king's hunt. Uncultivated pastureland would be common in the areas where sheep were being raised for milk, for sheepskins, and for wool. Social life centred around the church and the manor. Entertainment included dances and beauty contests, while the church organized pilgrimages to local shrines, holy celebrations, and religious plays.

cycle brought good seasons more often. A better diet produced better health, better fertility, and a better survival rate among infants resulting in population increases across Europe. From the late eleventh century there is evidence of widespread demand for new areas of settlement because the existing ones were overcrowded. Areas that had been forested were cleared and tilled; marginal soils in the valleys and uplands that had not been needed by a smaller population were now ploughed and settled. In some areas the settlement of new lands was the spontaneous initiative of peasant families with their lord's consent. In other places such as northern Germany between the rivers Elbe and Oder and further east on the German plain, it was a planned enterprise. Huge areas, which became new principalities as powerful as those in the German heartland, were opened up to colonial settlement much as the American mid-West and the prairies were developed in the nineteenth century. The small Slav population that inhabited the region was killed, enslaved, or driven from their land as members of the German nobility and clergy were given territories for development. They recruited peasant cultivators as far west as Flanders and offered them larger holdings and freer tenures than they could find at home. The German monarchy fostered this enterprise, not only because it reinforced the security of the kingdom against the Slavs, but because they hoped that these newly created feudal principalities would offset the doubtful loyalty of the established **duchies** and counties, which frequently challenged royal authority.

The eastern frontier of Germany was the most striking example of colonial expansion in the twelfth century, but it was not the only one. Anglo-Norman lords crossed into Ireland where they carved feudal feoffs out of Irish tribal lands, while earlier Normans had sailed to southern Italy and there established the Norman kingdom of Sicily. The Christian kingdoms, which had held the foothills of the Pyrenees in Spain when Muslim invaders of the eighth century almost swept them away, took the first steps in the eventual reconquest of the Iberian peninsula. Even the Crusades themselves, which began in A.D. 1095, were in one aspect a response to a hunger for land, which could not be satisfied nearer to home.

The Rise of Towns

While the changes addressed above were quite significant it was the rise of towns and the recovery of urban life that truly transformed the existing social structure. Even when towns remained partly rural with orchards and pasture within their walls or limits, they depended for food on rural produce brought in from outside. This further stimulated production on the manors. The town offered a market for the sale and exchange of produce and goods and attracted tradespeople and craftspeople, many of whom worked in woollen textiles and different kinds of metalwork and leather. The rise of towns injected a whole new class into the feudal hierarchy. In the period between 1000 and 1200 the more successful urban communities attracted not just local produce but long distance and international trade in luxuries. This kind of trade was further stimulated by the Crusades, which created a demand among those who had journeyed to the Near East and had seen its wealth. The Crusades also helped to establish a source of supply through the permanent depots that Italian seafaring cities like Pisa, Genoa, and Venice had established in the new Christian principalities along the coast of the Holy Land.

These trading ports served as the **bridgeheads** for overland trade from the Far East, which brought the caravans of oriental spices, cloths, weapons, precious metals, and stones that Europeans desired. Because this trade was primarily for the rich, much of it was small in bulk but large in profit. The risks that the merchant faced were many: storms, shipwreck, piracy at sea or attacks by bandits on land, theft, and political instability along the trade routes. In addition to the physical risks, the long period which separated the capital outlay to purchase and transport goods and the point of sale in Europe meant that the profit to be made on a successful enterprise could be large. A new class of merchants who traded internationally arose to meet these needs. Italians dominated the Mediterranean link, but the stimulus and the demand spread north of the Alps, from where most of the Crusaders had come. By the twelfth century the Alpine passes, markets at Lyon, Geneva, and Troyes, the Rhine Valley, and the cloth towns of Flanders constituted a busy trading axis.

Capitalism

A new range of business activities was required by the scale of this international trade, which was so different from the local markets that had flourished earlier. The resources needed were too large for most single merchants, so partnerships were developed. In addition to partnerships, loans were sought and advanced, and ingenious steps were found to sidestep the church's distrust of material wealth earned without the sweat of the brow. Credit, letters of exchange, and rudimentary banking services steadily grew to complete the emerging capitalism. The widespread, wealthy communities of Jews, with cosmopolitan connections across Europe and into the Near East and Africa, made them an alternative source of financial services. Outside of Spain the Jews were tiny minorities and vulnerable in society. They relied heavily on royal protection for the recovery of their loans and for security against racial and religious hostility.

In feudal society, trade had no recognized place. Merchants, traders, and townspeople in general, did not fight; they were not the clergy who prayed, and they were not oppressed by physical labour like the peasantry. Politically the towns and the merchants who lived in them were given a recognized place in the twelfth century as the **Third Estate**, after the clergy and the nobility. It was a position that could be turned to their advantage, not by themselves but by the king. European kings in the twelfth century quickly recognized the opportunities that this new, social class offered them. In France, England, Germany, Spain, and eastern Europe kings offered cities and towns privileges of self-regulation in return for support against periodic opposition from their greater nobles and contributions in tolls and taxes.

Chartered Towns

As towns were the product of a revival in trade it is not surprising to find most situated on a major waterway or at a major crossroads. Feudal warring and the presence of roving bandits were still a factor in the twelfth century, and thus it was also necessary for towns to be situated near a defensive fortification such as a castle, monastery, or royal palace. Over time the new, urban class freed itself from a dependence on defensive fortifications (such as keeps) by building walls around the towns. As the city grew and expanded old walls were torn down to make room for new streets and new walls. The average town of the High Middle Ages had a population of 2500, while a town of 20 000 was considered large. Only a few towns such as Paris, Venice, and Milan had populations of over 100 000.

As towns grew in size they came to have increasingly more economic clout. Eventually towns began to press for political and social freedom and were often able to achieve their goals through peaceful negotiations, but at times were forced to resort to insurrection. Towns were granted their freedom through charters that guaranteed the rights of the inhabitants. As independent bodies, towns governed themselves by a council made up of members of business groups. This council levied taxes and market tolls, maintained walls and roads, and established a militia for defence. A separate body was responsible for the administration of justice in towns. To reflect the new social order of the towns new laws related to marriage, inheritance, liens, debts, and settling business were created. Petty crimes were punishable by being placed in the stocks while violent crimes such as rape or murder were punished by castration, the amputation of limbs, decapitation, or hanging.

Medieval Towns

The towns of medieval Europe held little of the charm that historic cities of Europe today have. The streets, which were often no more than two or three metres wide, were crammed with wooden houses that were built as a solid block along the street. In the rear of the houses people often kept a small garden as well as pigs and chickens. Pigs were an important element of the medieval town as they provided the most efficient garbage disposal. At a time when garbage was simply dumped into the streets and picked up on an infrequent basis, pigs rummaging in the street provided an essential service.

As people jostled for space, stories were added to the houses with each jutting out further than the one beneath it. The result can still be seen in cities such as York, England where a person can literally shake hands with someone across the street by leaning out of an upper-story window. Strolling down the streets of a medieval town was not without its hazards. At your feet you would have to be constantly watching for rooting pigs while from above you needed to be on the look out for slop which was thrown from the windows above.

Merchant and Craft Guilds

The birth of an urban middle class was accompanied and nurtured by the development of **guilds**. The primary purpose of guilds, whether merchant or craft, was to provide economic protection for their members. While economics lay at the root of guilds their purpose went much further. They created a bond between members and provided important social benefits. When a guild member was ill others in the guild made sure food and clothing were provided, and when a member died all others prayed for their soul. Guild funds were also used to assist members in paying their debts, bailing members out of jail, providing dowries for their daughters, and supporting the widows of members. Guilds also provided important opportunities for social interaction by hosting banquets, pageants, festivals, and parades.

The earliest guilds to develop were the merchant guilds that grew out of the practice of long distance traders joining together in caravans to ensure safety. Eventually the advantages gained by banding together were extended to the towns of Europe where merchants formed guilds to regulate and dominate commerce. As specialized trades developed a new kind of guild emerged known as the craft guild. Each craft or trade was represented by a number of guilds. For example the textile industry had guilds for wool, flax, and hemp merchants, wool combers, spinners, weavers, dyers, and so on.

Guilds provided both protection for their members and stringent regulations for them to follow. No person could engage in a craft or sell goods in the marketplace unless they were a member in a guild. In exchange for this protection members had to abide by the regulations of the guild. To join a guild you had to complete an apprenticeship of two to ten years, depending on the craft. During this time the apprentice lived with the master and had to obey, without question, their orders. Following the apprenticeship, the artisans had to pass an examination set by guild officials before being allowed to become masters and establish their own shop. The regulations set by the guilds were quite strict. Generally they insisted on a high quality of work from all members. The durability of some of their work is evident today in the magnificent cathedrals of Europe. Poorly made articles were refused the guildhall's seal of approval. To ensure against poor quality of work, guild members were always watching for unscrupulous merchants or sloppy work in the craft shops. If caught, members could either be fined or expelled from the guild.

The regulations set by the guilds were aimed not only at ensuring the quality of the articles produced but also at limiting competition. Guild members were not allowed to work longer hours than others in the industry nor could they pay higher wages, employ more apprentices, or advertise in any way. Even the prices members could charge were regulated by the guild.

Over time the power of the merchant class steadily grew. Kings eventually gave a voice to the merchants in the affairs of the nation, recognizing the vital role they played in raising revenue. Despite their increase in economic and political power, the nobility continued to snub wealthy merchants viewing them as lowborn *nouveaux riches*, or the new rich. Nonetheless, the rising bourgeois or middle class became a permanent fixture in Europe and were able to build opulent mansions, wear expensive clothes, and educate their children. The wealth of the middle class was also channeled into beautifying cities, commissioning artists, and building cathedrals and public monuments. To a large degree it was the wealth of this new urban middle class that produced many of medieval Europe's greatest artistic achievements and eventually led to the Renaissance.

Women in Medieval Society

In an age when wealth and power were determined by military strength, it is hardly surprising that women were perceived as having a limited role. It has been suggested that women's role in the High Middle Ages was largely limited to producing heirs and consummating political alliances. In fact members of the clergy even went so far as to suggest that there was no evil equal to a woman as they were the greatest barrier to salvation luring men to sins of the flesh. The irony of this belief is particularly evident when we pause to remember that in an age plagued with war and violence, women did not slay or oppress people, destroy cities, poison water supplies, or set fires. Despite the male dominance in medieval society and the limited role women were allotted by law and custom, women in all classes did play a vital role in the society of medieval Europe.

When considering the attitudes towards women that were prevalent during the High Middle Ages it is important that the nature of the time period be remembered. This was an age when power was determined by brute strength and hence was concentrated in the hands of the militaristic aristocracy. As a consequence the role assigned to women and the ideas about women that prevailed were those imposed by the aristocracy. The other body of people who had a major impact on shaping medieval ideas about women were the clergy. As one of the few literate groups in society members of the clergy had a great deal of influence.

The divergent nature of these two groups produced contradictory images of women. While the clergy portrayed women as evil temptresses, as depicted in the Bible, the romantic literature of the aristocracy placed women on a pedestal as semi-divine creatures. According to the romances of the period the ideal woman was beautiful, intelligent, fair, and delicate. She was the beautiful damsel in need of being rescued by a brave knight, thus attaching, at least in the ideal, the actions of a warrior class to an honourable deed. Whether a member of the clergy or the aristocracy, most men of influence in medieval Europe seem to have agreed on the subjection of women. As a result neither law nor customs acknowledged women as complete individuals. Instead they were perceived as inferior to men simply because of their sex.

The Lady of the Manor

If the attitudes towards women were shaped by the aristocracy, the concept of the ideal medieval woman was based on the upper-class lady of the manor. It is of the women of this class that the most is known and one fact is certain: aristocratic women were, as Frances and Joseph Gies noted, "customarily a pawn in the game of politics and economics as played by men."

Throughout most of their lives women lived under the guardianship of men, first their fathers and next their husbands. If a woman had not married by the time of her father's death she was placed under the wardship of her father's lord. Women did have legal rights such as the right to own land, inherit it, and sell it; however, once they married they were legally under the power of their husband. This included the right to sell land held in his wife's name except for her dower, without her consent. Women enjoyed the greatest legal rights as widows, at which point they were no longer under male guardianship.

From Birth to Marriage

A daughter of a lord was usually brought up away from home in a castle or manor of another noble family or in a convent where she might have to spend her entire life. The education of the daughters of the aristocracy differed little from the boys other than an emphasis on more refined talents such as embroidery and poetry. Both men and women of the aristocracy shared an enjoyment in riding, hawking, and playing chess.

Childhood was brief for women in medieval Europe. Girls were often married between the ages of 12 and 14 and as early as age 5 may have had their hand promised in marriage. Among the upper class marriage was an important means to establishing alliances with other prominent families and therefore arranged marriages were common. Personal attraction was seldom the basis for marriage as marriage was considered too important to leave to the whims of young lovers. It was common in the Middle Ages for women to have had several children by the age of twenty and to be grandmothers by the age of thirty, assuming they had not succumbed to the dangers of childbirth.

Women in Towns

It is generally fair to say that the importance of women in society was greater among the lower classes than among the aristocracy even though fewer records exist. The presence of women in the workforce in medieval Europe resulted from the need to supplement the family's income or the need of single women to sustain themselves. Not all women could expect to marry even though most women sought the opportunity. The higher mortality rate among men, resulting from plague and war, combined with the large numbers of men who elected to enter monasteries resulted in many women not being able to find a spouse.

Many of the married women who worked found employment alongside their husband in his trade. It must be remembered that this was an age when goods were manufactured by craftspeople in their homes and workshops and thus it was assumed that wives and daughters would assist in the trade. Often widows carried on their dead husbands' trade and the effectiveness with which they did so suggests a great familiarity with the business. It was not unusual for families to send young children, boys and girls, out to work at an early age. In some cases this would lead to an apprenticeship for both sexes, although girls were usually apprenticed under the master's wife.

Women played a considerable part in the economy of medieval Europe. They filled the roles of butchers, chandlers, ironmongers, net-makers, shoe-makers, glovers, girdlers, haberdashers, purse makers, cap makers, skinners, bookbinders, gilders, painters, silk weavers as well as many other trades. Perhaps the most important contributions made by women to the economic vitality of Europe, aside from homemaking, were in the industries of spinning wool, silk production, weaving, and brewing. From these industries titles such as spinster, webster, and brewster are derived.

Women in the Countryside

The least prominent group in the historical records of medieval Europe is the large class of working women in the countryside. Their role seems to have been taken for granted. Women in the countryside shared in the labours of the land as well as running the household. In the home, aside from preparing the food and tending to the children, they also made cloth and clothing, for use by the family and for sale. Outside the home peasant women assisted in virtually all of the work except ploughing. This included planting, weeding, reaping, threshing, and winnowing as well as milking the cows, looking after the poultry and doing much of the sheep shearing. The hardest worked class of all were the women who held land in their own name. This was most often the case with women who were widowed. Women, who were legally serfs, were required to perform so many days work per week on the lord's land as well as supply the lord with produce. This served to intensify the difficulties faced by peasant women who were widowed. Regardless of class or marital status women of medieval Europe faced numerous obstacles that restricted their participation in society. Despite such limitations they played a critical role in many aspects of medieval life.

Investitures and Reform

The effects of a vastly improved economic condition in Europe were also felt by the church. The improved channels of communication, along which trade flowed, also had consequences for the rulers of the church. As the isolation between regions in Europe lessened, the church in different kingdoms and regions became better informed of what was happening elsewhere and the papacy at the centre was better able to influence local trends. Although the church tried to offset feudal violence, there was a constant danger that bishops might assume the values and interests of feudal society. Bishops were often drawn from the nobility and feudal authorities frequently tried to apply the church's landholdings to the political tasks of defense and order. Kings tried to attach the church to their interest by controlling the appointment of bishops. For feudal nobles the leading positions of the church provided a career for those not destined to inherit the family estate. As a result, leading church officials were drawn into worldly, feudal aims as was particularly evident in the case of Germany where, by the middle of the eleventh century, the pope often seemed to be the emperor's minister and not necessarily the church's.

Reforms

Resistance to this secularizing trend came from different quarters in the church, including bishops and others. The bishops who made collections of the church's law, called **canon law**, stressed that the church should be different from secular society. For example the clergy should not marry like laymen, offices in the church should not be sought for gain, and to buy them for money was the sin of **simony**.

Furthermore, bishops should be chosen by the clergy of their cathedral city, not appointed by secular rulers. Decrees forbidding priests to marry, requiring that bishops be freely elected, and condemning bribery or pressure in appointments to any church office were promoted in papal decrees in the eleventh century and were picked up in regional **synods** thereafter. Not that reforms in any of these matters took effect instantly, but a process to reverse the corruption of standards had begun.

The distinctive character of the church and its moral standards were reinforced by the monastic reforms that had spread from the **Abbey of Cluny** in the tenth and eleventh centuries. A succession of great abbots was able to extend the influence of this reformed Benedictine abbey in rural Burgundy to more than a thousand dependent monasteries throughout western and central Europe. Abbots Odilo and Hugh of Cluny exercised enormous influence on the German emperors of the eleventh century, with the result that reformers replaced corrupt Romans in the papacy at the orders of the emperor. This in turn had the effect of raising the quality of popes and of their advisers. In the middle of the eleventh century steps were taken to assist the church in asserting its independence from secular rulers. In A.D. 1059 a papal decree enacted that the election of a pope was confined to the senior clergy of Rome—the cardinals. No longer could an emperor name the successor to St. Peter's chair, any more than Roman nobles could force their candidate into office.

One of the most influential reformers of the eleventh century was an Italian monk named Hildebrand, who was elected Pope Gregory VII in A.D. 1075. Gregory VII extended the church's independence claiming the right to dispose of crowns, even of the imperial crown. When the emperor, Henry IV, resisted such claims as unheard of, he was dethroned by the pope and his subjects were encouraged to rebel. The emperor finally came to the pope at Canossa in A.D. 1077 begging forgiveness. He was forced to wait three days in the snow before being reconciled.

The War of Investitures

The two leading institutions of Latin Christendom, the papacy and the Holy Roman Empire, were engaged in a struggle which lasted, with interruptions, for two centuries. From time to time there was outright war as well as the ongoing battle for people's minds. The costly conflict, which placed the papacy and some bishops in opposition to the kings of France, England, and Germany, could not be allowed to continue. Eventually the broader issue of the claim of being the superior authority in Christendom was reduced to a more manageable question: Who had the right of investiture or the right to appoint bishops and abbots?

Even that was not straightforward. As well as being the key figures in carrying out the policies of a reformed papacy, the bishops were also subjects of a king and were his feudal vassals. Thus, their role was both influential and essential to the implementation of royal policies. An agreement based on an arrangement worked out between the king of England and the archbishop of Canterbury was eventually reached. The compromise was sealed in A.D. 1122 in the German city of Worms between the Emperor Henry V and Pope Calixtus II. This agreement stated that while bishops should be elected by the clergy according to the church's law the election should also allow for the emperor's wishes regarding the candidate to be elected. Furthermore, although symbols of the bishop's spiritual office should be conveyed to him by the church, the lands that he held as subject and vassal were handed over by the king. This did not conclude the larger struggle between empire and papacy but it did bring to an end the **War of Investitures**, as it has come to be known.

Beliefs and Heresy

The popular imagination was peopled by angels and devils, saints and demons. The world was full of conflict and danger: you had to be on guard. Between you and your destination there were dark paths through the forest and dangerous passages across rivers or mountains. Indeed, this was the case in fact as well as in imagination, for, despite the growth of population and settlement, deep woodland and marsh was a common part of country people's experience, unless they lived among mountains. Such places were favoured by robbers who seized your goods or snatched your baby, leaving another in its place. Forces of good and evil shared equal sway in this world. This conflict between good and evil is richly illustrated in a twelfth century priory church in France. There, on a plateau high above the Durance River, the mosaic pavement depicts some boldly designed beasts. Some bite their own tails, two lions share one ferocious head, the flanks of others are branded with a cross. At one end St. Michael, the archangel, mounted as a knight, spears a writhing dragon through the mouth. The struggle between good and evil was the source of much of the heresy that was a continual concern for the medieval church.

Heresy is an imprecise subject because it embraces any belief or practice that the church could not reconcile with its own beliefs and practices. It often included the best-intentioned reforms, which grappled with abuses within the church. At a time like the twelfth century when better standards were being pursued by popes, bishops, and reformed monastic orders, there were a good many grounds for conservative church officials to fear changes from old ways. In the eleventh and twelfth centuries anxious people tried to escape from the pressures of changing standards, the competition for material prosperity, the uncertainty of the struggle of good and evil in the world, by picking their own path to what seemed a surer salvation. In some cases the result was very successful for the official church. Cistercian monks built a reformed order which in forty years expanded to three hundred monasteries. This expansion was partly due to the reputation of Saint Bernard of Clairvaux, the greatest Cistercian, but it rested also on a renewed adherence to the letter of Saint Benedict's Rule. In some cases the reputation of individuals attracted followers in large numbers like Robert of Arbrissel in the Breton forest of Craon; and in some cases charismatic leaders made extravagant claims for their own authority and for the absence of any restraint on the passions of their followers. Religious fanatics have been good subjects for spectacular reporting in all ages, and in this period the church came down on them with all the considerable force that it could command.

The Albigensians. The most spectacular case of heresy and its suppression in the Middle Ages was provided by the **Albigensians**, who followed Cathar beliefs. According to these beliefs the struggle between light and darkness, and good and evil would be uncertain in its outcome until the end of time. What was material and created by humans was inevitably infected with the evil principle. The path of virtue was to escape from this world to a spiritual existence with as little physical contamination as possible. The elect among the Albigensians were the *cathari*, or pure, whose final initiation in the sect was effectively an undertaking to end their own lives. This extremity was only for the few: the perfect. Their followers continued normal lives, but holding to beliefs about the created natural order that were destructive to social values.

In A.D. 1208 Pope Innocent III proclaimed a Crusade against the Albigensians. When the Crusaders, comprised of northern barons and sol-

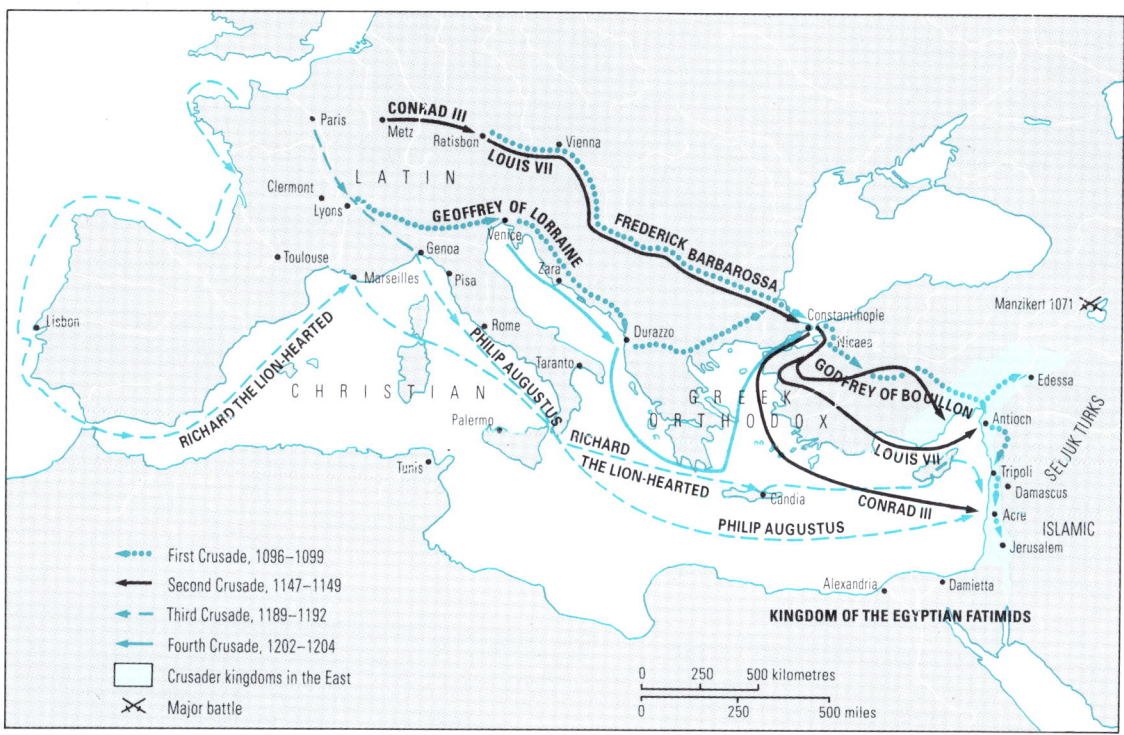

The Crusades 1096–1204

diers of fortune, arrived in the region of Languedoc they were resisted by virtually the entire population. The Crusaders offered to spare the city of Beziers the horrors of war in exchange for the surrender of all heretics, but the city leaders refused. In response to this refusal the Crusaders scaled the walls, captured the town, and 20 000 men, women, and children both of the Albigensian sect and orthodox Christians were killed. Following the assault at Beziers the Crusaders went on to capture the fortified city of Carcassone and to assault numerous towns. In each town the people were given the opportunity to swear allegiance to the Catholic Church or to die as heretics. While thousands chose to take the oath of allegiance many others preferred death. Eventually, following the death of Innocent III, the Crusade was suspended.

Impact of the Reformed Church and Papacy

Although Pope Innocent III had authorised the Albigensian Crusade he had done so with some misgivings. Nonetheless, his pontificate (1198-1216) represents the pinnacle of the papal monarchy in the Middle Ages. This high point was the result of active papal leadership of the church which had continued almost without interruption since the reforms of the mid-eleventh century. The reputation of Innocent III and his successors in the thirteenth century was most clearly expressed in their claim to be the Vicars of Christ meaning Christ's earthly representative; a title widely acknowledged.

The Albigensian Crusade was neither the first nor the last crusade called by Innocent III and his successors. The papacy continued to be an active promoter of crusades which they used to eclipse the Holy Roman Empire as the centre of leadership for western Christendom.

Between 1050 and 1250 papal influence raised the level of the church's activity in many ways. The establishment of parish churches throughout rural Europe, although not directly the work of the papacy, was guided by the standards set by the popes. Popes of this time were often nobles and had been trained in the law. Also intellectual training in religion or theology was becoming increasingly common among bishops. Despite the increase in the level of education among the church hierarchy, church authorities retained reasonable expectations of what could be expected of the people. What was important to them was that there should be standards and that they should be uniform in all parts of Christendom. Popes accomplished this by calling bishops into council and by an unending flow of letters and decrees to clarify problems and to correct abuses. These decrees clearly established guidelines for regulating the life of the church and outlined the minimal duty expected of the Christian lay person.

The unity provided by the Catholic church in the twelfth and thirteenth centuries is a critical feature of the High Middle Ages. The leadership of the church is often credited as a major factor in the achievements of this period as it allowed for a reintegrated, orderly, wealthy and intellectually alert Christendom. In fact it is the unity of the High Middle Ages which distinguishes it from the chaos of the Dark Ages, the fragmentation into the national politics of the late Middle Ages, and the diversity of modern periods.

The Crusades

The **Crusades**, or the Holy War against the Muslims in Palestine, were a fundamental feature of the Middle Ages. While the hunger for land, created by an increase in population and the revival of trade, contributed to sustaining the crusading movement the true motive of the Crusades was religious. They were, to a large degree, a product of the papal and ecclesiastical reforms discussed above.

The First Crusade

The first Crusade was proclaimed at the Council of Clermont in France in A.D. 1095 by Pope Urban II. The object of the Crusade was to recover the Holy Land in Palestine from the Muslim Arabs who had held this area since the seventh century. Pilgrimages by Christians to the Church of the Holy Sepulchre, where Jesus was believed to be buried, and to Bethlehem, where he had been born, had continued despite Muslim control of Palestine. Then, late in the eleventh century, Turks took control and imposed restrictions on Christian worshippers. The Turks had come close to destroying the Byzantine Empire by that time, leading Byzantium to put aside its long-held suspicion of Franks and westerners and prompting the Greek emperor to appeal for help against the **infidel**.

The response to Urban II's call was overwhelming. Armies of Crusaders marched or were transported by sea to the Holy Land. Simple peasants, townspeople, and even children set off on foot. The crux of the crusading effort was the feudal knights from France, Germany, England, Italy, and Spain. What drove so many to join in such an arduous journey? The reasons were numerous and varied, ranging from the quest for glory and adventure to a profound reverence for the land that Christ walked

upon. Certainly one of the crucial attractions for the Crusaders was the church's promise of a remission of penance for past sins. It seems somewhat ironic that the Crusaders, fighting for the holiest of reasons, were the most brutal of people.

The fervor of the Crusades extended beyond the papacy and the aristocracy. Common people from all walks of life set forth to take part in the Crusades. One of the most interesting leaders of the "People's Crusade" was a hermit from Amiens, France, named Peter. With his wild hair, rolling eyes, and fiery speeches he was able to mesmerize crowds in marketplaces throughout Europe. Peasants, including whole families, flung down their tools and joined Peter's rag-tag band of crusaders destined for the Holy Land. Eventually the "People's Crusade" were reported to number as many as 500 000.

The obsession to kill the infidel took its toll even before the Crusaders left central Europe. Jews were often attacked and as the motley band of crusaders moved east into Bulgaria they decided that the Bulgars were heathen. This led them to repeatedly attack the Bulgers who eventually struck back by slaying many of the western Crusaders in their sleep and by poisoning the wells.

By the time Peter's band of Crusaders reached Constantinople in 1096 their numbers had been greatly reduced by sickness and exhaustion. Those who remained were immediately sent into battle against the Turks in Asia Minor where they were mowed down. Few of the civilian mob led by Peter the Hermit ever returned home to Europe.

While the "People's Crusade" ended in disaster the Crusader knights enjoyed much greater success. After waging three years of war the Christian armies amassed outside the walls of Jerusalem. By this time their numbers had been reduced from 30 000 to 12 000, but they remained undaunted in their resolve. Employing a huge battering-ram and two large siege towers, the Crusaders were able to fight their way over the walls and into the city. Once inside of Jerusalem the Christian Crusaders proceeded to commit what is considered to be one of the great crimes in history. They killed nearly the entire population of the city, which is estimated to have been between 40 000 and 70 000 people. One priest who was present at the fall of Jerusalem left this description:

> Numbers of the Saracens were beheaded...others were shot with arrows, or forced to jump from the towers; others were tortured for several days and then burned in flames. In the streets were seen piles of heads and hands and feet. One rode about everywhere amid the corpses of men and horses.[1]

Following the capture of Jerusalem in 1099 Crusader states were established along the shore of the eastern Mediterranean. Although these states were strengthened by the ports through which Italian fleets from Amalfi, Pisa, Genoa, and Venice supplied them, Christian control was to be short lived. Crusaders fought with Byzantium and among each other as often as against the Turks and within a century of its recovery Jerusalem had been lost again.

Despite the fact that two of Christendom's greatest warriors, Frederick Barbarossa, the Emperor and King of Germany, and Richard the Lionheart, King of England, fought in the Third Crusade (1189–1192) they were unable to reverse the losses suffered since 1099. There was too little unity among Crusaders, who were often more interested in their personal gain than in the joint crusading effort. They were in an alien environment, fighting far from their bases in western Europe. Beyond

---

[1] Steven Runciman, A History of the Crusades (Middlesex: Penguin, 1954).

what could be provided from the small principalities that they established in the Near East, they depended on the Italian fleets for supplies and reinforcements. Almost inevitably the Crusaders who settled in Palestine and Syria went "native" while warriors like Richard the Lionheart and Saladin, the Sultan of the Egyptian Mamluks, held each other in mutual respect.

*I*ntellectual Revival

The economic reinvigoration of Europe, the expansion of the boundaries of Latin Christendom and the growing independence of a reformed church were accompanied by an intellectual revival. The term often used for it is the twelfth century Renaissance.

The term renaissance, or rebirth, was coined to describe the recovery of the literature and art of the Greeks and Romans as models for the Italian Renaissance of the fourteenth and fifteenth centuries. Carolingian Renaissance is regularly used to describe the revival of letters in the time of Charlemagne and his successors. The revival of the twelfth century has a bit of the character of both of these other renaissances.

One of the major achievements of the twelfth century revival lay in the extension of basic education in literacy and numeracy. The revival of trade, towns, and the consolidation of power under feudal lords created a demand for clerks who could keep records, write charters or letters, and keep accounts. To meet this need the old Roman curriculum of late antiquity was revived. The *trivium*, as it was called, laid the groundwork for literacy. Its three parts were grammar; logic, or the ability to form a coherent argument; and rhetoric, or the art of persuasion. On this foundation there followed a series of studies of which measure or relationship was the common element: arithmetic, geometry, music, and astronomy. Much of this methodology was reinforced by the recovery, in Latin translation, of the texts of Aristotle, the Greek observer of nature. In the Middle Ages Aristotle provided the model for systematic, logical explanation and was often referred to simply as "Philosophous," the philosopher. In this regard the twelfth century was similar to the respect of the Italian Renaissance for the intellectual achievement of the classical past.

Although modern advances in natural science have caused the achievements of medieval scholars in the study of physics and motion to be belittled it was the **theologians** who provided the chief intellectual achievements of the time. By taking the natural observations of Aristotle and adapting them to that which was recorded in the sacred word of the Bible, the masters of the twelfth century probed the nature of the universe and of human existence. Over the years a series of original thinkers discussed a range of different possibilities. Where some, like Anselm of Canterbury, were pessimistic about human nature, others were optimistic. When Abelard (d. A.D. 1142) who was a free-thinking scholar from northeastern France, emphasized reason as the key to understanding and faith, St. Bernard helped to silence him with the authority of revelation as taught by the church and the Bible.

*M*edieval Universities

The universities where these questions were debated did not emerge overnight. A university was an incorporated body that held a charter from the king, the pope, or a bishop. The charter designated the university's officials, their powers and the assemblies to which they were responsible. The incorporated body usually comprised all the masters active in the university. Students everywhere sought out teachers with the highest reputations. Even before universities in a formal sense had appeared, teachers banded together in one city or town because of the

greater security they gained from each other.

Even at this early date there was considerable mobility among scholars, which increased with the expansion of trade. Lanfranc, William the Conqueror's choice for archbishop of Canterbury, was brought over from the Norman abbey of Bec. Lanfranc had been attracted to Bec from his studies in Pavia by the monastery's reputation for learning and discipline. The Englishman, John of Salisbury, became bishop of Chartres in the kingdom of France, in the twelfth century on the strength of his reputation in the schools at Notre Dame in Paris. A century later those schools were the fully fledged University of Paris, and its leading light was the Dominican friar St. Thomas Aquinas from Italy. Learning was already international.

Universities grew with the intellectual revival of the twelfth century and like it they were centred in Italy, France, and southern England. Bologna was notable for the study of canon and civil law; Salerno and Montpellier were best known for medicine; Paris and Oxford were the chief centres of theological and philosophical speculation. Each of these, and the few other universities established before A.D. 1300 offered the basic training of the Faculty of Arts. The universal mode of instruction, even after the appearance of printed books, continued to be the lecture.

Each university drew its students from across western Europe. They were lively, often riotous communities. Not only did students come from different backgrounds, but until the later thirteenth century, when colleges were founded, they had no choice but to make their own arrangements for board and lodging. There was the additional expense of fees and texts, and there were numerous distractions, including the taverns that produced many of the rhythmic and satirical *carmina burana*, or student songs. Then, as now, students were regularly short of cash. Occasions for dispute and stress were not lacking. Control of discipline, as well as of the curriculum and standards required to graduate, were reasons that universities acquired a tradition of self-regulation.

Cathedrals in Medieval Europe

In the twelfth century the revival of urban society and the growth of cities, resulting from increased manufacturing, the expansion of trade, and the rise of universities produced economic stability. This new prosperity allowed for the huge investment of capital and labour in large scale undertakings such as the building of cathedrals. Between 1180 and 1270, 80 cathedrals and thousands of parish churches were built. During this period more stone was quarried than for the pyramids of Egypt. **Gothic architecture** began in the northern regions of France in the royal monastery of Saint Denis near Paris, in the first half of the twelfth century. Abbot Suger was the first to encourage this new style of pointed arches, tall windows, and cross-ribbed vaults. Once taken up this style spread via cathedrals and parish churches throughout France and Europe including Germany, and England. This tide of building continued to the end of the Middle Ages. Its purpose was to give greater glory to God in worship. Churches in the earlier Romanesque style, which preceded Gothic, were often cramped and dark with small windows. The ponderous solidity was due to the fact that the walls and the columns had to carry the weight of the entire building.

Gothic Architecture

The builders of Gothic architecture strove to increase the size of the windows, to reduce the number of structural supports, and to open up the interior for an overall effect of height and vast, bright open spaces. The architectural features that made this possible were: the compound support or pier, which appeared less massive than one solid column; the pointed arch, which emphasized upward movement and made height possible; the rib vault, which carried the thrust to pillars and walls and appeared light and graceful; and the flying buttress, the huge external stone supports that extended well beyond the sides of the buildings. These buttresses carried the main load of the building and kept the structure in shape while removing the need for heavy stone walls. Instead the walls became skeletal supports and the space was filled by huge windows of stained glass. (See photograph of Notre Dame, in Paris, one of the most famous Gothic Cathedrals, on page 460.)

Stained Glass

This medieval art form flourished in conjunction with Gothic architecture from the twelfth to the sixteenth century. Stained glass was remarkable for its extent, forms, and colours. In Chartres, a cathedral in France, 100 windows contain over 2000 square metres of glass. In form stained glass was either figurative or geometrical. Since a large part of the population was illiterate the decorations illustrating Biblical scenes, religious symbols, and pictures showed these people what to believe. Biblical scenes such as the Resurrection of Christ, Moses and Golden Calf, depictions of Biblical figures, saints, martyrs caught the eye for a purpose—namely to instruct and to help recall incidents, stories, and lessons from the Bible.

The famed rose windows, huge round expanses of stained glass, were purely geometrical. The challenge to the designer was to create eye-catching beauty by arranging the coloured glass in symmetrical forms. As can be imagined the effect of light streaming through these coloured glass windows, creating a glittering effect of many colours in the lofty interior of the church must have had an emotional effect on the worshippers, contributing to their sense of the glory of God.

The essential Gothic style had many regional variations which fascinate engineers, architects, and tourists today. What is fundamental to all of them is that they reflect the change in the centre of Christendom during the Dark Ages. The high points of Gothic achievement are found in places like Paris, Chartres, Amiens. Canterbury, Lincoln, York, Cologne, and Prague. Towns competed against each other to see who could build the largest and most splendid churches. In 1163, the people of Paris built Notre Dame, which rose to a height of 35 m, Chartres attained a height of 36.5 m, and Beauvais cathedral built in 1247 attained a height of 48 m, but the tower collapsed because it was too high and too heavy. In the Mediterranean region Gothic architecture seldom appeared while the rounded Romanesque arch continued to dominate through the Renaissance.

Medieval Art

The explosion of art which occurred in the High Middle Ages is reflected in the Gothic cathedrals of Europe. Both the interior and the exterior artistic forms and ornamentations of the cathedrals expressed the prominence of medieval faith, aspirations, and knowledge.

Sculpture

A renewed interest in sculpture developed and the stone masons began to adorn the buildings with decorative arcades, capitals, and doorways. They also carved the gargoyles, stone spouts at the ends of gutters, which were shaped into bizarre and grotesque forms designed to shoot the rainwater clear of the walls. As stone decorations became more extensive, whole sides were carved and decorated with symbols and statues. These decorations often were intended to convey medieval beliefs and religious ideas to the viewer. Depicted were stories from the Old and New Testaments and figures of saints, martyrs, and confessors. Chartres cathedral in France contains 10 000 of such figures and scenes in stone and in stained glass.

Another visible development is the sculpting of religious themes using the strict conventions of the times progressing to a realistic human image with a life-like presence. In later medieval cathedrals the subject matter becomes increasingly realistic and the sculptor effectively portrays not only appearance but also personality. The decorations that were a part of so many of these great churches were designed to show religious teachings, yet have become along with the cathedrals great works of art.

Painting

The painting of the Middle Ages was also for church or cathedral ornamentation. Inside the cathedrals, walls and sometimes ceilings were plastered to a smooth finish. Bright murals and patterns were then painted over this finish. Carved tombs and wooden sculptures were often painted as well. As fashions changed the plaster was often removed and the paintings or the painted surface vanished. A few murals and painted altar panels remain, as do scraps of paints in corners and between carvings. The medieval painters ground their own colours and mixed their own paints using small millstones or mortar and pestles. Paint was applied with brushes very similar to our own with hair bristles from hogs, badgers, or squirrels. Church and cathedral accounts indicate that large amounts of money were allotted to painters, indicating that much painting was done and that it was an important form of church ornamentation.

Manuscript Illumination

Another form of painting that developed in the Middle Ages was that of manuscript illumination. The religious nature of the times fostered this art form, which usually added visual attraction and information to a text. Uplifting pictures would be combined with funny scenes or bizarre creatures to add comic relief for the reader. The illumination (or illustration), might simply be a decorated enlarged initial beginning a text, or borders that were alive with little human and animal figures, to extensive illustrations of the text such as scenes from the Bible. The illuminators used the challenge of the flat page to bring the text to life, never allowing the illustrations, no matter how detailed and skillfully wrought, to dominate the text. A keen eye for nature resulted in exquisitely multicoloured borders, including vines and foliage to house lively little animals that perched on or hid behind the leaves. The intense colours

ARCHITECTURE

Gothic Cathedrals

Among the greatest lasting achievements of the High Middle Ages were the numerous Gothic cathedrals. In a span of 90 years, from 1180 to 1270, 80 cathedrals, 500 abbey churches, and thousands of parish churches were built in Europe using up more stone than the pyramids of Egypt. The features which clearly distinguish Gothic architecture are the use of pointed arches and vaults, flying buttresses on the outside to carry the weight, and enormous amounts of glass in the walls allowing for an interior lightness never before achieved. The overall sensation you experience when standing in a Gothic cathedral is one of great height and lightness. The following excerpt from Ken Follett's *Pillars of the Earth* gives a vivid description of a newly completed Cathedral in the High Middle Ages.

He reached the top of street and turned into the priory close; and there, before his eyes, was the reason for the rise of Kingsbridge and the decline of Shiring: the cathedral.

It was breathtaking.

The immensely tall nave was supported by a row of graceful flying buttresses. The west end had three huge porticos, like giants' doorways, and rows of tall, slender, pointed windows above, flanked by slim towers. The concept had been heralded in the transepts, finished eighteen years ago, but this was the astonishing consummation of the idea. There had never been a building like this anywhere in England. . . .

The church was even more impressive inside. The nave followed the style of the transepts, but the master builder had refined his design, making the columns even more slender and the windows larger. But there was yet another innovation. William had heard people talk of the colored glass made by craftsmen Jack Jackson had brought over from Paris. He had wondered why there was such a fuss about it, for he imagined that a colored window would be just like a tapestry or a painting. Now he saw what they meant. The light from outside shone through the colored glass, making it glow, and the effect was quite magical. The church was full of people craning their necks to stare up at the windows. The pictures showed Bible stories, Heaven and Hell, saints and prophets, disciples, and some of the Kingsbridge citizens who had presumably paid for the windows in which they appeared—a baker carrying his tray of loaves, a tanner and his hides, a mason with his compasses and level.

Flying Buttresses ①

Perhaps the most distinguishing external feature of a Gothic cathedral are the flying buttresses. These graceful supports bear the weight of the stone vault lessening the need for massive walls and thick pillars. This allowed medieval architects to design and build soaring cathedrals whose interiors drew visitors, eyes to the heavens and bathed them in the sunlight which penetrated the stained glass.

Clerestory ②

The use of flying buttresses to carry the weight of the structure allowed walls to become mere skeletons. This allowed the clerestory, or the uppermost part of the church, to increasingly contain less and less stone and more and more glass. The huge windows of stained glass flooded the interior of church with magical blending of light and colour.

Piers ③

This is the column or the pillar that supports the arch. The piers were the only internal support for the high vaulting sharing this job only with the exterior buttresses.

Vaulting ④

The high vaulting of the ceiling or roof is of brick or stone. The great height of the cathedrals was achieved through the use of ribs which directed the weight onto the piers and the exterior buttresses.

such as bright golds, luminous blues, glowing reds, and deep greens effectively enlivened the text. Medieval books were handmade from start to finish. Scribes in monasteries or priests would purchase parchment made of stretched animal skins. The scribe would cut them to size and rule margins and lines. Then the text would be copied. Usually the book would be decorated and the illuminators, talented scribes or artists, would paint borders, guild and decorate the letters, or paint the pictures. The finished sheets would be passed to the binder who would sew them together and enclose them in leather-covered boards. These illuminated books were used as altar copies of the Bible and the church's services. A precious luxury item containing some of the most beautiful examples of illumination are the individual prayerbooks (Book of Hours) created for the medieval nobility. The markets among university students and the increasingly literate populace created a guaranteed market for books.

No facet of the Middle Ages better reflects the resurgence of European culture than the art and architecture of the period. The soaring cathedrals, beautiful stained glass windows, numerous statues, and ornately decorated manuscripts remain as a testimony to the creativity and vitality of the High Middle Ages. While the art and architecture was a product of the increase in wealth it also depicted the deeply religious nature of the people. Much of the artistic outpouring of this period was dedicated to the glory of God.

By the end of the thirteenth century western Europe, led by France, predominated over eastern Europe. A significant change had taken place in the centuries between the end of the Carolingian dynasty and the thirteenth century. By the thirteenth century no king could claim to control an empire as vast as the former German Empire. Following the death of Frederick Barbarossa in 1190 the political structure of Germany began to dissolve, as rule fell into the hands of the leading princes, who established almost independent principalities. Italian loyalties were directed to the papacy as much as to any secular ruler, and the papacy's concern was to preserve its political independence from the domination of any monarch. The popes found support in the recently enlarged and enriched Italian cities like those of the Lombard League. In Spain the kingdoms that had nearly been obliterated by Islamic invaders focused their energies on the task of reconquest. The divisions among Islamic rulers after the collapse of the Ummayad Empire, and the reliance of the Arabs in Spain on military help from Africa, made the Christian task easier.

Expansion was part of the feudal history of the British Isles. Norman barons carved out feoffs in Wales, Ireland and lowland Scotland. In none of these three border regions were they capable of bringing the whole country under English subjection but a hereditary dynasty with royal title continued only in Scotlad. In Celtic Wales and Ireland there was no tradition of a hereditary single crown and it was preserved in Scotland only because of the penetration of Norman feudalism. Aquitaine, which comprised the provinces from the Loire River to the Pyrenees in southwestern France, was added to England by the marriage of Eleanor of Aquitaine to Henry II. Except for Gascony in the southwest of this region, the responsibilities of the English crown were centred on the British Isles from the thirteenth century to the end of the Middle Ages.

Saint Louis represented the epitome of the Capetian dynasty in France and the ideal feudal king and lord. As king, Louis IX (1226–1270) protected popes, led crusades, and dispensed justice internally and externally. He supported the ambitions of his brothers to rule in southern France and in southern Italy. In Louis' reign France led Europe, not only politically but also in culture. France led the way in learning and literature, Gothic architecture, and in courtly life. None of this could have been achieved without the immense wealth of France.

In the course of the High Middle Ages these countries; France, Italy and Spain, England and Germany established themselves as the political and cultural powers in Christendom. They came to overshadow the Slav and Magyar Kingdoms of eastern Europe, Scandinavia and the decaying Byzantine Empire.

Suggested Sources for Further Research
▼▼▼

Please see pages 514 and 515 for complete list for Chapters 14, 15, and 16.

Focus Your Knowledge
▼▼▼

1. Describe the response to the second wave of invasions and how order was restored.
2. Provide a description of a medieval knight. Include how he fought, what he wore, and his code of ethics (the chivalric code).
3. Describe the relationship between the serf and the lord, the mutual obligations and the distribution of manorial lands.
4. Prepare a chart which illustrates the rights and obligations of the lords and their vassals under the feudal system.
5. How did the rise of trade and towns begin to alter traditional feudal society?
6. Outline the various roles played by women in medieval society.
7. What examples of a resistance to secularization were evident in the church?

Apply Your Knowledge
▼▼▼

1. What evidence was there to suggest that medieval Europe was a violent, male dominated society rooted in inequality?

2. Assuming that you were not a member of the aristocracy would you have preferred to have lived in a medieval monastery, manor, or town? Justify your answer.

3. In what ways did the church play a contradictory role in feudal society?

4. What was the purpose of the Crusades? What degree of success did they achieve?

5. Why was the twelfth century considered a period of intellectual revival?

6. How did the beliefs of the common people reflect their insecurities, superstitions, and ignorance?

7. How does Gothic architecture reflect the values of medieval society?

Extension Activities

1. Research medieval castles and build a scale model of a typical castle from the period.

2. Choose a Gothic cathedral and prepare a pamphlet outlining its features and significant architectural details. (Include a floor plan and historical details.)

3. Based on what you have learned from this chapter as well as further research assume you are a student attending a medieval university. Write a letter to your parents or a diary entry explaining your daily routine. Be sure your account includes descriptions of classes, evenings at the tavern, your lodgings, and your acquaintances.

4. Organize a panel discussion where students represent various classes of feudal society. Panelists are responding to the question, "Who is the true backbone of medieval society?" Prepare a response and state your case. This discussion could be held in costume.

5. Drawing on your personal talents either create a tavern song that might have been sung by students at a medieval university, write a medieval romance or epic which reflects chivalric ideals, or recreate a page from a medieval manuscript with calligraphic lettering and colourful illumination.

CHAPTER 16

The Late Middle Ages

Chapter Highlights

- the Black Death

- discontent and peasants' revolts

- war and fighting methods

- Joan of Arc

- the Avignonese papacy

- the origins of our parliamentary system

The late Middle Ages are usually defined as the two centuries before the European arrival in the Americas and the Protestant Reformation, or approximately A.D. 1300–1520. Historians have seen this as a period of decline in the papacy and the kingdoms of western Europe, in the universities and intellectual curiosity, and in towns, and trade. These had been the regions and institutions that had been responsible for the achievements of the High Middle Ages. This chapter will consider the impact of the plague and of a prolonged war, which were responsible for much of the depression of this period, particularly during the hundred years from 1350 to 1450 when France and England were fighting. Problems encountered by the Catholic church will be discussed, focusing on abuses that were not handled radically enough to achieve reform. At the same time, the transformation of feudalism and a review of social and institutional developments, which directed Europe into a more controlled and wealthier modern society, will be considered.

Key Concepts

Black Death
buboes
Peasants' Revolt
contract army
The Great Schism
Inquisition
Commons
Isabella and Ferdinand

▼▼▼

Plague and Hardship

For the late Middle Ages the most universally traumatic event was the **pandemic** plague known as the **Black Death**, which swept across Europe in the middle of the fourteenth century and recurred periodically during the next three hundred years. By A.D. 1400 the plague had catastrophically reduced the population of Europe by between one third and one half. Its impact varied from place to place and between classes, but barely anyone escaped its effects. The result was a severe and prolonged economic recession.

The Hundred Years' War between France and England, which frequently involved Flaunders, Scotland, and Castile as allies, also contributed to the devastation in the late Middle Ages. Although the war, which began in 1337 and ended in 1453, was not continuous it did spread destruction, mainly in France which was Europe's richest country in agricultural production. The war also distorted and interrupted trade, and generally it wasted resources and human energy in non-productive activities.

The institutions whose reputation suffered the most in the late medieval world were the papacy and the church. The papal claim to supremacy in Christendom reached its peak in the time of Innocent III. Thereafter, the papacy's reputation declined as the monarchies of France and England insisted that their needs had first priority on the resources of their subjects. From 1378 to 1417 the competing interests of secular rulers across Christendom led to a scandal in the papacy, dividing the loyalties of Catholics for a century.

Despite this long list of negative features, there was a brighter side to life in the late Middle Ages.

The surplus lands left by death due to the plague gave many struggling peasants the opportunity to achieve economic security, which some even managed to turn into wealth. War squandered resources, but not before royal governments had been forced to explore new ways of assembling them. That added to the expertise of governments and increased the habit of accepting government as normal. Many people responded to the public breakdown in church authority by personally assuming the responsibility for a more individual piety and more reflective morality.

The Black Death

The decisive factor in fourteenth-century Europe was the Black Death and its consequences. As has been noted it was not the only factor in the prolonged recession; there was also war and a change in the weather pattern, which brought colder winters and wetter summers. Between 1314 and 1317 and at six similar periods in the same century there was a sequence of disastrous harvests across Europe that brought starvation to many. Nevertheless, the plague was what claimed everyone's attention.

The spread of the plague known as the Black Death was unavoidable and its symptoms were painful and often deadly. The black swellings called **buboes**, which were the visible sign of infection, spread fear among the population. The plague arrived in Europe from the ports on the Black Sea, where Italian ships traded, and from there it moved along the commercial routes of Europe with a demoralizing speed. In the winter of 1347–1348 it infected the inhabitants of the Mediterranean basin, and in the late summer of 1348 it reached England and spread to Scotland later that winter.

The medical knowledge of the Middle Ages, based on the four elements of earth, air, fire, and water, and the corresponding humours, provided neither explanation nor remedy. The plague was caused by a complex ecological situation that was beyond the comprehension of the time. An imbalance in the rodent population on the borders of China led to the infection of the Black Sea ports. The plague was quickly spread by fleas that carried the bacillus. The fleas were transported by the rats that infested the docks and ships which carried goods from east to west. When a flea carrying the bacillus fed on the blood of a rat, the bacillus was transferred to the rat's bloodstream causing the rodent to die. This forced the flea to jump to a new host to feed on, which may have been another rat or a human.

In time the effectiveness of quarantining became apparent, but that was not done on a community-wide scale before the seventeenth century. In the fourteenth and fifteenth centuries those who could afford it learned to stay away from congested cities and towns in the summer, when bubonic infection was most common. Stone buildings were inhospitable to rats, and hygiene and cleanliness helped to reduce the presence of rats and fleas. So it was the poor, living in wooden and thatched buildings without sanitation, who suffered the most.

There were various forms of the infection. Besides the swollen glands called buboes, which appeared as painful swellings in the groin or armpit, the bacillus transmitted by the fleabite could enter the bloodstream and kill in hours. Death from this form of plague was close to one hundred percent. In winter, droplet infection spread a pneumonic form of plague, which was also more deadly than the more common bubonic form. Victims of the pneumonic plague drowned in their own fluids as their lungs became infected. Fear of the plague was neither imaginary nor unfounded.

The Effects of the Black Death. Those who survived the Black Death of 1347–1349 gained a natural immunity, but there were epidemic

LITERATURE

GEOFFREY CHAUCER'S CANTERBURY TALES

Geoffrey Chaucer provides us with a vivid picture of medieval people in *The Canterbury Tales*. These tales are told by a motley collection of pilgrims from all levels of society who have but one thing in common. They are visiting the shrine of Thomas Becket in Canterbury. These tales, recounted on the pilgrimage, usually suit the character and range from courtly romances to bawdy anecdotes. The characters themselves are just as fascinating and Chaucer describes them so picturesquely that the reader has little trouble picturing them. The following is an excerpt of two of these character sketches which make up The Prologue to *The Canterbury Tales*.

The Wife of Bath

There was a housewife come from Bath, or near,
Who—sad to say—was deaf in either ear.
At making cloth she had so great a bent
She bettered those of Ypres and even of Ghent.
In all the parish there was no goodwife
Should offering make before her, on my life:
And if one did, indeed, so wrath was she
It put her out of all her charity.
Her kerchiefs were of finest weave and ground:
I dare swear that they weighed a full ten pound
Which, of a Sunday, she wore on her head.
Her hose were of the choicest scarlet red,
Close gartered, and her shoes were soft and new.
Bold was her face, and fair, and red of hue
She'd been respectable throughout her life,
With five churched husbands bringing joy and
    strife,
Not counting other company in youth:

---

recurrences of plague in the 1360s, 1370s, and 1390s and periodically in the fifteenth century on a more local scale. It was the recurrences of plague, which felled subsequent generations who had no immunity that so depressed the populations of affected regions. The moral effect of such a prolonged and widespread disaster was considerable, and many people became preoccupied with death. The shadowing of living men and women by their skeletons in the *danse macabre*, the concern with purgatory, the importance of doing penance as a routine discipline, and the elaborate monuments to the dead, many of which portrayed rotting corpses, were all evidence of the late medieval preoccupation with death and the rituals that surrounded it.

The catastrophic decline in population was to have an equally great effect on Europe's economic and social structure. It took Europe nearly one hundred and fifty years to begin to recover from the demographic effects of the plague. Land, especially the most recently settled holdings, stopped producing because there were not enough peasants to work even long-settled tenements. Towns shrank and whole quarters of cities were abandoned, the ranks

But thereof there's no need to speak, in truth.
Three times she'd journeyed to Jerusalem;
And many a foreign stream she'd had to stem;
At Rome she'd been, and she'd been in Bologne,
In Spain at Santiago, and at Cologne.
She could tell much of wandering by the way:
Gap-toothed was she, it is no lie to say.
Upon an ambler easily she sat,
Well wimpled, aye, and over all a hat
As broad as is a buckler or a targe;
A rug was tucked around her buttocks large,
And on her feet a pair of sharpened spurs.
In company well could she laugh her slurs.
The remedies of love she knew, perchance.
For of that and she'd learned the old, old dance.

The Miller

The miller was a stout churl, be it known,
Hardy and big of brawn and big of bone;
Which was well proved, for when he went on lam
At wrestling, never failed he of the ram.
He was a chunky fellow, broad of build;
He'd heave a door from hinges if he willed,
Or break it through, by running, with his head.
His beard, as any sow or fox, was red,
And broad it was as if it were a spade.
Upon the coping of his nose he had
A wart, and thereon stood a tuft of hairs,
Red as the bristles in an old sow's ears;
His nostrils they were black and very wide.
A sword and buckler bore he by his side.
His mouth was like a furnace door for size.
He was a jester and could poetize,
But mostly all of sin and ribaldries.
He could steal corn and full thrice charge his fees;
And yet he had a thumb of gold, begad.
A white coat and blue hood he wore, this lad.
A bagpipe he could blow well, be it known,
And with that same he brought us out of town.

---

of the clergy were depleted, and the volume of trade showed a sharp decline.

A natural result of the recession was a reversal of the economic enterprise that had invigorated the twelfth and thirteenth centuries. Merchants and their guilds became more restrictive, anxious to protect their existing share of the market and to preserve familiar products and familiar ways of doing business. In defence of established interests, they kept out newcomers to their craft and blocked the advance of apprentices who wanted to become masters. Innovations in technique became suspect, which lead to a decline in enterprise.

At the same time, there was a shift in economic power. The country generally did better than the town. In England the restrictions in the various textile guilds in the towns, among them weavers, fullers, and dyers, led to the transfer of these activities to favourably situated villages, where cleaning and spinning wool had always been done. Where the wool merchants lost, the cloth merchant prospered, supplying the raw wool and coordinating the many processes through which it passed in the course of being woven into cloth. The prosperity of many small villages and towns in late medieval Europe is evident in the construction of marketplaces or crosses, stone houses, in rebuilt churches and church towers as well as charitable institutions. Such communities were generally healthier than larger cities, which could only adapt by shrinking.

The Changing Countryside. With the decline of large urban markets, landlords found less profit in selling serf produced crops, and increasingly they rented their land to smallholders. In manorialized England in particular, economic advantage passed

ASPECTS OF DAILY LIFE
The Black Death

The course of the Black Death or bubonic plague can be traced from China around 1331. The next fifteen years saw it spread by merchants, soldiers, and traders along caravan routes in Asia until it reached southern Russia in 1346. From here it was again spread the same way along trade and shipping routes to Europe in 1347. Within a few years Italy, Germany, France, and England were also affected.

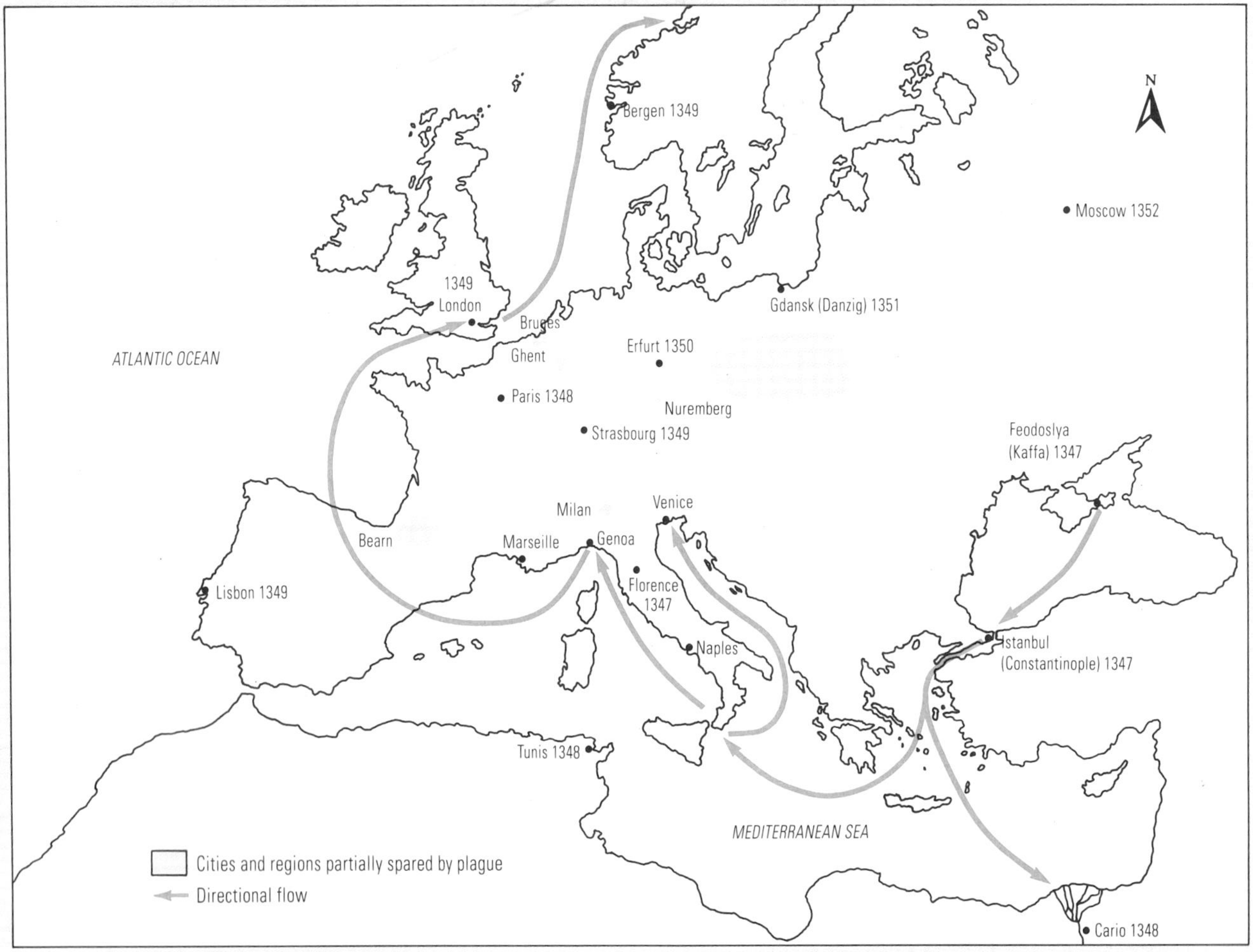

Symptoms of the Black Death

The causes and course of the plague have been researched and are understood much better now. The bacillus that causes the plague lived in the bloodstream of an animal, preferring the flea, which lived on rats or squirrels. The "host black rat" moved around and hence often travelled by ship. It would live in the cargo hold and depart the ship at the next destination. Cities, unsanitary and overpopulated as they were, harboured diseases easily in the rubbish. The close proximity of living and sleeping quarters and the lack of personal hygiene allowed fleas to run rampant. Everyone from the priest to the peasant had them. The symptoms began with a nut-sized growth in the groin, armpit, or neck. This boil, called the bulba, was agonizingly painful. If this bulba was lanced and completely drained there was a chance the victim might recover. On the second stage, black spots, caused by bleeding under the skin, appeared. Then the victim began to cough and to spit blood because the bloodstream had been thoroughly infected. At this stage the agony was increased by the fetid stench exuded from the body. Mercifully, death followed in 2-3 days, which was usually within 5 days of infection.

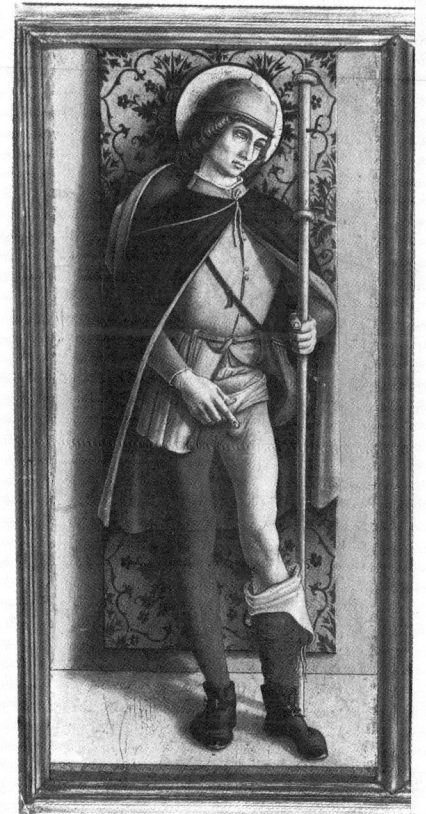

Ring Around the Rosie

This pessimism is reflected in the macabre nursery rhyme describing symptoms and effects of the plague. Children still recite today;

"Ring around the rosies,
A pocket full of posies
Achoo! Achoo!
We all fall down."

Can you explain what the real meaning of this rhyme is?

Reactions to the Plague

Since the plague was not understood it could not be treated effectively. People believed that the infection was carried through the air so they covered their faces; when that didn't work scapegoats such as the Jews were found and persecuted. The dead were buried and the sick were quarantined. Physicians could sometimes lessen the pain but once infected there was usually no escape and no cure. Some people seeing that the plague ravaged urban centres, moved to the countryside to escape it. However, the scourge continued to sweep through Europe leaving a grim trail of death, destruction, and decay so horrible that many believed this was the end of the world.

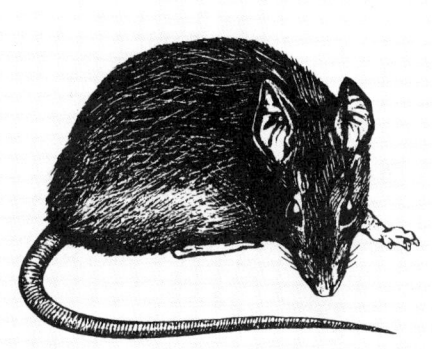

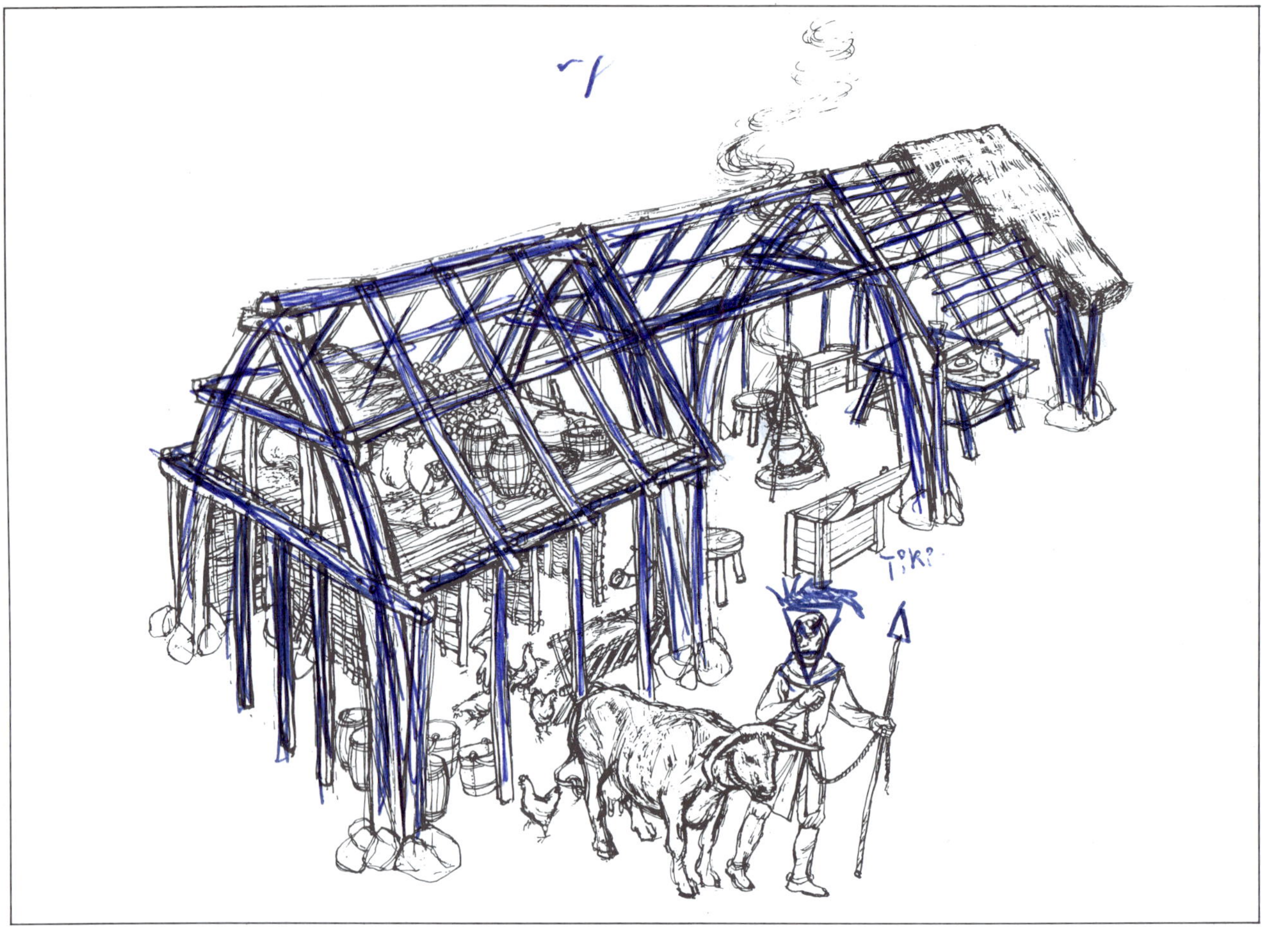

A peasant's cottage consisted of two rooms, combining both living quarters and a stable. The room on the left was where the livestock were kept and might also have been used for storage. The larger room on the right was where the family lived, ate, and slept, allowing for little privacy.

from the landlord to the peasant as a result of the changes brought about by the reduced population. Unoccupied land profited no one, so an energetic peasant family, having survived the plague, could take land on more favourable terms than had been available before 1348. Peasant fortunes thus showed a greater variety as some made use of these opportunities and added the cash returns from participation in the growing English cloth trade. The fourteenth and fifteenth centuries brought the **yeoman**, the richer and more progressive tenant farmer, into the foreground of English rural life.

Rising Discontent. The late Middle Ages saw plenty of occasions for adjustment in industry and in the countryside. It did not, however, always come easily. Landlords, like merchants, strove to maintain their advantage. In much of Europe they succeeded. In England they used the law to try to hold the level of wages to what they had been before the plague, to control prices and to retain the old manorial obligations to labour services. This led to widespread discontent. When a poll tax (a tax on every head) was added between 1377 and 1380 to previous economic grievances, there was an explosion. The **Peasants' Revolt** of 1381, particularly affecting the counties around London, totally disrupted the king's government for a week. It persuaded the ruling class of the cost of not adapting to change, but otherwise had little effect. Around this same time there were also revolts in the industrial centres of Florence and Ghent, which aimed to redress the grievances of artisan weavers. These protests also failed to make any permanent change. In 1358 and for several years after, peasant uprisings in central France created a reign of terror, showing a substantial level of rage against the upper class, whom the peasants blamed for their problems. The grievances and discontent expressed throughout Europe following the Black Death were primarily the result of the plague, but the actions of those in positions of power frequently made things worse.

The Hundred Years' War

After the plague, the war, known as the Hundred Years' War, between England and France was the most influential experience of the leading kingdoms of the period. The cohesion and organization that was the result of feudalism in France and England left them as the two monarchies best able to develop and apply their resources. It was the recovery by France of the French territories, which had been held by the English, that provided many occasions for the two kingdoms to engage in war.

Causes of the War

At the end of the thirteenth century, Philip IV ruled France and Edward I ruled England. Both were masterful and ambitious rulers who made repeated demands on their subjects for taxation and military service and continually worked towards bringing local interests under central control. As a result, each king faced rebellions.

One of the reasons for their excessive demands was that Philip IV and Edward I were at war with each other from 1294 to 1303. The basic cause of this war was that Edward, who controlled the duchy of Gascony in southwestern France, was therefore a vassal of Philip. Since the time of the Albigensian Crusade the French kings had gradually extended control over their subjects in the south and southwest of their kingdom. French officials wished to extend this control to Gascony, thus placing the Gascons and the English under Edward I on the defensive.

In addition, Gascony was economically tied to England by the wine trade. The duchy's economy concentrated on wine, most of which was shipped to England. Medieval rural economy was generally mixed farming and largely self-sufficient in every region; with its emphasis on wine production, Gascony was atypical. Furthermore, the Gascons relied on imports from England for their needs in grain, cloth, and other staples. Moreover, every change of ruler on either the French or English throne raised the delicate question of the king of England, as duke of Gascony, doing homage to the king of France as a vassal.

The so-called Hundred Years' War began in A.D. 1337 with Edward III ruling England and Philip VI ruling France. In addition to the concerns of Gascony, Edward III had another complaint against France. Since the time of Edward I, England's main battlefront had been in the North against the Scots, who insisted on maintaining their independence against English claims to sovereignty over Scotland. Just prior to 1337 Philip VI had allied with the Scots to prevent the ambitious young Edward III from launching a successful attack against them. In retali-

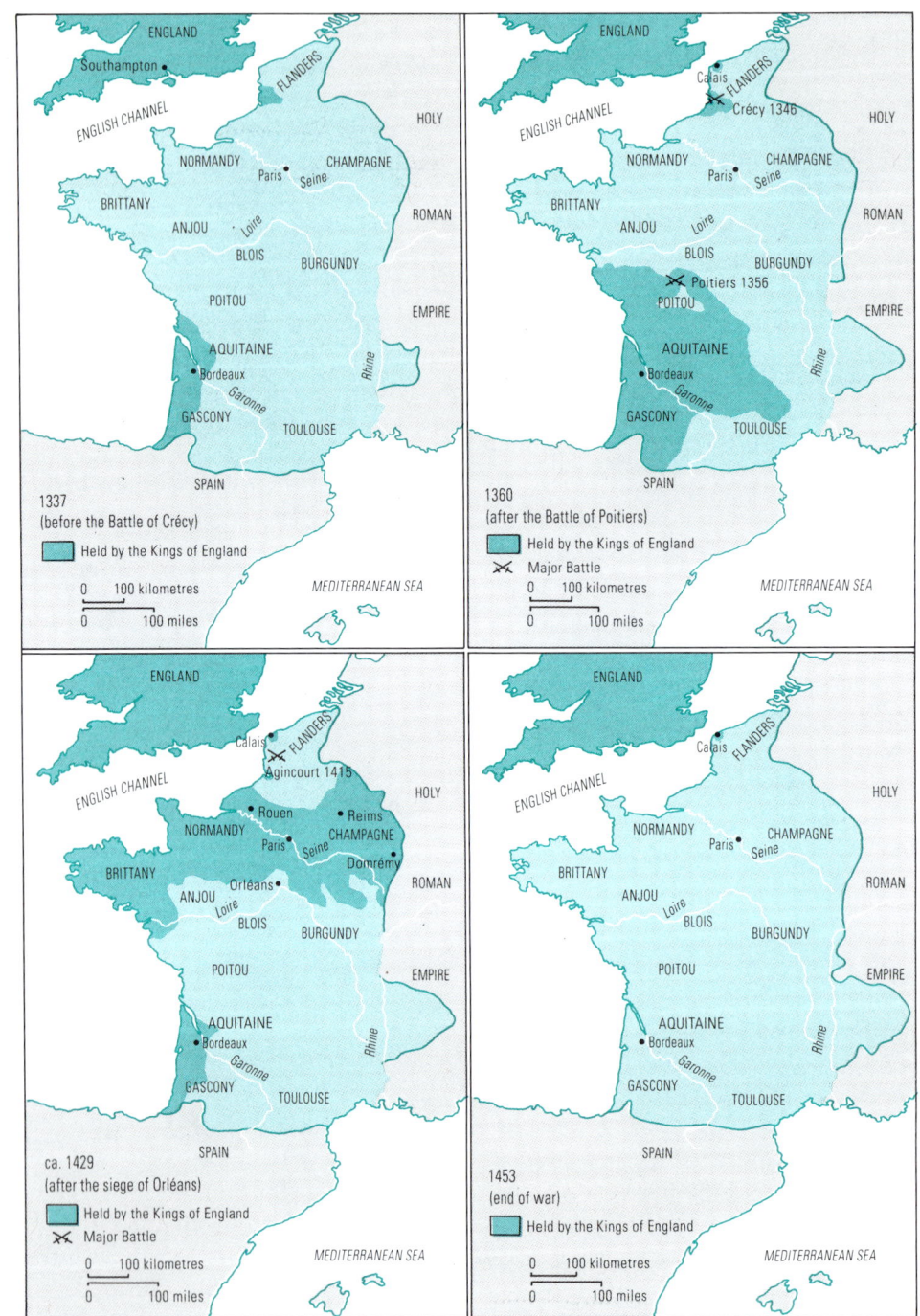

The Hundred Years' War

These maps indicate the various land holdings and stages of the Hundred Years' War.

ation Edward III challenged Philip's claim to the throne of France. Edward argued that by virtue of his mother, who was the sister to the three previous kings of France, he had a stronger claim to the throne than Philip whose claim was through an all male, but junior line. Although the issue had already been settled in Philip's favour in the highest French court, the *parlement*, the claim was still valuable to Edward as a means to rally allies against France. Most important among these allies was Flanders, which was linked to England by its dependence on English wool for the manufacture of cloth. The English found other supporters among the neighbours of Flanders, a region bordering the northeast frontier of France. These small duchies and counties, which were formally part of the German Empire, had suffered from French aggression, and were happy to accept the subsidies that Edward III was prepared to pay in exchange for their support of his claim.

The Conduct of War

Although there were the makings of a coalition surrounding France, medieval Europe had neither the capacity nor the communications to coordinate a grand alliance. War was not decided by a grand strategy, but by the result of particular battles that were fought as isolated actions. It is important to recognize that the fighting between the French and the English took place on French soil. It was a sign of France's natural wealth that the country emerged from the war victorious in A.D. 1453 with a royal treasury vastly richer than England's.

Control of the English Channel was a key factor in the war. The English established that control in a battle on the Flemish coast in A.D. 1340 by using **impressed** merchant and fishing vessels. They continued to use them to transport their forces and supplies as the weather allowed. Although the English built some royal ships of larger capacity than usual there was no real coordinated naval policy or action during the Hundred Years' War. Fighting at sea could only take place at close quarters and was an extension of fighting on land, using the same weapons.

For much of the fourteenth century the English held on to ports at Calais, Cherbourg, Brest, and Bordeaux, and in 1415 Henry V seized Harfleur as a preliminary to gaining control of all of Normandy. Once the English had their forces ashore the usual objective was to spread destruction, demoralize the population, and to acquire as much portable booty and as many prisoners for ransom as possible. This was accomplished by mounted raids, some of which ranged all the way from Calais to Gascony. After some notable defeats in pitched battles the French learned to shadow the raiding force, and in the 1370s and 1380s they kept the English military from expanding its territory. When the armies did meet in a regular battle the English used the tactics that they learned fighting the Scots and generally they won decisive victories. These tactics were displayed by Edward III at Crecy in 1346, the Black Prince at Poitiers in 1356, and Henry V at Agincourt in 1415 who all had battles forced on them and put their smaller forces in a defensive position with protected flanks. The knights dismounted to fight on foot with men-at-arms and archers, and the rest of the English army waited, usually in three divisions with some defensive depth, for the French to attack along a restricted front.

Arms and Armour

The strategy of the English was to use their archers to break up the lines of advancing knights. Then, when the charge reached the English line, it was more easily held. Once the charging knights had been halted, the dismounted English of all ranks and arms attacked with swords and knives to plunder the dead and to take the living prisoner. The extent of the losses in these encounters demoralized the French, and this was one reason that there were few full-scale battles in the long war. Until the French improved the use of artillery in the final years of the war, the longbow remained the decisive weapon. The English took full advantage of the range of the longbow, a weapon introduced by the Welsh. Measuring nearly two metres in length and requiring extensive practice if it was to be drawn completely, the longbow was a specialist's weapon capable of a high volume of fire. With its great range the longbow proved to be a superior weapon to the crossbow. The crossbow, which was used by the mercenaries recruited by the French, had a greater initial velocity and penetrating power against armour at close range, but was less effective as a long range weapon. The rain of arrows, through which the French knights had to ride, probably interfered more with the horse than their armoured riders, but it was effective just the same.

Personality and leadership also made a contribution to the outcome of battles. In the early phase of the war the English had the advantage under the command of Edward III and the Black Prince leading the assaults. Between 1389 and 1415 there was a long truce as neither the French nor English monarchs of that time were military leaders and both were preoccupied with problems at home. Eventually, in 1415, Henry V renewed English confidence in the glories of war, only to have the balance tipped in France's favour after his death by the leadership of Joan of Arc.

Joan of Arc

Joan of Arc was an illiterate, 16-year-old shepherdess when she declared she had been called upon by God to save France. Born about 1412 in a village called Domremy in northeastern France, she was a typical peasant youth except for her exceptional piety. Joan spent long hours praying in the parish church and first claimed to have seen visions and heard voices at the age of 13. These voices eventually told her to go and rescue Orléans from the English. In May 1428 she set out with her uncle to go to a French stronghold where she intended to offer her services. The captain she met there was unimpressed, but she remained undaunted. Upon her return to the fortress the following January, the captain sent her to meet the Dauphin (the heir to the French throne). When Joan was presented to Charles, the Dauphin, she was able to immediately pick him out from among his courtiers despite his efforts to hide among them. She informed the Dauphin that God had ordered her to fight the English and to see that he was crowned king at Rheims. Although he was initially doubtful of this young peasant woman dressed in men's clothing, Charles was convinced by the theologians to allow her to try to lead the army at Orléans. Their examinations had revealed no signs of either heresy or insanity.

Immediately following her appearance before the Dauphin, Joan of Arc set out with an army of 4000 men. Accompanied by priests chanting psalms, she arrived at Orléans at the end of April and within a few days her troops had overrun the main English earthworks. This initial success was soon followed by a series of stunning victories that raised the morale of the French and earned Joan of Arc her fame. The leadership provided by Joan, and her claim of divine inspiration, led many of the French to believe that they were fighting a holy war.

Joan of Arc was finally captured during a skirmish in May 1430. The chronicler Enguerrand de Monstrelet noted that the English "had never been so afraid of any captain or commander in war as they had been of the Maid." While she was not always merciful in battle, at least once ordering the beheading of an enemy commander who had been captured, it was the believed presence of the supernatural that instilled fear in the English. Prior to the arrival of Joan of Arc the English had seemed invincible and they took each victory as a sign that God was with them. Joan's successes on the battlefield not only were costly to the English but also threatened the English claim to the French throne. It was imperative that this woman, dubbed "the witch of Orléans" be found guilty of heresy and disposed of.

The trial of Joan of Arc began on February 21, 1431 after nearly a year of lengthy and unscrupulous investigation by church lawyers. During the trial Joan was accused of rejecting the authority of the church in claiming a personal revelation from God and in asserting that she was assured of salvation. These charges were accompanied by a number of lesser charges including the wearing of male dress, which the English felt was perverse. After much bullying and misrepresentation Joan of Arc was found guilty and sentenced to be executed in the marketplace at Rouen as a heretic. She was burned at the stake on May 30, 1431. Her charred corpse was pulled from the fire before being destroyed so that people could see that it was the body of a young woman.

Throughout her trial, the Dauphin, Charles, made no attempt to rescue her. Although she had won him the opportunity to be crowned at Rheims as Charles VII and had rallied the French troops she had been but an instrument and not an end in herself. Joan of Arc has been accorded more respect since her death. Twenty years after being found guilty of heresy the papacy annulled the sentence and nearly five centuries later, in 1920, the young shepherdess from Domremy was canonized and became St. Joan.

The Contract Army

While weapons and personality are factors in war so is military organization. The French were conservative in their reliance on the traditional levy of feudal nobles. By the outbreak of the war in A.D. 1337 the English had tried out an alternative method of raising armies. They did not call on the feudal levy for service in France, for under the feudal levy the formal requirement was 40 days military service. That was not sufficient for the needs of the English kings in their wars against the Scots, Welsh, and French, and so they began to use what is known as the **contract army**. Its essence was payment for military service. The king contracted with leading nobles that they should provide a force of a certain size and composition for a particular campaign on prearranged terms which included the weapons to be used, their replacement, and who should have the spoils of war. In turn, that leading noble contracted with captains to raise the force that he had undertaken to bring to the campaign. While these units and sub-units held together during the length of the contract, they did not have the permanence of a modern regiment.

The contract army brought a greater professionalism to military service. The stay-at-home landowners were no longer obliged to take up arms just because they held land. The contract army also built in a structure of command and responsibility where experience would be recognized more readily than under the feudal system. Numerous successful captains, many from modest social beginnings, made a rewarding career during the course of the Hundred Years' War. The negative side of the contract army was that the captains and soldiers looked for employment as mercenaries during the long lulls in the war. These free companies, for lack of regular employment, preyed on the countryside until their next commission came along. It was the French countryside that suffered from these roving marauders. On the other hand the wages paid to these soldiers during times of war, and the booty they collected, contributed substantially to the redistribution of wealth. The English archer, for example, was paid six pence a day, as much money as a peasant might handle in six months.

Changing Forms of Feudalism

The contract army altered the character of traditional feudalism. Earlier in the thirteenth century land had come to be treated as a unit of economic production and not for the political purpose of supplying labour and soldiers. The sale, purchase, and inheritance of land had led to the fragmentation of knights' fees, which led to confusion over the corresponding obligations. Because the feudal levy could not deliver the military service that was due, Edward I turned to the contract army and this soon became the norm.

The new military arrangements of the contract army had social consequences that offered greater flexibility in relationships between the classes. In England the feudal hierarchy had changed to the point that it ran from prices of royal blood, such as the house of Lancaster, which combined five earldoms and more than one hundred manors, to simple knights who struggled to maintain their status on the revenue generated by a single manor. In France and Germany noble rank remained more formally attached to the bloodline and as a result social status was less flexible. In all European countries service to kings or princes was the surest means to acquire wealth and to advance socially. As the general economic situation led to reduced revenues from landholding, office under the king, with its rewards in salary and influence, became the main key to social position and mobility.

The history of the Paston family of Norfolk, England provides an excellent example of the penalties and opportunities available through patronage appointments under the new form of feudalism. For much of the fifteenth century the family lived with the constant fear that they would be on the losing side in the competition for local leadership. At the same time their social standing steadily advanced from yeoman Clement, who in Edward III's reign rode with his corn to his lord's mill, to his grandsons, who were county gentry in Norfolk and Suffolk and place-seekers at the court.

Merchants and Towns

As a concept, the "middle class" seems to have grown in size and power in every period. In the later Middle Ages the great wealth of some merchant families, like the banking dynasties of Fugger in Augsburg or Medici in Florence, raised them to the same level of power as nobles. England and France did not match these examples from the Holy Roman Empire, nor did Spain. In England the middle class were drawn from yeomen and richer peasants, the lesser gentry and professional bureaucrats, and the leading citizens of the towns.

By the fourteenth century the period of urban growth was over. With some exceptions towns suffered from the general recession of the late Middle Ages. Few new urban communities with powers of self-government were established after the middle of the thirteenth century. Some cities grew, such as Bristol and Antwerp, but most diminished with the decline in trade that resulted from the devastation of the population because of the plague. Across Europe oligarchies took control of towns to ensure that those in power retained their share of surviving profitability. The vigour of urban life shrank, and towns everywhere pleaded with their rulers that poverty made it impossible for them to carry the share of taxation which they had borne in the past; ports had silted up, towns had suffered in war, or markets had been lost. Despite the prevailing hard times, some urban construction of streets, civic halls, and churches continued all over Europe.

When clerics, around A.D. 1000, listed the classes of feudal society they had not recognized the existence of townspeople and merchants. This changed considerably by the late Middle Ages when towns and trade had an established place in the politics of all European countries. Nevertheless, aristocratic and military values still dominated society and the greatest merchants continued to take second place in the social order, except in Venice and Florence.

Women

Women in later medieval society were in a position not unlike that of the merchants, in that they played a crucial role but without corresponding status. By the late Middle Ages, however, more opportunities existed for women to make their mark in society. In the twelfth century, Hildegard, abbess of Bingen, had been a prolific if eccentric author, expressing a very individual and feminine view of God's creative bounty in nature. In the same period the Beguines, who were a women's movement, created a loosely structured ministry in the service of the sick and the poor. The men who ruled the church, both locally and in the papacy, suspected any lay movement, particularly one formed of uneducated lay women, of bordering on heresy and they did all they could to discourage the Beguines.

In the fourteenth century, women, although excluded from an ecclesiastical office outside a nunnery, could achieve considerable religious influence. The exiled popes in Avignon listened to Saint Catherine of Sienna when she, among others, pleaded with them to return to their traditional see in Rome. Her contemporary, Juliana of Norwich, was a leading figure among the English mystics of the fourteenth century, the rest of whom were men. Her *Revelations*, copied and perhaps edited and distributed by men, showed a definite feminine emphasis in her devotion to Christ's humanity and the bodily aspects of his suffering.

Moral direction of a more conventional and political nature was the life work of Christine de Pisan, who wrote early in the fifteenth century. Christine was French but of Italian extraction. She supported herself by her writing, which enjoyed considerable success due to its appeal to wealthy patrons. For example, she translated and adapted into French for the French king a sequence of moral or political texts which had gained a reputation in Latin. Every so often she wrote tracts of her own that condemned the divided politics of the court. Henry IV of England was so enamoured of her work that he tried to convince her to move across the Channel.

Christine de Pisan was the daughter of an Italian physician. Others born at the top of the political ladder had opportunities for greater influence. Margaret of Anjou, for example, moved from France to England to become Henry VI's queen. Within a year or two of her arrival, even before she had provided her husband with an heir, she was the centre of political influence in her new country. Margaret's prominence was the result of the withdrawn personality of the king and her presence at the English court showed that queens could have real power.

In society at large the individuality of particular women was recorded more often and in more detail than earlier in the Middle Ages. Chaucer's unforgettable vignettes from the end of the fourteenth century depict contrasting types of English women, from the well-mannered prioress to the worldly, wise, and much-married Wife of Bath. Among the Pastons, who were mentioned earlier, there was Margaret, the **matriarch** of the family, who by influencing her husband, sons, and grandsons, was central to the management of her family's business and property affairs. More typical may be Felicia de Whelton who was the heiress to a very small estate close to the centre of England early in the reign of Edward I. Her immediate lord was another woman who held a barony in her own right. Felicia successfully beat off challenges to her father's title to the manor of Whilton after the upheavals of Henry III's reign, and was able to transmit her rights to her own daughter.

Women below the upper class generally achieved greater equality with the men. The patriarchal authority of the man in marriage was never questioned and was reinforced through the teaching of the church and the laws of the age. Regardless of restrictions, women married to peasants or merchants played an active role in their husband's livelihood. In the fields women shared the backbreaking work with the men, and after a husband's death a widow continued to hold the land if there was no adult male heir. Similarly, a merchant's widow continued her husband's business though she was usually excluded from the social life of the guilds. Although the late medieval world remained in many ways a man's world, women were increasingly coming to play a prominent role.

The Church in the Late Middle Ages

The Avignonese Papacy

During the time of Pope Innocent III in the early part of the thirteenth century, the papacy established its authority in spiritual and temporal matters. When, a century later, Pope Boniface VIII (1294–1303) reiterated the church's claims, both Philip IV of France and Edward I of England promptly challenged the power of the church. The collision that occurred was over the kings' claim to tax the clergy. When Boniface decided that taxation of the clergy required his approval, Philip reacted so severely that he broke the spirit of the elderly pope and shattered a tradition of respect and obedience towards the papacy. To avoid a hostile enquiry into the conduct of Boniface, Pope Clement V (1305–1314) agreed to relocate the papal court within easy reach of the French king. The papacy moved to Avignon, where it stayed until 1378. Avignon was on the east bank of the Rhone River, facing the kingdom of France on the opposite bank, where Philip's successors built the castle of St. Andre. The new papal residence at Avignon was more a fortress than the residence of the spiritual leader of Christendom.

As a result of the papacy relocating in Avignon, enemies of France suspected the popes of favouring French interests. Though the facts did not completely support this impression, French ambitions were feared above all in England (France's traditional enemy) as well as in Italy, Germany, and Aragon. Italians continually bemoaned what they called the "Babylonian captivity" and looked for its end with the return of the papacy to Rome. By 1378 the rebellious condition of the Papal States, which had provided a reason for the pope to stay in Avignon, had improved sufficiently for Pope Gregory XI (A.D. 1370–1378) to move the papal court back to Rome. In the seventy years or so since Clement V's election, much had happened to change the character of the papacy besides a prolonged period of residence outside Italy.

The Great Schism

No sooner had Gregory XI returned to Rome in 1378 than he died. The election that followed provided an Italian as his successor, but was quickly challenged as invalid. A second pope was chosen by a dissident group of French cardinals. These cardinals claimed to have been under duress during the first election, as the Roman crowd shouting in the streets and breaking into the election, had terrified them. The pope elected by the dissidents immediately returned to Avignon and there established a separate papal administration in rivalry with Rome. The Spanish rulers alone appear to have made a careful examination of the opposing claims, while other

When Clement VI moved the Papacy to Avignon in 1309, he had a new papal residence built. This fortress-like structure was sumptuously decorated with frescoes of hunting and fishing scenes. This was an unusual theme considering the religious significance of the papal palace.

rulers of Christendom chose sides based on their feelings towards France. France with its allies backed the pope at Avignon, while the enemies of France and neutrals supported the pope at Rome. So began **The Great Schism** in which two popes claimed Christian obedience as the Vicar of Christ. This debate, which left the church with two rival heads, was not resolved until November 1417.

First and foremost this was a problem for the clergy, for the bishops of the church, and the universities which advised them. Above all, since the schism had rapidly become entrenched in national and regional loyalties, it could not be settled until there was sufficient common interest among the leading rulers of Europe. For most of the forty years of the schism much effort was spent trying to negotiate the withdrawal of one of the two popes, or both.

Repeatedly frustrated efforts led the cardinals of both sides to agree upon calling a general council to consider the problem. When a council met at Pisa in 1409, it isolated the two contending popes and elected its own candidate. This compounded the problem as neither of the initial two rivals relinquished their claim, and thus the church was temporarily saddled with three opposing popes. It took another council to remove these three contenders. This was the council that assembled north of the Alps at Constance from 1414–1418.

The Council of Constance

The Council of Constance succeeded in removing the three rivals and elected a pope, Martin V (1417–1431), who was accepted by all parties. As well as restoring unity, the council had been given the task of reforming the church. A number of modifications to the central administration of the church were approved, but no substantial reforms were implemented. The failure to address problems within the church would prove serious a century later when reformers, led by Martin Luther, broke the church apart.

The third task proposed for the Council of Constance was the elimination of heresy. The heresy in question was not as widespread as the movement that had concerned the church around 1200, but it was still linked to calls for reform which authorities within the church would not accept. Typically of the late Middle Ages the movements that were of greatest concern to the church had a distinct national or regional flavour. John Wycliffe (d. 1384) was a teacher at Oxford whose very conservative position in the faculty of theology made him an independent and original thinker. He responded to the Great Schism with a torrent of outspoken works on the nature of the church, attacking the pope's authority and the doctrine of **transubstantiation**. At a late stage in his career he seems also to have found a concern for the spiritual salvation of his readers and listeners, whom he believed to be in jeopardy. Through his sermons and translations from the Bible, and with the help of a handful of disciples, the thrust of some of his very academic arguments had some impact on pious laypeople. Although these people, who were called Lollards (or mumblers), provoked repressive measures in England they were not perceived as a problem for the church at large.

Students from Prague came to Oxford and took home Wycliffe's criticisms and writings. In Bohemia, Wycliffe's doctrines inflamed an established tradition of criticism of the church's hierarchy. During the early 1400s the Bohemian protests were fanned by the fervent preaching of the charismatic Jan (John) Hus. He managed to generate a movement that neither the Czech church nor the monarchy could contain. Hus and the Hussites became the target of the orthodox church and of the Council of Constance. It took armed intervention and a bitter social conflict to bring the Hussites under control of the church.

The Inquisition

The means used by the church for controlling heresy was the **Inquisition**. This was a special office, staffed by **friars** who developed a technique of examination that tended to elicit the answers which the inquisitors sought and which would condemn the accused. It was this abusive aspect of the Inquisition in Spain during the fifteenth century and during the witch-hunts in Germany at the end of the Middle Ages that brought discredit to the office. In Spain the usual targets were converts to Christianity from Islam or the Jewish faith and who had maintained or returned to their old faith and its ways. The examination of Joan of Arc after her capture was typical of inquisitorial procedure. Relentless interrogation by skilled questioners finally forced her to admit to the offences of which she was accused. For the inquisitor the eternal salvation open to a confessed and repentant heretic was more important than the pain of the examination and the punishment of being burned at the stake.

The people of the later Middle Ages were not any less attached to their religious faith than earlier periods, and in fact there was probably a better understanding of its meaning. There was, however, much less sense of a common purpose and more mutual suspicion and disrespect between the common lay members of the church and the clergy who controlled. As the fifteenth century gave way to the sixteenth century there was a growing number of people who were listening to the reformers who would lead the Protestant Reformation.

Society and Government

Throughout Europe during the late Middle Ages war was as much a principal activity between organized communities as it had been between the disorganized communities in the Dark Ages and in the feudal principalities of the High Middle Ages. War generally was the business of the aristocracy and for this reason political and social life in late medieval Europe continued to be dominated by the nobility.

The point of this statement is to emphasize that a country's government reflected the structure of its society. Since institutions varied from country to country, generalizations about them can be misleading. Yet there is no doubt that in Europe at the end of the Middle Ages the aristocracy were still dominant in society, politics, and government as they had been from the start. Society also continued to be violent. Tempers were short, and because weapons were easy to obtain, quarrels were often settled by force. When reading court records of the fifteenth century it might seem that there had been little improvement since the time of the Viking raids. At the same time there is plenty of evidence that suggests much greater efforts were being made to impose central authority.

Local Officials

In England, the sheriff retained a prominent position as the link between the local community and the national community. Their function, however, had become more a channel of communication between the local community and the seat of royal government at Westminster in London than that of the universal executive, which they had been in the twelfth century. The old tasks in tax collection, in justice, and in the supervision of the county's military resources were now carried out by other officials. Local gentry, accompanied by clerks, undertook the tasks of government. The justices of the peace were typical of such officials, and their survival to this day is a sign of their effectiveness. Their origins in the middle of the fourteenth century lay in a variety of commissions, as a result of which they relieved the central government of concern for the numerous petty crimes. The justices of the peace were often guilty of enforcing the interests of their propertied class, the gentry, but nonetheless they provided an influential lobby for royal interest in the local community.

Parliament

The use of an elected representative body, such as Parliament or Congress, has become the core of democratic governments in the western world. Parliamentary government, which originated in England during the Middle Ages, was not a bold departure from the past but instead was an adaptation based on existing institutions and practices. Edward I, throughout his reign, established the routine of summoning representatives of the communities of England to join the periodic parliaments usually at Westminster and by doing so was making sensible use of resources at hand. Earlier events had shown ways to put pressure on the central government. For example, in 1215, disgruntled barons had been able to force King John to sign the famous Magna Carta. This document placed limits on the monarch's powers. England was not unique. Governments in all countries needed popular support to balance the forces that opposed them. The only theories concerning the practice of representation came later from the church, as it learned from the consultative councils during the time of the Great Schism.

The development of the English parliament was not unparalleled. French estates, German diets, and Argonese cortes met less frequently, but they all began to be called upon in the same general period. All these consultative bodies depended on basic practicalities for their operation. There had to be a means for summoning their members. Those members had to have the means to travel to the assembly, including assurances of security. To serve a useful purpose they had to be confident that they would be listened to and would be given some responsibility in the decisions that they brought back to their communities.

A comparison of these institutions will show that, though the English parliament was far from unique, it had certain distinctive features that contributed to its endurance. It met in two unequal groups: the Lords, who were less numerous; and the ***Commons***, who, though greater in number had less power. It was possible for the two bodies to exchange views, but ordinarily Lords and Commons met separately although at the same time. The Lords themselves comprised two groups who met together: the lords temporal and lords spiritual. The first group was comprised of the leading nobles of the realm while the second was made up of bishops and important abbots. In the Middle Ages the Lords and Commons were not known as "Houses," and the Lords were

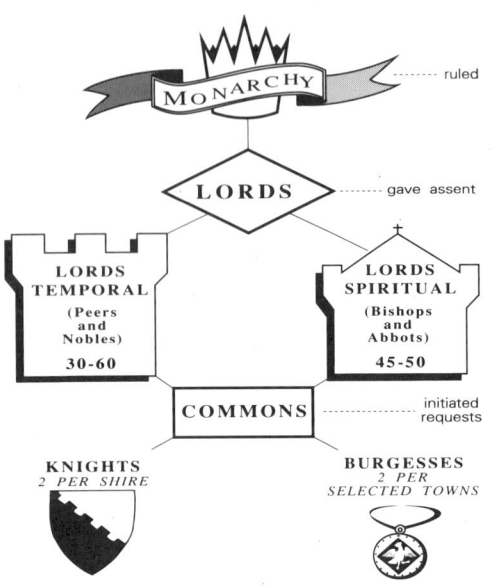

Parliamentary Government of Medieval England

English parliamentary government, which evolved during the late Middle Ages, laid the foundation for our modern parliamentary system. The workings of medieval parliamentary government can best be explained by the phrase "the monarch rules with the assent of the lords and at the request of the commons." What this meant was that the commons, or those representing the people, petitioned or asked for laws to be passed; for the request to be granted required the assent of the lords, who would then advise the monarch. Of course the King or Queen had the perrogative to reject the advice of the lords, thereby maintaining ultimate authority. Obviously our system of government has changed a great deal—or has it? What elements of medieval, parliamentary government are retained to this day? What parallels do you see? Be sure to consider both the theory and practice of our government. For example, who still has tultimate authority? Where are laws initiated? Who can block laws?

distinguished from the Commons by the fact that each lord was sent an individual summons to attend parliament. The individual summons reflected the Lords' regular association with the king, which in turn reflected their wealth and territorial power. The numbers of temporal lords attending Parliament before 1500 varied between 30 and 60 and there were 45 to 50 spiritual lords, although not all came to every parliament. The Commons, on the other hand, were representatives and were summoned by an order to each sheriff to elect two knights in his county court and two **burgesses** from each designated town. Despite the fact that there were more than twice as many burgesses elected as knights, they remained subordinate to the 74 elected knights. The English parliament was peculiar because the landholding aristocracy was represented in the Lords and in the Commons. The greatest landholders, the nobles or barons, sat in the Lords. The lesser landholders were elected to the Commons as knights of the shire, where they mingled with the non-aristocratic element from the towns. In the late Middle Ages the Lords formed a restricted group of peers, but the lesser aristocracy of knights and gentry had close associations, socially and in parliament, with the groups above and below them. This enabled England to avoid the social polarization that was common throughout Europe.

Framing and passing laws was one of the functions of parliament. Towards the end of the fourteenth century a growing proportion of English legislation arose from petitions generated by the Commons. Commons' petitions kept the king informed of the concerns of his subjects, at least of the politically influential subjects. In exchange, the representatives of the Commons carried an explanation of the king's needs back to their constituents. During the Hundred Years' War the king's chief need was for money to pay for his soldiers and ships. Thus, an agreement to a parliamentary subsidy, which was a tax on movable wealth, was a chief function of parliament. In

1407 the Commons won the recognition that the declaration of the agreement to a subsidy should come first from their Speaker who, before 1500, was chosen from the knights of the shire. Taxation was always something of an exception, however, to the usual relation between the Lords and the Commons. In most other respects the medieval Commons took their lead from the Lords who were their social leaders and in many cases their immediate superiors. Lords were also born into a position of political leadership.

The medieval English parliament was the king's parliament. It met only when the king summoned parliament to deal with business that he or his ministers brought up. Parliament in England met for several weeks each year in times of difficulty and generally was a more constant part of royal government than the representative assemblies in other countries. In France, the size of the country made the Estates-General (equivalent to the English parliament) a more unwieldy body which only met on an infrequent basis. Meetings of provincial estates had a greater coherence and were more effective but were only summoned by the French king when he was driven to acknowledge the need for a broader basis of support. In Germany the Diet, which was an assembly of princes rather than a truly representative body, was called only when the ruler of the kingdom saw the chance of using it to improve national unity, which Germans found so elusive. Finally, the Cortes in Spain met by estates as in France, and in Aragon the nobles were divided into higher and lower to make four estates rather than three.

The New Monarchy

Although representative assemblies had a part in late medieval government, which they had not held earlier, the late fifteenth century remained an age of monarchies not of representative institutions. The term "new monarchy" has been coined to convey the late medieval, early modern idea that the fortunes of the people were closely connected with the interests of the monarchy and were not to be swayed by a self-interested nobility. Discontented nobles had disrupted royal rule in England under Richard II and during the Wars of the Roses, in France under Charles VI, and in Germany throughout the fifteenth century. The dominant instrument of the "new monarchy" was the king's council; there the king's wishes were paramount. Even if chosen nobles were on the council, they shared power with men from the lesser nobility and the professional class, and none of them could seriously challenge the will of the monarch.

Following the Wars of the Roses, which ended in 1485 with the triumph of Henry Tudor over King Richard III, the new king strengthened the English throne by employing the best fiscal and administrative measures of his predecessors. The end of the Hundred Years' War, earlier in the same century, had made it easier for English monarchs to live off their own revenues and not to have to rely on Parliament for taxes. The French also benefited from the absence of war. Similarly in Spain the union of the crowns of Castile and Aragon in 1474 followed closely on the heels of the marriage of **Isabella** of Castile and **Ferdinand** of Aragon. Political unity was aided by the wealth of riches that poured into Spain from its overseas empire. The unity and wealth of the late fifteenth century Spanish monarchy helped to consolidate its power.

Towards a New Age

By the beginning of the sixteenth century a balance of power was taking shape in Europe. Yet around 1500 the concepts of state and nation were still ambiguous. The legacy of long wars, different institutional traditions, divergent economic interests, and most obviously the advance of **vernacular** languages shared by all classes of a country, had done much to promote national consolidation. On the other hand, allegiance to a single faith and church, common cultural values, and the international chivalry that still prevailed among dominant aristocracies meant that nationalism was not the major force that it would later become. Policy was still dictated by dynastic interest. It was the security of the royal house and the advance of the ruling family that decided a country's policies. If the interest of the state or nation were involved they were secondary to the needs of the ruling family. The era that followed the fifteenth century was governed by the rivalry of the Hapsburgs, ruling Spain, the German Empire, and the Low Countries, and the Valois House of France.

The emergence of power politics and religious divisions, which characterized the sixteenth century, was indicative of the fading ideals of medieval Europe. The wars of the Middle Ages had been wars of survival, to defend rights, but rarely to secure territorial advantage and never to secure power as an end in itself. Despite the deep distrust between Orthodox and Catholic, Christians throughout Europe held a common faith and recognized a common heritage of belief and church order. All classes accepted the existing social order. It is the unity of European Christendom that distinguishes the Middle Ages from the Ancient World and the Modern Period.

Suggested Sources for Further Research

Gies, Joseph and Frances, *Life in a Medieval Village* (Harper and Row Publishers, 1990).

Gies, Joseph and Frances, *Life in a Medieval Castle* (Harper and Row Publishers, 1974).

Gies, Joseph and Frances, *Women in the Middle Ages* (Harper and Row Publishers, 1978).

Hibbert, Christopher, *The English: A Social History* (W.W. Norton & Co., 1987).

Hollister, C. Warren, *Medieval Europe: A Short History* (McGraw-Hill Pub., 1990).

Holmes, George, *The Oxford Illustrated History of Medieval Europe* (Oxford University, 1988).

Huizinga, J., *The Waning of the Middle Ages* (St. Martin's Press, 1924).

Matthew, Donald, *Atlas of Medieval Europe* (Facts on File, 1983).

Morgan, Gwyneth, *Life in a Medieval Village* (Cambridge University Press, 1975).

Morgan, Kenneth, *The Oxford Illustrated History of Britain* (Oxford University Press, 1984).

Myers, A.R., *England in the Late Middle Ages* (Penguin Books, 1971).

Power, Eileen, *Medieval Women* (Cambridge University Press, 1975).

Seward, Desmond, *The Hundred Years War* (Atheneum, 1978).

Trevelyan, G.M., *Illustrated English Social History: 2* (Penguin Books Ltd., 1960).

Tuchman, Barbara, *A Distant Mirror* (Alfred A. Knopf, 1978).

Watson, Percy, *Building the Medieval Cathedrals* (Cambridge University Press, 1990).

Wood, Michael, *In Search of the Dark Ages* (Facts on File, 1987).

Focus Your Knowledge

1. Outline the causes of the Hundred Years' War and explain how the direction of the war was determined by the interests of different monarchs.
2. Describe the causes and symptoms of the bubonic plague.
3. Compare the effectiveness of the longbow to the crossbow.
4. What contribution did Joan of Arc make to the Hundred Years' War? Why was she burned at the stake?
5. Prepare a chart that illustrates the social classes of the late Middle Ages. Be sure to clearly explain the rise of the middle class.
6. Describe the role played by women in the late Middle Ages. Had their role altered significantly from earlier periods?

Apply Your Knowledge

1. What elements exist in our system of government that are derived from the parliamentary system of fourteenth century England? Compare the role of the monarch and the upper and lower houses.
2. The loss of lives resulting from the Black Death profoundly altered the society of medieval Europe. Describe the changes that occurred and assess the positive or negative impact these had on society.
3. To what degree was the Hundred Years' War the product of developing national monarchies? What effects did the war have on England and France?

4. The fourteenth century was a century of change throughout Europe. Assess the social, economic, and demographic changes that occurred in Europe during this century.

5. Comment briefly on the role of women in the male-dominated medieval society. How would you respond to a historian who claimed that the woman's lack of power means the study of women in medieval Europe is unimportant?

6. How did the Great Schism divide Christendom and with what degree of success was the Council of Constance able to mend divisions?

7. Describe various levels of government in medieval England. To what degree was this a democratic government?

Extension Activities

1. In groups, prepare a special edition newspaper covering the Black Death. Articles could include accounts of the deaths, descriptions of cures, eye witness reports from citizens, reports from doctors, priests, and prominent citizens. Include advertisements as well.

2. Choose one of the significant battles of the Hundred Years' War and do a recreation. This might include work on Bristol board, a video, a staged battle outside, or animation. Your research should focus on the impact of weapons, personalities, and strategies on the outcome of the battle chosen.

3. As a class project prepare and host a medieval banquet. Groups of students should be responsible for such activities as: recreating the banquet hall, entertainments, table settings and decorations, clothing, food, and etiquette.

4. Choose a character who has particularly appealed to you in this chapter. Research this character and prepare a biographical sketch. The results of your research could be presented by a portrayal of this character on video, in a taped interview, or in a class skit.

CHAPTER 17

The Foundations of Early Modern Europe

Chapter Highlights

- the Italian Renaissance

- the ideal individual of the Renaissance

- the genius of Leonardo da Vinci

- what caused Christendom to splinter and divide

- the role of Martin Luther, Ulrich Zwingli, and John Calvin in directing the course of history

In the two and a half centuries from 1350 to 1600 Europe was radically transformed. During this period three major occurrences combined to hurdle Europe from its medieval past: the **Renaissance** redefined learning and Europe's view of the world; the **Reformation** divided Christendom; and the emergence of a capitalist world economy provided the impetus for Europeans to explore and colonize new lands. The changes wrought by these movements would ultimately transform not only Europe, but the entire world. By 1600, Europeans were exporting their manufactured goods, their religion, and their culture to all corners of the world. In return they were receiving a vast array of raw materials, new foods, and sources of cheap labour.

The fifteenth and sixteenth centuries undoubtedly marked an epoch for Europe as it moved from medieval to modern times. The changes were evident in virtually all aspects of life, from government and religion to art and education. While Christianity remained central to the lives of many it became fused with classical ideas leading to an explosion of artistic and intellectual achievements. Advances in science and technology allowed for the dissemination of knowledge and ideas. At the same time, major changes in economic systems reshaped social divisions, led to a rise in towns, and provided the stimulus for the building of global empires.

Key Concepts

Renaissance

Reformation

humanism

David

indulgences

Luther's 95 theses

Counter-Reformation

Jesuits

The Renaissance

It is difficult to define the Renaissance in terms of a specific time period, as it overlaps both the late Middle Ages and the Reformation; although it is generally regarded as the period from approximately 1350 to 1550. It is more useful to define the Renaissance by the changes in attitudes and ideas and the resulting artistic changes and intellectual achievements that occurred.

Before proceeding further it is imperative that the term renaissance be clearly defined. Literally, "renaissance" means revival or rebirth and is most often used in relation to culture and learning. During the period known as the European Renaissance, for example, there was a renewed focus on the writers from antiquity, such as Plato, Aristotle, and Cicero whose works were being studied in their original forms. Graeco-Roman culture, which is referred to as classical, came to the fore during the Renaissance. Throughout the Middle Ages classical ideas and art forms were rejected as pagan while the absolute authority of God and the church was emphasized. By the end of the fourteenth century a renewed interest in classical art, ideas, and the works of ancient writers was laying the foundations for a revival of classical culture in Italy. Along with the rebirth of classicism came a renewed focus on the study of humans and human achievements. In the end classical ideas became fused with Christianity producing new and exciting ideas and works of art.

The Emergence of the Renaissance

The 1300s have been aptly described by historian Barbara Tuchman as "the calamitous, 14th century." As noted in Chapter 16, this was a century dominated by famine, disease, and war. Throughout Europe, people, weakened by the recurring crop failures, were devastated by the onslaught of the Black Death in 1348. Further heightening the miseries of the population in the fourteenth and early fifteenth centuries was the Hundred Years' War lasting from 1337 to 1453. It is no wonder that the period from 1300 to 1450 was an age of pessimism; an age when people began to lose faith in established institutions. It was from this age of pessimism and misery that the Renaissance emerged.

There is no doubt that Italy, and in particular northern Italy, was the origin of the Renaissance. Why was Italy home to the greatest cultural revival of the fifteenth century? Certainly other areas such as France and the Holy Roman Empire had led Europe in terms of wealth and power throughout the Middle Ages. To fully understand Italy's emergence as the leading cultural and intellectual centre of Europe, it is first necessary to understand the society from which the Renaissance sprang.

Perhaps the most obvious reason a revival of classical ideas occurred in Italy first is that the traditions of the Italians were inextricably tied to the achievements of ancient Rome. Throughout much of the medieval period Italy played a less significant role than the kingdoms of northern Europe. One must remember, however, that much of the cultural tradition of the Middle Ages was Gothic and Italy's roots were not Gothic. If any nation was going to lead a revival in classical culture then Italy would be that nation.

A vital factor in the success of the Renaissance was the peace and stability of the second half of the fifteenth century. This stability resulted from the Treaty of Lodi, which was signed in 1454 by the three most important cities of northern Italy: Milan, Venice, and Florence and later by Naples and the papal states. The treaty, which lasted until 1494, allowed Italian culture to flourish as the resources of the people were poured into the arts and civic projects rather than costly wars.

Cities. The feature that most distinguished Italy from its European counterparts in the fourteenth and fifteenth centuries was the degree of urbanization. By the late fourteenth century, a significant percentage of the population in northern Italy lived in urban centres whereas only a marginal number of the English population lived in cities at this time. Furthermore, the cities of northern Italy were relatively large, many of them exceeding 100 000 inhabitants. This urban concentration affected Italian culture in many ways. Unlike the agriculturally based economies of northern Europe, many Italians relied on urban industries and commercial trade. The secularization of education that occurred during the Renaissance stemmed from the needs of an urban society, as the diversity of urban occupations required a greater degree of training than was needed in agriculture. Many Italian cities established publicly supported schools in response to this need. Finally, the political organization of the city-states allowed for active participation of the citizenry.

The Middle Class. Traditionally in Europe the nobility was comprised of large landowners whose income was derived from renting out their land. In

Italy, following the Black Death, a new nobility of the city began to emerge. These people, called the patriciate, made the middle class way of life, that being trade and commerce, the ideal. For the new aristocracy of the Italian city-states wealth, carefully arranged marriages and active participation in civic affairs were the keys to power and prestige. It was these wealthy merchants and tradespeople who not only became rulers of the Italian cities, with the exception of Rome, but also the patrons of the arts and learning. Free from the pretentious traditions of the "Old Nobility," the patriciates encouraged the new trends in art, literature, and philosophy.

The Italian City-States

Florence. In many ways, Florence is synonymous with the Renaissance. On a leisurely stroll through modern-day Florence visitors experience the grandeur and majesty of the Cathedral, the Pitti palace, the Ponte Vecchio, and a host of other sites, all of which are a lasting testimony to the greatness of Renaissance Florence. Its stature as the leading cultural and intellectual centre of the late fifteenth century is also reflected in the names of the people who made Florence their home: Francesco Petrarch, Filippo Brunelleschi, Lorenzo de Medici, Sandro Botticelli, Michelangelo Buonarroti, and Niccolo Machiavelli were but a few of the Florentines whose genius contributed to establishing their city as the home of the Renaissance.

Renaissance Florence, with its economy rooted in trade and banking, was the richest and fourth largest city of Italy. By placing a tax on income the municipal government was able to construct impressive buildings such as the Palazzo Vecchio, to house the government, and the Ponte Vecchio, which still spans the Arno River. Most impressive of all was the new Duomo cathedral with its soaring dome and its stunning marble exterior.

During the latter half of the fourteenth century, repeated disasters befell Florence. In 1348 Florence lost perhaps as many as 45 000 of its 90 000 inhabitants to the Black Death. Compounding Florence's woes were the repeated famines that struck in 1352–1353, 1369–1370, and 1373–1375. The recurring

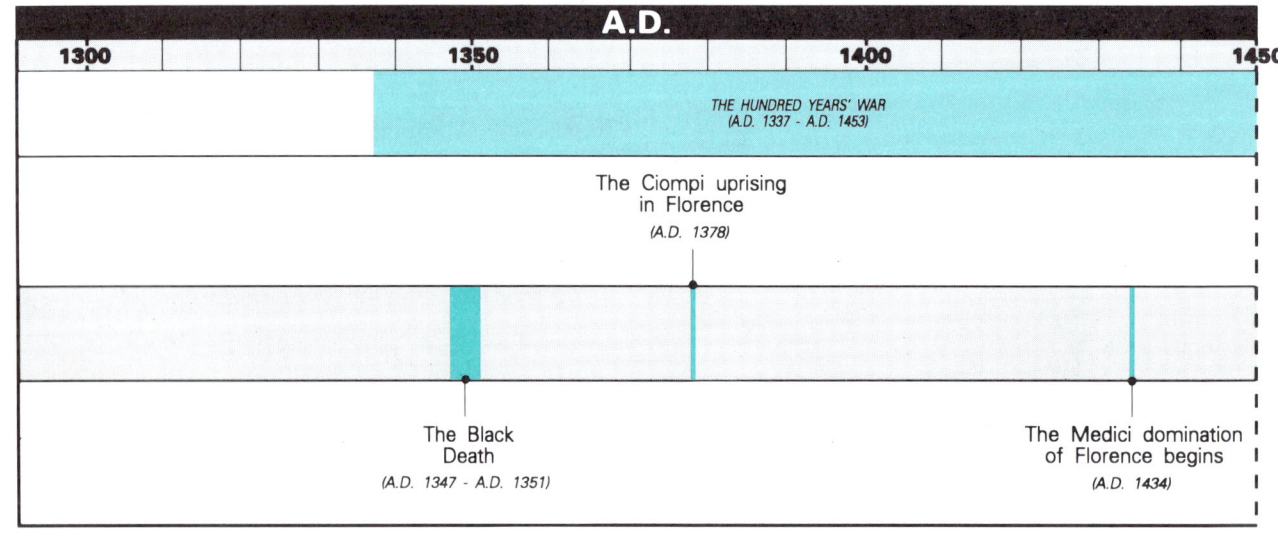

MAJOR EVENTS IN EUROPEAN HISTORY: A.D. 1304 - A.D. 1588

disasters culminated in the Ciompi revolt of 1378. The Ciompi revolt was an uprising of the poor in an attempt to gain rights for the unorganized workers, and to establish a fair judicial system and equitable tax laws. The Ciompi captured the Palazzo Vecchio in July, 1378 and held it for one month. Then, in August the building was stormed and all members of the Ciompi were captured and hung from the windows of the Palace. The end result of the uprising was the further restriction of democracy and the emergence of a few powerful ruling families.

In 1434 Cosimo de Medici was appointed the head of the Florentine government. For the next three centuries the Medici family would dominate Florentine politics. The Medicis, although part of the aristocracy of Florence, were favoured by the commoners ever since Salvestro de Medici had supported the Ciompi revolt. The incredible wealth of the Medicis, gained through banking and trade, much of which was done with the papacy, also contributed to their power and influence. Financial records from the mid-fifteenth century clearly show that the Medicis were by far the wealthiest family in Florence. Aside from the dominant role he played in Florentine politics, Cosimo was also a patron of the arts and literature. The stability he brought to Florence, coupled with the financial support he gave to many Renaissance artists and writers, was crucial to the leading role Florence would play in the Renaissance.

Florence reached its zenith under the guidance of Cosimo's grandson, Lorenzo de Medici (the Magnificent). Lorenzo managed to provide continued stability for Florence and in fact expanded its influence and control through much of Tuscany. Like his grandfather, Lorenzo was a great patron of the arts and sponsored artists such as Ghirlandaio, Botticelli, and the young Michelangelo. He also sponsored poets such as Pulci and Politian and the philosopher Marsilio Ficino, and was known for his own vernacular poetry. When he died in 1492, Lorenzo left the family fortunes in decline due to his neglect and preoccupation with politics. Even more damaging, he left Florence in the hands of his incompetent son, Piero.

When Charles VIII of France attacked Naples,

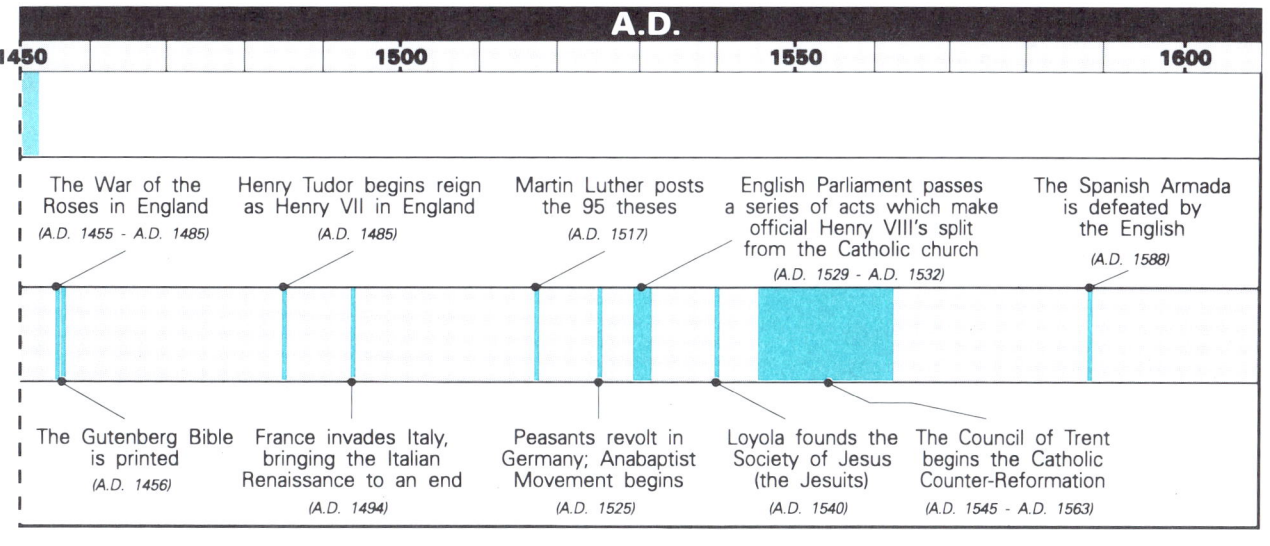

No city has better retained the essence of Renaissance than Florence. This panorama of the day shows several historical landmarks. To the left is the Ponte Vecchio, perhaps the most famous bridge in Europe. Moving to the right, the first tower one sees is the town hall or the Signoria. In the centre of the picture is the Florentine cathedral, crowned by Brunelleschis's famous dome. On the extreme right is the medieval church of Santa Croce where Michelangelo is buried.

Piero ignored the traditional friendship between France and Florence and sided with Naples. This incurred the wrath of Charles VIII who turned on Florence and threatened to attack the city. Piero then begged forgiveness and ceded Florentine territories including Pisa to placate the French. This earned him the hatred of all of Florence and he was driven from office by an angry crowd. Thus ended the first period of Medici rule and began the period of foreign domination in Italy.

The period of peace and stability brought by the Treaty of Lodi, which had allowed for the vitality of the High Renaissance, was drawing to a close. Ultimately, the French would be driven out by an alliance between Spain and Florence. In allying themselves with Spain, the Florentines had not found a liberator but had simply replaced one dominating power with another. By 1525 Spain was in control of much of Italy and the Italian Renaissance was nearly over.

Humanism

Underlying all that defined the Renaissance was **humanism**. The humanists were primarily concerned with humaniora or the humane studies and thus embraced the liberal arts, which included grammar, rhetoric, poetry, history, and moral philosophy. In many ways the early humanists, who were the teachers of the liberal arts, carried on a medieval tradition of the professional teachers or dictators. The way in which the humanists differed from their medieval predecessors was in their close adherence to the classical models studied. They were not only interested in antiquity but sought to relate it to the present. For the Renaissance humanists the study of the ancients provided them with classical forms of thought as well as new norms by which to judge one's thoughts and deeds. It was the humanist's love of classical ideas and their focus on the earthly actions and concerns of humans that clearly set them apart from the medieval philosophers.

Petrarch. Francesco Petrarch (1304–1374), is considered the first humanist and consequently is an important figure in the transition from the medieval period to the Renaissance. Both his education and his relationship with the church reflect his dual nature, as a man of both the Renaissance and medieval Europe. Although Petrarch studied for seven years in preparation for a career in law he never found it a satisfying challenge. Instead his interest drifted towards the study of classical literature. In 1326 Petrarch moved to Avignon where he benefited from the patronage of various high-ranking church officials and in fact took minor orders, although he was never ordained a priest. On April 26, 1327 Petrarch first laid eyes on a woman whom we know only as Laura. He was so struck by her beauty and grace that he immediately fell deeply in love with her and she became the focus of his poetry. As Laura was married Petrarch was only able to adore her from a distance and to immortalize her in the 400 sonnets he wrote in her honour. Alas, Laura fell victim to the Black Death in 1348 and Petrarch was left only the hope of a heavenly reunion.

In many ways Petrarch was the first to move in a new direction. The earthly love of women was, to Petrarch, to be encouraged for he felt it would lead you to love God as the creator of women. He also questioned the value of the contemplative life led by monastic orders, believing that members of the clergy were more useful working in society to save souls. Petrarch's most significant break with medieval attitudes and ideas was his emphasis on life on earth and the stress on an active life. In many of his poems Petrarch accentuates the virtues of earthly, physical love and emphasizes how to live on this earth. Petrarch was the first to reject many medieval ideas and open the door for later Renaissance writers. He provided the important connection between the medieval and Renaissance mentality.

Niccolo Machiavelli. Of all the literary works written during the Renaissance none was, or has been, as controversial as Niccolo Machiavelli's *The Prince*. This short work, intended as a guide for governing, shocked many by its pragmatic approach, which emphasized that the end justifies the means. The Renaissance humanists ushered in a new concept of the nature of humanity and placed a new emphasis on the works of the ancients, which had been shunned throughout the Middle Ages. Machiavelli's *The Prince*, while having little in common with the literature of the Middle Ages, was in many ways a departure from the works of his contemporary humanists. Rather than focusing on the essential goodness of humanity Machiavelli stressed the need for a ruler to act pragmatically to succeed in government. For example, *The Prince* clearly states that it is better to be miserly rather than incur a large debt by the government.

Although Machiavelli's pragmatic views often contrasted sharply with the idealistic views of earlier humanists there is no doubt he was a product of the Renaissance; in presenting his ideas Machiavelli drew heavily on the works of ancient writers and throughout his life Machiavelli worked for the city of Florence. He was greatly troubled by the turmoil created by the divisions within the city and the upheaval caused by the invasions that occurred at the beginning of the sixteenth century. It was Machiavelli's firm belief that a strong ruler was necessary to Florence if the city was to rise above the problems that plagued it.

Machiavelli's notion of an ideal ruler was someone who realized what must be done to unite the people under a single rule, and then carry out the necessary actions to establish themselves firmly as the head of state. Machiavelli's ideal ruler, as outlined in *The Prince*, was to be neither an aloof idealist, nor a power-hungry autocrat only after personal glory. Machiavelli believed a ruler should be ruthless only when it was necessary to unite and preserve the state. There is no doubt that Machiavelli adopted an amoral stance in his political philosophy. Perhaps he is best remembered for the phrase "the end justifies the means." Machiavelli certainly advocated ruthlessness and deception if it was necessary to effectively manage a state, and cautioned rulers that it is better to be feared than loved. Yet, despite this apparent cynicism, Machiavelli's essential goals were similar to earlier civic humanists: the glory, unity, and perfection of the state.

Renaissance Art and Architecture

The rise of new ideas is often reflected in the art and architecture of a culture. During the Renaissance, the ideas of Petrarch and the civic humanists found expression in the works of the great artists of the age. A hallmark of the Renaissance was the resurgence of fountains and immaculate gardens to adorn the grounds of the wealthy. Formal gardens such as those at the Pitti Palace in Florence were later copied by Louis XIV in his construction of Versailles.

Similarly, Renaissance art rejected the conventions of the Middle Ages choosing instead to glorify humans. In the Middle Ages people were purposefully dwarfed by religious figures to show the insignificance of humanity. The humanists, with their emphasis on the individual and the accomplishments of individuals, placed humans at the centre of the universe. Portraiture, seen as vain in the Middle Ages, became very popular in the Renaissance. Perspective was also rediscovered, allowing artists to make their paintings highly realistic. By adding windows to their paintings artists were able to give their pictures depth, moving away from the flat, two dimensional works of the Middle Ages. Finally, the influence of classical antiquity can be seen in the rebirth of nudes, as the Renaissance artists began to focus on the ideal human form and the perfectibility of humans rather than their imperfections.

Renaissance Architecture. The greatest achievement of fifteenth-century Florence was the completion of the Duomo (Cathedral). By 1400 the Duomo was complete except for the massive dome. Traditional methods were not sufficient to span the 42 m and none of the architects working on the Duomo could solve this architectural problem. Filippo Brunelleschi managed to solve the dilemma in a typically Renaissance fashion: he looked to the ancients for his answer. By closely studying the Pantheon in Rome, Brunelleschi learned the Romans' method of spanning such a wide area and was able to submit a workable plan in 1417. Once his plan was approved, Brunelleschi began his daunting task under the watchful eye of the Florentine crowds. As the dome took shape the population watched with a mixture of awe, disbelief, curiosity, and scepticism. In the end Brunelleschi's dome made the Duomo the most lasting and dominant feature of the Florentine skyline. The Duomo was truly a transitional building as its scale made it medieval, but the construction of the dome had boldly set a new standard and direction for architecture.

The civic pride of the Renaissance was also reflected in the changes in architecture. The haphazard and unplanned streets of medieval Europe were no longer seen as adequate, instead urban planning was stressed with an emphasis on efficient human-oriented cities. In most cases the idealistic plans were never implemented due to the exorbitant costs. The Renaissance also brought a renewed emphasis on the homes of individuals. The stability of the High Renaissance allowed leading merchants, bankers, and others to build impressive palazzos, which were quite unlike the traditional fortress-like structures of earlier centuries. Palazzos such as the Pitti Palace in Florence or the Doge's Palace in Venice reflected the wealth and power of the new urban aristocracy as well as the source of their wealth; the ground floor of these impressive structures often served as a storefront for the family business. The three-tier design of these palaces was a mark of the Renaissance, as was the use of Greek columns and sculpture in their design. Impressive though they were, the palazzos were not overwhelmingly opulent as the Gothic architecture had been. The construction of these large new homes for the patriciate was a boon for artists as it generated a great demand for works of art. The patriciates became the leading patrons of the arts, commissioning leading sculptors and painters to produce works for their homes.

Painting and Sculpture. During the Renaissance artists were equivalent in stature to artisans such as leather workers; in other words, because they worked with their hands they were considered lower middle class, and well beneath the aristocracy who employed them. The artists received their training as apprentices in workshops that produced paintings, sculptures, and other works of art on a commission. Initially, these commissions came mainly from churches, however, as a wealthy middle class emerged merchants and bankers became important patrons of the arts. Throughout the Renaissance art remained primarily religious although the secular influence is apparent in the move towards naturalism.

One of the most renowned artists of the mid-fifteenth century was Sandro Botticelli (1444–1510). Botticelli was a favourite artist of the Medici family and thus enjoyed their patronage; both *Spring (Primavara)*, painted in 1478, and *Birth of Venus*, completed after 1482 were done for the Medici. *Birth of Venus* was one of the first female nudes of the Renaissance and depicts the goddess of love emerging from the sea on a shell. The painting combines medieval mysticism, a pagan allegory, and Renaissance naturalism to produce an enchanting picture.

Sculptures were also heavily influenced by a renewed interest in classical works as well as a move towards naturalism. Two of the great sculptors of the fifteenth century were Lorenzo Ghiberti and Donato Bardi (Donatello). Ghiberti's (1378–1455) fame and lifelong work were the Bronze doors he sculpted for the Baptistery in Florence. The bronze panels sculpted by Ghiberti, over a period of fifty years, depicted scenes from the Old Testament and once completed the two doors were among the most famous and costly works of their time. The realism and clarity Ghiberti managed to achieve is startling. The panels, no more than half an inch deep clearly depict foregrounds and backgrounds and set the standard in bronze work for centuries to come.

The undisputed master of sculpture throughout the first half of the fifteenth century was Donatello (1386–1466). Donatello worked with both Ghiberti and Brunelleschi, studying the Roman statues at the Pantheon, while Brunelleschi studied its dome. His careful study of human anatomy allowed him to accurately portray the human body in a variety of poses. Donatello's most famous work is his bronze sculpture *David*, completed about 1430. It was the first nude sculpture of the Renaissance and the first life-size sculpture of modern Europe. Donatello's *David* is a slender youth who appears quiet and meditative, and is relaxed with one foot resting triumphantly on the head of Goliath. In this sculpture

Donatello's appreciation of antiquity and his knowledge of human anatomy were blended to create a work that redefined sculpture in the Renaissance.

Leonardo da Vinci. During the Renaissance the ideal individual was one who was well rounded in all their abilities. No individual fulfilled the ideal of the "universal man" better than Leonardo da Vinci (1452–1519). He was a gifted painter, sculptor, and engineer with an interest in anatomy, geology, mathematics, and botany. Leonardo was also gifted with horses, a genial courtier, and a superb organizer of fetes and celebrations.

Leonardo is best remembered for his paintings of which, ironically, few survive. Of those that have survived almost all are unfinished, damaged, altered, or are decaying. The disastrous state of the works of Leonardo is in large part due to two facets of his character; his willingness to experiment, and his perfectionism. Many of the technical experiments tried by Leonardo proved disastrous for the preservation of his art while his perfectionism led him to set aside tasks for years, often never returning to those he felt he could not complete to his satisfaction. *The Last Supper*, considered a masterpiece, made Leonardo famous in his own time. In this painting Leonardo captured the moment at which Jesus had just announced that one of his disciples will betray him. Unfortunately Leonardo's reputation was somewhat damaged by his experiment with a new approach to frescoes. Instead of using plaster, which dries quickly, Leonardo tried using a clay base that allowed him to achieve fine details. The experiment failed, as the paint became discoloured and cracked and peeled off the clay.

The most famous of Leonardo's paintings, and arguably the most famous painting in the western world is the *Mona Lisa*. Francesco del Giocondo, a wealthy Florentine merchant, commissioned Leonardo to do a portrait of his wife, Madonna Lisa Gherhaedini. After spending four years on the paint-

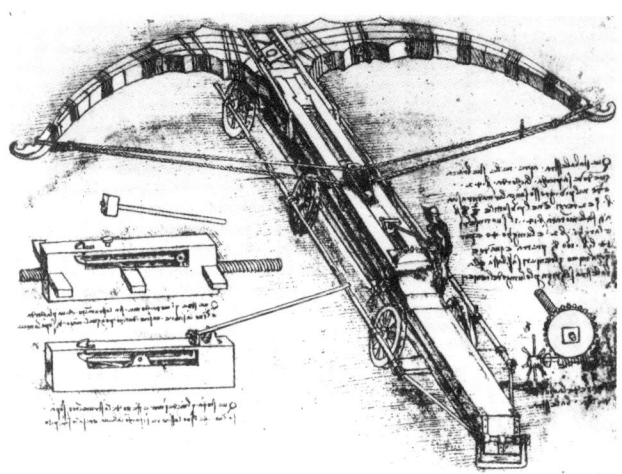

Leonardo da Vinci best exemplifies the concepts of Renaissance man. Although most famous for the Mona Lisa and The Last Supper, he was also a great sculptor, writer, and inventor. This illustration of Leonardo's giant crossbow is somewhat impractical for the times, but does reflect the genius of his mind.

ing Leonardo decided not to part with it and instead took it to France when he moved there. The most famous element of the painting is the model's mysterious smile, which has been described as "more divine than human." The background is typical of many of Leonardo's paintings, with misty landscapes and towering rocks adding a romantic element to the picture.

One of Leonardo's personal passions was the study of human anatomy. He endeavoured to understand the human body and spent endless hours dissecting corpses, and making meticulous notes and superbly accurate drawings. In his notebooks, which ran to thousands of pages, Leonardo recorded detailed sketches of bone structure, muscles, and anatomical drawings of the human torso, as well as the anatomy of animals and a brilliant treatise on water. These notebooks represent Leonardo's greatest contribution to science, but his reluctance to put his energies into the uncreative work of organizing his notes prevented their publication. Consequently much of his work remained unfinished and unknown for centuries.

Another of Leonardo's great passions was the study and design of military and civil machinery. Among the detailed drawings found in his voluminous notebooks are giant crossbows, flying machines resembling helicopters, chariots armed with flails, and sketches of submarines. Leonardo even went so far as to recommend himself to Duke Lodovico of Milan as a military expert capable of producing portable bridges, improved canons, catapults, and ships. In reality, Leonardo's military ideas reflected an active and creative mind more suited to an abstract dreamer than a practical strategist. None of his inventions ever made it beyond his notebooks, and in fact, few were practical in nature.

When Leonardo da Vinci died at the age of 67 he was buried in a Gothic tomb in Amboise, France. Throughout his life Leonardo had created great art that would influence the work of future masters such as Michelangelo and Raphael. In the process he had begun to earn artists the respect they deserved.

Michelangelo Buonarroti. Michelangelo Buonarroti (1475–1564) exemplified Renaissance humanism in his artistic expression. His greatness lay in his ability to fuse classical style with Christian themes. Works such as the **David** and the paintings in the Sistine Chapel represent the pinnacle of the Renaissance and are among the greatest achievements in the history of western art. Michelangelo was not a revolutionary figure in the world of art, as he did not bring about the radical changes that characterized the shift from medieval to Renaissance art. Instead he was a child of the Renaissance, inheriting the ideas of Donatello, Botticelli, and Leonardo da Vinci. Using these ideas Michelangelo became perhaps the greatest artist of the Renaissance. His achievements were not limited to one particular area for he excelled in painting, sculpture, architecture, and poetry. His art enveloped his entire life; in fact when he died at the extraordinary age of 89 he was still creating masterpieces.

Considered by some to be the greatest sculpture of the Renaissance, and one of the greatest in the history of art, was Michelangelo's *David*. In 1501 Michelangelo won the commission from the city of Florence to sculpt a statue of the biblical David from a 5.4 m block of marble, which had lain in a yard near the Duomo since the 1460s. Although the block was an impressive piece of marble it was flawed as the result of an earlier attempt to work it. Within three years of receiving the commission Michelangelo had completed the *David*. When it was unveiled in September of 1504, at the entrance to the city hall, it brought immediate fame to both Michelangelo and Florence.

David had long been a favourite theme of Renaissance sculptors, but Michelangelo's was a significant departure from earlier representations. Michelangelo's *David* was no boy, but rather a glorification of male beauty portrayed as a young man. The pose of the statue is classical; relaxed with weight on one leg and the other slightly bent, thereby combining stillness with the promise of movement. Michelangelo, unlike earlier artists, chose the moment of decision rather than triumph. Others such as Donatello had portrayed a defiant David with his foot resting on Goliath's head exultant in triumph. Michelangelo chose instead to portray David as he wrestles with the decision to act. The look on the face of Michelangelo's *David* is intense and anxious as he looks to his inner self for the strength to face Goliath. The slight twist to the body with the sling over his left shoulder tenses the body, revealing the perfect male form.

The fame accorded Michelangelo as the result of the *David* brought him both rewards and frustrations. His title as the greatest living artist in Europe went undisputed. This, he believed, would bring him more commissions for sculptures. As he prepared to make a permanent home in Florence he

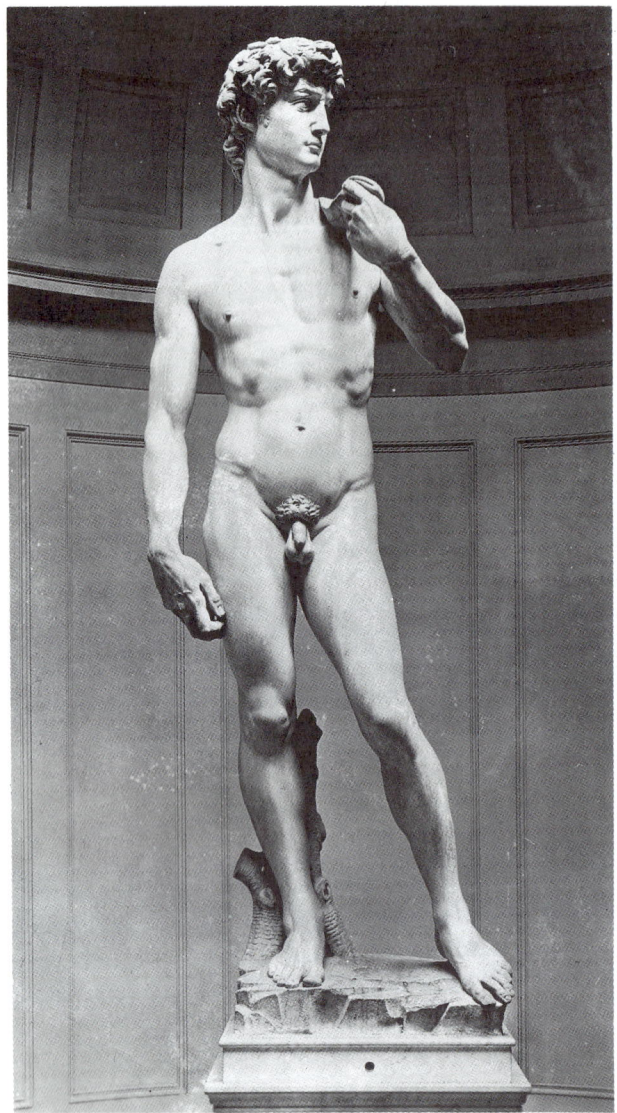

Michelangelo's David, *which stands today in the Accademia in Florence, continues to impress viewers with its power.*

was summoned by Pope Julius II to Rome to paint the ceiling of the Sistine Chapel at the Vatican. Julius was adamant that the work on the chapel be done by the best artist of the time and so, despite all of Michelangelo's efforts to turn down the commission, he was coerced into accepting the job. Michelangelo not only undertook the mammoth task but singlehandedly transformed the commission from a painting of the twelve apostles and a series of relatively quick and easy ornamental designs of circles and rectangles to 520 square metres of figures, scenes, and architectural elements. The execution of this task convinced many that the 37 year old Michelangelo was truly superhuman. To complete the painting of the ceiling of the Sistine Chapel required four years, most of this time Michelangelo spent atop specially constructed scaffolding with his head thrown back and paint dripping in his eyes. Although the scenes are all biblical, the work is most definitely Renaissance. The pictures that adorn the Sistine Chapel are human centred, with the figures presenting both physical and spiritual beauty. Many of the figures, such as the famous *Creation of Adam*, are nudes that would have been unheard of two centuries earlier.

The completion of the Sistine Chapel ceiling in 1512 firmly established Michelangelo as the premier artist in both sculpting and painting, and his life was but half over. The Renaissance ideas first expressed by humanists such as Petrarch received their clearest expression in the art of Michelangelo. By successfully combining classical style with Christian themes Michelangelo Buonarroti's art became a lasting testimony to the vibrant culture of Renaissance Italy.

The Ideal Renaissance Individual

The political stability of the High Middle Ages, the rise of the Italian city-states, and the emergence of the new urban aristocracy all contributed to the rise of a new concept of the ideal man. This new ideal was the opposite of the medieval ideal. The universal man of the Renaissance was to be cultured, educated, and well versed in the classics; a gentleman comfortable both on the battlefield and in the ball-

A revival of sumptuous banquets accompanied the rebirth of classical ideas. This painting illustrates the elaborate clothing of the banqueters and the lively entertainment which accompanied the meal. The increased emphasis on the family is seen through the presence of men, women, and children.

room; a poet and artist; and a man of eloquence, wit, satire, and music. The leaders of the Renaissance rejected nobility by birth stressing instead the importance of intellect.

Gone also was the medieval concept of the ideal woman, who was placed on a pedestal and whose very presence stirred knights to war. Although the women of the Renaissance were not to participate in physically demanding sports, they were, on the whole, more equal than their medieval predecessors. Many women of the Renaissance were educated and cultured, and participated in activities such as dance, theatre, and music. It also appears that the women of the Renaissance had more say about whom they married, for they were often advised not to fall in love unless it was likely to lead to marriage. The average age of marriage during the Renaissance was 27 for males and 18 for females. This had important implications for the role women would play in society. Most women were widowed by the age of 40–50 and many inherited large sums of money or thriving businesses. This made these women important individuals in society and gave them some sway in establishing the new values of the Renaissance.

The Spread of Renaissance Ideas to Northern Europe

The rebirth of classicism, which fueled the Italian Renaissance, eventually spread northward and laid the foundation for a modern Europe. The new ideas and ideals came to pervade all aspects of life from England and France through to Spain and Portugal. Essential to the spread of the Renaissance were two technological innovations: the printing press, invented by Johann Gutenberg in 1453, and the introduction of paper. These two developments allowed for the production of cheap and readily available books, and therefore the circulation and preservation of humanist thought. It also meant that many people could now read the works of the ancients, learn Greek and Latin, and partake in the new secular learning that characterized the Renaissance. In the end, it was the printing press that ensured the Italian Renaissance would not be transient, as had been the eighth century Renaissance under Charlemagne, but would extend its influence throughout Europe. The countries north of the Alps had sprung from different roots and hence developed humanistic ideals appropriate to their character, history, and culture. In essence, this was not a "renaissance" or rebirth of classical ideals, but a northern version of humanism.

The Art of the Northern Humanists.

The beginnings of this movement occurred when northern Europe was still entrenched in the traditional Gothic style with its rigid religiousness and medieval conventions. When the new humanistic and renaissance trends emerged they manifested themselves in many forms of art. Some examples are the elaborate wooden altarpieces such as the magnificent carvings by Tilman Riemenschneider, which were sponsored by wealthy patrons. The realistic detailing from the pallets of Jan Van Eyck and other Flemish masters set the standards for the realistic and interpretive portraiture of Hans Holbein, and the sensitive landscapes and the domestic scenes by Pieter Brueghel. The woodcuts, which suited themselves to the deft genius of Albrecht Dürer, became popular with the printing press. The other genres of art at this point were little more than Italian imitations.

The development of a humanistic trend in northern European art began with a break in the Gothic tradition. Conventions were disregarded and a sincere attempt at realism was made. Jan Van Eyck, in his portraits and scenes, exemplifies this style. He was painting for a new audience in the flourishing commercial centres, such as Brugges and Ghent, where the merchant class commissioned secular paintings and portraits. One of the most famous

Dürer, in his woodcuts, characterizes the fear felt in a society convinced that the world was ending. In "The Four Horsemen of the Apocalypse", Death, Want, Sickness, and War trample their victim — humanity.

examples of this art is the wedding portrait of Giovanni Arnolfini and his Bride.

Hans Holbein the Younger, an artist from Basel exemplifies northern humanism in his complete break from the Gothic tradition. His fame comes from the purity of the artistic form; and with this uniqueness northern art reached its peak. In Basel he encountered leading humanists such as Erasmus who encouraged him to abandon religious painting. This he did and travelled to the court of King Henry VIII to paint and to design clothes and costumes.

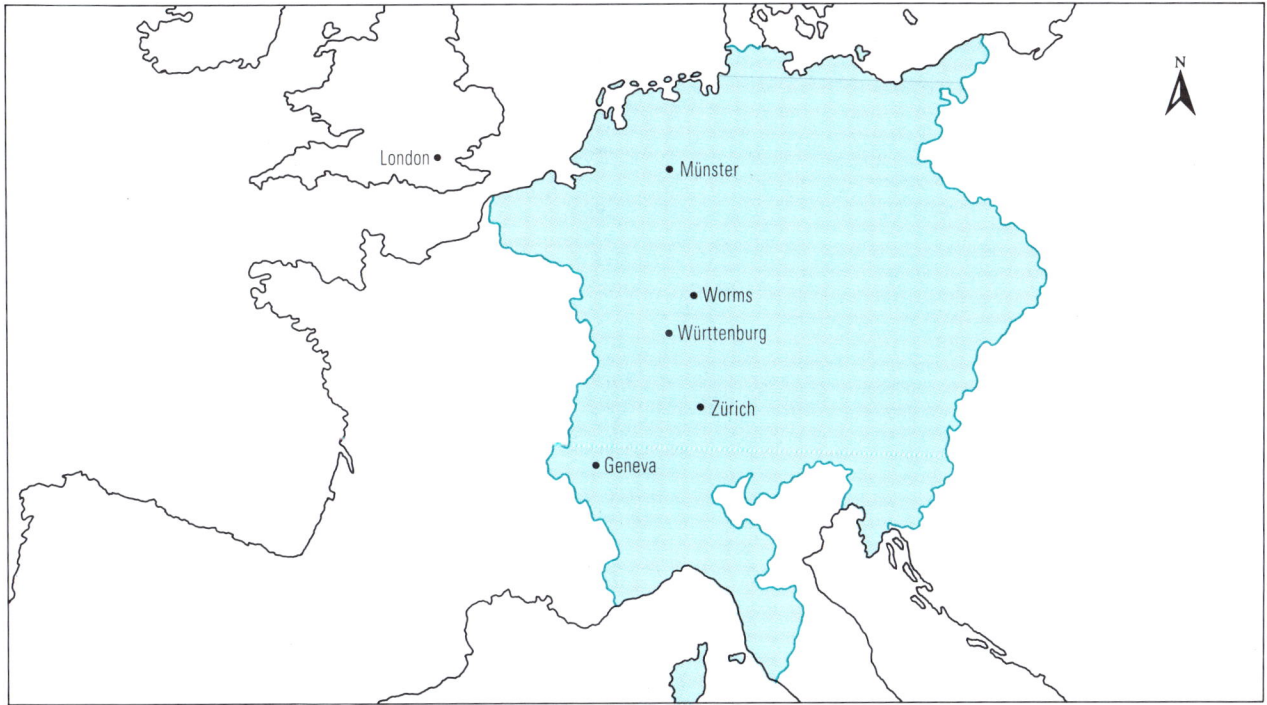

The Holy Roman Empire During the Reformation
Central Europe was home to the Reformation, partially because of the fragmented nature of the Holy Roman Empire. Note the areas of particular significance to the Reformation.

While Holbein chose to dodge the effects of the Renaissance the German artist Albrecht Dürer managed to remain northern in character despite developing a new approach. His approach synthesized the meticulous portrayal of detail from the Eyckian school with the ideas of proportion and mathematical reason of Renaissance art. The Renaissance spirit of inquiry is obvious in his detailed scientific observations of people and landscapes, which he encountered on his journeys. Some of the first pure landscapes evolved from these sketches where the landscape is no longer just a backdrop. To him nature became art and in his fresh and accurately insightful renditions he drew people and places as they were. He also struggled to free art from the restrictions of religion and to make it a mirror of humanity. His works cover a wide range of subject matters from traditional themes, to new concepts of concern, to the introspective humanistic psyche. He strove for a new and individual approach, combining Gothic symbolism and the tradition of line, with the humanistic beliefs of the Renaissance, and the use of mass to increase the sense of reality.

The Reformation

At the outset of this chapter it was noted that there were two major movements that marked the epoch between medieval and modern history in Europe: the Renaissance and the Reformation. These two

BELIEFS

MISOGYNY AND THE EUROPEAN WITCHCRAZE

During the late fifteenth century the church was becoming increasingly concerned about heresy in society. So, to find out what people believed and to stamp out pagan beliefs and practices, the papacy sent out inquisitors who identified and brought people to trial for acts of witchcraft. Two of the most famous inquisitors were Heinrich Kraemer and Jacob Sprenger. These two men were the inquisitors in Upper Germany and gained a great deal of fame from the publication of their book called *Malleus Maleficarum* in 1486. The *Malleus Maleficarum* was the first comprehensive book of witch-beliefs and attempted to clearly explain how witches were found, convicted, and executed. The thoroughness of Kraemer's and Sprenger's book made it the most respected and consulted source on witches and witch practices by both Catholics and Protestants down to the eighteenth century.

The publication of the *Malleus Malificarum* was to have a devastating effect on thousands of women in Europe. Heinrich Kraemer, who wrote a great deal of the book, was a blatant misogynist, or women-hater. Throughout much of the book there is ample evidence of Kraemer's hatred of women with the result being that women were far more likely to be found guilty of witchcraft and to be executed for it than were men. The excerpts below are intended to illustrate Kraemer's misogyny. As you read the passages consider to what degree attitudes such as these have negatively influenced society's views towards women and to what degree such sexist and dangerous attitudes still exist.

WHY SUPERSTITION IS CHIEFLY FOUND IN WOMEN

° **women are naturally more impressionable, and more ready to receive the influence of a disembodied spirit...**

° **they [women] have slippery tongues, and are unable to conceal from their fellow-women those things which by evil arts they know...**

° **since they are feebler both in mind and body, it is not surprising that they should come under the spell of witchcraft.**

° **And it should be noted that there was a defect in the formation of the first woman, since she was formed from a bent rib, that is, a rib of the breast, which is bent as it were in a contrary direction to a man. And since through this defect she is an imperfect animal.**

° **There is no man in the world who studies so hard to please the good God as even an ordinary woman studies by her vanities to please men.**

° **All witchcraft comes from carnal lust, which is in women insatiable.**

OF THE POWER OF WITCHES

For they raise hailstorms and hurtful tempests and lightnings; cause sterility in men and animals; offer to devils, or otherwise kill, the children whom they do not devour.... They can also, before the eyes of their parents, and when no one is in sight, throw into the water children walking by the water side; they make horses go mad under their riders; they can transport themselves from place to place through the air, either in body or

> in imagination; they can affect Judges and Magistrates so that they cannot hurt them; they can cause themselves and others to keep silence under torture; they can bring about a great trembling in the hands and horror in the minds of those who would arrest them...they can see absent things as if they were present; they can turn the minds of men to inordinate love or hatred...cause abortion, kill infants in the mother's womb by a mere exterior touch; they can at times bewitch men and animals with a mere look, without touching them, and cause death....

movements are often studied in tandem not only because of chronology but also because in many ways the Reformation was a product of the new ideas unleashed by the Renaissance. For instance the Reformation owed an equally large debt to Gutenberg's invention to movable type as did the Renaissance. Many people before Martin Luther had sought reform in the church only to be branded heretics, and often burned at the stake. By 1520 Martin Luther had published a couple of books and was able to command a great deal of respect from people over a wide area. Some of his supporters were powerful German princes, who would play a significant part in the Reformation. As with the Renaissance, the success of the Reformation depended largely on the rapid spread of ideas, which was facilitated by the printing press.

Although the drastic changes that rocked the Catholic church throughout the sixteenth century were the product of the thoughts and actions of Martin Luther, it was the socio-economic and political conditions existing in northern Europe at the time that allowed the ideas to take root and spread. During the early years of the sixteenth century food shortages and famines were becoming more frequent as a result of the population returning to pre-Black Death levels and the repeated occurrences of hailstorms. It was also a period when the rich were getting poorer and the poor were becoming much poorer.

Causes of the Reformation

Often, when dealing with the causes of the Reformation the abuses and corruption within the church are cited as the primary cause. Although corruption in the church was widespread it is too simple an explanation for the events that occurred in the sixteenth century. Cries for reform of the church were not new to the latter part of the fifteenth century. As early as the last quarter of the fourteenth century John Wycliffe, a brilliant lawyer from Oxford, England, challenged the authority of the hierarchy within the church, the doctrine of transubstantiation, and the sale of indulgences. Johann Hus (1371–1415), the Czech reformer, carried on this struggle for reform. His fight against the Roman Catholic hierarchy, and abuses within the church, provided a link between the reformers of the fourteenth century and the leaders of the Reformation in the early part of the sixteenth century. After being twice excommunicated, Hus was condemned to be burnt at the stake.

The underlying causes of the divisions, which emerged in the sixteenth century, went far beyond the need to improve the image of the papacy, as they included doctrinal issues as well as changing political and economic factors. The abuses highlighted by Luther acted as the catalyst that set in motion a series of events that would forever change Christianity and the history of the western world.

The Impact of Humanism on the Reformation

Many of the leading proponents of reform, such as Martin Luther, were greatly influenced by the writing of early reformers such as Johann Hus as well as the humanist philosophy of the Renaissance. Most of the reformers rejected the opulence and extravagance of the papacy and were critical of the formalism of religious practice. Like the chapels built by Brunelleschi, the style of religion sought by the reformers was one that operated on a human level, rather than following doctrines that placed the word of God well above the masses. Reformers wished to bring about a religious revival, which was to be rooted in widespread education and would use the everyday language as the language of learning rather than Latin. The early reformers also challenged the concept of the church as the intermediary between God and individuals, instead stressing that humans could come to God on their own.

Doctrinal Divisions. On the eve of the Reformation the church had become bogged down in theological debates. When the split between reformers and conservatives in the church did occur the division ran much deeper than the perceived abuses of church officials. While corruption within the church hierarchy acted as a catalyst to the Reformation it was the differences over doctrine that ultimately divided Christendom. Issues such as the nature of the Eucharist, and the primacy of the papacy, came to the fore and drove a wedge between the church hierarchy and the leading reformers. Once the role of the papacy was questioned, people began to question the central authority of the church of Rome, which drained revenues from northern Europe and enriched Rome. Other factors including political and economic concerns came into play.

Why did the Reformation Begin in Germany?

Thus far it has been shown that the Reformation was the result of a multiplicity of causes including: corruption within the church, humanist ideas fused with Christianity, and doctrinal differences within various factions of the church. What remains to be answered is why the Reformation began in Germany rather than in France, England, or Spain.

By the sixteenth century the political map of Europe was being reshaped by the emergence of nation-states. England, united under the Tudor monarchs following the Wars of the Roses, France under the leadership of the "Renaissance King" Francis I, and Spain united under the joint rule of Ferdinand of Aragon and Isabella of Castille, all developed centralized governments during the sixteenth century. Germany, meanwhile, remained a patchwork of principalities with no central force to deal with the papacy. The local princes, who ruled the various regions of which Germany was comprised, eyed the church lands with envy and longed for the wealth that was siphoned by the church and sent to Italy. Protests against church taxes and a feeling of anti-Roman sentiment, although present elsewhere, was strongest in Germany where no centralized government existed that could resist papal taxation. Many people in Germany felt robbed by papal agents and resented the extravagance in Rome, which they believed was enjoyed by the popes at their expense. Many were just waiting for the opportunity to voice their displeasure.

Indulgences. The commercialization of **indulgences** provided the disenchanted people in Germany with the catalyst they needed to break with Rome. Indulgences had become a tool of the medieval papacy to raise armies and money for the Crusades. Initially they were remissions of punishment due for sins that were granted to those going on a crusade, a pilgrimage, or to someone who made a donation to the church. Those who could not, or would not, go on the Crusades often purchased an indulgence to gain the same remission from sins as the Crusaders. Over time the use and interpretation of indulgences changed rather dramatically. Special issues were authorized by various popes to help defray diverse costs, which ranged from the building of St. Peter's Basilicia in Rome to fighting wars to defend or expand the Papal States. Also indulgences came to be seen as a personal release from time served in the afterlife for sins committed; in fact some of the agents, or pardoners as they were called, went so far as to suggest that indulgences could be applied to future sins and thus seemed to encourage sinning. In 1476 Pope Sixtus IV expanded the sale of indulgences by stating that they applied not only to the living but also to souls in purgatory. Thus one of the greatest money-making devices of the church was made even better. The major drawback to indulgences, as the popes would discover only too late, was that they alienated and angered the poor as they were rightly perceived as a means for the wealthy to buy remission for their sins.

Martin Luther's Reformation

The Character of Martin Luther. While the underlying causes of the Reformation were many and diverse, the rebellion, which would ultimately transform the western world, was spearheaded by a single man, Martin Luther. His actions so profoundly altered the course of history that there is a danger of losing sight of the individual. Luther's character, although complex, reminds us that he was very human; often questioning his actions, showing fear, love, and above all a resolute determination to defend his beliefs. Martin Luther, the second son of

Martin Luther, the driving force behind the Protestant Reformation, was a complex character who, although filled with self-doubt, was firm and obstinate in his beliefs.

a self-made businessman, was born in the small German town of Eisleben in 1483. Luther received a good education, graduating from the University of Erfurt in 1502, after which he completed a master's degree and began to study law. Suddenly on July 16, 1505 Luther announced to a group of friends at a party that they would never see him again for it was his intention to enter a Augustinian monastery. The cause of such a drastic decision would seem to be the result of living in a fear-motivated medieval society, coupled with a series of freak occurrences immediately prior to his entering the monastery. On his return to Erfurt after spending Easter with his family

Luther cut an artery in his leg and nearly bled to death, shortly thereafter a classmate died of the plague, and on a subsequent visit home Luther was caught in a storm during which he was very nearly struck by lightning.

Luther entered the monastery in September of 1506 and within a year was ordained as a priest. He quickly earned a solid reputation for his theological studies and was soon recommended for a post at the new University of Wittenberg. Except for a brief stint at the University of Erfurt Luther would remain at Wittenberg for the rest of his life, earning his doctorate in theological studies and assuming the chair for biblical studies.

Martin Luther Breaks With the Church. The facet of Luther's character that has received the most attention and may well have been the most influential in shaping his break with the Roman Catholic church was his self-doubt. Luther appears to have been obsessed with his own sinfulness and sought every opportunity to overcome his sense of guilt and earn worthiness in the sight of God. He could see no way that mortal beings, as despicable and sinful as they are, could receive anything but fierce punishment from the Almighty. Ultimately, the spiritual peace and contentment he discovered in his study of the Bible would form the basis for the revolution in religion that Luther would lead. That revelation for Luther was the realization that God's mercy was as great as his justice and that salvation was achieved through the grace of God and faith alone.

Luther's first confrontation with the church came on October 31, 1517 when he posted his **95 theses** (statements), on indulgences, among other things, on the door of the university church in Wittenberg. This act was prompted by the sale of indulgences by a Dominican friar named Johann Tetzel. Tetzel had arrived in Wittenberg in the spring of 1517 to sell indulgences in order to raise money for the building of St. Peter's Cathedral in Rome. As part of his sales pitch Tetzel offered complete release from purgatory. This flew in the face of Luther's belief that salvation was achieved through faith alone and that the pope could grant pardons only for penalties he imposed. Luther argued that indulgences were dangerous as they induced a false sense of security and were a threat to salvation. For the peasantry, indulgences were a waste of their hard-earned money and nothing but worthless promises.

It did not take long for word to spread that a monk had challenged the sale of indulgences. The Dominicans, long-time rivals of the Augustinians, immediately launched an attack on Martin Luther, although the pope initially viewed the incident as little more than a quarrel between monks. Three years later Martin Luther made it clear that his actions were not merely a conflict between religious orders when he published three controversial pamphlets: *An Address to the Christian Nobility of the German Nation*, which appealed to Germans to reject the authority of the pope; *The Babylonian Captivity*, which attacked the basis of the church's power; and *The Liberty of the Christian Man*, in which Luther explained his doctrine of faith. These pamphlets constituted a direct attack on church doctrine and papal authority, which the pope could not ignore. When he was excommunicated in 1520 Martin Luther showed further contempt for the authority of the pope by publicly burning the papal bull (a seal affixed to a document from the pope). A year later Luther's battle with the church was brought into the secular realm when the emperor, Charles V, summoned Luther to Worms where he was to offer his defence at what has become known as the Diet of Worms. Dressed simply in his monk's robes, Luther was in stark contrast to the richly attired secular and ecclesiastical officials who gathered at the cathedral in Worms to hear his defence. When his opportunity to speak arose Luther eloquently and steadfastly refused to recant anything. Upon hearing Luther's defiant response Charles V declared the actions of the rebel monk to be wrong and issued an imperial edict calling for Luther's arrest. It was at this point that the power of the local princes in Germany and their resentment of the foreign interference of the popes came into play, Elector Frederick III of Saxony, who had never met Luther, came to his aid by having him taken to Wartburg Castle where he was safe from arrest.

Luther remained at Wartburg for nearly a year, during which time he worked with his close friend Philip Melanchthon at preparing a German translation of the bible and in developing the doctrines of Lutheranism, which the reformed church would be based upon. The Lutheran church would have no relics, saints, fasts, nor monasteries and would allow for the clergy to marry. Underlying all Lutheran doctrines is the conviction that God is merciful and that it is through God's mercy that salvation is granted. Aside from this belief there are three main concepts that form the basis of Lutheranism; *sola fide* (by faith alone), *sola scriptura* (by scripture alone), and *sola gratia* (by grace alone). Sola fide emphasizes that individuals are saved by faith alone and that no one is saved on their own merit, as humans have no merit. According to Luther, individuals have no control over their salvation and can do nothing to bring themselves closer to God, as salvation is only through the gratuitous mercy of God who alone mysteriously selects the few who are to be saved. Sola scriptura states that the only source of religious truth is the word of God, which is revealed in scripture. This doctrine challenged the authority of the pope and the clergy to interpret the word of God or to speak for God. Sola gratia maintained that all good and all virtue comes from God's grace while all wickedness, weakness, and evil comes from nature, especially human nature. Furthermore, as natural humans can know neither truth nor good without grace they must seek the help of Christ the Savior.

Ulrich Zwingli and the Reformation in Switzerland. Luther's political conservatism was typical of most of the church reformers of the early sixteenth century. Ulrich Zwingli was among the few reformers who were willing to broaden their convictions to the political realm. At the time of the Reformation Switzerland was in the midst of an economic crisis brought on by a rising population and high rates of inflation. The economic problems brought social disorder as the upper classes struggled to maintain their wealth at the expense of the peasantry, which led to a peasants' revolt in 1524.

Zwingli's greatest contribution to the Reformation was that he pushed the simplification of religion much further than Luther had been willing to. Zwingli's aim was to reduce religious practices to the bare essentials by doing away with many of the lavish rituals, which he felt obscured the true word of God. Aside from suggesting that Scriptures were open to all to interpret Zwingli also led a move to simplify the churches. In 1524 he had all the images in the Zurich churches taken down, the stained glass windows removed, and the walls whitewashed so that people would not ignorantly pray to images of a saint.

Ulrich Zwingli's death was ironically violent and untimely. In 1531 a group of Zwinglians numbering about 1500 clashed with 8000 Catholics. In the resulting melee 500 Zwinglians including Zwingli himself were killed. Although his life and his work were short-lived his influence was quite significant. His interpretation of the Eucharist (communion) as being merely a symbolic gesture in remembrance of the redemptive death of Christ caused a serious and irreparable rift with Luther, who maintained that the actual body and blood of Christ coexisted with the bread and wine and that Christ's presence during the Communion service was real not symbolic. This split led to the first major division among Protestants and would later be developed by John Calvin. Perhaps the most significant group to emerge from Zwingli's reforms were the Anabaptists.

John Calvin

By the 1530s the split with Rome, initiated by Martin Luther, had spread to many cities throughout Europe. In each area leaders of varying strengths and convictions led the struggle to establish new reformed churches. Among those leading the way was a determined young man named John Calvin. Calvin, along with Luther and Zwingli, is considered among the most influential leaders of the Protestant Reformation. Unlike Luther and Zwingli, who were innovators in the truest sense of the word, Calvin was a second generation reformer who built on the ideas of his predecessors. His greatest contribution to the reformation movement was to organize the Protestant doctrine into a clear system and to unite the ideas of earlier reformers. In so doing, Calvin created a third variety of Protestantism, which is midway between Lutheranism and Zwinglianism.

The situation in France in the 1530s was quite tense. The actions of Protestant reformers met stiff resistance from the French monarch Francis I and Calvin himself was imprisoned several times. In 1534, when Francis I pledged to purge France of Protestantism, hundreds of people were imprisoned and 35, including John Calvin's brother, were burned. Amidst the turmoil Calvin fled France for Basel, Switzerland. In 1536 Calvin made a secret trip back to France, after which he had determined to go to Strassbourg. Enroute to Strassbourg Calvin made what was supposed to be an overnight stop at a friend's house in Geneva. While there he was asked to stay on and to bring the Reformation to Geneva. This fortuitous visit led Calvin to adopt Geneva as his new home. Except for a brief period from 1538 to 1541 when enemies of his controlled the government and succeeded in driving him from the city, Calvin remained in Geneva for the rest of his life.

Upon his return to Geneva John Calvin set about reorganizing the church on a four-tier system. The first level were the pastors, who were ministers of the gospel; the second level were the doctors, who were put in charge of delivering a Christian education; the third level were the elders, whose job was to assist the pastors in looking after the spiritual welfare of the people and governing the consistory, which was primarily a morals court; and the final tier were the deacons, who administered civic charities. Aside from the four-tier organization of the church there were laypeople, usually elders, who acted as morals police by reporting on impenitent sinners. Transgressions such as dancing, wearing a dress with a low neckline, card playing, or drunkenness drew stiff penalties in Calvin's Geneva. Even taverns were closed and replaced with orderly cafes with Bibles available, although public pressure eventually led to the reopening of the taverns. Extreme measures were often taken in the enforcement of strict moral behaviour. Torture was used to extract confessions and 58 people were reported executed in a four year period.

In many areas of theology including original sin and the doctrine of faith, John Calvin agreed with other prominent reformers. He did, however, differ significantly in some areas. Calvin agreed with Luther that Christ was present during communion, but suggested it was only a spiritual presence. On predestination, there was again a connection with Luther, although Calvin stated that God knew in advance who is to be saved and who is to be damned, and that people could in fact be predestined to be damned, even before they were born. It was this doctrine of predestination that would later be stressed by the English Puritans and in some cases would create serious psychological problems. Perhaps the area in which Calvin's ideas would have the greatest impact on society was in relation to one vocation. Calvin saw in history a divine plan in which the work of all people fit. Other reformers felt that to earn salvation you must do God's work, which often meant withdrawing from the secular world. Calvin stressed that each individual must follow a calling, by doing their chosen vocation and work on earth under the knowledge that there was a divine plan in which all vocations are equally important. Calvin rejected the notion that parents should determine a child's future and the Renaissance belief that one type of life is better than another. This emphasis on following a chosen vocation would become one of the hallmarks of Protestantism.

Despite remaining in Geneva from 1541 until his death in 1564, the ideas of John Calvin spread far and wide. Refugees from other parts of Europe visited Calvin's Christian commonwealth and returned to their homelands inspired by Calvinist doctrine. Thus it was that Calvinism spread to many countries including France (Huguenots), Scotland (Presbyterians), and Holland (Dutch Reformed Church), and impacted on Germany (Baptists), and England (Anglicans and Puritans). Of all the forms of Protestantism that arose during the sixteenth century none were to be as aggressive and influential as Calvinism.

The Catholic Response to The Reformation

Thus far it would seem that as Christendom splintered the Catholic church sat idly by. This was by no means the case. In fact there were two distinct movements connected to the Roman Catholics' response to the Reformation movement; the Catholic Reformation and the **Counter-Reformation**. The Catholic Reformation took place during the 1520s and 1530s and was largely an attempt on the part of the Catholic church to implement reform. The 1530s became a period of extensive renewal in spiritual, moral, and ecclesiastical affairs quite independent of Protestantism. The Counter-Reformation was a movement directed against the spread of Protestantism. Using a variety of weapons including the Roman Inquisition, censorship, and the growth of new militant orders, the Catholic church successfully fought to stem the tide towards Protestantism.

The Counter-Reformation. Centuries of conflict with Muslims, and the struggle to drive them out of Iberia, had developed in Spain a militant and fanatical Christian orthodoxy. Under Ferdinand and Isabella, effective controls were developed to deal with anyone who deviated from the norm. The most famous of these controls was the Holy Inquisition. Adopting its organization, Pope Paul II sanctioned the Holy Inquisition in 1542 and extended its authority throughout Christendom. Ultimately, the success of the Holy Inquisition depended on the support it received from secular rulers throughout Europe.

Effective thought control required that heretical books, as well as their authors, be burned. Beginning in 1521 the Catholic church prepared and distributed lists of forbidden books. The first complete list for the entire church, published in 1559, was called *Index librorum prohibitorum*. This list included Protestant writings as well as the works of renowned humanists, including highly respected Catholics such as Erasmus.

The Jesuits. Another important development of the Counter-Reformation was the establishment and rapid growth of new orders, which sought to convert Protestants in Europe and non-Christians overseas. The most important of these new orders was the Society of Jesus, better known as the ***Jesuits***.

The Jesuit order was founded by one of the most dramatic characters in the history of Christendom; Ignatius Loyola (1491–1556). As the son of a Basque noble, Loyola served as a page at the court of King Ferdinand and was educated in courtly manners and military strategy. While defending against a French invasion, Loyola was struck by a cannonball that shattered his right leg and wounded his left leg. The injuries left the young soldier lame for the rest of his life. While recuperating at the family castle, Loyola read Carthusian's *Life of Christ*, which proved to be such a great religious inspiration that he decided to turn his military training and chivalric ideals to the realm of faith. The Society of Jesus, which Loyola founded, was eventually sanctioned by the Catholic church in 1540. The order would become, in a spiritual sense, the militant and aggressive arm of the renewed Catholic church.

The Jesuits are perhaps best remembered for the world missions they undertook, such as the one at Saint Marie Among the Hurons, near present day Midland, Ontario. These missions spread Christianity to the four corners of the world and often acted as a counter balance to the materialistic imperialism of European explorers. The eye-witness accounts and scholarly reports of the Jesuits form an important body of documents for historians wishing to examine the contact period, as they are not economic assessments of the regions. The reports of the Jesuits, known as *The Jesuit Relations* introduced Europeans to a great variety of customs and beliefs and forced them to rethink their Eurocentric views of non-Europeans.

The Council of Trent. The advent of the Reformation caused the Catholic church to do more than weed out abuses and become more militant. It forced the church to go through a period of introspection that resulted in a more clearly defined doctrine, which laid the foundations for modern Catholicism. The church of the Middle Ages was much more flexible and accommodating with regards to doctrinal divisions than either the Protestant churches or the Catholic church of the late sixteenth century. In fact many of the ideas put forth by Protestant reformers had co-existed with traditional Catholic theology in the Middle Ages. It was the development of Protestantism based on a systematic theology, resulting from the work of Martin Luther and John Calvin, that forced Catholics to redefine and reorganize Catholic doctrine in order to clearly set Catholicism apart from Protestantism.

The task of redefining and reorganizing Catholicism was carried out by the Council of Trent (1545–1563). The Council of Trent was dominated by hard-line conservatives and as a result was essentially a backlash against the Renaissance, humanism, and especially Protestantism. The Council of Trent did much to reassert the power and prestige of the church. It stressed the exclusive right of the Catholic church to interpret scripture, decreed that individuals were saved through a combination of faith and good works and emphasized the role of the church as the intermediary between God and humanity. The Council also insisted that the mass be said in Latin and made the church the only sacred meeting place, insisting that baptisms, weddings, and funerals be held in a church.

The Council of Trent reaffirmed many of the beliefs and practices that even Catholic humanists of the early sixteenth century had considered superstitions such as a belief in purgatory, the invocation of saints, the power of relics, and the validity of indulgences. It also placed an emphasis on the Virgin Mary and the Saints, both of which were rejected by Protestant churches. Finally, the post-Trentine churches did everything possible to make Catholic churches and services resplendent. The richly decorated Catholic churches of the late sixteenth century and the ritualistic services contrasted sharply with the simple whitewashed churches of many Protestant denominations and served as a visual reminder of the enormous gulf that now separated Christendom.

By 1560 the religious unity of Europe had been irreparably shattered. It was replaced with a highly charged competition for human souls between a reinvigorated Catholic church, the Lutheran church, the Zwinglian and Calvinist churches, the Anglican church, and a variety of other sects. Combined with an expanding worldview (resulting from

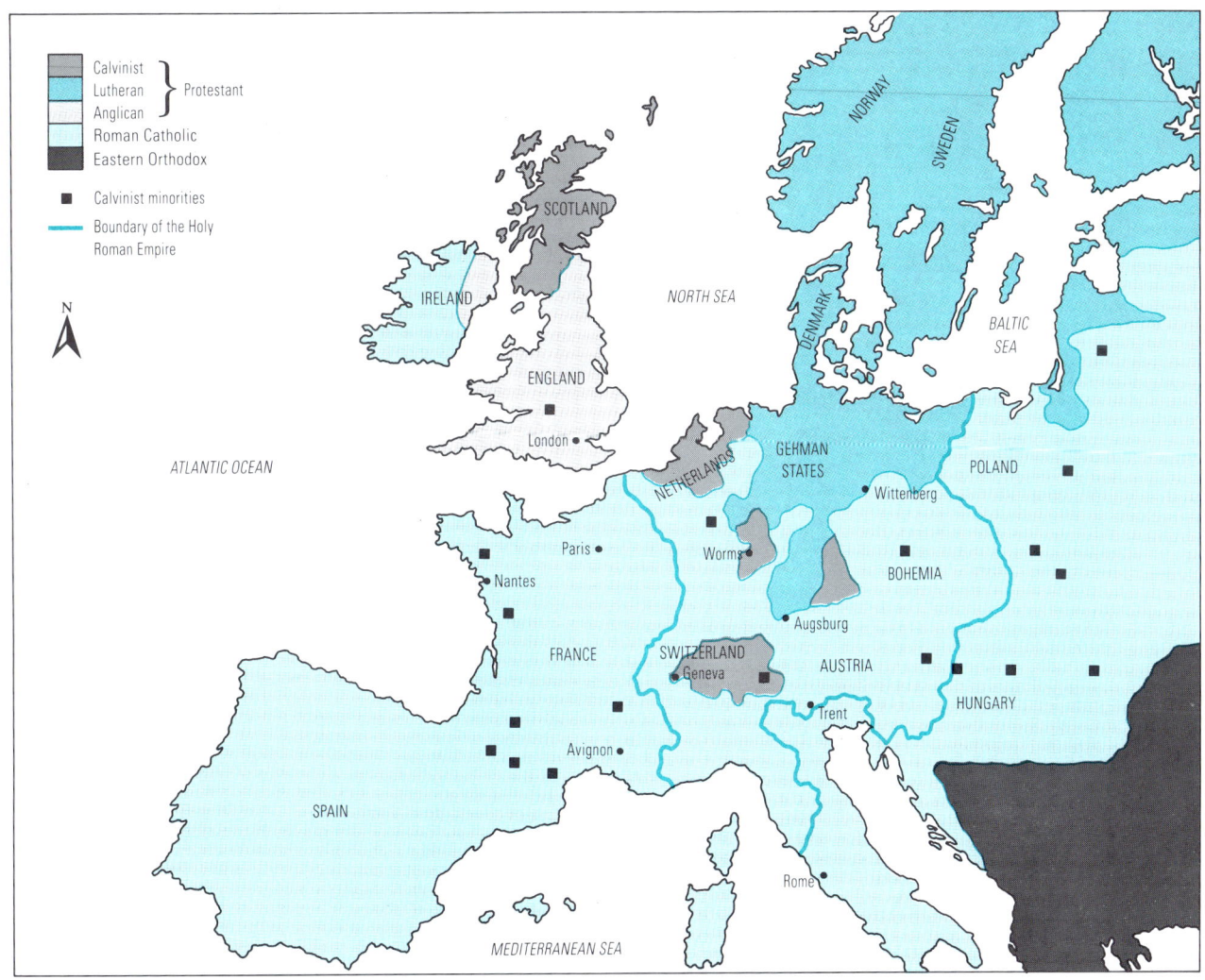

Religions in Europe in 1600

By 1560, the religious map of Europe had been radically transformed. While western Europe, including England, had embraced Protestantism. Only the orthodox faiths remained unchanged in their beliefs.

the advent of overseas exploration) and an increase in secular learning (resulting from Renaissance humanism), Europe by the mid-sixteenth century was poised on the edge of a new age. The rebirth of classical ideas, fused with influences of various parts of the world, set western civilization on a new and exciting course which would ultimately create the modern age.

The Foundations of Early Modern Europe   CHAPTER 17   541

Suggested Sources for Further Research

Burckhardt, Jacob, *The Civilization of the Renaissance in Italy* (Harper and Row, 1975).

Chartier, Roger (ed.), *A History of Private Life: Passions of the Renaissance* (The Belknap Press of Harvard University Press, 1989).

Cole, Bruce and Adelheid Gealt, *Art of the Western World* (Summit Books, 1989).

Durant, Will, *The Story of Civilization Volumes V & VI* (Simon and Schuster, 1957).

Harris, Nathaniel, *The Art of Michelangelo* (The Hamlyn Pub. Group, 1989).

Hibbert, Christopher, *The English: A Social History 1066–1945* (W.W. Norton & Co., 1987).

Levack, Brian P., *The Witch-Hunt in Early Modern Europe* (Longman Group UK Ltd., 1987).

Mannering, Douglas, *The Art of Leonardo da Vinci* (Hamlyn Pub. Group, 1989).

Morgan, Kenneth O., *The Oxford Illustrated History of Britain* (Oxford University Press, 1984).

Simon, Edith, *The Reformation* (Time Incorporated, 1966).

Spitz, Lewis W., *The Renaissance and Reformation Movements* (Concordia Publishing House, 1971).

Focus Your Knowledge

1. Define the term Renaissance and use aspects from Renaissance Florence to illustrate this concept.

2. Why did the Renaissance occur in Italy? Why was it not as much a northern European phenomenon?

3. The Renaissance has been referred to as "a time of outsized men and a culture studded with geniuses." Select one artist or literary figure, one political or military figure, and one reformer and prepare a list of their major achievements.

4. Drawing on the information above, prepare a time line listing the major works of art and literature produced during the Italian and Northern Renaissances.

Apply Your Knowledge

1. To what degree were the fortunes of Florence tied to the Medici family?
2. Show that art of the Renaissance was truly a rebirth of classical ideas by describing the achievements of various artists. Your answer should touch on a variety of art forms.
3. Assess the impact of the printing press in history. To what degree does it parallel the computer revolution of today?
4. It has often been argued that the term "Northern Renaissance" is a misnomer. By comparing and contrasting the works of northern humanists to the works produced during the Italian Renaissance show that the two movements were similar and yet distinct.
5. Prepare a brief summary of the major causes of the Reformation. If you had lived at the time would you have followed Luther, Calvin, Zwingli, or remained with the Catholic church? Explain your answer.
6. Assess the Catholic church's response to the Protestant Reformation. Was the Council of Trent the product of progressive or regressive minds?

Extension Activities

1. Recreate the persona of one of the following characters of the Renaissance and the Reformation. Be sure to capture their nuances, appearances, ideas, and reasons for their prominence. This could be presented live to the class or on video.

Francesco Petrarch	Albrecht Dürer	Martin Luther
Michelangelo Buonarroti	Jan Van Eyck	Ulrich Zwingli
Leonardo da Vinci	John Calvin	Ignatius Loyola

2. Prepare a modern-day news report of the Diet of Worms. Be sure that the major issues are discussed and key personalities are interviewed.

SKILLS FOCUS

Unit Overview

1. This unit opens with European civilization at a low point and closes with Europe at an artistic and cultural high point. Review the elements of a civilization and decide which elements had declined in the Dark Ages and conversely, which elements rebounded so dramatically in the Renaissance.

2. What did the decline of civilization in the Dark Ages and its resurgence mean for the role that women would play in Europe. Did the resurgence of culture, learning, and political stability improve women's standing in society? Provide specific examples to support your statements.

3. To what degree can the church be credited with preserving and nurturing western civilization? To what degree was it a limiting factor?

4. As stability returned to Europe and trade began to increase new ideas and new products were imported. Assess the impact of trade and cross-cultural influence in medieval Europe.

5. Medieval and Renaissance Europe was an age of giants, when individuals commanded great power, often at the expense of the general population. Select one character from each of the four chapters and explain why you feel this character was a dominant figure of their time.

Art: A Window to Our Past

Refer to the colour-plate section for Unit 4.

1. The Renaissance is defined as a period of rebirth of classical ideas. By examining various works of art from medieval and Renaissance Europe trace this rebirth. Compare the nature of the progression from medieval to Renaissance art.

2. How does the art of medieval Europe reflect the religious and militaristic nature of the society?

3. Take a careful look at the works of art contained in this unit. Choose one work of art that you find the most impressive and justify why.

Testing a Hypothesis

Medieval and Renaissance Europe was an age dominated by larger-than-life figures. Historians often debate whether great individuals shape history or are shaped by history. For example, was Michelangelo the product of the Renaissance or was he a catalyst fueling the Renaissance. Similarly, was Charlemagne a great leader or simply a man at the right place, at the right time.

Select one character who seemed to dominate

her/his time period and state whether they were the product of their age or whether they helped shape their age. Prepare an argument that defends your statement, or hypothesis. To do this, review the skills developed at the end of each unit to organize and analyze your research.

Use this gathered research to write a short essay of 500–700 words. Your essay should include an effective introduction that clearly states your thesis. Your thesis should set out what you are attempting to prove. The body of the essay should include sound factual support for the argument you are developing. The essay should end with an effective conclusion that clearly summarizes the argument you have made.

Epilogue: The Emergence of the Global Village

CHAPTER 18

Towards the Modern Age

The world of today is often referred to as a global village. Our stores are filled with products from around the world; many of the foods we eat are imported from a variety of nations; and the variety of cultures which make up Canada reflects our multicultural heritage. The foundations of this global interdependence lie in the age of exploration which began over five centuries ago.

The development of a capitalist economy created a desire among Europeans for new sources of raw materials and markets for their manufactured goods. This sent them exploring the four corners of the world. The results of their voyages were to have profound implications for both themselves and the cultures they encountered. Unfortunately, the changes were seldom as beneficial to the peoples encountered by the Europeans: many of those encountered were exploited; some cultures were decimated by disease and warfare.

This final chapter is designed to draw together the various societies studied throughout the text. By the eighteenth century few areas of the world remained in isolation. Hence, this chapter attempts to examine the impact of contact between various peoples and the process of acculturation. This concluding chapter to the study of world civilizations provides a bridge to the era referred to by western historians as the *modern age*.

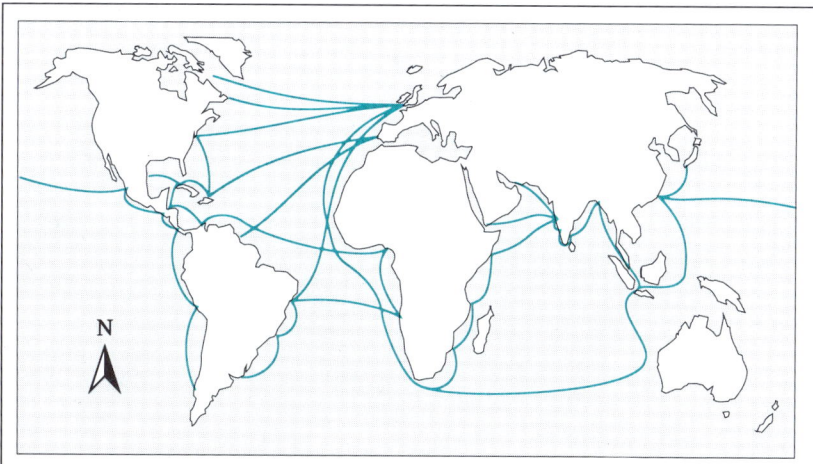

EUROPEAN VOYAGES OF EXPLORATION

CHAPTER 18

Towards the Modern Age

Chapter Highlights

- distinguishing between the Medieval and Modern Eras

- European exploration

- the emerging capitalist system

- early contact between civilizations

- acculturation and its effect on various societies

Our long journey through civilizations of the past has reached a critical juncture in the history of humanity. We began our odyssey by tracing the origins of humans and the development of complex societies. Throughout the course of this book we have traced the rise of various cultures from village to empire and have repeatedly seen how interaction between cultures has helped to create unique and diverse societies worldwide. And yet, what distinguishes the time period since A.D. 1500 from all earlier periods of history, is the degree of **globalization** that has occurred. While it may be true that the cultures and civilizations studied in this book were not homogeneous, regions of the world remained relatively isolated before 1500. The five centuries since Columbus's exploration of the Americas have profoundly changed the world in which we live. During the three centuries from 1480 to 1780, European voyages of exploration, and attempts at colonization, brought the four corners of the world into contact with each other. The impact of these voyages, and of the increased contact between all areas of the world, was to be felt by all peoples of the earth. The purpose of this chapter is to briefly explore the impact of European exploration on the world by considering such issues as trade, **acculturation**, and the growth of the slave trade. As an epilogue, the task before us is to raise a number of provocative questions that may form the basis for further exploration. The pitfall we hope to avoid is that of presenting the Modern Age as an age of modernization led by Europeans. Instead we need to address this period of history from a broader perspective, taking into account the impact of contact on all the cultures involved.

Key Concepts

globalization

acculturation

world-economy

modern era

Europeanization

Christopher Columbus

capitalism

Amerindians

▼▼▼

Early Trading Networks

Extensive trading networks and contact between civilizations is by no means a phenomena particular to the sixteenth century. Far reaching commercial networks had existed for thousands of years. Whenever an area had surplus produce the people sought markets through which they could trade their surpluses for goods or services. Prior to the sixteenth century, transport facilities were limited to beasts of burden, which hauled goods overland, or to ships that could accommodate low tonnage. Because of these limitations trade in luxury goods, which could earn the merchant enormous profits, tended to dominate long-distance trade. Goods for everyday use were only traded among the towns and villages in a restricted area.

During the five hundred years prior to the advent

of European exploration, trade between Asia and Europe was maintained along overland routes. This period was the heyday of the caravan trade, and of the pastoral nomads who lived on the land between the civilizations of Asia and Europe. The pastoral nomads specialized in raising livestock by continually moving their herds in search of pasture and water. They generally relied on trade to obtain grains and other crops and manufactured products. These people, which included Turks, Mongols, Arabs, and Berbers, played a major role in the transcontinental caravan trade, as they were able to demand tribute in exchange for safe conduct. The emergence of long-distance trade by sea routes relegated the pastoral nomads to a marginal role in world affairs.

The pastoral nomads are an indication of the degree to which all societies prior to the sixteenth century existed in some interconnectedness with other societies. Whether we are examining the highly centralized Chinese civilization, the loosely independent city-states of Greece, or the Maya lowlands, no societies existed in complete isolation, and therefore all cultures were the product of some interaction between societies. In fact, on the eve of the age of European exploration there existed at least three world-economies. A ***world-economy***, like a world war, does not include all countries of the world, but is called a world-economy because it involves a number of states and is larger than any defined political unit. In the fifteenth century the Asian and Russian world-economies co-existed with the European world-economy. What occurred in the centuries following 1500 was that long-distance trade developed and brought cultures from around the world in contact with each other.

*E*urope in Transition

The period 1480 to 1780 was very much a watershed, both in terms of European history and in the history of the world. The period referred to as medieval was drawing to a close as Europe rebounded from the Black Death and the Hundred Years' War. The rise of towns, the shift towards centralized nation-states, the split in the Christian church, and a commercial revolution all helped to radically alter the nature of Europe; hence the concept of the **modern era**. The term "modern era," applied by historians to this period of history, reflects very much a **Eurocentric** bias, as it implies that progress and the export of European civilization were connected. In the past, many have assumed that European conquests were bound to happen and that the long-term effect of European world expansion has been to allow more human beings to share in the benefits of European civilization. In fact, one historian has stated that "the Europeanization of a country was to be synonymous with its modernization" and went on to suggest that those who followed and accepted European civilization have received the benefits of modernization, while those areas isolated or reticent to follow Europe's lead have been left behind as the world continues to progress. The danger in accepting this sort of view of history is that it ignores the fact that rich and vibrant civilizations flourished throughout the world prior to contact with the Europeans and that in fact **Europeanization** was detrimental to many cultures.

The belief among westerners that their civilization is superior to all others is neither new nor unique to westerners. Most, if not all, societies place themselves at the centre of their universe and see themselves as the pinnacle of civilization. Where cultures seem to differ is the degree to which they accept foreigners in their society and on what basis. For example, the Chinese allowed outsiders to become Chinese, meaning that newcomers were permitted if they fully assimilated. India, conversely, often tried to exclude foreigners, as they feared their culture would be contaminated through contact with other people. Finally, although the people of medie-

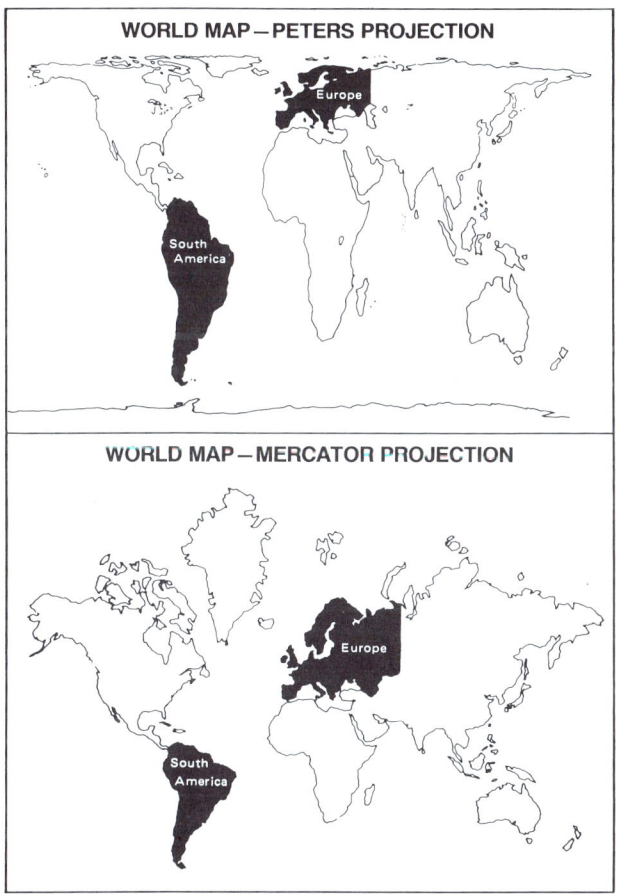

For years the Mercator projection has been widely used and remains an excellent navigational tool. Recently the Mercator projection has been criticized for distorting the middle latitudes and thereby diminishing the land mass of many third world nations. The Peter's Projection, which attempts to redress this problem, compresses the upper latitudes, with the result that North and South America and Africa appear as long narrow continents. As all projections distort, it is necessary to decide on which distortions are acceptable for your purpose.

val Europe were aware of other people including Muslims, Jews, and other non-Christians, they did not impact considerably on their world view. Medieval Christians considered themselves the chosen people and believed that central Europeans represented the pinnacle of civilization. Thus, the belief that one's culture is superior to all others was a common feature throughout the world.

The fact that European civilization was exported around the world, and that western culture has been dominant for the past few centuries, is by no means indicative of its superiority over any other culture. A number of factors including disease, regional wars, and the slave trade allowed Europeans to establish themselves as a leading force in the world. Despite the dominance of the western world other civilizations operating under different religions, as well as different economic and political institutions, were equally viable and progressive.

Foundations for European Exploration

The famous voyage made by **Christopher Columbus** in 1492 was but one of many European voyages of exploration that took place between 1487 and 1780. During these three centuries of exploration and colonization, Europe was to undergo profound changes to its economic system while altering the histories of many peoples worldwide. What were the factors that both incited and allowed Europeans to sail around the world? The four most important changes that occurred were a resurgence in learning led by the Florentine humanists, a number of technological advances related to seafaring, the closing of the overland trade routes to the Orient by the Ottoman Turks, and the development of capitalism.

Medieval Europe's preoccupation with spiritual and religious learning left little room for exploring the world. The Crusades, which greatly expanded medieval Europe's view of the world, played an important role in reopening trade routes that had existed between the Roman Empire and the Orient. Of equal importance in laying the foundations for

European exploration were the Renaissance humanists, who ushered in a new age of learning. The humanists, with their focus on ancient texts and their faith in the ability of humanity, took the lead in devising means to explore the world with the stars as their guide. Rather than seeing far-off lands as simply being inhabited by pagans, Europeans were beginning to assess the material worth of Africa and the Orient.

By the late Middle Ages trade with India and the Orient was supplying Europe with spices for flavouring and preserving foods, silks for fine clothing, and herbs essential for medicine. The exotic nature of the goods imported from Africa and the Orient led many to imagine that a Terrestrial Paradise existed. This land of splendour was thought to be enclosed by a high wall of crystal or diamonds and was believed to be the source of all the great rivers of the world. Over the rivers hung branches of balsam, cinnamon, myrrh, cardamom, and benzoin. While the Terrestrial Paradise was a mythological land it was a reflection of people's view of the East and the increasing importance of trade between Europe and the Orient. The Turkish conquest of Constantinople in 1453 created a serious problem for European merchants who imported goods from the East. Although the Ottomans did not intend to close trade between the East and West, they did attempt to regulate it by imposing duties on goods. The result was that trade goods from the Orient were either not available or became too expensive, causing western merchants to look elsewhere for their supplies.

One of the solutions made possible by the advances in seafaring technology was to establish trade routes with India and the Orient by water rather than by land. The technological changes made to sea travel during the fifteenth century allowed for greater distances to be travelled with much less risk. Among the changes that helped to revolutionize sea travel in the fifteenth century were changes in sails; the use of a Catalan rudder, which was mounted on the sternpost instead of two side rudder oars; compasses; nautical charts; and pilots' books. The net result of these advancements was that navigation of the open seas became possible. No longer was it necessary to be constantly within sight of land, nor were clear skies essential for navigation. Without technical changes such as these, voyages like those undertaken by Christopher Columbus and Vasco da Gama would have been less possible and may have ended in disaster.

While the growth of secular learning and the expansion of the European world view, the closing of the land routes to Asia, and the changes in naval technology all contributed to the exploration of the world, it was economic forces that sustained Europeans in their voyages of discovery. The driving force behind European expansion between 1480 and 1780 was the quest for new markets and sources of raw materials to fuel the emerging ***capitalist*** economy.

The Development of Capitalism

Throughout the Middle Ages the society and the economy had been organized around the feudal order. By the late Middle Ages feudalism was in crisis as the rise of towns and the revival of commerce and trade had brought about a new middle class and a new means of earning wealth. The rise of a strong merchant, or middle, class in Europe signaled the beginning of the end for the feudal system, as merchants did not fit into a feudal society that was rooted in land-based wealth. Similarly, the growth of towns, the proliferation of markets, and the organization of capital all served to radically alter the economy and society of the Middle Ages thus ushering in what has become known as the early modern period of history.

The features of the capitalist economy that emerged in the late Middle Ages should sound familiar to most, as they remain the pillars of our economic system to this day. Paramount in capitalism is the use of money to make money. In the pre-capitalist era, **usury** was against church law and was frowned upon by most people. Furthermore, land was viewed as the only form of secure wealth, while capital (money) was seen as liquid and volatile. The emergence of powerful banking families such as the Medicis in Florence and the Fuggers in northern Europe began to alter this view of wealth. Capitalism, which relies on the organization of capital, labour, and raw materials to produce surplus wealth, provided the impetus for powerful merchants to sponsor voyages of exploration and attempts at colonization. This brought about a radical change in the nature of long-distance trade, from the predominance of luxury items to raw, unprocessed goods that could be refined by European manufacturers. Finished products would, in turn, be used in trade with the regions supplying the raw materials. Thus, as European countries adopted the capitalist mode of production their economies became increasingly tied to the use of cheap raw materials, and cheap labour, extracted from various parts of the world. As Eric Wolf noted:

> In less than two centuries...the European powers expanded the scope of their trading activities to all the continents and made the world their battleground. The quest for American silver, the fur trade, the trade in slaves, and the search for Asian spices drew people into new and unforeseen interdependencies and profoundly changed their lives.[1]

---

[1] Eric Wolf, Europe and the People Without History (Berkeley: University of California Press, 1982).

Globalization

The age of European exploration and expansion began in 1414 when the Portuguese captured the Muslim port of Ceuta on the African side of the Straits of Gibraltar. While the primary objective of the Portuguese had been only to secure access to the Mediterranean, their presence on the North African coast opened the door to European exploration of the southern Atlantic. The need for raw materials to fuel the emerging capitalist economy of Europe, and the blockade of the overland routes, prompted Europeans to search for a sea route to the riches of Asia. The Atlantic would prove to be the key.

During the two centuries that followed the Portuguese seizure of Ceuta, Europeans set sail for the four corners of the world. By 1487, the Portuguese had established settlements at Madeira and on Arguin Island, had explored the mouth of the Congo River, and had rounded the Cape of Good Hope. With Vasco da Gama's voyage around the Cape to East Africa and the Indian Malabar coast in 1497, the Portuguese had opened the road to India.

The Portuguese were not alone in the quest for new sources of wealth. In 1492, Columbus (sailing west in search of a route to the East) came upon the islands of the Caribbean. The Spanish followed up on Columbus's discovery by exploring the mainland of South and Central America. In 1513 Balboa reached the Pacific Ocean by crossing the Isthmus of Panama; in 1519 Cortés began the conquest of Mexico; and in 1530 the Spanish, under Pizarro, set out to conquer Peru. Despite their fortuitous discovery of the Americas the Spanish continued with their original quest to discover a western route to Asia. This route was discovered by Magellan who, between 1519 and 1522, completed the first circumnavigation of the globe. In his journey around the world Magellan located a route around the southern tip of South America, which later were named the Straits of Magellan, thereby crossing the Pacific and reaching the Philippines and Moluccas.

The Portuguese voyages around the Cape of Good Hope and the Spanish voyages westward around the southern tip of South America proved that the oceans of the southern hemisphere were connected, thereby opening up sea routes to the East. Throughout the sixteenth century the Spanish and Portuguese zealously guarded the passages to the East, using force to maintain their monopoly on the spice trade. Anxious to partake in the lucrative trade with Asia, other countries (including England, France, and the Netherlands) sought alternate routes. This search led men, such as John Sebastian Cabot (1497); Jacques Cartier (1534 and 1535); Martin Frobisher (1574); and Henry Hudson (1610) to explore the coastline of North America. While they were unsuccessful in finding a passage to the East their voyages did reveal the extent of the North American landmass and opened up the exploration and settlement of eastern North America.

The richness of the resources to be found in Asia, Africa, and the newly discovered Americas meant that from the sixteenth century onward clashes between European powers would take place on a global level. Herein lies the essence of the modern age—an age when events in one part of the world have repercussions in other parts, and when several continents are drawn into a global system of interdependence.

Early Contact

Before proceeding further with our study of European exploration and the resulting globalization, it is important that it be fully realized that throughout the world perfectly viable alternatives to European culture and economic systems existed. Many of the cultures the Europeans came into contact with (and with whom they established trading relationships) have been the focus of earlier chapters. What should be apparent to anyone who has studied various civilizations of the world is that several advanced societies existed world wide and that the eventual dominance of Europeans was neither inevitable nor the product of cultural or racial superiority. In many cases Europeans were only superior in their ability to travel great distances and in fact possessed weapons less suited to many of the environments they found themselves in. The eventual dominance of Europeans in the Americas was largely the result of the decimation of the **Amerindian** population from disease. As Karen Kuperman pointed out:

> European diseases did more than European technology to vanquish the American Indian in the early years of colonization.[2]

Estimates of the scale of this disaster place the number of deaths in the range of 75 percent to 90 percent of the Amerindian population. This means that in North America alone as many as eight to ten million Amerindians may have died as a result of contact with Europeans; the vast majority succumbing to diseases for which they had no natural immunity.

Europeans enjoyed varying degrees of success in penetrating the regions of the world. Because they were seldom technologically superior, the primary aim of most European expeditions was to establish trading relationships with the societies they encountered. In all regions, European explorers found that in order to establish such relationships they had to agree to mutually beneficial terms. It is false to assume that, in the initial stages of contact, Europeans were able to take advantage of naive natives. If, for example, we are to consider trade between Euro-

---

[2] *Karen Kuperman*, Settling with the Indians (Totowa NJ: Rowan and Littlefield), p. 186.

peans and the Amerindians of North America, we come to realize that the fur trade was in the interest of both parties involved. Amerindians did not receive worthless beads for valuable furs. The furs, to the Amerindians were easy to obtain and therefore of little value. In fact, the Europeans preferred furs that had been worn by the Amerindians for some time, as this loosened and helped remove the coarse outer fur. The Amerindians, therefore, were receiving glass beads and metal utensils, which to them were rare and of value, in exchange for plentiful furs. This same argument in terms of relative value can be applied in reverse to the Europeans making the initial stages of the fur trade a truly mutually beneficial trading relationship.

As the driving force behind European expansion was the quest for new markets and new sources of raw materials to fuel their economy, European reaction to the peoples they encountered was largely shaped by the role these people would play in the European world economy. This often led to a tragic irony in the relationships of Europeans and other cultures. While the peoples encountered were often classified as barbaric pagans, albeit noble barbarians who made suitable targets for conversion to Christianity, the actions of many of the Europeans were much more savage and inhumane. When reading accounts of the Spanish conquests in the Americas one is horrified by the atrocities committed by the **conquistadors**. Bartolome de Las Casas, who took part in the conquest of Cuba in 1513, recorded some of the atrocities committed by the Spanish:

> The Spaniards with their Horses, their Speares and Lances, began to commit murders, and strange cruelties: they entred into Townes, Borowes, and Villages, sparing neither children nor old men, neither women with childe...[3]

---

[3] John Carey, *Eyewitness to History (Massachusetts: Harvard University Press, 1987)*, p. 82.

In the mid-nineteenth century Japan re-established trade with numerous foreign nations. As a result the Japanese developed an insatiable appetite for things foreign, especially prints of foreign ships which were called Kurofune (Black ships). These prints, such as the example shown here by Utagawa Yoshitora, depicted foreign ships and reflected the Japanese view of a typical westerner. The writing for this print was supplied by the famous Japanese writer Kanagaki Robun and tells of the ship's dimensions, construction and about the country of origin.

In an attempt to justify the enslavement of the Amerindians, Spanish intellectuals classified them as "natural slaves." According to the Greek philosopher, Aristotle, there were two types of slaves: civil slaves, who were captured in war and became slaves in exchange for their lives being spared; and natural slaves, who were subhuman beings, whose purpose was to be enslaved. By being enslaved to the Spanish, so the argument went, the Amerindians fulfilled their lot in life and, in fact, were believed to be better off because of the influence of European civilization. In time this argument was repudiated and the Amerindians came to be viewed as fully human, but a younger civilization. By this time, however, their numbers had been greatly reduced through disease and through Spanish atrocities.

In areas such as China, Japan, and India, where disease was not a factor, Europeans were less able to establish themselves on their own terms. China, unlike Europe of the seventeenth century, was a highly centralized and bureaucratized nation, which strictly followed the directives of the central government in Peking. This was a source of much frustration to the Dutch, who repeatedly tried to establish a base for trade in China. The Chinese limited the Dutch to the role of transporters of goods in an already established trade circle and at no point allowed them to become essential to trade. In fact, once the Manchu dynasty was firmly established, and the threat of Japanese piracy lessened, the Chinese decided to limit contact with foreigners to commercial relations only; this was to take place only on selected coastal sites. Furthermore, no European power was ever allowed to establish a monopoly trade with the Chinese.

West Africa: A Case Study of Contact

For centuries Africa remained remote and mysterious and its people and their customs appeared strange to Europeans. Eventually, Europeans, who failed to assess other cultures in terms other than their own, classified Africans as savages and as inferior beings; perhaps a partial justification for the perpetuation of the slave trade, which became an integral part of the European world economy. This simple-minded view belies the western ignorance of Africa and its people. Contrary to such racist beliefs, Africa's past is resplendent with rich cultures and civilizations. Cities such as the legendary Timbuctu, which is reputed to have had so many scholars that merchants made their greatest profits from books; and Benin, which was a thriving commercial and cultural centre, bespeak the richness and vitality of the civilizations of West Africa.

When Muslims, in the ninth and tenth centuries, and Europeans in the later part of the fifteenth century, visited West Africa, they found not a savage wilderness but prosperous city-states linked by a vibrant system of trade. The cities' inhabitants, which included merchants, artisans, clerks, and labourers, lived comfortable lives. Although the Africans may have been behind the Europeans in their technical knowledge, they excelled in many other areas such as mining, metalworking, and tropical farming techniques. They were also astute businesspeople and had established sophisticated social and political systems.

Early Portuguese voyages to West Africa were prompted by the search for gold and spices. At the beginning of the relationship between the Portuguese and the kingdoms of West Africa there was a mutual investigation of each other's resources and a joint decision to enter into trade was made. In exchange for textiles, wheat, brass utensils, and glass beads the Portuguese received gold, pepper, ivory, gum, beeswax, leather, and timber as well as slaves.

Initially the slave trade was only of secondary concern. In time, as the demand for cheap labour grew on the new plantations in the Americas, the slave trade came to dominate African-Portuguese relations. It has been argued that Europeans did little more than enter into an existing system of trade for which the Africans were responsible. Although it is true that trade in people was not new, in either

Africa or Europe, the scale of the trade was. In the century between 1701 and 1801 over 6 million people were forcibly removed from Africa to supply the demand for slaves in Europe and the Americas. Also, the concept of **chattel slavery**, which was predominant throughout the western hemisphere, was absent in Africa. Prior to contact with the Portuguese, there were three ways a person in West Africa may have become a slave: through pawnship, through crime, and through warfare. Pawnship was a means to settle a debt, whereby an individual who owed money transferred their rights over the produce from their labour for a set period of time. Those captured in war or enslaved as a form of punishment, despite their status as a slave, could become functioning members of society. This was not to be the case once Europeans entered into the slave trade in Africa. It is the European who must accept much of the blame for the slave trade, for it was they who introduced chattel slavery, they who provided an insatiable market for slaves, and they who brought on and encouraged a century of civil war between African kingdoms, which produced the prisoners to be sold into slavery. The net result of the Portuguese exploitation of West Africa was massive depopulation, particularly of young males, and the conscious underdevelopment of the region. No contribution to West Africa's infrastructure was made, only cheap manufactured goods were exchanged for slaves, thus contributing to West Africa's Third World status today.

The Process of Acculturation

Throughout the world European expansion and the resulting globalization brought about significant change to most cultures. Can you imagine Italian food without tomatoes? The tomato, which is indigenous to South America, was not introduced to Europe until the sixteenth century. All areas in which distinct cultures met were altered by the process of acculturation. Acculturation is the blending of two or more cultures to create a new culture. It is distinct from **assimilation**, in that one of the cultures is not overwhelmed by a stronger or superior culture, but rather elements of both cultures are preserved. While the thought of a new culture, created by the synthesis of cultures, may sound appealing, it must be remembered that the process of acculturation has not always been kind.

Acculturation is very evident in North America. As a result of European contact with the Amerindians a new culture, most aptly termed Euro-American developed. The Euro-American culture was neither European culture transplanted to North America nor native American culture embraced by the Europeans; rather it was a blending of the two cultures. The early European colonists brought with them the Christian religion, a new concept of landownership, European government and law, Old World customs, traditions, and foods, and introduced a number of plants and animals to North America. Horses, sheep, cattle, and pigs were all imported, as was the dandelion, which was brought over as a food source, and the starling, which was brought over to make Canada seem more like England. Survival for the early colonists meant adapting to a new environment, which was most often done by learning from the native inhabitants. Hence, the Old World customs came to be blended with elements of the New World culture. Maize became a regular part of the diet, tobacco a favorite pastime, and canoes and snowshoes an integral part of travel. Canadian culture has continued to evolve as our multicultural heritage becomes increasingly diverse.

The process of acculturation was not so positive for the Amerindians. While they initially benefited from trade with the Europeans, in time they were drawn into a market economy that contributed to a growing dependence on European traders. Many of the nomadic tribes altered their traditional patterns of hunting in order to enter in a trading relationship with the Europeans. This led to clashes between tribes and to tribes being ill-prepared for winter, as they had been preoccupied with the fur trade rather than their winter food supply. As disease ravaged the native population, the shamans increasingly lost their prestige as they appeared powerless to deal with the tragedy that gripped the native villages. Traditional native religions were supplanted by Christianity, which served to undermine the social structure of the Amerindian society. The introduction of alcohol helped to further erode Amerindian society. Thus, while the Europeans successfully blended elements of Old World and New World cultures to create a strong Euro-American culture, the Amerindians suffered from their experience with acculturation.

Some regions of the world initially resisted contact with other cultures, wishing to remain pure. Throughout its history, China, which had always viewed itself as the centre of the universe, had maintained relatively extensive contacts with the outside world. Under the Tang dynasty (A.D. 618–906) China increasingly developed its contact with India allowing Buddhism to make major in-roads. Later, under the Song dynasty there had been a great expansion of trade with the southern seas, and under the Mongols contact with the West was reopened through the old silk roads, which brought Muslim, Jewish, and Christian merchants to China. The increasing contact with the outside world came to an abrupt end in 1367 when the Mongols were driven out of China and the Ming seized power. The Ming, seeking to return China to its traditional roots, withdrew from foreign exploration and contact with the outside world, in favour of stability at home.

The Chinese never completely stamped out foreign trade, but rather imposed restrictions. The European demand for spices and especially tea, which had become a favourite drink in the West, brought European merchants back in search of trade. The advent of the Manchu dynasty in 1644 brought a return to East–West trade, but with very strict imperial control. The commercial activity that did develop under the Manchu dynasty, and earlier, was to have important repercussions within China. Already by the sixteenth century Portuguese and Spanish trade along the southern coast had led to the production of sugar, textiles, porcelain, and metal wares specifically for export to the West. In exchange the Chinese received tobacco, sweet potatoes, and peanuts, all brought from the Americas. Thus, despite China's reluctance to engage in extensive foreign trade its culture too, was altered by trade. China, like many regions of the world, had been drawn into a very complex international economy. As Eric Wolf noted:

> To pay for tea, otter skins from the Northwest Coast of North America, sea cucumbers and sandalwood from the Pacific, silver from America, and Indian raw cotton and opium all began to flow toward China in a gigantic escalation of mercantile activity.[4]

With the worldwide exchange of goods and the increasing interdependence of nations upon trade with other nations the global village was born. Not only had economies become integrated, but cultures from various regions of the world were influenced by, and had influence on, other cultures. By the nineteenth century, food, clothing, music, art, and many other facets of life, in many areas of the world, had taken on an international flavour.

We have now come full circle in our odyssey through the ages. After tracing human origins into the heart of Africa we saw how people migrated and

---

[4]*Eric Wolf,* Europe and the People Without History *(Berkeley: University of California Press, 1982).*

eventually populated the entire earth. The chapters that followed "Humanity Before Civilization" examined a number of the world's great civilizations from their earliest beginnings to the eve of what we have termed globalization. While each chapter has focused on a specific civilization all have acknowledged the importance of outside influences on the culture studied. Hence, contact between peoples and the process of acculturation were not new in the fifteenth century. What was new was the extent of the contact and the corresponding changes that occurred as a result of the meeting of very distinct worlds. The modern era is perhaps best defined as the age in which the world ceased to be the home to distinct cultures, which existed in relative isolation, and became an interconnected, global village. No country better exemplifies the modern age than Canada. As home to a multiplicity of cultures, tolerant of a wide variety of religions and customs, Canada is truly a microcosm of the events that have reshaped the world since the fifteenth century. One needs only to stroll through cities such as Vancouver, Calgary, Toronto, Montreal, or Halifax to experience the cosmopolitan flavour of this country. Within Canada exists the product of millenniums of cultural development. Here, East and West, New World and Old World, are joined in a rich and vibrant multicultural nation. Consequently, the best foundations for Canadians who wish truly to understand and appreciate the histories and cultures that have combined to make up this nation is to study the civilization of the world. In this way we become educated, not only in the history of the world, but also in the heritage of Canada.

Suggested Sources for Further Research

Barraclough, Geoffrey, *The Times Atlas of World History* (Hammond Incorporates, 1984).

Cardini, Franco, *Europe 1492* (Facts on File, 1989).

Davidson, Basil, *African Kingdoms* (Time Incorporated, 1966).

Diaz, Bernal, *The Conquest of New Spain* (Penguin Books, 1963).

Hakluyt, Richard, *Voyages and Discoveries* (Penguin Books, 1987).

Tyler, S. Lyman, *Two Worlds: The Indian Encounter with the Europeans 1492–1509* (University of Utah Press, 1988).

Wallerstein, Immanuel, *The Modern World-System 1* (Toronto Academic Press Inc., 1974).

Wolf, Eric, *Europe and the People without History* (University of California Press, 1982).

Topics for Further Research

▼▼▼

The preceding chapter is the product of a highly successful and rewarding meeting of many of the contributors to *Odyssey Through The Ages*. This meeting, which brought together a number of scholars from a wide variety of backgrounds, focused on the question "What happened when the East and West met; when the Old World collided with the New World?" Our intent, both at the meeting and in this chapter was to draw together several of the civilizations examined in earlier chapters and to introduce a number of new concepts, which were the result of the increasing globalization that occurred after the fifteenth century. The ambitious nature of this task, with the inherent limitations imposed by the length of the chapter, left us with little opportunity to delve deeply into any of the areas covered. Instead we have simply introduced the main ideas that came out of the meeting and have chosen to leave the in-depth study of this fascinating and diverse topic to the students. Hence, below are a number of suggested topics and activities that are well suited to Independent Study projects, Research papers, Seminars, or Presentations. Once completed, this chapter and the research topics will act as an excellent introduction to future courses in either Modern Western civilization or World history.

The topics are of a challenging nature and will require some fairly extensive research and planning. To enjoy the greatest success students should review the "Skills Focus" at the end of each of the Units in *Odyssey Through the Ages*. By drawing on the skills developed throughout the book students will be able to define and focus their topic, gather and organize their research, and effectively present the information in a logical and coherent fashion.

Topics

1. Acculturation, or the blending of cultures, occurs when two societies come into contact with each other. Choose one of the cultural groups from below and assess the degree to which acculturation has changed or reshaped the culture. Also assess whether the culture has experienced a net gain or loss as a result of acculturation.

Amerindians	Europeans
Maya	Aztecs
Chinese	Japanese
Muslims	Indians

2. As pointed out in the chapter, many historians have linked the concept of Europeanization with modernization. After clearly defining modernization, select one region of the world covered in Chapter 18 or previous chapters and assess the impact of European contact on that region. Be sure to consider religion, disease, trade, warfare, food, and technology as well as other relevant factors. Also, attempt to view the impact of contact from the standpoint of the culture studied as well as the European point of view.

3. The key to European voyages of discovery were the many advancements made in naval technology. On page 552 several of these are mentioned briefly. Construct a model of a ship from the fifteenth or sixteenth century which shows these changes. Prepare an informative guide to accompany the model so that a viewer could become fully aware of the major changes and their significance.

4. Resulting from the three centuries of exploration, between 1480 and 1780, were far-flung empires of European powers. All corners of the world came to be affected in one way or another by European expansion. Listed below are a number of topics related to European imperialism. Select one of the topics from the list on which to do a research paper, independent study, or presentation.

   Chinese Drug Wars
   The British in India
   Gandhi and India's Independence Movement
   Caribbean Independence Movements (Select one movement.)
   Slave Trade of West Africa
   The Zulu Wars
   Canada's Role in Louis XIV's French Empire
   The Boer War

5. It was suggested in the concluding paragraph of the chapter that Canada is a microcosm of the changes brought about by globalization. To test this statement prepare a list of 10 food items and 10 other items (such as clothing, stereos, furniture, and cars). For each of the items selected find their origins. Based on this random survey and your own personal observations assess the degree to which Canada is truly representative of the "global village." What are the benefits of such diversity? What are the drawbacks and how can they be addressed?

Illustration Credits

pages 10 and 11 The Mary Rose Trust; **page 22** The Bettmann Archive; **page 30** William Sturgis Bigelow Collection. Courtesy, Museum of Fine Arts, Boston; **page 35** Painting by Jay H. Matternes © National Geograhic Society; **page 40** Illustration by Hugh Nachamie, reprinted from John Fleagle *Primate Adaptation and Evolution* published by Academic Press, 1988; **page 41**(both) © Sisse Brimberg/Woodfin Camp, Inc. By Sisse Brimberg © 1988 National Geographic Society; **page 45** © English Heritage; **page 51** (detail) Royal Ontario Museum, Toronto, Canada; **page 61** The Ancient Art and Architecture Collection; **page 66** Royal Ontario Museum, Toronto, Canada; **page 71** (bottom) Royal Ontario Museum, Toronto, Canada; **page 72** Royal Ontario Museum, Toronto, Canada; **page 73** Illustration by Lloyd K. Townsend, © National Geographic Society; **page 74** Reproduced by Courtesy of the Trustees of the British Museum; **page 77** Courtesy of the Egyptian Museum, Cairo; **page 79** Illustration by Lloyd K. Townsend, © National Geographic Society; **page 80** Photo by Victor R. Boswell, © National Geographic Society; **page 81** (photo) Reproduced by Courtesy of the Trustees of the British Museum; **page 86** The Bettmann Archive; **page 94** (detail) Courtesy of the Government of India Tourist Office, Toronto; **page 98** Robert Harding Picture Library Ltd.; **page 100** Reproduced by permission from *Indian Architecture* (Vol. 1: Hindu and Buddhist Period) by Percy Brown (Bombay: D.B. Taraporevala Sons & Co. Private Ltd.), 1991; **page 105** Reproduced from *An Introduction to the Study of Indian History* (2nd ed.) by Damodar Dharmanand Kosambi, published by Popular Prakashan Pvt. Ltd., 35-C, Pt. M.M. Marg, Tardeo, Bombay 400 034, India, in 1975; **page 106** By permission of the British Library; **page 114** © Rijksmuseum—Stichting Amsterdam; **page 116** (photo) Courtesy of ACSAA; **page 118** Courtesy of ACSAA; **page 122** Courtesy of the Government of India Tourist Office Toronto; **page 129** (detail) Courtesy of The Palace Museum; **page 136** Courtesy of the Royal Ontario Museum, Toronto, Canada; **page 142** E. McNabb, National Film Board of Canada; **page 144** Courtesy of the Royal Ontario Museum, Toronto, Canada; **page 148** Photo by Dorothy Hoover, courtesy of the Royal Ontario Museum, Toronto, Canada; **page 151** Calligraphy courtesy of Charles Wing-hoi Chan; **page 153** The Nelson-Atkins Museum of Art, Kansas City, Missouri (Nelson Fund) 47-71; **page 156** Courtesy The Palace Museum; **page 176** Greek National Tourist Organization; **page 177** Photo: G.P. Schaus; **page 180** Courtesy of the Royal Ontario Museum, Toronto, Canada; **page 185** Courtesy of the Royal Ontario Museum, Toronto, Canada; **page 188** From *The Pageant of the Past*, (Trueman & Trueman, 1965), published by McGraw-Hill Ryerson Limited; **page 193** From *The Pageant of the Past*, (Trueman & Trueman, 1965), published by McGraw-Hill Ryerson Limited; **page 207** Reproduced by Courtesy of the Trustees of the British Museum; **page 209** (lower right), From the Archives of the American School of Classical Studies of Athens; **page 212** Adapted from *Great Commanders and Their Battles*, by Anthony Livesay, published by Macmillan Publishing Company. Reprinted by permission of Marshall Editions Developments Limited; **page 213** *Great Commanders and Their Battles*, by Anthony Livesay, published by Macmillan Publishing Company. Reprinted by permission of Marshall Editions Developments Limited; **page 216** *Greek Everyday Life*, by Roger Nichols and Sarah Nichols, published by Longman Group UK Limited; **page 217** (photo) Reproduced by courtesy of the Trustees of the British Museum; **page 218** (left) Delphi Museum; **page 218** (right) Photo: G.P. Schaus; **page 238** The Bettmann Archive; **page 239** The Bettmann Archive; **page 246** Painting by Louis Glanzman © National Geographic Society; **page 250** From *Great Commanders and Their Battles*, (Anthony Livesay), published by MacMillan Publishing Company. Reprinted by permission of Marshall Editions Developments Limited; **page 268** John E. Stambaugh, *The Ancient Roman City*, The John Hopkins University Press, Baltimore/London, 1988, fig. 22, p. 202; **page 270** The Mansell Collection; **page 271** Scala/Art Resource, NY. K62275 Gismordi, ricostruzione plastica di Roma Antica. Roma, Museo della Civilita Romana; **page 274** From *The Roman World*, by Boardman, Griffin & Murray © Oxford University Press, 1988; **page 283** The Roman aqueduct at Segovia, still being used today after 2000 years. Courtesy of the Tourist Office of Spain; **page 289** The NY Carlsberg Glyptotek, Copenhagen; **page 292** *World History 1*, by Jerome R. Reich, Mark M. Krug, and Edward L. Biller. Copyright © 1987 by Harcourt Brace Jovanovich Canada Inc. Original Edition copyright © 1984 by Coronado Publishers. All rights reserved. Reproduced by permission of the publisher; **page 300** (photo) Tony Morrison/South American Pictures; **page 302** Courtesy of the Israel Government Tourist Office, Toronto; **page 307** Reproduced by courtesy of the Trustees of the Chester Beatty Library, Dublin; **page 316** Courtesy of the Israel Government Tourist Office, Toronto; **page 325** Courtesy of the Royal Ontario Museum, Toronto, Canada; **page 327** The Bettmann Archive; **page 335** From *The Japan of*

Today, Vol. B1 No. 11; **page 342** Courtesy of the Royal Ontario Museum, Toronto, Canada; **page 346** Calligraphy courtesy of Charles Wing-hoi Chan; **page 348** The Tokugawa Art Museum; **page 355** From *The Japan of Today*, Vol. B1, No. 11; **page 356** Hanging Scroll of Samurai, Edo Period (1615-1868); ink and colours on paper. Gift of Howard Roloff, Art Gallery of Greater Victoria; **page 358** Eastern Images Picture Library; **page 360** Ikenobo Ikebana Society of Toronto; **page 367** Stela 22 in enclosure, Group E, Tikal; Courtesy of Dr. David M. Pendergast, Department of New World Archaeology, The Royal Ontario Museum, Toronto, Canada; **page 369** Drawing by Emil Hustiu; **page 372** Stela 22 in enclosure, Group E, Tikal; Courtesy of Dr. David M. Pendergast, Department of New World Archaeology, The Royal Ontario Museum, Toronto; **page 373** Drawing by H. Stanley Loten and Michael P. Closs. Courtesy of The Royal Ontario Museum, Toronto, Canada; **page 375** Courtesy of The Royal Ontario Museum, Toronto, Canada; **page 378** Drawing by Emil Hustiu; **page 380** (photo) Peabody Museum, Harvard University; **page 380** Drawing by Emil Hustiu; **page 381** Deer, monkey, longtailed creature—Drawings by Georgina Hosek; Courtesy of the Royal Ontario Museum, Toronto, Canada. Jaguar with bundle—Redrawn by E. Hustiu from Thompson, *The Rise and Fall of Maya Civilization*; Courtesy of the Royal Ontario Museum, Toronto, Canada; **page 385** Photo courtesy of Elizabeth Graham; **page 386** Drawing by Mariana Hustiu. Courtesy of The Royal Ontario Museum, Toronto, Canada; **page 387** Drawing by Emil Hustiu; **page 396** Tony Morrison/South American Pictures; **page 396** Tony Morrison/South American Pictures; **page 399** Map by Emil Hustiu; **page 404** Map by Emil Hustiu; **page 408** Drawing by Emil Hustiu; **page 415** Drawing by Emil Hustiu; **page 417** (top four drawings) by Emil Hustiu; **page 420** Neg. no. 326597—Great Temple of Tenochtitlan. Courtesy of the Department of Library Services, American Museum of Natural History; **page 421** Tony Morrison/South American Pictures; **page 422** Drawing by Emil Hustiu; **page 423** The Bettmann Archive; **page 424** Drawing by Emil Hustiu; **page 426** Akademische Druck—u. Verlagsanstalt, Graz, Austria; **page 432** The Bettmann Archive; **page 434** GEKS; **page 437** *World History 1*, by Jerome R. Reich, Mark M. Krug and Edward L. Biller. Copyright © 1987 by Harcourt Brace Jovanovich Canada Inc. Original Edition copyright © 1984 by Coronado Publishers. All rights reserved. Reproduced by permission of the publisher; **page 442** GEKS; **page 444** John P. McKay, Bennett D. Hill and John Buckler, *A History of World Societies*, Second Edition. Copyright © 1988 by Houghton Mifflin Company. Used with permission; **page 446** From *Arthur's Britain*, by Leslie Alcock (Allen Lane, The Penguin Press, 1971), copyright © Leslie Alcock, 1971. Reproduced by permission of Penguin Books Ltd.; **page 454** Courtesy of the Royal Ontario Museum, Toronto, Canada; **page 460** Courtesy of Douglas Newman; **page 467** *The Observer's Book of Castles*, by Brian Davison, Copyright © Frederick Warne & Co., 1979, 1986. Reproduced by permission of Frederick Warne & Co.; **page 468** John P. McKay, Bennett D. Hill and John Buckler; *A History of World Societies*, Second Edition, Copyright © 1988 by Houghton Mifflin Company. Used with permission; **page 472** (top) John Pearson, Historical Illustrator; **page 481** John P. McKay, Bennett D. Hill and John Buckler, *A History of World Societies*, Second Edition, Copyright © 1988 by Houghton Mifflin Company. Used with permission; **page 485** The Bodleian Library, University of Oxford; MS Canon. Misc. 416, fol. 1R; **page 489** Andromeda Oxford Ltd.; **page 493** Mansell Collection; **page 499** Courtesy Soprintendenza per i Beni Artistici e Storici, Venezia; **page 500** G. Morgan, *Life in a Medieval Village*, New York: Cambridge University Press, 1975; **page 502** John P. McKay, Bennett D. Hill, and John Buckler, *A History of World Societies*, Volume A, Second Edition. Copyright © 1988 by Houghton Mifflin Company. Used with permission; **page 517** The Bettmann Archive; **page 522** The Bettmann Archive; **page 526** The Bettmann Archive; **page 528** The Bettmann Archive; **page 529** The Bettmann Archive; **page 530** Print Collection, Miriam and Ira D. Wallach Division of Art, Prints and Photographs; The New York Public Library; Astor, Lenox and Tilden Foundations; **page 535** The Bettmann Archive; **page 546** Giraudon/Art Resource, N.Y. CRL 5.884/LAC 108.081 Edition d'ulm 1486: Carte du Monde de Ptolomee, planch I, vue d'ensemble, Paris, Bibl. Nationale; **page 548** The Bettmann Archive; **page 551** World Map: Peters Projection, distributed in North America by Friendship Press, New York. Copyright Akademische Verlangstalt. Used by permission; **page 555** Courtesy of the Royal Ontario Museum, Toronto, Canada.

We would like to thank Garfield Newman for contributing numerous photographs.

Acknowledgements

pages 8 and 9 Adapted and redrawn from *The Hamilton Spectator*, Tuesday April 24, 1990, p. AA5. Courtesy of *The Hamilton Spectator*; **pages 18 and 19** From *A Vision of Light* by Judith Merkle Riley. Copyright © 1989 by Judith Merkle Riley, (pages 1-8). Reproduced by permission of New English Library Limited. Used by permission of Delacorte Press, a division of Bantam Doubleday Dell Publishing Group, Inc.; **pages 36 and 37** Reprinted from *Science and Religion: Opposing Viewpoints* by permission of Greenhaven Press, Inc. PO Box 289009, San Diego, CA 92198-0009; **page 42** Excerpt abridged from *Sarum*, by Edward Rutherford, published by Hutchinson. Copyright © 1987 by Edward Rutherford. Reprinted by permission of Crown Publishers, Inc.; **page 112** *Sanskrit Poetry* by Daniel H. Ingalls, Harvard University Press, 1972. Reprinted by permission; **pages 190 and 191** "The Gods of Greece." Harry N. Abrams, Inc.; **pages 216 and 217** *Greek Everyday Life*, by Roger Nicholsand Sarah Nichols, published by Longman Group UK Limited; **page 284 and 285** Recipes from *The Roman Cookery of Apicius*, by John Edwards, 1984. Hartley & Marks Ltd. Revised as *Roman Cookery: Elegant and Easy Recipes from History's First Gourmet*, 1986; **page 309** From *The Tale of the Reed Pipe*, by Massud Farzan. Copyright © 1974 by Massud Farzan. Used by permission of the publisher, Dutton, an imprint of New American Library, a division of Penguin Books USA, Inc.; **page 323** The font used to print this in Arabic is available from Linguist's Software, Inc. P.O. Box 580, Edmonds, WA 98020-0580; Tel. (206)775-1130. Prepared by George Sawa; **page 382** Reprinted from *Landa's Relacion De Las Cosas De Yucatan, A Translation*, (Alfred M. Tozzer, ed., 1941). Courtesy of the Peabody Museum of Archaeology and Ethnology, Harvard University; **page 406** From *The Conquest of New Spain*, by Bernal Díaz, translated by J.M. Cohen (Penguin Classics, 1963), page 217 copyright © J.M. Cohen, 1963. Reproduced by permission of Penguin Books Ltd.; **page 410** From *The Conquest of New Spain*, by Bernal Díaz, translated by J.M. Cohen (Penguin Classics, 1963) pages 225 227 copyright © J.M. Cohen, 1963. Reproduced by permission of Penguin Books Ltd.; **pages 450 and 451** From *A Sourcebook For Medieval History*, by Oliver J. Thatcher and Edgar Holms McNeil (Charles Sccribner's Sons, New York, 1905); **page 467** *The Observer's Book of Castles*, by Brian Davison, copyright © Frederick Warne & Co., 1979, 1986. Reproduced by permission of Frederick Warne & Co.; **pages 488 and 489** Ken Follett, Pillars of the Earth, Copyright © 1989 by Ken Follett, published by William Morrow and Company, Inc. Used with permission by William Morrow and Company, Inc. Publishers, New York, Penguin USA, New York; **pages 532 and 533** From *Witchcraft in Europe 1100–1700* Philadelphia: University of Pennsylvania Press, 1972, pp 113-132.

Care has been taken to trace ownership of copyright material contained in this text. The publishers will gladly accept any information that will enable them to rectify any reference or credit in subsequent editions.

Glossary

acculturation The blending of two or more cultures resulting in the creation of a new culture. For further explanation see Chapter 18.

adze A heavy hand tool with a steel cutting blade attached at right angles to a wooden handle. Used for squaring timber.

alluvial plain Extensive accumulations of clay, silt, sand or gravel deposited by running water forming a level or gently sloping surface.

alms Food, money, clothing or other items given as charitable gifts to help the poor.

amalgamation An independent whole which results from the uniting and combining of various factors or elements.

ancestor veneration Honouring the spirits of dead ancestors with the intent of avoiding evil and being granted good fortune.

animism The belief that everything, every object such as plants or stones, any natural phenomena such as thunderstorms have a soul or spirit and life inside, being able to affect situations by exerting a positive or a negative influence.

anthropology The study of the anatomical and mental make-up of humanity, examining also historical and present geographical distribution, cultural history, acculturation, cultural relationships and racial classification.

anthropomorphic The idea of attributing either in description or representation, human characteristics and appearance to something non-human.

apostate One who has abandoned their religious faith or given up moral allegiance.

assimilation The cultural absorption of one group into another.

autocracy A form of government where one person holds absolute and unlimited power and authority.

autonomy The degree of political control and moral freedom possessed by a political unit, community or group as it relates to the larger political picture of which it is a part.

beneficium Property bestowed on a person by a lord in return for unspecified work; in a religious context it can also mean the granting of a church benefice or office.

benevolent Being kind and generous and taking pleasure in doing good works which may result in the happiness and prosperity of others.

bishopric The administrative area under the jurisdiction of a bishop, the office of a bishop, or the bishop's seat or residence.

borough A group of fortified houses forming a town in medieval times, having duties and privileges, courts, representatives in council or parliament, and holding an inheritable charter from the king.

bridgeheads An area seized in hostile territory and used as a foothold in further advancements.

Bronze Age The period of human culture between the Stone and Iron Ages, distinguished by the use of bronze tools and weapons and intensive trade beginning in the Middle East about 4500 B.C. and lasting in Britain from about 2000 to 500 B.C.

bureaucracy A structured, centralized and inflexible system of government or rule characterized by a hierarchy of authority with a powerful group of officials basing their actions on fixed rules.

burgess The small minority who held full legal rights in a town or a city. The obligations which accompanied the position of a burgess included: holding public office, entertaining visiting officials, and granting loans to the king. The status of a burgess was given by the governing body of the town and the basis for this was prescribed in a town's charter. An equivalent office would be a more restricted version of a modern chamber of commerce.

canon law A written group of religious laws for the government of a church or for the members of a particular faith.

capitalism An economic system based on the private ownership of the means of production, distribution, and exchange. Also characterized by the use of money to earn money through usury or trade.

caste Divisions within a society based on wealth, inherited rank or privilege, profession or occupation.

Caucasoid Of, resembling, or related to the Caucasoid race; the race of humanity which has a light complexion.

chattel slavery A type of slavery which assumes the slaves to be items of personal and moveable property. Slaves and their descendants are held as slaves in perpetuity and are not held in lieu of debt for a specified period of time.

chivalry The system of knighthood based on the character of the ideal knight, who exhibits in manners and mind: honour, protective kindness to the weak, generosity to friends as well as enemies, and flawless gallantry.

Classical Age While all civilizations have periods referred to as "Classic" the term "Classical Age" is accepted by most historians as referring to the civilizations of Greece and Rome despite the Eurocentrism attached.

confederacy A group or league formed by people or political units for mutual support or for achieving common goals.

conquistador Usually refers to the Spanish conquerors of the Americas in the sixteenth century.

cosmopolitan Being sophisticated, urban, knowledgeable and aware of the world; having a wide vision and not being restricted by regional beliefs, attitudes, prejudice or interests.

cultural diffusion The spread of the characteristics and traits of a culture to other cultures and inhabitants in other areas.

deify To give the status of a god and divine power to something or someone.

demigod A divine or semi-divine being, perhaps the offspring of a mortal and a god, who carries less power than a god.

desiccation The process of drying out or having dried out.

despotism A system of government where the ruler has absolute power and authority.

diaspora A dispersion of people of a common national origin or of common beliefs into other countries; often used with reference to the dispersion of the Jews.

diocese An administrative division of the Roman Catholic church, usually the district where the bishop has authority.

duchy The dukedom or the territories or lands ruled by a duke or a duchess, who are nobles of the highest hereditary rank.

dynasty A succession of rulers coming from the same family or the same line of descent.

ecosystem A unit which combines the living and non-living elements of an ecological system.

egalitarian A belief that everyone is equal and is equally entitled to the rights and privileges of society.

enfranchisement To free and to give political rights to a town or a city; under feudal law to free lands previously held as a fiefdom.

entrepreneur A person who organizes, owns or manages an economic venture and who usually assumes all the risks, financial or otherwise.

ethnohistory A means of studying the past through the use of aspects of culture such as folklore, religion, oral traditions, and customs.

ethnology The science which deals with the racial divisions of humanity and which compares and analyzes their respective origins, distribution, relations, characteristics, cultures, and societies.

etymology Tracing the historical development of a sound or a word to its earliest recorded use; identifying cognates or similar words in other languages and examining their development.

eunuch A castrated man often in charge of a harem or otherwise employed in a palace.

Eurocentric A world view that measures aspects of civilization in relation to European standards. Implies a belief in the intrinsic superiority of European culture.

faience Pottery or porcelain that is decorated with coloured opaque glazes.

feudalism A social system or society which represents the legal and society organization of medieval Europe. This includes the granting of fiefs and a series of contractual obligations between the lord and his vassals. For further explanation see Chapters 14 and 15.

fief (also feoff) A grant of land held in return for a specified service (usually a military one).

fiefdom A feudal estate or territory held by a vassal.

fluvial deposit The deposits produced by the flowing action of a river.

fratricide The act of murdering either brother or sister or someone who is very close.

fresco The painting of fresh moist plaster with water-based paints often done on large surfaces resulting in brightly-coloured murals.

friar A member of a religious order where monastic life and religious activity are combined, and the possession of property is forbidden.

genealogy A historical account, in the order of succession of the descent of a person, a family or a group of people.

gentry The people of the upper class wielding large economic and social influence. Wealth and power generally derived from political appointments as they are not part of the nobility. Although of the upper class, their position is more volatile than members of the aristocracy.

genus A class or group marked by one or several common characteristics.

hieroglyph A picture or a symbol that represents an object, an idea or a sound.

hominid Any primate belonging to the family Hominidae (includes modern humans).

humanoid Resembling a human in appearance.

iconoclasm The attacking of established and traditional beliefs and often included the destruction of religious icons or sacred objects.

iconography The symbols used in a work of art or an art movement i.e. a pregnant woman to represent fertility.

ideologies A body of ideas and concepts.

impress To commandeer or coerce people or their property into government service.

indigenous Having originated, developed or been produced in a particular land, region, or environment.

infidel A person who has no religious belief and who rejects a specific religion especially Christianity or Islam.

insular Being remote or isolated.

investiture The act of granting an office or a title. This act is often accompanied by a ceremony and by the transfer of the symbols of this particular office or position.

jurisprudence The science or philosophy of law.

lord A male member of the nobility or someone of whom a fee or estate is held in feudal tenure; often the master of the manor or a person who holds power and authority over others.

manumission Formal release from slavery or from feudal obligations.

martyrdom The suffering or death of a person, caused by a refusal to renounce beliefs or adherence to a particular religious faith.

matriarch The female head of a family, tribe, community, or dynasty who rules by dictatorship and without male influence.

mausoleum A building which serves as a tomb, usually for a number of people.

megalomania A mental illness where one believes one has the ability to perform great feats, characterized by delusions of grandeur, power, and wealth.

mendicants People who beg and who live by begging.

mercenary A soldier hired into foreign service into an army he holds no allegiance to.

metaphysical Deals with ideas or elements which are outside the realm of everyday life.

millennium A period spanning 1000 years.

Mongoloid Related to or belonging to one of the major groups of humanity characterized by a yellowish complexion, straight black hair, slanting eyes, short nose, a flat face, and little facial hair.

monolithic Consisting of a large, complete unit which is uniform and has no diversity or variation.

monotheism The belief or doctrine that states that there is only one god.

myth A story about superhumans, involving the lives of gods, which was seen by early humanity as being a true account of how natural phenomena or social customs came into being.

Neolithic The latest period of the Stone Age, characterized by: grinding stone, making pottery, domestication of animals, cultivating grain, weaving linen, and the beginnings of a settled village life.

ochre Earth containing natural pigments that are used in creating yellow, orange, or red colours for paints.

oracle An agent of divine or supernatural communication. It can also be the place where this communication occurs.

pagan A person who follows a polytheistic religion. The term was generally applied to worshippers of religions other than Christianity, Judaism, or Islam.

paleoanthropology The branch of anthropology relating to primitive humanity.

Paleolithic The second period of the Stone Age where primitive humanity emerged and manufactured chipped unpolished stone tools. The time period was from about 2.5 to 3 million years ago until about 12 000 B.C.

paleontologist A person who studies prehistoric life forms through the study of plant and animal fossils.

pandemic Affecting an exceptionally large percentage of the population and affecting people over a wide geographical area; often an extensive epidemic.

pantheon A collection of all the gods in a religion; the temple built to all the gods.

papal see The jurisdiction such as the seat or the centre of the power and authority of a pope.

pastoral nomadism A nomadic lifestyle based on the search for pasture land.

patriarchy A system based on the male head of a family, community, tribe or dynasty.

patrimony An inheritance from one's father or ancestor.

peasant The term peasant is a broad term which encompasses both free peasants and servile peasants. Free peasants could own their own land and legally owed no obligation to a lord other than the king. Servile peasants also known as serfs or villeins did not own their own land but held a tenement from a lord. These people were tied to the soil in that they owed feudal obligations to a lord and were not free to leave the manor. Serfs could obtain the status of freemen if the lord chose to grant manumission. This may have been in return for a payment or a service, or as an act of generosity.

philanthropy Goodwill towards humanity demonstrated by performing charitable or benevolent actions.

pi The ratio of the circumference of a circle to its diameter.

polity Refers to a political organization, a form of government, or the constitution of a political unit.

polyandry A form of marriage where a woman has more than one husband at the same time.

polytheist A person who believes in or worships more than one god.

pottage Oatmeal or vegetables cooked to the consistency of a stew or a thick soup.

primates An order of mammals that includes humans, apes, monkeys, and lemurs.

primeval Relating to or being from the earliest stages of the world or human history.

primogeniture The exclusive right of the first child of the same parents to inherit the property or estate of their ancestors.

priory A community of religious people lead by a prior living under the jurisdiction of an abbey.

proto-human Any of the prehistoric primates that were related to or resembled early modern humans.

realpolitik Politics based on practical and material factors, on political realities, or on the realities of national interest and power.

regionalism The development of a political or social system based on smaller political units or regions that may divide the country.

relief Sculpture where figures are distinguished by being raised from or sunk into the surrounding flat surface.

rhetoric The art of expressive speech and effective communication.

secular Relating to worldly as opposed to sacred things; not concerned with or related to religion.

Semitic A branch of the Afro-Asiatic family of languages that includes Arabic, Hebrew, Aramaic, Amharic as well as such ancient languages as Akkadia and Phoenician. Also another word for Jewish.

sericulture Producing raw silk by cultivating silkworms.

servility Being obedient or dominated by a person or thing, usually as a slave.

shamanist A person who practices or believes in the powers of a shaman, a priest doctor who uses magic to cure the sick, to divine, to control the good and evil spirits of the world.

simony The selling or buying of a church office.

social contract An agreement that results in the creation of an organized society with a ruler and a community, and defines the rights and duties of its people.

species A biological class of related living organisms having common attributes and being capable of interbreeding.

strata A succession of deposits one on top of another, so that the uppermost deposits are later in date than the lower ones.

suzerain A feudal lord or a political state or sovereignty exercising some degree of control over a dependent state, often in the control of its foreign affairs.

synod The meeting of an ecclesiastical council, a church governing or advisory body, usually of a diocese to discuss church matters.

tectonic plates It is believed that the earth's crust is made up of a number of plates known as tectonic plates. Since the core of the earth is fluid these plates will occasionally shift which creates mountain ranges, volcanic activity, earthquakes, or tidal waves.

temporal Relating to secular as opposed to spiritual or religious affairs; of or relating to a particular time.

tenement Usually land or permanent property held in tenure by one person or another.

theocracy A government or a state under religious rule, directed by or administered by God or religious officials such as priests or clergy.

theologian A specialist in or a person engaged in the study of religion.

Third Estate In medieval Europe society was broadly broken into three estates: the First Estate being the Estates Temporal (the aristocracy); the Second Estate being the Estates Spiritual (religious leaders); and the Third Estate being the Estates Common (the common people including the gentry). Later the journalists were called the Fourth Estate and the television program *The Fifth Estate* suggests that the electronic media is the fifth estate.

tithe A tenth of the yearly agricultural yield, personal income or profits contributed as a tax or voluntarily for religious purposes and for the support of the church or the clergy.

transubstantiation The doctrine or belief that the whole substance of bread and wine changes into the substance of the body and the blood of Christ when consecrated by the Eucharist.

tribute Homage or payment paid by a vassal to his lord; a sum of money or valuables paid by one ruler or nation to another as acknowledgement of submission and often as payment for peace and protection.

triremes Greek warships from the fifth century B.C. which were fast and manoeverable and were operated by 180 rowers.

usury The practice of loaning money and charging interest for its use.

vassal A person who holds a feoff from a superior lord. This does not include a peasant as they held a tenement.

vernacular The commonly spoken language or dialect of a particular people of a region or a country which contrasts to the literary or cultured form of the language.

xenophobic To be afraid of or to hate strangers or foreigners, their politics and their culture; fear or hatred of anything strange or foreign.

yeoman A member of the most respected class of common people, the small freeholders who ranked below the gentry and cultivated and farmed their own land.

Index

Page references in italics indicate illustrations, maps or charts. **Entries in boldface indicate key concepts**

Aachen, 454, 455
Abbasid caliphate, 311–313, 315
Abbey of Cluny, 479
Abelard, 484
Abraham, 321
Acculturation, 123, 125, 549, 557–559
Actium, Battle of, 265
Acupuncture, 155, 158
Adze, 98
Aediles, Roman, 242
Aegyptopithecus, 36
Aeneid, 267
Aeschylus, 195, 206
Aesop, 182, 183
Age of the Earth, 25
Agora of Athens, 219, 220
Agriculture. *See* Farming
Agrippa, Marcus, 264, 265
Agrippina (mother of Nero), 278
Ainu, 338
Akbar, 120–121
Akhenaton, 65–66
Akkadians, 55
Alans, 291, 293
Alaric (Gothic leader), 293
Alberuni, 123
Albigensian Crusade, 480–481, 482
Albigensians, 480–481
Alcibiades, 204–205
Alcuin, 454, 455
Alexander the Great, 211–214, 245
Alfred the Great, of England, 462, 463
Algebra, 324, 330
Alhazen (Muslim scientist), 329–330
Ali (son-in-law of Muhammad), 307, 311
Alla-ud-din Khalji, 120
Alluvial plain, 53
Alphabet, 85, 184
Alps, 234
Altun Ha, 385
Alvares, Jorge, 363
Amon-Re, 64, 65, 68
Amerindians
 effects of contact with Europeans, 554–555
 process of acculturation, 557–558

Ammianus Marcellinus, 291
Amorites, 55
Amphitheatres, Roman, 269, *269*
Amphorae (pottery containers), 281
Anabaptists, 537
Analects of Confucius, 138
Ancestor veneration, 135, 158
Andron, 223–224
An Lu-Shan, 150
Anselm of Canterbury, 484
Anthropomorphism, 67, 136, 224
Antigonus, 214, 245
Antony, Mark, 252, 259, 264–265
Apennine Mountains, 234
Appian Way, 246
Apprenticeship, 475, 478
Apuleius (Roman writer), 280
Aqueducts, Roman, 282–283, 286
Aquinas, St. Thomas, 310, 485
Aquitaine, 490
Arabian Nights, 324, 326–327
Arabic language, 322, 323
Arabic numerals, 324
Arabic script, 323
Archaeology
 analyzing data, 13–16
 Ball site, 5–7
 importance to historian's work, 3
 nature and purpose of, 4–5
 search for King Arthur, 11–12
 underwater archaeology, 7–11
Archimedes, 222
Architecture
 Aztec, 418–419
 of the European Renaissance, 524–525
 Gothic architecture, 486, 488–489, 490
 Greek, 208–209, 219, 227
 in the Islamic world, 325, 328–329
 Mayan, 385–387
 Roman, 268–272, 273–274, 279–280, 282–283, 286, 295
 the Taj Mahal, *122*, 123
Archons, 188
Aristeides, 201
Aristophanes, 206–207, 225
Aristotle, 214, 215, 222, 555–556

Armour, medieval, 467
Art. *See also* Architecture; Painting; Pottery; Sculpture
 Arabic script, 323
 the Carolingian Renaissance, 454
 Egyptian, 73–75
 the European Renaissance, 524–528
 Greek, 196, 215, 218, 227
 Paleolithic, *41*, 43
 Song dynasty, 150, 152–153
Arthashashtra, 104–105
Arthur, King
 knight in time of, *446*
 legend of, 11–12
Artifacts, analyzing, 14–15
Aryabhatta, 111
Aryans, 99, 101
Ashikaga shogunate, 354–362
Ashikaga Takauji, 354
Ashoka, 105–106
Ashura, 322
Assemblies in ancient Rome, 241
Assimilation, 557
Assyrians, 56
Athens, 188
 imperialism of, 201–202
 Peloponnesian War, 202, 203 (map), 204–206
 rivalry with Sparta, 203–204
Atlantis, 177
Attila the Hun, 293
Augustine of Hippo, Saint, 294, 438–439, 443
Augustus Caesar, 255, 260, 264, 265, 277
 administrative skills, 265, 267
 establishment of the Roman Empire, 265
Aurangjeb, 123
Australopithecus afarensis, 34, 35, 37
Australopithecus africanus, 35, 37
Averroes, 308–309
Ayisha (Muhammad's youngest wife), 320
Aztec civilization
 agriculture, 423–424
 architecture, 418–419
 beliefs, 405–409
 calendar, 422–423

clothing, 416–418
daily life and customs, 413–418
feasting, 410–411
geography, 398–399, 401
gods, 407–409
human sacrifice, 405–407
literature and music, 418
maps, 399, *404*
markets, 425–426
medicine, 421–422
migrations, 403
Nahuatl language, 400
origins, 401–403
sculpture, 420, *421*
social structure, 409, 412–413
Spanish Conquest and depopulation, 426–427
trade and tribute, 424–425
writing and painting, 421
Aztlan, 403

Babylonia, 53, 55–56
Baghdad, sacked by Mongols, 315
Bakufu, 351
Ballard, Robert, 9
Ball site, 5–7
Baniwa, 340
Barbarians
confrontation with the Roman empire, 291, 293, 294, 435, 437–438
description of ancient Germans by Tacitus, 290–291
sacking of Rome, 293
Barter, 226
Baths, Roman, 268–269
Bayeux Tapestry, 465
Beagle (ship), 32
Beguines (women's movement), 507
Beliefs and morals
Chinese zodiac, 132–133
Egyptian gods, 68–69
the European witchcraze, 532–533
Greek gods, 190–191
organization of the Catholic Church, 440
Roman gods, 254
Stonehenge, 44–45
yin-yang, 141
Zen meditation, 352
Benedict, Saint, 449, 450
Benedictine Rule, 449, 450–451, 480
Beneficium, 463
Berbers, 438
Bernard of Clairvaux, Saint, 480, 484

Bhagavadgita, 108
Bhakti, 125
Bias, historical, 16, 17
Bible. *See also* Old Testament
story of creation in, 31
Bipedalism, 34, 35, 37
Bishopric, 463
Black Death, 494, 495–496, 498–499, 506, 519, 520
Boethius (Roman philosopher), 294
Bo Juyi, 149, 150
Boniface, Saint, 452
Books
illuminated manuscripts, 487, 490
printed, 529, 530
Botticelli, Sandro, 525
Bow and arrow, 41
Brahmagupta, 111
Brahmins, 99, 100–101
Bridgeheads for trade, 473
Bronze, 175, 234
Brueghel, Pieter, 530
Brunelleschi, Filippo, 524, 525
Bryan, William Jennings, 36, 37
Buboes, 495
Buddha, 95, 101, 102–103
Buddhism, 95, 148
in Japan, 341, 342, 343, 344
in Kamakura Japan, 351–353
spread of, 108–109
Bureaucracy in ancient China, 144, 146
Bureaucratic-patrimonial states, 316–317
Burgesses, 511
Bushi code, 356–357
Bushido, 356–359
Byzantium, 287, 288, 294, 435
under Justinian, 439, 441

Caddy, John, 370
Caesarion, 264, 265
Cairo, 313, 315
Calendar
Aztec, 422–423
Julian, 252
Mayan, 375–376, 390
Caligula (Roman emperor), 277
Caliphates, 310–313
Calvin, John, 538–539, 540
Canaanites, 85
Canada today, 559
Cannae, Battle of, 244
Canopic jars, 72
Canossa, 479

Canterbury Tales (Chaucer), 496–497
Capitalism, 474, 552–553
in the Song dynasty, 152
Capitoline, 239
Caracalla (Roman emperor), 281, 286
Caravanserai, 328
Carolingian House, 452–455, 457
Carthage, 85
Carthaginians, 242, 243–245
Castles in Medieval Europe, 466, 467, 468–469
Cathedrals in Medieval Europe, 485–487, 488–489
Catherine of Sienna, Saint, 507
Catherwood, Frederick, 370
Catholic Church. *See* Roman Catholic Church
Catullus, 259
Cave painting, 43
Cenotes, 369
Censors, Roman, 242
Centuries (of Roman soldiers), 251
Chaeronaea, Battle of, 211
Champollion, Jean Francois, 81
Chance mutation, 33
Chandragupta II, 110
Chandragupta Maurya, 103–104
Chapel of the Lioness, 43
Charlemagne, 447, 452, 453, 454, 455
Charles Martel, 452, 453, 463
Charles VII of France, 504, 505
Charles VIII of France, 521, 522
Chattel slavery, 557
Chaucer, Geoffrey, 496–497, 507
Chichen Itza, 370, 376
Childbirth
in ancient Rome, 253, 255, 257
among Aztecs, 413
in medieval Europe, 471
Children
in ancient Egypt, 76, 77
in ancient Rome, 253–254
among Aztecs, 413–414, 415
China
Chinese world view, 163–164
classical age, 136–140
contacts with foreigners, 558
creation stories, 27
First Empire, 140, 142–148
formative period, 134–136
geography, 131–133
Last Empire, 161–163
limits contact with foreigners, 556

maps, *131*, *145*, *160*
origin of civilization along Yellow River, 47
Second Empire, 148–150
Third Empire, 150, 152–161
time and history in, 133–134
Chinampas, 398, 423–424
Chingghis Khan, 119–120, 159, 315
Chivalry, 464, 467
Chocolate, 414
Christian Century in Japan, 363
Christianity. *See also* Jesus Christ; Papacy; Reformation; Roman Catholic Church
effect on the Roman Empire, 294
explanations for Christianity's spread, 276–277
persecution of Christians, 276, 277, 287
rise of, 274–277
similarities with mystery religions, 289
Christine de Pisan, 507
Chromosomes, 33
Cicero, 259
Cimon, 202, 203
Ciompi revolt, 521
Circus, Roman, 269, 272
Circus Maximus, 271, 272
Cities. *See also* Towns
in Islamic Middle East, 319
Mayan, 372
City of God (Augustine), 439
City-states
Greek, *174* (map)
Italian, 324, 330, 519, 520–522
Civilizations
fundamental elements in, 47
and rivers, 23, 47
Civil service examinations in China, 146
Classical revival, 518–519, 523
Class structure
in ancient India, 100, 101, 102
in Aztec civilization, 409, 412–413
among Maya, 378–379
in medieval Europe, 464, 469, 474, 475–476, 506–507, 519–520
Class system in neolithic society, 46, 47
Claudius (Roman emperor), 273, 277
Cleisthenes, 189
Cleopatra, 224
Cleopatra VII, 264–265
Clergy, influence in medieval Europe, 476
Climate
Greece, 181
Italy, 234–235

Clothing
in ancient Egypt, 77, 79
Aztec, 416–418
Greek, 216
Roman, 256, 257
Clovis, 444, 445
Cohorts, Roman, 251
Coinage
Greek, 226
in the Roman Empire, 281
Colonial expansion
ancient Greece, 186–187
Europe of High Middle Ages, 471, 473
Colosseum, 269, 271, 272
Columbus, Christopher, 551, 553
Comitia Centuriata, 241
Comitia Curiata, 241
Comitia Tributa, 241
Commons, 511, 512, 513
Concilium Plebis, 241
Concrete, 234, 295
Confucius, 138–139
Conquistadors, 555
Constantine the Great (Roman emperor), 277, 281, 287, 288
Constantinople (Byzantium), 287, 288, 317
Consuls, Roman, 241
Contract army, 505–506
Copan, 370
Corinth, 204, 210, 245
Cortés, Hernán, 397, 405, 425–426, 427
Cosmetics in ancient Egypt, 79–80
Cosmopolitanism of Tang dynasty, 149
Council of Constance, 509–510
Council of Five Hundred, 189
Council of Four Hundred, 188–189
Council of Plebeians, 242
Council of Trent, 540
Counter-Reformation, 539
Court of the Lions, 325
Covenant, 86, 87
Crassus, M. Licinius, 251
Creation stories, 25, 26–31
Crete, 173. *See also* Minoans
Crick, Francis, 33
Crossbow, 504
Crusades, 309, 313, 314, 473, 482–484, 551
map, *481*
Culhua, 403–404
Cult of beauty, 348–350
Cult of Isis, 288–289
"Cultural amnesia", 2
Cultural diffusion, 63

Cuneiform, 56–57, 58–59, 80
Cypselus, 188
Cyrus the Great (Persian king), 192
Daily life
Aztec clothing, 417
an Aztec feast, 410–411
a banquet from the Song dynasty, 156–157
Black Death, 498–499
food in India, 116–117
food of the Maya, 382–383
life in ancient Greece, 216–217, 219–220
life of a Mughal gentleman, 124–125
medieval knights and castles, 467
a medieval village, 472
raising a daughter in 16th-century Yucatan, 377
a Roman banquet, 284–285
Roman clothing, 256, 257
Viking raids, 456
Daimyo, 355, 363
Damascus, 304, 331
Daoism, 140
Darius, king of Persia, 192–193, 194
Dark Ages, Europe in, 433, 434–457
Barbarian invasions, 437–438
Carolingians, 452–455, 457
the Church, 438–439, 440, 448–452
daily life, 445–446, 447
Justinian's Byzantium, 439, 441
law, 446–447
Ostrogoths and Franks, 441–445
Darrow, Clarence, 36–37
Darwin, Charles, 32–34
Dating artifacts, 13
David (sculpture by Michelangelo), 527, 528
Delhi Sultanate, 119
Delian League, 201–202
Delphic Oracle, 192, 224
Demesne, 469
Democracy, 187, 189, 202–203
in Rome, 260
Desert regions, in Middle East, 304, 319
Despotism, 132, 162
Dessication, 70
Dhamma policy of Ashoka, 105–106
Dharma shastras, 108, 114
Díaz del Castillo, Bernal, 397, 406, 410, 419
Dictator, Roman, 241
Diet in Germany, 513
Diet of Worms, 536

"Dig team", 5–6
Diocletian (Roman emperor), 286–287
Diogenes (Greek philosopher), 214
Dionysius Exiguus, 289, 291
Disease
  effects of foreign diseases on Japan, 344
  effects of European diseases on American Indians, 426, 554, 558
  in medieval Europe, 471. *See also* Black Death
Divination, 135
Dome of the Rock, 316, 323, 325
Domitian (Roman emperor), 278
  Palace of Domitian, 271
Doña Marina, 397
Donatello (sculptor), 525–526
Donation of Constantine, 451, 453
Dorians, 183
Doric order (Greek temple design), 208, *209*
Drama
  Chinese, 160–161
  Greek, 196, 227
  Japanese (Noh), 359, 361
Duomo (cathedral in Florence), 524
Dürer, Albrecht, 530, 531
Dynasties of China, 133, 134

Earthquakes in Aegean area, 177
Economic recession in medieval Europe, 494, 495, 496–497, 500, 506
Education. *See also* Universities
  among ancient Aztecs, 414
  in ancient Egypt, 77
  in ancient India, 113, 114–115
  in ancient Rome, 253–254, 255
Edward III of England, 501, 503, 504
Egalitarian structure of pastoral nomadic society, 318
Egypt, 62–84
  art, 73–75
  creation stories, 27
  development along Nile River, 47
  geography, 62–63
  life among the ancient Egyptians, 75–80
  maps, *60, 83*
  Middle Kingdom, 64–65
  New Kingdom, 65–66
  Old Kingdom, 63–64
  religion, 65–66, 67–73
Elgin Marbles, 210
Ennius (Roman poet), 258–259
Epic, 179, 182
Epictetus (Roman philosopher), 281

Epicureanism, 259–260
Epicurus (Greek philosopher), 259–260
Equites, 248
Estates-General in France, 513
Etruscan League of Twelve Cities, 236, 238 (map)
Etruscans, 235–239
  monarchy, 237, 239
Eunuchs, 146
Euphrates River, 52–53, 54
Euripides (Greek dramatist), 206
Europe. *See also* Dark Ages, Europe in; High Middle Ages; Reformation in Europe; Renaissance in Europe
  geography of medieval Europe, 436–437
  map of medieval Europe in A.D. 1360, *437*
Europeanization, 550
Europeans in Japan, 362–363
Evolution, theory of, 25, 32–34
  history of human evolution, 34–41
Exploration, European, *547* (map), 551–552, 553–554
Fables, 182, 183
Fabliaux, 464
Fa-hsien, 110
Family life in ancient Rome, 253–254
Farming, 46
  in ancient Egypt, 77–78
  in Tigris-Euphrates Valley, 53, 54, 57
Fatimid dynasty, 313
Felicia de Whelton, 507–508
Feof, 463, 464, 469
Fertile Crescent, 52, 55
Festivals
  in ancient Egypt, 78
  Greek, 225
  in the Islamic Middle East, 321–322
Feudal agreement, 464
Feudalism, 448, 463–470
  changing forms, 506–507
  in China, 137, 142
  and the church, 465–466
  values, 464–465
Fiefdom, 265
Filial piety, 138–139
First Triumvirate, 251
Flanders, 503
Flavius Aetius (Roman general), 293
Florence, 520–522
Flower arranging, Japanese art, 359–360
Fluvial deposits, 234
Flying buttresses, 489

Food
  in ancient Egypt, 78
  an Aztec feast, 410–411
  food gathering, 41, 43
  Greek, 217
  in Heian Japan, 349–350
  in India, 116–117
  Mayan, 379, 381–384, 391–392
  Romans, 284–285, 286
  of the Song dynasty, 154–155, 156–157
Footbinding, 154
Forum, Trajan's, 278
Forums, Roman, 271
France, formation of, 455
Franks, 435, 442, 443–445, 448, 452, 455, 456
Fratricide, in legendary origins of Rome, 237
Frauds, archaeological, 13–14
Frederick Barbarossa, 483
Frescoes, 176, 236
Fujiwara, 345, 347, 350
Funerals, Egyptian, 72–73
Fur trade in North America, 555, 558

Galla Placidia (Roman empress of the West), 293
Games
  Aztec, 409, 415–416
  Mayan, 380
  Olympic, see Olympic Games
Gardens
  feudal Japan, 359
  Renaissance Europe, 524
Gathering of food, 41, 43
Gauls, 242
Geisha, 359
Gemmyo, 343
Genetics, 33
Genghis Khan. *See* Chingghis Khan
Geoffrey of Monmouth, 12
Germanic migrations (map), *444*
Germans, ancient, 290–291. *See also* Barbarians
Germany, formation of, 455
Ghiberti, Lorenzo, 525
Gladiators, Roman, 269, 273
Globalization, 549, 553–554
Global village, 558
Go-Daigo, 354
Gods. *See also* Religion
  Egyptian, 68–69
  Greek, 28–29
  Roman, 254

574 *Index*

Gordion knot, 214
Gotama the Buddha, 101, 102–103
Gothic architecture, 486, 488–489, 490
Government
    Greek, 187–190
    importance to civilization, 47
    in late Medieval Europe, 510–513
Gracchus brothers, 248
Great Chain of Being, 32
"Great Leap Forward", 39–41, 46
Great Rift Valley, 36–37
Great Schism, 508–509
Great Wall of China, 143, 144
Greece
    Alexander the Great, 211–214
    classical moment, 206–210
    colonization, 186–187
    creation stories, 28–29
    culture, 195–196
    daily life, 216–217, 219–220
    the dark ages, 183–184
    Delian League, 201–202
    geography and climate, 181–183, 226
    government, 187–190
    greatness of the Greeks, 226–228
    Greek culture, 214–215, 218–219
    literature, 182–183, 184, 196
    maps, *174, 186, 193, 203*
    medicine, 220–221
    Peloponnesian War, *203* (map), 204–206
    philosophy, 196, 214–215, 227
    religion, 190–191, 224–225
    rivalry of Sparta and Athens, 203–204
    science and technology, 196, 221–222
    trade, 225–226
Gregory I, Pope, 449–450
Gregory of Tours, 445
Gregory VII, Pope, 479
Guilds, 475–476, 497
Gunpowder, 152
Gupta Empire, 110–111, 113–115, 118–119
    daily life in, 114–115
Gutenberg, Johann, 529

Hadrian (Roman emperor), 276, 278, 282
Hadrian's Wall, 278, 279
Hagia Sophia, Church of, 279, 288, 325, 441, 442
Haiku, 361, 362
Hamilton and Scourge Project, 8–9
Hammurabi, 56
Han dynasty, 143–147

Han Fei Zi, 142
Hangzhou, 152, 153–154, 155, 158, 159
Hannibal, 243–244
Hara-kiri, 357
Harappa, 96
Harsha, 115, 118–119
Hastings, Battle of, 465, 466
Hatshepsut, 65
Hebrews, 85–90
    religion, 86, 87–90
Heian-kyo (Kyoto), 344, 345
    daily life in, 347–350
Heian Period in Japan, 344–350
Hellenistic Age, 214
Helots, 190
Henry V of England, 503, 504
Herculaneum, 15–16, 235
Heresy, 480–481, 509–510, 532
Herodotus, 62, 173, 193, 194, 224, 228
Hesiod, 187, 219
Hieratic writing, 82
Hieroglyphs
    Aztec, 421
    Egyptian, 80, 81, 82
    Mayan, 390–391
High Middle Ages in Europe, 460–491
    art and architecture, 485–490
    Crusades, 482–484
    feudalism, 463–470
    investitures and reform, 478–482
    map, *462*
    towns, 473–475
    villages, 469, 470–471, 472
    women in medieval society, 476–478
Hildegard, 507
Himeji (Japanese castle), 355
Hind bint Utba, 320
Hindi language, 107
Hinduism, 95, 113–114
    Hindu-Muslim interaction, 123, 125
Hippias (tyrant of Athens), 189
Hippocrates (Greek physician), 221
Historical fiction, 17, 18–19, 42
History
    difficulties in writing, 3
    foundations in Greece, 228
    legends and, 3–4
    reconstructing the past, 17–20
    science, anthropology, and, 15–16
    what is history?, 3
Hittites, 84–86
Hiuen Tsiang, 113, 115, 118, 119
Holbein, Hans, the Younger, 530–531

Holy Roman Empire, 455
    during the Reformation (map), *531*
Homer, 4, 179, 182–183, 184
Hominids, 34, 35, 37–41
Homo erectus, 35, 37–38
Homo habilis, 37
Homo sapiens, 34, 37, 38–39
Homo sapiens sapiens, 38–46
Homosexuality in ancient Greece, 221
Hoplites, 187–188
Horace (Roman poet), 267
Horyuji Temple, *342, 343*
Houses
    in ancient Egypt, 76, 78–79
    in ancient Rome, 273–274
    in Dark Ages of Europe, 447
    in Heian Japan, 349
    in the Islamic world, 328–329
    peasant's cottage in late medieval Europe, *500*
Huitzilopochtli, 404
Human evolution, 34–41
Humanism, 522–524, 552
    impact on the Reformation, 534
Human sacrifice, 376, 405–407
Hunas, 111
Hundred Years' War, 494, 501–506, 512, 513, 519
    arms and armour, 503–504
    causes of the war, 501, 503
    conduct of war, 503
    contract army, 505–506
    Joan of Arc, 504–505
    maps, *502*
Huns, 143, 291, 293, 437, 438
Hunting, 40, 41, 42, 43
Huron villages, 5–7
Hurrians, 55, 56
Hus, Jan (Johann), 510, 533, 534
Husayn (grandson of Muhammad), 322
"Hydraulic societies", 132
Hyksos, 64–65

Ice Ages, 46
Iconoclasm, 451–452
Ideograms, 57, 59, 80
Ikebana, 359–360
Iliad, 179, 182, 184
Il-Khans, 315–316
Impressed vessels, 503
Index librorum prohibitorum, 539
India
    Buddhist period, 101–103

contributions to the world, 125–126
creation stories, 27–28
development of civilization in Indus River Valley, 47
education, 113, 114–115
food, 116–117
formative period, 106–110
geography, 95
Gupta Empire, 110–111, 113–115, 118–119
Hinduism, 113–114
Hindu-Muslim interaction, 123, 125
Indus Valley civilization, 96–99
maps, 96, 97, *111*, *121*
Mauryan Empire, 102, 103–106
Mughal Empire, 120–123
regional kingdoms, 119–120
science, 111
Vedic Age, 99–101
Indo-European peoples, 55, 84
Indulgences, 534–535, 536
Indus Valley civilization, 96–99 "Infidels", 482
Ink, in Roman times, 258
Innocent III, Pope, 480, 481
Innovations
Chinese writing, 151
chocolate, 414
Hindi language, 107
Japanese writing, 346
Maya mathematics, 389
Mesopotamian writing, 58–59
mummification, 71
the Rosetta Stone, 81
Silphium, 258
underwater archaeology, 8–9
Inquisition, 510, 539
Ionic order (Greek temple design), 208, *209*
Iran, 317
Iraq, 315
Isabella and Ferdinand, 513
Isis, Cult of, 288–289
Islam, 161, 305–310
creation stories, 29
growth, 441, 448
Hindu-Muslim interaction, 123, 125
Islamic philosophy, 308–310
Islam today, 331
Shi'ites, 322
Sufi mysticism, 308, 309
Sunni and Shi'i, 307–308
Islamic Middle East
the arts, 323, 324–329

cross-cultural influences, 322, 324
economy, 330–331
geography, 303–304, 318–319
growth of empire, 310–317
map, *312*
religious beliefs, 305–310
science and technology, 329–330
social history, 318–324
trade and commerce, 304–305
Israelites. *See* Hebrews
Itzcoatl (Aztec ruler), 405, 407

Jade, 387, 388
Jahangir, 121
Japan
Ashikaga Shogunate, 354–362
creation stories, 29–30
early civilizations, 339–342
emperors, 336
Europeans in Japan, 362–363
formative age, 338–339
geography, 337
Heian period, 344–350
Kamakura Shogunate, 350–354
late Yamato and Nara periods, 342–344
maps, *341*, *354*
periods of history, 337, 338
writing, 346
Jason Project, 8, 9
Jerusalem
conquest by the Crusaders, 313
destruction of Temple, 276
Jesuit Relations, 540
Jesuits, 539–540
in China, 162
Jesus Christ, 255, 275–276, 291
Joan of Arc, 504–505, 510
Johanson, Dr. Donald, 34, 35
John of Salisbury, 485
Jomon culture, 338, 339
Judaism, 87, 89–90
Julian (Roman emperor), 291
Juliana of Norwich, 507
Julius Caesar, 251–252, 259, 267
Justices of the peace, 511
Justinian, 439, 441
Justinian's Code, 441
Juvenal (Roman writer), 280

Kamakura Shogunate, 350–354
Kami, 340, 341
Kamikaze, 353
Kana, 347

Kanishka, 106–107
Karma, 113
Kautilya, 104–105
Khadija (Muhammad's first wife), 320
Khubilai Khan, 159, 160, 353
Knights, feudal, 463–464, 467
Knossos, 176, 177, 180
Kojiki, 339, 344
Koken, 344
Koran, 29, 306, 320, 323
Kuge, 347
Kushans, 106–108
Kyoto, 344, 345, 356

Labyrinth, 178
Lady of the manor, 477
Laetoli Beds, 34, 35
Landa, Bishop, 382
Lanfranc, 485
Las Casas, Bartolome de, 555
Lascaux Caves, 43
Latin language, 294
in medieval Europe, 453
Latin Rights, 246, 248, 249
Leakey, Dr. Mary, 34, 35
Leakey, Richard, 35
Legalism, 140, 142
Legends
and history, 3–4, 16
King Arthur, 11–12
Legions, Roman, 250–251
Leo III, Pope, 455
Lepidus, Marcus, 264
Leprosy, 471
Levees, 53–54
Libby, Willard F., 13
Linear A (Minoan script), 176, 180
Linear B (Mycenean script), 177, 180
Li Si, 142, 143
Literature
of ancient Greece, 182–183, 184, 196
Aztec, 418
Chaucer's Canterbury Tales, 496–497
haiku, 362
in the Islamic Middle East, 309, 324, 326–327
Mayan, 384–385
Roman, 258–259, 266–268, 280, 291
Sanskrit poetry, 112
Livy, 237, 239, 266–267
Lollards, 510
Lombards, 452
Longbow, 504

Lords, 511
Lothair, 455, 456
Lottery system for selecting civic officials, 202
Louis IX, king of France, 490
Louis the Pious, 455
Loyola, Saint Ignatius, 539–540
Lucretius, 259, 260, 259, 260
"Lucy," 34
Luther, Martin, 509, 533, 534, 535–537, 540
Luther's 95 theses, 536
Lydians, 192
Lyric poetry, Greek, 196
Lysander (Spartan general), 205

Maat, 70
Macellum (Roman market), 278
Machiavelli, Niccolo, 523–524
Macrobius (Roman writer), 291
Maecenas, 267
Magellan, Ferdinand, 553–554
Magistrates, Roman, 241–242
Magna Carta, 512
Magyars, 456
Mahabharata, 108
Malleus Maleficarum, 532–533
Malory, Sir Thomas, 12
Malthus, Thomas, 32
Mamluks, 315
Mandate of Heaven, 144–145
Manor, 468, 469–470
Manumission, 282, 470
Manuscript illumination, 487, 490
Manyoshu, 344
Marathon, Battle of, 192–193
Marco Polo, 153, 160
Marcus Aurelius (Roman emperor and philosopher), 281, 286
Mardonius, 195
Margaret of Anjou, 507
Margaret of Ashbury, 18–19
Marinatos, Spyridon, 177
Marius, Gaius, 249, 250–251, 260
Marriage. *See also* Women
  in ancient Egypt, 76–77
  among Aztecs, 414–415
  in medieval Europe, 471
  in Rome, 253, 255
Martial (Roman writer), 280
Martyrdom, 287
Mary Rose (ship), 7, 10–11
Masako, 351
Mastabas, 72–73

Mathematics
  in ancient Greece, 221
  in the Islamic world, 330
  Mayan, 389, 390
Mauryan Empire, 102, 103–106
Mausoleum of Hadrian, 270
Maya highlands and lowlands, 368–369
Mayan civilization
  architecture, 385–387
  calendar, 375–376
  "collapse" of Classic period, 373–374
  creation stories, 30–31
  cross-cultural influences, 384
  customs and festivals, 379
  discoveries and inventions, 390
  food and drink, 379, 381–384
  government and law, 370–371
  literature, 384–385
  map, 369
  mathematics, 389, 390
  medicine, 388
  morals and values, 376–377
  mythology, 374–375
  painting, 388
  religion, 371, 372, 373, 374, 375–376, 379, 386
  rise to dominance, 371–374
  roles of men and women, 377–378
  sculpture, 387–388
  social structure, 378–379
  sources of information, 369–370
  sports and leisure, 379, 380
  trade, 391–392
  writing system, 390–391
Mecca, 305, 306
  pilgrimages to, 321–322
Medici, Cosimo de, 521
Medici, Lorenzo de, 521
Medici, Piero de, 521, 522
Medicine
  ancient Egypt, 82
  ancient Greece, 220–221
  Aztecs, 421–422
  Mayan, 388
  of the Song dynasty, 155, 158
Medina, 306, 307
Mediterranean Sea, 63
Megalomania of Julius Caesar, 252
Megasthenes (Greek historian), 104
Melanchthon, Philip, 537
Mendel, Gregory, 33
Mental baggage, 16

Mercenary armies
  in the Hundred Years' War, 504
  of Justinian, 441
Merchant class
  in Aztec civilization, 412
  in medieval Europe, 474, 475–476, 506–507, 519–520
  in Renaissance Europe, 525
Mesopotamia, 52–61
  creation stories, 26
  development along rivers, 47
  geography, 52–54
  growth of the empire, 55–56
  lasting influence, 61
  people, 54–55
  religion, 57, 60–61
  science and technology, 57
  writing, 56–57, 58–59
Metals, 175–176, 234
  for coinage, 226
Michelangelo Buonarroti, 527–528
Middle class. *See* Merchant class
Middle Kingdom
  division of Carolingian Empire, 455
  of Egypt, 64–65
Milleniums, 449
Miltiades, 193
Minamoto Yoritomo, 350–351
Ming dynasty, 161–163
Ming-huang, 149–150
Minoans, 173–178
Minotaur myth, 178
Mirazama, 124–125
Misogyny and the European witchcraze, 532–533
Missing link, 13
Mithraism, 288, 289
Modern era, 550
Mohen-jo-daro, 96
Monarchies
  Greek, 187
  in Mesopotamia, 55
  "new monarchy" in late medieval Europe, 513
Monasticism, 449, 450
Mongols, 119–120, 159–161, 315–316
  invasions of Japan, 353, 354
Monotheism, 66, 87, 158
Montezuma, 397, 406, 409, 410, 411
Moses, 86, 87, 90
Mosques, 316, 325, 328
Mountain regions in Middle East, 303–304, 318

Mo Zi, 139–140
Mughal Empire, 120–123
 life of a Mughal gentleman, 124–125
Muhammad, 29, 305–306, 321
Muhammad bin Tughluq, 120
Mummification, 70, 71, 72
Murasaki Shikibu, Lady, 347–348
Muslims, 305. *See also* Islam; Islamic Middle East
 rule in India, 119–120
Mycenaeans, 177, 178–180
 Trojan War, 181
Mystery religions, 288–289
Myths, 3–4
 creation stories, 25, 26–31
 Greek, 190–191
 Mayan, 374–375

Nahuatl language, 400
Nara, 343, 344
Nationalism, 514
Natural selection, evolution by, 32–33
Naumachiae, 273
Neanderthals, 38, 39, 40
Nebuchadnezzar, 61
Neo-Confucianism, 150
Neolithic Revolution, 43, 46
Nero (Roman emperor), 276, 277–278
Nicene Creed, 292
Nile River, 62, 77, 303
Nirvana, 102, 103, 148
Noh drama, 359, 361
North China Plain, 131
Novel
 Chinese, 160
 Tale of Genji, 347–348
Nur Jahan, 121, 123

Oases, 304, 319
Obsidian, 391
Octavia, 264, 265
Octavian. *See* Augustus
Odyssey, 179, 182–183, 184
Old Testament, 85, 86, 87, 88–89
Oligarchy, 187
Olympic Games, 184, 185, 225
 abolished, 292
Onin War, 362
Oracle bones, 135, 136
Origin of Species, 32, 33
Ostracism, 189–190
Ostrogoths, 291, 435, 439, 441, 442, 443
Ottomans, 317, 552
Ovid, 267–268

Painting, 40, 43
 Aztec, 421
 Egyptian, 75
 Greek, 218
 in the Islamic world, 329
 Mayan, 388
 in the Middle Ages, 487
 in Renaissance Europe, 525, 526
 Song dynasty, 152–153
Pakistan, 123
Palaeopathology, 14
Palazzo Vecchio, 520, 521
Palenque, 370
Paleoanthropology, 34–35
Paleontology, 34
Pandemic plague, 494. *See also* Black Death
Pantheon, 270, 278, 279–280
Papacy, 288, 449, 481–482, 490
 Avignonese papacy, 508
 Great Schism, 508–509
 in late medieval Europe, 494
Papal see, 448
Paper, 529
Papermaking, 152
Paper money, 152
Papyrus, 257
Parchment, 257
Parliament in medieval England, 511–513
Parthenon, 207, 209, 210
Paston family, 506, 507
Pastoral nomads, 304, 550
Patolli, 409
Patriarchy in the Islamic Middle East, 321
Patricians, 239, 242, 246, 248–249
Paul, Saint, 255, 276
Pax Romana, 282
Peasants' Revolt, 501
Peisistratus, 189
Peking Man, 130
Peking Opera, 160–161
Peloponnesian League, 203
Peloponnesian War, 202, *203* (map), 204–206
"People's Crusade", 483
Pepin, 452, 453
Pergamum, 245, 246
Pericles, 202, 203, 204, 223, 224
Perioikoi, 191
Perry, Commodore Matthew, 363
Persian Wars, 192–195
Peter the Hermit, 483
Petrarch, Francesco, 523
Petronius (Roman writer), 280, 286
Phalanx, 210

Pheidias, 207, 210
Philippi, Battle of, 264
Philip the Great, 210–211, 221
Philosophy. *See also* Religion
 Aquinas, St. Thomas, 310, 485
 Confucius, 138–139
 Greek, 196, 214–215, 227
 Islamic, 308–310
 Lao Zi, 140
 Mo Zi, 139–140
 Neo-Confucianism, 150
 Roman, 259–260, 280–281
 yin-yang, 141
Phoenicians, 85, 225
Phonograms, 80, 82
Pictographs, 56–57, 59, 80
Piltdown man, 13–14
Pimiko, 340
Piracy, 179–180
Pirates, 245
Pitti Palace, Florence, 524, 525
Plataea, Battle at, 195
Plato, 215, 227
Plautus, 259
Plebeians, 239, 242, 246, 248–249
Pliny the Elder, 280
Pliny the Younger, 280
Plutarch, 214
Poll tax, 501
Polyandry, 320
Polybius, 245
Pompeii, 15, 235
 houses at, 273, 274
Pompey, Sextus, 264
Pompey the Great, 251, 269
Pontius Pilate, 276
Pope. *See* Papacy
Population increases, 46, 473
Porcelain, 152
Po River, 234
Portuguese in Japan, 362–363
Pottery, 15, 179
 Mayan, 375, 378, 379, 388
Praetors, Roman, 241–242
Predestination, 538
Primary data, 4, 14
Primary documents
 analysis of, 16
 Benedictine Rule, 450–451
 Herodotus, 194
 Old Testament, 88–89
 Scopes' monkey trial, 36–37
 Tacitus, 290–291
Primary source, 3

Primates, 34, 36
Primogeniture, 471
Prince, The (Machiavelli), 523, 524
Principate, 265, 267
Printing, 152
Printing press, 529–530
Proscriptions, Sullan, 249
Protagoras, 215, 225
Ptolemy, 214, 245
Punic Wars, 243–245
Puranas, 113–114
Pyramids, Egyptian, 22, 64, 72–73

Qing dynasty, 161
Quaestors, Roman, 242
Quetzalcoatl, 397

Rabi'a al-Adawiyya, 320
Radiocarbon dating, 13
Ramapithecus, 34
Ramayana, 108
Ramses II, 66, 86
Reformation in Europe, 510, 531, 533–540
    beginnings in Germany, 534–535
    Calvin, 538–539, 540
    Catholic response, 539–540
    causes of the Reformation, 533
    Holy Roman Empire during the Reformation (map), *531*
    impact of humanism, 534
    Luther, 535–537
    religions in Europe in 1600 (map), *541*
Regionalism in China, 133
Religion. *See also* Buddhism; Christianity; Hinduism; Islam; Judaism; Papacy; Philosophy; Roman Catholic Church
    in ancient Greece, 190–191, 224–225
    Aztec, 407–409
    beliefs and heresy, 480–481, 509–510, 533
    Egyptian, 65–66, 67–73
    of Hebrews, 86, 87–90
    in Heian Japan, 349
    Mayan, 371–376, 379, 386
    Mesopotamian, 57, 60–61
    in neolithic times, 44–45, 46, 47
    in paleolithic times, 43
    Roman, 253, 254, 288–289
    in the Song dynasty, 158–159
Remus, 237, 266–267
Renaissance in Europe, 518–531
    art and architecture, 524–528
    emergence of the Renaissance, 519–520
    humanism, 522–524
    ideal Renaissance individual, 528–529

Italian city-states, 520–522
    spread to Northern Europe, 529–531
    twelfth century Renaissance, 484–485
Republican Wall, 271
Richard I, king of England, 314, 483
Riemenschneider, Tilman, 530
Rig-Veda, 99–100, 101
Ritual suicide, 357
River basins in Middle East, 303, 318
Rivers: importance to development of civilizations, 23, 47, 131–132
Roads, Roman, 246
Roman Catholic Church
    in the Dark Ages, 438–439, 440, 448–452
    decline in reputation, 494
    in late medieval Europe, 508–510
    reforms, 478–479, 539–540
Roman civilization
    army, 250–251
    buildings, 268–272, 273–274, 279–280, 282–283, 286, 295
    creation stories, 28–29
    daily life, 252–260
    dating of time, 289, 291
    decline of the Republic, 260
    enfranchisement of Italy, 249
    Etruscans, 235–239
    expansion and colonization, 245–246, *247*
    First Triumvirate, 251
    geography, 234–235
    the Gracchus brothers, 248
    houses, 273–274
    Julius Caesar, 251–252
    legacy of Rome, 294–295
    literature, 258–259, 266, 267–268, 280, 291
    maps, *233, 243*
    non-Christian religions, 288–289
    philosophy, 259–260, 280–281
    Punic Wars, 243–245
    republican government, 239, 240, 241–242, 246, 248–249
    rise of Christianity, 274–277
    sacking of the city (A.D. 410), 293
Roman Empire
    in A.D. 200 (map), *436*
    collapse of the Western Empire, 294, 435
    confrontation with barbarians, 291–293
    division into East and West, 287
    establishment of, 265
    maps, *275, 292, 436*
    Rome in the fourth century, 288
    successors of Augustus, 277–278
    survival of the Eastern Empire, 294

Romulus and Remus (Livy's story), 237, 266–267
Rosetta Stone, 81
ROV system for underwater archaeology, 8, 9
Rule, Dr. Margaret, 9, 10

Sabi, 359–360
Sacred Band of Thebes, 221
Sadducees, 276
Safavids, 317
Sainte-Marie Among the Hurons, 17
Saladin, 313, 314
Salamis, Battle of, 195
Samurai, 350, 351, 353, 356–357, *358*, 359
San Clemente, Basilica of, 271
Sankan, 355
Sanskrit, 107
    poetry, 112
Sappho, 221, 223
Saracens, 456
Schliemann, Heinrich, 4, 179
Science and technology
    in ancient Egypt, 80, 82
    in ancient Greece, 196, 221–222
    in ancient India, 111
    in the Islamic world, 329–330
    Mesopotamian, 57
Scipio Africanus, 244–245
Scopes, John T., 36
Sculpture, 40, 43
    Aztec, 420, *421*
    Egyptian, 75
    Greek, 210, *218*, 219, 227
    Mayan, 387–388
    in the Middle Ages, 487
    in Renaissance Europe, 525–526, 527, 528
Seafaring, technological advances, 552
Seals from Indus culture, 96–97, 98
Seclusion Policy (Japan), 363
Secondary sources, 3, 16
Second Dark Ages, 456–457
Second Triumvirate, 264
Seleucus, 214, 245
Senate, Roman, 241
Senatus Populusque Romanus, 241
Seneca (Roman philosopher), 278, 280–281
Serf, 469–470, 472
Shaft graves at Mycenae, 179, 180
Shah Jahan, 122, 123
Shajar al-Durr, 320
Shakas, 106
Shang dynasty, 135–136

Index   579

Shatavahanas, 106
Sheriffs, 511
Shi Huangdi, 142–143
Shi'i Islam, 307–308
Shinto religion, 340, 341–342
Shishiki, 355
Shogun, 351
Shosoin, 344
Shotoku, 343
Shrines in Japan, 336, 342
Silphium, 258
Sindbad the Sailor, 305, 326–327
Sistine Chapel paintings, 527, 528
Site reports of archaeologists, 6–7
Slavery
    of Africans by Europeans, 556–557
    of Amerindians by Europeans, 555–556
    in ancient Greece, 188
    in Aztec civilization, 413
    in China, 136
    in the Roman Empire, 260, 281–282
Social contract, 103
Socrates, 215, 225
Solon, 188–189
Song dynasty in China, 150, 152–159
    art, 150, 152–153
    beliefs, 158–159
    daily life, 153–154
    food, 154–155, 156–157
Song of Roland, 453
Sophists, 215, 225
Sophocles, 206
Spain: conquest by the Crusaders, 313, 314
Spanish Conquest, 374
Sparta, 190–192
    Peloponnesian War, 202, *203* (map), 204–206
    rivalry with Athens, 203–204
Spartacus, 251, 282
Stained glass, 486
Statius (Roman writer), 280
Stelae, 372–373, 387
Stephens, John L., 370
Steppes, in Middle East, 304, 318–319
Stilicho (Roman statesman), 293
Stoicism, 215, 280–281
Stola, 256
Stonehenge, 44–45
Strata, 98
Stratigraphy, 13
Suetonius (Roman historian), 280
Sufi mysticism, 308, 309
Suiko, 343

Sui Wendi, 148–149
Sulla, L. Cornelius, 249–250
Sumayya bint Khubbat, 320
Sumerians, 54, 55, 56, 60
Sun Goddess (Japan), 340
Sun-line, 340
Sunna, 307
Sunni Islam, 307 "Survival of the fittest", 32–33
Suzerain, king as, 464
Swaddling, 471
Symposion, 216–217
Syracuse, 204

Tacitus (Roman historian), 280, 290–291
Taiho Code, 343
Taika, 343
Taizong, 149
Taj Mahal, 122, 123, 328
Tale of Genji, 347–348
Tang dynasty in China, 149–150
Taoism. *See* Daoism
Tarquin the Proud, 237, 239, 241, 260
Tea ceremony in Japan, 360–361
Tectonic plates, 177
Temple of Jerusalem, 86, 87
Temples
    Aztec, 418
    Egyptian, 73
    Greek, 208–209, 224
    Indian, *118*
    Japanese, *342*, 343
    Mayan, 372, 376, 385–387
Tenochtitlan, 398, 404, 405, 418, 419, *420*
Teotihuacan, 373, 384, 402
Terence, 259
Tetzel, Johann, 536
Thales of Miletus, 192
Theatre of Epidaurus, *205*
Theatre, Roman, 259, 269
Thebes, 210
Themistocles, 194, 195
Theodoric, 293–294, 439, 443
Theodosius the Great (Roman emperor), 291, 292
Theologians, 484
Thermopylae, Battle of, 193–195
Theseus and the Minotaur, 178
Third Estate, 474
Thirty Tyrants, 206
Thucydides, 202, 204, 208
Thutmose III, 65
Tiberius (Roman emperor), 277

Tiber River, 234
Tigris and Euphrates Rivers, 52–53, 54, 303
Time. *See also* Calendars
    B.C. to A.D., 289, 291
    Chinese view, 133–134
Time lines
    Aztec history, *402–403*
    Chinese history, *134–135*
    Egyptian history, *63*, *64–65*
    European history A.D. 1304 to A.D. 1588, *520–521*
    Greek history, *175*
    Indian history, *98–99*
    Islamic history, *310*
    Japanese history, *338–339*
    Mayan history, *370–371*
    Middle Ages in Europe, *438–439*
    Middle Eastern history, *53*
    Roman history, *236–237*
Tithes, 470
Titus (Roman emperor), 276, 278
Tlacaelel, 406, 407
Tobacco, 412
Toga, 256, 257
Tokugawa Shogunate, 363
Toltecs, 402, 403, 402, 403
Tomoe, 357
Tools, 37, 40, 43, 46
Tortilla, 379, 381
Tournaments, 467
Tower of Babel, 61
Towns, 46. *See also* Cities
    in feudal Japan, 361
    in medieval Europe, 473–475, 506–507
Trade, 40
    in ancient Egypt, 63, 82–83
    in ancient Greece, 225–226 in ancient India, 109–110
    ancient trade routes (map), *109*
    Aztecs, 424, 425
    China, 152
    early trading networks, 549–550
    between Europe and the Far East, 473–474
    Greeks, 184, 225–226
    in the Islamic world, 304–305, 330, 331
    among Maya, 391–392
    of Phoenicians, 85
    in the Roman Empire, 281
    tribute, 163–164
Trajan (Roman emperor), 278
Trajan's column, 278

Transubstantiation, 509
Treaty of Lodi, 519, 522
Tribunes, Roman, 242
Tribute, 163–164, 399
    Aztecs, 424–425
Trojan War, 4, 179, 181
Troubadours, 465
Troy, 4
Tsumi, 341
Tula, 402, 403–404
Tunic, Roman, 256
Tyranny, 188, 189

Uji, 340
Ukiyoe, 361
Umayyad caliphate, 310–311
Underwater archaeology, 7–11
Universities
    in ancient India, 113
    in medieval Europe, 484–485
Upanishads, 101
Upper Paleolithic Age, 25
    daily life in, 41–43
Urban planning, 524–525
Ussher, James, 32

Valens (Roman emperor of the East), 291
Valley of the Kings, 73
Vandals, 437, 438, 439, 441, 443
Van Eyck, Jan, 530
Vedas, 28, 99–100, 101
Ventris, Michael, 177
Vespasian (Roman emperor), 278
Vestal Virgins, 257
Vesuvius, 234, 235
Vikings, 438, 456
    defence of England against, 462, 463
Village in medieval Europe, 469, 470–471, 472
Vinci, Leonardo da, 526–527

Virgil, 267
Visigoths, 291, 293, 439, 441, 443, 444–445
Vision of Light, A, 18–19
Vitruvius (Roman architect), 220

Wabi, 359
Walker, Alan, 35
Walker, Patrick, 370
Warfare. *See also* particular wars
    in medieval Europe, 514
War of 1812, 8
War of Investitures, 479
War of Unification (Japan, 1573–1600), 363
Warrior culture in Japan, 359–361
Wars of the Roses, 513
Watson, James, 33
Weapons, 40
West Africa, contact with Europe, 556–557
Wheel, 57, 61
William the Conqueror, 463, 466
Witchcraft, 532–533
Wolf, Eric, 553, 558
Women
    in ancient Egypt, 76
    in feudal Japan, 357, 359
    Greek, 216–217, 223–224
    in Heian Japan, 350
    in the Islamic Middle East, 319–321
    in Kamakura Japan, 351
    in late medieval Europe, 507–508
    Mayan, 377–378
    in medieval Europe, 18–19, 476–478
    in Renaissance Europe, 529
    in Rome, 253–254, 255, 257
    in the Song dynasty, 154
    Spartan, 192, 223
    in the Tang dynasty, 149
    the witchcraze in Europe, 532–533
World-economy, 550
World War II, 342, 345

Writing
    in ancient Egypt, 77, 80–82
    Aztec, 421
    Chinese, 151
    importance to civilization, 47
    Japanese, 346
    Linear A script, 176
    Linear B script, 177
    lost during Dark Ages of Greece, 184
    Mayan, 390–391
    in Mesopotamia, 56–57, 58–59
    Phoenician alphabet, 184
    in Rome, 257–258
Written records, importance to historian, 16
Wu, 149
Wudi, 144, 147
Wycliffe, John, 509–510, 533

Xavier, St. Francis, 363
Xerxes, king of Persia, 193, 195

Yahweh, 86, 87, 89
Yang Guifei, 149–150
Yangzi River, 131
Yayoi, 339
Yellow River, 131
Yeomen, 500
Yin-yang, 141
Yoshimitsu, 356, 359
Yoshinori, 356
Yuan dynasty, 159–161
Yugen, 359

Zama, Battle of, 244, 245
Zazen, 352 **Zen**, 352–353, 359
Zheng He, 163
Zhou period in China, 136–140
Ziggurats, 61
Zodiac, Chinese, 132
Zwingli, Ulrich, 537